The Battle of Kursk: The Red Army's Defensive Operations and Counter-Offensive, July-August 1943 offers a peculiarly Soviet view of one of the Second World War's most critical events. While the German defeats at Moscow and Stalingrad showed that Hitler could not win the war in the East, the outcome of Kursk demonstrated beyond a doubt that he would lose it. This study was compiled by the Red Army General Staff's military-historical directorate, which was charged with collecting and analyzing the war's experience, and issued as an internal document in 1946-47. The study languished for more than a half-century, before being published in Russia in 2006, although heavily supplemented by commentary and other information not contained in the original. The present work omits these additions, while supplying its own commentary in places deemed necessary. The book is divided into two parts, dealing with the defensive and offensive phases of the battle, respectively. The first begins with a strategic overview of the situation along the Eastern Front by the spring and summer of 1943 and the Soviet decision to stand on the defensive. This is followed by a detailed examination of the Central Front's efforts to counter the expected German attack out of the Orel salient, and the Voronezh Front's attempts to do the same against the German concentrations in the Belgorod—Khar'kov area. The rest of this section is devoted to an exceedingly detailed day-by-day, tactical-operational account of the struggle, particularly along the southern face of the salient, where the Germans came closest to succeeding. The second part will be more of a revelation to the Western reader, who is likely to be more familiar with the defensive phase of the battle. Here the authors once again, in great detail, lay out the Red Army's preparations for and conduct of a massive counteroffensive to clear the Orel salient, which soon degenerated to a grinding struggle, which while ultimately successful, cost the Soviets dearly. Likewise, the authors detail the Voronezh Front's preparations to reduce the Belgorod salient and seize the industrial center of Khar'kov. This offensive, in conjunction with a simultaneous offensive in the Donets industrial region, pushed the German lines to the breaking point and set the stage for the follow-on advance to the Dnepr River and the eventual liberation of Ukraine.

Richard W. Harrison earned his undergraduate and master's degrees from Georgetown University, where he specialized in Russian area studies. In 1994 he earned his doctorate in War Studies from King's College London. He also was an exchange student in the former Soviet Union and spent several years living and working in post-communist Russia.

Dr. Harrison has worked for the US Department of Defense as an investigator in Russia, dealing with cases involving POWs and MIAs. He has also taught Russian history and military history at college and university level, most recently at the US Military Academy at West Point.

Harrison is the author of two books dealing with the Red Army's theoretical development during the interwar period: *The Russian Way of War: Operational Art, 1904–1940* (2001), and *Architect of Soviet Victory in World War II: The Life and Theories of G.S. Isserson* (2010). He has also authored a number of articles on topics in Soviet military history. He is currently working on a history of the Red Army's high commands during World War II and afterwards.

Dr. Harrison currently lives with his family near Carlisle, Pennsylvania.

THE BATTLE OF KURSK

THE BATTLE OF KURSK

The Red Army's Defensive Operations and Counter-Offensive, July-August 1943

Soviet General Staff

Edited and translated by Richard W. Harrison

AUSA
ASSOCIATION OF THE UNITED STATES ARMY

Helion & Company

Published in cooperation with the Association of the United States Army

Helion & Company Limited
Unit 8 Amherst Business Centre
Budbrooke Road
Warwick
CV34 5WE
England
Tel. 01926 499619
Email: info@helion.co.uk
Website: www.helion.co.uk
X (formerly Twitter): @Helionbooks
Facebook: @HelionBooks
Visit our blog at https://helionbooks.wordpress.com/

Published by Helion & Company 2016, in cooperation with the Association of the United States Army.
This new edition 2025
Designed and typeset by Mach 3 Solutions (www.mach3solutions.co.uk)
Cover designed by Paul Hewitt, Battlefield Design (www.battlefield-design.co.uk)

ISBN 978-1-806720-64-4

British Library Cataloguing-in-Publication Data.
A catalogue record for this book is available from the British Library.

Contents

List of Maps

List of Tables

Preface to the English-language edition

This study was originally compiled on the basis of materials gathered during 1943-44 by the Red Army General Staff's historical section. It was published in 1945 for internal use in the form of a short study. However, it never saw the light of day until it was published, with a number of editorial comments, in 2006, under the title of *The Battle of Kursk* (*Bitva pod Kurskom*). This volume also contained a number of editorial comments and documents—mostly orders and reports, which are not printed here.

The study contains a number of terms that may not be readily understandable to the casual reader in military history. Therefore, I have adopted a number of conventions designed to ease this task. For example, a *front* is a Soviet wartime military organization roughly corresponding to an American army group. Throughout the narrative the reader will encounter such names as the Southwestern Front and the Voronezh Front, etc. To avoid confusion with the more commonly understood meaning of the term front (i.e., the front line); italics will be used to denote an unnamed *front*. Similar German formations (i.e., Army Group Center) are also spelled out in full.

I have chosen to designate Soviet armies using the shortened form (i.e., 13th Army). German armies, on the other hand, are spelled out in full (i.e., Fourth Panzer Army). In the same vein, Soviet corps are designated by Arabic numerals (35th Guards Rifle Corps), while German units are denoted by Roman numerals (e.g., LII Army Corps). Smaller units (divisions, brigades, etc.) on both sides are denoted by Arabic numerals only (8th Rifle Division, 57th Infantry Division, etc.).

Given the large number of units involved in the operation, I have adopted certain other conventions in order to better distinguish them. For example, Soviet armored units are called tank corps, brigades, etc., while the corresponding German units are denoted by the popular term *panzer*. Likewise, Soviet infantry units are designated by the term rifle, while the corresponding German units are simply referred to as infantry.

Many of the place names in this study are hyphenated, such as Novo-Oskochnoe and Dmitrovsk-Orlovskii. In these cases, the names are separated by a single hyphen, which is to distinguish them from a number of such locales along a particular line, such as Vedenskaya—Gotnya—Krasnyi Pochinok—Rakitnoe. In the latter case, the individual villages and towns are separated by two hyphens.

The work subscribes to no particular transliteration scheme, because no entirely satisfactory one exists. I have adopted a mixed system that uses the Latin letters ya and yu to denote their Cyrillic counterparts, as opposed to the ia and iu employed by the Library of Congress, which tends to distort proper pronunciation. Conversely, I have retained the Library of Congress's ii ending (i.e., Rokossovskii), as opposed to the commonly-used y ending. I have also retained the apostrophe to denote the Cyrillic soft sign.

The published work contains a number of footnotes inserted by the authors, in order to explain this or that technical question. These have been retained as endnotes and have been supplemented by a number of appropriately identified editorial notes, which have been inserted as an explanatory guide for a number of terms that might not be readily understandable to the foreign reader.

Elsewhere, I have taken some small liberties as regards the book's overall organization, although there is nothing here that deviates in a major way from the original. These liberties primarily involve leaving out some maps, copies of orders, and tables, the inclusion of which would have made the final product too long. On the other hand, I do not take issue with some of the claims made in the text, and any errors or interpretations should be disputed after examining the relevant documents in the two countries' military archives. Nor have I attempted to make the language more "literary," and have striven throughout to preserve the military-bureaucratic flavor of the original.

BOOK ONE

THE DEFENSIVE BATTLE (JULY 1943)

Introduction

The Overall Situation at the End of March, 1943

The overall situation along the central and southern sectors of the Soviet-German front by the end of March 1943 had come about as the result of the conclusion of the offensive operations of the Bryansk, Central, Voronezh, Southwestern and Southern fronts during the winter and spring of 1943.

In January-February the forces of the Bryansk and Voronezh fronts defeated a large German group of forces in the area of Voronezh and Kursk. During the course of subsequent operations the bridgehead captured by our forces in the Kursk area was expanded significantly. By the end of the spring fighting the Red Army's units had consolidated along the following lines:

Kirov—Zaprudnoe—Dumshichi—Chernyshino—Ozhigovo, by formations of the Western Front's left wing.

Excluding Ozhigovo—Troitskoe—Gorodilovo—Krasnogor'e, by forces of the Bryansk Front.

Excluding Krasnogro'e—Maloarkhangel'sk station—Chern'—Korenevo, the Central Front;

Excluding Korenevo—Khoten'—Gotnya station—Belomestnaya station—Volchansk, the Voronezh Front.

The Southwestern Front had gone over to the defensive along the line of the Severskii Donets River.

Further to the south, the Southern Front was defending along the Mius River.

The so-called Kursk salient was created, which jutted deeply into the enemy lines.

At the end of March our forces' front had stabilized. Both sides began to forcibly prepare for summer operations.

The Situation in the Area of the Kursk Salient by the End of March 1943

By the end of March the Central Front, which consisted of the 48th, 13th, 70th, 65th, 60th and 2nd Tank armies, was defending the northern sector of the Kursk salient, from Gorodishche to Sheptukhovka. The overall length of its front was 312 kilometers.

The 48th Army[1] was defending the front Gorodishche—Panskaya (36 kilometers);

The 13th Army[2] was defending the front excluding Panskaya—excluding Gremyach'e (58 kilometers);

The 70th Army[3] was defending the front Gremyach'e—excluding Asmon' (36 kilometers);

The 65th Army[4] was defending the front Asmon'—Selino (88 kilometers);

1 Five rifle divisions, three tank regiments, eight artillery regiments, seven anti-tank artillery regiments, and six mortar regiments.

2 Nine rifle divisions, three tank brigades, nine artillery regiments, two anti-tank artillery regiments, six mortar regiments, two guards mortar regiments, and one guards mortar battalion.

3 Five rifle divisions, three tank regiments, seven artillery regiments, one anti-tank artillery regiment, two mortar regiments, and two guards mortar regiments.

4 Nine rifle divisions, one rifle brigade, two ski brigades, three cavalry divisions, three tank brigades, one motorized-rifle brigade, four tank regiments, one artillery regiment, four anti-tank artillery regiments, five mortar regiments, and two guards mortar regiments.

The 60th Army[5] was defending the front excluding Selino—excluding Sheptukhovka station (94 kilometers).

The following units were located in the *front* reserve in the Fatezh—Kursk area: the 2nd Tank Army,[6] 6th Guards Rifle Division, 2nd Anti-Tank Artillery Division (six anti-tank artillery regiments), a mortar regiment, two guards mortar regiments, and the 9th Tank Corps.[7] The *front* headquarters was located in the area of the town of Svoboda.

Facing the Central Front were the forces of the German Second Panzer Army's right flank (299th Infantry Division), the Ninth Army (LV Army, XLVI Panzer, XX, XXIII, and Hungarian VIII army corps, and Manteuffel's[8] group[9]), and the Second Army's XIII Army Corps.

The 299th Infantry Division occupied the defensive line Nikol'skoe—excluding Zmievka.

The Ninth Army's corps were defending as follows:

The LV Army Corps (two infantry and one panzer divisions)—along the front Zmievka—excluding Tagino;

The XLVI Panzer Corps (two panzer and two infantry divisions), with Manteuffel's group (four *Jager* battalions)—along the front Tagino—Plosskoe;

The XX Army Corps (three howitzer regiments and one SS cavalry division)—along the front excluding Plosskoe—Yevdokimovo;

The XXIII Army Corps (three infantry and one panzer divisions)—along the front excluding Yevdokimo—Lipnitsa;

The Hungarian VIII Army Corps (three light infantry divisions) was operating against the partisans in the area Navlya station—Lokot'—Seredina Buda.

The Second Army's XIII Army Corps (four infantry divisions) faced the Central Front's left wing along the sector excluding Lipnitsa—Korenevo.

The Voronezh Front, consisting of the 38th, 40th, 21st, 64th, and 69th armies was defending the southern sector of the Kursk salient from Sheptukhovka station to Khotomlya. The overall length of the front was 264 kilometers.

The 38th Army[10] occupied the sector Sheptukhovka—Ugroedy (80 kilometers);

The 40th Army[11] occupied the sector excluding Ugroedy—Sumovskaya station (50 kilometers);

The 21st Army[12] occupied the sector excluding Sumovskaya station—Melekhovo (64 kilometers);

The 64th Army[13] occupied the sector excluding Melekhovo—Khotomlya (70 kilometers);

---

5 Three rifle divisions, four rifle brigades, two cavalry divisions, one ski brigade, one tank brigade, two artillery regiments, five anti-tank artillery regiments, four mortar regiments, two guards mortar regiments, and one battalion of anti-tank rifles.

6 Four tank brigades and one tank regiment.

7 Three tank brigades and one motorized-rifle brigade.

8 Editor's note. Hasso von Manteuffel (1897-1978) joined the army in 1916 and fought in the First World War. During the Second World War he rose from battalion commander to commander of a panzer army in the USSR, North Africa and Western Europe. Following the war, Manteuffel enjoyed a career in West German politics.

9 Following our troops' elimination of the Demyansk bridgehead, the Ninth Army was transferred in March 1943 from around Rzhev to the Orel area.

10 Four rifle divisions, one rifle brigade, two tank brigades, two artillery regiments, five anti-tank artillery regiments, two mortar regiments, one guards mortar regiment, and one guards mortar battalion.

11 Five rifle divisions, two tank brigades, one motorized-rifle brigade, two tank regiments, six artillery regiments, five anti-tank artillery regiments, two mortar regiments, and two guards mortar regiments.

12 Six rifle divisions, three artillery regiments, 3 guards mortar regiments, one guard mortar brigade, and one battalion of anti-tank rifles.

13 Nine rifle divisions, one cavalry corps, two tank brigades, three tank regiments, two artillery regiments, four anti-tank artillery regiments, and five battalions of anti-tank rifles.

The 69th Army[14] comprised the *front* reserve and was located in the Novyi Oskol—Nikitovka—Gotov'e area.

The 1st Tank Army,[15] which was at the disposal of the Deputy Supreme Commander-in-Chief, Marshal of the Soviet Union Zhukov,[16] was concentrated in the Oboyan' area. The *front* headquarters was located in the Novyi Oskol area.

Facing the Voronezh Front were the German forces of the Second Army's VII Army Corps and the Fourth Panzer Army (LII Army Corps, an SS Panzer Corps, and the XI Army Corps' 320th Infantry Division.

The VII Army Corps (four infantry divisions) was defending along the front Snagost'—Bol'shaya Chernetchina.

The formations of the Fourth Panzer Army, which had gone over to the defensive, were deployed as follows:

The LII Army Corps (five infantry divisions) occupied the front excluding Bol'shaya Chernetchina—Butovo with four divisions; the SS Panzer Corps (four panzer divisions) occupied the line Butovo—excluding Murom.

The XI Army Corps' 320th Infantry Division occupied the area Ternovaya—Staryi Saltov. The LII Corps' 168th Infantry Division comprised the army reserve and was located in the Akhtyrka area.

Thus the German group of forces facing the Central Front consisted of 19-20 infantry and 4-5 panzer divisions, and a single cavalry division, with an overall strength of about 125,000 men and officers, 290 tanks, 1,600 guns of various calibers, and 1,500 mortars.

The correlation of forces between the Central Front the enemy facing it was as follows:

Men—1:2.3 in our favor
Tanks—1:2.2 in our favor
Guns of all calibers—1:1.8 in our favor
Mortars of all calibers—1:3.3 in our favor

The German group of forces facing the Voronezh Front had ten infantry and four panzer divisions; this group of forces consisted of up to 76,000 men and officers, 375 tanks, 500 guns of various calibers, and 530 mortars.

The correlation of forces along the Voronezh Front's sector was as follows:[17]

Men—1:2.4 in our favor
Tanks—1:2.4 in our favor
Guns of all calibers—1:2.8 in our favor
Mortars of all calibers—1:4.1 in our favor

14 Five rifle divisions, one tank brigade, three artillery regiments, two anti-tank artillery regiments, and one mortar regiment.

15 Five tank brigades, three mechanized brigades, one motorized-rifle brigade, three anti-tank artillery regiments, two mortar regiments, one guards mortar regiment, and one guards mortar battalion.

16 Editor's note. Georgii Konstantinovich Zhukov (1896-1974) joined the Russian imperial army in 1915 and the Red Army in 1918. He defeated the Japanese at the Khalkhin-Gol River in 1939 and at the beginning of the Great Patriotic War was Red Army chief of staff. During the war he commanded a number of *fronts* and also served as deputy supreme commander-in-chief, immediately under Stalin. The dictator turned against him in 1946 and Zhukov returned to power only after his death. Zhukov was appointed defense minister in 1955, but was dismissed two years later by Nikita Sergeevich Khrushchev.

17 In determining the correlation of forces, the 1st Tank Army, which was in the process of concentrating, and two of the 64th Army's divisions, which were on the march, were not counted.

As a result of the preceding fierce battles, the German forces operating opposite the Central and Voronezh fronts suffered heavy losses. The strength of more than a third of the infantry divisions had fallen significantly and varied between 2,500 and 4,000 men and officers; these divisions were either not capable of combat, or only partly so. All eight panzer divisions were also of limited combat value, each having 50-80 tanks remaining.

A Brief Military-Geographical Description of the Battle Area. The Significance of the Kursk Salient and the Orel and Belgorod—Khar'kov Bridgeheads

The borders and extent of the area

The area, in the territory of which in July-August 1943 combat activities unfolded, is located within the bounds of the Orel, Kursk, Khar'kov and Sumy oblasts. The boundaries of the area are as follows: to the north—the line Yepifan'—Belev—Zhizdra; to the south—Novaya Kalitva—Roven'ki—Zmiev—Poltava; to the west—the Bolva and Desna rivers, and then the line Novgorod-Severskii—Sumy—Akhtyrka, and; to the east—the Don River.

In the northern part of the area, the distance between the eastern and western borders is 320 kilometers, and 300 kilometers in the southern part. The distance between the northern and southern boundaries is about 450 kilometers. The size of the area exceeds 135,000 square kilometers.

Large-scale fierce fighting occurred in a more limited area: in the northern part of the area—in the Bolkhov—Karachev—Orel—Novosil' triangle; in the southern part—in the territory defined by the line of the Severskii Donets in the east, and the line Oboyan—Graivoron—Bogodukhov—Valki—Merefa in the west.

The operational significance of the area

This area had great operational significance for our troops and the enemy. In its territory were located the powerful Orel and Belgorod—Khar'kov enemy bridgeheads, which were valuable for carrying out the summer offensive operation planned by the German command.

In its turn, the Kursk salient could serve as a launching pad for the organization of a large-scale offensive by the Red Army. Significant enemy forces, concentrated along the Moscow strategic direction, were tied down along the sector opposite the Kursk salient.

Within the boundaries of the area were located major industrial and administrative-political centers, and the major rail and road junctions of Orel, Kursk and Khar'kov. A developed road network served both sides as a secure connection with the rear, as well as in terms of broad operational maneuver.

The significance of the Orel and Belgorod—Khar'kov bridgeheads

The Germans' Orel bridgehead was an enormous salient pointing east. The bridgehead's boundaries from the northeast, east and southeast was the front line, which ran south of Kirov to Duminichi and then to Novosil', Zmievka, Tagino, and Dmitrovsk-Orlovskii. The Orel bridgehead, one of the most powerful and well fortified in the enemy's defensive system had great operational importance. It could serve as the jumping-off area for a German attack on Moscow, as well as for an attack on Kursk from the north. Simultaneously, the Hitlerite command considered it the chief bastion of the German defense along the entire Soviet-German front.

The enemy's second fortified area was the Belgorod—Khar'kov bridgehead. As was the case with the Orel bridgehead, it was in the shape of a salient facing east. The northern and eastern boundaries ran along the line Gotnya station—Belgorod, and then south along the Severskii Donets as far as Zmiev.

While holding the Belgorod—Khar'kov bridgehead, the Germans could threaten by an attack toward Kursk from the south to reach our important Yelets—Kastornoe—Staryi Oskol—Valuiki lateral railway. On the other hand, the Belgorod—Khar'kov bridgehead served as the key to the Donbass[18] and to the entire left bank of Ukraine. Without eliminating it, it was impossible to launch a blow from the north against the German Donets group of forces, as our forces, in turn, would expose themselves to attack.

Within the boundaries of these bridgeheads were located such powerful and heavily fortified strong points as Orel, Bolkhov, Mtsensk, Belgorod, Khar'kov, and Merefa. They were all simultaneously major railroad and road junctions, connecting the front with the rear and enabling the Germans to carry out wide-ranging maneuver with their forces and equipment. The Khar'kov railroad junction, which connected the Belgorod—Khar'kov and Donets enemy groups of forces, was especially important.

The retention of the Orel and Belgorod—Khar'kov bridgeheads offered the enemy the opportunity of launching a simultaneous attack on Kursk from the north and south, for the purpose of capturing Kursk, to destroy our forces located within the Kursk salient, and to subsequently develop the offensive into the depths of the Soviet Union on Moscow.

The elimination of the Germans' Orel bridgehead would completely remove the threat of an enemy offensive on Moscow and the Kursk salient from the north, and would create favorable conditions for our offensive on Bryansk. With the elimination of the Belgorod—Khar'kov bridgehead, the threat to the Kursk salient from the south would be eliminated and our forces would have the opportunity for operations against the enemy's Donets group of forces and the subsequent development of operations to liberate all of left-bank Ukraine.

The Kursk salient's operational significance

The Kursk salient, which deeply cut into the German's defense, had a particularly important strategic significance for us. Our large forces concentrated there not only tied down the enemy's Orel and Belgorod—Khar'kov groups of forces, but also presented a serious danger to them. The Central Front, which occupied the northern part of the Kursk salient, had the opportunity, along with the forces of the Bryansk Front and the left wing of the Western Front, of launching an attack against the rear and flanks of the Germans' Orel group of forces. The same opportunity existed for the forces of the Voronezh Front, which would be able to launch an attack from the north and east against the flanks and rear of the enemy's Belgorod—Khar'kov group of forces.

The Kursk salient, which had been transformed into a powerful bridgehead, enabled our forces to successfully deploy for a general offensive for the purpose of defeating the most important German groups of forces and subsequently developing operations for clearing the enemy out of Ukraine and Belorussia.

The German command also attached great operational significance to the Kursk salient. This is confirmed by captured enemy documents.

"The Kursk salient," according to a description of combat activities by the 19th Panzer Division, "represented a ready-made jumping-off point for the Russians and the gates for an invasion of Ukraine. For the German armed forces, it offered the opportunity to easily carry out the encirclement of the enemy."

It's completely natural that the elimination of the Kursk salient was an important objective in the German command's plans for the summer of 1943. In the event of successfully achieving this

18 Editor's note. The Donbass (Donetskii Bassein) is an important industrial region in the area of the Donets River in eastern Ukraine.

goal, the enemy would have encircled and destroyed the forces of the Central Front and the right wing of the Voronezh Front, thus eliminating the danger of an attack into the rear of the Orel and Belgorod—Khar'kov groups of forces, reducing their frontage by 250 kilometers, and would then have had the subsequent opportunity of developing the offensive toward Moscow.

A description of the area's surface

The area's terrain is divided into two parts—forested and swampy, located in the Belev—Zhizdra—Trubchevsk triangle, and steppe. The eastern part of the area, lying between the Orel—Kursk—Belgorod—Khar'kov railroad and the Don River, is open and slightly hilly. To the south of the Seim River along the Poltava—Zmiev line, the terrain is covered 15-20 percent by woods and shrubs.

In the Orel—Maloarkhangel'sk—Fatezh area, the terrain is very hilly and cut by a large number of gullies, trailing off in various directions. The gullies' width usually does not exceed 600-800 meters or more than 40-70 meters deep. Their sides are precipitous. Rivers and creeks flow along the bottoms of the gullies. Heights, which reach 280-290 meters above sea level, lie between the gullies. The heights' slopes are gentle.

To the west of the Kursk—Oboyan'—Khar'kov line the terrain is less broken. The elevation varies between 80 and 240 meters above sea level. There are large wooded areas in the area of Khar'kov, Chuguev, Lyubotin, Shebekino, Volchansk, Sumy, and Poltava.

The rivers, gullies, heights, and woods offer great advantages for the organization of a defense. The hills and heights along the rivers and gullies, as well as the widespread inhabited points, were used by the Germans for creating strong points and centers of resistance.

The open character of the terrain created great difficulties for the concealed deployment of our forces in the area of Orel and the Kursk salient. The enemy's artillery had the opportunity to conduct observed fire over great distances. In rainy weather the gullies and river valleys made the maneuver of tanks and artillery exceptionally difficult, as well as that of auto transport.

The terrain relief in the eastern and southern parts of the area was very favorable to the employment by both sides of large mechanized forces and aviation. The exception was the extreme northwestern part of the area. The basins of the Resseta, Zhizdra, Snezhed', Bolva, and Desna rivers were almost completely covered with woods (the Bryansk woods) and swamps, which made it significantly more difficult to employ large motor-mechanized formations and aviation. Tanks could operate only in small subunits, or even individual vehicles, and only along the roads. Artillery could not freely maneuver on wheels and conduct aimed fire. All of this created difficulties in organizing cooperation. As a result, the infantry was often forced to attack without the support of tanks and artillery, which extremely complicated its activities. At the same time, the woods created favorable conditions for the hidden accumulation of forces and concealed them well from the enemy's aviation.

The area's soils vary, with clay soil predominating and black earth often encountered. In the Belgorod—Tomarovka—Borisovka area, lime soils are met up with. In rainy weather the roads become difficult for auto transport; in the summer, during the dry season, they dry out and become dusty, giving away the movement of troops and transport during the daytime.

Rivers

The area is intersected by a large number of rivers, flowing in various directions. The largest of these are the Desna, Oka, Zusha, Bolva, Neruch', Zhizdra, Vytebet', Resseta, Seim, Severskii Donets, Vorskla, and Psel. The Oka, Zusha, Zhizdra, and Resseta flow to the northwest and the remainder to the south. Relying on the rivers, the enemy had the opportunity to create in the area a series of important defensive lines.

The width of the majority of rivers is comparatively small—from 80 to 130 meters; the depth is 0.7-3 meters; the rate of flow is 0.2-0.7 meters per second. In the Orel area the width of the Oka River does not exceed 80 meters and its depth 2.5 meters.

Of the rivers cited, the most significant river obstacle is the Desna, the width of which reaches 220 meters and is 2-4 meters deep south of Bryansk; its rate of flow is 0.2-0.7 meters per second.

In the northern part of the area of combat activities the banks of the majority of rivers slope gently and are sandy, while in the Orel area they are steep and precipitous. The rivers have a hard bottom. The Zhizdra, Resseta and Vytebet' rivers flow through solid wooded areas and swampy terrain. Their banks are quite swampy and in many areas are overgrown with bushes. The insignificant distance between the Vytebet' and Resseta rivers enabled the enemy to organize fire cooperation along these lines and made it easier for him to wage a mobile defense.

The Zusha, Oka and Neruch' rivers were employed by the enemy for constructing powerful defensive lines. These rivers' broad valleys and the presence of hollows and favorable heights enabled the Germans to create a highly developed fire system; in the river valleys various engineering obstacles were erected. At the same time, the rivers' completely open banks made it difficult to prepare for a crossing and to cross our forces. The enemy air force, which was constantly in the skies, would immediately attack our crossings.

The Severskii Donets was part of the Voronezh Front's zone of combat activities only along its upper course. Its width along this sector does not exceed 20-25 meters, and its depth 1-3 meters, and its flow 0.2-0.5 meters per second; the banks are very swampy. The great operational significance of this river was that it covered Khar'kov from the east and the powerful enemy group of forces located there. The Uda, Lopan' and Khar'kov rivers were less significant, but very convenient for creating defensive lines.

In the rear of the Belgorod—Khar'kov group of German forces, the enemy took advantage of the Vorskla and Psel rivers, with their broad right-bank flood plains and high western bank; powerful defensive lines were constructed along the rivers.

However, despite the difficulties of attacking to the west, the north-south flow of these rivers created favorable conditions for our forces to outflank the Orel and Belgorod—Khar'kov enemy bridgeheads from the north and northwest. In this case, our attacking units did not only not encounter serious water barriers along their route, but quite the opposite—their flanks were covered by these water lines during the advance.

Lines for defense

In the Kirov—Chernyshino and Volosovo area the terrain is predominantly wooded and swampy. In the Bryansk Front's sector the Oka (from Belev to Voronets) and the Zusha rivers (from the headwaters to its junction with the Oka) served as convenient lines for creating the main defensive zone. They covered the Tula axis and the Uzlovaya—Yelets—Kastornoe lateral railroad. Further to the rear, as far as the line of the Don River, there were no significant water obstacles. Thus the second and third army lines and the *front* rear line had to be built on open, slightly hilly, terrain.

In the sector of the Central Front and the right wing of the Voronezh Front, where in July our forces waged intensive defensive battles, the terrain is open. The Seim River had been configured by our forces as a defensive line along only a small sector (from Bukino to Korovino). Along the remaining sectors, the river could be use only for building switch positions.

The Svala (along the sector from Nikol'skoe to its mouth) and Psel (along the Prokhorovka and Miropol'e sectors) rivers were convenient defensive lines covering Kursk from the west and south.

The eastern bank of the Severskii Donets River, along the Belgorod—Chuguev sector, is low-lying, but nevertheless the river served as a convenient line for creating the forward edge of the Voronezh Front's main defensive zone and for covering the axes to Novyi Oskol and Valuiki.

The Tim and Oskol rivers, which flow from north to south, could serve as a convenient line for creating the main resistance zone for the forces of the Steppe Front and for covering the axes toward Yelets and Voronezh. The Sosna River, which flows to the northeast, was a convenient line for creating switch positions.

Along the Don River, along the Yepifan'—Boguchar sector, ran the most favorable natural rear line. Here lay the state defensive line, which in the north linked up with the defensive line of the Moscow zone.

The enemy had the more favorable terrain. The line of heights, stretching in a general direction from the north to the south along the Oka, Zusha, Nugr', Neruch', Optukha, Seim, Severskii Donets, Lopan', and Uda rivers, in conjunction with their steep western banks, facilitated the creation of powerful defensive lines for covering the major strong points of Orel, Bolkhov, Mtsensk, Belgorod, Khar'kov, and Ryl'sk.

The Psel and Vorskla rivers, which flow in the rear of the Belgorod—Khar'kov bridgehead, with their high and steep western banks, were used by the enemy for the construction of powerful rear defensive lines.

Population and local resources

Before the war the Orel, Kursk, Khar'kov, Poltava, and Sumy oblasts were thickly populated. By the summer of 1943 their population had sharply fallen. A significant majority of the working-age population had left for the Red Army as early as 1941. Those residents capable of work who remained on German-occupied territory were either physically exterminated or forcibly sent to hard labor in Germany; the only ones who survived were those who managed to hide or join the partisan detachments.

Agricultural products (bread, meat, fats), as well as manufactured articles, which the area was so rich in, had been taken by the Germans to Germany; the remaining small enterprises, which had not been evacuated into the interior of the Soviet Union, had been either destroyed or burned by the enemy.

All of this made the materiel supply of our forces during the offensive extremely difficult. Their supply was primarily carried out by deliveries from state and military bases in the deep rear.

A description of the inhabited locales

The inhabited locales are most thickly located in the area of Orel and Kursk, and within the confines of the Khar'kov, Poltava and Sumy oblasts. On the average, there is one inhabited locale every 8-9 square kilometers. The northwestern corner of the area of combat activities is less thickly inhabited.

The majority of the inhabited locales are located along the rivers, gullies, and in the hollows. Only in the northwestern wooded and swampy area of the area are they located in the heights.

Khar'kov, Kursk, Orel, Poltava, Sumy, Bryansk, and Belgorod are the largest cities in the area and the most important rail and road junctions. During the German occupation these cities lost their previous significance as industrial centers. Their enterprises were either evacuated into the interior of the Soviet Union or destroyed by the enemy, but they nevertheless retained their important operational significance.

In the cities that became the main centers of resistance in the enemy's defensive system, there were located not only the rear organs, but military-economic enterprises. Orel, Belgorod, Khar'kov,

Bryansk, Sumy, and Poltava are located along natural favorable lines and were transformed by the Germans into powerful fortified strong points. In the Orel, Khar'kov and Poltava areas the enemy disposed of major airfield junctions.

A significant part of the inhabited locales had been burned by the Germans. Khar'kov, Poltava, Orel, and Belgorod had been subjected to a great deal of destruction. However, the enemy was not able to completely destroy the cities and part of the inhabited points; many of them were saved from destruction and ruin by the Red Army, which was swiftly driving the Germans from its native land.

The location of the inhabited locales along the rivers, ridges and heights offered the enemy the opportunity to transform them into powerful centers of resistance and configure them for perimeter defense. In the southern and southwestern parts of the area this was facilitated by the type of structures (stone and mixed clay). There were a particularly large number of stone structures in the Orel area. Stone houses, barns and cellars were easily transformed by the Germans into strong points, with an insignificant expenditure of men and materiel.

Communications routes

By the start of combat operations our forces had the single Tula—Yelets—Kastornoe—Staryi Oskol—Valuiki two-track lateral railroad, with a capacity of 40-45 pairs of trains per day. From this lateral railroad in the direction of the front ran the following railroads: a) Tula—Kozel'sk—Sukhinichi; b)Tula—Mtsensk; c) Volovo—Belev; d) Yelets—Verkhov'e; e) Kastornoe—Kursk—L'gov, and; f) Valuiki—Kupyansk. Each line's capacity did not exceed 12-18 pairs of trains per day. A two-track railroad runs from Liski station through Ostrogozhsk and Alekseevka to Valuiki and Kupyansk, which, due to heavy destruction, had a very limited capacity.

The Yelets—Valuiki and Liski—Valuiki lateral railroads and the Staryi Oskol—Tim—Kursk, Staryi Oskol—Korocha—Volchansk, Novyi Oskol—Belgorod and Novyi Oskol—Volchansk dirt roads, and the Kursk—Fatezh, Kursk—L'gov and Kursk—Ternovka paved roads were very important for supplying the troops of the Voronezh and Steppe fronts, and the Tula—Mtsensk road for the Bryansk Front. The main troop supplies moved along these roads. The necessity of two-way traffic (to the front and from the front) on the single-track railroads significantly reduced supply effectiveness.

The enemy disposed of a more developed network of railroads and roads. The junctions of the Orel, Bryansk, Vorozhba, Poltava, and Khar'kov railroads and roads had great importance for the enemy, both in the immediate front zone, as well as in the rear. The railroads and roads that branched from these junctions in various directions completely covered the operational shipments of enemy troops and supplies from the rear and maneuver along the front. Khar'kov was connected by rail and road with Dnepropetrovsk, Poltava, Sumy, Vorozhba, and Belgorod. Along the main roads (two-track railroads and paved roads) connecting Orel and Bryansk were airfield junctions and large enemy bases, which fed his Orel and Belgorod—Khar'kov groups of forces.

The Bryansk—Navlya—Khutor-Mikhailovskii—Vorozhba—Sumy road was an important lateral railroad for the Germans, which connected their Orel and Belgorod—Khar'kov groups of forces; this lateral railroad enabled the enemy to maneuver troops and equipment along the front.

During the occupation the enemy had altered the gauge of a significant part of the railroads and shortening the ties, which later (following the liberation of this territory) made it more difficult for our troops to restore and use them. While retreating, the enemy blew up a large part of the railroad bed, destroyed bridges, and destroyed and burned station structures.

For supply by auto transport, the Germans used the following roads: the Bryansk—Orel, Orel—Kromy, Orel—Kursk, Kromy—Dmitrovsk-Orlovskii, Khar'kov—Belgorod, Khar'kov—Sumy, Khar'kov—Poltava; Sumy—Vorozhba; Ryl'sk—Glukhov, and Ryl'sk—Putivl' paved roads, and Orel—Bolkhov, Bolkhov—Zhizdra, Orel—Sevsk, Sevsk—Fatezh, Belgorod—Borisovka—Graivoron—Akhtyrka—Zen'kov—Poltava, and; and the Khar'kov—Krasnograd and other dirt roads.

Movements of our troops and supplies were primarily carried out along the following paved roads: Tula—Mtsensk, Chukino—Yefemov—Yelets—Voronezh, and Kursk—L'gov. In the areas closer to Khar'kov, small portions of the paved roads were employed. The Orel—Khar'kov paved road was mostly in enemy territory; our forces could only use the Kursk—Fatezh and Kursk—Ternovka sections.

The Kaluga—Velizh, Yefemov—Novosil', Yelets—Livny—Maloarkhangel'sk, Kastornoe—Kursk, Staryi Oskol—Korocha—Belgorod, Novyi Oskol—Volchansk, Korocha—Shebekino—Volchansk, and Valuiki—Kupyansk dirt roads and others were maintained in good condition and widely used for moving troops and supplies to the front line. However, during the rainy period they all became difficult for wheeled transport.

The condition of local communications means

In falling back under the blows of our troops in the winter of 1943, the Germans almost completely destroyed the local communications means in the territory abandoned by them. However, by the start of the operation units of the Red Army had restored a large part of the communications means and employed them widely during the fighting.

In enemy-occupied territory communications had been almost completely destroyed. The German command restored the permanent telegraph and telephone lines along the railroads and highways. The enemy carried out communications along the remaining axes with the aid of radio communications and field cable. In withdrawing in the summer of 1943, just as in the winter of 1942-43, the Germans destroyed 80-90 percent of the local communications network; they tore down lines, blew up telephone stations, and destroyed telegraph and telephone poles along many sectors. Thus our forces were forced during the offensive to build new lines and only partially, along certain sectors, were they able to restore the old ones. This made the communications troops' work very difficult.

Meteorological conditions

June 1943 was rainy and cold. The average air temperature did not exceed 15-17 degrees Celsius. The visibility on certain days was reduced to 2-4 kilometers. Dirt and graded roads became very sodden and along many sections became difficult for auto and horse-drawn transport. All of this made the concentration of our forces and their preparation for defense more difficult.

At the end of June warm and sunny weather set in. The condition of the roads improved. This weather, interrupted from time to time by short summer rains, was the norm for the entire period of the battle.

PART ONE

THE ORGANIZATION OF THE DEFENSE

1

The Decision by the *Stavka* of the Supreme High Command and the *Front* Commanders

The Evaluation of the Situation by the *Stavka* of the Supreme High Command

The overall forecast by the *Stavka*[1] of the Supreme High Command as to the Germans' possible actions in the summer of 1943 arose from Stalin's[2] instructions that the enemy was still sufficiently strong enough to organize a serious offensive along some single direction.

In selecting a line of strategic conduct for the summer campaign of 1943, there were two possible variants for the high command of the German army:

First. Proceeding from a realistic appraisal of the situation and the correlation of forces, the German armies on the Soviet-German front could go over to the strategic defensive. Putting such a decision into practice would result in difficult consequences for Germany and its satellites: taking up the strategic defensive would mean an admission by the German-Fascist government of the fact that the possibility of a German victory in this war had been lost for good.

Second. In order to restore its authority and shaky prestige among its allies, the Hitlerite command needed a major victory; thus it sought at any price to show the ability of the German army to carry out major offensive operations, to slow up the process of the fascist bloc's disintegration, to frighten its enemies, and to put off the formation of a second front as much as possible.

The second variant was adopted—to prepare a new offensive operation. By the summer of 1943 the enemy had a number of favorable prerequisites for this. As a result of carrying out a "total" mobilization, which had begun as early as January 1943, the German command had managed by the summer to raise the strength of the divisions operating along the southern sector of the Soviet-German front to 70-80 percent of their authorized strength, to restore a reserve for replacement units and to form 15-16 new infantry and up to three panzer divisions. Moreover, the lack of a second front in Europe enabled the German command to retain a great deal of strategic freedom and, without a great deal of risk, to throw the main mass of its forces against the Red Army.

1 Editor's note. The *Stavka* of the Supreme High Command/*Stavka* of the Supreme Commander-in-Chief (*Stavka Verkhovnogo Glavnokomanduyushchego*) was the highest Soviet military body during the Second World War. It was formed on 23 June 1941 and disbanded following the war with Japan in 1945.

2 Editor's note. Iosif Vissarionovich Stalin (Dzhugashvili) (1879-1953) joined the Russian Social Democratic Worker's Party as a young man and soon aligned himself with the Bolshevik faction under V.I. Lenin. Following the Bolshevik coup, Stalin was appointed people's commissar for nationalities and was a political commissar during the civil war. In 1922 Stalin was appointed general secretary of the party and used this position to increase his power and eliminate his rivals. During the Great Patriotic War he was simultaneously general secretary of the Communist Party, chairman of the Council of People's Commissars, people's commissar of defense, supreme commander-in-chief, and chairman of the State Defense Committee. Following Stalin's death, his successors denounced him as a mass murderer.

The measures carried out by the German command in the spring of 1943, most of all the concentration of a major group of forces in the southern sector of the Soviet-German front, suggested that the enemy would not try to carry out an offensive simultaneously along several strategic directions. He no longer had the necessary forces for this.

During the first stage of the summer campaign of 1943 the German high command evidently put forth a limited aim—by powerful attacks along the Orel—Kursk and Belgorod—Kursk axes, to defeat our forces defending the Kursk salient and eliminate the latter.

The successful accomplishment of this operation could, in the German command's opinion, create favorable prerequisites for the subsequent development of the offensive by the German armies into the depth of our country for the purpose of capturing the capital of the Soviet Union—Moscow.

Such were the strategic and military-political goals that the German high command, entering upon the summer campaign, laid down for its armies.

In order to study in detail the situation that had arisen in the area of the Kursk salient, comrade Stalin in March 1943 dispatched there the Deputy Supreme Commander-in-Chief, Marshal of the Soviet Union Zhukov, who delivered a detailed evaluation of the enemy's group of forces and his likely intentions. Zhukov, in his reports to the *Stavka* at the end of March and the beginning of April, pointed out that along the portion of the southern sector of our front (facing the Central, Voronezh and Southwestern fronts), there was a German group of forces consisting of up to 59 divisions: about 23-24 divisions facing the Central Front, of which 15-17 were infantry and 6-7 panzer, one cavalry and one motorized divisions; up to 16-17 divisions facing the Voronezh Front, of which 12-13 were infantry and four panzer (the SS Panzer Corps), and; up to 18 divisions facing the Southwestern Front, of which 7-9 were infantry and up to nine panzer.

A characteristic feature of the German group of forces facing the southern sector of our front was the presence of a large number of panzer divisions: of the overall number of 59 divisions, 20 were panzer (34 percent). Besides this, in this sector of the front the strengthening of the enemy's combat aviation was noted, as well as the presence of a significant number of self-propelled guns.

The concentration of a large number of panzer and air formations, given the absence of significant enemy strategic reserves, forced us to assume that the enemy was making his main bet on the massed employment of tanks and aviation, as well as the broad employment of maneuver.

According to the German command's plan, the summer offensive operation was to consist of a series of consecutive stages.

The goal of the first stage was the defeat of the Central and Voronezh fronts' forces, the elimination of the Kursk salient and to reach the line Droskovo—Tim—Korocha—Volchansk.

It was assumed that in order to achieve this goal the Germans' Orel group of forces would launch its main attack in the direction of Maloarkhangel'sk and Shchigry, bypassing Kursk from the east, with supporting units reaching the Droskovo—Tim line. The possibility was not excluded that the enemy would launch supporting attacks along the following axes: a) Kromy—Fatezh—Kursk; b) Dmitrovsk-Orlovskii—Mikhailovka—Fatezh, and; c) Ryl'sk—L'gov, at the junction of the Central and Voronezh fronts. The main blow by the Germans' Belgorod group of forces would be launched along the Belgorod—Oboyan'—Kursk paved road to the north, with supporting units reaching the line of the Korocha and Donetskaya Seimitsa rivers.

A supporting enemy attack in the direction of Sudzha and Oboyan', along the northern bank of the Psel River, was also possible.

The task of the second stage was evidently the defeat of our reserves west of the Kastornoe—Novyi Oskol railroad, as well as the defeat of units of the Southwestern Front to the west and south of Kupyansk, and the arrival of enemy forces at the line Novosil'—Livny—Kastornoe—Staryi Oskol—Novyi Oskol—Valuiki—Svatovo—Lisichansk.

The following likely axes of attack during this stage were as follows: a) Maloarkhangel'sk—Livny; b) from the Shchigry—Tim area toward Kastornoe and Staryi Oskol; c) from the Korocha area toward Gniloe and along the Korocha—Budennyi graded road; d) from the Volchansk—Staryi Saltov area toward Urazov, and; e) from the Slavyansk—Lisichansk area toward Svatovo and Urazov.

The chief goal of the third stage could have been the capture of the line Yefemov—Yelets—Voronezh—Liski—the Don River from Liski to Novaya Kalitva and then Kantemirovka—Belovodsk—Verkhne-Teploe.

Upon arriving at this line the enemy could go over to the defensive along the front from Voronezh to Taganrog and, along the Moscow direction, having grouped his main forces in the area Yefremov—Livny—Kastornoe—Voronezh—Yelets, launch an attack toward Ryazan' and Vladimir, bypassing Moscow from the southeast.

Possible axes of attack during this stage were as follows: a) from the Novsil'—Verkhov'e area toward Yefremov; b) from the Livny—Volovo area toward Yelets; c) from the Kastornoe—Gorshechnoe area toward Voronezh; d) from the Staryi Oskol and Volokonovka areas toward Korotoyak and Liski; e) from the Pokrovskoe—Svatovo area toward Rossosh', and; f) from the Lisichansk area toward Starobel'sk and Kantemirovka.

The decisions by the *Stavka* of the Supreme High Command

During the second half of March 1943 the *Stavka* of the Supreme High Command adopted the basic decisions that determined the activities of our forces for the spring and first summer months.

The further continuation of our offensive operations, for the purpose of foiling the offensive being prepared by the enemy, was recognized as inexpedient. The decision was made for the Central and Voronezh fronts to go over to a static and stubborn defense for the purpose of exhausting and bleeding the enemy white, should he undertake an offensive. It was planned that the Western and Bryansk fronts would attack in the general direction of Orel. The goals of this offensive were as follows: a) an attack the rear of the Germans' Orel group of forces, in case it should attack the Central Front; b) the defeat of this group of forces, and; c) the elimination of the enemy's Orel bridgehead. The close cooperation with the forces of the Central and Voronezh fronts was foreseen. Their counteroffensive was to begin immediately, as soon as it became clear that the Germans' attacking Orel and Belgorod—Khar'kov groups of forces had been bled white in the preceding defensive battles.

In order to impart the maximum firmness to the defense of the Kursk salient, it was planned to create a number of defensive lines. The entire area from the front line to the Don River (to a depth of up to 300 kilometers) was to be put into a defensive state. The defense being erected had the task of withstanding the concentrated attacks of large tank groups, supported by aviation.

Based upon the likely deadlines for the beginning of the expected German offensive, a schedule for completing the defensive works was established. It was planned to begin the work on all the defensive lines simultaneously and complete the first round by 15 April; the local population was widely employed in constructing the rear lines, as well as the Directorate for Defensive Construction (UOS).

Units of the Central and Voronezh fronts were brought up to authorized strength. The strength of the divisions was raised to 8-9,000 men and that of the rifle companies to 120-130 men. Measures were adopted to supply the units with all kinds of armaments in short supply, particularly anti-tank weapons and the necessary engineering equipment.

Large reserves were created in the rear of the Kursk salient. Their task consisted of securely covering the Kursk—Voronezh axis, as well as supporting a sufficiently powerful blow once the forces of the Central and Voronezh fronts went over to a general counteroffensive. On 6 April the

Map 1 The Situation by the Beginning of the Battle of Kursk, 5 July 1943.

Stavka ordered the creation of a reserve (later the Steppe) *front*. It included the 2nd Reserve, 24th, 66th, 46th, 47th, 53rd, and 5th Guards Tank armies, as well as the 1st Guards Don, 3rd Guards Kotel'nikovo, 4th Guards Kantemirovka, and 10th tank corps, and the 1st and 5th mechanized corps. Voronezh was the center of the reserve *front's* location.

In the event the German forces broke through our front along the Kursk salient, the reserve *front* would occupy a defensive line along the Kshen' River, on the Livny—Volokonovka sector.

The 1st Tank Army, which by this time was concentrated in the Oboyan' area, was subordinated to Marshal of the Soviet Union Zhukov, as a powerful and mobile shock reserve. From 28 April the army was subordinated to the Voronezh Front. In accordance with these decisions, directives were issued to the *fronts'* military councils. At the same time, the *front* commanders received instructions that along with the thorough training of the troops for defensive activities, it was necessary to train them for a decisive offensive.

The actions of the forces defending the Kursk salient were to be supported from the air by two air armies—the 16th and 2nd, which were part of the Central and Voronezh fronts, respectively. The air force's overall task was as follows: to secure air superiority and, in conjunction with the ground forces, facilitate their firm retention of the defensive lines. The most important local tasks were the secure covering of the ground forces against the enemy's aviation; the destruction of the enemy's aviation on his airfields; the foiling of any of the enemy's regroupings and railroad movements; the destruction of the enemy's forces and equipment in their concentration areas, and; covering our airfields from the air, as well as the rail lines and junctions.

The overall control of the Central and Voronezh fronts on the spot, as well as the responsibility for carrying out *Stavka* orders, was entrusted to the Deputy Supreme Commander-in-Chief, Marshal of the Soviet Union Zhukov.

The overall structure of the Kursk salient's defense

In carrying out the decision adopted, the *front* commanders received instructions to create no less than 5-6 defensive lines along the most important axes. In addition to these, the following could be employed: a) the so-called State Defensive Line, which ran along the eastern bank of the Don River, and; b) the Livny—Staryi Oskol defensive line, which was later built by the forces of the Steppe Front.

The structure of the Kursk salient's defensive system is as follows:

Each army in the first *front* echelon was to build three defensive lines: a main defensive zone, a second defensive zone, and a rear army zone. In certain sectors these zones were augmented by a series of switch and intermediate lines, such as along the Voronezh Front's right flank and center.

Moreover, each *front* was to build three defensive lines: the first, second and third *front* lines, which in places were augmented by intermediate lines and reinforced along the most important axes by centers of resistance, which were built around large inhabited locales (Kursk, Staryi Oskol, Novyi Oskol, and others).

In this way, inside the *fronts* along the axes of the assumed enemy main attacks (Maloarkhangel'sk—Shchigry on the Central Front and Belgorod—Oboyan' on the Voronezh Front), up to six defensive lines were to be built, which were consecutively echeloned to a depth of up to 110 kilometers along the Central Front and up to 85 kilometers along the Voronezh Front. The defensive system was less developed along the *fronts'* boundaries. At the tip of the Kursk salient the distance between the rear army zone and the first *front* defensive line was 60 kilometers, at the same time that along other sectors of the salient the distance of the defensive lines from each other did not exceed, on the average, 15-20 kilometers.

Maximum use was made in the defensive construction of natural obstacles—the Severskii Donets, Psel, Seim, Svapa, Tim, Kshen', and Don rivers, as well as the wooded expanses in the areas of L'gov, east of Sumy, Belgorod, Shebekino, and Nechaevo.

A characteristic feature of the defense of the Kursk salient was as follows: the troops occupied four defensive lines beforehand—the main defensive zone completely, and most of the second, and along the axes of the assumed main enemy attacks the troops occupied the rear army zone and the first *front* line. Moreover, from 16 May the forces of the Steppe Front (Military District) occupied the defensive line along the Kshen' River (Livny—Kshen' station—Zalomnoe).

The decisions by the front commanders and preparations for the defensive operation

The main decisions by the commander of the Central Front, General (now Marshal of the Soviet Union) Rokossovskii[3] and the commander of the Voronezh Front, General Vatutin,[4] as well as their instructions to their forces for preparing for the defensive operation, are laid out in a series of directives, issued at the end of March 1943. The instructions on the creation of defensive lines and the manner of carrying out defensive work were given in the *front* commanders' orders: order no. 00123/op of 21 March for the Central Front, and order no. 0087/op of 27 March for the Voronezh Front. The disposition and tasks for the forces, as well as their employment in the course of the defensive battle were noted in the Central Front commander's directive of 29 March, and the commander of the Voronezh Front's order no. 0093 of 31 March.

These basic directives and orders were late augmented by a series of local orders and combat instructions, as well as the personal instructions of the *front* commanders.

The decision by the commander of the Central Front. The disposition and tasks of the front's forces

The Central Front's main task was to defend the Kursk salient in the sector between the following boundary lines: from the right (with the Bryansk Front's 3rd Army): Yefremov—Mikhailovskoe—Verkhov'e—Nikol'skoe—Stish' (all locales, except for Stish', were within the Central Front); from the left (with the Voronezh Front's 38th Army): Staryi Oskol—Dezhovka—Verkhnii Reutets—Lokinskaya—Korenevo station—Bruski (all locales, except for Staryi Oskol were within the Central Front). The overall length of the front was 306 kilometers.

In adopting the decision to defend, the *front* commander believed that the likely axes of the enemy's attack might be as follows:

1. Zmievka—Droskovo—Livny;
2. Glazunovka—Shtyri—Zolotukhino—Kursk;
3. Kromy—Fatezh—Kursk.

3 Editor's note. Editor's note. Konstantin Konstantinovich Rokossovskii (1896-1968) served in the Russian imperial army and joined the Red Army in 1918. Rokossovskii was arrested in 1937, but managed to survive and return to the army in 1940. During the Great Patriotic War he commanded a mechanized corps and an army, as well as several *fronts*, including the Second Belorussian Front from late 1944. Following the war, Rokossovskii commanded the northern group of Soviet forces and served several years a Polish defense minister. Upon his return to the USSR, he commanded a military district and held posts in the central military apparatus.

4 Editor's note. Nikolai Fedorovich Vatutin (1901-44) joined the Red Army in 1920. During the Great Patriotic War he served as chief of the General Staff's operational directorate, deputy chief of staff and a *Stavka* representative. From 1942 he commanded a number of *fronts* along the southwestern strategic direction. He died from wounds received in a partisan attack.

The second of these axes was considered the most likely for the enemy's main attack.

Based on this, the *front* commander believed that the *front's* right wing was the most important defensive sector. The main forces and equipment were concentrated here.

By the beginning of July 1943 the disposition of the *front's* forces was as follows:

There were five armies in the *front's* first echelon—48th, 13th, 70th, 65th, and 60th.

This echelon included 41 rifle divisions, four rifle brigades, two tank brigades, 15 independent tank regiments, 27 field artillery regiments from the High Command Reserve, six regiments of self-propelled artillery, two heavy artillery brigades, three anti-tank artillery brigades, six independent anti-tank artillery regiments, three independent guards mortar brigades, nine independent guards mortar regiments, one independent guards mortar battalion, 16 army mortar regiments, and five battalions of anti-tank rifles.

The *front* reserve included the 2nd Tank Army and the 9th and 19th tank corps.

The *front* reserve included 13 tank brigades, two motorized-rifle brigades, two heavy-caliber artillery brigades, one cannon artillery brigade, three anti-tank artillery brigades, four independent anti-tank artillery regiments, one mortar brigade, and six army mortar regiments.

The *front's* activities were to be supported from the air by the 16th Air Army,[5] which by the start of combat included 455 fighters, 241 *Shturmoviks*,[6] 260 daylight and 74 night bombers, and four reconnaissance aircraft: or more than 1,000 combat-ready planes.

The 48th Army, along with reinforcements, was defending a sector of the front between the following boundary lines: from the right: the *front* boundary line; to the left: Droskovo—Stepanishchevo—Verkhnyaya Gnilusha—2nd Five-Year Plan (all points within the 48th Army). The army's overall front was 38 kilometers.

Three rifle divisions defended in the army's first echelon;[7] the remaining four divisions[8] constituted the second echelon and occupied the second defensive zone. The 2nd Anti-Tank Brigade, which was in the army reserve, was concentrating in the Vorovo—Vyazovoi area. Three tank regiments were deployed behind the army's left flank between the second and rear army defensive zones. The army headquarters was located in the village of Perekhozhee.

48th Army's Strength

Combat Arm	Number of Formations and Units	Name of Formations and Units
Rifle Troops	7 rifle divisions	73rd, 143rd, 137th, and 170th rifle divisions; 4th Rifle Corps (16th Latvian, 399th and 202nd rifle divisions)
Tank Troops	3 tank regiments	45th, 193rd and 299th independent tank regiments
Artillery	1 cannon artillery regiment	1168th Army Cannon Artillery Regiment
	3 self-propelled artillery regiments	1434th, 1456th and 1540th self-propelled artillery regiments
	1 anti-tank artillery brigade	2nd Anti-Tank Artillery Brigade (449th, 1323rd and 1329th anti-tank artillery regiments
	1 anti-tank artillery regiment	220th Guards Army Anti-Tank Artillery Regiment
Mortar Units	1 mortar regiment	479th Army Mortar Regiment

5 The air army included the 3rd and 6th bomber corps, and the 6th Night and 5th Fighter corps.

6 Editor's note. *Shturmovik* was the popular name for the Il-2 dive bomber, which first entered service in 1941 and quickly became one of the most popular aircraft of the war. The aircraft carried a two-man crew and had a top speed of 414 kilometers per hour. One version was armed with two 23mm cannons, two 7.62mm machine guns, and a single 12.7mm machine gun. The aircraft could carry up to 600 kilograms of bombs and several rockets.

7 73rd, 143rd and 16th Latvian rifle divisions.

8 137th, 170th, 399th, and 202nd rifle divisions.

The 13th Army, along with reinforcements, occupied the most important sector of the front and was defending a sector about 32 kilometers in breadth, bordered on the right by the boundary line with the 48th Army, and on the left by the boundary line Zubarevka—Vozy—Teploe—Podolyan'—Tagino (all locales, except for Teploe and Tagino were within the 13th Army).

Four rifle divisions were defending in the army's first echelon;[9] the remaining eight rifle divisions occupied the second defensive zone (three rifle divisions),[10] the army rear zone (three rifle divisions,[11] and part of the first *front* line (two rifle divisions).[12]

The 129th Tank Brigade and five tank regiments, which were reinforcing the army, were deployed along the rear army line.

The army's artillery reinforcement was mainly achieved by employing the 4th Artillery Corps, consisting of the 5th and 12th artillery divisions.

13th Army's Strength

Combat Arm	Number of Formations and Units	Name of Formations and Units
Rifle Troops	12 rifle divisions	15th Rifle Corps (8th, 148th and 74th rifle divisions); 29th Rifle Corps (81st, 15th and 307th rifle divisions); 18th Guards Rifle Corps (2nd, 3rd and 4th guards airborne divisions); 17th Guards Rifle Corps (6th, 70th and 75th guards rifle divisions)
Tank Troops	1 tank brigade	129th Tank Brigade
	5 tank regiments	27th, 30th, 43rd, 68th, and 237th guards tank regiments
Artillery	6 artillery regiments	540th, 768th, 697th, 700th, 1007th, and 1214th light artillery regiments
	5 cannon artillery regiments	19th Guards, 642nd, 753rd, 125th, and 155th cannon Artillery regiments
	6 howitzer regiments	208th, 393rd, 876th, 469th, 539th, and 872nd howitzer regiments
	3 self-propelled artillery regiments	1441st, 1442nd and 1541st self-propelled artillery regiments
	1 anti-tank artillery regiment	374th Army Anti-Tank Artillery Regiment
	2 heavy artillery brigades	86th and 89th heavy howitzer brigades
Mortar Units	3 guards mortar brigades	16th, 22nd and 23rd guards mortar brigades
	5 guards mortar regiments	6th, 37th, 65th, 86th, and 324th guards mortar regiments
	8 mortar regiments	106th, 124th, 139th, 208th, 224th, 232nd, 476th, and 477th army mortar regiments

The 70th Army, with reinforcements, was defending a sector 62 kilometers in length, bordered on the right by the boundary with the 13th Army, and from the left by the line 1st Vorob'evka—Shmarnaya—Mikhailovka—Razvet'e—Bryantsevo—Rublino (all locales, except for 1st Vorob'evka were within the 70th Army).

9 8th, 148th, 81st, and 15th rifle divisions.
10 71st, 307th and 6th Guards rifle divisions.
11 2nd, 3rd and 4th guards airborne rifle divisions (18th Guards Rifle Corps).
12 70th and 76th guards rifle divisions.

Four rifle divisions[13] were defending in the army's first echelon, while the remaining four[14] occupied the second defensive zone. Three tank regiments of reinforcements were grouped behind the army's right flank along the second defensive zone. The army's headquarters was in the woods north of Radogoshcha.

70th Army's Strength

Combat Arm	Number of Formations and Units	Name of Formations and Units
Rifle Troops	8 rifle divisions	28th Rifle Corps (280th, 211th and 132nd rifle divisions); 19th Rifle Corps (116th, 102nd and 162nd rifle divisions); 175th and 140th rifle divisions
Tank Troops	3 tank regiments	240th, 25th and 259th tank regiments
Artillery	3 artillery regiments	200th, 206th and 167th light artillery regiments
	2 cannon artillery regiments	201st and 205th cannon artillery regiments
	3 howitzer regiments	169th, 203rd and 399th howitzer regiments
	1 anti-tank artillery regiment	378th Army Anti-Tank Artillery Regiment
	1 anti-tank brigade	3rd Independent Anti-Tank Artillery Brigade/2nd Anti-Tank Artillery Division
Mortar Units	2 guards mortar regiments	84th and 92nd guard mortar regiments
	1 mortar regiment	136th Army Mortar Regiment

The 65th Army, with reinforcements, was defending a sector bordered on the right by the 70th Army and on the left by the boundary line Kursk—Bol'shaya Gorodykova—Selino—Rashkovichi (all locales, except for Kursk, were within the 65th Army). The overall length of the army's front was 82 kilometers.

Six rifle divisions and a single rifle brigade[15] were defending in the army's first echelon. The remaining three rifle divisions[16] occupied the second defensive zone. The tank regiments were grouped behind the army's right flank between the second and rear army defensive zones. The army headquarters was in the village of Snizha.

65th Army's Strength

Combat Arm	Number of Formations and Units	Name of Formations and Units
Rifle Troops	9 rifle divisions	18th Rifle Corps (149th, 246th and 69th rifle divisions); 27th Rifle Corps (193rd and 60th rifle divisions, and the 115th Rifle Brigade); 37th Guards Rifle Corps (114th, 334th and 181st rifle divisions)
Tank Troops	4 tank regiments	40th, 84th, 255th, and 29th guards tank regiments
Artillery	2 anti-tank artillery regiments	543rd and 120th anti-tank artillery regiments
Mortar Units	1 guards mortar regiment	94th Guards Mortar Regiment
	2 mortar regiments	143rd and 478th army mortar regiments

13 280th, 211th, 106th, and 102nd rifle divisions.

14 132nd, 175th, 140th, and 162nd rifle divisions.

15 149th, 246th, 69th, 194th, 334th, and 193rd rifle divisions, and the 115th Rifle Brigade.

16 37th Guards, 181st and 60th rifle divisions.

The 60th Army was defending a 92-kilometer sector along a front bordered on the right by the boundary with the 65th Army, and on the left by the *front* boundary.

Three rifle divisions and two rifle brigades were defending in the army's first echelon.[17] Two rifle divisions and one rifle brigade[18] made up the second army echelon and were disposed as follows: one rifle division was in the Vasil'evskoe area, one rifle brigade in the Skovorodnevo area, and one rifle division in the Iznosovka—Blagodatnoe area. Along the boundary with the Voronezh Front, the 14th Anti-Tank and 130th Tank brigades were in the Zhuravlya—Kremyannovo—Pogrebki area. Army headquarters was in the town of L'gov.

60th Army's Strength

Combat Arm	Number of Formations and Units	Name of Formations and Units
Rifle Troops	5 rifle divisions 3 rifle brigades	24th Rifle Corps (112th Rifle Division, 42nd and 129th rifle brigades); 30th Rifle Corps (121st, 141st and 322nd rifle divisions); 55th Rifle Division and 248th Rifle Brigade
Tank Troops	1 tank brigade	150th Tank Brigade
Artillery	1 cannon artillery regiment	1156th Cannon Artillery Regiment
	1 anti-tank artillery regiment	1178th Anti-Tank Artillery Regiment
	1 anti-tank artillery brigade	14th Anti-Tank Artillery Brigade
Mortar Units	1 guards mortar regiment	98th Guards Mortar Regiment
	1 guards mortar battalion	286th Independent Guards Mortar Battalion
	3 mortar regiments	128th, 138th and 497th army mortar regiments

Part of the *front's* reserves were concentrating behind the right flank of the 13th Army in the Verkhnyaya Sosna—Pokrovka area (13th Anti-Tank and 68th Cannon Artillery brigades), with the main mass in the Kursk area and to the north.

The 2nd Tank Army (3rd and 16th tank corps),[19] the 11th Guards Tank Brigade, two anti-tank artillery regiments,[20] two mortar regiments,[21] and an anti-aircraft artillery regiment[22] were concentrated in the Vereitinovo—Banino—Konevo area. Headquarters was in Skorodnoe.

The 19th Tank Corps (19th, 101st and 202nd tank brigades) was located in the area Lobazh—Staryi Buzets.

The 9th Tank Corps (23rd, 95th and 108th tank and 8th motorized-rifle brigades) was located in the Tsvetovo area.

The 2nd Anti-Tank Division's 4th Anti-Tank Brigade and the 100th and 104th heavy caliber artillery brigades[23] were concentrating in the Kursk area, and the 1st Anti-Tank Brigade in the Vereitinovo area.

On the whole, the Central Front's main forces and equipment were grouped along the axis of the presumed enemy main attack; that is, in the 13th Army's sector.

17 112th, 322nd and 141st rifle divisions; 42nd and 248th rifle brigades.
18 55th and 121st rifle divisions and the 129th Rifle Brigade.
19 The 3rd Tank Corps consisted of the 51st, 103rd and 50th tank and 15th motorized brigades; the 16th Tank Corps consisted of the 107th, 164th and 109th tank brigades.
20 130th and 563rd anti-tank artillery regiments.
21 236th and 234th army mortar regiments.
22 121st Anti-Airraft Artillery Regiment.
23 From the 4th Artillery Corps.

Out of an overall number of 41 rifle divisions in the *front's* first echelon, 12 were in the 13th Army. If, on the average, along the entire front there was a rifle division for every 7.5 kilometers, in the 13th Army each rifle division occupied a front of only 2.7 kilometers (including the divisions located in the depth of the army's defense).

Of the 68 reinforcement artillery regiments[24] in the *front* 25, regiments (37 percent) were attached to the 13th Army.

Of the two independent tank brigades and 15 tank regiments at the disposal of the *front*, one tank brigade (50 percent) and five tank regiments (33 percent) were to reinforce the 13th Army.

Of 22 mortar regiments, eight (37 percent) formed part of the 13th Army.

Of nine guards mortar regiments and three mortar brigades, five regiments (55 percent) and all three brigades formed part of the 13th Army.

The defense's degree of saturation of fire from field anti-tank artillery in the area of the presumed main German attack is clear from the next table.

The maximum depth of the defense occupied by the troops of the 13th Army was 30 kilometers.

The main attack and anti-tank weapons, which comprised the *front* reserve (tank formations and units, as well as anti-tank brigades), were grouped in two areas: one part (main) was located in the Verkhnyaya Sosna—Berezovets—Pokrovka area; the other part in the Banino—Nikol'skoe—Lyubazh area. Thus, in the event of an enemy offensive along the Ponyri—Zolotukhino—Kursk axis, we had the ability to launch attacks against both flanks of the attacking enemy group of forces, without complex preliminary maneuvers.

The Central Front's headquarters was deployed in the area of the town of Svoboda.

The Central Front's Artillery Strength

Weapon	Central Front (306 km)		13th Army (32 km)	
	Absolute number of tubes[1]	Per kilometer of front	Absolute number of tubes[2]	Per kilometer of front
All calibers of field artillery (including 76mm field guns)	3,312	10.4	1,537	48.4
All calibers of anti-tank guns, including the rifle units' small-caliber artillery	2,400	7.3	776	24.3
Mortars of all calibers	8,606	24.8	2,245	70

Table Note:

1 Counting all the artillery and mortars subordinated to the *front*.

2 Counting the artillery and mortars subordinated to the 13th Army, as well as the *front* reserve.

The plan, drawn up by the Central Front staff, in case of enemy attack, foresaw the activities of the *front's* forces unfolding according to three variants.

The first variant was that the enemy would launch his main attack along the front of the 48th Army along the Zmievka—Droskovo—Livny axis.

In this case, the task of the *front's* armies was as follows:

The 48th Army was to hold the army rear zone with all its forces.

24 Including field and anti-tank artillery.

The 13th Army, with the forces of the 18th Guards Rifle Corps (2nd, 3rd and 4th guards airborne divisions) and the 2nd Tank Army's 3rd Tank Corps, would launch a counterblow from the morning of the second or third day of the operation from the Verkhnyaya Sosna—Ivan'—Andreevka area in the direction of Alekseevka and, having defeated, in conjunction with the 48th Army and the 16th Air Army, the attacking enemy group of forces, would restore the position along the 48th Army's front.

The 13th Anti-Tank Brigade would be moved up to the 48th Army's rear defensive zone and there, in the Fedorovka area, would reinforce the anti-tank defense.

The 16th Air Army would launch a massive blow with bomber and air assault aviation against the main attacking German group of forces. On the second day of the operation our fighter aviation, from 0500 to 2000, would cover the 18th Guards Rifle and 3rd Tank corps in their jumping-off areas, as well as during their counterblow.

In the second variant, the enemy would launch his main attack along the front of the 13th Army in the direction of Ponyri, Zolotukhino and Kursk.

According to this variant, the 13th Army, in the event of an enemy breakthrough of the main defensive zone, was to firmly hold the second defensive zone, and from the morning of the second or third day of the operation, having occupied the Maloarkhangel'sk—Ostrov—Ponyri line with the 18th and 17th (75th and 70th guards rifle divisions) guards rifle corps, was to go over to a decisive counteroffensive with all its forces in the general direction of Krivye Verkhi and Boranovskii Lozovets.

Simultaneously with the 13th Army, the 48th Army's left-flank divisions would attack in the general direction of Zmievka, and the 70th Army's right-flank divisions in the general direction of Kromy.

On the night of the second day the 2nd Tank Army would concentrate as follows: 3rd Tank Corps in the Berezovets—Gorodishche area; the 16th Tank Corps toward Ol'khovatka, and; the 11th Guards Tank Brigade toward Vozy. On the morning of the operation's second or third day the army was to go over to a decisive offensive in the general direction of Krivye Verkhi and Boranovskii Lozovets and, in conjunction with the 13th Army and 16th Air Army, would fall upon the attacking enemy group of forces in the Ponyri—Arkhangel'skoe area.

Before the start of our counteroffensive, the 16th Air Army would launch a night bomber attack against the enemy's headquarters and communications centers to disrupt his command and control; bomber and air assault aviation would support the counterblow by the 16th and 3rd tank corps; attacks by bombers and *Shturmoviks* would prevent the arrival of enemy reserves, while fighter aviation would cover the main forces of the 13th and 2nd Tank armies from 0500 to 2000 on the second (or third) day of the operation.

In the third variant the enemy would launch his main attack along the 70th Army's front in the direction of Fatezh and Kursk. According to this variant, the 70th Army, in case of an enemy breakthrough of the main defensive zone, was to firmly hold the second defensive zone and from the morning of the operation's second or third day attack in the general direction of Trosna.

The 13th Army, with the forces of the 17th Guards Rifle and 16th Tank corps, as well as the 2nd Tank Army, would launch a counterblow on the operation's second or third day from the line Gorodishche—Khmelevoi in the general direction of Nikol'skoe and Malakhovo and, in conjunction with the 70th Army, destroy the German group of forces, thus restoring the situation along the 70th Army's front. With the attack by the 17th Guards Rifle and 16th Tank corps, the 16th Air Army would launch a bomber and assault air attack against the main group of attacking enemy tanks; from 0500 to 2000 on the operation's second or third day, fighter aviation would cover the 17th Guards Rifle and 16th Tank corps in their jumping-off positions and during the counteroffensive.

The decision by the commander of the Voronezh Front. The disposition and tasks of the front's forces

The Voronezh Front had the task of defending the Kursk salient in the sector between the following boundary lines: from the right (with the Central Front's 60th Army) Staryi Oskol—Dezhovka—Verkhnii Reutets—Lokinskaya station—Korenevo station—Bruski (all locales, except for Staryi Oskol, were within the Voronezh Front); from the south (with the Southwestern Front's 57th Army) Volokonovka—Volchansk—Khar'kov (all locales within the Voronezh Front). The overall length of the defensive front was 244 kilometers.

In adopting his decision for defense, the *front* commander considered the following axes as most likely for the enemy's attack: a) Belgorod—Oboyan'; b) Belgorod—Korocha, and; c) Volchansk—Novyi Oskol. Based upon this, the *front's* left wing was defined as the most important sector.

By the beginning of July 1943 the disposition of the Voronezh Front's forces was as follows.

The *front's* first echelon consisted of four armies: 38th, 40th, 6th Guards (formerly the 21st Army), and the 7th Guards (formerly the 64th Army).

There were 27 rifle divisions, six tank brigades, three independent tank regiments, 15 High Command Reserve field artillery regiments, three self-propelled artillery regiments, five anti-tank artillery brigades, 22 independent anti-tank artillery regiments, eight guards mortar regiments, nine army mortar regiments, 16 battalions of anti-tank rifles, and three independent armored train battalions in the first *front* echelon.

The *front* reserve contained the 69th and 1st Tank armies, the 35th Guards Rifle and 2nd and 5th guards tank corps. The *front* reserve contained eight rifle divisions, 14 tank brigades, three motorized-infantry brigades, three mechanized brigades, two independent tank regiments, three howitzer regiments (including two heavy-caliber howitzer regiments), one anti-tank artillery brigade, nine independent anti-tank artillery regiments, three guards mortar regiments, one guards mortar battalion, seven army mortar regiments, and 11 battalions of anti-tank rifles.

The *front's* operations were to be supported from the air by the 2nd Air Army, which contained the following units: 3rd and 4th fighter, 1st Assault Air, and 1st and 2nd bomber corps, the 291st Assault Air and 208th Night Air divisions, and the 454th Bomber and 50th Reconnaissance regiments. In all, by the start of the fighting the army numbered 389 fighters, 276 *Shturmoviks*, 172 day and 34 night bombers, and ten reconnaissance aircraft, for a total of 881 combat-ready aircraft.

The 38th Army was defending the sector of the front between the following boundary lines: from the right the boundary line between the *fronts*, and from the left Pavlovka—Belaya—Zabuzhevka—Krasnopol'e—Boromlya (all locales, except Zabuzhevka were in the 38th Army's zone). The overall length of the army's front was 80 kilometers.

Five rifle divisions[25] defended in the army's first echelon; one rifle division[26] comprised the second echelon and was located in the army's rear defensive zone in the Sudzha area. The 29th Independent Anti-Tank Brigade was in the army's reserve and was concentrated in the Belovody—Yunakovka area. The tank formations were located as follows: 180th Tank Brigade behind the army's center, ten kilometers southwest of Sudzha, and; the 192nd Tank Brigade behind the junction of the 38th and 40th armies, in the Preobrazhenskoe area.

The army headquarters was located in the village of Ulanka.

25 240th, 180th, 167th, 340th, and 232rd rifle divisions.
26 204th Rifle Division.

38th Army's Strength

Combat Arm	Number of Formations and Units	Name of Formations and Units
Rifle Troops	6 rifle divisions	51st Rifle Corps (240th, 180th and 204th rifle divisions); 50th Rifle Corps (167th, 340th and 232nd rifle divisions)
Tank Troops	2 tank brigades	180th and 192nd tank brigades
	1 tank regiment	an independent breakthrough tank regiment
	3 anti-tank rifle battalions	124th, 125th and 126th independent anti-tank rifle battalions
Artillery	1 cannon artillery regiment	112th Guards Cannon Artillery Regiment
	1 howitzer regiment	111th Howitzer Regiment
	1 anti-tank artillery brigade	29th Independent Anti-Tank Artillery Brigade
	4 anti-tank artillery regiments	222nd, 483rd, 1658th, and 1660th anti-tank artillery regiments
Mortar Units	1 guards mortar regiment	66th Red Banner Guards Mortar Regiment
	1 guards mortar battalion	441st Independent Guards Mortar Battalion
	2 mortar regiments	491st and 492nd army mortar regiments

The 40th Army was defending the sector of the front bordered on the right by the boundary line with the 38th Army and on the left by the line Ivnya—Melovoe—Sumovskaya station—Khotmyzhsk (all locales, except for Sumovskaya station were within the 40th Army). The length of the army's front was 50 kilometers.

Four rifle divisions[27] were defending in the army's first echelon, while two rifle divisions[28] comprised the army's second echelon and were located in the second defensive zone: one rifle division[29] occupied the switch position Shmyrevo—excluding Melovoe. The 32nd Independent Anti-Tank Brigade (the army reserve) was located in Rakitnoe, near the junction of the 40th and 6th Guards (formerly the 21st) armies.

The tank units were concentrated as follows: 86th Tank Brigade behind the army's center in the Seleznevka area, with one of the tank regiments in the Mokrushino area and the other in the Zinaidino area.

Army headquarters was located in the village of Mokrushino.

27 217th, 206th, 219th, and 100th rifle divisions.

28 161st and 309th rifle divisions.

29 184th Rifle Division.

40th Army's Strength

Combat Arm	Number of Formations and Units	Name of Formations and Units
Rifle Troops	7 rifle divisions	47th Rifle Corps (237th, 206th and 161st rifle divisions); 52nd Rifle Corps (100th, 309th and 184th rifle divisions); 219th Rifle Division
Tank Troops	1 tank brigade	86th Tank Brigade
	2 tank regiments	69th and 60th tank regiments
	3 anti-tank rifle battalions	127th, 128th and 129th anti-tank rifle battalions
Artillery	3 cannon artillery regiments	76th Guards, 453rd and 1001st cannon artillery regiments
	2 howitzer regiments	805th and 839th howitzer regiments
	1 anti-tank artillery brigade	32nd Independent Anti-Tank Artillery Brigade (1850th, 1852nd and 1854th anti-tank artillery regiments)
	6 anti-tank artillery regiments	4th Guards, 869th, 1663rd, 1664th, 1244th, and 12th anti-tank artillery regiments
Mortar Units	1 guards mortar regiment	36th Guards Mortar Regiment
	4 mortar regiments	9th, 10th, 493rd, and 494th army mortar regiments

The 6th Guards (formerly 21st) Army was defending a sector bordered on the right by the boundary line with the 40th Army, and on the left by the line Mikhailovka—Nechaevo—Sheina—Belgorod (all locales, except for Nechaevo and Sheina were in the 6th Guards Army). The overall length of the army's front was 64 kilometers.

Four rifle divisions[30] defended in the army's first echelon; three rifle divisions[31] occupied the second defensive zone.

The 27th and 28th anti-tank brigades, as well as the 49th Tank Brigade (3rd Mechanized Corps), which constituted the army commander's reserve, were concentrated behind the army's center behind the second defensive zone in the Sukho-Solotino area. The army's tank units occupied the following areas: 96th Tank Brigade: the defensive line Dal'nyaya Igumenka—Blizhnyaya Igumenka, behind the junction of the 6th and 7th guards armies; two tank regiments were in the areas of Lukhanevo and Bykovka, behind the main defensive zone.

The army headquarters was in Kochetovka.

6th Guards Army's Strength

Combat Arm	Number of Formations and Units	Name of Formations and Units
Rifle Troops	7 rifle divisions	22nd Guards Rifle Corps (71st, 67th and 90th guards rifle divisions); 23rd Guards Rifle Corps (51st and 52nd guards and 375th rifle divisions); 89th Guards Rifle Division
Tank Troops	1 tank brigade	96th Tank Brigade
	2 tank regiments	230th and 245th tank regiments
	5 anti-tank rifle battalions	133rd, 134th, 135th, 136th, and 137th anti-tank rifle battalions

30 71st, 67th and 52nd guards, and 375th rifle divisions.
31 90th, 51st and 89th guards rifle divisions.

Combat Arm	Number of Formations and Units	Name of Formations and Units
Artillery	5 cannon artillery regiments	628th, 93rd, 142nd, 159th, and 163rd cannon artillery regiments
	1 self-propelled artillery regiment	1440th Self-Propelled Artillery Regiment
	2 anti-tank artillery brigades	27th and 28th independent anti-tank artillery brigades (1837th, 1839th, 1841st, 1838th, 1840th, and 1841st anti-tank artillery regiments
	8 anti-tank artillery regiments	611th, 694th, 493rd, 496th, 868th, 1666th, 1667th, and 1240th anti-tank artillery regiments
Mortar Units	4 guards mortar regiments	5th Red Banner, 16th, 314th, and 316th guards mortar regiments
	2 mortar regiments	263rd and 295th army mortar regiments
	1 battalion of armored trains	60th Independent Armored Train Battalion

The 7th Guards (formerly the 64th) Army was defending a sector of front bordered on the right by the boundary with the 6th Guards Army, and on the left with the *front's* boundary line. The length of the army's front was 50 kilometers.

Four rifle divisions[32] were defending along the army's first echelon; three rifle divisions[33] occupied the second defensive zone.

The 30th Independent Anti-Tank Artillery Brigade was concentrated behind the army's center in the Starikovo—Kupino area. The tank formations and units were located as follows: 27th Guards Tank Brigade in the Nezhegol' area; the 201st Tank Brigade and a tank regiment behind the junction of the *fronts* in the Yefremovka area; another tank regiment in the Blizhnyaya Igumenka area, and; the third in the Belovskaya area.

The army headquarters was in Starikovo.

7th Guards Army Army's Strength

Combat Arm	Number of Formations and Units	Name of Formations and Units
Rifle Troops	7 rifle divisions	25th Guards Rifle Corps (81st, 78th and 73rd guards rifle divisions); 24th Guards Rifle Corps (72nd, 36th and 15th guards rifle divisions); 213th Rifle Division
Tank Troops	2 tank brigades	27th Guards and 201st tank brigades
	3 tank regiments	148th, 167th and 262nd tank regiments
	5 anti-tank rifle battalions	1st, 2nd, 3rd, 4th, and 5th anti-tank rifle battalions
Artillery	3 cannon artillery regiments	109th, 161st and 265th cannon artillery regiments
	2 self-propelled artillery regiments	1431st and 1529th self-propelled artillery regiments
	1 anti-tank artillery brigade	30th Independent Anti-Tank Artillery Brigade
	4 anti-tank artillery regiments	114th, 115th guards, 1669th and 1670th anti-tank artillery regiments
Mortar Units	2 guards mortar regiments	97th and 315th guards mortar regiments
	1 mortar regiment	290th Army Mortar Regiment
	2 armored train battalions	34th and 38th independent armored train battalions

32 81st, 78th, 72nd, and 36th guards rifle divisions.
33 73rd Guards, 213th and 15th Guards rifle divisions.

The *front's* reserves were located as follows: all of the 69th Army's[34] five divisions occupied the army rear zone along the sector Ol'khovatka—Yefremovka; the army's headquarters was in Korocha.

The 35th Guards Rifle Corps[35] occupied the first *front* defensive zone along the sector Krivosheevka—Stolbishche.

The 1st Tank Army consisted of the 6th Tank,[36] 31st Tank[37] and 3rd Mechanized[38] corps, three anti-tank artillery[39] and two mortar[40] regiments, and one guards mortar regiment and a guards mortar battalion.[41] The army was concentrating in the Belaya—Kurasovka—Vykolov area, behind the center of the Voronezh Front. Army headquarters was in the woods two kilometers northeast of Potopakhino.

The 5th Guards Tank Corps[42] was located in the Marino area, and the 2nd Guards Tank Corps[43] was in the Korocha area.

Besides this, there were in the *front* reserve three artillery regiments,[44] five independent anti-tank artillery regiments,[45] two guards mortar regiments,[46] four mortar regiments,[47] and eight independent anti-tank rifle battalions.[48]

The 31st Anti-Tank Artillery Brigade, which was also part of the *front* reserve, was in the Korocha area.

In evaluating the overall disposition of the Voronezh Front's forces, the following circumstance should be taken into account.

1. At the same time that on the Central Front the defensive depth along the axis of the assumed enemy's main attack was being created from the 13th Army's resources, on the Voronezh Front this was done using the *front* reserves—the 69th Army and the 35th Guards Rifle Corps, which were occupying defensive lines along the axes of the enemy's likely attacks. Thus in determining the operational and tactical defensive densities on the Voronezh Front, it is necessary to take into account the forces and weapons of the 69th Army and the 35th Guards Rifle Corps.
2. The front of the likely enemy attacks along the Voronezh Front was significantly broader than on the Central Front, where it was limited only to the 13th Army's sector; here it included the defensive zones of two armies—6th and 7th guards—and reached 114 kilometers (46 percent of the overall frontage).

---

34 48th Rifle Corps (183rd, 305th and 107th rifle divisions), 111th and 270th rifle divisions, 496th Mortar Regiment, 1661st Anti-Tank Artillery Regiment, and the 13th, 131st and 132nd anti-tank rifle battalions.
35 93rd, 92nd and 94th guards rifle divisions.
36 22nd, 112th and 200th tank and 6th Motorized Rifle brigades.
37 100th, 237th and 242nd tank brigades.
38 1st, 3rd and 10th mechanized, 1st Guards and 49th tank brigades.
39 35th, 538th and 1008th anti-tank artillery regiments.
40 265th and 270th army mortar regiments.
41 79th Guards Mortar Regiment and the 405th Independent Guards Mortar Battalion.
42 20th, 21st and 22nd guards tank and 6th Guards Motorized Rifle brigades, and the 48th Independent Guards Heavy Tank Regiment.
43 4th, 25th and 26th guards tank and 4th Guards Motorized Rifle brigades, and the 47th Independent Guards Heavy Tank Regiment.
44 1528th Howitzer and the 522nd and 1148th heavy-caliber howitzer regiments.
45 1076th, 1689th, 1177th, 1207th, and 1212th independent anti-tank artillery regiments.
46 80th and 309th guards mortar regiments.
47 189th, 201st, 204th, and 206th army mortar regiments.
48 138th, 139th, 140th, 141st, 142nd, 121st, 122nd, and 123rd independent anti-tank rifle battalions.

Of 35 rifle divisions in the *front*, 22 occupied defensive positions along the axes of the likely enemy attack. If, on the average, each rifle division occupied a front of ten kilometers in width, this was only 5.2 kilometers along the axes of the main attack.

Of 70 reinforcement artillery regiments, 44 (63 percent) were employed in the 6th and 7th guards armies' sectors; that is, along the axes of the assumed enemy attacks.

Half of the tank units (out of six tank brigades and ten tank regiments) were employed for reinforcing the 6th and 7th guards armies.

Eight guards mortar regiments (73 percent) out of 11 were designated for operations in the two armies' sectors.

The degree of saturation with field and anti-tank artillery, as well as mortars, is evident from the following table:

The Voronezh Front's Artillery Strength

Weapon	Voronezh Front (244 km)		6th and 7th guards armies (114 km)	
	Absolute number of tubes[1]	Per kilometer of front	Absolute number of tubes[2]	Per kilometer of front
All calibers of field Artillery (including 76mm field guns)	2,513	10.3	1,724	14.2
All calibers of anti-tank guns, including the rifle units' small-caliber artillery	1,776	7.2	1,000	8.8
Mortars of all calibers	6,618	27.0	3,542	31.0

Note:

1 Counting all the artillery and mortars subordinated to the *front*.

2 Counting the artillery and mortars of the 6th and 7th guards and 69th armies, the 35th Guards Rifle Corps, and those units at the disposal of the *front* commander.

Along the threatened sector of the front, it was not possible to create a significant tactical density. We had to increase the defense's resilience by maximally increasing its depth, which in the case at hand was done to a depth of 60 kilometers; four defensive lines were occupied by the forces of the first *front* echelon and the *front* reserves (69th Army and the 35th Guards Rifle Corps).

In the depth of the front along these axes were concentrated the *front's* main mobile shock weapons: the 1st Tank Army, 5th and 2nd guards tank corps, and other units, for an overall total of 14 tank brigades, three mechanized brigades, 3 motorized rifle brigades, 11 anti-tank artillery regiments, eight battalions of anti-tank rifles, 66 army mortar regiments, and three guards mortar regiments.

The Voronezh Front's headquarters was first deployed in Bobryshevo, and was then moved to Rzhava.

Based on the three main axes of the enemy's expected attacks, the order of employing the *front* reserves was as follows:

1. In case of an enemy attack from the Tomarovka—Belgorod area in the general direction of Oboyan', the enemy group of forces that broke through the main defensive zone was to be attacked by: the 1st Tank Army from the Oboyan' area in the general direction of Voznesenovka and Belgorod; the 5th Guards Tank Corps from the Vyshnyaya Ol'shanka area in the general direction of Belgorod; the 2nd Guards Tank Corps from the Bekhteevka area in the general direction

of Gostishchevo, and; by formations of the 69th Army from the Aleksandrovka area in the general direction of Pokrovka.

2. Should the enemy launch his attack from the Belgorod area in the general direction of Korocha, his group of forces must be attacked by: 1st Tank Army from the Oboyan' area in the general direction of Korocha; the 5th Guards Tank Corps from the Vyshnyaya Ol'shanka area toward Korocha; the 2nd Guards Tank Corps from the Bekhteevka area toward Belgorod, and; formations of the 69th Army from the Alekseevka area toward Belgorod.
3. Given an enemy attack from the Murom—Ternovaya area in the general direction of Volchansk and Volokonovka against the juncture of the Voronezh and Southwestern fronts, his group of forces should be attacked by: the 5th Guards Tank Corps from the Vyshnyaya Ol'shanka area in the general direction of Korocha and Volchansk; 2nd Guards Tank Corps from the Bekhteevka area toward Volchansk, and; formations of the 69th Army from the Alekseevka area toward Volchansk.

Aside from these main axes, the possibility was considered that the enemy might attack from the Sumy area in the general direction of Sudzha and Kursk, as well as from the Stanovoe area in the general direction of Rakitnoe and Oboyan', against the juncture of the 40th and 6th Guards armies. The possibility of a simultaneous enemy offensive along two of these axes was also foreseen.

In the first case, the enemy would be counterattacked by the 1st Tank Army and the 5th Guards Tank Corps from the Oboyan' area in the general direction of Sudzha; in the second case, by the 1st Tank Army from the Oboyan' area toward Rakitnoe.

The disposition and tasks of the strategic reserves

By the end of April the formation of the Reserve Front (from 13 April, the Steppe Military District) had been completed.

By 8 May the *Stavka* of the Supreme High Command possessed information that the enemy might launch his offensive during 10-12 May along the Orel—Kursk or Belgorod—Oboyan' axes, or along both axes simultaneously. In order to strongly reinforce the defense of the Kursk salient and securely cover the Kursk and Voronezh axes, the *Stavka* on that day ordered the forces of the Steppe Military District to occupy by 10-12 May the defensive line Rossoshnoe—Belyi Kolodez' (which partially runs along the eastern bank of the Kshen' River). The overall length of the line was about 250 kilometers. At the same time, these forces were given the assignment of preparing counterattacks in the general directions of Maloarkhangel'sk, Kursk and Oboyan'.

On the basis of these instructions the line along the eastern bank of the Kshen' River was occupied by 16 May by the 27th, 53rd and 5th Guards (formerly the 66th) armies of the Steppe Front (Steppe Military District). Immediately upon arriving at this line, the *front's* (district's) troops began to carry out defensive works.

By the beginning of the German offensive, on 4 July 1943 the disposition and composition of the Steppe Front was as follows.

The *front's* three armies (27th, 53rd and 5th Guards) occupied the defensive line Rossoshnoe—Kruty—Korotysh—the eastern bank of the Kshen' River—Krestishche—Rogoztsy—Nikolaeva—Maslovka—Belyi Kolodez'.

The 27th Army[49] along the line Rossoshnoe—Nikol'skoe;

The 53rd Army[50] along the line excluding Nikol'skoe—Prilepy;

49 155th, 147th, 241st, 163rd, 166th, and 71st rifle divisions and the 93rd Tank Brigade.

50 84th, 252nd, 214th, 233rd, 116th, 293rd, and 28th guards rifle divisions and the 1st Mechanized Corps.

The 5th Guards Army[51] along the line excluding Prilepy—Belyi Kolodez';

The 47th Army[52] was concentrated in the area Ol'khovatka—Krivonogovka—Kamenka;

The 4th Guards Kantemirovka Tank Corps was located in the Staraya Veduga area;

The 10th Tank Corps was in the Staryi Oskol area.

The 5th Guards Tank Army[53] was concentrated as follows: 29th Tank Corps in the woods west of Ostrogozhsk; 5th Guards Zimovniki Mechanized Corps in the Kamenka area, and; the 18th Tank Corps in the Nikolaevka area. The 3rd Guards Stalingrad Mechanized Corps was in the Kuzmenkov area.

The cavalry formations were located as follows: 7th Guards Cavalry Corps in the Belogor'e—Pavlovsk area; 3rd Guards Cavalry Corps in the Staraya Kalitva—Novaya Kalitva area and; the 5th Guards Cavalry Corps in the area of Novo-Markovka—Kirovo—Nikol'skoe.

In the event of the *front's* (district's) forces being committed into the battle, they were to be supported by the 5th Air Army.

51 13th, 66th, 97th, 95th, and 42nd guards rifle, and the 6th and 9th guards airborne divisions.

52 29th, 30th, 38th, 337th, and 23rd rifle divisions.

53 29th Tank, 5th Guards Zimovniki Mechanized and 18th Tank corps.

2

The Preparation of the Defense

The Preparation of the Central and Voronezh Fronts' Defensive Lines

The overall course of defensive works

The systematic preparation of the Kursk salient's defense by the forces of the Central and Voronezh fronts began in April 1943 and continued until 5 July; that is, to the start of the German offensive. Throughout this entire period the defense was developed and improved.

The "Instructions on the Reconnaissance and Construction of Field Defensive Lines," of 27 April 1943, which had been drawn up by the chief of the Red Army's engineering troops, Colonel General (now Marshal of Engineering Troops) Vorob'ev[1] and confirmed by the chief of the Red Army General Staff, Marshal of the Soviet Union Vasilevskii,[2] lay at the heart of the construction of the defensive lines. These instructions laid out the basic principles of organizing modern field defenses. The manual paid particular attention to the organization of anti-tank defense, the construction of battalion defensive areas and company centers of resistance as the bases of each defensive line, to the broad development of a trench system and communications trenches as measures that would maximally facilitate maneuver by fire and personnel, to the maximum employment of the terrain in the interests of organizing powerful and easily controlled fire in front of the forward edge and in the defensive depth, with the broad employment of the advantages of flanking and oblique fire.

Detailed plans for the engineering support of the defense were drawn up by the *fronts'* engineering directorates.

The key question of all these directives and combat orders by the *front* staffs was the idea of organizing a firm, deeply-echeloned field defense, with the maximum development of engineering structures throughout the entire operational depth. The defense was to be constructed in order to withstand the pressure of large tank groups of forces.

The defensive depth, which at first was calculated at five defensive lines, was defined at 120-130 kilometers. During the course of further preparation it was increased along certain axes to 150-190 kilometers, by creating yet another (third *front*) defensive line.

1 Editor's note. Mikhail Petrovich Vorob'ev (1896-1957) was drafted into the Russian imperial army in 1916 and joined the Red Army in 1918. During the Great Patriotic War he commanded a sapper army and from 1942 until the end of the war he served as chief of the Red Army's engineering troops. Vorob'ev continued in this position until 1952, when he was mysteriously reduced in status, and he continued to serve in a lesser capacity until his death.

2 Editor's note. Aleksandr Mikhailovich Vasilevskii (1895-1977) served in the Russian imperial army and joined the Red Army in 1919. During the Great Patriotic War Vasilevskii served in the General Staff apparatus and was appointed chief of staff in 1942, and in 1945 was made a member of the *Stavka* of the Supreme High Command. Vasilevskii also served as the *Stavka* representative to a number of *fronts*, charged with coordinating their activities. In 1945 he commanded the Third Belorussian Front and was commander-in-chief of Soviet Forces in the Far East, where he supervised the Soviet invasion of Manchuria and Korea. Following the war, Vasilevskii again served as chief of staff and minister of the armed forces.

The *front* commanders demanded that the troops occupy not only the first and second defensive lines, but the rear lines as well. This, for example, is what the commander of the Voronezh Front did. On 31 March 1943 he ordered the troops to occupy not only the main defensive zone, but also the second and rear army zones.

In all their directives, the *front* commands emphasized that the basis of the forthcoming operation must be active defense, with the possibility not only to launch counterblows, but to go over to a counteroffensive as well. Thus, powerful reserves were to be created in both the *fronts* and armies. The commander of the Voronezh Front (combat order no. 0093), for example, demanded that the army commanders "possess powerful shock groups for carrying out counterblows and going over to a counteroffensive."

The advantages of such a defensive method were displayed with full clarity as early as the battle of Stalingrad in defending the southern face of the Stalingrad perimeter along the 64th and 57th armies' sectors. These principles subsequently became mandatory for organizing the defense.

In three months of preparation (April-June) the forces of the Central and Voronezh fronts outfitted six main defensive lines, as well as several intermediate and switch lines. Thus the most important axes were intersected by 6-7 defensive lines, the length of which by the start of the operation is shown below:

Main defensive zone—550 kilometers
Second defensive zone—640 kilometers
Rear army zone—540 kilometers
First *front* line—300 kilometers
Second *front* line—310 kilometers
Third *front* line—310 kilometers
Total—2,590 kilometers

Moreover, intermediate lines and switch positions were constructed stretching hundreds of kilometers. However, as it later became clear, an insufficient number of switch positions were constructed; there was a shortage of these positions in the confines of the Central Front's main and second defensive zones, as well as along the sectors of the Voronezh Front's 6th Guards and right flank of the 7th Guards armies. The absence of switch positions along the right flank of the 7th Guards Army enabled the enemy that broke through from the Belgorod area to subsequently launch an attack to the north in the flank of the 6th Guards Army.

The construction of the main defensive zone was carried out by military units; for work on the second and rear army zones, besides the military, the civilian population was also drawn in. *Front* lines were constructed by the Directorate for Defensive Construction (UOS).

First of all, defensive structures were erected that enabled us to organize a fire system and the distribution of combat formations along the defensive lines occupied by the troops (rifle trenches, trenches with the main and reserve rifle and machine gun positions, earth and timber pillboxes, and firing positions for the mortars and artillery, etc.), and troop control (command posts and observation posts). Along the most important axes and the approaches to the forward edge and in the depth of the main defensive zone, anti-tank and anti-personnel obstacles and mine fields were established; specially laid cross-country routes of march and tread roads secured the troop rear's normal work.

Secondly, defensive structures were built in the depth of the defense, trenches and communications trenches were improved, as well as firing positions for the artillery and mortars, while communications trenches were developed in depth and along the front, and shelters and dugouts were built.

In three months a great deal of work was done for the engineering reinforcement of both the army and *front* lines. Here are some figures that illustrate this.

The Central Front's forces dug up to 5,000 kilometers of trenches and communications trenches, laid about 400,000 mines and land mines; 112 kilometers of wire obstacles, of which 10.7 kilometers were electrified, were built along the 13th and 70th armies' sectors, as well as more than 170,000 mines laid. The Voronezh Front dug 4,240 kilometers of trenches and communications trenches, laid more than 600,000 mines, and built up to 500 kilometers of anti-tank obstacles, while the amount of rifle and machine gun trenches reached 60,000.

The zone, which had been prepared for defense along the Central Front's sector, was 190 kilometers wide, and 130 kilometers along the Voronezh Front. The most important inhabited locales in the fortified zone, in accordance with the *Stavka* directive of 21 April 1943, were configured for defense. Bridges were prepared for demolition. The destruction of several inhabited locales along the most important axes was also foreseen, for the purpose of creating operational obstacles.

Thus by the start of the German offensive the defensive zone represented a serious obstacle, with the appropriate development of field fortifications. In the engineering sense, the defense was prepared throughout the entire depth. Thanks to this, during the defensive fighting the troops were able to carry out any kind of maneuver and always find on the ground support for a firm defense, as well as for going over to a counterattack. By 5 July the main part of the defensive works had been carried out from 80-100 percent. The plan was over fulfilled by 120-35 percent as concerns such types of work as the construction of machine gun trenches, earth and timber pillboxes, and command and observation posts.

The preparation of defensive lines was carried out at an increasing rate, and was especially fruitful in May and June. The greatest share of defensive work was carried out in these months: 82 percent for trenches and communications trenches, 70 percent for earth and timber pillboxes, and 90 percent for laying mines. Mining was particularly intensive during these months. On some days up to 6,000-8,000 mines were laid in the 6th and 7th guards armies.

The *front* commanders devoted special attention to the creation of a firm and resilient defense along the most likely axes of an enemy offensive. Along the Central Front's sector these axes were as follows: a) Orel—Kursk (along the railroad); b) Kromy—Fatezh. Along the Voronezh Front's sector they were: a) Tomarovka—Oboyan'—Kursk; b) Belgorod—Korocha, and; c) Volchansk—Novyi Oskol. The most likely axes were considered Orel—Kursk and Belgorod—Kursk, which were defended by the forces of the 13th and 6th Guards armies, respectively.

In organizing the defensive work along these most important axes, the *front* commands mainly concentrated on the creation of a firm and effective anti-tank defense. The necessity of such a defense during the preparation process became more obvious, because it was namely along these axes that the enemy was concentrating his tanks. It was clear that the Germans were preparing their main blow here, which is why particular attention was paid to the defensive sectors of the 6th Guards and 13th armies. This is also clear from a simple comparison of numerical data.

Of the overall number of 10,643 anti-tank mines and 104 kilometers of anti-tank obstacles, which were laid in April in the Voronezh Front's sector, 4,500 and 48 kilometers of these (about 50 percent of all mines and anti-tank obstacles) were in the 6th Guards Army's sector. The Central Front's 13th Army was also taken care of in the engineering sense. By July 50,755 mines had been laid in its sector, while at the same time the 65th Army counted only 13,000.

The likely axes of the enemy's attacks were reinforced by erecting additional intermediate lines before Kursk in the Central Front's sector, and before Oboyan' in the Voronezh Front's sector, as well as through the appropriate configuration of the *front* lines and the location of the *front* reserves. It was for this purpose that the 6th Guards and 13th armies received more anti-tank weapons (artillery and anti-tank rifles).

Along with the preparation of defensive zones, in accordance with *Stavka* directive no. 1706663 and its special instructions of 27 April 1942, the removal of the civilian population from the immediate 25-kilometer front zone was also carried out. A similar measure, which was first carried out in accordance with the *Stavka's* orders, in the summer of 1942, justified itself as a method that allowed the troops to fully take advantage of the inhabited locales in a defensive battle and broadly engage in maneuver. Besides this, it was an effective method of combating enemy espionage.

The course and quality of the defensive works was systematically controlled by the *Stavka* of the Supreme High Command, the General Staff, and the *front* commands. Mistakes were uncovered in a timely manner and immediately eliminated.

The troops' readiness for carrying out their forthcoming tasks was simultaneously checked. In three months the staff of the Voronezh Front carried out an inspection of all the armies three times: in the second half of April, at the end of May, and in the middle of June. The inspection included a large number of units and formations. For example, in May a battalion in each regiment was checked along the Voronezh Front. The Central Front's staff organized a special commission, headed by a member of the military council; the commission's task was the control over the organization of the defense in all the formations and units, down to and including the battalion level. Surveys of the defense and the system of organizing rifle fire in the companies, and even in platoons, were carried out; army commissions carried out this work.

The results of these inspections were transmitted to the troops through special orders for each army separately. The orders laid out in detail the shortcomings uncovered and issued instructions for eliminating them.

Among the most characteristic shortcomings found in the organization of the defense were:

- not everywhere was the forward edge of the main defensive zone selected successfully; its shape along certain sectors was unsatisfactory from the point of view of locating weapons and the organization of control of the battle;
- the linear character of the defense, the frontal siting of firing structures, and the poor development of flanking and oblique fire;
- the low saturation of fire in the zone in front of the forward edge (3-4 bullets per minutes for one linear meter of front);
- the poor cover of units' boundaries, particularly in the defensive depth;
- the lack of correspondence, in certain cases, of the depth and width of trenches and communications trenches to field manual requirements, the poor configuration of trenches and communications trenches for firing and carrying out counterattacks, all of which limited the maneuver of men and weapons;
- a certain slighting of the development of engineering obstacles, which were primarily built in front of the forward edge, in the defensive depth;
- the poor masking of defensive structures, which enabled the enemy to discover the character of our defense;
- the absence of sufficient fire cover of the minefields and engineering obstacles along some sectors.

The course of the defensive works was a subject of particular concern and attention of both the *Stavka* of the Supreme High Command and the *front* commands.

The *Stavka* representatives—the Deputy Supreme Commander-in-Chief, Marshal of the Soviet Union Zhukov, and the chief of the General Staff, Marshal of the Soviet Union Vasilevskii, exercised direct control on the spot, systematically travelling to the troops of the Central and Voronezh fronts. In acquainting themselves there with the course of the work and the defensive construction down to the organization of a fire system along the forward edge, and checking the troops' combat readiness, they would immediately and on the spot eliminate these or other shortcomings and abnormalities. All of this significantly sped up the completion of the defensive work and the troops' combat readiness.

We see the same kind of concrete leadership on the part of the *front* commands. The military councils undertook regular trips to see the troops. Reports by division commanders on the course of defensive work were usually heard along with reports by the chiefs of the engineering service and artillery. Shortcomings in the organization of the defense were corrected immediately. The necessary help to the lower-level commanders and staffs was on a daily basis.

Alongside all of this, General Staff officers and specially assigned representatives from the central directorates controlled the defensive preparations of the Kursk salient.

The main part of the detected shortcomings and organization of the defense was eliminated by the start of July through the common efforts of the command and staffs at all levels. We managed to achieve fire densities in front of the forward edge of 8-10 bullets per minute per linear meter of front, and to create in the main defensive zone along the most important axes 3-4 lines of trenches and to cover the tank-endangered axes with minefields, with a density of from 1,600 to 2,500 mines per kilometer of front. On the average, there were up to 25 earth and wooden pillboxes per rifle battalion.

A firm and deeply echeloned defense, with a highly developed network of field structures, covered the Kursk salient. Such a defense could withstand the most powerful attacks by the enemy's tanks and infantry.

Features of the main defensive zone

The main defensive zone of the Central and Voronezh fronts represented an enormous bulge, 550 kilometers long and 5-6 kilometers wide. At its base, the bulge was traversed by the Orel—Belgorod railroad, while the salient part of the bulge ran near the line Sevsk—Ryl'sk—Sumy. The terrain in this zone is somewhat broken, but basically open. There are a few wooded expanses: a) along the Bryantsevo—Kuban' sector, occupied by the right flank of the 65th Army; b) along the line Alekseevka—Krasnopol'e, where the left flank of the 38th Army was defending; the Banishche area, which entered the 60th Army's zone, and; in the Shebekino area in the 7th Guards Army's territory.

The terrain was favorable to the organization of a defense. The relief along the majority of sectors of the defensive front of the Kursk salient sloped down toward the enemy, and only some sectors proved the exception: for example, on the territory of the 7th Guards and 70th armies the terrain on the enemy's side towered above our main defensive zone.

The forward edge of the main defensive zone, which had arisen by the end of the March fighting, ran along the heights and lacked any significant natural lines of cover. Only along the Voronezh Front's left flank, the Belgorod—Volchansk sector of the 7th Guards Army's defense was protected by the Severskii Donets River. The forward edge of the defense ran mostly along the slopes facing the enemy. The twisting shape of the forward edge was employed to create "pockets of fire" and for the organization of flanking and oblique fire.

There was combat security in front of the forward edge only along the 6th Guards Army's front and partially along the 38th Army's right flank. Along the remainder of the front the main defensive zone immediately bordered on the enemy's line and was guarded by field guards and patrols.

The main defensive zone consisted of battalion defensive areas, anti-tank strong points (PTOP) and a system of engineering obstacles.

A battalion defensive zone occupied a front of 2-2.5 kilometers, with a depth of 0.8-1.0 kilometers. Company and platoon strong points were created in the battalion areas. Two to three battalion defensive areas, located in one or two echelons, formed a regimental sector, the width of which reached 4-5 kilometers, with a depth of 3-4 kilometers.

In all, there were more than 350 battalion defensive areas in the main defensive zone of both *fronts*.

There were 37 battalion areas in the 6th Guards Army's main defensive zone; each of these consisted of a system of rifle trenches, machine gun and gun earth and wooden pillboxes, overhead covers, trenches and communications trenches, engineering obstacles and obstructions. On the average, there were in such an area 42 rifle trenches, 38 anti-tank rifle trenches, 40 artillery trenches, 47 mortar trenches, 55 machine gun trenches, nine earth and wooden pillboxes,[3] 8.3 kilometers of trenches and communications trenches, 2,000 anti-tank mines, 1,840 anti-personnel mines, 3.3 kilometers of wire obstacles, and two kilometers of anti-tank obstacles.

In the Voronezh Front's main defense zone about 100 anti-tank strong points had been outfitted; on the average, there was a strong point for every 2.5 kilometers of front. An anti-tank strong point was a powerful fire fist, consisting predominantly of artillery weapons. Besides this, it also included anti-tank rifles, automatic riflemen and, in some cases, even tanks. The terrain was augmented by engineering structures, mine obstacles and obstructions.

Anti-tank ditches, post obstacles, escarpments, tank traps, wire obstacles, booby-traps, mines, rolling barrages, bottle and mine fields, flooded lowlands, and brides, dams and buildings prepared for demolition formed part of the system of engineering obstacles.

By the start of the German offensive the main defensive works along the main defensive zone had been completely finished. During this time 30,673 rifle and machine gun trenches had been dug, 10,049 anti-tank trenches, and 2,593 kilometers of trenches and communications trenches, 4,983 command and observation posts and 604 anti-tank obstacles built, 434,667 anti-tank mines laid, and about 700 kilometers of wire obstacles built.

It was on the Voronezh Front that flame mines (MOF)[4] of bottles with a flammable mixture were first employed by making "fields" out of them similar to minefields. Such flammable bottle fields, which stretched from 200 to 2,000 meters along the front and, to a depth of 80 meters, were part of an overall system of anti-tank and anti-personnel obstacles. Within these fields the mines were located in chessboard order. By the start of the defensive operation the overall length of the flame mine fields (MOF) was 47.6 linear kilometers; overall, up to 300,000 bottles with a flammable mixture were employed. The greatest saturation of these fields was along the 6th and 7th guards armies' sectors.

The flame minefields completely justified themselves during the course of the defensive battle. Their effect was great, not only against the infantry, but against tanks as well. For example, in the area of Kreida station, in the 7th Guards Army's defensive sector, eight enemy tanks burned up on the flame minefields. For the entire period of the defense the enemy lost more than 70 tanks on the flame minefields laid by the Voronezh Front.

On the average, for every kilometer in the main defensive zone there were: 0.65 battalion areas, about 1,600 anti-tank and anti-personnel mines,, 1.2 kilometers of wire obstacles, 25.7 rifle trenches, 18.2 anti-tank trenches, about 30 machine gun trenches, 4.7 kilometers of trenches and communications trenches, 1.1 kilometers of anti-tank obstacles (minus the mine fields), and nine command and observation posts.

Along the most important axes the density of defensive structures was significantly higher. An example of this is the defensive zone of the 7th Guards Army's 81st Guards Rifle Division. Here, along its left flank, in the area of the village of Mikhailovka, the enemy managed to retain a

3 Earth and wooden pillboxes, as a rule, were of the light variety; they protected only against shrapnel and the impact of 75mm shells.

4 A flame mine consists of a case with 19 flammable bottles, in the center of which was a mine with a diminished charge, or a TNT explosive. A slight pressure on the top of the case and the mine blows up, breaking open the bottles, and the flammable mixture ignites.

bridgehead along the eastern bank of the Severskii Donets. The command of the 7th Guards Army was ordered to gird this bridgehead with such a defense as the enemy would not be able to use it as a jumping-off place for an offensive from the Belgorod area to the east and northeast. The army successfully carried out this task. The 81st Guards Rifle Division's defensive zone was endowed with such firmness, from both the front and flanks, that the enemy was not able to break through from the Mikhailovka bridgehead, either on 5 or 6 July. The defensive density in the divisions' sector is illustrated by the following indices. Per kilometer of front there were: 28 rifle trenches, 38 machine gun trenches, 16 machine gun anti-shrapnel nests, 6.6 earth and wood pillboxes, 20 artillery trenches, 22 anti-shrapnel artillery nests, 54 shelters, 2.6 kilometers of wire obstacles, 2,133 anti-tank mines, and 2,126 anti-personnel mines.

Of the two fronts occupying the Kursk salient, the greatest density of defensive structures in the main defensive zone was created along the Voronezh Front's sector. This is clear from the following table.

Trenches, which were the basis of the location of our troops and the organization of the infantry's fire system, were particularly developed in the main defensive zone. As a rule, 2-3 lines of trenches were located along the front, connected between themselves with communications trenches (on the average of 5-6 per kilometers of front, which amounted to 2-3 communications trenches per company defensive area). Four, and in some places five[5] trench lines were constructed along the most important axes. The distance between them was, on the average: 100-150 meters between the first and second lines, 200-250 meters between the second and third, and 150-200 meters between the third and fourth.

Thus the trench network completely embraced the depth of the company defensive areas, intersecting them along the front and in depth with 2-4 lines.

The first line of trenches was usually occupied by automatic riflemen and tank destroyers. The infantry's heavy weapons were located in the second trench line, where the main mass of structures had been prepared for them. The heavy weaponry's location in the second line significantly increased the defense's tenacity.

The Fronts' Density of Defensive Measures

Front	Per Kilometer of Front						
	Anti-Tank Mines	Anti-Personnel Mines	Wire Obstacles (per km)	Anti-Tank Rifle Trenches	Machine Gun Trenches	Mortar Trenches	Artillery Trenches
Central	680	450	1.0	13.5	22.5	16	8.8
Voronezh	923	1,120	1.5	22.1	35	37	15

The construction, within the trenches, of shelters, such as slit trenches, recess trenches, and covers under the breastworks, was widely practiced.

A thick network of trenches and communications trenches eased the creation of a firm and stable fire system, and enabled us to maneuver weapons and personnel along the front and in depth during the battle. Besides this, the troops using the trenches had the opportunity of easily avoiding massed fire onslaughts by the enemy's artillery and aviation.

On the average, each rifle division defending in the main defensive sector had 66 kilometers of trenches and communications trenches. In the Voronezh Front's 6th Guards Army's divisions their

5 The Voronezh Front's 6th Guards Army and the Central Front's 13th Army.

overall length exceeded 70 kilometers. The construction of trenches was closely connected with the establishment of engineering obstacles. Great firmness was imparted to the defense by the location of wire obstacles, minefields and anti-tank obstacles; they were situated not only in front of the first trench line, but also in the defensive depth.

Features of the second and rear (third) army defensive zones

The second defensive zone, at 540 kilometers in length, and the rear army zone, at 580 kilometers, represented lines completely prepared for defense, consisting of rifle, machine gun, mortar, and artillery trenches, trenches, communications trenches, artillery anti-tank strong points and a number of switch positions. On the average, the second zone was 10-15 kilometers from the main one; on some sectors of the front, depending on the terrain, this distance rose to 20-25 kilometers. Along the main axes both zones, according to the number of defensive structures, differed little from each other. We can see this by comparing the zones along the 6th Guards Army's front.

The Number of Defensive Structures in the Sixth Guards Army's Defensive Zones

	Rifle Trenches	Anti-TankRifle Trenches	Machine Gun Trenches	Wood and Earth Pillboxes	Trenches and Communications Trenches (in km)
Main Defensive Zone	1,478	1,344	1,920	327	290
Second Defensive Zone	1,333	1,120	1,540	207	249

However, the second zone was significantly inferior to the main one in the density of engineeing obstacles. If the main zone in the 6th Guards Army contained 69,688 mines, there were only 20,200 in the second; at the same that 64,340 anti-personnel mines had been planted in the main zone, there were only 9,097 in the second zone.

The average density of defensive structures in the second defensive zone was as follows:

The Fronts' Density of Defensive Structures in the Second Defensive Zone

Front	Per Kilometer of Front						
	Anti-Tank Mines	Anti-Personnel Mines	Rifle Trenches	Anti-Tank Rifle Trenches	Machine Gun Trenches	Artillery Trenches	Trenches and Communications Trenches (in km)
Central	–	–	20	8.6	11	7	2.7
Voronezh	170	74	24	16	9	8.4	2.8

The troops occupied the second defensive zone, as a rule, along its entire length, with a solid front along the main axes, while only the most dangerous sectors were occupied along the secondary axes. For example, in the 38th Army's main zone there were five divisions, with two brigades (anti-tank artillery and tank) in the second zone, covering Sudzha. Along the 60th Army's front of more than 90 kilometers, there was only one division in the second zone, which was covering the L'gov axis. In the 70th Army there were four divisions each in the first and second zones. In the 40th Army four rifle divisions occupied the first zone, with two occupying the second. In the 6th and 7th guards and 13th armies there were four divisions apiece in the first zone, and three apiece in the second.

The army rear zone ran at a distance of 20-40 kilometers from the front edge of the main zone and, along some sectors, in the interests of employing the advantages of terrain, it was moved to the depth as far back as 35 kilometers, and in places even 45 kilometers. The forward edge of the second zone was, on the average, 10-25 kilometers from the rear zone; only along the 60th Army's sector did they nearly touch one another. Natural lines, such as the Psel, Svala and other rivers were used in constructing the rear zone at a significant distance.

In the rear army zone the troops were deployed only along the operationally important axes in the 13th Army's sector, where three rifle divisions had been concentrated, and on the Voronezh Front's left flank (in the 6th and 7th guards armies' sectors), where five rifle divisions were located. It was in this zone that the main part of the *front* reserves were being concentrated: the Central Front's 16th and 19th tank corps, and the Voronezh Front's 1st Tank Army. The army rear zone was most fully prepared along the Voronezh Front's sector. In the *front's* 6th Guards, 38th and 40th armies, aside from the main line, there was also an intermediate line and a series of switch positions, one of which was along the sector Shmyreva—excluding Melovoe, was occupied by our troops.

The overall length of the Voronezh Front's army rear zone was 384 kilometers, of which 164 consisted of switch positions.

The density of the defensive structures in the army rear zone is visible from the following table.

The Voronezh Front's rear army zone exceeded that of the second defensive zone in the density of structures, which is explained by the presence there of a significant number of switch positions.

The Density of Defensive Structures in the Fronts' Army Rear Zone

Front	Per Kilometer of Front					
	Rifle Trenches	Anti-Tank Rifle Trenches	Machine Gun Trenches	Artillery Trenches	Mortar Trenches	Trenches and Communications Trenches (in km)
Central	13	8	11	3.3	5.1	2.3
Voronezh	32	28	13	10	35	4

In all, during the three-month preparatory period, in the Kursk salient's second and rear army defensive zones, the following were built and outfitted: 21,136 rifle trenches, 16,048 anti-tank rifle trenches, 14,092 trenches for heavy machine guns, 7,575 artillery trenches, 20,221 mortar trenches, 4,350 command and observation posts, and 3,399 kilometers of trenches and communications trenches.

Features of the *fronts'* lines

On the Kursk salient's territory three *front* lines were outfitted, which formed a zone 40-75 kilometers in width and 300 kilometers in length. The first *front* line, the right flank of which touched the center of the 13th Army's rear line in the area of Novaya Slobodka, was 50-100 kilometers from the main defense zone and 20-30 kilometers from the army rear zone; along the Central Front's central sector this distance increased and reached 60-65 kilometers. This line was prepared not only in the engineering sense, but a large part of it was directly occupied by troops; such was the case along the line's flanks: along the right flank from Novaya Slobodka to Anakhino (22 kilometers southwest of Kursk) and along the left flank from Kondrovka to Bogdanovka. Besides this, the second echelons of the *front* reserves were located along this line.

The second *front* defensive line was 300 kilometers long and consisted of three sectors: two of them connected the first and third *front* lines, thus forming switch positions north and south of Kursk; the third sector—the southern part of the second defensive line—ran along the Seim and Oskol rivers.

The third *front* line was outfitted along the eastern banks of the Tim, Seim and Oskol rivers. Moreover, obstacles had been constructed in the areas of Kursk, Staryi Oskol and Novyi Oskol.

By the start of the German offensive the main part of the defensive works had been completed or was being wrapped up. For example, along the Voronezh Front's sector, machine gun and mortar trenches, trenches for anti-tank rifles, and trenches and communications trenches had been dug, and command and observation posts outfitted. Remaining unfinished was work on building wood and earth pillboxes, anti-tank ditches and artillery trenches. Nevertheless, the volume of the work accomplished proved to be quite significant; along only three of the Voronezh Front's lines there had been constructed 7,418 rifle trenches, 5,148 anti-tank rifle trenches, 13,545 machine gun trenches, 6,394 artillery and mortar trenches, and 1,541 kilometers of trenches and communications trenches.

Thus, by the beginning of July the forces of the Central and Voronezh fronts had constructed six defensive lines and a series of switch positions. This enabled them to carry out any kind of maneuver and always find support in the prepared terrain, both for defense as well as going over to a counterattack.

The Kursk salient was girded with a secure defensive zone with an average depth of 60-100 kilometers; its greatest depth reached 190 kilometers. The entire zone was prepared in the engineering sense. The number of structures along both *fronts'* three army lines reached the following: 39,600 rifle trenches, 20,095 anti-tank rifle trenches, 32,753 mortar trenches, 14,244 artillery trenches, 37,024 machine gun trenches, 4,992 kilometers of trenches and communications trenches, and 503,063 anti-tank and 439,348 anti-personnel mines were laid.

The Armies' Organization, the Units' Combat Formation, and Boundary Security

The armies' organization

The disposition of the armies defending the Kursk salient arose from the demand for organizing a firm, deep and resilient defense, capable of not only withstanding the massed attacks by enemy tanks and infantry, but also to secure the complete defeat of the enemy in the subsequent offensive operations.

The Central and Voronezh fronts' armies, as a rule, were deployed in two echelons. Those armies defending the most important axes had a three-echelon formation. An example of the latter is the 13th Army's formation on the Central Front. Its first echelon consisted of four rifle divisions, with powerful artillery reinforcement; the second consisted of three rifle divisions and three tank regiments, while the third consisted of five rifle divisions, two tank regiments, and a tank brigade.

The Voronezh Front's 40th Army also had a three-echelon deployment, but only a single rifle division was located in its third echelon.

The 6th Guards Army, which was defending the decisive Belgorod—Kursk axis, along the Voronezh Front, had only two echelons. The *front* command created a third echelon along this axis with its reserves. The 69th Army was concentrated in the 6th and 7th guards armies' rear army zone. In defending, it was simultaneously covering two of the main likely axes of the enemy attack: Belgorod—Kursk and Belgorod—Korocha.

Thus all three echelons of the army defensive zones of both *fronts* were occupied by troops along the most important axes.

The armies' first echelons along the most important axes consisted of rifle divisions, plentifully supplied with artillery; usually all of the reinforcement artillery worked for the first echelon. For example, the 6th Guards Army's first echelon included eight anti-tank artillery regiments (out of 14) and four guards mortar regiments. In the 13th Army the first-echelon forces had 520 field guns. The 40th Army's first echelon included ten reinforcement artillery regiments (out of 14). Reinforcement field artillery, which mainly supported the first-echelon divisions, had firing positions in the depth of the main defensive zone.

Tanks were not attached to the first echelon. The exceptions were the 6th and 7th guards armies. Their first echelons included tanks: two tank regiments and a tank brigade in the 6th Guards and one tank regiment in the 7th Guards armies.

In all, there were in both *fronts'* first army echelons 37 rifle divisions, three rifle brigades, three tank regiments, and one tank brigade. The first echelons occupied the main defensive zone.

The second army echelons consisted of rifle units, artillery and tanks. As opposed to the first echelons, there were significantly fewer artillery and mortar weapons, and so the second echelons were inferior to the first in firepower. However, they were superior to the first echelons in shock force, because the main part of the tank troops were part of the second echelons. According to the number of infantry, the second echelons along the main axes differed little from the first echelons. The 6th Guards Army had in its first echelons four rifle divisions and three in the second, while the 70th Army had four divisions in each echelon. The number of rifle divisions in the second echelon was twice as less as in the first along the secondary axes.

The second echelons were sharply different according to their makeup and strength. The most powerful of these were located along the Central Front's right flank and along the Voronezh Front's left flank, while the less powerful ones were at the tip of the Kursk salient.

For example, the 48th Army, which was defending the highly important Orel—Maloarkhangel'sk axis, had in its second echelon four rifle divisions, three tank regiments and one anti-tank artillery brigade; the 70th Army, which was covering the Fatezh axis also had four rifle divisions and three tank regiments in its first echelon. At the same time, the second echelon of the 38th Army, which was defending the tip of the Kursk salient, consisted only of one rifle division, two tank brigades and an anti-tank artillery brigade.

The tasks of the second echelons along the front's different sectors varied. For example, the second echelons of the 6th Guards, 48th and 13th armies, which were occupying the second zone, were to firmly defend it along its entire length, while the second-echelon divisions occupied almost the same front as the first-echelon divisions. At the same time, the 60th Army's first echelon, which consisted of two rifle divisions, a rifle brigade, a tank and an anti-tank artillery brigades, which were deployed separately from each other along a front of nearly 100 kilometers and along different defensive lines (along the second and rear army zones) had the mission of covering only the most important axes in the army's zone.

The formations of the 65th Army's second echelon were deployed in the second defensive zone: one rifle division with a tank regiment along the right flank, and one rifle division with two tank regiments behind the center, and one rifle division with a tank regiment behind the left flank. The second echelon's overall front was more than 60 kilometers. Part of the second echelon had the task of covering the most important axes—along the flanks and the boundaries of the army defensive zone.

An army's second echelons, as a rule, were located in the second defensive zone. Their distance from the forward edge of the main zone was determined by the configuration of the second defense zone. Along the Central Front's sector the distance of the second echelons from the forward edge of the main defensive zone varied from six kilometers (along the 13th Army's front) to 20 kilometers (along the 65th and 60th armies fronts); along the Voronezh Front's sector the second echelons were, on the average, 8-12 kilometers from the forward edge of the main defensive zone.

On the 60th and 38th armies' fronts the second echelons were partially located in the second defensive zone and partially in the rear zone. Their distance from the front line reached 20-25 kilometers.

In all, there were 25 rifle divisions, one rifle brigade, six tank brigades, 17 tank regiments, and seven anti-tank artillery brigades in the second echelons of both *fronts'* sectors.

Only two armies had third echelons: the 13th Army had here five rifle divisions, two tank regiments, and a tank brigade, while the 40th Army had one rifle division in its third echelon.

The distribution of forces between the first, second and third army echelons along both *fronts*, in percentage terms, is clear from the following table.

The Distribution of Forces in the Armies' Echelons

Echelon	Rifle Divisions %	RifleBrigades %	Tank Regiments %	TankBrigades %	Anti-TankArtillery Brigades %
First	54.1	75	14	12.5	–
Second	37	25	77	75	100
Third	8.6	–	9	12.5	–

The units' combat formations

The rifle divisions, which were defending along a normal front, had a two-echelon formation: the first echelon contained two rifle regiments and the second echelon one. In the divisions defending along a 12-kilometer or greater front, the single-echelon formation was practiced. In this case, as a rule, the division commander retained a rifle battalion and part of the anti-tank weapons as a reserve.

Typical was the formation of the 6th Guards Army's divisions. Here, of seven rifle divisions, six, including four rifle divisions occupying the main defensive zone, had a single-echelon formation. The absence of second echelons in the rifle divisions occupying the main defensive zone was compensated for, to a certain extent, by the attachment of two tank regiments and a tank brigade to these divisions, as well as the overall greater depth of the defense.

In the 13th Army all four rifle divisions located in the main defensive zone were deployed in two echelons.

The depth of the divisions' combat formations deepened as the defense was being prepared. For example, in April all of the 40th Army's first-echelon rifle divisions had a single-echelon formation; by June of two rifle divisions already consisted of two echelons. The 100th Rifle Division, by extending its rifle regiments' defensive front, was able to pull back two battalions to its second echelon.

The divisions' first-echelon rifle regiments occupied a 5-7 kilometer front. The second-echelon regiments, which occupied a 6-8 kilometer front, were located 3-5 kilometers from the forward edge of the main defensive zone, and in certain cases 6-8 kilometers. The regiments' and battalions' combat formations were also organized into one or two echelons, depending upon the width of the defensive front and the importance of the axis.

The 13th Army was distinguished by the echelonment of its combat formation, in general, and of its regiments and battalions in particular. In this army the echelonment of combat formations often began at the company level. The platoons of the companies' second echelons were deployed in individual trenches from behind and were linked by communications trenches with the first line of trenches. The companies of the second-echelon battalions occupied the second line of trenches, while the battalions of the regiments' second echelons occupied the third line of trenches.

In the 6th Guards Army the rifle battalions' combat formations also had a two-echelon organization: in the first echelon two companies were each located along an 800-1,000 meter front, with one company in the second echelon along a front up to 1,000 meters. The distance between the echelons varied from 300-500 meters and depended on the terrain relief.

Alongside this, the combat formations of some of the divisions' first-echelon rifle regiments were organized in a single echelon. In this case, the division's second-echelon regiments were located no more than 4-5 kilometers from the forward edge of the main defensive zone.

The combat formation of the 40th Army's 219th Rifle Division was organized according to this principle.

The combat orders of the Central and Voronezh fronts' units and formations during the defense of the Kursk salient were distinguished by the deep echeloning of forces. All the armies had a two-echelon formation and, in the armies defending along the most important axes, there were third echelons as well. The second and third echelons, which swallowed up up to half of all the infantry and the main part of the tanks at the armies' disposal, and also up to 20-25 percent of the artillery, represented a serious force.

Securing the boundaries

In accordance with the instructions of the *Stavka* of the Supreme High Command, the staffs of the Voronezh and Central fronts carried out a great deal of important work for securing their boundaries during the preparatory period. In the plan for organizing cooperation of the troops, which had been drawn up by the *front* staff, the formations responsible for the boundary were indicated, a system of artillery and rifle fire was foreseen, as was the axis of counterattacks by formations located along the boundary, as well as measures for organizing engineering-mining obstacles, and cooperation signals, etc.

Specially delegated commissions observed the fulfillment of the plan for securing the boundaries between the *fronts* and armies and for cooperation between them. The *front*-level commissions were designated by order of the *front* commander, while those at the army level were designated by the army commanders and confirmed by the *front* commander. The commissions were usually headed by one of the *front* commander's deputies (*front* level) or the army commander (army level). The commissions were made up of representatives of the staffs of all the combat arms—officers and generals of artillery, tank troops, aviation, engineering troops, anti-aircraft defense, and others.

The commissions' work was conducted constantly among the troops. Along with the commanders of the formations and units, who had the tasks of securing the boundary on the ground, they marked the forward edge of the defense, the subsequent lines, and switch positions, the locations of the reserves, artillery, guards mortar units, and the tasks of the reinforcements. At this time particular attention was paid to the creation of interlocking fire, the location of minefields, and engineering and anti-tank obstacles. Upon completion of the work, the commission would draw up a survey, to which was attached a map showing the location of the units and a listing of their tasks, an engineer-mine obstacle plan, a map showing the organizing of communications along the boundary, and a signals table for the troops.

The basis of securing each boundary was powerful artillery and mortar fire, engineering-mine obstacles, and counterattacks by tanks and infantry.

The most prepared and combat-ready units and troop formations were allotted for securing the boundaries. They disposed of a large amount of artillery and tanks; according to the defensive plan, the necessary amount of aircraft could be thrown into the battle for the boundary at any moment.

Most typical of the securing of the boundary between the Voronezh and Southwestern fronts the 7th Guards and 57th armies. The commission for securing the boundary included the commander of the 7th Guards Army, Lieutenant General Shumilov,[6] the commander of the 57th Army, Lieutenant General Gagen,[7] the deputy chief of staff of the Voronezh Front's military road directorate, Major General Venskii, the commander of the 7th Guards Army's artillery, Guards Major General Petrov, the 57th Army's artillery commander, Colonel Novitskii, the chief of the 7th Guards Army's engineering troops, Guards Major General Plyaskin, the chief of the 57th Army's engineering troops, Colonel Onuchin, the deputy of the 7th Guards Army's tank and motor-mechanized troops, Colonel Bogdanov, the 7th Guards Army's chief of staff, Major General Lukin, and the chief of the 57th Army staff's operational section, Major General Afanas'ev.

The commission, which worked about ten days among the troops, organized the securing of the *fronts'* boundary in the following fashion. For this the 7th Guards Army allotted the 15th and 36th guards rifle divisions, the 27th Guards Tank Brigade, an independent battalion of armored trains, and a mobile anti-tank reserve consisting of a tank regiment, an anti-tank artillery regiment, an engineering company, and four artillery regiments. These formations and units were assigned the following tasks.

15th Guards Rifle Division:

- employing the fire of no less than two battalions, to prevent the enemy's buildup along the eastern edge of the woods along the western bank of the Severskii Donets River near the crossings across from 1st Sovetskoe and Pisarevka;
- to destroy with artillery and mortar fire the enemy's tanks and personnel when they try to cross the Severskii Donets River along the sector 1st Sovetskoe—Pisarevka;
- to prepare the fire of two artillery battalions against the inhabited locales of 1st Sovetskoe and 1st Krasnoarmeiskoe, and the fire of two battalions against the northern exits from the villages of Shestirivka and Petrovka;
- to prepare the fire of two heavy artillery battalions for supporting the counterattacks of the second-echelon division (36th Guards Rifle Division) and tanks in the direction of Ukrainskoe;
- for defending from the south and southwest the approaches to the town of Volchansk, which is located in the 57th Army's zone, and to allot from the 15th Guards Rifle Division two battalions, reinforced with anti-tank guns and anti-tank rifles;

Both battalions were to prepare for anti-tank defense the following areas: a) Sinel'nikov—Oktyabr'skoe—marker 147.6 (one battalion), and; b) excluding the bridge over the Volch'ya—marker 137.2 marker 133.6 (the other battalion).

The 36th Guards Rifle Division was to prepare counterattacks along two axes: a) Volchanskie Khutora—Petrovka—Ukrainskoe, and; b) Volchanskie Khutora—Belyi Kolodez':

- the division's artillery regiment was meanwhile to prepare fire against the northern exits from the village of Zemlyanoi Yar and along the northern slopes of heights 182.7 and 189.7

The 27th Guards Tank Brigade received orders to prepare counterattacks from the Voznesensk area through Volchanskie Khutora in the direction of Ukrainskoe and through Pokalyanoe toward Belyi Kolodez'.

6 Editor's note. Mikhail Stepanovich Shumilov (1895-1975) joined the imperial army in 1916 and the Red Army in 1918. During the Great Patriotic War he commanded a corps and, from 1942, the 64th (7th Guards) Army until the end of the war. Following the war, Shumilvo commanded several military districts.

7 Editor's note. Nikolai Aleksandrovich Gagen (1895-1969) joined the imperial army in 1914 and the Red Army in 1919. During the Great Patriotic War he commanded a division, corps and armies. Following the war, Gagen commanded a corps and served in the Soviet Far East.

The armored train battalion was to cover the line Belyi Kolodez'—Volchansk and to support the counterattacks by the 36th Guards Rifle Division and the 27th Guards Tank Brigade.

It was planned to use the anti-tank reserve for destroying enemy tanks that broke through south of Volchansk.

The 57th Army was to prepare its artillery fire against the town of Volchansk and to the west, as well as to occupy with one rifle regiment the anti-tank area along the line Arbuzovskii station—height 175.1—height 173.3.

The 19th Rifle Division (the 57th Army's second echelon) was to occupy defensive positions along the line Pokalyanoe—Belyi Kolodez'.

Aside from this, the commander of the 57th Army was ordered to prepare counterattacks with one rifle division and an anti-tank artillery brigade along the following axes: a) Belyi Kolodez'—Volchansk, and; b) Belyi Kolodez'—Pokalyanoe—Mar'in.

The 24th Guards Rifle Corps of the Voronezh Front's 7th Guards Army was responsible for the boundary.

Thus the boundary between the Voronezh and Southwestern fronts was to be covered by four rifle divisions, two tank brigades, an anti-tank artillery brigade, and a battalion of armored trains. It was planned to use more than half of these forces for counterblows.

All possible crossings over the Severskii Donets River and the exits from the woods along its western bank were to be under fire from artillery and mortars.

Tank-accessible axes were securely covered by continuous minefields. On the *fronts'* boundary (south of Volchansk) the adjoining divisions were preparing powerful anti-tank areas, relying upon which, our forces could more successfully carry out their counterattacks.

In selecting the axes for the second echelons' counterblows, it was assumed that the enemy, having broken through the forward edge of the defense, would try to penetrate toward Zemlyanoi Yar (six kilometers from the forward edge), in which area he would arrive already significantly exhausted. It was planned to completely destroy him here by decisive and powerful attacks by our reserves.

Thus the boundary between the *fronts* was firmly secured and the units defending it were supported by a sufficient amount of reinforcement weapons. The success of both *fronts'* defense was obliged, to a significant degree, to the durability of the boundary between them.

Along the northern sector of the Kursk salient, the boundary between the Central and Bryansk fronts ran along the line Dolgoe Gorodishche—Ol'khovets. This boundary was also securely covered by the following: in the 3rd Army (Bryansk Front)—by the left-flank 41st Rifle Division, reinforced with an artillery regiment and tank regiment; in the 48th Army—by the right-flank 73rd Rifle Division, with an artillery regiment, a High Command Reserve artillery battalion, and a battalion from an artillery regiment.

In both neighboring armies' second echelon the following units were located: two rifle divisions (one each from the 3rd and 48th armies) and a tank regiment, which, with the support of two howitzer regiments, a light artillery and two motorized artillery regiments, were ready to launch counterattacks (all reinforcements belonged to the 48th Army).

Of no less significance were the boundaries between the armies, particularly between those which were defending along the likely axes of the enemy's expected attacks.

The defense was most secure along the boundary of the Voronezh Front's 6th and 7th guards armies. The boundary was defended by four rifle divisions: two (375th and 73rd guards) immediately along the forward edge and two (89th and 81st guards) in the second echelon. A powerful artillery barrage was to be created along the approaches to the forward edge. Six anti-tank areas were being outfitted in the defensive depth behind the boundaries, and a large network of minefields and various obstacles was being established. The counterblows by the armies' second echelons were aimed at Staryi Gorod and were not called for by the plan in the defensive depth.

Thus the reliably covered boundary between the 6th and 7th guards armies was just as secure as the boundary between the 7th Guards Army and the Southwestern Front.

The boundaries between divisions and regiments were secured chiefly by specially-allocated machine guns, mortars and anti-tank guns. These weapons, concentrated along the divisional or regimental boundaries, created a continuous zone of interlocking fire in front of the front line and in the depth. The subunits defending along the boundary maintained lateral liaison between each other.

The units securing the boundary were reinforced with 1-2 batteries of divisional artillery. For example, in order to directly secure the boundary with the 8th Rifle Division (Central Front), the 16th Latvian Rifle Division allotted four 45mm and two 75mm guns, four anti-tank rifles and three heavy machine guns. For the same purpose (the boundary with the 67th Guards Rifle Division), the 71st Rifle Division employed one artillery battery (151st Guards Artillery Regiment), a battery of regimental artillery, two batteries of 82mm mortars, 11 anti-tank guns, 14 anti-tank rifles, three heavy and nine light machine guns. The 67th Guards Rifle Division disposed of somewhat fewer weapons.

The 71st and 67th guards rifle divisions' enumerated weapons were located southwest and south of the village of Cherkasskoe and secured the division's boundary. A minefield and an anti-tank ditch barred the approaches to the forward edge. The employment here of infantry subunits for counterattacks was not foreseen by the defensive plan. The division and regimental reserves were designated for this task.

The examples cited show that the Central and Voronezh front commands, in organizing the defense of the Kursk salient, attached great significance to the securing of their boundaries and employed all means to securely cover them. As a result, the degree of the defense's ability to resist was significantly increased. Our troops, relying on such a defense, withstood the Germans' vicious pressure in the July fighting.

The organization of anti-tank defense

The defense of the Kursk salient was prepared, first of all, as anti-tank defense. Its basis consisted of a series of anti-tank defensive lines with powerful anti-tank strong points along the tank-accessible axes, maximally saturated with anti-tank artillery. The anti-tank defense, which had been created for the purpose of repelling a mass attack by the enemy's tanks and motorized infantry, had as its main task the destruction of the enemy's tanks in front of the forward edge and, in the event they should break into the defensive zone—to split them up and destroy them in detail.

All of both *fronts'* artillery, including anti-aircraft artillery, which, depending on its technical and tactical specifications, was to engage the enemy's tanks from hidden positions and over open sights, was designated for repelling the enemy's tanks. The artillery's main forces were to be employed along the axes of the enemy's likely tank and infantry attack.

The number of artillery tubes among the Central Front's armies and the density of their saturation along individual sectors are visible from the table below.

Thus the Central Front's main artillery forces were directed at supporting the defense of the 13th and 70th armies, in whose zone the German forces' main attack was expected.

The Central Front's Artillery Strength

Army	Front Width (in km)	45mm and 76mm Guns (regimental and divisional artillery)	Density per Kilometer
48th	38	428	11.3
13th	32	979	30.6
70th	62	637	10.3
65th	82	562	6.8
60th	92	335	3.6
Total	306	2,941	12.5

The same principle formed the basis of the Voronezh Front's employment of artillery. The following table gives an idea of the distribution of artillery among the *front's* armies.

The Voronezh Front's Artillery Strength

Army	Front Width (in km)	45mm and 76mm Guns (regimental and divisional artillery)	Density per Kilometer
38th	80	296	3.7
40th	50	515	10.3
6th Guards	64	638	9.9
7th Guards	50	571	11.4
Total	24	2,020	8.81

Note: Both tables fail to include that part of divisional and reinforcement artillery that was also employed in anti-tank defense.

Anti-tank strong points, which comprised the basis of the anti-tank defense, were created throughout the entire depth of the army defense: in the main zone by order of the division commanders, and in the depth by order of the army commanders. The status and tasks of the strong points were precisely foreseen by the overall plan for the army's anti-tank defense. For the better organization of cooperation between the strong points and for convenience in management, the latter were united into anti-tank areas on the Central Front. By 4 July 1943 the depth of the anti-tank defense along the *front's* right wing reached 30-35 kilometers and was based on three main lines: a) Yegor'evka—2nd Protasovo—Podolyan'; b) Maloarkhangel'sk—Ponyri—Snova, and; c) Verkhnyaya Sosna—Nikol'skoe—Ol'khovatka.

Along the 13th Army's first anti-tank line there were 15 anti-tank areas, consisting of 45 anti-tank strong points. There were 1.4 strong points per kilometer of front. Along the army's second line there were nine anti-tank areas with 34 strong points (one strong point per kilometer of front), and along the third line—14 areas with 70 strong points (two strong points per kilometer of front).

The saturation of the 13th Army's lines with anti-tank artillery varied from 3.2 to 12.2 guns per kilometer of front: 7.5 45mm and 76mm guns per kilometer along the first line; 3.0 guns along the second line, and; 12.2 along the third line.

Along the Voronezh Front the most highly developed system of anti-tank defense was in the 6th and 7th guards and 40th armies.

In the 6th Guards Army the number of anti-tank strong points reached 43 and they were distributed along the defensive zones as follows: 19 in the main zone, nine in the second zone, and 15 in the army rear zone. Besides this, the defense was strengthened by tanks dug into the ground, which had been configured for firing over open sights; two tank regiments and a tank brigade were employed for this purpose. The army's chemical subunits created fire walls out of dry tall weeds and straw along the most tank-accessible axes, laid out mine-bottle fields, and covered the most important axes with flamethrowers.

For anti-tank defense, the army commander retained a powerful anti-tank reserve, consisting of two anti-tank artillery brigades, two anti-tank artillery regiments, and one independent battalion of anti-tank rifles, for an overall amount of 90 guns, 31 mortars, 468 anti-tank rifles, 3,000 anti-tank mines, and 78 anti-tank dogs.

The overall artillery density per kilometer of front in the 6th and 7th guards armies' zones was 15.6 guns: six anti-tank guns and 9.6 anti-tank guns from regimental and divisional artillery, and the High Command Artillery Reserve. By including the artillery from the second-echelon formations (1st Tank Army, 69th Army, 2nd Guards Tank Corps, and the 35th Rifle Corps), which were located in the 6th and 7th guards armies' zone, the artillery saturation increased almost two times and reached 12.3 anti-tank guns and 16.7 guns from divisional artillery and the High Command Artillery Reserve, or 29.5 guns per kilometer of front.

The overall density along the tank-accessible axes was not the same. For example, along the Krasnopol'e—Ugroedy axis along the boundary between the 38th and 40th armies, there were 14.0 guns per kilometer of front, while along the Terebreno—Ilek axis there were 18 guns, and seven guns per kilometer of front along the Berezovka—Krasnaya Yaruga axis.

Along each line the anti-tank strong points were located in chessboard fashion and formed anti-tank sacks, blundering into which the enemy tanks would be fired on from two, three and more directions.

Our troops' anti-tank defense was distinguished by great vitality. The strong points' close fire cooperation between each other, the broad fire maneuver and wheels, and the powerful engineering fortification of the strong points made the defense resilient and capable not only of withstanding, but of repelling large enemy tank forces. Reserve positions were selected and prepared beforehand on the calculation that while one subunit was changing its position it would be supported by no less than two others.

An anti-tank strong point usually consisted of anti-tank artillery guns, anti-tank rifle crews, mortar subunits, groups of automatic riflemen, tank destroyers, and sappers, and sometimes of small groups of tanks. The strong points' composition and armament were not the same and chiefly depended on the importance of the axis, on the terrain and on the presence of artillery weapons along this axis, etc. For example, the anti-tank artillery strong points in the 38th Army had the following: No. 3 in the 240th Rifle Division—three guns and nine anti-tank rifles; No. 7 in the 180th Rifle Division—12 guns and 32 anti-tank rifles; No. 5 in the 232nd Rifle Division—24 anti-tank rifles, and; No. 5 in the 206th Rifle Division (40th Army)—16 guns and nine anti-tank rifles.

The anti-tank strong points covered the tank-vulnerable axes and were located either in the infantry's combat formations, or independently. In this and other cases close cooperation with the infantry subunits was organized. This gave the defending forces the opportunity not only to repel the attacks by enemy tanks, but also to destroy his personnel. This was the main advantage of the anti-tank defensive system in the Kursk salient.

The combined-arms commander was responsible for the outfitting of the anti-tank strong point and for the organization of cooperation with the troops. The organization of a fire system of anti-tank and anti-personnel weapons, as well as fire control in battle was the responsibility of the senior artillery chief, who was the commander of the artillery strong point.

As a rule, an anti-tank strong point included artillery of various calibers, so that it could engage any kind of enemy tanks.

The spaces between the anti-tank areas, along the front and in depth, varied from 200-300 meters, if the defense was built around the fire of anti-tank rifles, and up to 400-800 meters if anti-tank guns were present in the defense. Each anti-tank strong point and area was prepared for perimeter defense. The guns and anti-tank rifles had 2-3 well-prepared reserve firing positions, which were selected so that in moving this or that gun in the firing position the overall fire system would not be disrupted.

Lines along the axes where enemy tanks were most likely to appear were scrupulously registered beforehand by all the guns. The strong points' artillery chiefs compiled firing charts and dispatched them to each subunit forming part of the strong point. These showed the lines for destroying tanks, the weapons being employed for firing along this or that line, the sequence for moving guns within the strong point, and signals for calling in fire, etc.

Highly visible and easily remembered reference points were selected on the terrain and were learned by all the gun crews and served as the chief means of target designation. In those places where there were no natural reference points, artificial ones were set up. The distance to each reference point was exactly measured with a measuring tape.

Permanent minefields or mines, prepared for burial in the event of danger from tanks, were located in front of the anti-tank areas and strong points. The number of minefields and the number of mines within them varied. In the Voronezh Front's 7th Guards Army, around the anti-tank strong point near Blizhnyaya Igumenka, which consisted of a tank company from the 167th Tank Regiment and a company of sappers, the following had been laid: 250 anti-tank mines, 300 anti-personnel mines, 300 kilograms of mines, and 100 kilograms of controlled landmines. In the anti-tank area near Shebekino (also the 7th Guards Army), occupied by the 730th Rifle Regiment, a battery from the 193rd Anti-Tank Battalion and two sapper platoons, the following were laid: 1,700 anti-tank mines, 500 anti-personnel mines, 500 kilograms of mines, and 200 kilograms of controlled mines.

Aside from the structures set up in the anti-tank strong points, as well as the engineer-mine obstacles around them and along the tank-accessible axes, a complete zone of anti-tank obstacles was established in front of the forward edge and in the defensive depth. In this zone, aside from a large number of minefields, anti-tank ditches had been dug, post obstacles set up, and dams built for flooding the area, etc. For example, the by 4 July the Central Front's 13th Army had laid 50,750 anti-tank and 28,805 anti-personnel mines. Along the 70th Army's sector about 60,000 of both types of mines had been laid, six kilometers of anti-tank ditches and escarps built, eight kilometers of forest obstacles prepared, reinforced with mines, and ten dams built for flooding an overall surface of 3.81 linear kilometers of terrain.

A significantly greater amount of minefields were laid by the troops of the Voronezh Front. Here there were 89,888 anti-tank and 63,843 anti-personnel mines; there were 66,746 anti-tank and 85,140 anti-personnel mines along the 7th Guards Army's sector.

Along both *fronts'* threatened axes the number of anti-tank mines per kilometer reached 1,400-1,500 and the number of anti-personnel mines 1,000-1,700. Such a large saturation of the terrain with mines caused heavy casualties in enemy tanks and personnel, when he attacked.

A captured German tank officer, an *oberleutnant*, testified under interrogation:

> Our tank losses were huge and are caused, for the most part by the minefields. We never expected that the Russians could plant so many mines. Because of the minefields the tank crews are afraid to operate and this significantly affected the development of military operations.

Besides the authorized mines, the engineers employed a large number of captured artillery shells and laid anti-tank fields with them. No additional explosive devices were required when mining with these shells: the explosive charge of the shell itself served as the fuse. 30,426 of these mines were laid along the Voronezh Front.

It was along this *front* that fire mines (MOF) were first used in large quantities; they were widely used in particular along the 6th and 7th guards armies' zones.

By 4 July 1943 sappers had prepared 361 bridges for demolition along the Voronezh Front's sector, using various devices. They laid 315 delayed-reaction mines in groups, with different reaction times, on the main roads and bridges. The mining of bridges with delayed-reaction mines pursued the goal of a repeat explosion: when our forces would withdraw, a bridge was blown up the usual way, and then a repeat explosion followed some time later, which was calculated to strike the troops engaged in repairing it.

27 airfields along this *front* were prepared for destruction and blocking. The airstrips, various structures and approach roads were mined. The number of mines laid on the airfields was as follows: anti-tank—1,284, anti-personnel—1,500, and delayed reaction—134.

Specially organized teams of sappers and miners were in constant readiness to bring the obstacles laid down into combat readiness, as well as for carrying out destruction on each airfield.

Railroad lines were also mined. Up to 500 kilometers of line, using 1,630 delayed-reaction mines, which had not yet been activated, were laid along the Voronezh Front. On some sectors of the railroad approaching the forward edge of the defense (110 kilometers in length), 109 delayed-reaction mines were laid.

Each gun, each mortar and anti-tank rifle had already adjusted for fire the lines of the likely appearance of the enemy's tanks. In the gun commanders' firing maps the lines of fire, distances and aiming were noted. The gun crews carried out numerous fire training exercises against tanks.

In the middle of May 1943, when information had been received about the enemy's possible employment of the T-VI "Tiger"[8] and the "Ferdinand"[9] assault gun, our artillery officers put all their efforts into inculcating into the troops a feeling of confidence in their victory over this new enemy weapon. The troops trained to fight these tanks, familiarized themselves with their vulnerable areas, and trained in hitting them with special shells. According to the plan drawn up by the army and division staffs, the anti-tank crews and infantry would "roll" with their tanks. During training each gun crew sought to achieve the ability to relieve each other fully. All batteries had anti-tank destruction teams.

Communications between the anti-tank strong points were carried out by telephone, which was backed up by radio and mobile means. A strong point commander was required to be in the immediate vicinity of the combined-arms commander.

Various light and sound signals were primarily employed for directing the anti-tank weapons' fire. Non-stop observation was carried out for the subunits' timely warning of the appearance of enemy tanks in the anti-tank strong points.

Forward paired observers were moved up into the infantry's formation along tank-accessible axes. Upon the appearance of enemy tanks, they were to warm their subunits, either by visual signals or by telephone, about the approaching danger. The observers in the strong points and the forward observers maintained communication.

Anti-tank defense was not limited to the creation of anti-tank strong points and obstacle zones. All kinds of weapons were employed in the anti-tank battle: artillery, mortars, rocket artillery, and

8 Editor's note. The Panzer VI ("Tiger") was a German heavy tank which first appeared in 1943. One model weighed 54 tons and carried a crew of five. It was armed with an 88mm gun and two 7.92 machine guns.

9 Editor's note. The Ferdinand was a German heavy tank destroyer, named in honor of the designer Ferdinand Porsche, which first saw action at Kursk. The Ferdinand had a crew of six and weiged 65 tons. It was armed with an 88mm gun.

infantry. Division and corps artillery, as well as guns from the High Command Reserve, prepared fire and anti-tank obstacles along the entire defensive front.

Along the Central Front's main axis the artillerymen prepared and registered 49 distant fire attack areas (DON), 38 concentrated fire areas (SO), and up to 27 mobile fire obstacles (PZO). An artillery regiment had its field of fire sector, within the confines of which it was fully responsible for the destruction of enemy tanks appearing there. Lines of immobile fire obstacles (NZO) were also prepared in the defensive depth—for example, along the 13th Army's first and second defensive lines there were 18 of these. These lines were not only marked, but registered as well.

Artillery firing positions were also configured for anti-tank defense and for firing at tanks over open sights, and were included in the overall anti-tank defense plan.

Anti-aircraft artillery, which correspondingly organized its own firing positions, was also brought into the anti-tank defense. In the training firing carried out with the crews of the anti-aircraft guns, the employment of armor-piercing shells against land targets was foreseen. Bringing in anti-aircraft guns to the anti-tank defense would significantly increase the effectiveness of our defense against the German tanks. The Central Front alone disposed of 25 anti-aircraft artillery regiments. Ten of these were located along the sector of the enemy's expected attack, while 11 were in the *front* commander's reserve. From the start of the Germans' July offensive, all of these were employed in the 13th and 70th armies' sectors. Thus there was an average of 5.5 anti-aircraft guns, prepared for resisting the enemy tanks, alone along the Germans' likely attack axis.

Aircraft warning posts, aside from their immediate task, also observed the enemy's tanks. Employing small barrage balloons and objects towering over the surrounding landscape, the observers were to warn of the enemy's tank movements.

The employment of guards mortar units for fighting tanks was not foreseen by instructions, but nevertheless guards mortar regiments were brought in to carry out this mission. According to the anti-tank defensive plan, they were assigned positions (up to seven positions for each rocket-artillery vehicle) and lines indicated, along which they were to prepare salvos. Training fires with the mortar crews showed a high degree of hits against dummy tanks.

Mobile obstacle detachments, which during the battle would lay down mines, anti-tank mines and mobile obstacles, and blow up bridges, were broadly employed in the fight against tanks. The mobile obstacle detachments consisted of 1-2 sapper companies or an engineer battalion, reinforced by automatic riflemen. Such a detachment would have its combat zone indicated beforehand for fighting with the enemy's attacking tanks. For example, the 13th Army mobile obstacle detachment no. 1 was to defend the axis toward Ol'khovatka, no. 2 the axis toward Ponyri, and detachment no. 3 the axis toward Maloarkhangel'sk. The 209th Engineering Battalion was given the task of covering the Oboyan' axis with obstacles. It had 3,000 anti-tank mines, three motor vehicles and ten horse-drawn wagons for this. The 109th Engineer Battalion, which had 3,500 anti-tank mines, 500 anti-personnel mines, 300 kilograms of explosives, five motor vehicles, and ten horse-drawn wagons, had a similar assignment along the Prokhorovka axis. The 47th Engineer Battalion, which was to cover the Korocha axis, disposed of 4,700 anti-tank mines, 500 kilograms of explosives, three motor vehicles, and ten horse-drawn wagons. The 105th Engineer Battalion was in reserve and also in readiness to operate along any axis, and disposed of 2,000 anti-tank mines and 500 kilograms of explosives.

Depots with a sufficient number of mines (from 10,000 to 20,000) and explosives were created within the *fronts'* and armies' engineering directorates for supplying the mobile obstacle detachments with the necessary engineering equipment. These depots had in constant readiness ten motor vehicles apiece, which could immediately delivery supplies at the first summons of this or that detachment.

Army mobile obstacle detachments (POZ) were subordinated to the chief of the army's engineering troops, and divisional (divisional POZ) ones to the chiefs of divisional engineering service.

Control over the mobile obstacles detachments was exercised by the commanders of the engineer battalions from which these detachments were allotted. As a rule, the rifle division commanders issued orders to the mobile obstacle detachments.

Sapper-hunters were widely employed in the battle against the enemy's tanks. These hunters, operating in small groups of 2-7 men, armed with grenades and anti-tank mines, would approach the enemy tanks in the battle and destroy them, and also penetrate into the enemy's immediate rear and in concentration areas for his tanks, mine the roads, blow up vehicles and fuel depots, etc. The best, most prepared sappers were picked for these groups and were most often volunteers, brave and cunning soldiers with great willpower.

Dog tank destroyers, on whose backs were strapped up to six kilograms of explosives, were an active means of combating the enemy's tanks. Soldiers with well-trained dogs were located in the anti-tank traps.

Aside from the mobile obstacle detachments, the division, army and *front* commanders had anti-tank reserves of various composition. For example, the commander of the 40th Army's 237th Rifle Division had four 45mm guns and 44 anti-tank rifles in reserve; the commander of the 38th Army's 180th Rifle Division had four guns; the commander of the 13th Army had the 874th Anti-Tank Artillery Regiment in reserve, and; the commander of the Voronezh Front's 40th Army had the 32nd Independent Anti-Tank Artillery Brigade. The commander of the 6th Guards Army had in reserve two independent anti-tank artillery brigades, two anti-tank artillery regiments, and a battalion of anti-tank rifles. The reserve of the commander of the 7th Guards Army consisted of an independent anti-tank artillery brigade and one anti-tank artillery regiment. The reserve of the commander of the Voronezh Front consisted of three anti-tank artillery brigades (eight anti-tank artillery regiments) and eight independent battalions of anti-tank rifles. In the commander of the Central Front's reserve there were three anti-tank artillery brigades (12th, 1st and 4th) and two anti-tank artillery regiments.

The anti-tank reserves, being completely motorized, were highly maneuverable; they were usually located along tank-accessible axes and in anti-tank strong points, in readiness to operate by fire and wheels in any direction. The deployment lines for the anti-tank reserves, which had been previously reconnoitered, had been prepared for firing.

Each reserve was assigned several lines. For example, the 7th Guards Army's anti-tank reserve (30th Independent Anti-Tank Artillery Brigade), located behind the army's center, had five prepared lines with open trenches for guns, outfitted with fire control means. The Central Front's 13th Anti-Tank Artillery Brigade, which was located along the boundary between the 48th and 13th armies, was based on six previously prepared deployment areas; the 1st Anti-Tank Artillery Brigade on five areas, and; the 4th Anti-Tank Artillery Brigade on 14 areas; the latter's activities were planned for along three axes: Kursk—Oboyan'; Kursk—Fatezh, and; Fatezh—Dmitriev-L'govskii. The presence of powerful and mobile anti-tank reserves in the hands of the army and *front* commanders enabled them to broadly maneuver these weapons on the battlefield and launch attacks on the enemy tanks where the threat was greatest.

Thanks to the all-round scrupulous preparation of the anti-tank defense by the Central and Voronezh fronts, our forces were able to halt the masses of enemy tanks within the confines of the tactical defense zone and inflict a heavy defeat on the Germans on the first day of their offensive. On the following days the anti-tank defensive weapons, employing broad maneuver with fire and movement, constantly exhausted the enemy's forces and, finally, bled him white and halted him.

Organization of the fire system

In organizing the defense of the Kursk salient, the *front* headquarters devoted particularly attention to the fire system. At the base of its organization lay the principle of massing all weapons along the most important axes, with the broad employment of maneuver on the battlefield both of fire and weapons. The fire system was calculated on fully employing the firing capacity of all types of weapons.

All of these problems were successfully resolved. According to the massing of weapons and density of fire, the defensive battle along the Kursk salient was far greater than all the defensive operations known to us in the history of warfare. Along the Central Front's decisive axis, in the 13th Army's zone, about 2,700 guns and heavy and medium mortars were concentrated along a 32-kilometer front, which yielded up to 85 tubes per kilometer of front; if one takes into account the *front* reserve's weapons, then the average saturation rises to 95 tubes per kilometer of front; this figure amounted to about ten guns per kilometer of front along the secondary axes.

The fire system was organized in such a way that it called for the following:

- a zone of complete fire in front of the forward edge of the defense, 400 meters wide, and with a density of up to ten bullets per linear meter of front;
- the deep echeloning of weapons with the necessary fire density along the most important axes throughout the entire depth of the army defense;
- the broad maneuver of fire during the battle, so as to guarantee its great concentration along the threatened sectors;
- the maximum employment of flanking and oblique fire, both in front of the forward edge and in the defensive depth;
- the simplicity and reliability of fire control, with the creation of the necessary number of observation posts and uninterrupted communications;
- the covering of boundaries with dense fire, and;
- the possibility of the troops conducting a perimeter defense.

The troops received special instructions on the necessity of putting all the heavy infantry weapons (heavy machine guns, mortars, anti-tank and regimental guns) into the organization of a permanent barrage (NZO) in front of the forward edge of the main defensive zone.[10]

The system of infantry fire

Rifle sections had 2-3 basic sectors for observing and firing, as well as 1-2 additional sectors for fire communications with their neighbors. Sections and platoons of automatic riflemen were used for keeping dead spaces under fire and securing gaps and boundaries between rifle subunits. Machine gun sections, as a rule, were located in wood and earthen firing points, yielding frontal and flanking fire to a distance of 500-2,500 meters, and having 1-2 open reserve platforms near the firing point. In some armies traditore machine guns were emplaced at a distance of 100-150 meters in front of the line of the first trenches. These machine guns had open but skillfully masked positions. About 100 of these positions were prepared along the 6th Guards Army's sector.

A large part of the light and heavy machine guns were registered by lines and prepared for night firing. Each firing point had 2-3 reserve positions, which enabled us to broadly maneuver weapons during the fighting.

Platoon defensive areas were mostly located so as to facilitate keeping under fire a 400-meter zone in front of the forward edge. Fire coordination within the platoon area was achieved through mutual fire support by the sections and the maneuver of weapons. The positioning of platoon areas

10 The *front* staffs received these instructions on the basis of a directive (no. 11845 of 18 April 1943) by the chief of the Red Army General Staff, Marshal of the Soviet Union Vasilevskii.

at an angle forward or back enabled us to wage flanking, oblique and cross fire and also facilitated the creation of firing sacks within the company defensive area. The gaps between the platoon areas were covered by fire from the neighboring sections and by specially allotted heavy machine guns, located in the depth of the company area, and by automatic riflemen.

Company defensive areas, like the jumping-off areas, were located at an angle in front or behind, which facilitated the coverage of fire of the entire area inside the battalion area and the favorable employment of flanking and oblique fire. Machine gun companies were employed by machine gun in wood and earthen firing points, with several reserve open platforms, for firing in front of the forward edge, along the flanks, and along the most important axes in the defensive depth. Before the start of the German offensive the greater part of the battalion had prepared barrage and concentrated fire from heavy machine guns, both in front of the forward edge and in the depth of the battalion areas and regimental sectors.

Mortar areas also had previously registered zones and lines. Light mortars were located directly in the trenches, while the heavy ones were located in specially outfitted firing positions in the gaps between the trenches.

Anti-tank rifle companies, as a rule, operated compactly in platoons or sections along tank-accessible axes. They were located like the mortars (in the first line of trenches or in specially outfitted firing positions behind them). Sometimes part of the anti-tank rifles were moved beyond the first line of trenches, according to the terrain conditions. In order to increase their tenacity, automatic riflemen were included in these companies. Along particularly tank-accessible axes the anti-tank rifles were employed together with the anti-tank guns. For example, in the 38th Army's 180th Rifle Division such a group consisted of 3-4 anti-tank rifles and one gun.

The following density of weapons per kilometer of front was created directly along the forward edge along the most important axes: 160 rifles, 70 automatic rifles, 11 light machine guns, 4-5 heavy machine guns, and 8-10 mortars. Such a density of weapons covered the 400-meter zone in front of the forward edge with fire at a density of ten bullets per linear meter of front per minute.

The overall saturation of infantry weapons in the main defensive zone along the most important axes is illustrated by the following data:

Density of Infantry Weapons in the Main Defensive Zone

Army	Per Kilometer of Front				
	Rifles	Automatic Rifles	Heavy Machine Guns	Mortars	Anti-Tank Guns
13th	312	74	8.2	19	3.4
6th Guards	261	136	7.6	9.4	2.3

The fire system for infantry weapons in the second and rear army defensive zones was organized according to the same principle, with the difference being that these zones were only partially occupied along the most important axes. According to the density of fire, the second zone (along the sectors occupied by troops) was no less than in the main zone, while the rear zone was significantly weaker than the first two, as may be judged from the following data:

Density of Infantry Weapons by Defensive Zone, 6th Guards Army

	Per Kilometer of Front			
Zone	**Men**	**Rifles**	**Automatic Rifles**	**Light Machine Guns**
Main (5th Guards Rifle Division/6th Guards Army)	631	280	168	25
Second (90th Guards Rifle Division/6th Guards Army	445	205	124	18.3
Rear Army (305th Rifle Division/6th Guards Army)	360	214	84	11

	Per Kilometer of Front			
Zone	**Heavy Machine Guns**	**Mortars**	**Anti-Tank Weapons**	**Anti-Tank Rifles**
Main (5th Guards Rifle Division/6th Guards Army)	9.8	9.2	2.8	16.7
Second (90th Guards Rifle Division/6th Guards Army	7.2	8.3	2.0	13.9
Rear Army (305th Rifle Division/6th Guards Army)	3	7	1.7	9.8

Along the sector of the Central Front's 13th Army the rear zone was significantly stronger, according to the number of weapons, than not only the second zone, but of the main defensive zone as well. The density of the defensive zones along the 13th Army's sector is shown by the following data:

Density of Infantry Weapons by Defensive Zone, 13th Army

Zone	Rifles	Automatic Rifles	Heavy Machine Guns	Mortars (not counting 50mm)	Anti-Tank Guns (only 45mm)
Main	10,600	2,500	271	642	115
Second	8,500	4,600	268	268	101
Rear	11,300	11,500	729	480	213

Such a correlation of weapons, located along the defensive zones, existed only along the 13th Army's sector and was not, of course, typical of the Central Front's entire defensive system, and even more so of the Voronezh Front.

The overall depth of a rifle division's fire system reached an average of 6-8 kilometers, and in some cases more. For example, the 38th Army's 180th Rifle Division had a fire system depth (including the combat security zone) of 12 kilometers. This depth consisted of three firing zones: the combat security zone's firing zone, the firing zone in front of the forward edge, and in front of the division's second echelon. All of this was augmented by the following strong points: a) Vodolagi; b) Varachin, and; a branch of the Molotov State Farm—height 210.6. The latter was configured for perimeter defense.

The artillery fire system

At the heart of organizing a system of artillery fire lay the principle of massing artillery and mortars along the main axes. Massing was achieved by means of the corresponding distribution of these weapons, as well as by employing broad-ranging maneuver by fire and movement.

Having determined the likely axes of the enemy's operation, the *front* and army commanders sought to create along these axes powerful artillery groupings, capable of withstanding ramming blows by the enemy's tanks and infantry. If the overall artillery density on the Central Front was 6.2 field and 6.8 anti-tank guns per kilometer of front, then along the most important axis—the 13th Army's sector—it increased by 3-4 times and reached 25.2 field and 18.3 anti-tank guns per kilometer of front. The commander of the 13th Army, in his turn, created a denser grouping of artillery weapons along the tank-accessible axes. Thus there were 87 tubes per kilometer along the Ponyri axis, 68 along the Arkhangel'sk axis, and 36 along the Fatezh axis.

The overall distribution of artillery by army along the Central Front is clear from the following figures:

Artillery Distribution Along the Central Front

Army	Width of Front (in km)	82mm and 120mm Mortars		Divisional Artillery and Anti-Tank Guns (45mm, 57mm, 76mm)	
		Number	Per km	Number	Per km
48th	38	487	12.8	321	8.4
13th	32	1,325	41.4	587	18.3
70th	62	768	12.4	411	6.6
65th	82	541	6.6	392	4.8
60th	92	508	5.5	219	2.1
Front Reserve	–	155	–	152	–
Total	306	3,787	12.4	2,082	6.8

Army	Width of Front (in km)	Divisional Artillery and Reinforcements (76mm 122mm, 152mm, 203mm)		Total Guns and Mortars	
		Number	Per km	Number	Per km
48th	38	183	4.8	991	26.0
13th	32	806	25.2	2,718	85.0
70th	62	406	6.5	1,585	25.5
65th	82	251	3.1	1,187	14.5
60th	92	178	1.9	905	9.8
Front Reserve	–	81	–	391	–
Total	306	1,908	6.2	7,777	25.4

This table clearly illustrates the Central Front command's measures for the artillery reinforcement of the troops defending the most important axes. The 13th Army, occupying 14 percent of the overall length of the front, had 2,718 guns and heavy and light mortars, which comprised 35 percent of the Central Front's entire artillery.

The same distribution of artillery was carried out by the Voronezh Front command, as is clear from the following table:

Artillery Distribution Along the Voronezh Front

Army	Width of Front (in km)	82mm and 120mm Mortars		Divisional Artillery and Anti-Tank Guns (45mm, 57mm, 76mm)	
		Number	Per km	Number	Per km
38th	80	551	6.9	159	2.0
40th	50	869	17.4	393	7.9
6th Gds	64	779	12.2	418	6.5
7th Gds	50	653	13.0	426	8.5
Total	244	2,852	11.7	1,396	5.7
38th & 40th	130	1,420	11.0	552	4.2
6th & 7th gds	114	1,432	12.6	844	7.4
69th	–	590	–	309	–
1st Tank	–	249	–	20	–
2nd & 5th gds tank corps	–	190	–	40	–
35th Gds Rifle Corps	–	362	–	184	–
Front Reserve	–	87	–	20	–
Total	244	1,330	17.7	1,969	8.0

Army	Width of Front (in km)	Divisional Artillery and Reinforcements (76mm 122mm, 152mm, 203mm)		Total Guns and Mortars	
		Number	Per km	Number	Per km
38th	80	194	2.4	904	11.3
40th	50	371	7.4	1,638	32.7
6th Gds	64	477	7.4	1,674	26.2
7th Gds	50	391	7.8	1,470	29.4
Total	244	1,433	5.9	5,681	23.3
38th & 40th	130	565	4.3	2,537	19.5
6th & 7th gds	114	868	7.6	3,144	27.6
69th	–	155	–	1,054	–
1st Tank	–	68	–	337	–
2nd & 5th gds tank corps	–	48	–	278	–
35th Gds Rifle Corps	–	112	–	658	–
Front Reserve	–	104	–	211	–
Total	244	1,920	7.9	8,219	33.6

A denser artillery grouping was created in the 6th and 7th guards armies' sectors. Taking into account the *front* reserves in these armies' sectors, the average density per kilometer of front here was raised to 50 tubes.

The artillery's combat formation was deeply echeloned. 45mm anti-tank and 76mm field guns were located along the forward edge of the defense. Behind them, at a distance of 3-5 kilometers from the forward edge, were located the firing positions of the divisional artillery and reinforcement artillery. Even further behind them the heavy artillery's firing positions were established. The overall depth of the artillery's firing system reached 15 kilometers, not counting the artillery units that were occupying some sectors of the rear defensive zone.

The artillery positions were well outfitted in the engineering sense of the word; the equipment was located in the trenches and the rank and file had slit trenches and overhead covers. A large portion of the artillery positions was covered by anti-tank obstacles and barriers.

For the purpose of increasing the artillery's survivability, its firing positions were covered by anti-tank weapons and rifle subunits. Special guns and batteries, which fired from reserve positions, were allotted for repulsing the enemy's reconnaissance parties. As a rule, the artillery batteries had no more than 2-3 reserve positions. Firing from roving guns was widely practiced; each rifle division had 2-3 batteries of such guns. All these measures deprived the enemy of the opportunity of uncovering our fire system before the start of the offensive.

As General Schmidt, the commander of the German 19th Panzer Division wrote:

> We knew little about these fortifications before the start of the offensive and it was not expected that we would encounter a quarter of what the Russians built.

A system of fire was drawn up in each army: NZO, PZO, SO, and DON.[11] For example, in the 7th Guards Rifle Army's zone 18 PZO sectors were planned, of which ten were in front of the forward edge and six in the defensive depth; in the 13th Army there were 35 PZO sectors, of which 17 were in front of the forward edge and 18 in the defensive depth.

Data prepared beforehand for firing from hidden positions was systematically checked by firing single rounds. This data, which was noted for each gun, made it easier for the gunners to work out systems by target.

The concentration of fire along the important axes reached 5-7 artillery battalions. Some separate sectors were reinforced by artillery by transferring it from less important sectors, and the corresponding movement of reserves.

An extremely important measure—the organization of the artillery counterpreparation—was planned out beforehand by armies along both *fronts* (in some armies, for example, in the Voronezh Front, this was done two months before the start of the defensive battle). The plans included planned targets that were to be suppressed, as well as the tasks of independent artillery units and subunits. According to this plan, the divisional artillery and reinforcement artillery were to take a full part in the counterpreparation. The review of the plans and the preparation for the tightening up of separate details were carried out systematically during the entire process of preparing for the battle.

Along the sector of the Voronezh Front's 6th Guards Army up to 1,000 targets were established. In each rifle division's sector there were 2-3 NZO sectors, 2-4 DON areas, and 20-30 SO areas. The first order of business was the fire against the enemy's areas for concentrating infantry and tanks and the firing positions of his more active batteries, as well as his observation posts. Fire registration was carried out along this sector on 22 June.

---

11 DON was not widely employed, as there was no forward area; the main defensive zone fronted on the enemy line almost everywhere.

In all, 208 guns, 95 rocket-artillery vehicles, and about 400 mortars took part in carrying out the counterpreparation in this army. All the forces of the infantry weapons and tank fire were included for increasing the strength of the fire. The anti-tank artillery regiments and artillery subunits, which were located in the strong points, as well as the anti-tank reserves, did not take part in the artillery counterpreparation. The other armies prepared for the artillery counterpreparation in approximately the same manner. A particularly important moment was the decision to start the artillery counterpreparation. For this, it was necessary to carry out continuous reconnaissance of all kinds.

In the process of the artillery units' combat training, the plan for the counterpreparation was held in strictest secrecy. The officers and soldiers systematically trained for firing according to their orders, although none of them knew the true designation of this fire.

The employment of tanks in the fire system

Tank fire was organized in the following manner: a) stationary (from previously prepared firing positions, and; b) on the move. With the appearance of the German T-VI and, taking into account its technical-tactical specifications, special emphasis was on the organization of tank ambushes. Tank units and formations along the main axes of the enemy's presumed operations prepared firing positions with fully-developed trenches for each tank.

Tank regiments and brigades that were attached directly to the armies were employed for reinforcing the second defensive zone and, with part of their forces, the main defensive zone. The tanks were deployed by platoon and company—directly in the troops' combat formation along the tank-accessible axes; the combination of tank fire from the main positions and on the move (mobile firing points) increased to a significant degree the flexibility of the firing system.

In the 6th Guards Army part of the tanks, in groups of 10-15 machines, operated within the anti-tank strong points. Such an employment of tanks justified itself during the course of the defensive fighting.

The bedrock of the defensive fire system in the Kursk salient was the fire from the artillery and infantry. Artillery and mortar fire was the main means that determined the fire strength of our defense. The percentage of artillery weapons increased significantly: the number of tubes per kilometer of front along the most important axes reached 80-90; that is, the density of fire was approaching that which was necessary for an offensive operation. The method of the massed employment of weapons along the decisive axes is instructive.

The organization of anti-aircraft defense

The German command, in preparing its summer offensive on Kursk, by the beginning of July had concentrated along this direction large aviation forces. According to intelligence data, which was confirmed by the testimony of captured German fliers and captured documents, the Central Front was faced by the Fourth Air Fleet, under the command of General Field Marshal Richtofen,[12] and consisting of the I, IV and VIII air corps. The I Air Corps was based on the Bryansk airfield network; the VIII on the Khar'kov airfield network, and; the IV in the Dnepropetrovsk area. The aviation formations of Group *Ost*, under the command of Colonel Ritter von Greim,[13] also operated along this axis.

12 Editor's note. Wolfram Freiherr von Richtofen (1895-1945) joined the German army in 1913 and fought in the First World War, when he joined the air force. During the Second World War he commanded air corps and air fleets in the west, the Balkans, Italy, and in the Soviet Union. Von Richtofen died of illness in Allied captivity.

13 Editor's note. Robert Ritter von Greim (1892-1945) joined the German army in 1911 and fought in the First World War, when he joined the air force. During the Second World War he commanded an air wing and was

In these air formations operating against our forces in the Kursk salient, there were 1,850 aircraft: 1,000 bombers, 600 fighters, 100 assault aircraft, and 150 reconnaissance aircraft. Besides this, from the beginning of the German offensive up to 200 bombers operated from distance airfields, located in Smolensk, Orsha, Stalino, Zaporozh'e, and Kirovograd. Thus the overall number of enemy planes concentrated for the support of the forthcoming offensive reached more than 2,000.

In April, May and June the German air force sharply increased its activity. In the first two months the enemy's planes systematically launched concentrated raids against railroad junctions, large inhabited locales and airfields located in the shallow rear of our forces. At the same time, the enemy aviation carried out aerial reconnaissance of the forces defending the Kursk salient.

The railroad junctions of Kursk, Yelets, Kastornoe, Livny, and Marymzhi were subjected to particularly heavy air raids. In June the enemy air force shifted its raids to the Orel—Kursk railroad. The Ponyri, Vozy, Zolotukhino, and Svoboda stations were subjected to repeated bombings. On 2 June the Germans launched a powerful converging attack by air against the city and railroad junction of Kursk. 824 enemy planes attacked the city from different directions. Echelons of planes, following one after the other, encountered the stiff resistance of our fighter aviation and the powerful fire of anti-aircraft artillery; such a reception forced the German fliers to drop the main part of the bombs erratically, outside the city. The Germans lost 160 planes in this raid. In June enemy reconnaissance flights were replaced by systematic bombing of our artillery firing positions, rear communications and control centers. Incidents of group dive bombing attacks by enemy planes became more frequent against our forces in the main zone, and the minefields, in order to destroy them.

Beginning in April, the German air force's activity within the confines of the Kursk salient increased daily. Attacks from the depth of the salient were shifted closer and closer to its center. In June our defending troops began to be systematically subjected to bombing raids. This forced the Central and Voronezh front command to broadly maneuver the men and materiel of our anti-aircraft defense. In March, April and May the *front* commanders assigned up to 70 percent of their anti-aircraft resources to cover rail communications and road junctions. A significant part of our fighter aviation was drawn into this as well. Such a measure completely justified itself. Before long the German aviation, when attacking rear targets, began to suffer heavy losses; in connection with this, they sharply curtailed their daylight raids and shifted their activities to the nighttime. In the June raid on Kursk 300 sorties out of 824 were carried out at night.

With the shift in enemy air activity to our troops' combat formations, our anti-aircraft units were quickly shifted from rear targets to ones nearer the front.

The threat of the Germans' forthcoming summer offensive and, in this regard, the concentration of a large amount of enemy aviation, forced the *front* commands to everywhere increase and strengthen the *front* and army anti-aircraft units. In July the armies of the Central and Voronezh fronts were reinforced by 14 anti-aircraft artillery regiments and one anti-aircraft division from the High Command Reserve.

By 5 July among the units of the Central Front's anti-aircraft defense were the following: five anti-aircraft divisions from the High Command Reserve,[14] five medium-caliber anti-aircraft artillery regiments, 23 small-caliber anti-aircraft artillery regiments, four anti-aircraft battalions, and 12 anti-aircraft machine gun companies.

appointed commander-in-chief of the *Luftwaffe* during the final days of the war. He committed suicide in Allied captivity.

14 16th, 1st, 25th, 12th, and 10th High Command Reserve anti-aircraft divisions.

These weapons were distributed among the armies as follows:[15]

The Central Front's Distribution of Anti-Aircraft Weapons

Army and Air Formation	Anti-Aircraft Units			
	Medium-Caliber Artillery Rgts	Small-Caliber Artillery Rgts	Battalions	Anti-Aircraft Machine Gun Companies
48th Army (16th Anti-Aircraft Division of the High Command Reserve)	1	4	1	2
13th Army (1st and 25th anti-aircraft divisions of the High Command Reserve)	2	7	–	1
70th Army 12th Anti-Aircraft Division of the High Command Reserve	–	4	–	1
65th Army	–	1	–	–
60th Army	–	1	–	–
Total	3	17	1	4
Front rear and *Front* Reserve (10th Anti-Aircraft Division of the High Command Reserve	2	6	2	8
Total	5	23	3	12

Army and Air Formation	Armament			
	Medium-Caliber Artillery	Small-Caliber Artillery	ShVAK*	Anti-Aircraft Machine Guns**
48th Army (16th Anti-Aircraft Division of the High Command Reserve)	28	60	–	93
13th Army (1st and 25th anti-aircraft divisions of the High Command Reserve)	32	110	–	128
70th Army 12th Anti-Aircraft Division of the High Command Reserve	–	64	12	64
65th Army	–	15	–	16
60th Army	–	16	–	16
Total	60	265	12	317
Front rear and *Front* Reserve (10th Anti-Aircraft Division of the High Command Reserve	68	86	48	162
Total	128	351	60	479

* Editor's note. The ShVAK was a 20mm cannon, often mounted on Soviet aircraft.

** Editor's note. The DShK was a Soviet heavy 12.7mm machine gun.

15 This table does not include two anti-aircraft regiments from the tank corps, consisting of 28 small-caliber anti-aircraft guns, 16 DShK machine guns, three airfield anti-aircraft regiments, and four companies of ShVAK cannons, consisting of 48 small-caliber guns, 48 ShVAK and 80 DShK machine guns, which were part of the 16th Air Army.

Army and Air Formation	Density Per Kilometer of Front		
	Medium-Caliber Cannons	Small-Caliber Cannons	Machine Guns
48th Army (16th Anti-Aircraft Division of the High Command Reserve)	0.5	1	2
13th Army (1st and 25th anti-aircraft divisions of the High Command Reserve)	1	3.5	1
70th Army 12th Anti-Aircraft Division of the High Command Reserve	–	1	1
65th Army	–	0.2	0.2
60th Army	–	0.2	0.2
Total	–	0.8	1
Front rear and *Front* Reserve (10th Anti-Aircraft Division of the High Command Reserve	–	–	–
Total	–	–	–

As is clear from the table, the greatest density of anti-aircraft fire was created along the axis of the likely enemy attack—along the Orel—Kursk railroad. The 1st and 25th anti-aircraft divisions covered this axis.

The Voronezh Front disposed of the following: four anti-aircraft artillery divisions from the High Command Reserve, six army anti-aircraft artillery regiments, two anti-aircraft artillery regiments from tank units, three airfield anti-aircraft artillery regiments, two independent anti-aircraft battalions from the High Command Reserve, one anti-aircraft artillery battalion from tank units, and five anti-aircraft batteries from tank units.

In all, there were 25 anti-aircraft artillery regiments, three anti-aircraft battalions and five anti-aircraft batteries. These weapons were distributed among the armies in the following manner:

The Voronezh Front's Anti-Aircraft Units

Army	Anti-Aircraft Rgts	Anti-Aircraft Bns	Anti-Aircraft Divs	Anti-Aircraft Rgts and Bns
38th	2	1	–	1288th and 981st anti-aircraft rgts, 93rd Anti-Aircraft Bn from the High Command Reserve
40th	4	–	9th Anti-Aircraft Div from the High Command Reserve (minus the 981st Anti-Aircraft Rgt)	1488th Anti-Aircraft Rgt
6th Gds	5	–	26th Anti-Aircraft Div	1487th Anti-Aircraft Rgt
7th Guards	6	–	5th Anti-Aircraft Div from the High Command Reserve	162nd and 258th anti-aircraft rgts
69th	1	1	–	225th Gds Anti-Aircraft Rgt, 332nd Independent Anti-Aircraft Bn From the High Command Reserve
1st Tank	4	–	8th Anti-Aircraft Div from the High Command Reserve	–
2nd Air	3	–	–	1554th, 1555th, 1605th airfield anti-aircraft rgts
Front rear and targets	-	1	–	22nd Gds Independent Anti-Aircraft Bn from the High Command Reserve

Along the Voronezh Front's sector the main forces of the anti-aircraft guns were employed in the 6th and 7th guards armies' zones. Besides this, national air defense forces' weapons, stationed in the Kursk salient were brought in to protect the forces deployed in the Kursk salient. By 10 June 1943 these forces consisted of two mixed anti-aircraft regiments, a small-caliber anti-aircraft regiment, six battalions of anti-aircraft machine guns, ten anti-aircraft armored trains, ten anti-aircraft machine gun companies, and two fighter divisions.

All of these anti-aircraft units were designated for defending the Kursk railroad junction and the Kursk—Kastornaya railroad.

Thus the following units were concentrated for the defense of our forces in the Kursk salient: nine anti-aircraft divisions, 40 anti-aircraft artillery regiments, 17 anti-aircraft artillery battalions, five anti-aircraft artillery batteries, 22 anti-aircraft machine gun companies, two fighter divisions, and ten anti-aircraft armored trains.

The anti-aircraft units' chief task was to cover the infantry and the tanks' and artillery's concentration areas. As a rule, in the armies two-thirds of all the anti-aircraft artillery covered the troops' combat formations. For example, in the 6th Guards Army three out of five anti-aircraft regiments carried out this mission; the fourth regiment was covering a supply station and army depots, while the fifth covered an airfield. In the 7th Guards Army, of six anti-aircraft regiments, five were covering the infantry and one the Volokonovka supply station.

Two and three layers of anti-aircraft fire, predominantly small caliber, covered the infantry. Artillery positions and concentrations of tanks were covered by a single layer of fire from medium caliber weapons.

From the beginning of combat activities, when the axis of the enemy's main attacks had already been discerned, the commander of the Voronezh Front carried out a large-scale regrouping of anti-aircraft forces from the north and south toward the areas where the enemy was concentrating his aviation efforts. Upon the completion of the regrouping, some formations began to be covered by a four-layer fire from all the anti-aircraft artillery's systems.

Thus along the axis of the enemy's main attack on the Central Front, by 9 July the power of our anti-aircraft fire had increased significantly, as shown by the following data.

The Central Front's Anti-Aircraft Coverage

Layers of Fire	Area Covered (in square kilometers)	
	Small Caliber Fire	Medium Caliber Fire
One	52.8	131.0
Two	61.9	155.9
Three	57.6	143.7
Four	45.1	163.8
Five and More	80.5	221.5
Total	207.9	815.9

We see that more than 60 percent of the territory occupied by our forces was covered with a multi-layer (three and more) fire from small and medium-caliber anti-aircraft artillery. For example, during an overflight by one enemy aircraft along the front, our anti-aircraft artillery could fire on him 41,642 small-caliber rounds and 1,350 medium-caliber ones; during an overflight from the front to the rear, the corresponding figures would be as follows—1,161 small-caliber rounds and 476 medium-caliber ones.

The density thus created guaranteed the anti-aircraft fire's high results. In only two days (June 9-10) 103 enemy planes were shot down or damaged along the 13th and 70th armies' sectors.

The troop anti-aircraft system was built according to a plan drawn up by the *front's* artillery staff; in this plan, aside from anti-aircraft measures, the employment of anti-aircraft artillery in the interests of anti-tank defense was foreseen. In the army plans several variants for the employment of anti-aircraft artillery, depending on the axis of the enemy's attacks, were drawn up. The necessary documentation was drawn up for each variant.

The Central Front's anti-aircraft system was built on the basis of three variations of the likely axis of the enemy's attacks:

a) along the Orel—Kursk paved road;
b) along the Orel—Kursk railroad;
c) in the general direction of the town of Livny.

The 12th Anti-Aircraft Division covered the first axis; the 125th and 1st anti-aircraft divisions covered the second, and; the 16th Anti-Aircraft Division covered the third. Along the remainder of the front (60th and 65th armies) the troops' operations were covered from the air by only two artillery regiments.

Along the Voronezh Front the combat formations of the 40th and the 6th and 7th guards armies were covered by the 9th, 26th and 5th anti-aircraft divisions, while the remainder of the front was covered by only two anti-aircraft regiments. The Belgorod—Oboyan' axis was the most securely covered. The 8th Anti-Aircraft Division was located in the Oboyan' area. The gap between the operational zones of the 26th and 8th anti-aircraft divisions was supported by the 848th and 1487th anti-aircraft artillery regiments, whose main efforts were directed at the defense of the Oboyan'—Belgorod paved road.

The *front's* anti-aircraft weapons were just as deeply echeloned in the area of the Belgorod—Kursk railroad. Here the 1369th Anti-Aircraft Artillery Regiment was located in the area of Prokhorovka station; the 22nd Guards Independent Anti-Aircraft Battalion in the area of the Rzhava junction station, and the 1555th Anti-Aircraft Artillery Regiment in the area of Solntsevo station. Thus along the Voronezh Front's sector, along the likely axis of the enemy's main attack, there was a completely sufficient amount of anti-aircraft weapons, both along the front and in the rear. For example, the enemy's planes heading for Oboyan' were under continuous fire from our anti-aircraft artillery for more than 30 kilometers.

The anti-aircraft divisions had zones of 15-20 kilometers in width and 5-7 in depth carved out for them, within which it was necessary to protect the ground forces from enemy air attacks. In order to preserve fire communication between the anti-aircraft divisions and the reliable cover of the most important defensive targets by fire, the latter were reinforced with batteries and, in some cases, with battalions of small-caliber anti-aircraft artillery. A complete fire zone was guaranteed by the deployment of these reinforcements in the gaps between the anti-aircraft divisions' combat formations.

The anti-aircraft divisions most often deployed small-caliber anti-aircraft regiments in a single line, and less often in two; a single regiment was usually located in the second line. The regiment's batteries were deployed, as a rule, in three lines, by which the fire coverage of a zone 7-8 kilometers deep was guaranteed.

The anti-aircraft artillery's firing positions were usually selected for firing on tanks over open sights along a 360 degree radius at a distance of 800-1,000 meters. The batteries were assigned a firing sector. Each battery had an anti-tank defense plan. All anti-aircraft gun systems were sufficiently supplied with armor-piercing shells for fighting the enemy's tanks.

Teams of tank destroyers were trained in all the batteries from the rank and file of the command platoons and the instrument sections, which were armed with anti-tank grenades, bunches of hand grenades and bottles with flammable liquid.

The deputy artillery commander, whose command post was located in the area of the army artillery commander's command post, directed the operations of the anti-aircraft divisions and other anti-aircraft weapons.

Aside from authorized anti-aircraft weapons, a large number of infantry weapons were prepared to wage battle with the enemy's aviation. These included on the Central Front 581 heavy machine guns, 992 light machine guns, 1,302 anti-tank rifles, and 69 guns; on the Voronezh Front these included 2,132 rifle groups, 829 heavy machine guns, 1,551 light machine guns, 2,160 anti-tank rifles, and 50 guns.

The broad employment of infantry weapons for anti-aircraft purposes completely justified itself. Along the Central Front's 48th, 13th and 70th army sectors alone, our rifle units shot down 35 enemy planes during 5-10 July 1943.

During the organization of our anti-aircraft defense, serious attention was devoted to the masking of the anti-aircraft weapons. Before the beginning of the defensive fighting a strict fire regime was established for our anti-aircraft units; fire was to be opened only in two cases—against planes bombing our combat formations or some other target, and against reconnaissance aircraft. Special batteries were allotted for these purposes. While shifting our positions, the firing positions were outfitted with gun crews beforehand; the move itself was carried out only at night. After the batteries left them, the old positions were uncamouflaged and outfitted as new ones.

The intensified combat training carried out among the anti-aircraft crews, had a quick effect on their fire effectiveness. Proof of this are the data on shot down enemy planes; along the Central Front the percentage of planes shot down to those fired upon was as follows: in March—5.2 percent; in April—8.7 percent; in May—12.5 percent, and; in June—13.0 percent.

The *front* commands devoted a great deal of attention to the organization of cooperation between anti-aircraft artillery and fighter aviation.

The boundaries of the areas being supported by medium-caliber anti-aircraft artillery, as well as the main areas being supported by small-caliber anti-aircraft fire, were known to the entire air force rank and file, and particularly to the fighter pilots. This enabled our bombers, in case they were being pursued by enemy fighters, to take cover in the complete destruction zone, where the German planes would come under anti-craft artillery fire; the fighters, well knowing these boundaries, would break off their attacks on the enemy aircraft and resume them following their exit from the anti-aircraft artillery zone.

The anti-aircraft gunners employed examples of silhouettes and the appropriate descriptions of their signature features for identifying aircraft. Special observation of our air operations was carried out at the command posts of the anti-aircraft divisions, regiments and batteries. The observers, either by telephone or voice, constantly reported to headquarters on our planes that had entered the zone of an anti-aircraft division's fire, or which was flying within its boundaries.

In cases in which our fighter aviation had a good chance of destroying the enemy, it was allowed to radio to the ground the signal "I'm attacking" and enter the anti-aircraft fire zone after the enemy plane. Upon receiving this signal, the artillery would immediately cease fire or shift its fire to other targets not being attacked by our fighter aviation.

Given an unfavorable correlation of forces, when our planes were being pursued by enemy aviation, our planes would retreat and lure the enemy planes into our anti-aircraft artillery fire and then break contact with the pursuing enemy planes.

At the same time, routes were designated for the free passage of our aviation over the front, which were indicated in daytime by clearly displayed local landmarks and at night by light signals.

In the army, rifle and anti-aircraft division headquarters were representatives from the 16th Air Army, who maintained direct radio communication with its headquarters. The representatives were called upon to immediately call upon fighter aviation and direct it to the target.

A system of complete observation underlay the aircraft warning service. Each rifle regiment set aside non-organic aircraft warning posts. In the rifle divisions two posts were deployed by using an army aircraft warning company, of which one post was located along the forward edge and the other in the area of the division command post. The army aircraft warning service's company's posts were also set up with the rifle corps' command posts, on airfields, air ambushes, and with the army command, posts, etc.

The *front* aircraft warning services company's posts carried out their work between the army and *front* headquarters, on airfields and *front*-level targets.

Regimental and divisional aircraft warning posts were employed for informing the troops about danger from the air, with the assistance of troop telephone communications. Company posts of the air warning service were connected by radio directly with fighter aviation's airfields. Upon the appearance of enemy planes, they immediately informed the airfields of this. The main company radio station would transmit this information on the warning wavelength.

There were radio receivers, tuned to the warning wavelength, located on all the fighter airfields. They were specially designated for receiving reports from the aircraft warning service's posts.

Radio communications, which were maintained by independent air warning service posts with the airfields, were duplicated by telephone. All reports from the posts were relayed only in code.

Communications with *front* artillery headquarters with the armies' anti-aircraft sections were carried out by telegraph. When necessary, and for a short time, the main radio stations of the aircraft warning service's control points, which usually worked in the warning network, would be switched for working in the command network, duplicating the latter's work; thus the reception of telegraph correspondence was quickened. Army anti-aircraft sections maintained communications with the headquarters of the anti-aircraft divisions through a permanently active command radio network, over wire through the army company's air warning service posts, through communications officers, and personal contact.

Guidance radio stations (2-3 per army) played a big role in the warning service. The task of these radio stations was to inform the fighter aviation airfield of the air situation in a timely manner. Upon fighter aviation's taking off to intercept enemy planes, the stations would guide them to their targets. For this the guidance radio stations, using code, would communicate the type of enemy plane, their number, height (approximately), and their direction, defined by the cardinal points (course).

In guiding a plane directly to its target, the radio stations communicated in the clear, naming the type of plane, and communicated to the pilot only the direction or location of the enemy plane as related to itself: behind, to the right, to the left, higher, lower, etc.

Practice confirmed the viability of employing guidance radio stations in all types of combat. For example, just on the Central Front's sector, 12 enemy planes were shot down and seven damaged with the assistance of these stations.

The scrupulous training for anti-aircraft defense, conducted by the troops of the Central and Voronezh fronts, made it possible to inflict heavy aircraft losses on the enemy during the July fighting from the outset and to weaken the enemy's air activity to a significant degree.

The Troops' Combat Training

Taking advantage of the lull in combat activity, the forces of the Voronezh and Central fronts, alongside their defensive preparations, conducted intensive combat training.

Regular exercises in the combat and political training of the troops and staffs were conducted from April 1943 according to diagrammatic plans, confirmed by the *front* and army commanders.

In order no. 003/op of 6 April 1943, the commander of the Voronezh Front ordered:

> For the purposes of raising the troops' combat training to a higher level, as of 6 April 1943 exercises in combat and political training are to be organized with the rank and file in all of the *front's* units and formations.... Combat training is to be planned and conducted with the staffs and command element at all levels, proceeding from a plan for organizing the defense and a plan for conducting the defensive battle. The basis of this training should be the *Field Regulations*, *Infantry Field Regulations*, and People's Defense Commissariat orders nos. 306 and 325.
>
> The following problems are to be practically worked out during the period to April 20 1943:
>
> - the organization of all types of fire in the defense;
> - the organization of an anti-tank defense plan;
> - the organization of an anti-aircraft defense plan;
> - the engineering support of the position;
> - fire control of all types;
> - the repulse of the enemy's tank attack, cutting the infantry off from its tanks and destroying it;
> - the maneuver in defense of anti-tank weapons, artillery, rocket artillery units, tanks, second echelons, and reserves, for the purpose of creating a dense defense and a superiority of force along the axis of the enemy's attack, as well as for the purpose of preparing counterblows and a counteroffensive;
> - the organization and conduct of flank counterblows and a counteroffensive for the purpose of encircling and destroying the enemy's attacking forces.

Troop training was not limited to defensive matters. The order also contained the following task: "During the 20 April-1 May time period, elaborate the problems of organizing and conducting the offensive battle and operation."

In carrying out these instructions in the units and formations, the command immediately undertook to teach the troops and prepare their staffs. A great deal of attention was devoted to training the troops for operations at night. It was planned to conduct no less than a third of all exercises at night.

Preparing the staffs

During the period of constructing the defense all the staffs, without exception, were completely brought up to strength with well-trained, in the tactical sense, officers possessing staff work culture. Three basic questions formed the basis of training the staffs: the working out of the staff officers' functional duties, the compilation of combat documentation and inculcating in the officers firm habits of employing secret methods of troop control. Teaching the staff officers was carried out against the background of the real situation by means of staff exercises in conformity with the developed plans and defensive variations.

During these exercises the staffs' sections compiled the necessary combat documents (combat charts, plans for regroupings, combat orders, etc.), which were then verified in the exercises by the troops, confirmed by the command, and served as the basic documents during the defense.

Each staff exercise was preceded by a cycle of lectures on such themes as "the staff's support of the troops' regrouping," "the staff's support of the commitment of mobile reserves into the defense," "the organization of anti-tank defense," and others. The lectures were read by generals and officers.

On 23 June the 1st Tank Army staff conducted a conference of corps and brigade commanders and their staffs. Two reports were widely discussed at the conference: "the counterblow by a tank corps in a *front* operation," and "the commitment of a tank army's tank corps into the breakthrough." Both reports took into account the situation that had arisen along the front. During the examination of the reports, *front* commander General N.F. Vatutin and member of the military council, General N.S. Khrushchev,[16] who were present at the conference, issued detailed and concrete instructions on the order of employing tank formations in the defensive and offensive battles. All of this aided to a significant degree the 1st Tank Army staff and the corps staffs to correctly organize their work and to prepare for the forthcoming battle.

In order to assist the *front* and army commanders to study the terrain relief in their sectors, by order of the chief of the General Staff of the Red Army, the *front* and army staffs prepared 1:50,000 relief maps. Such maps were widely used by operational workers in their practical work and for conducting war games.

During the initial period of organizing the defense (the end of March-end of April) the *front* staffs drew up a number of orders and operational planning documents defining the *fronts'* tasks during the defensive preparation period, and also prepared all the combat orders and instructions necessary for troop control according to various defensive variations.

Part of the officers from the *front* staff's operational section, following the study of the questions connected with organizing the defense within the staff, was dispatched to the front and there took part in training the army and division staffs.

Infantry training

In training the rifle units for defense, the chief emphasis was on eliminating the fear of tanks among the troops. All of the infantry was fully trained to handle the anti-tank rifle, the anti-tank grenade and a bottle with flammable liquid. The troops trained to wage combat against the enemy's infantry attacking behind the tanks, to cut it off from the tanks and then destroy it.

Infantry training was carried out on specially outfitted training sites, which were located 6-7 kilometers from the forward edge of the defense. Training in firing from infantry weapons and infantry anti-tank weapons was carried out on these sites' firing ranges. The first-echelon rifle units were taken out daily, by company, to the rear to the training site for exercises. Second-echelon units trained in their permanent locations.

As a rule, tactical themes were worked through during two-side exercises. For inculcating firmness in the defense and eliminating the fear of tanks, T-34[17] tanks were passed through the trenches occupied by the troops, which moving in different directions, "lambasted" the trenches and showed in a practical manner that the enemy's tank was not scary if the trench has been skillfully prepared for defense.

16 Editor's note. Nikita Sergeevich Khrushchev (1894-1971) was born into a peasant family and served as a political commissar during the civil war. He later entered full-time party work and rose rapidly in its ranks, becoming a protégé of Stalin and party boss of the Ukraine in 1937. During the Great Patriotic War he served as a member of the military council of a high command and a member of the Voronezh Front's military council. Following the war, Khrushchev continued his rise during Stalin's final years and following the dictator's death in 1953. He presided over the Soviet party and state apparatus for several years, until his removal from power in 1964.

17 Editor's note. The T-34 was the Red Army's outstanding medium tank of the Second World War. One model weighed 26.5 tons and carried a crew of four. It was armed with a 76mm gun and two 7.62mm machine guns. A later model carried a crew of five and was armed with an 85mm gun.

In the process of knocking together companies and battalions, such themes were worked through: a) the repulse of the enemy's tank attack; b) the destruction of the enemy infantry that has broken into the forward edge of the defense; c) the battalion's withdrawal and occupation of an intermediate defensive line or switch position; d) the counterattack by our units and subunits against the enemy's infantry following behind his tanks, and; e) the battle in encirclement, etc.

Training the artillery

The combat training of the artillery units was conducted on the basis of the instructions of Marshal of Artillery Voronov.[18] The instructions emphasized that in the forthcoming battle the enemy was preparing to employ a large number of tanks and that among them are a large number of new heavy T-VI tanks ("Tiger").

Special firing ranges were set up in the armies for training artillerymen for firing on tanks. These contained dummy tanks that were both mobile and that appeared for a short time in various parts of the firing range. The anti-tank rifle crews and tank destroyer teams, created in each battery, carried out combat firing against the dummy tanks on these firing ranges. Battery fires were usually conducted in conditions close to combat.

The gun and battery crews' chief training, on the whole, was conducted in their permanent positions, in the prepared anti-tank areas and strong points. The commanders allotted individual tanks and armored vehicles for training the strong points' gun crews. Operating according to plan, they would appear in the designated sectors of the enemy's likely tank attack and carried out movement in various directions, etc.

A great deal of attention was devoted to studying the tactical-technical characteristics of the enemy's T-VI ("Tiger") tanks.

The artillery units' combat training transpired under the continuous control of the army and *front* commanders. The rapidity of calling fire and the artillery's opening fire, the knowledge of the artillery's tasks and signals for calling up artillery by the combined-arms commanders, and the fire cooperation of the anti-tank guns in the anti-tank areas—all of this was the subject of the army commands' special concern. The army artillery staffs created special commissions for verifying the artillery units' and subunits' combat training.

Gatherings were organized for artillery officers at the army level, the goal of which was predominantly to inculcate skill in fire control. At these gatherings the officers studied the new shell models being received by the artillery and became acquainted with their effects against the armor of a captured enemy tank.

Combat documentation was scrupulously worked out with artillery staff officers in staff exercises; everyone who studied developed concrete skills in formulating the documents. Part of the officers, specially set aside by their units, went through training in the techniques of correcting artillery fire from a tank.

In training the artillery units, the shifting of firing positions by batteries and battalions was practiced, as well as their moving from one line to another in accordance with the defensive plan. The necessary marches for this were mainly carried out at night.

In May representatives from the Red Army's Main Artillery Directorate carried out a scrupulous review of the artillery equipment in all the artillery units, and those guns requiring factory

18 Editor's note. Nikolai Nikolaevich Voronov (1899-1968) joined the Red Army in 1918 and made his way through the ranks of its artillery branch. During the Great Patriotic War he served as chief of the Main Anti-Aircraft Defense Directorate and head of the army's artillery branch. He also served as a *Stavka* representative with several *fronts*. Following the war, Voronov occupied a number of posts in the army's central administrative apparatus.

repair were replaced. These same representatives conducted exercises in the units, which helped the officers master new gun systems, optical equipment and the latest make of shells.

The anti-aircraft units and formations carried out intensive combat training during the lull. The task of all gun crews was systematic training in the ability to quickly open fire against a plane flying horizontally or in dive mode, in the ability to quickly shift from shooting at air targets to shooting at an enemy tank. Combined combat firing exercises against air and land targets were organized. Aside from this, gatherings of the commanders of anti-aircraft guns and machine guns and short-term radio operator courses were conducted. The war games (on maps) that were conducted at these gatherings pursued the goal of scrupulously working out the possible employment of anti-aircraft weapons in accordance with the variations foreseen by the overall defensive plan.

One of the important measures carried out by the artillery staffs of both *fronts* was the organization in each army of short-term courses for sergeants and soldiers of infantry subunits, who had been designated, along with their weapons, for anti-aircraft defense. Under the leadership of experienced instructors-anti-aircraft operators, they learned to fire on airplanes (mainly strafing ones), to organize group fire from rifles, and to employ the simplest anti-aircraft equipment in firing.

Training the tank troops

The training of the tank units and formations was carried out according to a plan confirmed by the commander of the armies' and *fronts'* tank troops. The tank crews, in undergoing this instruction, trained in the ability to deliver accurate fire from a tank hidden in a trench and to quickly and secretly change their position and, when convenient, leave the trench and attack the enemy on the move. The aiming of guns and combat firing, which were carried out on tank exercise fields, built in every corps area, were the main exercises. In the process of training the crews sought to replace each other fully; each crew member trained to fire accurately from a gun and machine gun, drive the tank, and to carry out the duties of the radio operator.

In training the tank troops, attention was mainly paid to knocking together the subunits, units and formations and for employing them in defense in accordance with the plan's variations.

All routes and lines, along which it was planned to, deploy tank units and formations were scrupulously reconnoitered. Reconnoitering was carried out by tank officers, under the leadership of responsible representatives from the staff of the commander of armored forces. Special teams drew up routes on the spot, and signposts were set up that sharply stood out and which were configured for both the daytime and nighttime movement of tanks. The engineering units did a great deal of work; in the march route of the 2nd Tank Army's formations alone during the defensive preparatory period they built 69 new bridges, repaired 29, improved 30,150 linear meters of roads, and prepared four collapsible heavy-duty bridges to be used in the Ol'khovatka area.

All the defensive variations were played out with the officers. War games and raids were carried out with the troops. Units or formations were usually roused at night by alarm and, by forced march along their designated road, moved up to the area designated by the plan. Having occupied this area as a jumping-off position for a counterblow, the tank troops immediately began to outfit their positions: they dug trenches for the tanks, built shelters for ammunition, disguised their position, and checked and outfitted the routes of possible counterblows. As a result of these exercises, the area designated for tank operations (the positions and exit routes to them) were completely prepared for defense. The commanders and troops knew their places well in their combat and march formations and their defensive tasks and could successfully carry them out.

Before the beginning of the operation (in the last days of June) the military council and staff of the 1st Tank Army carried out test command and staff exercises with the corps staffs. Brigade staffs, and partly, battalion staffs, were included in these exercises. The shortcomings revealed in these exercises were corrected on the spot, and the officers received instructions for organizing troop control and employing reinforcements.

The exercises conducted with officers and the troops gave the staffs the opportunity to check all their computed data, which they had compiled for each defensive variation, to tighten up the plan for employing their forces, and to check control signals.

During the entire combat training process, a great deal of attention was paid to developing endurance in the commanders and soldiers. For this purpose, besides daily physical training that consisted mainly of overcoming assault training grounds, forced marches of 20 kilometers with full pack and weapons were carried out.

Training the engineering troops

The engineering troops underwent varied training. Part of them passed through an intensive school of combat practice and carried out their tasks excellently. A significant number of subunits and units arrived at the front for the first time and were in need of prolonged training. In connection with this, the training of newly arrived units was the object of the greatest attention by the command of both *fronts'* engineering troops. The troops learned to lay anti-tank mines, bottle fields, employ captured shells as mines, employ mine detectors, and probing rods. A significant amount of time was devoted to carrying out earthworks.

The instruction program was not long; 10-15 hours were devoted to each subject. The carrying out of combat tasks was the basis for training sappers. Young soldiers, under the leadership of experienced sappers, laid mine field and set up barbed wire obstacles, built bridges and carried out demolition work. The most scrupulous training was carried out with newly formed mobile obstacle detachments and sapper subunits, set aside for accompanying the tanks. These detachments trained to lay movable anti-tank barriers along the tanks' routes of movements at special training sites. Sappers on tanks were moved up to the area of the training mine field and cleared the mines, blew up post obstacles, and learned to destroy the enemy's escarps by blowing them up, etc.

Once a week exercises were conducted with engineering officers; they involved such themes as "The study of the infantry field manual, parts 1 and 2"; "The construction of very simple types of fortification structures," and; "The mounting of structures on site." These exercises were conducted exclusively in the field and often right along the defensive constructions sectors.

Chemical training

In light of the fact that the Germans were preparing to employ poisonous substances, the chemical subunits of our units and formations outfitted ahead of time areas for degassing guns, equipment and uniforms, constructed decontamination-washing stations, and organized a network of chemical observation posts. All troops and officers received gas masks, anti-chemical packets and capes. Twice a week they carried out exercises in which they studied the workings of the gas mask, the rules for employing chemical packets, chemical decontamination, decontaminating weapons, and chemical alarm signals.

A great deal of attention was devoted to training soldiers and officers to wear their gas masks at work, during fire training, and on the march. The daily amount of wearing gas masks was raised to eight hours. A significant part of the soldiers underwent chemical fumigation.

Political training

Before the start of the German offensive party-political work in the units and formations was directed at the study and daily fulfillment of the latest orders of the Supreme Commander-in-Chief, Marshal of the Soviet Union Stalin.

These orders served as the basis for the entire work of the party-political apparatus, the party and Komsomol[19] organizations, and the officer complement. The main slogans in this work were as follows: "Glory to the hero, contempt for the coward," "Stand to the death, as the defenders of Stalingrad stood," and "Death to the German aggressors." The political organs published a large number of posters, messages and leaflets. *Front* and army newspapers made a significant contribution in aiding the defense. For example, the Central Front's political section issued prior to 1 July more than 100 messages popularizing the best scouts, tank killers, artillerymen, sappers, and tank troops. These messages were dedicated to studying the experience of their work. A series of booklets was issued: "Booklet for Fighting 'Tiger' Tanks," "Booklet for the Tank Killer," and "Booklet for the Grenade Thrower," etc. Work in acquainting the rank and file with the combat traditions of his unit and formation yielded good results. Many soldiers, although wounded, did not leave the battlefield; those discharged from hospitals asked to be sent back to those units in which they had fought earlier.

The Organization of Control

The location of command posts

Headquarters at all levels controlled their troops through a prepared system of command and observation posts, connected with each other through main and back-up communications means. As a rule, troop control was exercised from the main command posts. Along some axes, where the troops occupied defensive positions along a broad front, the commanders created auxiliary command posts (VPU). These posts, to a certain degree, eased control problems. For example, the Voronezh Front headquarters had one auxiliary command post and three reserve command posts, while the Central Front headquarters had one auxiliary command post and two reserve ones.

The main command posts of the *front* and army headquarters, in the majority of cases, were located behind the center of their troops' position, which under conditions of waging a defense significantly simplified troop control. The command posts were located as follows: the Central Front—within the confines of the second *front* line (Svoboda), and the Voronezh Front—within the first *front* line (Bobryshevo); their distance from the forward edge varied from 50-55 kilometers.

The armies' command posts were located between the second defensive zone and the army rear zone. The 13th Army's command post was located a bit further and was behind the rear army defensive zone (Lesostaevo), 28 kilometers from the front line. Such a remove can be explained by the fact that the 13th Army's defensive sector was the most deeply echeloned (up to 35 kilometers) and saturated with a large amount of equipment, as well as the fact that the main *front* reserves were concentrated in its zone. The distance of the remaining army command posts from the front line varied from 11 kilometers (70th Army north of Radogoshch) and 25 kilometers (7th Guards Army—Starikovo).

The armies' headquarters, besides the command posts, had one reserve and 1-2 auxiliary control posts and 3-4 observation posts for the army commander (6th Guards Army).

19 Editor's note. The Komsomol (*Kommunisticheskii Soyuz Molodezhi*), or Communist Youth League, was the communist party's youth auxiliary.

The corps and division headquarters had one each main and reserve command posts and two observation posts. Regimental and battalion headquarters had one main command post and one observation post.

With the onset of summer, as well as in connection with the enemy's increasing air activity, the command posts were moved from the villages to the woods, gullies and terrain contours. Strict camouflage measures and military secrecy were observed during these moves. It was forbidden to locate command posts in houses with the local population, or near one. The headquarters' sections and directorates were dispersed, often at a distance of 12-15 kilometers from each other.

Movement by automobile was forbidden within the confines of the headquarters' location, both during day and night. Cars were left in special places set aside for this purpose, 2-3 kilometers from headquarters. Airfields for communications planes were no closer than 4-5 kilometers from the *fronts'* headquarters and 1-2 kilometers from those of the armies.

The scrupulous observance of camouflage measures and discipline at the command posts deprived the enemy of the opportunity of discovering their location. This is borne out by the fact that with the beginning of the offensive, not one command post was subjected to a bombing raid, although the paralysis of our control system in this case was usually the enemy's main goal.

All the headquarters' sections were located in spacious overhead covers and dugouts, built and well outfitted by sapper subunits. Overhead covers and dugout were covered by 3-4 flat layers of logs and carefully disguised.

The organization of control and the staffs' work

Strict military secrecy was observed in the work of the *front* and army staffs, and the most scrupulous security measures were called for. Operational plans, as a rule, were drawn up by a strictly limited number of people. In the Central Front's headquarters the defense plan (all documentation, including maps) was personally compiled by the chief of the operational section and there was only one copy of each document. A small number of people were also drawn into putting together the operational plans in the armies' headquarters, and in each separate case a list of these people was submitted to the *front* headquarters for confirmation.

In the defense plans, in which everything was foreseen to the smallest detail, it was pointed out exactly which army was to carry out which assignment, the means of carrying it out according to each variation of the enemy's attack, what the reinforcements were to do, the method of their cooperation with the combined-arms formation, the jumping-off position for carrying out the mission and the time necessary to occupy it. A map, with a graphic depiction of the likely axes of the enemy's attack, our troops' (down to brigade level) location and their tasks, was attached to it.

The *front* commanders and their staffs carried out troop exercises according to all the defense variations. The divisions and brigades, carrying out training missions, carried out marches and occupied the positions set aside for them by the plan, etc. Staff officers, following the course of the exercises, checked the realism of the defensive plan and made the necessary changes to it. As a result of the large amount of work carried out by the command, troop control during the defensive battle was made much easier. For example, all the commander of the Central Front, General Rokossovskii, had to do on the night of 5-6 July was to order the army commanders to "operate according to variation no. 2," so that the formations, which knew their assignments well, sprang into action.

Operational plans were transmitted to lower headquarters in various ways. Usually the army commander was summoned to the *front* headquarters, where the *front* commander personally laid out the assignment on a map. After this, the army commander was sent an excerpt from the defensive plan and a map with the army's tasks indicated on it. Besides this, the commander of the Voronezh Front issued a combat order for the defense, which was distributed to the army staffs and some corps. The army commanders themselves often traveled to their subordinate formations and personally laid out the missions to the corps commanders, as well as to the division commanders defending along the main axis.

Subsequently, all necessary instructions toward carrying out the defensive plan were issued as local combat orders or instructions from the chief of staff. The issuance of general circular orders and directives was forbidden. Operational plans and instructions to them were sent out to the lower-level headquarters only in coded form and always with a special courier. Conversations involving questions of organizing the defense were conducted over the telephone, radio or telegraph only by prearranged message code. The duty officer at the communications center had the right, in cases involving violation of the conversation rules by officers, to report this by telephone to the chief of the operational section, and in those involving an obvious violation of military secrecy—to immediately end the conversation.

Operational documents, as well as all operational information about the troops, were sent out to the staff's operational sections. The remaining sections could only receive the necessary information from them.

During the defensive preparation period personal interaction, as one of the most effective means of control, was widely employed. A sufficient number of mobile means (planes, motor vehicles, motorcycles) at the disposal of the *front* and army commanders made it possible for them and the staff officers to visit subordinate headquarters and units at any time and to issue the necessary instructions and check their execution, to be personally in the know as to the course of the defensive work and troops' combat training, and to know the troops' real needs for weapons and engineering equipment, etc. For this purpose, almost every day the *front* commanders and the members of the military council visited the army headquarters, the divisions and the regiments and there carried out staff exercises and checked the troops' combat readiness.

Staff officers were attached to formations (chiefly to divisions) and spent a significant part of their time with the troops. Besides supervising the fulfillment of the command's instructions, these officers aided the officers and staffs on the spot in the organization of the defense, the fire system, and in troop control. Thanks to such a system of personal interaction, the command was also aware of all the preparatory work for organizing and strengthening the defense.

The boundaries of the *fronts* and armies were in the center of attention of the special commissions, specially created by the *front* commanders. These commissions had the task of coordinating on the spot all problems of securing the boundaries, as well as organizing there the system of infantry and artillery fire. Measures for organizing the defense of the boundaries were affixed in the commission's report.

In the days when engineering equipment arrived in heavy amounts, the *front* staff would dispatch its representatives to all the *front* depots. They assisted the depot directorates to precisely regulate the shipment of equipment and controlled the passage of automobile transportation with this equipment along the roads.

Representatives of the *front* and army staffs were dispatched during the exercises for the designated defensive variations. This measure was particularly favorably felt during the defensive battle. Staff officers who had thoroughly studied their formations' locations, their missions and routes, could arrive at the formation in all conditions and lead them to their jumping-off position, according to the commander's order, and facilitate the achievement of their mission.

Route maps, which were compiled on the basis of reconnaissance data, were prepared for the tank troops. On these maps each route was indicated with a corresponding color and broken up into kilometers; the unit's number was indicated on the map, showing the time necessary for it to pass. All the mine fields, laid by our forces inside their position, were indicated on the map, as well as a radio signals table. There was a combat order, previously drawn up, for each defensive variation. All calculations and the order and successiveness of the tank units' actions were made beforehand.

During combat the commanders exercised troop control mainly through high-frequency (VCh) communications. In this case the relaying of orders to the executors was significantly speeded up. Written documents were sent out only as an exception. Such communications method caused a certain difficulty in the work of those headquarters which had not been informed about the ongoing talks over the high-frequency telephone. As a result the headquarters did not always exactly know what mission this or that formation or units was carrying out at any given moment.

The location of the artillery, aviation and tank troops' commanders' control organs near the combined-arms commander's command post eased troop control. This territorial proximity enabled the *front* commander to issue orders to this or that specialist at any time and through him, quickly influence the course of the defensive operations.

In organizing troop control, attention was chiefly paid to securing the necessary combat communications, as well as the cooperation of the armies and divisions with the reinforcements, including those at the *front* level.

Most interesting was the organization of cooperation with the 16th Air Army. In the headquarters of the 13th Army, which was operating along the main axis, the deputy commander of the 16th Air Army was constantly on hand, along with operational workers and a radio station with direct contact with his headquarters; all problems of organizing cooperation with the commander of the 13th Army, General Pukhov,[20] were resolved on the spot. The air army's representatives (officers) were also present with all the division staffs of the 48th, 13th and 70th armies. Employing direct radio communications with their airfields, they would summon their planes, by request of the division commanders, and guide them to their targets; they also recorded the results of raids. Air force representatives, along with the combined-arms commanders and the commanders of the reinforcements, drew up a coordination plan for all the defensive variations, took part in reconnaissance and exercises. Aviation maps appeared as a result of this work, on which the following were clearly indicated: a) the forward edge of our troops' position and that of the security zone; b) possible intermediate lines and switch positions, which had been foreseen for occupation by the defensive plan; c) troop concentration areas, and; d) cooperation signals, etc.

According to the instructions of the air army headquarters, the aviation representatives marked on maps the enemy forces' concentration areas, which were to be suppressed by our aviation during the period of the artillery preparation, and designated air strikes in the tactical depth of the enemy's defense. The air army headquarters, in order to coordinate with the ground forces, dispatched a planning table and cooperation signals table to each army. All of this significantly eased cooperation between the air force and the ground forces and also increased the effectiveness of its actions. The necessity of sending requests to the air army headquarters and demands to dispatch aviation to the battlefield dropped off.

Responsible representatives of the tank formations operating along a given axis were at the army headquarters, as well as representatives of the *front* artillery commander.

For the purpose of speeding up the exchange of operational information, from the beginning of combat operations twice-daily telegraph conversations between the *front* and army headquarters were introduced. U-2[21] aircraft and motor vehicles were set aside in case of a break in wire commu-

20 Editor's note. Nikolai Pavlovich Pukhov (1895-1958) joined the Russian imperial army in 1916 and the Red Army in 1918. During the Great Patriotic War he commanded a rifle division, and from 1942 to the end of the war he commanded the 13th Army. Following the war, Pukhov commanded an army and several military districts.

21 Editor's note. The U-2, also known as the Po-2, first appeared in 1929. It carried a one-man crew and had a top speed of 152 kilometers per hour. It was armed with a single 7.62mm machine gun and could carry up to

nications. In order to fully facilitate the passage of combat documentation in cipher from the start of combat operations, some of the weight was taken off the cipher organs. All the secret and top secret documentation usually passed through their hands. The passage of correspondence slowed down greatly. On the instructions of the commander of the Voronezh Front, secret telegrams began to be passed along in code; only top secret and especially important telegrams were passed along in cipher. This order limited the number of people who had access to the passage of operational and other documents in cipher.

The reconnaissance activity of our ground intelligence organs was strengthened. In July, along the most important sectors of the front, the army headquarters (intelligence sections) organized reconnaissance groups, consisting of 15-20 men each. The groups were designated for conducting reconnaissance in the tactical depth of the enemy's defense, discovering his reserves, particularly tank reserves, as well as for capturing prisoners and documents. This reconnaissance was carried out on the orders of the *front* staff and conducted independently of the activities of the regimental and division intelligence organs. The creation of such groups, with a picked complement of soldiers and commanders, fully justified itself. The army commander could throw in scouts along one of the axes at any moment and discover the enemy's situation and the location of his reserves and headquarters.

Organization of communications

Wire communications (telephone, telegraph) were the chief means in defense. They were backed up by mobile means, chiefly planes and motor vehicles. Radio was used for communications with tank formations and aviation, as well as a backup means. The telephone and telegraph showed great stability in the defensive battle. This can be explained by the well thought out system of organizing communications, the scrupulous outfitting of communications centers in the command posts, and the correct laying of the lines. Thanks to this, in the days of the most intense fighting there was not one breakdown in communications, for example, in the 13th Army, lasting more than 15-20 minutes.

Communications in both *front* headquarters was organized in accordance with the plan for the defensive battle. The main mission of the communications troops in preparing for the defense was the creation of a foolproof communications system that would make it possible to control the troops in any variation of their activities, in accord with the defensive plan. There was a sufficient amount of the necessary apparatus and cable at the disposal of both *fronts'* communications troops. For example, the 1st Tank Army had on 5 July the following: up to 100 percent of line equipment, up to 150 percent of telegraph apparatus, up to 100 percent of telephone apparatus, and up to 100 percent of radio apparatus, and operational materials for 5-6 days of uninterrupted work. All of the armies operating along the main axis of both *fronts* (13th, 70th and 6th Guards armies, and others) had this amount of communications equipment.

Detailed plans for organizing communications, which had been drawn up by the *fronts'* communications directorates, were foreseen for each defensive variation. According to these plans, the communications troops built permanent lines, the main ones of which, together with the communications centers, had been completed by the end of June 1943.

It seemed that a large number of troop formations (rifle divisions and brigades) would demand a large number of communications lines. For example, in the 13th Army it was necessary to secure 16 lines and 14 in the 70th Army. In order to avoid building such a large number of lines and conserve communications equipment, communications in the defense was constructed according

six 50-kilogram bombs.

to the axis principle, employing communications centers. As a result, in the 13th Army, instead of 16 lines, five communications axes were created and more than ten centers. A thick set of wires, laid down along each axis, enabled us to organize communications with each formation along 2-3 channels.

The army and corps reserve command posts were outfitted with communications equipment beforehand and had direct telephone communication with the main ones. When the commander and his staff moved to a reserve command post, communications with subordinate formations and neighbors was not disrupted. For example, in the 22nd Guards Rifle Corps cable communications equipment was laid down in such a way that it enabled us to fully exercise communications from the main and reserve command posts. These posts had telephone and telegraph communications between each other; communications with the divisions from the reserve command posts were exercised over a wire, which had been included in the 90th Guards Rifle Division's communications center.

In the rifle divisions wire communications ran along lines. The headquarters of the rifle regiments did not have direct wire communications between each other, but maintained communications through the division center.

Radio communications in the 13th Army were organized according to the network principle: a cooperation network, a network for the armored and motor-mechanized troops, and an artillery network; besides this, direct radio communications was organized with the Red Army General Staff and Central Front headquarters, etc. During the defensive preparation period, radio stations worked on an extremely limited scale; operational conversations by radio were categorically forbidden. The full employment of radios for communications was allowed from 5 July, and in some armies (6th Guards) only from 2000 on 6 July. The radio stations of the corps and division headquarters carried out, above and beyond their usual work, the tasks of the aviation representatives for guiding our planes to the enemy's aircraft.

The army commanders created special groups for servicing radio communications, consisting of 2-3 radio stations, set up on motor vehicles, predominantly four-wheel drive ones. These groups included battalion radio station "Prima," and RBI "North" radio stations. The army commander, through these stations, could get in touch with *front*, corps and divisional headquarters from any location.

Reserve networks were foreseen for newly arrived units, and reserve lines were left for assigning them call signs in the combat journals.

The work of the radio stations and networks was scrupulously checked before the start of the battle.

Communications through mobile means were organized according to directions. For this purpose U-2 aircraft, motor vehicles and motorcycles were employed in the army headquarters, motor vehicles in the corps and division headquarters, and lower—messengers on horseback and motorcyclists. Mobile communications means were employed as a backup system for wire communications and mainly supported the delivery of combat correspondence to the troops.

Before the operation's start communications through mobile means was organized through field postal stations. The major part of the army mobile means (automobiles and motorcycles) had been conserved before the start of the battle.

Communications officers (with transportation equipment) from the formations were located with the army headquarters' operational sections. A permanent cadre of officers saw to their most effective employment. All the formations were supplied to a sufficient degree with prearranged message codes, coded maps and radio signal tables.

A reserve of radio stations was usually held for communications maneuver: in the armies one RAF and 2-3 RSBs, and 1-2 RSBs in the corps. The number of wire communications means in these formations' reserve varied. But in any case, this reserve's equipment was counted on for communications with no less than two formations newly subordinated to the army or corps.

The scrupulous preparation for defense and the correct organization of communications enabled the headquarters at all levels to facilitate the command's precise and unbroken troop control in the defensive battle.

The *Fronts'* Reinforcement and Maintenance During April-June 1943

In three months, from April through June 1943, the *Stavka* of the Supreme High Command carried out a series of measures to maximally reinforce the Central and Voronezh fronts. They received new formations and units. One may judge the process of gradually strengthening the *fronts* from the following tables.

Reinforcing the Central Front

Formations and Units	Number		Absolute Change (plus or minus)	Increase (in %)
	1 April	1 July		
Rifle divisions	33	44	+11	33
Cavalry divisions	2	–	-2	–
Rifle brigades	5	4	-1	–
Ski brigades	3	–	-3	–
Anti-tank brigades	3 (9 AT rgts)	6 (18 AT rgts)	+3 (9 AT rgts)	100
Independent anti-tank regiments	8	10	+2	25
Total anti-tank regiments	17	28	+11	65
Field artillery regimental reinforcements	27	35	+8	29
Heavy and high-power artillery brigades	–	4	+4	–
Army mortar regiments	25	22	-3	–
Guards mortar brigades	2	3	+1	50
Independent guards mortar regiments	10	9	-1	–
Guards mortar battalions	1	1	0	–
Armored trains	5	15	+10	200
Tank brigades	13	15	+2	15
Independent tank regiments	13	15	+2	15
Motorized rifle brigades	2	2	0	–
Anti-tank rifle battalions	1	5	+4	400

Reinforcing the Voronezh Front

Formations and Units	Number		Absolute Change (plus or minus)	Increase (in %)
	1 April	1 July		
Rifle divisions	29	35	+6	20.7
Rifle brigades	1	–	-1	–
Independent battalions	4	–	-4	–
Anti-tank brigades	4 (12 AT rgts)	6 (18 AT rgts)	+2 (6 AT rgts)	50
Independent anti-tank regiments	9	31	+22	222
Total anti-tank regiments	21	49	+28	133
Field artillery regiments	13	21	+8	51
Army mortar regiments	5	16	+11	220
Guards mortar regiments	8	11	+3	37.5
Guards mortar battalions	1	1	–	–
Armored train battalions	–	3	+3	–
Tank brigades	10	20	+10	100
Mechanized brigades	–	3	+3	–
Independent tank regiments	5	10	+5	100
Motorized rifle brigades	2	3	+1	50

Simultaneously with the reinforcing of the *fronts* with new formations and units, both *fronts* were being brought up to strength with personnel and equipment. As a result, the *fronts* were brought up to full strength, according to a number of indices. The results of this over two months, 1 from April through 1 June, are clear from the following table:

Reinforcing the *Fronts*

	Increase (in %)	
	Central Front	Voronezh Front
Men	136	105
Rifles	91	163
Machine gun pistols	246	470
All machine guns	174	454
Mortars (all calibers)	66	171
Field guns (including 76mm regimental guns)	63	160
Anti-tank guns (including rifle units' small-caliber guns)	125	240
Anti-tank rifles	98	357
Tanks	189	897

Personnel reinforcement was carried out not so much through new arrivals as from the *fronts'* internal resources. For example, in the Voronezh Front the overall demand for reinforcements was met by mobilizing men in the liberated territories by 27 percent, 9 percent from those who had recovered and been discharged from army and *front* hospitals, 33 percent from rear-area personnel fit for combat, and 31 percent from outside reinforcements. Of the other major measures for the maximum increase in the combat capability of the *fronts'* forces and the steadiness of the defense, one may note the following:

- for the purposes of effectively employing the guards formations, as the most experienced and steady, the *Stavka* of the Supreme High Command decided by 1 May to combine all the Voronezh Front's guards formations into two guards armies: the 6th (the former 21st Army) and the 7th (the former 64th);
- for better troop control, a large part of the rifle divisions were organized into rifle corps; by the beginning of June the Central Front had formed 11 corps headquarters, with ten such headquarters in the Voronezh Front;
- in order to increase the stubbornness of the defense and to improve the quality of fire control, as well as to support the subsequent transition to the offensive, for the first time major artillery formations were employed; the 4th Artillery Corps, consisting of two artillery divisions and one independent guards artillery division, was concentrated along the axis of the enemy's likely attack (in the 13th Army's sector and along the 70th Army's right flank).

The *front* reserve consisted of the 2nd Anti-Tank Division, with two anti-tank brigades and one sniper battalion.

3

The Enemy's Group of Forces by the Beginning of the Battle and the Corrrelation of Forces

Changes in the Strength and the Enemy's Group of Forces Facing the Kursk Salient During the Period April-June 1943

Following the conclusion of the spring 1943 operations and the stabilization of the front, the German-Fascist command began to hurriedly prepare for a new offensive operation, with the immediate task of eliminating the Kursk salient. For this purpose, the Germans began to concentrate formations and units from other sectors of the Soviet-German front and from the operational depth.[1] The changes in the enemy forces' strength facing the *fronts* during the period from 27 March to 4 July are shown in the table:

Changes in Enemy Strength Opposite the Central and Voronezh Fronts

	Number of Formations		Absolute Change	Increase (in %)
	27 March	4 July		
		Facing the Central Front		
Total divisions	24	33	+9	38
Of these:				
Infantry	19	24	+5	26
Panzer	4	6	+2	50
Cavalry	1	–	-1	–
Mechanized	–	2	+2	–
		Facing the Voronezh Front		
Total divisions	14	21	+7	50
Of these:				
Infantry	10	12	+2	20
Panzer	4	9	+5	125

1 The 36th and 10th motorized, 86th, 6th and 292nd infantry divisions were transferred from the area of our Western Front; the 9th and 2nd panzer divisions from our Bryansk Front; the 106th Infantry, 3rd, 11th, 6th and 19th panzer divisions from our Southwestern Front, and; the 377th Infantry, 203rd, 213th, and 221st security divisions from the operational depth, following their reconstitution.

	Number of Formations		Absolute Change	Increase (in %)
	27 March	4 July		
		Facing Both Fronts		
Total divisions	38	54	+16	42
Of these:				
Infantry	29	36	+7	24
Panzer	8	15	+7	88
Cavalry	1	1	–	–
Mechanized	–	2	+2	–

The German command had the task of bringing up to strength its combat formations and units that had been badly worn out in the preceding battles. As a result of a total mobilization, the Germans managed to bring up the strength of the majority of their divisions to 8-12,000 men and officers.

The German command was counting on the shock effect of the unexpected employment of its new weapons—a large number of super-heavy T-VI "Tiger" tanks and heavy "Ferdinand" assault guns. The units that contained these weapons were located in both the Orel and Belgorod—Khar'kov enemy groups of forces.

The changes that took place in the numerical strength of the enemy's forces during the April-June 1943 period are shown by the data in the table on the following table:

German Reinforcements Opposite the Central and Voronezh Fronts

	Number of Formations		Change in Absolute Numbers	Increase (in %)	Comments
	27 March	4 July			
			Facing the Central Front		
Men	125,000	267,000	142,000	111	
Tanks	290	1,455	1,165	400	Of the 1,445 tanks, 600 were from high command reserve battalions, including 150 T-VI "Tigers"
Guns	1,604	4,263	2,659	166	
Mortars	1,523	2,103	580	38	
			Facing the Voronezh Front		
Men	75,000	168,000	93,000	124	
Tanks	375	1,700	1,325	353	Of the 1,700 tanks, 400 were from high command reserve battalions, including 100 T-VI "Tigers"
Guns	500	2,500	2,000	400	
Mortars	500	1,100	600	120	
			Facing Both Fronts		
Men	200,000	435,000	235,000	111	
Tanks	665	3,155	2,490	371	
Guns	2,104	6,763	4,657	230	
Mortars	2,023	3,203	1,180	58	

The Enemy's Group of Forces by 4 July 1943

The enemy's group of forces facing the Central Front

The enemy's main group of forces had been created facing the 13th Army along the 32-kilometer Glazunovka—Tagino sector. Here the German command concentrated five infantry divisions (the XXIII Army Corps'216th Division, XLI Panzer Corps' 78th, 86th, 6th, and 292nd divisions), six panzer (the XLI Panzer Corps' 18th Division, the XLVI Panzer Corps' 20th Division, and the XLVII Panzer Corps' 2nd, 4th, 9th, and 12th divisions), and one motorized (the XLVII Panzer Corps' 10th Division) divisions. A large part of the reinforcement artillery and tank battalions from the high command reserve[2] were in these divisions—including three battalions of T-VI "Tiger" tanks, with 50 tanks in each battalion, and a regiment of "Ferdinand" heavy assault guns, consisting of 90 vehicles.

On the remaining 274 kilometers of front, 14 infantry and one mechanized divisions were operating.

A comparison of the density of the enemy's group of forces facing the Central Front, on the whole and along the axis of the main blow, is shown in the second table:

Change to Density of Enemy Forces per Kilometer of Front

	Front Average	Along the Sector of the Main Attack
Men	870	4,500
Tanks	4.7	42
Guns	13	70.3
Mortars	6.8	34

The following data shows the correlation of forces along the Central Front's sector:

The Correlation of Forces Along the Central Front

	The Entire Front	Along the Sector of the Main Attack
Men	1:2.6 in our favor	1:1.1 in our favor
Tanks	1:1.2 in our favor	1:1.1 in our favor
Guns	1:1.3 in our favor	1:1.1 in our favor
Mortars	1:4.1 in our favor	1:1.8 in our favor

Note: In determining the correlation of forces on our side, the following were included: 13th Army, 2nd Tank Army, 19th and 9th tank corps, and the *front's* mobile anti-tank artillery reserves.

2 The main group of forces includes those formations located in the operational reserve along the axis of the main attack.

The enemy's group of forces facing the Voronezh Front

At the beginning of July 1943 the following units were operating against the Voronezh Front:

a) the right wing of the German Second Army, consisting of the XIII Army Corps (88th Infantry Division), VII Army Corps (26th, 68th and 75th infantry divisions, and a combat group from the 323rd Infantry Division);
b) the Fourth Panzer Army, consisting of the LII Army Corps (57th, 225th, 332nd, and 167th infantry divisions), XLVIII Panzer Corps (3rd and 11th panzer divisions and the *Grossdeutschland* Panzer Division), and an SS Panzer Corps (*Adolph Hitler*, *Totenkopf* and *Das Reich* SS panzer divisions);
c) Army group Kempf, consisting of the XI Army Corps (168th, 106th and 320th infantry divisions) and the III Panzer Corps (6th, 19th and 7th panzer divisions). The group's XLII Army Corps (282nd, 39th and 161st infantry divisions) were facing the Southwestern Front's 57th Army in the area south of Volchansk.

The main enemy group of forces was facing the 6th and 7th guards armies along the Zybino—Bezlyudovka sector. The sector was 70 kilometers in width.

The German command concentrated along this sector five infantry divisions: 332nd and 167th from the LII Army Corps, the 168th, 100th and 321st from the XI Army Corps, as well as nine panzer divisions: 3rd and 16th from the XLVIII Panzer Corps, *Grossdeutschland*, *Das Reich*, *Totenkopf*, and *Adolph Hitler*—from the SS panzer corps, and the 6th, 7th and 19th divisions from the III Panzer Corps. Just as along the Central Front, a large number of reinforcements, including two battalions of T-VI tanks, with 50 tanks in each battalion, were operating with these divisions.

Seven infantry divisions were defending along the remainder (174 kilometers) of the front, while all their artillery along the Sumy—Zybino sector had been included in the shock group of forces.

The density of the enemy's forces facing the Voronezh Front, on the whole, and along main group of force's concentration sector was as follows:

Density of Enemy Forces per Kilometer of Front

	Average Along the Front	Along the Axis of the Main Group of Force's Concentration
Men	730	2,000
Tanks	7.4	34
Guns	10	32
Mortars	4.5	1 5.4

Density of Enemy Forces per Kilometer of Front Along the Main Attack Sectors

Men	2,500
Tanks	42
Guns	40
Mortars	19

The correlation of forces along the Voronezh Front's sector is characterized by the superiority of the Red Army's groups of forces concentrated here.

The Correlation of Forces Along the Voronezh Front

	The Entire Front	Along the Concentration Sector of the Main Shock Group
Men	1:2.5 in our favor	1:1.35 in our favor
Tanks	1:1.1 in our favor	1:1.6 in our favor
Guns	1:1.7 in our favor	1:1.1 in our favor
Mortars	1:6.0 in our favor	1:3.7 in our favor

Notes:

1. In determining the correlation of forces on our side, this includes the forces of the 6th Guards Army, four right-flank divisions from the 7th Guards Army, the 1st Tank Army, and the 5th and 2nd guards tank corps.
2. The figures for the enemy do not include the rank and file of the army reinforcement units. If one leaves out our similar units, then the correlation of forces would be 1:1.

The enemy's air group of forces and strength

The final regrouping of the enemy's air force before the start of the offensive was carried out 2-3 days before it began. During this period up to 50 percent of the aviation that took part in the July offensive was moved up from bases in the Donbass and Crimea.

The Germans' air force, which took part in the offensive against the Central and Voronezh fronts, by the start of the offensive numbered 17 squadrons from the Fourth Air Fleet's I, IV and VIII air corps; or about 1,850 planes. All of these planes were based on the airfield nets in the areas of Bryansk, Orel, Belgorod, and Khar'kov.

Aside from this figure, more than 200 bombers took part in the operation, operating from bases in Smolensk, Orsha, Stalino, Zaporozh'e, and Kirovograd. Thus more than 2,000 planes operated against the Central and Voronezh fronts; that is, 80 percent of the enemy aviation on the Soviet-German front.

By the beginning of July 1943 the correlation of forces in the air was as follows:

The Correlation of Air Strength

	Our Planes			Enemy Planes
	16th Air Army	2nd Air Army	Total	
Fighters	455/71	389/85	844/156	600
Assault	241/28	276/29	517/57	100
Day Bombers	260/14	172/18	432/32	1,000
Night Bombers	74/2	34/15	108/17	–
Reconnaissance	4/2	10/8	14/10	150
Total	1,034/117	881/165	1,915/272	1,850

Note: Our combat-ready planes are shown in the numerator, and non-combat ready planes in the denominator.

Quantitatively, the sides' forces were almost identical. However, we had a very significant superiority over the enemy in fighters and in assault aircraft, but were inferior to him in bombers and reconnaissance aircraft.

Our command constantly followed all the changes in the enemy's grouping of forces. Nothing here remained unnoticed by the *front* staffs and the *Stavka* of the Supreme High Command. This is shown by *Stavka* and Central and Voronezh front headquarters documents. For example, on 10 April the Central Front's chief of staff, Colonel General Malinin,[3] reported to the chief of the General Staff that there were up to 15 German infantry and three panzer divisions in the first line facing the Central Front and that the enemy was concentrating new divisions toward the front. The *front* staff at the time considered the most likely axis of attack to be the line Orel—Kromy—Kursk.

On 12 April the commander of the Voronezh Front, General Vatutin, in his telegram no. 0093/op, reported the concentration of six infantry and 11 panzer divisions before his *front*. On that same day, in a telegram to the chief of the General Staff, General Vatutin reported that the enemy's main group of forces was being created in the Borisovka—Belgorod—Murom area, consisting, evidently, of up to six infantry and ten panzer divisions, with an overall strength of up to 1,500 tanks. The most likely axes of attack were considered from the Belgorod area to Staryi Oskol and toward Oboyan' and Kursk; auxiliary attacks could be expected along the Volchansk, Novyi Oskol, Sudzha, Oboyan', and Kursk axes.

On 11 May General Vatutin, in a report to the Supreme Commander-in-Chief, Marshal of the Soviet Union Stalin, stressed that the enemy was continuing the process of concentrating a shock group and that at the present time the enemy had concentrated in the area Graivoron—Tomarovka—Belgorod—Mikoyanovka no less than seven panzer divisions; by 11 May up to 13 infantry divisions in the first echelon had been fixed facing the *front*. The enemy's main attack was expected along the Oboyan'—Kursk axis.

On 16 May the Deputy Supreme Commander-in-Chief, Marshal of the Soviet Union Zhukov, stated in a report to comrade Stalin that the Voronezh Front was facing up to 13-14 infantry divisions and, in the immediate rear—up to 900 tanks, despite the fact that the enemy was not yet ready for an offensive.

The June (1943) reports from the Central Front headquarters emphasized that all the German prisoners captured in the course of the month spoke of the concentration of the main German group of forces along the Pokhval'noe—Tagino sector and that one can evidently expect the Germans' main attack along the 13th Army's front. Our command undertook active measures to counter the ongoing concentration of enemy forces. For example, on 4 May the *Stavka* of the Supreme High Command issued a directive to the commander of the Red Army Air Force to destroy the enemy's aviation on the airfields and in the air in the areas of Belopol'e, Romny, Poltava, and Merefa, the destruction of his railroad deliveries along the Poltava—Khar'kov sector, and the disorganization of his automobile movement along the roads in the Belopol'e—Akhtyrka—Novaya Vodolaga area.

Nor was the assumption of the offensive by the enemy unexpected for us.

Reports by partisans and prisoner testimony spoke to the fact that the German command at first planned to begin its offensive on Kursk in the second half of May (20-25 May). However, as the result of the Belgorod—Khar'kov group's lack of readiness, as its panzer divisions had not yet been brought up to strength in equipment and personnel, it was necessary to delay the offensive to a later date—5 July.

On 2 July comrade Stalin, in a special telegram, warned the commanders of the Central and Voronezh fronts of the enemy's forthcoming offensive:

3 Editor's note. Mikhail Sergeevich Malinin (1899-1960) joined the Red Army in 1919. During the Great Patriotic War he served as chief of staff of a mechanized corps, an army and a number of *fronts*, including the Central Front. Following the war, Malinin served as chief of staff of the Group of Soviet Occupation Forces in Germany and as first deputy chief of staff of the Ground Forces.

According to the available data, the Germans could go over to the offensive along our front during the period 3-6 July 1943.

The *Stavka* of the Supreme High Command orders the following:

1. To strengthen reconnaissance and observation of the enemy for the purpose of uncovering his intentions beforehand.
2. The troops and air force are to be ready to repulse a possible enemy attack.
3. Report on orders issued.

I. Stalin
A. Vasilevskii

On the night of 4-5 July a sapper from the 6th Infantry Division was captured, who stated that on 5 July the German forces would go over to the offensive in the general direction of Kursk with both groups of forces—Orel and Belgorod.

Conclusions

1. The German-Fascist plan for the summer of 1943 was sufficiently accurately uncovered by our command as early as March 1943. The *Stavka* of the Supreme High Command not only made a precise forecast as to the overall character of the enemy's forthcoming actions, but also completely concretely determined the deployment areas of his main shock groups of forces and the likely axes of his attacks.

2. As the subsequent course of events showed, the Red Army high command made the absolutely correct and appropriate decision to meet the enemy attack along a well-prepared defensive bridgehead, to bleed the attacking German groups of forces and then, upon going over to a general offensive with the forces of the Western, Bryansk, Central, Voronezh, and Southwestern fronts, to finally destroy them, thus creating favorable prerequisites for the unfolding of new and wide-ranging offensive operations. Our defense was prepared in expectation of the subsequent assumption of the offensive. This is testified to by the concentration of our forces and their disposition along the Kursk salient.

3. The complete knowledge of the axes of the German command's forthcoming attacks, along with the definite possibility of our going over to a general offensive, made it possible to create a powerful defensive system, as well as to concentrate a powerful group of forces and equipment—both along the entire territory of the Kursk salient, as well as immediately along the axes of the assumed enemy attacks.

   A correct strategic forecast, the well-organized regrouping process, the presence of powerful strategic reserves and mobilization resources, and our industry's unfailing meeting of all the army's demands, enabled us in three months of operational pause to create in the area of the Kursk salient a powerful defense that proved impossible for the German army to overcome. The German command was unable to create on a single sector of the front—even along the axis of the main attack—a superiority of forces. Quite the opposite, by the start of the German offensive the correlation of forces, according to all indices, was developing in the Red Army's favor. It was only in tanks along the axis of its main attack against the Voronezh Front that the Germans managed to achieve an insignificant superiority.

   In no small measure was the creation of a favorable correlation of forces in the area of the Kursk salient facilitated by the circumstance that the German command, not without foundation, feared attacks from the direction of the Western and Bryansk fronts and was thus forced to maintain major forces north of Orel and thus deprived of employing them for an offensive on Kursk.

Nor did the enemy's intention of disorganizing our defense by the surprise employment of a large number of heavy T-VI "Tiger" tanks and heavy "Ferdinand" assault guns yield the expected success, because the Red Army command adopted the corresponding measures in a timely manner.

4. Without a doubt, the German command had been informed, in a general manner, as to the forces and degree of readiness of our defense. However, in repeating its main mistake, which was determined by the defectiveness of the German strategy, which came down to overestimating its own forces and capabilities and underestimating ours, the German command set out on a grandiose venture that became the July offensive.

5. The characteristic feature of the Kursk salient's defense was its great depth, which reached 110 kilometers along the axes of the enemy's main attacks (the line prepared by the Steppe Military District was not a part of this). The *fronts'* forces occupied up to four defensive lines ahead of time. Thus the defense occupied by our forces along the most important axes reached 60 kilometers.

6. The defense's firmness and active nature was supported by the presence of powerful mobile reserves, which were located at the disposal of the *front* commanders. These were the tank armies and tank corps, as well as a large number of mobile anti-tank reserves (anti-tank brigades and regiments, and battalions of anti-tank rifles).

7. The supreme high command's precise and confident forecast as to the axis of the offensive being prepared by the enemy made it possible for us to concentrate in the rear of the Kursk salient powerful strategic reserves and to assign them concrete combat tasks, both of a defensive nature (the occupation and preparation of a defensive line along the Kshen' River), as well as to the likely counterblows (their axes).

8. The timely and uninterrupted study of the enemy's group of forces, as well as the knowledge of his operational methods (hackneyed attacks against the bases of a salient) enabled the *front* commanders to concentrate the main mass of their men and materiel along the likely axes of the expected main attacks and to avoid dispersing their forces along the entire Kursk salient, and to leave the tip of the Kursk salient relatively weakly manned by our forces.

9. The German command, having once again overestimated the penetrating capability of its groups of forces and, having underestimated the strength of our defense's resistance, was relying mainly on the crushing strength of its first blow in the forthcoming offensive. Thus the formation of our forces was characterized by the lack of large operational reserves.

10. The offensive character of the enemy's groups of forces and the distribution of his reinforcements (mainly tanks) along the various sectors of the front, testified to the fact that the German command was striving to break through our defense through the ramming method—concentrated attacks along narrow sectors of the front by powerful groups, consisting to a significant degree of tank formations, supported by a large amount of air power.

11. The Red Army command's knowledge of the timetable for the Germans going over to the offensive deprived the enemy, from the very beginning of the operation, of all the advantages of surprise, on which the German command had placed such great hopes.

PART TWO

A DESCRIPTION OF COMBAT ACTIVITIES ON THE CENTRAL AND VORONEZH FRONTS

1

A Brief Survey of the Defensive Battle

The battle of Kursk began on 5 July simultaneously along the northern and southern faces of the Kursk bulge.

The German command threw into the offensive its main groups of forces—the Orel group against the Central Front and the Belgorod—Khar'kov group against the Voronezh Front. The enemy sought to eliminate the Kursk salient and encircle our forces defending it. Both enemy groups of forces, as a result of concentric blows, were to link up in the Kursk area and complete the encirclement of the main mass of the Central and Voronezh fronts' forces.

A brief description of the fighting along the Central Front

The battle along the Orel—Kursk axis unfolded along a 40-kilometer front and embraced the territory of the Kursk salient to a depth of up to 12 kilometers. The fighting here lasted for 13 days. On 5 July the enemy's Orel group of forces, consisting of the XLI and XLVII panzer, part of the XLVI Panzer and XXIII Army corps, went over to the offensive along the sector Krasnaya Sloboda—Verkhnee Tagino in the general direction of Kursk. The Germans launched their main attack with the forces of the XLI and XLVII panzer corps along the front Arkhangel'sk—Verkhnee Tagino toward Ol'khovatka.

Auxiliary attacks to secure the flanks of the main group of forces were directed by the forces of the XXIII Army Corps from the Krasnaya Sloboda—Vasil'evka—Glazunovka area toward Maloarkhangel'sk, and the other by the left-flank formations of the XLVI Panzer Corps from the Verkhnee Tagino area toward Gnilets. The fighting along the Central Front is divided into three stages.

First stage—the 5-6 July fighting along the main defensive zone.

During 5 July the enemy managed to penetrate along the axis of its main attack 6-8 kilometers into the depth of the 13th Army's defense and reach the second defensive zone. The enemy's attempts to break through our troops' front along the auxiliary axes were unsuccessful.

On the following day the forces of the Central Front carried out a counterblow with part of their forces against the Germans' main group of forces that had penetrated the 13th Army's defense. Although our forces did not manage to defeat it and restore the situation, this counterblow so shook the Germans' main group of forces that in subsequent days it proved incapable of continuing major offensive operations. As a result of serous major losses incurred on the battle's first day, the enemy was forced to significantly shorten his operational front and refrain from attacking in the directions of Maloarkhangel'sk and Gnilets.

Second stage—the 7-8 July fighting.

Having committed fresh reserves, the Germans attempted during these days to break through the 13th Army's second defensive zone in the direction of Ol'khovatka and Ponyri, for the purpose of further developing the offensive on Kursk.

Having run up against our troops' extremely stubborn defense, the enemy managed to advance only 2-4 kilometers and insignificantly break into the second defensive zone along the Ponyri—Saborovka sector. However, this small tactical success cost the enemy such enormous losses that by the close of 8 July the German command was forced to renounce further offensive action and go over to the defensive.

The third stage embraces the gap in time from 9-17 July. The Central Front prepared and carried out a counteroffensive, as a result of which by the close of this stage it had restored the situation. By the close of 17 July the *front's* right wing had again reached the line it occupied before the German offensive. The fulfillment of this mission was made significantly easier by the fact that on 12 July the forces of the Bryansk Front and the left flank of the Western Front went over to the offensive. The German command had to remove part of its forces from the Central Front's sector (two panzer and one motorized divisions) and throw them into the Orel area, and to also throw the main part of its air power, which had earlier been operating along the Central Front's sector, against our attacking armies.

A short description of the fighting along the Voronezh Front

The battle along the Belgorod—Khar'kov axis unfolded along a front about 90 kilometers in length and embraced the territory of the Kursk salient to a depth of up to 35 kilometers. Here the fighting continued uninterruptedly for 20 days.

The battle along the Voronezh Front began along two relatively independent axes. The Germans, in striving to break through to Kursk, launched their main attack along the Belgorod—Oboyan'—Kursk paved road along the Oboyan' axis against the 6th Guards Army and then the 1st Tank Army. The enemy launched a supporting attack along the Korocha axis against the forces of the 7th Guards Army, and then the 69th Army.

The main forces of the Germans' Belgorod—Khar'kov group of forces (Fourth Panzer Army: XLVIII Panzer Corps, SS Panzer Corps, and the LII Army Corps) deployed and operated along the axis of the main attack.

The enemy group of forces, consisting of the III Panzer and XI Army corps operated along the supporting axis.

The fighting along the Voronezh Front is broken up into three main stages:

The first stage involved the fighting during 5-9 July along the Oboyan' and Korocha axes.

The second stage involved the fighting during 10-12 July along the Prokhorovka axis.

The third stage involved the fighting during 13-15 July by the 69th and 5th Guards Tank armies in the Leski—Gostishchevo—Shakhovo—Rzhavets area and the Voronezh and Steppe fronts' offensive during 17-23 July.

The first stage was characterized by fierce fighting along the Oboyan' and Korocha axes. As a result of stubborn fighting on 5-6 July, the Germans broke through the 6th Guards Army's main defensive zone. As early as the close of 6 July the main German group of forces had reached the second defensive zone, occupied by the 6th Guards Army's second-echelon troops and the *front* reserves. Subsequently, during 7-9 July the enemy continuously attacked the second defensive zone, striving at all costs to break through to Oboyan' and open the road to Kursk. However, all these attempts to break through to Oboyan', both immediately in the area of the Belgorod—Oboyan' paved road and by means of turning the 1st Tank Army's left flank by attacking from the Greznoe area to Kochetovka, ended in failure. On 10 July the German command was forced to call off its subsequent offensive by its main forces along the Oboyan' axis and went over to the defensive here.

Simultaneous with this fighting, no less fierce battles unfolded along the Korocha axis. The enemy sought to reach the area of the town of Korocha and thus secure the attack of his main force toward Kursk from the east. As a result of successive attacks, by the close of 6 July the Germans had forced the Severskii Donets along the sector Solotino—Pristan' and had reached the 7th Guards Army's second defensive zone.

The meager results of the fighting along both axes, and the impossibility of breaking through to Korocha through a short but powerful blow, forced the German command to limit its operations. On 8 July enemy forces went over to the offensive to the north, with the mission of encircling the 6th Guards Army's left-flank formations, which were defending along the Lipovyi Donets River. The enemy was counting on creating a crisis situation in this area to disperse our reserves there; moreover, he planned to broaden the breakthrough to the east, in order to secure the main group of forces' rear against our forces' attacks from the line of the Lipovyi Donets River.

By the close of 9 July the enemy along this axis had managed to reach the Melekhovo area along a thin wedge; our units were pushed back directly to the Lipovyi Donets River. In order to reinforce our forces operating along this axis, on 9 July the entire force of the 69th Army, to which the defense of the Prokhorovka axis was entrusted, was committed from the *front* reserve.

If one remembers that as early as 8 July the German offensive against our Central Front had ended in a complete collapse, the expediency of continuing the offensive against the Voronezh Front fell away or, at any rate, was in doubt.

The second stage embraces the fighting for Prokhorovka.

With the failure of the Germans' attempts to break through to Oboyan', they shifted their main efforts to the Prokhorovka axis, for the purpose of reaching Kursk by a more roundabout way—through Prokhorovka. The German command prepared to capture the Prokhorovka area by coordinated attacks by the main group of forces from the area Kozlovka—Yasnaya Polyana—Greznoe, and by the III Panzer Corps from the Melekhovo area toward Verkhnii Ol'shanets and then to Prokhorovka. Simultaneously, the German command calculated on encircling the 69th Army and thus significantly broadening to the east the pocket that had formed as a result of the German offensive.

On 11-12 July fierce tank battles unfolded along the Prokhorovka axis. During these battles the enemy suffered enormous losses and, having nearly completely exhausted his offensive possibilities, was forced here to give up further attempts to continue the offensive.

12 July was the day of the German offensive's final crisis. The Hitlerite command was forced to renounce the idea of carrying out its stated mission—the capture of Kursk from the south.

To top it off, the forces of the Western, Bryansk and Central fronts went over to a decisive offensive on that day, for the purpose of eliminating the Germans' Orel group of forces. The initiative had completely passed to the Red Army command.

The third stage includes the fighting by the 69th and 5th Guards Tank armies in the area Leski—Gostishchevo—Shakhovo—Rzhavets; the purpose of these battles was to parry the Germans' attempts to encircle the 69th Army's 48th Rifle Corps, which was defending the narrow salient formed by the course of the Lipovyi Donets and Severskii Donets rivers.

On 14-15 July the enemy, by launching concentric attacks from both sides from the Yasnaya Polyana area and from the Shchelokovo area toward Shakhovo, sought to encircle the 48th Rifle Corps' divisions. The Germans planned to eliminate the salient occupied by the corps' forces and broaden the pocket, which had formed as a result of the German offensive. On 15 July the corps' divisions exited the pocket, after heavy fighting, under the cover of rearguards. The task that the enemy had set for himself was also unfulfilled here.

As a result of the complete failure of the offensive operation on Kursk from the south, by 16 July the German forces facing the entire Voronezh Front were forced to give up the continuation of active operations and went over to a rigid defense.

On 16 July the German command, under the cover of powerful rearguard units, began to pull out the Fourth Panzer Army's main forces from the pocket to the line previously held by them.

Subsequently, during 17-23 July, the forces of the Voronezh and Steppe fronts, having gone over to the offensive, completely cleared the enemy out of the territory seized by him during the course of his ten-day offensive. The Red Army restored the situation that it had occupied at the start of the German offensive.

2

The Central Front's Defensive Battle

The Fighting for the Main Defensive Zone on 5-6 July 1943

The start of the battle

At the end of June 1943 the German command began to earnestly prepare its forces for the offensive. Our intelligence repeatedly observed the concentration of large groups of the enemy's tanks and self-propelled artillery in the forests north of Sen'kovo and Verkhnee Tagino. Motorized infantry was also being brought up here. The *front's* forces began to be subjected to sudden fire attacks by artillery and mortars. The enemy's reconnaissance aircraft were constantly in the air. Ground intelligence increased its activity. At night groups of German sappers would clear their minefields, and they also tried to make passages in our minefields and wire obstacles.

On the night of 4-5 July a reconnaissance detachment of the 15th Rifle Division discovered in the Verkhnee Tagino area a group of enemy sappers, numbering 17 men, busy making passages in our minefields. Bruno Formel, a Polish sapper from the 6th Infantry Division, was captured and related under interrogation that:

"The German forces have been brought to a condition of complete combat readiness, and on 5 July, following a short artillery preparation, at 0200 European time, will go over to the offensive in the general direction of Kursk. Simultaneously, an offensive along the Kursk axis will begin from the Belgorod area."

Based on this data, it could be assumed that the Germans were preparing to launch an offensive within the next few days.

The *Stavka* of the Supreme Command, possessing exact information as to the German forces' forthcoming offensive, as early as 2 July specially warned the Central Front command.

> Within the next few days the enemy's assumption of the offensive is possible. It is necessary to bring the forces along all the defensive lines to a state of complete combat readiness.

The combat activities that began on 4 July along the Voronezh Front also indisputably confirmed that on 5 July the enemy would undoubtedly go over to a general offensive.

Having received the instructions from the *Stavka* of the Supreme Command, the *front* commander ordered the army commanders to warn the troops of the possible assumption of the offensive by the enemy and to immediately bring all their equipment to a state of complete combat readiness. By this order all the mine-explosive obstacles in front of the forward edge of the defense were readied for action. The mobile obstacle detachments, in accordance with the plan, moved into their jumping-off areas. The *front's* artillery prepared to begin a counterpreparation. On the airfields the fighter and bomber crews were in readiness to take off immediately. The army and division commanders occupied their forward observation posts on the night of 4-5 July.

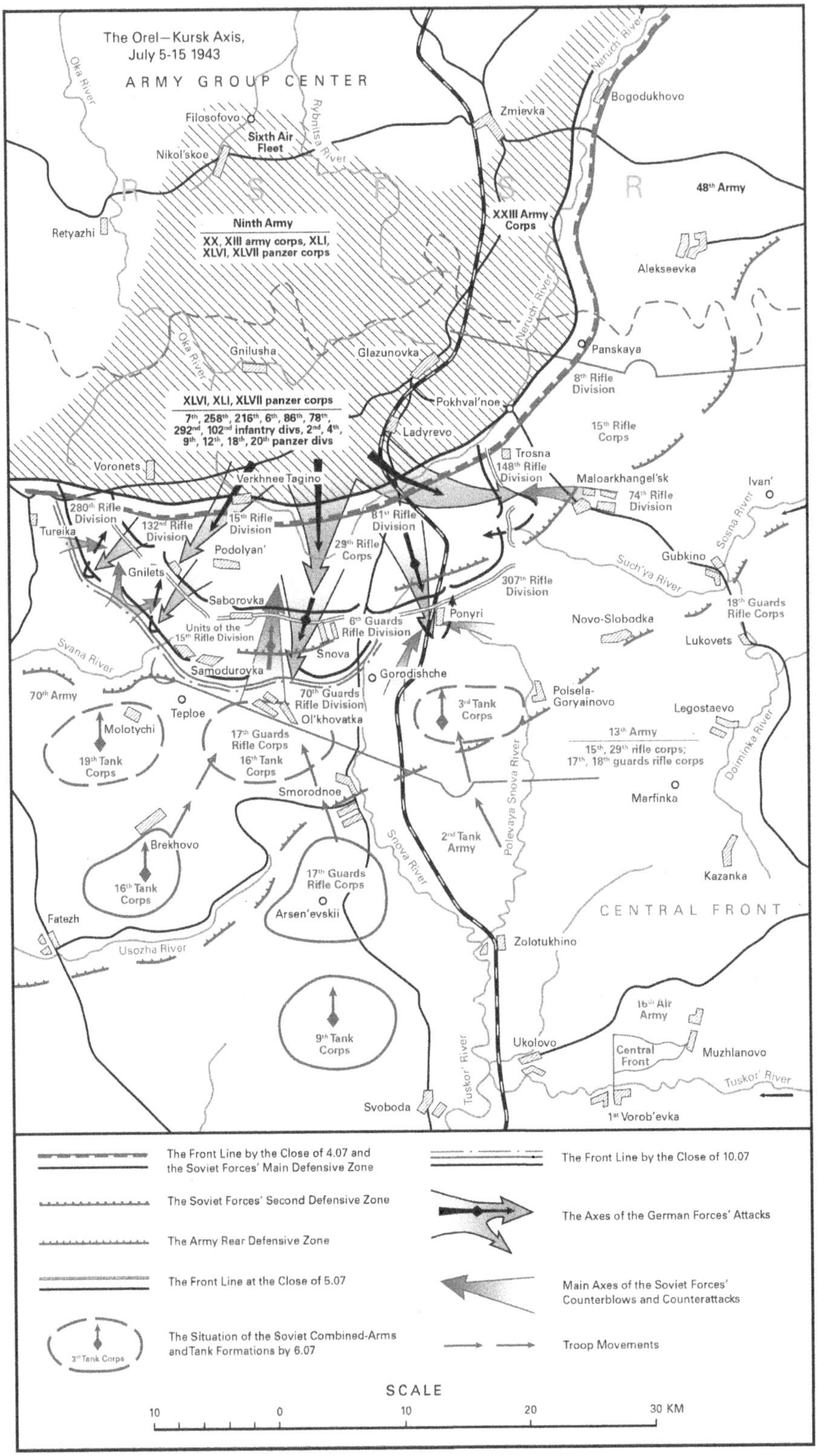

Map 2 The Orel—Kursk Axis, 5-15 July 1943.

At 0210 on 5 July, by order of the *front* commander, a powerful artillery counterpreparation began unexpectedly for the enemy along the *front's* right wing. The enemy line was covered with a solid wall of shell and heavy mortar explosions. As the result of a direct hit by our shells, several German depots with munitions blew up at a short distance from the enemy's forward edge. Large fires broke out.

The enemy's artillery answered weakly. The enemy's searchlights began working in the predawn darkness; the Germans began to intensely illuminate the terrain with rockets. As was discovered later, the enemy took the artillery fire for the beginning of an artillery preparation and decided that our forces had preempted their offensive.

The artillery counterpreparation lasted 20 minutes. As a result, more than 80 enemy artillery and mortar batteries were suppressed, six ammunition depots blown up, and heavy personnel losses inflicted on the enemy. The enemy's combat formations and control over them were to a significant degree disorganized by our fire. The German command was forced to delay the start of the offensive by 1½ -2 hours.

At 0430 the Germans began their artillery preparation. Their fire was mainly directed against our artillery and mortar batteries, and particularly against the infantry's first echelons.

The *front* commander ordered the artillery counterpreparation to be repeated. At 0435 our artillery interrupted the enemy's artillery preparation and immediately severely disorganized it. The enemy's fire began to weaken quickly. Many of the enemy batteries stopped firing altogether and were able to resume firing only at 0800.

At 0530 on 5 July the Germans went over to the offensive, considerably behind their original plan, launching attacks simultaneously along three axes.

The main attack by the forces of the XLI and XLVII panzer corps (2nd, 4th, 9th, 12th, and 18th panzer divisions, and the 78th, 86th, 6th, and 292nd infantry divisions, and the 10th Motorized Division) was directed at Ol'khovatka.

Two of the XXIII Army Corps' divisions (216th Infantry and 36th Motorized[1]), reinforced by tanks, launched a supporting attack toward Maloarkhangel'sk.

Another supporting attack by the forces of the XLVI Panzer Corps (7th Infantry and 20th Panzer divisions) was aimed at the boundary of the 13th and 70th armies in the direction of Gnilets.

The fighting along the Ol'khovatka axis

At 0730 on 5 July, when the enemy's artillery was still firing, the German aviation appeared in the sky. The enemy planes, in waves of 50-100 aircraft, continuously approached the forward edge of our defense and dropped a large number of bombs. Our artillery and the troops, located in the second army defensive zone, were also subjected to heavy air attacks. The German forces, covered by fire, went over to the offensive along the front Soglasnyi—Arkhangel'skoe—Novyi Khutor. The main attack, with forces up to four infantry and three panzer divisions, numbering about 500 tanks, was launched in the general direction of Ol'khovatka.

Heavy "Tiger" tanks, at high speed and in groups of 10-15 vehicles, reached the northern bank of the Ochka River and opened a heavy fire on our forces' lines. Behind them there appeared medium and light tanks, which at high speed and in groups of 50-100 vehicles, quickly approached the forward edge of the defense. Infantry followed behind the tanks in armored transports. A large number of infantry was observed in the combat formations of the tank units and in the immediate rear, which under the cover of the tanks, moved forward quickly.

1 The XXIII Army Corps' 36th Division had been reformed as an infantry division shortly before the battle.

Our artillery, mortars and machine guns opened a heavy fire against the attacking enemy. Guns firing over open sights, and anti-tank rifles, firing at point-blank range, shot up the enemy tanks. Our fighter and assault aviation reached the battlefield. Dogfights broke out in the sky.

The German tanks, upon reaching our minefields, began to blow up one by one. The vehicles following behind would drag the damaged tanks back and continued to overcome the mined sectors along their path. T-VI "Tiger" tanks and "Ferdinand" self-propelled guns covered their medium tanks and infantry with heavy fire.

Fire from our artillery and mortars and the increasing attacks by our aviation from the air significantly slowed down the German tanks. The enemy's infantry began to hit the ground more often. A large number of enemy vehicles were already burning on the battlefield.

Only at 0900 did the enemy manage to attack the forward edge of the main defensive zone and break into the positions of the 13th Army's 81st and 15th rifle divisions. These division's units, fighting stoutly, beat off four fierce enemy attacks. Only as the result of the fifth attack, when the German command committed fresh forces into the fighting, did the enemy tanks and infantry manage to break into our defensive positions at several points. Heavy fighting broke out. Our troops, fighting bravely, defended every foot of ground. Our anti-tank artillery, firing over open sights, shot up the enemy's tanks. The sappers and tank destroyers, risking their lives, threw themselves on the German vehicles under a hurricane of fire, placed mines under them, attacked them with anti-tank grenades, and set fire to the enemy vehicles with bottles containing flammable liquids.

Taking into account the situation developing in the 13th Army's center, the *front* commander threw more than 200 fighter planes and about 150 bombers into that sector. Before 1200 our aviation carried out 520 sorties. Our bombers launched serious attacks against the enemy's tanks and reserves, held up their advance to the battlefield, and disorganized their control to a significant extent.

The 13th Army was reinforced. It received from the *front* reserve the 1st and 13th independent anti-tank and 21st Independent Mortar brigades, which were hurriedly thrown into the areas of Ponyri and Snova.

Following two hours of fierce fighting, during which more and more tank and infantry reserves were thrown into the battle, the enemy broke our forces' resistance and pushed back the 15th and 81st rifle divisions. Units of these divisions, supported by powerful artillery fire and aviation, made wide use of the developed trench network and switch positions. Wearing down the attacking enemy's forces, they fell back in an organized manner.

By 1030 the enemy forces managed to take height 254, Ozerki and Yasnaya Polyana. Units of the 81st and 15th rifle divisions, coming under heavy attacks from large groups of tanks and infantry, could not hold on to this line for long and were split up. The enemy's tanks streamed to the south: up to 60 tanks broke through to Ponyri; more than 70 tanks attacked through Butyrki toward Snova; about 40 tanks and up to two regiments of infantry reached the Podolyan' area, threatening to outflank the 70th Army on the right.

In order to destroy the tanks that had broken through, the commander of the 13th Army moved two mobile obstacle detachments, a tank regiment, and several sapper elements into the battle. The divisional and anti-aircraft artillery (the larger caliber weapons) entered the battle against the enemy vehicles, firing from open positions.

The enemy began to suffer heavy losses. By 1300 our units had destroyed up to 40 percent of those tanks that had broken through. The remainder, having slowed down their rate of advance, began to operate indecisively; a significant portion of the tanks fell back to shelter.

Our infantry, while hanging onto each prepared line in the depth, put up stout resistance to the enemy. Using the powerful artillery support, it fell back slowly to the south and southeast. Units of the 15th Rifle Division, having suffered heavy casualties, by the close of 5 July had approached the second defensive zone, occupied by the 6th Guards Rifle Division, and there dug in. The 81st Rifle Division was engaged in heavy fighting along the line excluding Semenovka—Buzuluk—Ponyri. The enemy's forces, which had been bled heavily, were not in a condition to continue the offensive; having reached the second army defensive line, the enemy was forced to end his attacks to the morning of the following day.

The fighting along the Maloarkhangel'sk axis

At 0530, two hours before the enemy's main forces launched their offensive toward Ol'khovatka, the German command tried to launch a supporting attack to the east—toward Maloarkhangel'sk, in order to split our 48th and 13th armies. Up to two divisions (216th Infantry and 36th Motorized), reinforced by tanks, attacked the positions of the 8th and 148th rifle divisions.

At about 0600 the Germans broke into our troops' position along some sectors. Heavy fighting broke out in the area Aleksandrovka—Soglasnyi and Maloarkhangel'sk station. However, the 13th Army command managed to quickly determine the axis along which the enemy had thrown the main mass of his infantry and tanks. All our artillery fire was immediately concentrated along these sectors, and the divisional anti-tank reserves and guards mortar units entered the battle.

The German tanks, fired upon from several directions and suffering heavy casualties, were forced to turn back. Before long, units of the 8th and 148th rifle divisions completely destroyed the enemy infantry that had penetrated into our position and restored the forward edge of the defense. Thus the forces of the 13th Army's right flank successfully paralyzed a powerful enemy attack. The German units not only did not manage to break through the defense here, but in many places they were not even able to reach its forward edge.

The enemy forces, having smashed themselves against the impregnability of our defense along this sector, were not able to punch a secure wedge along the Maloarkhangel'sk axis—along the boundary of the 48th and 13th armies. The left flank of the main force of the enemy's Orel group of forces, which were attacking toward Kursk, remained unsecured against the forces of the 48th Army overhanging it from the north. The latter's cooperation with the 13th Army was not disrupted. Our forces retained complete freedom of maneuver along this sector. The fighting confirmed the enormous significance of the *front* commander's measures for securing the boundaries between his formations. The enemy's attempt to use the boundary between the 48th and 13th armies for breaking through our defense was a failure.

The fighting along the Gnilets axis

At 0930 on 5 July the enemy, with the forces of the 7th Infantry and 20th Panzer divisions, and supported by aviation, launched a powerful attack against the right flank of the 70th Army (132nd and 280th rifle divisions). However, the Germans were not able to break through the 132nd Rifle Division's defense. They repeated their attacks along this sector several times, threw into the fighting a significant number of tanks and aircraft, but each time they fell back with heavy losses. The units of the right-flank 280th Rifle Division just as successfully beat back the enemy attacks.

Despite this, the situation along the boundary of the 13th and 70th armies became more difficult with each minute. A large group of enemy tanks with motorized infantry, which had broken through to the Podolyan' area began to quickly spread to the south and southwest, pushing back the 13th Army's left flank. The 15th Rifle Division, having suffered heavy losses, was falling back to the south, thus exposing the 70th Army's right flank. The commander of the army's 132nd Rifle Division, in attempting to eliminate the possibility of the enemy outflanking the army from the east, threw in the 712th Rifle Regiment to the east of Gnilets. But this did not change the situation. The Germans, in up to a regiment in strength, with 40 tanks, turned from the Podolyan' area to the west and attacked the 712th Rifle Regiment, which had already suffered heavy losses. The regiment, while holding off the enemy pressure, began a fighting retreat in the direction of Gnilets. By 1230 the regiment's subunits, exerting their last bit of energy, delayed the enemy along the line marker 232—the eastern outskirts of Gnilets—Krasnyi Ugolok.

Almost simultaneous with the outflanking of the 132nd Rifle Division, the German forces attacked along the front for the second time and broke through the division's defense and began to spread out in the direction of Gnilets from the north, threatening the 712th Rifle Regiment with encirclement. Units of the 132nd Rifle Division, heroically fighting the enemy, could not withstand the pressure of significantly superior enemy forces, and in the second half of the day began to fall back.

The German aviation, supporting the advance by its units, shifted its attacks from the 13th Army's sector to the 70th Army's right flank. Dive bombers, in spite of our heavy anti-aircraft fire, uninterruptedly dropped bombs on the defending units of the 132nd and 280th rifle divisions.

The retreat of the 132nd Rifle Division was covered by the 605th Rifle Regiment's 1st Battalion. Having deployed north of the village of Gnilets, the battalion entered the fighting against the numerically superior enemy. The soldiers cut the infantry off from its tanks with powerful fire from mortars and machine guns. Within a few minutes six enemy tanks were burning on the battlefield. The battalion commander, Captain Kozmenko, ordered his men "to stand to the death, but not a step back!"

Suffering enormous losses, the Germans lunged forward. Following three unsuccessful attacks, the German command dispatched 80 planes to the battlefield, which in the course of 20 minutes incessantly bombed the 1st Battalion's defensive area. Many men died from the bomb explosions, while those who remained alive were more than once buried by the earth. The heroes continued to fight. The Germans, following the bombing attack, threw 15 tanks and a battalion of infantry into the attack. By night the enemy had managed to encircle Kozmenko's battalion. However, in these difficult hours the soldiers continued to carry out their combat mission with honor. On orders of the division commander, the battalion, summoning up its last reserves of strength, broke through the encirclement ring and linked up with friendly units.

As a result of the 132nd and 280th rifle division's stubborn resistance, the German forces, which had begun the offensive against the 70th Army's right wing, were bled white and could only penetrate an insignificant distance into our defensive position.

By 1900 our units had fallen back to the southwest and had securely consolidated their position as follows: the 132nd Rifle Division—along the line of the southern outskirts of Bobrik—northeastern outskirts of Probuzhdenie—Obydenki—northern outskirts of Izmailovo. The 280th Rifle Division's left flank remained along its previous line. All further attempts by the enemy to break through our defense along the 70th Army's right flank were unsuccessful.

Results of the 5 July fighting

Thus on the offensive's first day the German forces, despite a great superiority in force along the attack axis, were not able to break through the defense of the Central Front's right flank. At the cost of huge losses, they only pierced the defense along the Ol'khovatka axis to a depth of 6-8 kilometers, and were forced to halt there.

Due to the stubborn resistance of the 13th and 70th armies' forces, the enemy was seriously worn down and exhausted. In one day of fighting the Germans lost along the 13th Army's sector alone 15,000 men killed and wounded, more than 110 tanks, 106 planes, and a large amount of other equipment. As early the first day of its general offensive, the German command was forced to make an extended pause, regroup its forces, put them in order, and bring up fresh reserves.

The front commander's decision to launch a counterblow

The first day of the Germans' offensive completely uncovered the axis of their main attack. As the *front* commander had supposed, the German command had directed its main forces along the railroad to Kursk. By attacking on Maloarkhangel'sk, the Germans sought to split the Central Front's armies and secure from the east the offensive by its main forces to the south.

In the first part of 5 July the *front* commander issued the following orders to his army commanders over the high-frequency telephone: "At dawn on 6 July begin operations according to variation no. 2."

This variant of the defensive plan called for the launching of the main attack by the forces of two armies: the 13th (17th and 18th guards rifle corps) and the 2nd Tank along the front Mamoshino—Orlanka—Prilepy—Bityug—Kashara in the general direction of Ladyrevo and Koshelevo. This attack was to be supported by the 48th Army's left flank with an attack toward Zmievka, and the 70th Army's right flank, with the mission of attacking toward Kromy.

The commander of the 2nd Tank Army received additional instructions: "Begin operations immediately. Advance in company and battalion groups. The 19th Tank Corps is operationally subordinated to you."

The commander of the 9th Tank Corps received orders to concentrate his forces in the area Arsen'evskii—Trubitsyn—Sergeevskoe and be ready from the morning of July 6 for operations along the following axes: a) Verkhnee Smorodnoe—2nd Ponyri, and b) Stanovoe—Samodurovka.

In this way, the *front* commander, while keeping in place the plan for the counterstroke according to variation no. 2, only moved the 9th Tank Corps a little to the north and deployed it behind the 13th Army's center.

In carrying out the order, the troops immediately left for their jumping-off areas. By 1900 on 5 July the 2nd Tank Army had deployed as follows: 3rd Corps in the area Berezovets—Brusovoe, and the 16th Corps north of Ol'khovatka. The 9th Tank Corps occupied the defensive line Molotychi—Novoselki—Yasenok. The 18th Guards Rifle Corps was marching with the task of concentrating in the Maloarkhangel'sk area by the morning of 6 July. The 17th Guards Rifle Corps, which was delayed somewhat in its movement, was concentrating by the end of the day in the area Bityug—Kashara—Ol'khovatka.

By the close of the first day's fighting, it had finally become clear that the enemy was not directing his main efforts along the railroad, as had been supposed by the second variation of the defensive plan, but somewhat to the west, attacking in the general direction of Ol'khovatka. Under these conditions, the troops actions, had they been exactly directed at carrying out the second variation of the plan, would not have conformed to the situation, and thus the *front* commander made the necessary fine tuning to it.

At 2200 on 5 July the commander of the 2nd Tank Army was ordered to go over to the defense with his 3rd Tank Corps along the line Polsela—Goryainovo—southern outskirts of Gorodishche; the 16th Tank Corps, in conjunction with units of the 17th Guards Rifle Corps, were to attack at dawn on 6 July in the general direction of Butyrki—Gnilusha, with the task of restoring the situation along the 13th Army's left flank. The 19th Tank Corps was to attack toward Saborovka and Podolyan'. The 70th and 13th armies, taking advantage of the tank corps' attacks, were also to go over to the offensive and restore the situation. The 18th Guards Rifle Corps, while remaining in the army's second echelon, was to securely cover the Maloarkhangel'sk axis.

All our air efforts were also directed at destroying the enemy's tanks and infantry concentrated in the areas of Podolyan', Bobrik (three kilometers south of Podolyan'), Step' and Butyrki.

Thus, the *front* commander, by making timely corrections to the plan for the counterstroke, decided to launch a meeting attack with his main forces against the enemy's main group of forces.

He was forced to renounce any kind of complex maneuvers with his reserves, in connection with the developing situation. A good deal of time was necessary to carry out regroupings.

The *front* commander decided to launch a short but powerful attack as soon as possible against the enemy forces that had penetrated our defense, in order to finally bleed them white and deprive them of the capability of continuing the offensive. The moment for doing this had been fortuitously chosen: the enemy had not yet recovered from the heavy losses he had suffered and had not succeeded in restoring his disrupted command and control, and had not prepared his second echelons for commitment into the battle.

The Fighting on 6 July. The Central Front's Counterstroke

The counterstroke by the 17th Guards Rifle Corps and the 16th and 19th tank corps

During the night of 5-6 July the enemy uninterruptedly conducted intensified reconnaissance in small groups along the entire front. German sappers stubbornly sought out our minefields and tried to make passages through them. Night aircraft uninterruptedly illuminated the roads with rockets, along with wooded areas in the defensive depth, and bombarded them. The enemy's artillery and mortars did not cease firing along the forward edge of the second defensive zone the entire night. The loud sound of motors was heard coming from the enemy's positions. All this testified to the fact that the enemy was preparing for a new attack; his tanks and infantry could once again go over to the attack in the coming hours.

In accordance with the *front* commander's decision, units of the 17th Guards Rifle Corps and 2nd Tank Army set out to prepare a counterstroke. The 16th Tank Corps took up position in the area 2nd Ponyri—Kutyrki. Units of the 17th Guards Rifle Corps, which had been subjected to repeated attacks on the march by German aviation, was held up in its movement to its jumping-off area; its main forces had concentrated along the line Snova—Kashara and that only at 2030 on 5 July. This could not but affect upon the organization of cooperation with the tank formations and the corps' preparations for the offensive.

The 19th Tank Corps, having received orders to attack along a new axis, spent a lot of time reconnoitering the area, preparing passages through its infantry's combat formations, and mainly—on making passages in the minefields and other anti-tank obstacles, which had been set up by our forces in the defensive depth. As a result of this, the corps was not only not ready to attack by morning, but also by midday, and thus did not take part in the counterstroke together with the 17th Corps.

The 4th Artillery Corps and the 1541st and 1441st self-propelled artillery regiments were to support the troops' offensive. By the close of 5 July they were completely ready to carry out their assignments.

The 17th Guards Rifle Corps' offensive was supposed to begin at dawn on 6 July, in order to preempt the enemy and inflict a surprise attack on him.

At 0350 our artillery opened up a heavy fire. During the course of ten minutes the enemy position was covered with a large number of explosions. At 0400 our air force reached the front line. The bombers dive bombed in groups the enemy's tank and infantry, which had prepared for the offensive, and dropped bombs on them. The German artillery answered weakly, from time to time firing on our artillery's firing positions. Before long the enemy's fighters appeared. Heavy fighting broke out in the sky. At this time the tanks of the 16th Corps' 107th and 164th tank brigades, operating with the 75th and 6th guards rifle divisions, went over to the attack. The 107th Brigade's tanks advanced in front, followed by the 164th Brigade's vehicles echeloned to the left.

Despite our artillery fire and air action, the enemy put up stubborn resistance to our forces. The German artillery and self-propelled guns opened up a hurricane of fire on the 107th Brigade's tanks as soon as they set out. Our infantry, which was advancing behind the tanks, while suffering heavy losses, began to hit the ground more often and lag behind the tanks.

Firing on the move, our tanks destroyed one enemy firing point after another and stubbornly pressed forward. Sometimes individual tank elements were forced to return to their infantry, which was pinned down by the enemy fire. By covering the soldiers with their armor, the tanks helped them to advance.

At 0600 units of the 17th Guards Rifle Corps crushed the enemy's resistance and, having inflicted a defeat on him, reached the line 1st Ponyri—Druzhovetskii—Bobrik. To the right, units of the 148th, 74th and 81st rifle divisions, which had also gone over to the offensive, were fighting for the southern outskirts of Soglasnyi and Maloarkhangel'sk station.

The 107th Tank Brigade, continuing its movement from the line Druzhovetskii—Step' toward Butyrki, unexpectedly encountered an ambush of German heavy tanks, which had been carefully buried in the earth and camouflaged. The brigade got into a fight with them and, having lost more than 30 tanks, fell back on its infantry. In order to avoid further losses, the tank corps commander, who had been personally observing the fighting, ordered the 164th Tank Brigade, which was advancing behind and to the left of the 107th Brigade, to fall back to its jumping-off position.

Units of the 17th Guards Rifle Corps halted their attack and began to consolidate along the line achieved. On orders of the 13th Army commander, the 237th Tank Regiment, 1st Guards Artillery Division and the 378th Anti-Tank Artillery Regiment, were thrown into the fighting to help the corps. Mobile obstacle detachments immediately set out to lay mines along the tank-accessible axes.

The German forces, having halted our 17th Corps' attack, immediately went over to the attack. They renewed their attack to the south, toward Ol'khovatka. Up to 300 tanks and a large number of enemy infantry attacked the corps' positions along a broad front. Our infantry put up stubborn resistance to the enemy.

All of the 13th Army's artillery strength was concentrated to support the 17th Corps. On 6 July our artillery men destroyed more than 80 enemy tanks and self-propelled guns. However, the Germans, paying no heed to their heavy losses, pushed forward. At 1300 the enemy committed the fresh 292nd Infantry Division, with tanks, into the fighting from the Aleksandrovka area.

Units of the 17th Guards Rifle Corps, having failed to withstand the enemy's new attack, abandoned their line and fell back to their jumping-off position. The Germans' attempts to break into the second army defensive zone on the heels of the retreating units enjoyed no success that day.

Having completed its preparations for the offensive by 1700, the 19th Tank Corps launched an attack in the general direction of Podolyan'. By 2000 its units had reached the line two kilometers west of Saborovka—height 232. However, this attack, which was launched late, was not successful. The neighboring formations (17th Guards Rifle and 16th Tank corps) on the right had by this time been forced to fall back to their jumping-off positions, where they continued to repulse the enemy's fierce attacks. In order to avoid excessive losses, the 19th Tank Corps was pulled back to its jumping-off position and took up a defense along its previous line.

The fighting along the Ponyri axis

The Ponyri strong point, around which the fighting unfolded on 7 July, cut the Orel—Kursk railroad. By anchoring on it, our forces had the opportunity to launch flank attacks against the enemy group of forces attacking both along the Maloarkhangel'sk axis, as well as the Ol'khovatka axis.

From the front and flanks the Ponyri center of resistance was girded by continuous minefields, including radio-controlled ones. Part of these minefields was saturated with aerial bombs, operating according to the tension principle of action. Continuous rows of barbed wire ran in front of the trenches; tank-accessible axes were reinforced with post obstacles. The center of resistance disposed of a large number of tanks, buried in the ground, and anti-tank artillery. The commander of the 307th Rifle Division, which was defending the center of resistance from 6 July, disposed of an army mobile obstacle detachment.

The German command, perceiving the significance of the center of resistance, decided to capture it at any cost and secure for itself a free passage to the south. The enemy, having thrown into the battle simultaneously more than 170 tanks, with motorized infantry, supported by uninterrupted and powerful attacks from the air, broke through the 81st Rifle Division's defense along the line Semenovka—Buzuluk—1st Ponyri and began to rapidly spread out to the south.

However, the enemy did not manage to break into the army's second defensive zone on the heels of the retreating division. Units of the 307th Rifle Division, which occupied defensive positions here, while relying on the powerful strong points, halted the Germans. The enemy attacked the 30th Rifle Division's sector three times in great strength, but fell back each time with heavy losses.

Results of the 6 July fighting

As a result of the fighting on 6 July, the Central Front's right-flank forces, in spite of all their efforts, did not carry out the mission laid down by the *front* command. The front was not restored along the 13th and 70th armies' sectors. The enemy was in direct contact with the second defensive zone and was readying himself for new attacks. However, the sudden and powerful counterstroke by the *front* reserves foiled all the German command's plans. It did not even dare to throw into the battle its reserves (12th Panzer and 10th Motorized divisions), which had been designated for developing the offensive. During the 5 July fighting, and particularly following our counterstroke on 6 July, the Germans' main group of forces had been so powerfully shaken and had suffered such heavy losses, that in the following days it proved incapable of fighting and continuing major offensive operations.

If on the offensive's first day, the enemy managed to advance into the 13th Army's defensive depth 6-8 kilometers, then by the second day his advance did not exceed 1-2 kilometers. The enemy in the 70th Army's sector had been pinned down by our forces' attack from the south and did not undertake any active operations. On 6 July our forces killed up to 10,000 German officers and men and destroyed over 110 tanks and 113 planes.

It should also be noted that on 6 July the enemy had already been forced to significantly shorten his attack front and give up continuing the offensive along the axes toward Maloarkhangel'sk and Gnilets.

The 7-8 July Fighting for the Second Defensive Zone

The fighting along the Ponyri axis

On 7 July the fighting was renewed with new strength along the 13th Army's front. The German forces, supported by a large number of tanks and planes, attempted as before to break through the army second defensive zone. Their main efforts, as was the case on 6 July, were directed along the railroad to Ponyri and to the west, on Ol'khovatka.

The *front* and army command adopted all measures to halt the enemy along these axes. The 11th Mortar and 46th Light Artillery brigades were thrown into the Ponyri area from the *front* reserve, as well as the 2nd Independent Anti-Tank Brigade's 12th Artilllery Regiment from the 48th Army.

The 81st Rifle Division, which had been moved up into the army reserve on the night of 6-7 July, occupied defensive positions directly behind the 17th Guards Rifle Corps. The 13th Anti-Aircraft Division was moving up from the Maloarkhangel'sk area to cover the corps' units from the air.

Taking into account the experience of the preceding battles, the *front* commander ordered that all tanks be buried in the ground and were to engage the enemy's heavy tanks only from stationary firing points; the employment of tanks for counterattacks was authorized only against the enemy's infantry and light tanks.

At dawn on 7 July the enemy, having concentrated large infantry and tank forces in the 1st Ponyri area, once again went over to the attack in the direction of Ponyri. The attack was begun by heavy tanks, which advanced in the first echelon. The medium and light tanks remained in the hollows, in readiness to be thrown into the battle. The enemy's heavy tanks and self-propelled guns, having advanced to the defense at distance of a direct shot, opened up a hurricane of fire against our anti-tank weapons and infantry combat formations. Believing that our anti-tank system had been safely suppressed, the medium and light tanks went into the attack shortly thereafter. Behind them advanced the heavy tanks, in groups of 2-3 vehicles at intervals of 100 meters.

German aviation, operating in groups of 4-5 planes, uninterruptedly approached the front and dropped their bombs on our defense. However, its attacks this time proved to be significantly weaker than in the preceding days.

The Germans' assumptions were not justified. They did not manage to suppress the 307th Rifle Division's fire. The division's unexpected and massed fire from heavy-caliber artillery and fire over open sights, during the battle's first minutes, knocked out ten T-VIs and 12 medium tanks.

The radio-controlled minefields were activated. Mobile obstacle detachments entered the fighting against the tanks. Northwest of Ponyri an obstacle detachment, under the command of Guards Senior Lieutenant Artamonov, by skillfully maneuvering over the battlefield, laid mines along the attack routes of the enemy vehicles. Two tanks were knocked out and the remainder sought to bypass the minefield. However, the sappers had taken into account the possibility of such detours; mines had been laid in echelon along the flanks. The enemy tanks, believing that they had managed to bypass the minefield, increased their speed and advanced. Soon powerful explosions were heard. Four tanks halted on the spot and the rest turned back.

Five times the Germans attacked, trying to break through the 307th Rifle Division's defense near Ponyri and take the center of resistance; but each time they fell back with heavy losses.

At 1000 two battalions of enemy infantry, with 50 tanks, managed to break through to the northern and western outskirts of Ponyri. The division commander immediately committed his reserve into the fighting. Our soldiers' impetuous counterattack, supported by tanks and artillery fire, destroyed the enemy and restored the situation. Within an hour up to two enemy battalions, supported by 12 tanks, again attacked Ponyri from the northeast. In the fierce fighting that followed, which was often hand to hand, the Germans managed to capture the village of First of May and advance to the outskirts of Ponyri.

Taking advantage of this success, the German command threw fresh forces into this sector. Simultaneously, along the resistance center's flanks, infantry and large groups of tanks were concentrating. However, as had been the case in the previous days' fighting, the Germans, while disposing of great opportunities for maneuver (thanks to a large number of armored forces), continued to stubbornly attack only along the same axis. This significantly eased our forces' battle against the enemy.

The 307th Rifle Division commander, having received information about the new attack being prepared by the enemy, regrouped his forces and brought up all his anti-tank artillery to the Ponyri area; heavy-caliber guns, tank destroyers and obstacle detachments were prepared for the encounter with the enemy.

At 1530 a large number of enemy planes appeared over the battlefield. The German planes subjected our forces' combat formations to a heavy bombardment, and the enemy's artillery and mortars opened a fierce fire on them. Using the fire for cover, the enemy tanks and infantry attacked. The Germans threw the 18th Panzer Division and the 86th Infantry Division into the attack, as well as part of the 78th and 292nd infantry divisions, and launched a simultaneous attack from three directions: from the north, east and west. However, this attack did not yield the expected effect. Following several hours of fierce fighting, the Germans penetrated insignificantly into our position. The battlefield was littered with enemy corpses, while enemy tanks and vehicles burned.

The German command, with no regard for its enormous losses, continued to commit newer and newer forces into the fighting. At 1900 the Germans threw into the battle two infantry regiments and about 60 tanks. The enemy desperately lunged forward. Units of the 307th Rifle Division, following the intensive daytime battle, could not withstand the new attack by superior enemy forces and, abandoning the forward edge of the defense, fell back to the line excluding Bazhenova—excluding First of May—southern half of Ponyri. Using the previously prepared trenches here, our units consolidated and halted the attacking enemy with organized fire.

The next day (8 July), having regrouped their forces, units of the 307th Rifle Division attacked at 0600. They threw the Germans out of the northern part of Ponyri with a brief but powerful attack and restored the previous day's situation along the entire front.

On this day the Germans repeatedly tried to capture the Ponyri center of resistance and break through to the south, but failed to achieve success. The front stabilized.

The 7-8 July fighting along the Ol'khovatka axis

Particularly fierce fighting occurred during 7-8 July along the 13th Army's center and left flank. The German command concentrated up to 300 tanks along the 17th Guards Rifle Corps' front, as well as a large amount of artillery and infantry, and repeatedly tried to break through to Ol'khovatka.

On the night of 6-7 July our sappers, with the help of the infantry, restored the engineering obstacles in front of the forward edge and carried out the complete mining of these sectors. The 42nd and 53rd tank regiments, which had arrived at the commander's disposal from the army's right flank and reserve, occupied positions in the infantry's first echelons. Before beginning his attack along this axis, the enemy waited out the results of the fighting in the Ponyri area. By 1100 the situation there was already clear: the failure of the German attack had become obvious. After this, the German command issued orders to attack toward Ol'khovatka.

At 1200 two battalions of infantry, supported by 50 tanks, attacked the 17th Guards Rifle Corps' right flank, seeking to drive a wedge between our Ol'khovatka group of forces and the Ponyri center of resistance. Units of the 6th Guards Rifle Division, which were defending along this sector, put up stubborn resistance to the enemy. However, in spite of this, the Germans managed to push back our units and insignificantly advance: by 1230 the German infantry had captured the northern part of the woods west of Berezovyi Log, where it was halted. At 1500 the corps' center and left flank had come under a powerful air attack. The enemy bombers, in groups of 50-70 planes, uninterruptedly dropped bombs on the forward edge of our defense during the course of 30 minutes. The areas of Bityug, Kashara and Teploe came under powerful air attacks. At 1330 the enemy, with 200 tanks and two infantry divisions, opened a decisive offensive along the corps' entire front, launching the main attack along the sector height 257—Kashara.

Units of the 17th Guards Rifle Corps met the enemy tanks with organized anti-tank fire and inflicted heavy losses on him. The Germans could not withstand the fire and before long turned back, trying to tow away their knocked-out vehicles. More than 40 enemy tanks remained on the battlefield. The German infantry hit the ground and, suffering heavy losses, began to hurriedly entrench. Individual groups of enemy tanks, which had broken through to the area of height 257 and the village of Kashara, were destroyed.

The Germans, having put their units in order, attacked at 1700 against the corps' right wing. Following fierce fighting, they were able, at the cost of heavy losses, to push units of the 6th Guards

Rifle Division to the south and reach the southern part of the village of Berezovyi Log. Taking advantage of this success, the Germans hurriedly began to concentrate their tanks and infantry in the woods west of Berezovyi Log, and as early as 1930 once again went over to the attack. They launched the attack along the axis 2nd Ponyri—height 257, against the flank and rear of the 75th Guards Rifle Division, which was defending to the west of the village of Snova.

However, this attack failed to yield the enemy success. The divisional boundaries were heavily fortified and supported by crossfire. Units of the 75th Guards Rifle Division rapidly regrouped to the east, met the enemy attack with organized fire and repulsed it. The German forces, having lost up to 30 tanks and a large number of infantry, fell back to their jumping-off point.

With the onset of darkness, the fighting along all of the 17th Guards Rifle Corps' sectors ended. All the enemy attacks had been successfully repulsed by the corps' units, with the support of the 16th Tank and 4th Artillery corps. The enemy suffered huge losses.

According to data that is by no means complete, the 13th Army's forces on this day killed about 8,000 enemy officers and men and destroyed 98 tanks and several self-propelled guns.

At the cost of such losses, the enemy on 7 July managed to advance only insignificantly along the 17th Guards Rifle Corps' sector in the direction of Bityug and Kashara. Along the remainder of the 13th Army's front he had no success.

By the close of 7 July units of the 17th Rifle Corps occupied the following position: the 6th Guards Rifle Division was defending along the line excluding Ponyri station—southern outskirts of the village of Berezovyi Log—2nd Ponyri; the 75th Guards Rifle Division was defending along the line excluding 2nd Ponyri—height 257, and; the 70th Guards Rifle Division was defending along the line excluding height 257—Kutyrki.

7 July was the operation's day of crisis. A turning point had been reached in the defensive battle, with the initiative obviously shifting in favor of the Central Front's forces. On this day the *front* commander stated to the army commanders that "We have won the defensive battle, and our new mission is to finish off the defeated enemy by the launching of a decisive offensive."

Despite the difficulty of the first days of the defensive battle, the *front* commander retained significant reserves, which subsequently became the *front's* main shock force during the offensive. He retained the 18th Rifle and the 3rd and 9th tank corps.

However, the enemy still retained the capability of attacking and scrupulously prepared for it on the following day. Having brought more than two infantry divisions and tanks at night to the Snova—Podsoborovka—Saborovka area, at 0800 on 8 July he again attacked, trying to break through our defense along the 2nd Ponyri—Samodurovka sector. The enemy attacked our positions four times, but each time fell back with heavy losses. Our forces, employing intense rifle and machine gun fire, cut the infantry off from its tanks and forced it to cling to the ground. The tanks, cut off from the infantry, were shot up by our artillery from open positions; the number of knocked out vehicles on the battlefield grew.

The fiercest fighting unfolded for height 257, which was the 17th Guards Rifle Corps' central strong point. The enemy attacked this height three times simultaneously from the northeast and north. The attacks were carried out by groups of 60-100 tanks. The infantry climbed the height behind the tanks, in spite of the fire from the defending units. Hand to hand fighting broke out. Our troops would throw the enemy off the hill with audacious bayonet attacks and quickly restore the situation.

As before, the artillery men heroically fought the enemy's tanks, shooting up the enemy vehicles by firing over open sights. The guards artillery regiment, under the command of Major Konovalenko, which repelled 16 enemy tank attacks that day, particularly distinguished itself in battle. The regiment's firing position was ceaselessly attacked by German aviation, operating in groups of 20-30 planes. The guards troops bravely held their positions, destroying more than 40 enemy tanks.

By 1700 the enemy had captured height 257 and consolidated there. However, his further progress had been halted. The enemy had no success along the corps' remaining sectors. Thus on 8 July as well, despite the fierce fighting, the German forces were unable to achieve any kind of tangible results. The attempt to break through to Ol'khovatka remained without result.

Simultaneous with the attack toward Ol'khovatka, a large enemy group of forces attacked along the boundary of the 13th and 70th armies. Here units of the 132nd Rifle Division repulsed two furious attacks that day, involving up to 60 tanks.

The enemy launched his heaviest attacks against the boundary of the 175th and 140th divisions[2] near Samodurovka. Here the Germans threw more than 200 tanks and self-propelled guns into the battle. Units of the 140th Division repelled 13 attacks that day; it was only after the fourteenth attack that they, having suffered heavy casualties, began to fall back to the south. However, the neighboring divisions (70th and 175th) firmly held their positions. These divisions, having committed their reserves into the battle in the direction of Samodurovka, closed the breach and cut off the tanks and the infiltrated infantry from the enemy's main forces. The tanks sought more than once to link up with their forces near Samodurovka, but were unable to do this and were destroyed by our anti-tank units.

Along the right flank in the Ponyri area, the enemy's actions were limited to only inconclusive attacks.

Results of the 7-8 July fighting

The German forces, having lost 42,000 killed and wounded in four days of fighting, and more than 800 tanks and self-propelled guns, were incapable of continuing the offensive along the Central Front's right flank and went over to the defensive. On 9 July they undertook insignificant attacks along two sectors—in the area of height 257 and near Ponyri, and on 10 July only the activities of reconnaissance groups were noted along the entire front, with a weak crossfire exchanged.

Fierce enemy attacks were succeeded by the enemy's hurried defensive preparations along the entire front. The Germans, understanding the deleterious consequences of their unsuccessful offensive, began to intensively consolidate along the new line at night: they dug into the ground, mined the area, and erected wire obstacles; their artillery and mortars methodically fired on our lines.

The temporarily stabilized front ran along the line Trosna—Protasovo—Fedorovka—Ponyri—height 257—Samodurovka—hcight 250—Buzovo.

A favorable situation had arisen for abandoning the defense and going over to a decisive counteroffensive in order to defeat the German-Fascist forces and restoring the original situation. Moreover, it was necessary to go over to a counteroffensive in the next few days, in order to deprive the enemy of time to consolidate along the new line and put his units in order.

The Central Front's Counteroffensive, 15-17 July 1943

The *front* commander's decision for the counteroffensive

On 12 July the forces of the left flank of the Western Front and the Bryansk Front began their offensive. On that day the commander of the Central Front issued orders to attack on 15 July. Three days were left to prepare. All the Central Front's armies' combat formations, while still in the process of preparing the defense, were organized in such a manner that the armies' formations

2 On 6 July the 140th Rifle Division was transferred here from the left sector of the army second defensive line.

could shift from the defensive to a decisive counteroffensive at any moment. Aside from the 13th Army, the armies' combat formations had not been disrupted by the defensive battle, and thus their forces could freely begin their offensive operations on 15 July.

The 48th, 13th, 70th, and 2nd Tank armies, and the 16th Air Army, were allotted for assuming the offensive. The *front* commander assigned them the following mission: to destroy the enemy's shock group in the area Nizhnee Tagino—Probuzhdenie—Ponyri—Protasovo—Gremyachevo and by the close of 17 July reach the line Nagornyi—Shamshin—Novopolevo—Kamenka—Lebedikha—Morozikha—Katomki with their main forces. It was subsequently planned to develop the attack to the north in the general direction of Orel, in coordination with the Western and Bryansk fronts, the forces of which, according to the plan of the *Stavka* of the Supreme High Command, began their offensive as early as 11 July for the purpose of defeating the Germans' Orel group of forces and eliminating the Orel strategic salient.

The 48th Army had the following mission: by launching an attack with its left flank (42nd Rifle Corps), to attack the enemy along the sector Sondrovka—excluding Krasnaya Slobodka, in the direction of Yasnaya Polyana and Shamshin, and by the close of 17 July reach the line Nagornyi—Shamshin, with the idea of subsequently developing the offensive toward Zmievka. The army's boundary line on the left was: Aleksandrovka—Krasnaya Slobodka—Borisoglebskoe—Khvoshchino (all locales, except Aleksandrovka and Krasnaya Slobodka were in the army's boundary).

The 13th Army, consisting of the 15th and 29th rifle, 18th and 17th guards rifle, and 9th Tank corps, and the 143rd and 55th rifle divisions,[3] along with previously attached reinforcements, was ordered to go over to a general offensive from the morning of 15 July, and launch the following attacks:

The 15th Rifle Corps would attack from the line excluding Krasnaya Slobodka—Grinevka—Bazhenovo in the general direction of Kunach' and Staropolevo;

The 18th Guards Rifle Corps would attack along with the 9th Tank Corps from the line excluding Bazhenovo—Ponyri in the general direction of Kamenka;

The reinforced 17th Guards Rifle Corps would attack from the line Berezovyi Log—2nd Ponyri—Kutyrki—excluding Samodurovka in the general direction of Bogomolovka.

The army, in cooperation with the 48th and 70th armies, and supported by the 16th Air Army's entire strength, was to destroy the enemy facing it and by the close of 17 July reach the line Novopolevo—excluding Kamenka—Lebedikha; it was subsequently planned to develop the attack toward Staroe Gorokhovo, Filosovo and Nesterovo. The army's boundary line on the left was Samodurovka—Podolyan'—Nizhnee Tagino (all for the 13th Army) and further along the Oka River.

The 70th Army, consisting of the 28th and 19th rifle and 19th Tank corps, was to securely hold the line Katomki—Shepelevo—Verkhnyaya Grankina—Chern' with three rifle divisions, while the army's remaining forces and weapons were to attack on the morning of 15 July from the line Teploe—Muravl'. Attacking toward Gnilets and Nizhnee Tagino, the army was to support the 13th Army in destroying the enemy in the indicated area.

By the close of 17 July the main forces of the army's shock group were to reach the line Nizhnee Tagino—Lebedikha—Morozikha—Katomki. It was planned that the army would subsequently develop the attack in the general direction of Kamenets, Groznyi and Kromy. The army's boundary line was to remain as before.

3 The 143rd Rifle Division had been transferred from the 48th Army, and the 55th Rifle Division from the 60th Army.

The 2nd Tank Army (3rd and 16th tank corps) had the following mission: with the arrival of the 13th Army's infantry and tanks at the line Soglasnyi—Buzuluk—Druzhovetskii—Saborovka, the tank army was to attack with all its forces along the Ponyri—Bityug—Kashara sector (three kilometers southeast of Samodurovka) and, upon passing through the 13th Army's combat formations, develop the attack in the general direction of Snova, Sen'kovo and Gremyachevo; by the close of 17 July the army's main forces were to reach the Ol'gino—Gnilusha area; the army was to subsequently develop the attack toward Nikol'skoe and Nesterovo.

The 16th Air Army had the task of supporting the attack by the infantry and tanks of the 13th Army's shock group along the Protasovo—Ponyri sector with assault and bomber aviation; subsequently, by coordinating with the 13th and 2nd Tank armies, the air army was to assist them in defeating the enemy in the indicated area and prevent the withdrawal of the enemy forces to the north and northwest from the line Novopolevo—Gremyachevo—Voronets; fighter aviation was to cover the 13th Army's shock group, both in the jumping-off area for the offensive, as well as during the offensive.

The 16th Air Army had the task, before the arrival of the 13th Army's forces at the line Soglasnyi—Buzuluk—Druzhovetskii—Saborovka, to assist with all its forces the 13th Army and to subsequently assist with part of its forces the 9th Tank Corps' offensive, and the 2nd Tank Army with its main forces.

Thus the *front* commander declined to employ any kind of complex maneuver in the forthcoming offensive; the troops were to switch from the defensive to the offensive directly from the positions they occupied.

The main attack was to be made in the center, along the 13th Army's sector, which was to be supported by the 2nd Tank and 16th Air armies.

In selecting such an axis for the main attack, the *front* commander from the very outset sought to achieve success along the nearest approaches to Orel and to split the enemy's main group of forces in half and throw its remains into the path of the neighboring armies. Finally, all of the main forces of the *front's* reinforcements had been concentrated here in the 13th Army's zone. All of these could be readied for the offensive as quickly as possible.

Preparing the troops for the offensive and the group of forces as of 15 July 1943

We began immediately to prepare the troops for the offensive. Reconnaissance was reinforced along the entire front. Day and night our scouts penetrated into the enemy's position, discovered the disposition of his forces, the location of his artillery, tanks and reserves. The sappers sought out the minefields laid by the enemy, destroyed them and made passages in our own minefields. The artillery intensively bombarded the enemy's lines, interfered with his defensive construction, and suppressed the enemy's artillery and mortars. The Germans were subjected to systematic attacks by our aviation.

The regrouping of forces within the army and *front* was carried out night and day. This was the most important task. The headquarters devoted their chief attention to this. The precisely organized regrouping was carried out in an in a very rapid fashion and the troops along the *front's* right wing had occupied their jumping-off position for the offensive by the close of 14 July.

The armies deployed as follows:

48th Army—the 15th Rifle Corps (16th Latvian, 399th and 137th rifle divisions) along the line Krest'yanka—southern outskirts of Panskaya—Krasnaya Slobodka.

13th Army—15th Rifle Corps (8th, 148th, 74th, and 143rd rifle divisions) along the line excluding Krasnaya Slobodka—Grinevka—Bazhenovo; the 18th Guards Rifle Corps (2nd, 3rd and 4th guards rifle divisions) along the line excluding Bazhenovo—First of May—Ponyri; the 17th Guards Rifle Corps (55th, 6th, 70th, and 75th guards rifle divisions) along the line excluding

Ponyri—Kutyrki. The 29th Rifle Corps, which comprised the 13th Army's second echelon, concentrated as follows: 81st Rifle Division—Maloarkhangel'sk, 15th Rifle Division—Berezovets, and the 307th Rifle Division—Ostrov.

70th Army—the 140th Rifle Division north of Teploe and the 28th Rifle Corps (211th, 160th, 102nd, and 132nd rifle divisions) along the line excluding Krasavka—Buzovo—Katomki.

The 2nd Tank Army's 3rd Tank Corps was concentrated in the Ponyri—Goreloe area, and the 16th Tank Corps in the area Ol'khovatka—Step', and the 11th Guards Tank Brigade in the area east of Molotychi.

By the close of 14 July the armies had completely finished their preparations for the offensive.

The enemy facing the *front's* right wing was not active and limited himself to reconnaissance activities. From time to time he carried out artillery and mortar fire along the forward edge of our defense.

The German command, concerned by the opening of the offensive on Orel by the Western and Bryansk fronts, began to shift part of its forces from the Central Front's right wing and hurriedly send them north.

On 13 July our aviation observed the continuous movement to the north of railroad shipments with artillery equipment and tanks toward Glazunovka and Zmievka stations. Columns of tanks, motor vehicles, artillery, and infantry were moving along this direction day and night.

On 14 July the enemy shifted the 36th Motorized and the 2nd and 18th panzer divisions from the Central Front and sent them by march to the Orel area. The amount of artillery in the Germans' combat formations decreased noticeably. The enemy aviation also became less active.

The course of the counteroffensive

At 0600 on 15 July, following a 15-minute artillery fire onslaught, our forces attacked the enemy along the entire front. Tanks and infantry, supported by powerful artillery fire and aviation, broke into the German defenses simultaneously along several sectors. The enemy put up stubborn resistance. He repeatedly tried to halt our attacking infantry with mortar and machine gun fire.

There were a large number of damaged and undamaged tanks buried in the ground and transformed into immobile armored firing points along the forward edge of the enemy's defense; relying on these, the Germans repeatedly counterattacked our units.

Despite all of this, our troops crushed the enemy's resistance and by 0800 had penetrated 2-3 kilometers into his line. By midday the forces of the 13th Army had already captured the inhabited locales of Snova, Podsoborovka (six kilometers northeast of Samodurovka) and Saborovka. Their further advance was halted. The Germans repeatedly launched counterattacks. For example, they twice counterattacked units of the 17th Guards Rifle Corps, with forces up to a division in size and tanks, from the area of Druzhovetskii and Bobrik. Enemy aviation systematically dive bombed our forces in groups, dropped bombs and strafed them with machine guns. On this day the other armies also advanced slightly.

The following morning the *front's* forces renewed the offensive. Carrying out the *front* commander's orders, the 2nd Tank Army entered the breach along the 13th Army's sector and overturned the enemy infantry's combat formations along the Sen'kovo axis, which had configured the 13th Army's old defensive structures for defense along this line. The tank troops began to quickly advance to the north.

In the meantime, units of the 70th Army's right wing along the flanks of the shock group defeated the enemy in the area of height 250 and reached the Gnilets area; the 48th Army's left flank advanced toward Kunach.

The enemy continued to resist stubbornly and, covered by powerful detachments of infantry and tanks, fell back on his jumping-off positions. The German command tried to concentrate its reserves and sought to halt our offensive here.

Day or night, the fighting did not cease. On the morning of 17 July units of the 2nd Tank Army reached the previous enemy forward line in the Arkhangel'skoe—Ozerki area and began fighting for it. At the same time, formations from the 13th and 70th armies were completing the destruction of individual enemy groups and by the end of the day had also restored their previous position.

Results of the fighting along the Orel—Kursk axis

In a fierce defensive battle, lasting from 5-14 July, the troops of the Central Front's right wing carried out their assigned mission. By stubborn resistance they bled the attacking enemy white, halted him, and then threw him back to his jumping-off position with a powerful counterstroke. The German forces' offensive along the Orel—Kursk axis was foiled. The enemy did not manage to break through to Kursk and assist the main group of forces attacking toward Kursk from Belgorod. Besides this, the German forces suffered enormous, irreplaceable losses and were faced with the fact of complete defeat.

On 15 July our forces launched a counteroffensive and in three days of fighting restored their previous position and, securely holding the initiative, continued to develop the offensive on Kromy.

The successful defensive operations by the Central Front's right-flank forces, and their subsequent offensive to the north, significantly aided the success of the Western and Bryansk fronts' offensive operations to eliminate the enemy's Orel strategic salient.

3

The Voronezh Front's Defensive Battle

The Battles Along the Oboyan' Axis, 5-9 July 1943

The beginning of the battle
The 4 July fighting by the security outposts with the Germans' forward detachments

The defensive battle along the Voronezh Front began on the second half of 4 July. The forward detachments of the German Fourth Panzer Army, which had gone over to the offensive, began fighting with elements of the 6th Guards Army's security outposts. The enemy was seeking to overthrow the security outposts and reach the forward edge of our defense. At 1600 on 4 July the enemy launched a 10-minute concentrated artillery-mortar onslaught against our security outposts. The onslaught was accompanied by an enemy bomber attack. During the course of ten minutes the enemy dropped 2,500 air bombs in the area Butovo—height 230.8, which was occupied by the 67th Guards Rifle Division's combat security outposts. At 1610 the enemy's forward detachments, under the cover of artillery-mortar fire and strafing bombers, went over to the attack.

Up to two battalions of the 332nd Infantry Division and the 11th Panzer Division attacked along the sector Gertsovka—Butovo—excluding Dragunskoe. By 2400 the enemy had defeated the combat outposts in the area Gertsovka rail siding—Butovo—height 230.8 and had arrived along this sector at the forward edge of the main defensive zone. The enemy's attempts to push back our combat outposts along the sector Dragunskoe—Yakhontov were unsuccessful.

Thus on 4 July the Germans were not able to fully realize their intentions. The fighting to eliminate the 6th Guards Army's combat outposts remained uncompleted; the jumping-off position for deploying the main forces immediately in front of the forward edge of our defense was not secured; for this reason, the enemy's main forces were not able to begin their attack at dawn on 5 July.

On 4 July the enemy carried out reconnaissance in small groups facing the 7th Guards Army, while along individual sectors the Germans tried to cross reconnaissance parties, up to a platoon or company in size, over to the eastern bank of the Severskii Donets River. During the first half of the day the enemy artillery registered targets. At 1830 the enemy carried out several artillery-mortar onslaughts against the Karnaukhovka, Maslova Pristan' and Priyutovka areas. The enemy fired about 2,500 rounds against the Karnaukhovka and Maslova Pristan' areas alone.

During the day the enemy brought up his units in small parties to the riverbank and also was intensely cutting wood—evidently for constructing crossings.

The greatest concentration of German forces, as before, was noted in the areas of Belgorod, Toplinka, Ivanovka, and Pokrovka. Enemy activity in front of the *front's* right wing on 4 July was no different than in the preceding days.

The enemy's measures in the first days of July (intensified reconnaissance, making passages in our minefields, removing his own mine obstacles along a number of sectors, etc.) and the testimony of prisoners and defectors gave our command more than enough basis to assume the Germans' likely

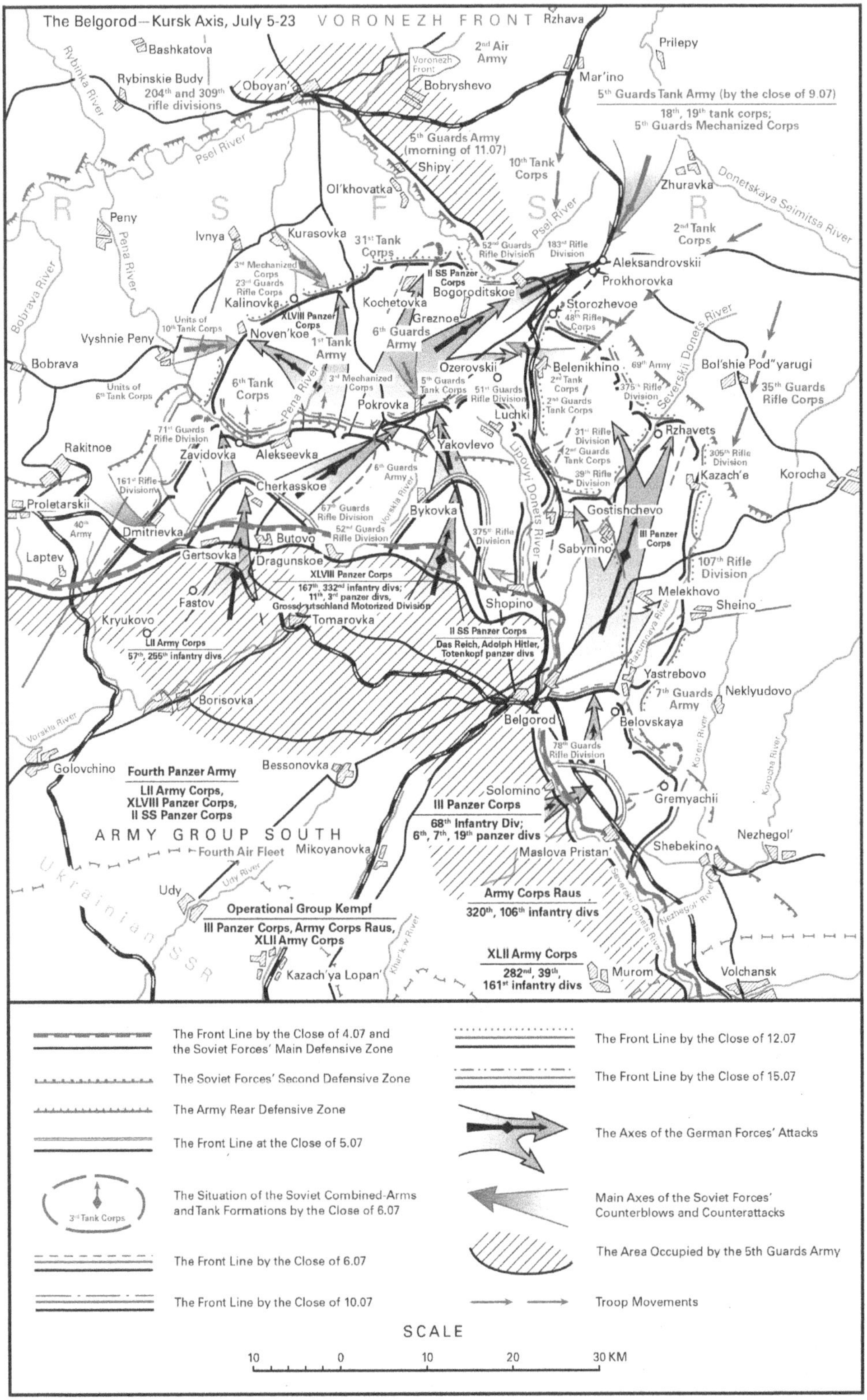

Map 3 The Belgorod—Kursk Axis, 5-23 July 1943.

offensive on 5 July. The actions of the enemy's forward detachments on 4 July finally confirmed the *front* command's assumptions that the enemy would begin his general offensive on 5 July.

Thus the *front* commander, as early as during the day of 4 July, made the decision to carry out an artillery counterpreparation along the 6th and 7th guards armies' front, and also employ the 40th Army's artillery. The first artillery counterpreparation along the 6th Guards Army's sector began at 2230 and continued five minutes. The beginning of the artillery onslaught was preceded by a salvo from the guards mortar units. 17 likely tank and infantry concentration areas were subjected to the artillery barrage, as well as 12 of the enemy's most active artillery batteries and 17 observation posts. This artillery counterpreparation did much to foil the attack by the Germans' forward detachments.

Combat activities on 5 July

Because the enemy was unable to overcome our combat outposts on 4 July along the entire front of the 6th Guards Army, the enemy forces on 5 July were not able to begin their general offensive with their main forces. At dawn they were forced to continue fighting to throw back and destroy the subunits along the combat outposts in the areas of Dragunskoe, Yakhontov and Zagotskot (facing the front of the 52nd Guards and 375th rifle divisions). The enemy offensive on 5 July began at 0200 with a 30-minute artillery and air preparation.

At 0300 the 6th and 7th guards armies repeated their artillery counterpreparation. Beginning with a 5-minute fire onslaught against areas of enemy concentration, it was continued during the next 15 minutes as methodical aimed fire against troop concentrations and the enemy artillery's firing positions. The counterpreparation concluded with a 10-minute fire onslaught against concentrations of the enemy's troops and tanks, as well as against active enemy batteries. Guards mortar units fired off two salvos—one before the beginning of the counterpreparation, and one at the end. As a result, more than 20 artillery batteries and 17 observation posts were suppressed and destroyed, and the enemy lost up to 2,500 men and officers, as well as a large number of tanks.

Hans Dorfel, a captured lieutenant from the 332nd Infantry Division, testified that his regiment lost 60 men to the Russian artillery barrage.

Both artillery counterpreparations significantly disrupted the enemy's command and control system. Thus the German units' offensive on the morning of 5 July did not begin simultaneously. The Germans' artillery counterpreparation was also organized very poorly and it was only along the 6th Guards Army's left flank (against the 375th Rifle Division's front) that it was more or less significant.

At 0420, almost simultaneously with the artillery counterpreparation, the 2nd Air Army's forces launched an attack against the German airfields and combat formations.

The fighting in the Korovino, Cherkasskoe and Krasnyi Pochinok areas

At 0600 on 5 July the enemy attacked along the 22nd Rifle Corps' (71st and 67th guards rifle divisions, which were defending in the first echelon) zone. The enemy launched his main attack with the forces of the 11th Panzer Division and the *Grossdeutschland* SS Panzer Division from the Gertsovka—Butovo area toward Korovino and Cherkasskoe.

In the 67th Guards Rifle Division's zone (along the Cherkasskoe axis), the enemy attacked with an infantry regiment, reinforced with 70 tanks. Besides this, the regiment's attack was supported by 70 planes. Our units beat back the enemy's first attack.

The Germans, having put their disorganized units in order and brought up reserves, attacked Cherkasskoe for the second time at 0710, this time with two infantry regiments and 100 tanks. However, thanks to artillery fire from an anti-tank strong point, which had been prepared in the

Cherkasskoe area, as well as divisional and army artillery, this attack was beaten back. The enemy, having suffered large losses, fell back to his jumping-off position. From 0800 to 1030 the enemy carried out a number of fierce attacks on Cherkasskoe, but they all invariably failed.

25 German tanks and up to 300 infantrymen blew themselves up on our minefields in front of Cherkasskoe. By this time the 27th Anti-Tank Brigade, had arrived from the army commander's reserve, in the Cherkasskoe area for securing the boundary between the 71st and 67th guards rifle divisions.

At 0900 the enemy, with up to an infantry regiment and 30 tanks, attacked from Gertsovka units of the 71st Guards Rifle Division, which was defending in the Korovino area. Up to 1000 all the enemy's attempts to break through to Korovino were unsuccessful.

The enemy, following the unsuccessful attacks on Cherkasskoe and Korovino, regrouped his units and at 1100 attacked between Korovino and Cherkasskoe from the area northwest of Butovo. Two infantry regiments, supported by 200 tanks and 100 planes, began to outflank Cherkasskoe from the west. The enemy air force's successive bombing raids cleared a road for the tanks and the infantry following behind them. The tanks advanced at low speed—no more than 5-10 kilometers per hour—with frequent stops, while waiting for the infantry to come up. As a result of the aviation support and repeated attacks, the enemy tanks managed to break through into the depth of our defense along the boundary between the 71st and 67th guards rifle divisions.

At 1200 the Germans attacked with an infantry regiment, supported by 30 tanks, from the Butovo area toward heights 244.5 and 237.8, in order to outflank Cherkasskoe from the east. Here the enemy penetrated into the 67th Guards Rifle Division's defense.

The fierce fighting for Voskhod, Korovino and Cherkasskoe continued throughout the second half of the day; by the close of the day the enemy, at the cost of heavy losses, captured these inhabited locales.

The fighting was particularly vicious for Cherkasskoe. All the Germans' attacks on this day were beaten back by units of the 67th Guards Rifle Division and fire from elements of the 27th Anti-Tank Brigade. The engineering technical service (TOS) helped our forces a great deal. While the enemy was concentrating his infantry in the area of the village of Cherkasskoe, an explosion by the TOS killed up to 150 Germans and the enemy attack broke down for a considerable time. Near height 244.5, where the enemy infantry was concentrating, delayed-action mines were set off. Those Germans who remained alive ran into a building located not far from the height. The building had also been mined (with a charge of 900 kilograms) and soon flew into the air. Along with it were killed up to a company of Hitlerites, as well as five tanks destroyed nearby.

At 1300 a group of 50 tanks, which had broken through along the boundary between the 71st and 67th guards rifle divisions, tried to attack Cherkasskoe from the west, but ran into a bottle minefield. 15 tanks were enveloped by fire from the flammable liquid. Four tanks burned up, while the remainder hurriedly fell back. Despite the enormous losses, the enemy continued to attack Cherkasskoe.

The troops of the 67th Guards Rifle Division stoutly repulsed the enemy's ceaseless attacks. After the division command ordered the garrison (a battalion from the 196th Rifle Regiment), which was defending an anti-tank strong point in the area of the village of Cherkasskoe, to fall back to the north, a platoon under the command of Guards Junior Lieutenant Alekov, which was covering the battalion's withdrawal, met the enemy's attacks. 15 valiant guards troops entered the unequal battle. Officer Alekov shouted: "The guard dies, but does not retreat!" The guards troops took off their forage caps and declared: "We will die, but we'll carry out the commander's order!"

Hundreds of Hitlerites fell under the fire of these brave men. The division commander's order was carried out. Under the guards forces, the battalion fell back in an organized fashion to a new line, while 15 sons of the motherland met the death of the brave. The enemy's further advance to the north was halted by our forces.

In the fighting near the village of Cherkasskoe the enemy employed for the first time "Tiger" tanks and "Ferdinand" self-propelled guns. They were employed by the Germans mainly for covering the combat formations of the advancing medium and light tanks, firing from a stationary position at distances up to 1,500 meters.

The enemy's overall loss of tanks in this battle reached 180 vehicles. The Germans suffered the greatest tank losses at the hands of our anti-tank artillery units. For example, in the first two hours of the battle alone the 1008th Anti-Tank Artillery Regiment, which occupied firing positions south of Cherkasskoe, knocked out eight tanks, of which six were "Tigers." Anti-tank dogs blew up 12 tanks. Several tens of tanks blew up in minefields.

By the close of the day our units had fallen back and occupied the defensive line Bubny—Novo-Ivanovka—Krasnyi Pochinok—Yarki—height 246—Trirechnoe.

The fighting in the Zadel'noe—Berezov—Koz'mo-Dem'yanovka area

Fighting along the Yakhontov—Berezov—Koz'mo-Dem'yanovka axis began at dawn on 5 July. The German units headed for Yakhontov and heights 228.6 and 218, which were held by forward outposts of the 52nd Guards Rifle Division. Following a 30-minute artillery preparation and a massed air attack, in which more than 180 planes took part, the Germans attacked at 0230: one infantry battalion attacked from the Rakovo area (north) toward Yakhontov, and one battalion from Rakovo toward height 218. The infantry's actions were supported by tanks and aviation, the latter of which cooperated with the infantry and tanks. The enemy's attacks along these axes were beaten off by fire from our units. At the same time, these attacks had been significantly weakened by our second artillery counterpreparation, which was carried out at 0300.

The Germans ceased their attacks. They replied to our artillery counterpreparation with an artillery onslaught against the positions of our forward outposts and the artilley's firing positions. The enemy renewed the attack only at 0400.

Stubborn fighting for the Yakhontov and height 228.6 strong points lasted 3½ hours. All the Germans' attempts to throw our subunits out of their strong points with artillery fire and bomber aviation ended in failure. Our infantry, which had firmly consolidated, held on stoutly.

Individual groups of tanks, which broke through the combat outpost's positions, were destroyed by anti-tank artillery firing over open sights. The German infantry, under fire from our rifle subunits, was forced to halt and hit the ground in front of the forward outpost's positions. Only at 0730 did the enemy seize height 228.6 and Yakhontov. The enemy needed up to an hour and a half to bring up his forces to the forward edge of our defense. This was carried out under a hurricane of fire from our artillery, which caused the Germans heavy losses in men and tanks. By 0900 the enemy had captured the line height 177.3—height 228.6—Berezov—height 218. On height 228.6 up to a company of infantry and 11 enemy tanks were destroyed on an electronically-controlled minefield in an explosion of anti-personnel mines-152.

The fighting for Berezov was especially fierce. Here up to two infantry battalions, reinforced with 20 tanks, including six "Tigers," attacked. From the air the attack was supported by the uninterrupted attacks of 80 planes. Our forces, which were occupying Berezov, put up stubborn resistance to the Germans. The crews of the anti-tank guns and the crews of tanks buried in the ground laid an accurate fire on the enemy tanks, which were moving under the cover of a smoke-screen. The soldiers of a mine-flamethrower subunit, which was fighting the enemy tanks on the approaches to Berezov, displayed particular valor. Allowing the German tanks to approach within 15-20 meters, they detonated the mine-flamethrowers on the platoon commander's order and immediately put seven tanks out of action. Overall, mine flamethrowers destroyed 11 tanks, four self-propelled guns and 260 enemy soldiers in the fighting near Berezov. Later, when the Germans threw large forces into the fighting, they reached Berezov and surrounded it. The strong point's garrison fought to the last man.

The enemy, having carried out a regrouping and having brought up reserves, committed into the battle at 1100 simultaneously more than 200 tanks, including a significant number of "Tiger" tanks and "Ferdinand" assault guns. The enemy attacked the forward edge of the 52nd Guards Rifle Division. This time the attack was preceded by a powerful air strike against the division's combat formations and artillery firing positions. The enemy planes did not leave the battlefield and constantly attacked our forces, clearing a road for their tanks.

By 1600 units of the 52nd Guards Rifle Division had fallen back under enemy pressure to the north to the line Lapin gully—Voznesenskii—Bykovka—Zhuravlinyi—Gonki. By this time the army commander had reinforced the division with the 28th Anti-Tank Brigade from his reserve.

The enemy, having regrouped his units and concentrated the main mass of his tanks in the Kamennyi Log area, again launched an attack during the second part of the day against the 52nd Guards Rifle Division's position along the eastern bank of the Vorskla River. This time the enemy attacked with a major tank group and, having broken through our defense, captured the Bykovka—Koz'mo-Dem'yanovka area by the end of the day, and his forward elements reached the southern outskirts of Solonets.

The 52nd Guards Rifle Division, while holding off the enemy's pressure, sought to prevent the enlargement of the breach along the flanks. On the corps commander's orders, two of the division's regiments occupied defensive positions along the western bank of the Vorskla River along the sector Lapin gully—Voznesenskii—Vorskla—Izotov woods. The third regiment's (155th Guards Rifle Regiment) subunits occupied defensive positions along the line Kamenskii—Gonki.

Simultaneously, the enemy sought to enlarge the breach with part of his forces to the northeast. For this purpose, he undertook attacks with several groups consisting of 30-40 tanks with motorized infantry. These attacks were directed at Kamenskii and the "Boldly to Work" Collective Farm. They were all beaten back by the 155th Guards Rifle Regiment and the 96th Tank Brigade along the line Kamenskii—Gonki.

In order to prevent a breakthrough by enemy tanks further to the north toward the line Solonets—height 218.3, our command moved up subunits from the 51st Guards Rifle Division, which was occupying a defensive sector along the second army zone. Thanks to these measures, the enemy's further attempts to advance to Yakovlevo were unsuccessful.

During the day's fighting units of the 52nd Guards Rifle Division and the artillery units destroyed 85 enemy tanks.

Simultaneously with the two main attacks, which were launched along the Cherkasskoe and Koz'mo-Dem'yanovka axes, the enemy on 5 July attacked along other sectors for the purpose of securing the shock group's flanks. For example, the enemy threw an infantry regiment and 15-20 tanks from the Nova Goryanka area toward Dmitrievka. Three attempts by this group of forces to break through the forward edge of the 71st Guards Rifle Division's defense were repulsed by artillery and mortar fire and were unsuccessful. Nor were the enemy's nine attempts, undertaken by forces up to an infantry regiment in strength, with 30 tanks, for the purpose of seizing Dragunskoe, successful. The 67th Guards Rifle Division's forward outposts threw back the enemy, which was striving to break through to Trirechnoe. Units of the 375th Rifle Division, beat off the enemy's attacks on Yerik, inflicting heavy losses, as well as from the area of Yachnev Kolodez' toward Chernaya Polyana.

Results of the 5 July fighting along the Oboyan' axis

In viewing the Oboyan' axis as the main one, the German command counted on quickly achieving a major operational success here; it planned to break through our defense by attacks of powerful tank rams along two narrow sectors of the front.

For this purpose, the enemy on the morning of 5 July launched a decisive offensive. Having deployed against the 6th Guards Army four panzer and two infantry divisions in the first echelon, he launched his main attacks along the 6-kilometer Korovino—Cherkasskoe sector, and along the 8-kilometer Zadel'noe—Berezov sector. The Germans had concentrated along these sectors a large part of their tanks and most of their aviation. Up to 300 enemy tanks were operating along the Cherkasskoe axis, and up to 400 in the direction of Bykovka. Out of the overall number of 700 tanks, 120-150 were heavy T-VI "Tiger" tanks, and a significant share were "Ferdinand" assault guns.

The German aviation, while operating with the attacking ground forces, carried out about 2,400 attacks by individual planes along the Oboyan' axis on the first day of the battle. Its attacks were mainly directed against our infantry's combat formations and the artillery's firing positions. On this day our aviation along this axis carried out 1,322 sorties and shot down 127 enemy planes in aerial combat; it destroyed another 34 enemy planes on their airfields.

Our command, which knew ahead of time about the Germans' forthcoming offensive, managed to adopt the necessary countermeasures. The troops met the attacking enemy fully ready to repel him.

Because the enemy was not able on 4 July to defeat our combat outposts and reach the forward edge of the main defensive zone directly, and the successfully conducted artillery counterpreparation disupted the enemy's plans, the Germans on 5 July were not able to carry out simultaneous mass attacks. The enemy's attacks began along different sectors of the front at different times. Along the 52nd Guards Rifle Division's sector the enemy was forced to expend almost half the day in order to throw the combat outposts from the line height 177.3—height 228.6—Yakhontov—height 218. The extremely brave and stubborn resistance by our forces and the correct employment of all types of anti-tank weapons (artillery, minefields, etc.) led to a situation in which the enemy suffered huge losses. In the first day's fighting the enemy lost up to 200 tanks, 180 planes, and more than 10,000 officers and men. At the cost of such colossal losses, the enemy had by the close of 5 July only penetrated insignificantly into the depth of our main defensive zone along the axes of the main attacks, but had not been able to break through it.

The enemy was not active along the 38th and 40th armies' fronts; his troops' operations were limited to carrying out reconnaissance with small groups and artillery-mortar fire against the army's first-echelon combat formations.

On 5 July along the 7th Guards Army's front the enemy forced the Severskii Donets along the Solomino—Maslova Pristan' sector and seized along the eastern bank a bridgehead up to ten kilometers in width and 3-4 kilometers in depth.

The command's measures

On 6 July the *front* commander assigned his forces the task of continuing to destroy the attacking enemy through stubborn defense. The *front* commander's measures that preceded this consisted of the following:

a) the timely organization of the defense along the second army defensive zone along the Oboyan' axis;
b) preventing the widening of the breach toward the flanks.

As early as the morning of 5 July the *front* headquarters warned the commander of the 1st Tank Army and the commanders of the 2nd and 5th guards tank corps of the possibility that they would be used on 5-6 July, along with units of the 6th Guards Army.

On the basis of these instructions, the command of the tank formations on 5 July established direct communications with the headquarters of the 6th Guards Army, to which, besides this, were dispatched responsible staff officers.

In the latter half of the day, when the axis of the enemy's main attacks had been clearly defined, the *front* commander, General Vatutin, issued orders for the movement of the 1st Tank Army and the 2nd and 5th guards tank corps. At 1600 he personally ordered over high-frequency telephone the commander of the 1st Tank Army to occupy with two corps by 2400 on 5 July the 6th Guards Army's second defensive zone behind the second echelon (90th and 51st guards rifle divisions): the 6th Tank Corps along the sector Melovoe—Rakovo—Shepeleika, and the 3rd Mechanized Corps along the sector Alekseevka—Syrtsev—Yakovlevo. The tank army's third corps (31st), in accordance with this order, was to move up to defend the Studenok—Vladimirovka line in the second echelon, in place of the 3rd Mechanized Corps. The army's main task was defined as "in no way to allow the enemy to penetrate in the direction of Oboyan'."

In order to reinforce the army, the 180th Tank Brigade (from the 38th Army), which by the close of July 5 occupied the Oboyan' fortified bridgehead along the Semenovka—Afanas'evka (five kilometers south of Oboyan') sector, was transferred to it.

By 2400 on 5 July the 1st Tank Army had reached the indicated lines.

At 1636 the commander of the 5th Guards Tank Corps received the following order: by 2400 on 5 July he was to move the corps to the line Luchki—Petrovskii, with the mission of preventing an enemy breakthrough in the direction of Prokhorovka.

Simultaneously, the commander of the 2nd Guards Tank Corps received orders to move by 2400 on 5 July from the Korocha area to the Sazhnoe—Novye Lozy—Gostishchevo area, preventing the enemy from advancing to the north and northeast.

Both corps were subordinated to the commander of the 6th Guards Army, on the orders of whom by the end of the day they had occupied the following line: the 5th Guards Tank Corps occupied defensive positions along the line excluding Yakovlevo—Nechaevka—Teterevino, and the 2nd Guards Tank Corps the line Rozhdestvenka—Novye Lozy—Druzhnyi.

At 1940 the commander of the 35th Guards Rifle Corps received orders from the *front* commander to move the 93rd Guards Rifle Division by 0300 from the Andreevskii—Kholodnoe—Tolstoe area to the Prokhorovka area, where it was to occupy the line Petrovka—October State Farm—Pravorot' (behind the 69th Army's 183rd Rifle Division), with the task of preventing an enemy breakthrough to the northeast. By the close of 5 July the division had reached the indicated area. Two other divisions (92nd and 94th) were being moved to reinforce the Korocha axis.

In order to prevent an enemy breakthrough to the west and northwest, the *front* commander ordered the reinforcing of the 40th Army's left flank and that the Korovino—Rakitnoe axis be securely covered. The 38th Army's 192nd Tank Brigade was to reinforce the 40th Army.

In carrying out the task assigned to him, the commander of the 40th Army reinforced his second defensive zone and at 1845 issued the following order: move to the Proletarskii—Kobylevka—Vengerovka sector a regiment from the 309th Rifle Division, the 59th Tank Regiment and the 86th Tank Brigade. The 192nd Tank Brigade from the 38th Army was to concentrate in the Rakitnoe area. Besides this, the 12th and 1689th anti-tank artillery regiments, as well as the 1461st Self-Propelled Artillery Regiment, were to be moved to reinforce this axis. By the close of 5 July all of these measures had been carried out.

Thus the 1st Tank Army and the 5th Guards Tank Corps, which had occupied the second army defensive zone together with the 6th Guards Army's second echelon, had significantly reinforced the Oboyan' axis.

The enemy's likely attempts to broaden the breach to the west and northwest could be parried by units of the 40th Army moved up to the line Proletarskii—Vengerovka. The repulse of the enemy's possible attempts to break through to the east, in the direction of Gostishchevo, was entrusted to the 2nd Guards Tank Corps.

Having adopted the enumerated measures, the *front* commander also called for active operations, given a favorable situation, to destroy the Germans' group of forces that had pierced the 6th Guards Army's defensive zone. For this he issued instructions to prepare a counterstroke: the 1st Tank Army in the general direction of Tomarovka, and the 5th Guards Tank Corps, together with the 2nd Guards Tank Corps, in the general direction of Teterevino, Bykovka and Rakovka, and the 2nd Guards Tank Corps (in conjunction with the 5th Guards Tank Corps) toward Bykovka, Berezov and Belgorod.

The 6 July fighting along the main defensive zone and the enemy's breakthrough to the second army zone

During the day on 5 July the enemy suffered huge losses in personnel and equipment. Thus neither at night nor on the morning of 6 July did he carry out any active operations, bringing up his reserves, making good equipment losses, and restoring his disrupted command and control. At 1000 on 6 July the Germans began an artillery and aviation preparation. However, the activity of the German aviation on 6 July declined sharply. On the previous evening our aviation inflicted heavy losses (in planes) and blockaded a part of his airfields.

The Germans sought to break through as rapidly as possible to the Oboyan' area. The Hitlerite command decided on 6 July to launch two concentric attacks along the Oboyan' axis: one—with the forces of three divisions (11th Panzer Division, the *Grossdeutschland* SS Panzer Division, and the 332nd Infantry Division) from the Cherkasskoe area to the northeast in the general direction of Pokrovka; the second—with the forces of the SS Panzer Corps and the 167th Infantry Division from the Koz'mo-Dem'yanovka—Bykovka area along the road to Oboyan'. Both of these attacks were to link up in the Pokrovka area, as a result of which they could complete the encirclement of the 6th Guards Army's 67th and 52nd guards rifle divisions. Subsequently, the united attacks would aim their blow at Oboyan'.

On the 7th Guards Army's front along the Solomino—Maslova Pristan' sector, the formations of the Germans' III Panzer Corps crossed over to the eastern bank of the Severskii Donets with part of their forces, and on the morning of 6 July began to develop the offensive in the direction of Korocha.

The fighting along the Cherkasskoe—Pokrovka axis

On 6 July the enemy along the Cherkasskoe—Pokrovka axis once again threw about 400 tanks into the battle. The Germans' attack began at 1130, following the completion of a 1½ hour artillery preparation.

Units of the 71st Guards Rifle Division, whose left-flank units were occupying defensive positions along the Bubny—Novo-Ivanovka—Krasnyi Pochinok—Mikhailovka sector were attacked by a group of up to 100 tanks and two regiments of infantry, supported by 200 planes. The enemy, while securing the left flank of his main shock group, continued his attacks with part of his strength from the area of the Korolevskii woods (two kilometers east of Bubny) toward Dmitrievka, and from the Voskhod area toward Novo-Ivanovka. The guards troops stubbornly resisted the enemy and inflicted heavy losses on him. The enemy, augmenting the attack, committed newer and newer forces into the battle—tanks and fresh infantry formations. His aviation ceaselessly bombed our combat formations. By 1200 the Germans had pushed back the division's units, seized Novo-Ivanovka, having pushed further toward Vasil'evka.

The enemy's first attack on the Krasnyi Pochinok strong point was beaten off by fire from the strong point's artillery and that of the 27th Anti-Tank Brigade, with heavy losses for the enemy. At 1300, following a lengthy massed air attack, the enemy once again repeated his attack on Krasnyi Pochinok and, having outflanked it from the west and east, by 1400 had captured it. Advancing to the north, by the close of the day the Germans seized Zavidovka.

All further enemy attempts to develop the offensive to the west were unsuccessful.

By the close of the day the 71st Guards Rifle Division's left flank had consolidated along the line height 217.9—Dmitrievka—Setnoe—Zarytoe—Podymovka.

In order to strengthen the axis being defended by the division, the commander of the 40th Army ordered at 1330 one of the 309th Rifle Division's regiments (294th Rifle Regiment) to occupy the defensive sector Kobylevka—Razdol (along the western shore of the lake), along which were located units of the 184th Rifle Division. By the close of the day the 294th Rifle Regiment, which had been transferred on motor vehicles, had occupied the indicated line.

At 1130 a German group of forces, with 200 tanks, motorized infantry and self-propelled guns, attacked from the Cherkasskoe area to the northeast in the direction of Lukhanino, Dubrovo and Ol'khovka.

Simultaneously, the enemy pushed back our combat outposts and seized Dragunskoe, and with a force of up to 50 tanks attacked along the western bank of the Vorskla River toward Trirechnoe and Ol'khovka, covering the right flank of its group of forces attacking from Cherkasskoe to the northeast.

As a result of stubborn fighting, by 1430 the enemy had seized the Alekseevka—Lukhanino area. Up to 80 German tanks arrived here. The Germans' further advance to the north was halted by units of the 90th Guards Rifle Division and the 1st Tank Army's tank corps, which had reached this line earlier. From 1500 the enemy occupied Trirechnoe and Novocherkasskoe (three kilometers north of Trirechnoe).

Along the Zavidovka—Alekseevka sector units of the 90th Rifle Division and the 6th Tank Corps beat back four German attacks, in which up to 100 tanks took part. The enemy lost up to 50 tanks in the fighting here.

During the latter half of the day the enemy dispatched his main forces to seize the Dmitrievka—Ol'khovka area: attacks were launched to the east from the area of height 237.7 and to the northeast from the Trirechnoe area. Fierce fighting also broke out on the approaches to these locales. The anti-tank artillery, anti-tank guns and guards mortar units opened an accurate fire on the tanks. The 2nd Battalion of the 5th Guards Mortar Regiment launched two salvos against a concentration of tanks in the area of heights 210 and 237.7. The battalion took out of action 22 of the 3rd Division's tanks and burned nine others with two salvos against a concentration of tanks in the area of height 237.7. The heavy losses suffered by the Germans in tanks and personnel delayed their offensive by several hours.

When the enemy, following fierce attacks, arrived at Dmitrievka the fighting on the approaches to the village became very intense. All the combat arms pitched into the battle with the tanks, while individual tank destroyers, armed with flammable liquid bottles and grenades, heroically repulsed the enemy attacks. The chief of the 199th Guards Rifle Regiment's chemical service, Captain Batanov, personally commanded a group of tank destroyers. The troops, letting the tanks advance within 15-20 meters, threw grenades at them, halted and then set them on fire with the bottles. In this manner 12 German tanks were destroyed.

By 1700 hours, as a result of new attacks from the west and southwest, the enemy captured both strong points—Dmitrievka and Ol'khovka.

The enemy's attempts to force the Vorskla River with attacks from the east, and from the west through Ol'khovka, and encircle the 67th and 52nd guards rifle divisions' units were unsuccessful. With the capture of Dmitrievka and Ol'khovka a threatening situation arose for the 52nd Guards Rifle Division; on the orders of the army commander, the division made a fighting withdrawal from the forming pocket to the second defensive zone. The 67th Guards Rifle Division fell back fighting to the Syrtsevo—Dubrova area.

The enemy, following the capture of the Dmitrievka—Ol'khovatka area, directed his efforts toward the north, for the purpose of arriving at the Belgorod—Oboyan' highway. Before nightfall, units of the 3rd Mechanized Corps and the 90th Guards Rifle Division repulsed eight tank attacks. Up to 100-150 tanks took part in each attack. In the area of height 247.2 individual groups of German tanks managed to break into the defensive zone and even flatten the combat formations of the 3rd Mechanized Corps' 3rd Mechanized Brigade. However, the brigade's elements did not waver and, cutting off the enemy infantry with their fire, used all means at hand to destroy the German tanks that had broken through to the defensive depth.

The enemy, having lost several tens of tanks, was forced to fall back to his original position. The attacking enemy units' considerable losses in this area were suffered at the hands of our guards mortars. In the Dubrova area a single salvo completely destroyed a column of enemy motorized infantry, consisting of 60 vehicles.

The fighting in the area of Yakovlevo and Luchki

At 1130 on 6 July, following a 1½ hour's artillery preparation, the enemy attacked toward Yakovlevo with a force of up to 400 tanks. The Germans, while securing the shock group's right flank, continued to attack with part of their forces to the east, toward the line of the Lipovyi Donets River. The 3rd Mechanized Corps' 1st Guards Tank Brigade, along with the 51st Guards Rifle Division's infantry, valiantly defended the Yakovlevo center of resistance. Despite the enemy's repeated attacks in groups of 40-120 tanks and uninterrupted bombing attacks from the air, the guards troops held the center of resistance in their hands until evening.

Having lost hope of capturing the Yakovlevo center of resistance through a direct attack from the south, the Germans during the latter half of the day shifted their main attack to the northeast in the general direction of Luchki (southern); they left a powerful tank screen against Yakovlevo. The enemy, in developing the offensive, ran into the stubborn resistance of the 5th Guards Tank Corps. The corps was occupying the Yakovlevo—Nechaevka—Teterevino line; its main group of forces was located along the right flank; the defense of the Luchki—Teterevino sector was being carried out by only part of the forces of the 6th Motorized Rifle Brigade and the 51st Guards Rifle Division.

The fighting for the line held by the 5th Guards Tank Corps lasted all day and part of the night of 6-7 July. Our tanks, buried in the ground, met the attacking enemy with accurate aimed fire and during the day's fighting knocked 95 enemy tanks and several "Ferdinand" assault guns out of action.

With the onset of darkness the enemy shifted his main forces to the corps' left flank; there he managed to break through our defense and seize Luchki. Part of the German forces began to outflank the combat formations of the corps' right flank, while advancing on Bol'shie Mayachki, while the remainder developed the offensive on Ozerovskii.

Elements of the 6th Motorized Rifle Brigade and the 51st Guards Rifle Division began to fall back on Sobachevskii and Kalinin under enemy pressure. Units of the corps, which ended up being half surrounded, were engaged in heavy fighting to the northeast of Yakovlevo until 2400 on 6 July. This time was well used by units of the 6th Guards Motorized Rifle Brigade, the 20th Guards Tank Brigade, and the 51st Guards Rifle Division's 158th Regiment, which had occupied and prepared a defense by the morning of 7 July along the Ivanovskii Vyselok—Belenikhino—Teterevino line. It was to this line that the 21st and 22nd guards tank brigades and the 48th Guards Tank Regiment withdrew to in fighting, having linked up with the corps' remaining units.

The commander of the 1st Tank Army, having established the enemy's intention of breaking through to Oboyan' along the boundary between the 1st Tank Army and the 5th Guards Tank Corps, by outflanking Yakovlevo from the northeast, at 1700 on 6 July decided to move up the 31st Tank Corps' 100th Tank Brigade to the Bol'shie Mayachki area, and the corps' remaining units (237th and 242nd tank brigades) to the Beregovoi—Krasnaya Polyana area, for the purpose of reinforcing the Yakovlevo axis.

After it became known that the 5th Guards Tank Corps' front had been penetrated and that the enemy was spreading out toward Luchki (northern) and Ozerovskii, the army commander ordered the 242nd and 237th tank brigades to make a forced march to that area, establish communications there with the 5th Corps and prevent the Germans from advancing further to the north.

By the close of the day the 100th Tank Brigade had occupied the defensive line Bol'shie Mayachki—Yablochki.

As a result of the premature blowing up of the bridges over the Solotinka River (near Kochetovka), the crossing of the corps' remaining brigades was delayed; only on the morning of 7 July did they cross along newly lay bridges and reached Yablochki—Malye Mayachki—Greznoe line. Having taken up defensive positions along this line, they threw out forward detachments in the direction of Ozerovskii and Teterevino. In the area of heights 255.9 and 224.5 the detachments got into a fight with newly-arrived groups of German tanks.

The fighting along the western bank of the Lipovyi Donets

The Germans' 167th Infantry Division, which was securing the enemy group's right flank, which was attacking toward Yakovlevo, attacked at 0800 with two regiments and 60 tanks toward Rozhdestvenka and Nepkhaevo, and one regiment, with 40 tanks, toward Visloe and Ternovka. By 0900, following a battle with the 52nd Guards Rifle Division's 155th Regiment and the forward elements of the 2nd Guards Tank Corps, which was occupying defensive positions along the eastern bank of the Lipovyi Donets River, along the Rozhdestvenka—Druzhnyi sector, the enemy reached Nepkhaevo and Soshenkov.

At 1500 the 2nd Guards Tank Corps received an order from the commander of the 6th Guards Army to cross over to the western bank of the Lipovyi Donets River and, together with units of the 5th Guards Tank Corps, attack in the direction of Smorodino and Bykovka and destroy the enemy units attacking toward Yakovlevo and Luchki. At 1630 the corps' units began to cross, and at 2050, having thrown the enemy back to the west, reached the Smorodino—Kamenskii area and the woods south of this area. During the night of July 6-7, by order of the *front* commander, the corps was pulled back to its former defensive line along the eastern bank of the Lipovyi Donets River.

To the south the enemy, following heavy fighting with the 96th Tank Brigade and units of the 375th Rifle Division, managed to break through to Shopino and Ternovka in individual groups of tanks. However, the 496th Anti-Tank Regiment inflicted significant losses on the German tanks here. Counterattacks by units of the 375th Rifle Division threw the enemy out of these locales to the west.

By the close of the day the right-flank units of the 375th Rifle Division and the 96th Tank Brigade had occupied a defensive position along the western outskirts of Visloe, Ternovka and Shopino.

Along the 7th Guards Army's front, the Germans' III Panzer Corps, while continuing to attack along the eastern bank of the Severskii Donets to the northeast, captured the area Razumnoe—Krutoi Log—the woods east of Generalovka.

Results of the 5-6 July fighting for the main defensive zone along the Oboyan' axis

In two days of fierce fighting the Germans, despite enormous losses, had not achieved a decisive success on any of their attack axes.

The mission of breaking through the entire depth of our operational depth through a short, powerful attack by major tank groups of forces and reaching the Oboyan' area in the first days of the battle—for developing the offensive on Kursk—was unfulfilled. The crushing effect of operations by powerful tank rams, including new types of heavy tanks and self-propelled guns, did not work out, although the Germans had counted on this. The tank rams broke up against the stoutness of our defense.

By the close of 6 July, along almost the entire front of the 6th Guards Army, our troops had halted the attacking enemy panzer divisions in front of the second army defensive zone. This was achieved as a result of its timely reinforcement by moving up the 1st Tank Army and the 2nd and 5th guards tank corps from the *front* reserve, which met the enemy tank attacks along previously prepared positions.

By the close of the battle's second day the enemy along the Oboyan' axis had overcome in stubborn fighting the depth of the 6th Guards Army's main defensive zone and had come up against the second army zone. Only along the Yakovlevo—Luchki sector had the units of the SS Panzer Corps penetrated into the second defensive zone and created the threat here of an operational breakthrough, because in the rear of the second army defensive zone there were no lines occupied by our forces along the Yakovlevo—Kochetovka—Oboyan' axis.

The 31st Tank Corps, which had previously been located along this axis, had already been drawn into the fighting for the second zone.

By the close of the battle's second day the enemy, although he had penetrated 10-18 kilometers into the depth of our defense, had nevertheless failed to achieve freedom of maneuver along any of the axes and had been forced to advance only through endless fighting with our units, which were consecutively occupying previously prepared positions, echeloned in depth.

The enemy's attempts to develop the success by maneuvering in the direction of both flanks—by attacking to the west and northwest, east and northeast—were also unsuccessful. The advance to the west was paralyzed by the stubborn defense of the 71st Guards Rifle Division (the 6th Guards Army's right-flank division), which occupied the Dmitrievka—Podimovka line, and the timely reinforcement of the 40th Army's left flank with the movement of units to the second defense zone along the Proletarskii—Kobylevka—Vengerovka sector.

As a result of analogous measures—the timely movement of the 2nd Guards Tank Corps to the line of the Lipovyi Donets River, as well as the result of the 375th Rifle Division's (the 6th Guards Army's right-flank division) stubborn defense—the enemy's attempts to develop his offensive to the east were parried. The enemy's personnel losses (especially in tanks) during the offensive's first days were so large, that beginning on the battle's second day the German command was forced to bring up a significant number of tanks from the deep rear to make good these losses. The tank columns, moving into the area of the fighting on 6 July, shocked us with their length: the *front* command had the impression that the Germans were bringing up at least two new panzer divisions to the battlefield.

The enemy air force's large losses, which it suffered on the battle's first day, led to a situation whereby as early as 6 July German air activity dropped sharply (3,600 aircraft attacks on 5 July versus 1,500 on 6 July).

By the close of 6 July the Voronezh Front's reserves were mainly already committed into the battle for the second defensive zone. An exception was three of the 69th Army's divisions, which were still occupying the rear army zone, and the 35th Guards Rifle Corps, which was moving up to the army rear zone.

A part of the 38th Army's reinforcements, which had not taken part in active defensive operations, was transferred to the 40th and 6th Guards armies.

Our units—the 6th Guards Army's 57th and 52nd guards divisions, the 7th Guards Army's 78th and 72nd guards divisions, and the 5th Guards Tank and 3rd Mechanized corps—had suffered significant losses. Along the Oboyan' axis only one defensive line remained occupied by our forces—the second defensive zone. Along the Prokhorovka and Korocha axes our forces continued to occupy two, and in places three, defensive lines.

Measures by the *Stavka* of the Supreme High Command and the *Front* and Army Commanders

The preparation of the 7 July counterstroke

At 1200 on 6 July the *front* commander made the decision to prepare flank counterstrokes for encircling and destroying the enemy's units that had broken through to the north and northeast of Tomarovka. It was planned to carry out the counterstrokes on the morning of 7 July. The main counterstroke—with the forces of two of the 1st Tank Army's tank corps (6th and 31st) and three of the 40th Army's rifle divisions—would be launched from the Vedenskaya Gotnya—Krasnyi Pochinok—Raktinoe area in the general direction of Tomarovka and Bessonovka (45 kilometers southwest of Belgorod). The second counterstroke by the forces of the 5th and 2nd guards tank corps and three of the 6th Guards Army's left-flank rifle divisions (92nd and 89th guards and 375th) was planned from the Gonki—Belomestnaya line in the general direction of Streletskoe.

From 1200 to 1230 the *front* headquarters transmitted the orders for preparing the counterstrokes to the armies.

The evaluation of the situation by the *front* command by the close of 6 July and the conclusions by Marshal of the Soviet Union Vasilevskii

At 1820 on 6 July the Voronezh Front's military council, in a report to the Supreme Commander-in-Chief Marshal of the Soviet Union Stalin, evaluated the situation in the following manner.

As of 1130 on 6 July The enemy has six panzer divisions, or 700 tanks, operating in front of the 6th Guards Army. Up to the present time all the enemy attacks have been beaten off in front of the forward edge of the second defensive line. The enemy's main tank attack was directed against the 6th Tank and 3rd Mechanized corps of Katukov's[1] army (1st Tank), which were deployed along this line, and Kravchenko's 5th Guards Tank Corps, and Burdeinyi's 2nd Guards Tank Corps.

The 7th Guards Army is being attacked by two panzer and three infantry divisions, containing up to 270 tanks, which by 1000 had captured Krutoi Log.

The enemy's air activity had dropped off sharply and our aviation has air superiority.

1 Editor's note. Mikhail Yefimovich Katukov (1900-76) joined the Red Army in 1919 and fought in the civil war. During the Great Patriotic War he commanded a tank brigade, a tank corps and a tank army on various fronts. Following the war, Katukov commanded a tank and mechanized armies and served in the central military apparatus.

The *front* commander emphasized that the enemy was bringing up fresh reserves, of up to two panzer divisions, which could be committed into the fighting from 8 July.

For the purpose of securing further active operations, the military council requested the Supreme High Command to reinforce the *front* with four tank and two air corps.

This report, which was transmitted to the *Stavka* by telegraph, was supplemented with the following notation by the representative of the *Stavka* of the Supreme High Command, Marshal of the Soviet Union Vasilevskii, who was with the Voronezh Front during the defensive battle:

> The situation at the front as of 1700 corresponds to what has been reported. For my part, I consider it expedient for future active operations to reinforce the front with two tank corps, with the dispatch of one of them to the Prokhorovka area (30 kilometers southeast of Oboyan'), and the other to the Korocha area; for this purpose we can employ the 10th Tank Corps from Zhadov[2] and the 2nd Tank Corps from Malinovskii[3] from Valuiki. Besides this, I would consider it expedient to move Rotmistrov[4] up to the Oskol River in the area south of Staryi Oskol. I await your instructions.

Measures by the *Stavka* of the Supreme High Command

On 6 July the *front* commander received by telephone a personal order by the Supreme Commander-in-Chief, Marshal of the Soviet Union, Stalin: "To exhaust the enemy along the prepared lines and prevent his breakthrough until our active operations along the Western, Bryansk and other *fronts* begin."

The *Stavka* of the Supreme High Command, having agreed with the opinion of Marshal of the Soviet Union Vasilevskii, issued an order to move by forced march the 5th Guards Tank Army to the western bank of the Oskol River in the Korobkovo—Melovoe—Orlik—Ivanovka area, in readiness to operate along the Oboyan' and Kursk axes.

At 0130 on 7 July the army moved out, and by the morning of 8 July its main forces had concentrated in the assigned area.

By a *Stavka* order the 10th Tank Corps (from the 5th Guards Army), which was located in the Staryi Oskol area, was subordinated to the Voronezh Front, and at 0400 on 7 July left for the Prokhorovka area, where it concentrated by 1900 that day.

The commander of the Voronezh Front received the 2nd Tank Corps, which by 0800 on 8 July had concentrated in the Kamyshevka—Pravorot' (east of Prokhorovka) area.

At 0040 on 7 July Marshal of the Soviet Union Vasilevskii issued orders to include the Southwestern Front's aviation for operations in the Voronezh Front's zone.

---

2 Editor's note. Aleksei Semyonovich Zhadov (before 1942, Zhidov) (1901-77) joined the Red Army in 1919 and fought in the civil war. During the Great Patriotic War he commanded an airborne and a cavalry corps, before being appointed commander of the 66th (later 5th Guards) Army in 1943. Following the war, Zhadov served in a variety of administrative posts.

3 Editor's note. Rodion Yakovlevich Malinovskii (1898-1967) joined the imperial army in 1914 and the Red Army in 1919. During the Great Patriotic War he commanded a corps and a number of armies and *fronts*, including the Southwestern Front during the Battle of Kursk. Following the war, Malinovskiii commanded Soviet forces in the Far East and in 1957 was appointed minister of defense.

4 Editor's note. Pavel Alekseevich Rotmistrov (1901-82) joined the Red Army in 1919. During the Great Patriotic War he commanded a tank brigade and then a tank corps. He later commanded tank armies, including the 5th Guards Tank Army during the fighting around Kursk. He was removed from command in 1944 and relegated to central administrative duties. Following the Great Patriotic War, Rotmistrov served with the Soviet occupation forces in Germany and worked in the central military-educational apparatus.

Thus on the basis of the evaluations of the first two days of the defensive battle, strategic reserves were being dispatched to the area of combat operations.

The Voronezh Front commander's measures for 7 July

On the basis of comrade Stalin's instructions, the *front* commander made the decision on the evening of 6 July:

> To defeat the enemy in a defensive battle along the previously prepared defensive line, having reinforced the 7th Guards Army's dangerous axis with units of the 35th Rifle Corps, and the Yakovlevo—Prokhorovka axis by moving two tank brigades and an anti-tank brigade to the boundary between the 1st Tank Army and 5th Guards Tank Corps.
>
> All of the Voronezh Front's air power will be directed at destroying the enemy's tanks and personnel along the Oboyan' axis, while the Southwestern Front's air power will be directed against the enemy operating against the 7th Guards Army.

Thus, due to the altered situation the counterstrokes planned for the morning of 7 July by the *front's* flanking formations fell by the wayside. The troops received instructions to hold at any cost their defensive lines on 7 July. In accordance with these instructions, on the morning of 7 July the 2nd Tank Corps was to concentrate in the Koshmanovka—Alekseevka—Korocha—Setnoe area, with the mission of preventing the enemy's advance on Khmelevoe, Novo-Slobodka and Zayach'e.

By the close of 7 July the 10th Tank Corps was to have concentrated in the Petrovka—Prokhorovka area, with the mission of preventing the enemy's breakthrough through the occupied area to the east and northeast.

The 1st Tank Army was to be reinforced by the 40th Army's 29th Anti-Tank Brigade, for use along the boundary between the 1st Tank Army and the 5th Guards Tank Corps.

The 7-9 July 1943 Fighting Along the Second Defensive Zone

During 7-9 July the German command continued to direct all its efforts toward carrying out its main task—a breakthrough in the Oboyan' area. Thus the direction of the enemy's main attacks during this time was concentrated along the Belgorod—Oboyan' paved road. In order to reinforce the group of forces operating along the Oboyan' axis, on 7 July the enemy committed his final reserve into the battle—the XLVIII Panzer Corps' 3rd Panzer Division.

On July 8-9 the fighting in the Oboyan'—Belgorod area reached the zenith of intensity. On 9 July the enemy carried out here his last attempt to break through to Oboyan' along the road from the south.

Following the unsuccessful fighting in the area east and northeast of Belgorod (along the 7th Guards Army's front) the German command lost hope of breaking through to Korocha by means of a short and powerful attack. From 8 July the Germans directed their operations to the north for the purpose of encircling the 6th Guards Army's left-flank formations, which were defending along the Lipovyi Donets River.

The enemy was seeking by such actions to, first of all, expand his breach to the east (which he had not been able to achieve by attacking the 6th Guards Army's left-flank formations from the west), and secondly—to create a crisis situation along the 6th Guards Army's left flank, in order to draw off part of our reserves there and secure the rear of his main group of forces attacking toward Oboyan' against our forces' attacks from the line of the Lipovyi Donets River.

On 9 July the enemy, by reinforcing the group of forces operating along the eastern bank of the Severskii Donets River, committed the 198th Infantry Division.

Their enormous losses and lack of reserves forced the Germans by 7 July to significantly shorten their front of active operations. For example, along the Trefilovka—Zavidovka and Teterevino—Shopino sectors, the enemy went over to the defensive, having begun defensive work. In the 7-9 July fighting along the Oboyan' axis the efforts of our forces were directed at retaining the second defensive zone.

Our forces from 8 July had gone over to counterattacks against the flanks of the enemy group of forces that had penetrated. Attacks against the flanks and rear of the main enemy group of forces had the purpose of reducing the enemy's pressure toward Oboyan'. It was planned that this would distract a part of his reserves from the Oboyan' axis to the sectors of the enemy front being attacked by us.

The forces of the 7th Guards Army were also engaged in fierce fighting. The army had the task of halting the enemy's offensive before the second defensive line. On 8 July the axis being defended by the army was reinforced with part of the 69th Army's forces and the 35th Guards Rifle Corps.

By the close of 7 July the strategic reserves (10th Tank Corps) began to arrive in the battle zone. On 8 July the 2nd Tank Corps had concentrated, and by the close of 9 July the 5th Guards Tank Army had concentrated in the Oboyan' area.

Thus by the morning of 10 July the Oboyan' and Prokhorovka axes had been reinforced with newly arrived reserves. Our defense along these axes now had the necessary depth.

The Fighting on 7 July

The situation by the morning of 7 July

Having brought up fresh reserves and reinforced his formations operating here, the enemy threw into the battle along the Oboyan' axis about 700 tanks on the morning of 7 July. The main mass of tanks was concentrated along the Syrtsevo—Yakovlevo line, for operations along the Belgorod—Oboyan' road.

By the morning of 7 July our forces along the Oboyan' axis occupied the following position.

The 40th Army received (from the 6th Guards Army) the 71st Guards Rifle Division, and by the morning of 7 July had a defense along its left flank, which had been organized in two echelons. In the first echelon, along the line excluding Trofimovka—Novo-Ivanovka—Podymovka, the 71st Guards Rifle Division was defending along a broad front. In the second echelon, along the line Vedenskaya Gotnya—Dmitrievka—Kobylevka—Melovoe, the 161st, 309th and 184th rifle divisions were defending, along with the 59th and 60th tank regiments, the 86th and 192nd tank, and 29th Anti-Tank brigades.

The 1st Tank Army's 6th Tank and 3rd Mechanized corps, together with the 6th Guards Army's 90th Guards Rifle Division, continued to hold the second defensive zone along the Melovoe—Lukhanino—Pokrovka sector. On the morning of 7 July, on orders of the commander of the 1st Tank Army, the 180th Tank Brigade was moved up from the Oboyan' area to the Krasnaya Polyana area to cover the boundary between the 3rd Mechanized and 31st Tank corps.

Along the line excluding Pokrovka—Yablochki—height 224.5 the 100th Tank Brigade and the forward detachments of the 237th and 242nd tank brigades (31st Tank Corps) were holding against the pressure of the enemy attacking to the northwest. On the morning of 7 July the main forces of the 237th and 242nd tank brigades had concentrated in the Malye Mayachki—Greznoe area.

The 69th Army's 183rd Rifle Division was occupying the army rear zone along the Bogoroditskoe—Vinogradovka—Novoselovka—Shipy sector, and on the morning of 7 July entered the fighting against the Germans' arriving forward detachments in the Teterevino farm—Yasnaya Polyana area.

The 67th, 51st and 52nd guards rifle divisions, which had been moved into the army reserve after heavy fighting, were putting themselves in order: the 67th in the Berezovka area; the 51st in the Sukho-Solotino area, and; the 52nd in the Nizhnyaya Ol'shanka—Kartashevka area.

The 5th Guards Tank Corps occupied defensive positions along the line Belenikhino—excluding Teterevino.

The 51st Guards Rifle Division's 158th Rifle Regiment was defending the Teterevino area.

The 2nd Guards Tank Corps, along with the newly arrived 93rd Guards Rifle Division (35th Guards Rifle Corps) occupied defensive positions along the eastern bank of the Lipovyi Donets River along the Rozhdestvenka—Druzhnyi sector.

The 375th Rifle Division and the 96th Tank Brigade were defending along the Visloe—Shopino—Chernaya Polyana sector.

The 89th Guards Rifle Division, which had been moved up from the second defensive zone, was completing its concentration in the wooded area to the east of Ternovka.

The 69th Army's 305th Rifle Division continued to occupy the rear army zone along the Vypolzovka—Aleksandrovka—Mazikino sector.

The fighting along the Oboyan' paved road

The Germans, having concentrated up to 500 tanks against the 3rd Mechanized Corps and the right flank of the 31st Tank Corps along the Syrtsev—Yablochki sector, began their attack on the morning of 7 July along two axes: they launched one attack by a group of 400 tanks and motorized infantry, continuously supported by aviation, from the Syrtsev—Yakovlevo sector in the general direction of Krasnaya Dubrava, and the other, with up to 100 tanks, from the Mikitino woods toward Bol'shie Mayachki.

The 3rd Mechanized Corps' 10th Brigade was defending the sector Spitsyn—northern outskirts of Lukhanino; the 1st Mechanized Brigade occupied defensive positions along the line excluding the northeastern outskirts of Lukhanino—Syrtsevo; the 3rd Mechanized Brigade was holding the sector excluding Syrtsev—excluding height 226, and; the 1st Guards Tank Brigade the Pogorelovka—Pokrovka area. The 31st Mechanized Corps' 100th Tank Brigade, which had been operationally subordinated to the commander of the 3rd Mechanized Corps, was defending the line excluding Pokrovka—Bol'shie Mayachki.

The Germans' attacks began at 0300 on 7 July. An attempt by an enemy group of 50 tanks, with automatic riflemen on board, to break through along the boundary between the 1st and 3rd mechanized brigades from the area of Dubrovo toward Syrtsev and to height 254.5, was beaten off. Only individual tanks reached the artillery firing positions, where they were destroyed. At 0430, following a heavy air strike, the enemy repeated his attack with a group of up to 170 tanks: the Germans were attempting to break through the brigades' front. Fierce fighting continued until 1500. At 1500 the enemy, having committed fresh reserves, broke through the 1st and 3rd mechanized brigades' front and began to spread toward the north and northwest.

The brigades conducted a fighting retreat, holding off the Germans' pressure. In the height 254.5 area the 3rd Mechanized Brigade got into a fierce fight with the pursuing enemy. A platoon of the 35th Anti-Tank Regiment's 3rd Battery occupied firing positions near the fork in the road in the area of height 254.5. A group of 37 tanks, among which were several "Tiger" tanks, advanced on the platoon.

The artillery men, having let the enemy vehicles to within 200-300 meters, began to fire on them at point-blank range. In several minutes they destroyed five heavy tanks. The remainder turned back. The enemy's attack along this axis was delayed for an extended time.

In the fighting near height 254.5 the commander of a machine gun platoon, Senior Sergteant Zinchenko, died a hero's death. When the German tanks had broken through to the machine gunners' trenches, Sergeant Zinchenko knocked the first tank out of action with an accurately thrown grenade. Despite a shoulder wound, the brave sergeant continued the fight. A "Tiger" tank approached his trench. Zinchenko, having girded himself with grenades, threw himself under the enemy vehicle's tracks. A powerful explosion sounded. The tank, with smashed up tracks, halted. The brave patriot died the death of the valiant.

In the area of the three burial mounds and height 230.1 (1½-2 kilometers north of Syrtsev) the attacking German tanks were subjected to a counterattack by the 112th Tank Brigade. This brigade had been transferred from the 6th Tank Corps' reserve on the morning of 7 July and subordinated to the commander of the 3rd Mechanized Corps, for the purpose of heading off the danger of a German breakthrough to the Verkhopen'e area. Having left the Tolstoe woods, it moved through Verkhopen'e toward Syrtsevo and then toward Syrtsev. The brigade, having encountered the attacking German tanks at 1530, deployed in the area of height 230.1 and began firing on the Germans from this spot. A fierce fight continued to the onset of darkness. The enemy lost 15 tanks, including six heavy ones. The brigade lost 20 tanks on this day.

The 1st Guards Tank Brigade, which was defending in the area Pogorelovka—Mikhailovka Collective Farm, was also attacked. At 0530 a group of enemy tanks (up to 60 vehicles with infantry) attacked from the area Koz'mo-Dem'yansk. The group's attack was supported by the air attacks of 100 planes. However, all the enemy's attempts to break into the brigade's position from the south were beaten back by fire from tanks and anti-tank artillery. Simultaneously, an enemy group of 30 tanks and an infantry battalion occupied Pokrovka and created a threat to the brigade's left flank. In order to restore the situation, the corps commander moved up his reserve 49th Tank Brigade from the Sukhaya woods. It was given the assignment of throwing the Germans out of Pokrovka and organizing the stubborn defense of this locale. The brigade carried out its assignment. However, at 2000 the enemy launched a second powerful attack and once again occupied Pokrovka, having forced elements of the 49th Brigade, which had suffered heavy losses, to pull back to the north.

The enemy, having taken advantage of the 3rd Mechanized Brigade's withdrawal, attacked the 1st Guards Tank Brigade (its right flank) with part of its forces along the direction toward height 226. Under threat of encirclement, the brigade abandoned the Pogorelovka area and conducted a fighting retreat to height 251.2, where it continued to fighting until the onset of darkness.

On 7 July the positions of the 31st Tank Corps' 100th Tank Brigade, which was defending along the line Ul'yanovka (one kilometer east of Pokrovka)—Bol'shie Mayachki—Yablochki, were subjected to numerous attacks by an enemy group of up to 100 tanks and motorized infantry. By evening the enemy had captured Pokrovka. An immediate threat to the brigade's right flank and rear arose. On the corps commander's orders, the brigade began a fighting retreat to the north and during the first part of the night of 7-8 July continued to beat off the Germans' ceaseless attacks along the line of the grove south of Krasnaya Polyana—height 252.5

By the close of 7 July the 6th Tank Corps' 6th Motorized Rifle Brigade continued to hold the Melovoe—Rakovo line. Units of the 3rd Mechanized Corps—10th and 1st mechanized and 112th Tank brigades—occupied defensive positions along the line Spitsin—excluding Syrtsevo—Shchenyachii woods (two kilometers west of Krasnaya Dubrava). The corps' 3rd Motorized Rifle, 1st Guards and 49th Tank brigades, which were conducting a fighting retreat to the north, were holding against enemy pressure along the line of Shchenyachii woods—the grove south of Krasnaya Polyana throughout the first half of the night of 7-8 July. The 100th Tank Brigade was defending the line of the grove south of Krasnaya Polyana—height 252.5.

Aerial photographs of the 3rd Mechanized Corps' fighting area, which were made at 1315 on 7 July, testify to the intensity of the fighting along the Oboyan' axis and the magnitude of the losses suffered by the enemy. The photographs show about 200 burning German tanks.

During the daytime of 7 July and the night of 7-8 July the commanders of the 1st Tank and 6th Guards armies took measures for creating a new intermediate screen in the rear of the 3rd Mechanized Corps, which was to bar the path of the enemy pushing toward Oboyan'. By the morning of 8 July the line of the machine-tractor station (Verkhopen'e)—Stanovaya woods (three kilometers east of Il'inskoe) had been occupied by the 6th Tank Corps' 200th Tank Brigade. The 67th Guards Rifle Division, which had been brought up from the Berezovka area, occupied defensive positions along the line of the southern outskirts of Verkhopen'e—Shchenyachii woods—Stanovaya woods. The 51st Guards Rifle Division, which was moving up on the night of 7-8 July to the line Krasnaya Polyana—height 252.5 (from the Sukho-Solotino area), upon approaching Krasnaya Polyana encountered the enemy's forward detachments, which before this had pushed out the 1st Guards Tank Brigade's elements from the village.

As a result of the fierce night fighting, the division's units, in conjunction with the brigade, threw the Germans out of Krasnaya Polyana and occupied their designated line. By morning the 40th Army's 192nd Tank Brigade, which had been included in the 31st Tank Corps, reached this line. The brigade stood directly behind the 51st Guards Rifle Division's combat formations. Simultaneously, the 86th Tank Brigade, which had been transferred by the *front* commander from the 40th Army, moved north to the line height 251.4—Sitnoe woods—height 248.3.

Moreover, both armies had been reinforced (by the *front* commander's 7 July order): the 1st Tank Army with the 309th Rifle Division, the 1244th and 12th anti-tank and 36th guards mortar regiments from the 40th Army, and the 222nd Anti-Tank and 203rd Tank regiments (a breakthrough regiment, consisting of KV[5] tanks) from the 38th Army; the 6th Guards Army with the 111th Howitzer Artillery Regiment, which had been transferred from the 38th Army. Thus the stubborn resistance by units of the 3rd Mechanized Corps, 112th Tank Brigade, 6th Tank Corps, and the 31st Tank Corps' 100th Tank Brigade helped up to win the necessary time for organizing by the morning of 8 July a stout defense along the line Syrtsevo—Verkhopen'e—Shchenyachii woods—height 251—height 252.5.

The 31st Tank Corps' battle in the Teterevino—Greznoe—Malye Mayachki area

Throughout 6 July the 31st Tank Corps' forward detachments fought with the Germans' tank units, which were attacking to the northwest. Pushed back by the enemy, they fell back on their main forces (237th and 242nd tank brigades), which were preparing a defense along the line Malye Mayachki—Greznoe.

By 1800 the German units had come into contact with the 31st Tank Corps' main forces. At 1900 the enemy threw about 120 planes against Greznoe. They bombed this area non-stop for two hours. After this, when it was already twilight, a powerful enemy group of tanks attacked, with the obvious goal of breaking through the corps' front in the Greznoe area.

As a result of the fierce fighting, the enemy pushed our forces back insignificantly and captured the eastern outskirts of Malye Mayachki and Greznoe.

Simultaneously with the attack on Greznoe, the enemy attacked with part of his forces to the north toward Krasnyi Oktyabr' and from Teterevino toward the Komsomolets State Farm. The enemy's attacks failed along both attack axes and were beaten back by units of the 69th Army's 183rd Rifle Division.

5 Editor's note. The KV (named after Soviet defense commissar K.Ye. Voroshilov) was a series of Soviet heavy tanks that appeared during the Second World War. Weighing between 42.5 and 47 tons and carrying a crew of five, these tanks were all armed with a 76mm gun and 2-4 7.62mm machine guns.

The piercing of our line by the enemy's attacking units along the boundary of the 51st Guards Rifle Division and the 5th Guards Tank Corps could have created the threat of a German breakthrough to the north. The enemy's subsequent operations to the northeast, for the purpose of capturing the Prokhorovka area, were possible. Foreseeing this, the *front* commander issued an order at 0040 on 7 July to move up by the close of 7 July the 10th Tank Corps, which had concentrated in the Prokhorovka area for securing the Prokhorovka axis, to the Petrovka—Pravorot' line. The corps was to occupy a firm defense here, which it carried out in time.

In connection with the arrival of the Germans in the Krasnaya Polyana—Teterevino farm—Ozerovskii area and the beginning of their attack on Greznoe and the Komsomolets State Farm, the threat of an enemy breakthrough toward Kochetovka, Oboyan' and Prokhorovka became even more real. Thus the *front* commander and the commander of the 1st Tank Army reinforced this axis: the 31st Tank Corps with the 29th Anti-Tank Brigade and the 1244th Anti-Tank Regiment; by the close of 7 July the 52nd Guards Rifle Division was defending along the northern bank of the Psel River along the Klyuchi—Polezhaev sector, with the task of preventing the enemy's breakthrough to the river's northern bank.

The enemy was also active along the 6th Guards Army's left wing. Throughout 7 July he sought to eliminate, with units of the 167th Infantry Division and tanks, our bridgehead along the western bank of the Lipovyi Donets River in the Visloe—Shopino area. All the numerous attacks were beaten back by the 375th Rifle Division defending here. The Germans suffered heavy losses in this.

Results of the 7 July fighting along the Oboyan' axis

On 7 July the enemy's main efforts were directed against the 1st Tank Army's center (3rd Mechanized Corps). Simultaneously, the enemy was developing the offensive from the area Teterevino farm—Ozerovskii toward Greznoe, striving to break through to the rear of the 6th Guards and 1st Tank armies, outflank the 1st Tank Army's left flank (31st Tank Corps) and open the road to Oboyan'. The Germans sought to secure their main group's right flank by operations along the front Komsomolets State Farm—Teterevino—Shopino. The enemy was not active against the 6th Guards Army's right flank.

By the close of 7 July our forces continued to hold the second defensive zone. The exceptions were the Lukhanino—Luchki and Bogoroditskoe—Komsomolets State Farm sectors. The enemy managed to penetrate 4-12 kilometers into our defense along the first of these sectors; on the second, the Germans reached the rear defensive zone with a narrow wedge along the front of the 69th Army's 183rd Rifle Division.

The most noteworthy actions that day were the operations of the 3rd Mechanized Corps and its attached 6th and 31st tank corps. Under the pressure of superior enemy forces, the corps abandoned its line. However, as a result of the subsequent skillful conduct of a mobile defense along the intermediate lines, the corps exhausted the enemy's units, inflicted huge losses on him and prevented him from breaking through our front on any sector.

By the close of the day the 1st Tank Army, along with units of the 90th Guards Rifle Division, occupied a defensive line along the line excluding Lukhanino—Syrtsevo—the southern outskirts of Verkhopen'e—Shchenyachii woods—Krasnaya Polyana—the western part of Malye Mayachki, and Greznoe. The 1st Tank and 6th Guards armies were reinforced with a number of formations from the 40th and 38th armies for the purpose of strengthening the combat capability of this line.

Along the 7th Guards Army's sector, the enemy, having gone over to the offensive on the morning of 7 July to the northeast, had by the close of the day penetrated 3-5 kilometers into our defense and captured the Belovskaya—Yastrebovo area.

The command's measures for 8 July

On the basis of the instructions by the *Stavka* of the Supreme High Command, the Steppe Military District's 47th Army moved out of the Ol'khovatka—Krivonosovka—Kamenka area for the Golubino—Bulanovka—Slonovka station area.

For the purpose of weakening the pressure by the main enemy group of forces along the Oboyan' axis, the *front* commander made the decision at 2300 on 7 July to launch counterstrokes on the morning of 8 July. The counterstrokes, to be undertaken by the *front's* tank formations and part of the 40th Army's left wing forces, were to be directed against the flanks of the main enemy group of forces. The 10th Tank Corps, moving out by the morning of 8 July to the line Bogoroditskoe—height 241.6, was to attack the enemy in the direction of Vasil'evka and Yakovlevo and reach the Yakovlevo area. The 2nd Tank Corps had the mission of attacking the Germans along the Komsomolets State Farm—Bykovka axis and reach the latter area. For this purpose, the corps was concentrating in the Vinogradovka—Storozhevoe area by the morning of 8 July. The 5th Guards Tank Corps had the task of attacking in the direction of Belenikhino, Luchki (southern) and Bykovka and reaching the Bykovka—Berezov—"Boldly to Work" Collective Farm. The 2nd Guards Tank Corps was ordered to attack toward Luchki.

Simultaneously with the attack by this main group of forces, which consisted of four tank corps, the 1st Tank Army's 6th Tank Corps was to attack the enemy from the Syrtsevo area in the general direction of Yakovlevo and subsequently reach the front Syrtsev—Yakovlevo. The 40th Army's left-flank divisions—161st and 71st Guards—were to attack in the general direction of Gertsovka and, if conditions were favorable, capture the Fastov—Gertsovka area. All of the *front's* air power was to support the planned counterstrokes.

It was planned to start the attack at 1030, following a 30-minute artillery preparation.

All of the *front's* remaining formations were to stubbornly defend their lines. The 180th Tank Brigade, which had been reinforced by two anti-tank regiments, constituted the army's reserve and occupied the line height 242.1—Stanovaya woods (three kilometers southeast of Il'inskii). The brigade had the task of preventing an enemy breakthrough toward Oboyan' along the road and be ready to counterattack to the southwest, south and southeast. The newly arrived 309th Rifle Division from the 40th Army, along with the 86th Tank Brigade and the 36th Guards Mortar Regiment, were ordered to occupy defensive positions along the line height 251.4—height 240.4—height 235.9—height 207.8—Peresyp', with the tank brigade along the sector height 251.4—height 240.4. The division had the task of preventing an enemy breakthrough toward Oboyan' along the Belgorod—Oboyan' road.

The 86th Tank Brigade occupied its designated area by the morning of 8 July, while the 309th Rifle Division was subordinated to the commander of the 1st Tank Army only on the morning of 9 July.

The 3rd Mechanized Corps (1st and 49th tank and 3rd Motorized Rifle brigades) was to be moved into the height 260.8—Il'inskii area by the morning of 8 July in the 1st Tank Army's reserve to put themselves in order. By that time the 100th Tank Brigade, on the orders of the commander of the 31st Tank Corps, had been pulled back into the reserve in the area of Veselyi village.

The 203rd Heavy Tank Breakthrough Regiment, along with the 222nd Anti-Tank Regiment, arrived in the Oboyan' area from the 38th Army. By the morning of 8 July the tank regiment was to occupy defensive positions along the near approaches to Oboyan' along the line southern outskirts of Semenovka—Goryanino.

The fighting on 8 July

Operating pretty much in their former grouping, the Germans on 8 July sought to develop their attacks against the center and left flank of the 1st Tank Army along the Syrtsevo—Greznoe sector. The enemy's main attacks were directed against units of the 1st Tank and 6th Guards armies, which were defending along the area of the Belgorod—Oboyan' paved road, and against the 31st Tank Corps and the 192nd Tank Brigade, which were defending along the Malye Mayachki—Greznoe line.

The fighting in the area of the Oboyan' paved road

On the morning of 8 July units of the 6th Tank and 3rd Mechanized corps were engaged in very intensive fighting. Overall, on this day the enemy committed up to 400 tanks in the area of the Oboyan' paved road. The Germans carried out uninterrupted attacks, striving to break through to Oboyan'; they sought with part of their forces to capture the area of Syrtsevo. The attacks by the enemy tanks were supported by aviation, which operated over the battlefield in groups of 40-50 planes.

The 6th Tank Corps 112th Tank Brigade and the 3rd Mechanized Corps' 10th and 1st mechanized brigades (operationally subordinated to the commander of the 6th Tank Corps), along with the 90th Guards Rifle Division's left-flank units, beat back during the day all of the enemy's attacks, which were trying to break through to Syrtsevo. By the close of the day they had completely held their positions.

The 3rd Mechanized Corps' 3rd Mechanized and 49th Tank brigades and the 6th Tank Corps' 200th Tank Brigade also were engaged in heavy fighting the entire day astride the Oboyan' paved road. While cooperating with units of the 67th and 51st guards rifle divisions,[6] they held off the pressure from the main enemy forces.

The anti-tank artillery units, which with their fire inflicted huge losses on the enemy and broke up his attacks, played a very important role in the fighting.

In spite of all the enemy's attempts to break through to the north, units of the 3rd Mechanized Corps and the 6th Guards Army continued to hold by evening a front along the southern outskirts of Verkhopen'e—Shchenyachii woods and then to the grove south of Krasnaya Polyana. Individual groups of German tanks, which had broken through the 3rd Mechanized Corps' combat formations in the direction of Oboyan', were destroyed by fire and counterattacks delivered by the 180th and 49th tank brigades from the area of Il'inskii village.

The 49th Tank Brigade, which had suffered significant losses, was withdrawn after the battle to the area of height 260.8, to put itself in order. During the day's fighting along the road in the area of height 242.1, our forces destroyed 104 German tanks, including 28 "Tigers."

The fighting for Greznoe and the withdrawal of the 31st Tank Corps to the Solotinka River

No less intense fighting unfolded along the front of the 31st Tank Corps and 192nd Tank Brigade. The enemy concentrated up to 300 tanks here and by attacking toward Kochetovka sought to get into the rear of the 1st Tank Army. Along the Greznoe—Kochetovka axis alone more than 200 enemy tanks were operating, supported by incessant air attacks. A number of repeated enemy attacks forced the corps' left-flank units to abandon the western part of Greznoe; during the latter

6 By 8 July both these divisions were severely understrength as the result of the preceding battles.

half of the day they began to fall back on Kochetovka, in order to take up a new defensive line along the Solotinka River.

The 29th Anti-Tank Brigade played a very important role in the fighting for Greznoe. During the first half of the day it beat off several attacks against the locale. As a result, the brigade covered the withdrawal of the corps' units to Kochetovka with its fire. In carrying out their combat assignment, the 184th Anti-Tank Regiment's 2nd Battery ended up being surrounded. The artillery heroes repelled the enemy attacks to the last shell and last bullet of the crews, and all died in the unequal fight. The 4th Battery, which destroyed 11 enemy tanks, fought just as valiantly. In all, during the daytime fighting the brigade destroyed 35 tanks, including three "Tigers" and one "Ferdinand" assault gun.

A group of enemy tanks numbering up to 100 vehicles, which had launched an attack against the boundary between the 3rd Mechanized and 31st Tank corps in the direction of Sukho-Solotino, managed during the latter half of the day to penetrate our defense. Under enemy pressure, units of the corp's right flank fell back toward Sukho-Solotino by the close of the day. Here they occupied defensive positions along the left bank of the Solotinka River along the sector of the grove southwest of Sukho-Solotino—Sukho-Solotino—Kochetovka—excluding Il'inskii along the Psel River.

All the Germans' attempts to develop the offensive further to the northwest were unsuccessful and were beaten back by our units. The enemy only pierced our defense in the Kochetovka area, occupying its eastern outskirts.

As a result of the penetration, units of the 192nd Tank Brigade bent their flank and occupied defensive positions along the line height 251—eastern outskirts of Krasnaya Polyana—the grove southwest of Sukho-Solotino, where they anchored their flank to the 31st Tank Corps' right flank.

The 192nd Tank Brigade's battle for the Krasnaya Polyana and Beregovoi (one kilometer north of Krasnaya Polyana) strong points continued all night into 9 July. By dawn our units were forced to fall back to the western bank of the Solotinka River, abandoning Beregovoi and Krasnaya Polyana.

The 51st Guards Rifle Division, which was defending along with the 192nd Tank Brigade, fell back in heavy fighting to the Sukho-Solotino area.

On that day our aviation was active along the Oboyan' axis and carried out more than a thousand sorties, was involved in 49 air battles, and shot down 93 enemy planes.

The 10th Tank Corps, which had deployed along the front excluding Krasnyi Oktyabr'—Vasil'evka—height 241.6, was beating off attacks by groups of enemy tanks, which had attacked along this axis from the morning of 8 July. All of the enemy's attempts to break through to the line of the Psel River ended in failure. However, the 10th Tank Corps, which had been preempted by the enemy, did not attack. Until evening the corps continued to wage defensive battles along the line, destroying ten enemy tanks that day.

The counterblows by the 40th Army and the 5th and 2nd guards tank corps

The counterblow from the west against the flank of the attacking enemy group of forces was organized by the 40th Army. According to the *front* commander's plan, the army's 161st and 71st Guards rifle divisions attacked in the morning along the Trefilovka—Voskhod sector. The 161st Rifle Division, after being relieved during the night of 7-8 July by units of the 71st Guards Rifle Division along the sector Trefilovka—excluding Voskhod, launched a demonstration attack in the morning and by the end of the day had captured the Papadino woods. The 71st Guards Rifle Division, which had also attacked with its right-flank forces, was fighting in the western outskirts of the village of Voskhod.

Two tank corps also attacked from the east against the flank of the attacking German group of forces. These corps attacked as follows: the 5th Guards Tank Corps at 1000 toward Kalinin, and the 2nd Guards Tank Corps at 1200 toward Nechaevka. After advancing slightly, they encountered powerful resistance and, coming under counterattack by enemy tanks and aircraft, fell back to their jumping-off position. Nonetheless, the corps' active operations distracted part of the enemy's forces. For example, the 5th Corps was counterattacked in the Kalinin area by a group of up to 100 German tanks.

On the 6th Guards Army's remaining sectors on this day the enemy was not active and continued his defensive works. He also limited himself to actions by small reconnaissance parties in front of the 38th and 40th armies along individual sectors of our defense and carried out fire onslaughts.

In the 7th Guards Army's sector, the enemy continued to develop his attack to the north. The Germans sought to reach the rear of the *front's* formations defending along the Lipovyi Donets River; by the close of the day, as the result of stubborn fighting, they seized Sevryukovo, Myasoedovo and Melekhovo.

Results of the 8 July fighting along the Oboyan' axis

During the offensive's fourth day (8 July) the enemy, despite continuous attacks and heavy losses, was also not able to carry out his main task and reach the Oboyan' area. All of his attempts to break through to Oboyan', both from the south along the Belgorod—Oboyan' paved road, as well as from the Greznoe area through Kochetovka, were unsuccessful. The enemy only pushed the 31st Tank Corps to the Solotinka River, advanced 4-6 kilometers along this sector, and widened the tip of his wedge to 8-10 kilometers in the area Krasnyi Oktyabr'—Kochetovka. The forces of the 1st Tank and 6th Guards armies mainly continued to fight along the second defensive zone.

The command's measures for 9 July

The *Stavka* of the Supreme High Command, taking into account the intensity of the situation along the Oboyan' axis, on 8 July ordered the 5th Guards Tank Army, which was concentrating that morning in the Korobkovo—Melovoe—Ivanovka area, to move on 9 July to the Bobryshevo—Srednyaya Ol'shanka (one kilometer east of Shipy)—Bol'shie Seti—Marino area, moving its forward detachments to the Psel River along the Oboyan'—Shipy sector. By 2300 on 9 July the army had concentrated in the designated area; its forward detachments reached the Psel River on the morning of 9 July.

Naturally, the *front* commander's chief attention was focused on maximally reinforcing the Oboyan' axis. For this purpose, at 0035 on 9 July he personally ordered the commander of the 10th Tank Corps by direct wire to turn over the defensive sector Vasil'evka—Komsomolets State Farm to the 2nd Tank Corps and operationally subordinate himself to the commander of the 1st Tank Army. The army commander ordered the corps commander to concentrate in the Vladimirovka area, in order to parry the enemy's attempts to break through to Oboyan' along the Belgorod—Oboyan' paved road.

The 38th Army's 20th Rifle Division was being transferred to the Oboyan' area in the *front* reserve.

By order of the *front* commander (those orders were issued from 1930 to 2200 on 8 July), the 1st Tank Army was further reinforced with the 59th and 60th tank, 4th Anti-Tank, and 38th Guards Mortar regiments from the 40th Army, as well as the 38th Army's 483rd Anti-Tank Regiment.

The overall increase in strength of our group of forces along the Oboyan' axis during 8-9 July was as follows:

- two rifle divisions;
- one anti-aircraft artillery division;
- three tank brigades;
- four tank regiments;
- three anti-tank brigades;
- eight anti-tank regiments;
- one cannon artillery regiment, and;
- four guards mortar regiments.

All of these units arrived from the 38th and 40th armies. Besides this, the 10th Tank Corps was being transferred to this axis. It was decided to reinforce the defense in the Belenikhino—Leski—Ivanovka area. For this purpose, at 2200 on 8 July it was suggested to the commander of the 69th Army that he move units of the 183rd Rifle Division's left flank from the Vinogradovka—Novoselovka—Shipy (the army rear zone) line to the railroad along the sector Komsomolets State Farm—Yasnaya Polyana—Teterevino. In this way the units of the 5th Guards Tank Corps located along the sector Belenikhino—Teterevino would be relieved.

The main task for the forces of the 1st Tank and 6th Guards armies, and the 69th Army's formations on 9 July remained the same: to firmly hold their positions and prevent the enemy's breakthrough to Oboyan' and Prokhorovka.

The armies carried out the necessary internal regroupings during the night of 8-9 July on the basis of the *front* commander's instructions to the army commanders.

The 309th Rifle Division, which had arrived from the 40th Army to the 1st Tank Army, had by the morning of 9 July taking up defensive positions along the line Malinovoe woods—Melovoe woods—southern outskirts of Ol'khovatka, as the army's second echelon.

The fighting on 9 July
The Germans' last attempt to break through to Oboyan' from the south

On 9 July the enemy's main forces were concentrated directly in the area of the Belgorod—Oboyan' paved road. The German command decided on that day to break through our defense at any cost and reach the Oboyan' area. During the night of 8-9 July the enemy grouped up to 500 tanks along the narrow 10-kilometer Verkhopen'e—Sukho-Solotino sector of the front. The average tank saturation was equal to 50 tanks per kilometer of front. Along the main attack axes the concentration of tank forces reach 100 vehicles and more. In order to ensure the success of his group of forces, the enemy threw all his available aviation into the battle, making more than 1,500 sorties that day.

Because the *front* command very clearly understood the enemy plan—to break through to Oboyan' from the south along the paved road, it adopted in a timely fashion all the necessary measures directed at parrying this attack. A powerful artillery anti-tank concentration was created in the area of the Oboyan' paved road, consisting of one anti-tank brigade, three independent anti-tank regiments and four guards mortar battalions. A significant part of the *front's* tank reserves were concentrated here.

On the night of 8-9 July the 1st Tank Army, on orders of the *front* commander, prepared and occupied the second defensive line Kruglik—Kalinovka—Melovoe woods (four kilometers south of Orlovka)—Safonovo along the axis of the expected attack.

In order to create more favorable conditions for the 9 July attack, the enemy decided to capture the village of Verkhopen'e, an important strong point in our defensive system, on the night of 8-9 July. At 0200 on 9 July an infantry regiment, supported by 60 tanks, attacked the 67th Guards

Rifle Division's subunits defending along the village's southern outskirts and pushed them back to the north.

At 0900, following a massive air strike, the offensive by the Germans' main forces unfolded. Along the sector Verkhopen'e—Stanovaya woods the enemy simultaneously committed about 250 tanks into the battle, with motorized infantry: 50 tanks and a regiment of infantry tried to break through from the southern outskirts of Verkhopen'e along the village to its northern outskirts; up to 200 enemy tanks attacked the subunits of the 3rd Mechanized Corps and 67th Guards Rifle Division, which were defending the southern slopes of height 242 (3.5 kilometers east of Verkhopen'e). 100 enemy planes, which uninterruptedly bombed the combat formations of the 67th Rifle Division and the 200th Tank Brigade, supported the tank attack.

The first German tank attack from the southern outskirts of Verkhopen'e was beaten back by the fire of our anti-tank artillery and tanks, buried in the ground. Having suffered significant losses, the enemy ended his attack. Having carried out a regrouping, at 1130 a group of 60 tanks attacked from the southeast (from the direction of the Shchenyachii woods) the Verkhopen'e center of resistance. Our units also successfully repulsed this attack.

Since the Germans were not able to take Verkhopen'e through direct attacks, they undertook a flanking maneuver: the enemy tanks moved east of Verkhopen'e, heading for Kalinovka. At the same time, the enemy renewed his attack from the village's southern outskirts and, as a result of fierce street fighting, reached the northeastern outskirts.

Units of the 67th Guards Rifle Division, which were defending the village, had by 1300 fallen back to the line southern outskirts of Kalinovka—height 251.4. By the close of the day, as a result of the fierce fighting and having suffered significant losses, the division fell back further to the north to the Kalinovka—Vladimirovka area to put itself in order.

The 200th Tank Brigade fell back to the western bank of the Pena River and during the latter half of the day repelled a number of attacks by the enemy attempting to force the river in the Verkhopen'e area.

The Germans' attempts to break through in the Kalinvoka area were repulsed by tank fire and the counterattacks of the 10th Tank Corps' units, which had reached the line Kruglik—Kalinovka—height 232.8 during the latter half of the day.

The 1st Tank Army's battle in the Novoselovka area

The enemy's main attack, which was launched along the road from the Krasnaya Dubrava area toward height 242.1 (four kilometers east of Verkhopen'e) and Novoselovka, was met by the 3rd Mechanized Corps, as had been the case on 8 July. Units of the 1st Guards and 49th tank brigades, which had been committed into the battle on the morning of 9 July, were reinforced by the 203rd Heavy Tank Regiment, which had been transferred from Oboyan', and the 180th Tank Brigade, and were engaged in stubborn fighting during the first half of the day along their lines, beating back the enemy's attacks with artillery and tank fire. Our assault aviation helped our units a great deal. The *shturmoviks* strafed the concentrations of enemy tanks.

At midday the enemy broke through our defensive front along the road. Our units began to fall back to the north. Until 1500 fierce fighting was waged for Novoselovka, which was defended by the 86th Tank Brigade. The enemy attacked the village from the south along the road, and with part of his forces sought to outflank it from the west. By 1630 units of the 3rd Mechanized Corps and the 67th Guards Rifle Division, as a result of their losses, were pulled back behind the 309th Rifle Division's combat formations. By the end of the day there were only two undamaged tanks in the 1st Guards Tank Brigade, and five in the 203rd Tank Heavy Regiment.

The enemy also launched a second attack from the Sukho-Solotino—Beregovoi area in the direction of Novoselovka by a tank group consisting up of to 200 vehicles. The attacks began from the Sukho-Solotino area at 1300 and from the Beregovoi area at 1630. Up to 100 tanks, supported by aviation, operated along each of these axes. Stubborn fighting broke out, as a result of which units of the 31st Tank Corps fell back by the end of the day behind the 309th Rifle Division's combat formations.

The 51st Guards Rifle Division occupied defensive positions along the line Melovoe woods (2½ kilometers west of height 207.8)—Il'inskii.

Beginning at 1700 the enemy attacked the 309th Rifle Division's combat formations along some sectors with groups of tanks; however, all the Germans attacks were unfailingly beaten back.

Simultaneously with the attack from the Krasnaya Dubrava area to the north, the enemy undertook several attacks with part of his forces against the 6th Tank Corps; the enemy attempted to force the Pena River along the Spitsino—Syrtsevo sector, operating in groups of 30-50 tanks. The attacks were repulsed by the fire of our anti-tank artillery and the tanks of the 112th Tank Brigade, as well as units of the 90th Guards Rifle Division.

The enemy attacked in infantry regiment strength, supported by 50 tanks, opposite the 52nd Guards Rifle Division along the Veselyi—Bogoroditskoe sector, pushed the division's forward outposts beyond the Psel River, and by 1600 captured the village of Krasnyi Oktyabr'. At 1900 up to a company of Germans, supported by ten tanks, unsuccessfully attempted to force the Psel River in the Krasnyi Oktyabr' area. At 2200 the enemy once again repeated his attempt to force the river, but this time with a battalion of infantry and 30 tanks. This attack was also unsuccessful.

During the day the enemy carried out reconnaissance by strong reconnaissance parties along the Prokhorovka axis along the Vasil'evka—Ivanovskii Vyselok sector.

The enemy continued to carry out defensive works in front of the 38th and 40th armies, as well as along the Belenikhino—Shopino sector.

Along the eastern bank of the Severskii Donets the enemy, while launching a concentric attack from the Melekhovo area toward Khokhlovo and from the Beloshchekaya area in the direction of Staryi Gorod and Shipino, captured the inhabited locales of Staryi Gorod, Blizhnyaya Igumenka and Dal'nyaya Igumenka.

Results of the fighting along the Oboyan' axis

On 9 July the last attempt by the German command to break through our defense by means of a powerful ram along a narrow 10-kilometer front and reach the Oboyan' area, for the purpose of subsequently attacking toward Kursk, failed. On this day the Germans, as a result of fierce fighting, managed to push back our units 6-8 kilometers to the north only along the axis of the main attack. However, this insignificant tactical success cost them huge losses that nothing could justify. In the 9 July fighting along the Oboyan' axis the enemy lost 295 tanks knocked out or burned. Our aviation made 660 sorties and conducted 31 air battles, shooting down 57 enemy planes. Besides this, the enemy lost a significant number of self-propelled guns, armored transports, motor vehicles, and personnel.

The enemy reached the Kalinovka—Melovoe woods—Il'inskii line already sufficiently bled and once again encountered here our forces' prepared defense and organized resistance. Besides this, on the night of 9-10 July the forward units of the 5th Guards Tank Army, which had concentrated in the Bobryshevo—Srednyaya Ol'shanka—Bol'shie Seti area, were arriving at the line of the Psel River along the Oboyan' axis. The town of Oboyan' was directly covered by the 204th Rifle Division,[7] which had arrived there toward the evening of 9 July, as well as by General Trufanov's detachment from the 5th Guards Tank Army.

7 Part of the 38th Army.

The Fighting Along the Korocha Axis, 5-9 July 1943

The 5 July fighting along the Severskii Donets River

Along the Korocha axis, which was being defended by the 7th Guards Army, as along the Oboyan' axis, on the night of 4-5 July, at 2230 and 0300 an artillery counterpreparation was conducted. Having been carried out successfully, it foiled a number of the German command's measures and interfered with the construction of crossings across the Severskii Donets River. In particular, the laying of a bridge in the Belgorod area was foiled. The bridge was designated for crossing heavy "Tiger" tanks from the 19th Panzer Division to the Mikhailovskii bridgehead southeast of Belgorod to the eastern bank of the Severskii Donets River.

On this note, the commander of the 19th Panzer Division, Gen. Schmidt, made the following comments in his report:

> The bridge for the "Tigers" was halfway finished. At that time the Russians began to pay attention and opened up a well-aimed harassing fire on the crossings with artillery, mortars and flanking machine guns. Despite the darkness, the fire was very accurate. One inflatable boat, loaded to the gills, sank as the result of a direct hit. The sappers also suffered heavy losses, because 40-50 men stood under each of the bridge's crossbeams. At exactly 0300 the Russians opened an artillery barrage from a large number of guns of all calibers, which testifies to their artillery's great concentration. The Russians peppered all the gullies that might be used as approaches with fire from 40 rocket-artillery launchers,[8] which had been committed into the fighting along the division's sector. There could now be no more talk about continuing the work of building a bridge for the "Tigers."

By the dawn of 5 July the enemy had deployed along the Belgorod—Grafovka sector the forces of the III Panzer Corps. There were five divisions in the corps' first echelon: three infantry (168th, 106th and 320th), two panzer (19th and 6th). The 7th Panzer Division formed the corps's second echelon. The Germans began their artillery preparation at 0330 on 5 July and it continued 30 minutes. At 0400 large groups of enemy bomber and fighter aviation appeared in the air. Covered by aviation and artillery fire, the Germans began to cross the Severskii Donets in infantry forward detachments. The crossing was carried out simultaneously along a broad front at eight points (Pushkarnoe, Dal'nie Peski, Dorogobuzhino, Solomino, Pulyaevka, Maslova Pristan', and Bezlyudovka).

By 0430 the enemy managed to cross to the river's eastern bank: in the Pushkarnoe area a battalion from the 168th Infantry Division; along the Dal'nie Peski—Solomino sector up to two battalions from the 106th Infantry Division; along the Pulyaevka—Maslova Pristan' sector two battalions from the 106th and 320th infantry divisions; in the Priyutovka area two battalions from the 320th Infantry Division, and; in the Bezlyudovka area two battalions from the 320th Infantry Division.

The enemy's attempt (with part of the 168th and 19th Panzer divisions' forces) to simultaneously attack from the Mikhailovskii bridgehead in the direction of Staryi Gorod and Kreida station were unsuccessful: our forces beat off all the enemy's attacks with fire. Despite their heavy losses, the German tanks could not break through the minefields with which our units had girded the Germans' Mikhailovskii bridgehead. General Schmidt complained that "Almost all the 'Tigers' were put out of action."

8 Belonging to the guards mortar regiments.

Having captured bridgeheads along the eastern bank of the Severskii Donets River, by 1100 the Germans had built a crossing near the village of Maslova Pristan', and by 1300 another one near Karnaukhovka. German tanks began to cross over to the eastern bank.

At midday the enemy began attacking along the eastern and northeastern axes. Our anti-tank strong points, which had been prepared in the areas of Razumnoe, Maslova Pristan' and Krutoi Log, met the enemy attack with stubborn resistance. For example, the Krutoi Log strong point, against which the Germans threw up to 100 tanks, beat back two German attacks and put 19 tanks out of action with fire from its anti-tank artillery; seven tanks were severely damaged in the minefield along the approaches to the strong point. The enemy could not take a single one of the strong points. Their garrisons, being already surrounded, stubbornly resisted throughout the entire day.

The German command was determined to encircle the 7th Guards Army's 81st and 78th guards rifle divisions by concentric attacks from the area of the Mikhailovskii bridgehead and from the Solomino—Ivanovka sector and, upon defeating the army's right flank, to open the way to Korocha. Thanks to our troops' stubborn defense, this plan could not be realized. The attack from the Mikhailovskii bridgehead did not yield the enemy any results; the attack by units of the 106th and 320th infantry and 6th Panzer divisions was halted by the stubborn resistance of the 78th and 72nd guards rifle divisions, as well as by a counterattack by the 213th Rifle Division and the 27th Tank Brigade.

At the cost of enormous losses, the enemy managed to only seize a bridgehead along the eastern bank of the Severskii Donets River 10-12 kilometers wide and up to 3-4 kilometers deep and to slightly dent the main defensive zone. Based on prisoner interrogations, the losses in the Germans' 320th Infantry Division, which was operating along the Maslova Pristan'—Bezlyudovka sector, reached as high as 50 percent.

By the close of the day our units occupied the following positions: 78th Guards Rifle Division: height 126.3—Razumnoe—Krutoi Log; 72nd Guards Rifle Division and units of the 213th Rifle Division: excluding Krutoi Log—eastern outskirts of Maslova Pristan'—Priyutovka.

The enemy's attack on the first day of fighting was supported by almost uninterrupted attacks by planes operating in groups of 20-40 aircraft. During the day they conducted up to 1,200 air attacks.

The command's measures on 5 July

During the latter half of 5 July the Korocha axis was reinforced with four divisions. The 111th and 270th rifle divisions (both from the 69th Army), which were occupying the rear army zone along the Belyi Kolodez'—Bol'she Troitskoe—Yefimovka (25 kilometers southeast of Shebekino) sector, were operationally subordinated to the commander of the 7th Guards Army. During the night of 5-6 July the 11th Rifle Division relieved the 15th Guards Rifle Division along the Shebekino—Volchansk (15 kilometers south of Shebekino) line.

By the close of 6 July the 270th Rifle Division had concentrated in the Shebekino—Krapivnoe area as the army commander's reserve. The other two divisions were taken from the 35th Guards Rifle Corps, which was occupying the first *front* defensive zone along the Belousovo—Yablonovo—Annovka—Bogdanovka—Afon'evka sector and covering the axis toward Novyi Oskol. Both of the corps' divisions were to concentrate as follows: the 94th Guards Rifle Division in the Korocha area by 0300 on 6 July, in order to defend the Novaya Sloboda—Golen'koe—Sennoe—Klenovets line, and the 92nd Guards Rifle Division southwest of Korocha in the Golen'koe—Alekseevka—Prokhodnoe area. The divisions' concentration in the designated areas was completed by 0500. The corps headquarters was to deploy its command post in Korocha.

The commander of the 7th Guards Army decided to restore the situation by two counterstrokes on the morning of 6 July to destroy the enemy that had crossed over to the eastern bank of the Severskii Donets River. Two shock groups were created from the army's second-echelon units.

The 25th Guards Rifle Corps' shock group, which consisted of the 73rd Guards Rifle Division, the 31st Anti-Tank Brigade and the 167th Tank Regiment, the 1438th Self-Propelled and 262nd Cannon Artillery regiments, and the 309th and 97th guards mortar regiments, was to attack from the line Belovskaya—Batratskaya Dacha State Farm in the direction of Krutoi Log and Nizhnii Ol'shanets.

The 24th Guards Rifle Corps' shock group, consisting of the 213th Rifle Division and 27th Guards Tank Brigade, was to counterattack from the area of the Shebekino woods in the direction of Maslova Pristan'. The corps' mobile group, consisting of the 201st Tank Brigade, 1529th Self-Propelled and 1669th Anti-Tank Artillery regiments, was to attack from the Gremyachii—Polyana State Farm area toward Krutoi Log.

The 15th Guards Rifle Division, following its relief by the 111th Rifle Division, was to be pulled back to the Neklyudovo—Churaevo area, along the eastern bank of the Koren' River as the army's second echelon.

It was decided to begin the counterattacks at 0330 on 6 July.

The 6 July fighting for Razumnoe and Krutoi Log

All of the enemy's attempts to launch an attack from the Mikhailovskii bridgehead on the morning of 6 July with the 19th Panzer and 168th Infantry divisions ended in complete failure. After this the III Panzer Corps command transferred the 19th Panzer Division's main forces to the south and in the Dorogobuzhino area crossed it over to the eastern bank of the Severskii Donets River. From here it was planned to organize an attack against the 81st Guards Rifle Division's left flank from the south in the general direction of Kreida station.

On the night of 5-6 July the Germans crossed the corps' main forces over to the river's eastern bank and on the morning of 6 July, following a powerful fire onslaught, renewed their attack, committing up to 300 tanks into the battle. The enemy's main attack was directed from the Nizhnii Ol'shanets area toward Krutoi Log; simultaneously, supporting attacks were launched with part of his forces: one from the Maslova Pristan' area to the Dacha Shebekinskaya woods, and the second from the Dorogobuzhino area toward Kreida station.

As a result of the stubborn fighting, by the close of the day the Germans captured the inhabited locales of Razumnoe, Generalovka and Krutoi Log.

Our counterattacks planned for 6 July did not yield the expected result. The 25th Rifle Corps' shock group (minus the 31st Anti-Tank Brigade, which was not able to arrive at the jumping-off position in time), which attacked along with the 78th Guards Rifle Division, halted the further advance by the enemy's main forces to the north (from Krutoi Log). His forward units were thrown back to the villages of Generalovka and Krutoi Log. The 24th Rifle Corps' shock group did not counterattack, because the 213th Rifle Division and the 27th Guards Tank Brigade had been drawn into the fighting as early as 5 July, and at dawn on 6 July the enemy went over to the offensive, which constrained the group's operations.

By the close of the day our units were holding the following line:

The 81st Guards Rifle Division's left flank (facing south)—the line of the prison—Harvest Day Collective Farm, while the right flank and center remained in place.

Units of the 78th and 73rd guards rifle divisions—the line of the southeastern outskirts of Belovskaya—Batratskaya Dacha State Farm—Korennaya Dacha.

Units of the 213th and 72nd Guards rifle divisions—the line Gremyachii—the northwestern edge of the Dacha Shebekinskaya woods—Rzhavets.

Thus, as a result of the second day's fighting the enemy only slightly deepened his bridgehead along the eastern bank of the Severskii Donets River to 10-12 kilometers. Along the 3-kilometer sector Batratskaya Dacha State Farm—Korennaya Dacha the enemy had reached the forward edge of the second defensive zone.

The enemy's air activity in the army's sector dropped sharply on the second day. Only 250 air attacks were noted on this day.

In the 6 July fighting the enemy lost about 10,000 officers and men, and up to 100 tanks and planes shot down by anti-aircraft artillery.

The 7 July Fighting

The situation on the morning of 7 July

During the night of 6-7 July, following stubborn fighting, our units abandoned Kreida station and the Harvest Day Collective Farm. By the morning of 7 July the forces of the 7th Guards Army continued to fight mainly along the first defensive line. Only along a 3-kilometer sector of the front, Batratskaya Dacha State Farm—Korennaya Dacha, had the Germans reached the forward edge of the second defensive zone.

From the enemy's actions on 6 July it had become clear that he was making his main attack to the north, striving to reach the Melekhovo area, along the Belgorod—Korocha paved road. Thus as early as the second half of the day the *front* commander adopted measures to reinforce this axis. The 92nd and 94th guards rifle divisions (from the 35th Guards Rifle Corps) and the 31st Anti-Tank Brigade were transferred to the commander of the 7th Guards Army. During the night of 6-7 July these formations marched from the Korocha area to the Melekhovo—Myasoedovo area.

On the morning of 7 July the 31st Anti-Tank Brigade, by order of the army commander, took up defensive positions along the line Sevryukovo—Solov'ev Collective Farm. As the army's second echelon, the brigade covered the main axis of the enemy offensive to the north—the space between the Razumnaya River and the woods west of Nikol'skoe.

The commander assigned the 7th Army's main task for 7 July as firmly holding the occupied positions and preventing the enemy from breaking through to the north and east.

The fighting in the Blizhnyaya Igumenka—Yastrebovo area

The enemy directed his attack against the 7th Guards Army on 7 July toward Yastrebovo and Sevryukovo, evidently for the purpose of securing the operations of his main shock group, which was attacking along the Oboyan' axis. The enemy was trying to reach the rear of the 6th Guards Army's left wing, the units of which continued to defend the Visloe—Belomestnaya—Chernaya Polyana area. For this purpose, the German command carried out a massed offensive against the units of the 81st, 73rd and 78th guards rifle divisions: along the sector Kreida station—the woods north of Krutoi Log the Germans command threw into the battle a group of forces consisting of 300 tanks and infantry. The enemy carried out the breakthrough of our defense with two groups. The first group, which consisted of the 6th Panzer and 106th Infantry divisions, was to attack from the Generalovka area and the woods west of the village toward Sevryukovo; part of this group's infantry would seek to capture the woods west of Nikol'skoe. The enemy attacks began at dawn on 7 July. The fighting immediately became fierce, particularly along the 81st Guards Rifle Division's sector.

The Germans' first attacks were beaten back by artillery and infantry fire, causing the enemy heavy losses. Besides this, the enemy suffered significant losses in tanks while overcoming our switch minefields in the area of Kreida station and the Harvest Day Collective Farm. A group of German tanks lost eight vehicles in a single mine bottle field. As a result of repeated attacks, supported by constant air raids, the enemy threw our units from their defensive line. While withdrawing to the north under the pressure of superior enemy forces, our units continued to put up stubborn resistance to the enemy along intermediate lines.

Describing the fighting in this area, the commander of the 19th Panzer Division, General Schmidt, wrote in his report:

> We knew too little about the Russians' fortifications in this area before the start of the offensive. We did not count here on even a fourth part of what we had to encounter. Each bush, each collective farm, all the groves and heights were transformed into strong points. These strong points were linked by a system of well-camouflaged trenches. Reserve positions for mortars and anti-tank guns were outfitted everywhere. However, what was most difficult to imagine was the Russians' stubbornness with which they defended each foxhole and trench.

During the latter half of the day the 81st Guards Rifle Division, having bent its left flank near Kreida station, occupied a new defensive line along the line excluding Kreida station—Blizhnyaya Igumenka; the enemy's further progress was halted.

The enemy's tank groups, which had reached the Yastrebovo area, entered into fierce fighting with the 31st Anti-Tank Brigade. The enemy's attempts to break through to the north toward Melekhovo were unsuccessful. By the close of the day the Germans managed to advance only insignificantly: they captured Sevryukovo and pushed back the 31st Anti-Tank Brigade to the line Myasoedovo—excluding Solov'ev Collective Farm. By the onset of darkness the 94th Guards Rifle Division reached this line. Almost at the same time the line of the woods east of Andreevskoe—excluding Myasoedovo was occupied by two of the 92nd Guards Division's regiments; another regiment occupied defensive positions in the Melekhovo area.

Simultaneously with the development of the attack to the north, the German 106th Infantry Division, reinforced with tanks, undertook an attack along the sector Solov'ev Collective Farm—Polyana State Farm, for the purpose of capturing the woods west of Nikol'skoe and reaching the Koren' River. As a result of stubborn fighting, the enemy managed to seize the Solov'ev Collective Farm and the Batratskaya Dacha State Farm, while part of his forces penetrated into the forest. However, the 15th Guards Rifle Division's 44th Guards Regiment threw the Germans out of the woods in a counterattack, and by the close of the day our units once again occupied both inhabited locales seized by the enemy.

The Germans were unable to capture the Gremyachii—Polyana State Farm area. Our forces beat back all the enemy attacks along this axis.

Thus the enemy attempts to break through to the Melekhovo area proved unsuccessful. As a result of significant losses, including about 90 tanks, the Germans only managed to push our units 3-5 kilometers to the north.

By the close of 7 July the forces of the 7th Guards Army continued to fight along the first defensive zone, and partially along the second.

In connection with of the 7th Guards Army's right flank being turned (the enemy had reached the Sevryukovo—Myasoedovo area, and the course of the fighting of the first half of the day showed that the Germans were trying to develop their main attack to the north), the army commander took the necessary measures during the latter half of the day (at 1430). The army's right flank was to be reinforced. The 111th Rifle Division was to move from the Shebekino—Volchansk area to the north, in order to occupy the defensive line excluding Churaevo—Shebekino. The 270th Rifle Division was to take up position north of this line (along the line Neklyudovo—Churaevo), relieving the 15th Guards Rifle Division. The latter was to move to the line Novo-Troevka—Neklyudovo. These measures by the army command were carried out by the 111th and 270th rifle divisions by the close of 7 July and the 15th Guards Rifle Division by the morning of 8 July.

The 8 July fighting for Melekhovo

On 8 July the enemy continued to develop his attack to the north, toward Melekhovo.

The 7th Guards Army's task on that day remained as before: to exhaust the attacking enemy in defensive fighting and prevent him from breaking through to the north and northeast.

By the morning of 8 July the Germans had concentrated up to 250 tanks, many of which were armed with flamethrowers, along a narrow 3-4-kilometer front in the Sevryukovo—Yastrebovo area. The enemy attacked the 92nd and 94th guards rifle divisions. At 1100 the enemy managed to break through our defense along the sector excluding Blizhnyaya Igumenka—Sevryukovo. A group of 160 tanks began to develop the attack toward Melekhovo, but, coming under our powerful artillery fire, was forced to turn back.

Having suffered heavy losses, the enemy broke off his attack here. The Germans directed their efforts at our center of resistance in the Dal'nyaya Igumenka area. However, this attack also failed. Our artillery fire and the counterattacks by the 96th Tank Brigade's elements forced the German tanks to halt their attack and fall back to the south; 15 burning vehicles remained on the field.

Having brought up reserves, at 1700 the enemy repeated his attack on Melekhovo and Dal'nyaya Igumenka. Following a fierce battle, the German tanks broke into Melekhovo at 1900. Fierce street fighting continued until darkness fell.

Along the 81st Guards Rifle Division's front the attacks by the enemy, who was striving to capture the villages of Staryi Gorod and Blizhnyaya Igumenka, were successfully repulsed by our units. Although by the end of the day a group of enemy tanks had managed to break into Blizhnyaya Igumenka, a night attack from three sides by our forces threw the Germans out. A large part of the tanks that had penetrated were destroyed.

Despite the breakthrough of our defensive positions and the arrival of the German tanks in the Melekhovo area, small groups and subunits defending the strong points in the depth of the 81st and 92nd guards rifle divisions' defense, continued to put up fierce resistance to the enemy; they heroically fought in conditions of complete encirclement. The actions of a group of brave men from the 81st Guards Rifle Division in the area north of the Harvest Day Collective Farm were described in the report by the commander of the German 19th Panzer Division:

> In spite of heavy losses suffered by the enemy defending north of the Harvest Day Collective Farm, as well as the fact that entire sectors of trenches and foxholes had been burnt out by our flamethrower tanks, we were not able to throw out of the northern part of the defensive line an enemy group of up to a battalion in strength, that had holed up there. The Russians ensconced themselves in the system of trenches, forced back our flame throwing tanks with anti-tank rifle fire and put up fanatical resistance to the motorized infantry attacking over open ground. During the night of 8-9 July this group managed to fall back to Blizhnyaya Igumenka.

Units of the Germans' 7th Panzer and 106th Infantry divisions carried out unsuccessful attacks all day along the sector Batratskaya Dacha—Polyana State Farm. The enemy was seeking to push back the units of the 73rd and 78th guards rifle divisions behind the Koren' River and thus secure his main group's right flank.

By the close of 8 July the 7th Guards Army's right-flank forces occupied the following line: the 81st Guards Rifle Division continued to hold Staryi Gorod and Blizhnyaya Igumenka, while the 92nd Guards Rifle Division, along with the 96th Tank Brigade, had consolidated along the line Andreevskoe—Postnikov Farm—Dal'nyaya Igumenka—excluding Shlyakhovo. The 94th Guards Rifle Division, along with the 31st Anti-Tank Brigade, having extended its right flank along the Razumnaya River from Myasoedovo as far as and excluding Sheino, continued to hold Myasoedovo.

The enemy's breach of our defense in the Yastrebovo—Sevryukovo area and his advance toward Melekhovo created a real threat to the rear of the formations defending with their front to the west along the Lipovyi Donets River along the Rozhdestvenka—Belomestnaya—Staryi Gorod sector. In order to prevent the enemy from spreading to the north and northeast, by order of the *front* commander, the commander of the 69th Army ordered at 0830 the 305th Rifle Division to leave its defensive line along the Vypolzovka—Mazikino sector and reach by forced march the prepared army second defensive zone along the Sabynino—Shlyakhovo—Sheino—Ushakovo line. The arrival of the 305th Rifle Division at this line had an immediate effect. Together with the units of the 92nd Guards Rifle Division, it halted the attack by the enemy, who was trying to develop his success from Melekhovo toward Shlyakhovo.

By the morning of 9 July, by order of the commander of the 69th Army, the 107th Rifle Division, which had been pulled from the Alekseevka—Liptsy defensive line and occupied the line Verkhnii Ol'shanets—Gremyachee—Ploskoe, which was located in the rear of this division. Thus by the morning of 9 July there were already two defensive lines occupied by our forces along the Korocha axis in the area of the Belgorod—Korocha paved road.

The Germans' tank group, although it had shoved a narrow wedge (its width did not exceed 5-6 kilometers and its depth 8-10 kilometers) into our defense and had seized the Melekhovo area, had not gained freedom of maneuver, because by the evening of 8 July it was outflanked on three sides by our forces' defensive positions. The important strong points of Blizhnyaya Igumenka and Myasoedovo, located at the base of the wedge, were being held by the units of the 81st and 94th guards rifle divisions.

The fighting on 9 July

To try to develop the attack further to the north along such a narrow wedge, which had formed as the result of the German units' breakthrough to the Melekhovo area on 8 July, was extremely risky: in the event of successful counterattacks by our troops from the areas of Blizhnyaya Igumenka and Myasoedovo, the German group of forces could be surrounded. Thus on 9 July the command of the German III Panzer Corps renounced continuing the offensive to the north. He directed all his forces' efforts to widening the resulting sack to the west, trying to reach the Severskii Donets River along the Khokhlovo—Staryi Gorod sector.

The four days of fighting had significantly exhausted the III Panzer Corps: it had suffered enormous losses. A large part of its forces were pinned down by the fighting along a broad front.

The corps commander no longer had the necessary men and equipment to create a shock group sufficiently powerful to develop the offensive further to the north. All this forced the German command to take measures to strengthen the main group of forces—the III Panzer Corps. For this purpose the 198th Infantry Division, newly arrived from the south, and was moved up on 9 July to the Batratskaya Dacha State Farm—Polyana State Farm line. It was to relieve the 7th Panzer Division here, which was to be transferred on the night of 9-10 July to the Melekhovo area to take part in the corps' offensive operations along the main axis.

The salient occupied by our forces (the 81st and 92nd guards divisions) along the eastern bank of the Severskii Donets River in the Staryi Gorod—Dal'nyaya Igumenka area, seriously concerned the III Panzer Corps command, which decided to eliminate it. For this purpose, it planned to make two concentric attacks. One attack, involving the main forces of the 6th and 19th panzer divisions from the Melekhovo area through Dal'nyaya Igumenka toward Khokhlovo and Shishino, was to capture these locales and reach the Severskii Donets River. The second attack by the 168th Infantry Division, reinforced by part of the 19th Panzer Division's tanks, was to be launched along a comparatively broad front from the Kreida station—Blizhnyaya Igumenka area toward Staryi Gorod and Shishino.

The enemy carried out unsuccessful attacks throughout the first part of the day, threw into the battle groups of infantry from one to two battalions in strength and reinforced by several tens of tanks. At 1600, by means of a concentrated attack by 100 tanks, supported by a powerful aviation group, the enemy managed to break through the front of our defense. By 1800 the Germans had captured the villages of Blizhnyaya Igumenka and Staryi Gorod and began to develop the offensive further to the north.

At the same time an enemy group of forces that was operating in the Melekhovo area also attacked. The Germans, in repeated attacks by 150 tanks, concentrated along a narrow front, broke through the 92nd Guards Rifle Division's front and, following a fierce battle, by 2000 had captured Dal'nyaya Igumenka. As the result of heavy losses suffered by the enemy during the day, his offensive capabilities were exhausted. By the end of the day the enemy had been halted in front of the Shishino—Khokhlovo line.

Thus the Germans' main task—to reach the Severskii Donets River—had not been completely carried out. However, the enemy managed to widen his pocket to the west and secure the left flank of his main group of forces. The enemy also sought to break through to the Mazikino area with part of his forces, but was unsuccessful.

By the end of the day our forces occupied the following positions:

- the 375th Rifle Division had pulled back its left flank, occupying the defensive line Belomestnaya—excluding Shishino;
- the 81st Guards Rifle Division, as a result of the daytime fighting, had fallen back and consolidated along the Shishino—Khokhlovo line;
- the 92nd Guards Rifle Division had carried out a fighting retreat to the line Kiselevo—the machine tractor station—Shlyakhovo.

The results of the fighting along the Oboyan' and Korocha axes during 5-9 July

The five days of stubborn fighting did not yield the Germans a decisive success along a single axis.

The enemy made a final desperate attempt along the Oboyan' axis on 9 July to break through with a powerful tank ram along a narrow front, toward Oboyan' and open the road to Kursk. The enemy created a powerful ram at the price of renouncing offensive operations along all the other sectors of the 6th Guards Army's front. This final attempt, like all the preceding ones, yielded no visible results and factually failed.

One may consider with complete confidence that 9 July was the day of crisis for the German offensive. On that day the German command was forced to finally renounce further attempts to carry out its main task—to reach Kursk through Oboyan'. The attacks in the area of the road were halted.

From 10 July, as the course of combat operations showed, the enemy began to rush about along our front, seeking out the most vulnerable places in it for carrying out a new attack. On 11 July the Germans shifted their main efforts to the Prokhorovka axis, in order to break through to Kursk by a roundabout way, through Prokhorovka. They began to prepare for a possible offensive operation along this axis several days before. This is supported by intelligence data. For example, from the morning of 9 July individual enemy groups, consisting of tanks and motorized infantry, carried out combat reconnaissance along the Krasnyi Oktyabr'—Komsomolets State Farm sector. They were seeking to penetrate to the northern bank of the Psel River. Besides this, a group of forces numbering more than 200 tanks was noted in the Greznoe—Ozerovskii—Yasnaya Polyana area.

By the close of July 9 the 6th Guards and 1st Tank armies continued to mainly fight along the first and second army defensive zones. Only along the 12-13 kilometer Il'inskii—Komsomolets State Farm sector did the Germans reach the rear army defensive zone.

As early as 5 July the German command was forced to renounce launching a deep attack to the northeast along the Korocha axis along the eastern bank of the Severskii Donets River (northeast of Belgorod), for the purpose of reaching the Korocha area. The III Panzer Corps was given a new mission: to reach the rear of the 6th Guards Army's left-wing units defending along the Lipovyi Donets River, for the purpose of enlarging the breakthrough and securing the right flank of their main shock group. The corps was to attract reserves from the other sectors of the front, including the Oboyan' axis, to the 7th Guards Army's sector by creating a crisis.

This task also proved to be impossible to fulfill. The Germans, as a result of offensive operations along the Korocha axis, managed to attract here no more than six of our rifle divisions from the *front* reserve.

It should be noted that by 9 July the enemy had fully exhausted the Fourth Panzer Army's reserves. The German command from this day was forced to transfer reserves from the other fronts in order to feed the offensive operation. For example, on 9 July the 198th Infantry Division, which had earlier been operating against our Southwestern Front, was thrown into the battle against the 7th Guards Army. On that same day the enemy began to bring up units of the 17th Panzer Division, which had also earlier been operating against the Southwestern Front, to the battle area. On 10 July this division was already operating along the main attack axis as part of the SS Panzer Corps.

The German forces suffered enormous losses during the recent fighting. There remained only 400 officers and men in some infantry (so-called grenadier) regiments, and in some companies—as few as 20 soldiers. Beginning on 6 July the German command was forced to transfer up to 160-200 tanks per day to make up for its losses in tanks.

It's necessary to remind one that on 8 July the German offensive against our Central Front ended in complete collapse. The enemy was forced to go over to the defensive along the Orel axis.

From this moment the expediency of continuing the offensive operation against the Voronezh Front as well was in great doubt.

The Command's Measures

Measures by the *Stavka* of the Supreme High Command

Because of the tense situation that had arisen along the Voronezh Front, as well as in connection with the first symptoms of the German offensive's crisis, the *Stavka* of the Supreme High Command on 9 July issued orders to the commander of the Steppe Military District to move three armies to the Belgorod—Kursk axis. The goal of this measure was to have shock groups ready in the event the Voronezh Front went over to a counteroffensive.

The 27th, 53rd and 5th Guards armies were to move from the Steppe Military District to the Belgorod—Kursk axis.

The 27th Army, earlier designated for operations along the Orel axis, carried out a march toward Maloarkhangel'sk; upon reaching the Dubovik—Kobzeevka—Pokrovka area on the evening of 9 July, it received orders to move to the Kursk area and take up the defense of the Kursk fortified area.

The 53rd Army, which received its orders on the morning of 9 July, was to abandon the defense of the Kshen' River (the Steppe Front's defensive line) and advance to the first *front* line along the Seim River. Here it was to occupy the Bunino—Solntsevo—Nechaevo defensive sector with three divisions. The goal of this movement was to create a powerful screen in the defense's operational depth along the Prokhorovka—Kursk axis. By the morning of 12 July the army had occupied its designated line.

The 5th Guards Army, which was defending along the sector excluding Stuzhen'—Rusanovka—excluding Skorodnoe along the Steppe Front's defensive zone, left this line on the basis of a *Stavka* order of 9 July, and by the morning of 11 July had reached the Psel River. The army was subordinated to the commander of the Voronezh Front and occupied the rear army defensive zone along the Oboyan'—Prokhorovka sector.

The *front* command's measures

On 9 July the *front* commander's entire attention was focused on strengthening the Oboyan' axis and organizing a strong defense along the Prokhorovka axis. The 5th Guards Tank Corps, which occupied defensive positions along the sector Belenikhino—excluding Teterevino was to be subordinated to the commander of the 1st Tank Army for strengthening the Oboyan' axis. The corps was ordered to turn over its sector to the 183rd Rifle Division (69th Army) and by 0100 on 10 July to concentrate in the Orlovka—Zarinskie Dvory area. Besides this, the commander of the 40th Army was ordered to move the 219th Rifle Division from the Raktinoe—Proletarskii area to the Kruglik—Kursakovka—Alisovka line. The division, which left its area at 2000 on 9 July, occupied its designated line by the morning of 11 July.

The 204th Rifle Division, which was located earlier in the *front* reserve in Oboyan', by the end of the day had occupied the line excluding Kruglik—Malinovoe woods and to defend it jointly with the 10th Tank Corps and 67th Guards Rifle Division.

Taking into account the Germans' powerful tank group, that had been noted in the Greznoe—Ozerovskii—Yasnaya Polyana area on 9 July, as well as the enemy's increased reconnaissance activities along the Prokhorovka axis and the continuing enemy pressure to the north from the area of Sevryukovo and Yastrebovo (two kilometers northeast of Belovskaya), the *front* commander decided that on 10 July the German command might attempt to launch an offensive with a major tank group of forces on Prokhorovka.

The possibility of the Germans' operations from the area of Ozerovskii and Yasnaya Polyana toward Rzhavets to the southeast was also not excluded, or an attack from the Melekhovo area toward Rzhavets to the north, for the purpose of surrounding the 6th Guards Army's left-flank formations.

In order to parry the expected attacks and maximally reinforce the defense along both the Prokhorovka and Korocha axes, the *front* commander decided to combine the command of all these formations operating along these axes in the hands of the commander of the 69th Army. At 1130 the *front* commander subordinated to the 69th Army commander the 183rd, 93rd Guards, 89th Guards, 375th, 81st Guards, 92nd Guards, 94th Guards, 306th, and 107th rifle divisions, the 2nd Guards Tank Corps, 148th Tank Regiment, 96th Tank, 30th Anti-Tank, and 27th Artillery brigades, two anti-tank regiments, and a guards mortar regiment.

The 69th Army was ordered to defend the front Vasil'evka—Belenikhino—Shopino—Belomestnaya—Shishino—Kiselevo—Shlyakhovo—Sheino—Myasoedovo.

By order of the *front*, the 2nd Guards Tank Corps, which was defending the Rozhdestvenka—Druzhnyi line with the 93rd Guards Rifle Division, was to concentrate in the Leski—Shakhovo—Dal'nii Dolzhik area.

Besides this, at 2350 the *front* commander personally instructed the commander of the 2nd Tank Corps, which was defending the Vasil'evka—Komsomolets State Farm sector that "The enemy along the front Vasil'evka—Belenikhino has concentrated no less than 250 tanks, and one must assume that on 10 July he will launch an attack along this axis."

The *front* commander warned the commander of the 7th Guards Army on the evening of 9 July of the possibility of the Germans attacking on 10 July in force against the 69th Army, and ordered the former to strengthen his right flank by the morning of 10 July, so that if necessary he could help the 69th Army with fire and (possibly) counterattacks, and to prevent the Germans from breaking through along the boundary of the 69th and 7th Guards armies.

The 10-12 July Fighting Along the Prokhorovka Axis

After the Germans failed to break through toward Oboyan', they subsequently ended their attempts to achieve a decisive success along this axis. The enemy then concentrated his main efforts along the Prokhorovka axis, having in mind reaching Kursk by the more roundabout way of Prokhorovka and Kursk. The German command hoped to carry out the seizure of the Prokhorovka area as the result of two coordinated attacks: a) by the main group of forces from the Krasnyi Oktyabr'—Greznoe—Krasnaya Polyana area along the road to Prokhorovka, and b) by the III Panzer Corps from the Melekhovo area to Verkhnii Ol'shanets, and then to the north to Prokhorovka. Simultaneously with the resolution of the main immediate task (reaching the Prokhorovka area), the German command also planned to achieve with these two attacks the encirclement of the 69th Army. In this way the Germans calculated on significantly expanding the "pocket," which had formed as a result of their offensive, to the east.

The German command, in order to carry out these tasks, on 10 July carried out a regrouping of its main forces operating before this along the Oboyan' axis, mainly grouping them to the east toward the Prokhorovka axis. Simultaneously, on 10 July and the first half of 11 July, the German command organized an attack, with part of its forces, from the Syrtsevo—Verkhopen'e area to the west, in order to cut off the salient occupied by our forces along the front Podymovka—Syrtsevo—Verkhopen'e—Kubasovskii gully (three kilometers north of height 258.5). From this salient our units threatened the flank and rear of the main German group of forces.

The Germans attacked toward Prokhorovka on 11 July from two sides: from the west (the forces of the main group) and from the south (the III Panzer Corps). On this day the enemy continued to develop the attack with part of his forces in the Berezovka—Verkhopen'e—Noven'koe area, along the so-called Dragunskoe axis. A fierce battle continued throughout the following day.

The Voronezh Front's main task during this period was to stoutly defend the occupied lines and to maximally exhaust the attacking enemy forces.

On 12 July the fighting along the Prokhorovka axis reached its greatest intensity.

On this day the *front's* forces, reinforced with the 5th Guards Tank and 5th Guards armies, launched a counterstroke against the main German group of forces, for the purpose of defeating it and depriving it of the capability of further offensive action. A major tank battle took place as the result of the counteroffensive by the formations of the 5th Guards Tank Army to the west of Prokhorovka.

The situation by the morning of 10 July

The forces of the 38th and 40th armies, and the right flank of the 6th Guards Army, continued to defend their previously occupied positions, foiling the attempts by the enemy's reconnaissance groups to approach the forward edge of our defense. By the morning of 10 July the *front's* formations occupied the following position:

- the 1st Tank Army's 6th Tank Corps, along with the 90th Guards Rifle Division, occupied the line Chapaev—Spitsin—Syrtsevo—the western outskirts of Verkhopen'e—Kubasovskii gully.

- the 10th Tank Corps, with units of the 67th Guards Rifle Division, occupied the line of the southern outskirts of Kruglik—Kalinovka—excluding Malinovoe woods.
- the 309th Rifle Division, 3rd Mechanized and 31st Tank corps occupied the Malinovoe woods—Melovoe woods (three kilometers south of Orlovka)—height 195.5 line.
- the 51st Guards Rifle Division occupied the line height 207.8—excluding Il'inskii.
- the 52nd Guards Rifle Division and the 2nd Tank Corps' 11th Motorized Rifle Brigade occupied the line of the northern bank of the Psel River from the village of Veselyi to the Voroshilov State Farm.
- the 69th Army's 183rd Rifle Division, along with the 2nd and 5th Guards tank corps, occupied the Bogoroditskoe—Komsomolets State Farm—Teterevino line. The tank corps were located as follows: the 2nd along the Bogoroditskoe—Ivanovskii Vyselok line, and the 5th Guards along the Belenikhino—Teterevino sector.
- the 93rd Guards Rifle Division, along with the 2nd Guards Tank Corps, along the line excluding Teterevino—Druzhnyi.
- the 89th Guards Rifle Division occupied the Visloe—Ternovka line.
- the 375th Rifle Division occupied the Shopino—Belomestnaya line.
- the 81st Guards Rifle Division occupied the line Shishino—Khokhlovo—excluding Kiselevo. The three divisions' line formed a sharp angle, which cut into the enemy's line.
- the 92nd Guards Rifle Division occupied the line Kiselevo—excluding Shlyakhovo.
- the 305th Rifle Division occupied the Sabynino (three kilometers northeast of Kiselevo)—Shlyakhovo—Sheino—Ushakovo line. The division was in direct contact with the enemy along the sector of the machine tractor station—Shlyakhovo—excluding Sheino.
- the 94th Guards Rifle Division occupied the Sheino—Myasoedovo line along the eastern bank of the Razumnaya River.

To the south along the front excluding Myasoedovo—the Solov'ev Collective Farm—Gremyachii—Rzhavets—Priyutovka, and then along the eastern bank of the Severskii Donets River, the front was defended by the 7th Guards Army.

By the evening of 9 July the 204th Rifle Division had concentrated in the Oboyan' area in the *front* reserve. The armies' second echelons occupied the following defensive positions: the 107th Rifle Division (69th Army) along the line Verkhnii Ol'shanets—Gremyach'e—the machine tractor station; the 16th Guards, 270th and 111th rifle divisions (7th Guards Army) along the eastern bank of the Koren' River along the Novo-Troevka—Shebekino sector.

By 2300 on 9 July the main forces of the 5th Guards Tank Army had concentrated in the Bobryshevo—Srednyaya Ol'shanka—Bol'shie Seti area.

On the morning of 10 July the forward units of the 5th Guards Army began to arrive in the Oboyan' area.

The fighting on 10 July

On 10 July the enemy had concentrated his main forces along the Syrtsevo—Verkhopen'e—Kubasovskii gully sector, along the so-called Dragunskoe axis. The Germans were operating with part of their forces along the Oboyan' paved road to the north; they were particularly active along the Prokhorovka axis opposite the 52nd Guards Rifle Division, where their individual detachments were striving to cross over to the northern bank of the Psel River. Throughout the day the enemy conducted intelligence activities with large reconnaissance parties along a number of sectors opposite the 6th Guards Army. Minor activity was noted opposite the 69th Army's left flank; small enemy detachments tried to attack from the Melekhovo area toward Shakhovo and Sheino.

In the first half of 10 July the enemy attacked the 6th Tank Corps and 90th Guards Rifle Division along the Syrtsevo—Verkhopen'e—Kubasovskii gully sector. Groups of 10-30 German tanks with motorized infantry and automatic riflemen tried to break into the area of the groves west of Verkhopen'e. Individual groups of automatic riflemen managed to infiltrate into the area of the grove two kilometers west of Verkhopen'e, but for the most part our units continued to hold their lines.

At 1500 the enemy, in groups of up to 160 tanks, with self-propelled guns, attacked from Verkhopen'e toward the Tolstoe woods (one kilometer west of height 258.5). Following a stubborn two-hour battle, units of the 6th Tank Corps fell back to the line western outskirts of Syrtsevo—height 258.5—Kubasovskii gully (four kilometers southeast of Kruglik).

Immediately after this (at 1700) the enemy renewed his attack with a group of 100 tanks from the area of Kubasovskii gully toward Noven'koe and Kruglik. A small group of tanks reached the eastern outskirts of Noven'koe and height 247. However, the tanks that broke through were destroyed by counterattacks launched by units of the 6th and 10th tank corps, and the attacking Germans fell back with heavy losses to their jumping-off position. The 6th Tank Corps, having restored the situation, once again occupied the line western outskirts of Syrtsevo—height 258.5—Kubasovskii gully.

Simultaneously with the attack on Noven'koe, the enemy made fierce attacks on Syrtsevo with a regiment of infantry and 30 tanks; his attacks were supported by aviation, which carried out several attacks on Syrtsevo. From 0900 to 1600 our units along the Spitsin—Syrtsevo sector beat back five enemy attacks; the enemy managed to push our subunits out of Syrtsevo. By the close of the day units of the 6th Tank Corps had consolidated along the line excluding Syrtsevo—height 258.5—Kubasovskii gully. The air force supported our operations the entire day. 25 air battles took place over the battlefield.

Throughout the day the enemy continually attacked units of the 67th Guards Rifle Division and the 10th Tank and 3rd Mechanized corps. Attempting here, west of the Oboyan' paved road, to advance along the Malinovoe woods—Kalinovka sector to the north, the Germans committed into the battle up to 100 tanks along this axis. However, all the enemy's attacks were beaten back and our units, by the onset of darkness, continued to hold their previous positions.

During the night of 10-11 July this area was reinforced. The following units were to move here: by order of the 40th Army commander, the 184th Rifle Division was to move toward the line Chapaev—Krasnyi Uzliv—excluding Kruglik, and by order of the *front* commander, the 219th Rifle Division was to move to the line Kruglik—Kurasovka—Alisovka.

To the east of the Oboyan' paved road, opposite the 52nd Guards Rifle Division, the enemy nearly managed to force the Psel River. Following a fierce air attack by 80 planes, an enemy force consisting of an infantry division, with 50 tanks, crossed the Psel River from the Klyuchi area (one kilometer northeast of Krasnyi Oktyabr') and broke through to the western slopes of height 226.8 (two kilometers northeast of Bogoroditskoe). However, counterattacks by the division's second echelon, supported by tanks from the 5th Guards Tank Army's forward units, which had reached this area by the morning of 10 July, the enemy was overthrown. By the morning of 11 July our forces had thrown the Germans back over the Psel River, inflicting heavy losses on him, and had completely restored the situation along this sector.

At 0830 on 11 July a group of 50 German tanks, supported by 200 planes, attacked the right-flank units of the 183rd Rifle Division and 2nd Tank Corps. By the middle of the day the enemy had broken into Vasil'evka and the Komsomolets State Farm. Counterattacking the enemy, our units threw the Germans out of Vasil'evka. Fighting continued until morning in the area of the Komsomolets State Farm.

German infantry, reinforced with tanks, attempted to push back units of the 305th and 94th Guards rifle divisions from the Melekhovo and Ushakovo areas, as well as from the Sevryukovo area back to height 206.9. However, our forces here also successful beat back the Germans' attacks and maintained their defensive positions.

Thus, as the result of the 10 July fighting the enemy managed to advance very insignificantly 1½-2 kilometers along the Dragunskoe axis.

The command's measures. Preparing the counteroffensive

The commander of the Voronezh Front, in evaluating the situation that had arisen by the close of 10 July, believed that the enemy, having halted his intensive attacks by his main group of forces in the area of the Oboyan' pavedroad, would regroup his forces and on the morning of 11 July would likely attack in force along the Prokhorovka axis, with the immediate objective of capturing Prokhorovka. The commander also believed that the enemy would continue his offensive operations along the Oboyan' axis and from the Melekhovo area north.

This was also confirmed by intelligence data, which the *front* commander possessed by the end of the day. This data enabled us to assume that up to 170 tanks were concentrated in the Greznoe—Malye Mayachki area, up to 200 tanks in the Prokhorovka area, and up to 200 tanks in the Yasnaya Polyana—Ozerovskii area. A large part of these forces were evidently designated for employment along the Prokhorovka axis. About 300 tanks, including the 6th Tank Corps' sector, were operating along the Oboyan' axis, and up to 350 tanks had been noted in the Dal'nyaya Igumenka—Melekhovo area.

Thus, by the close of 10 July it was clear that the enemy would most likely continue active operations along the Oboyan' and Prokhorovka axes. The German forces had already suffered enormous losses and the enemy command had expended his operational reserves. In order to continue his offensive operations, it would be forced to gradually take forces from the flanks, inevitably weakening the latter, to reinforce the shock groups. Taking all of this into account, the *front* commander made the decision on the night of 10-11 July as to the expediency of going over to a counteroffensive with part of the *front's* forces, in order to encircle and defeat the main German group of forces advancing toward Oboyan' and Prokhorovka.

The operational plan consisted of inflicting concentric attacks on the enemy, which it was planned to carry out in the following manner:

1. From the Melovoe—Noven'koe line in the general direction of Berezovka, Syrtsevo and Yakovlevo, with the forces of the 6th Guards and 10th Tank corps, under the overall command of the 1st Tank Army, as well as the 6th Guards Army's 22nd Guards Rifle Corps (90th Guards, 184th and 219th rifle divisions);
2. From the Veselyi—Mikhailovka—Yamki—Belenikhino line toward Greznoe, Bol'shie Mayachki and Yakovlevo, with the forces of the 5th Guards Tank Army and part of the 5th Guards Army. It was subsequently planned to develop this attack to the south, with the forces of the 5th Guards Tank Army, toward Bykovka;
3. From the line Kalinovka—height 244.8 in the general direction of Krasnaya Dubrava (one kilometer north of Gremuchii) and Pokrovka, with the forces of the 6th Guards Army's left-flank formations: 23rd Guards Rifle Corps (204th, 67th Guards and 309th rifle divisions);
4. From the line of the Melovoe woods (three kilometers east of height 244.8)—height 207.8 toward Sukho-Solotino and Krasnaya Polyana, with the 5th Guards Army's right-flank formations: 32nd Guards Rifle Corps (13th and 66th guards rifle divisions);
5. A holding attack from the line Batratskaya Dacha State Farm—Polyana State Farm toward Razumnoe and Dal'nie Peski, with the forces of the 7th Guards Army's 49th Rifle Corps (73rd Guards, 270th and 111th rifle divisions).

It was planned to carry out all the necessary measures on 11 July and during the night of 11-12 July. It was decided to begin the offensive on the morning of 12 July. By the morning of 11 July this decision had been communicated to the army commanders, in order to draw up army-level plans for the offensive.

The *front* commander, based upon the decision adopted at 0700 on 11 July, ordered the transfer of the 71st Guards, 184th and 219th rifle divisions from the 40th Army to the 6th Guards Army, and the 204th Rifle Division from the *front* reserve and the 309th Rifle Division from the 1st Tank Army.

The commander of the 69th Army decided on the night of 10-11 July to regroup his forces and to withdraw part of them from the dangerous sack that had formed as the result of the previous days' fighting in the area to the north of Belgorod. The Visloe—Ternovka—Belomestnaya—Petropavlovka—Khokhlovo sector was to be turned over to the 89th Guards Rifle Division. By the morning of 11 July it had occupied defensive positions in the area between the Lipovyi Donets and Severskii Donets rivers along the front Kalinin—northern outskirts of Belomestnaya—Kiselevo.

The 375th Rifle Division, which was occupying the Shopino—Belomestnaya sector, was to be pulled back on the night of 10-11 July to the Shakhovo—Zhilomestnoe—Novoselovo area, for the purpose of reinforcing the defense along this axis.

The 81st Guards Rifle Division, which had earlier been pulled back to the Krivtsovo area into the army commander's reserve, had occupied defensive positions along the western bank of the Severskii Donets River along the Krivtsovo—Ryndinka sector.

By order of the *front* commander, the 5th Guards Tank Corps abandoned its line at 1800 on 10 July and was subordinated to the commander of the 1st Tank Army, in order to strengthen the Oboyan' axis. By the close of 11 July it had concentrated in the 2nd Novoselovka—height 233 area.

The Fighting on 11 July

The fighting in the Berezovka area

On 11 July the enemy, while continuing to develop the offensive along the Dragunskoe axis, had concentrated his main forces directly along the Prokhorovka axis.

The *front's* forces were stubbornly defending their lines and preparing at the same time for an offensive, which they were to begin on the morning of 12 July. On 11 July a reconnaissance was conducted, army operational plans were drawn up, and partial regroupings carried out. On this day the 5th Guards Army was completing its concentrating along the Oboyan'—Veselyi—Prokhorovka line.

At 0100 on 11 July the commander of the 6th Tank Corps, without informing the commander of the 6th Guards Army or the commander of the 90th Guards Rifle Division, pulled the 10th Motorized Rifle Brigade from the Berezovka area and transferred it to Noven'koe for the purpose of reinforcing this axis, where the enemy had been making his heaviest attacks the previous evening. Thus the 90th Guards Rifle Division's left flank remained open.

At 0900 on 11 July the Germans, having concentrated up to 100 tanks against the 90th Guards Rifle Division's left flank and the 6th Guards Tank Corps, resumed the offensive from the area of the grove west of Verkhopen'e toward the northern outskirts of Berezovka and toward the village of Krasnyi Uzliv. Part of the enemy's forces attacked the 90th Guards Rifle Division's right flank from Zavidovka and Alekseevka toward Rakovo.

The enemy, having felt out a weak place in our defense along the 90th Guards Rifle Division's left flank, reached the division's rear with part of his forces. The division, which had taken up a perimeter defense, fought for six hours half encircled. The enemy sought to encircle the division at all costs and brought up reserves from other sectors of the front, fired on the division's defensive area with artillery and mortars, and constantly attacked its combat formations from the air. At 1400 the division commander issued an order to pull back the division's units to a new defensive line. While parrying the enemy's attempts to close the encirclement ring, the division, along with units of the 6th Tank Corps, by the end of the day had fallen back in fierce fighting behind the 184th Rifle Division's combat formations; by order of the army commander, it concentrated in the Melovoe—Noven'koe area to put itself in order.

The enemy was seeking to advance further to the west, but was halted by the 184th Rifle Division's fire.

The Germans were not active along the Kruglik—Kalinovka—Malinovoe woods—Il'inskii front, having gone over to the defense here. Only along the 51st Guards Rifle Division's sector did they seek to attack height 207.8, but unsuccessfully: the attack was beaten back by fire from the division's artillery and subunits.

The Germans' offensive operations against the 6th Tank Corps and the 90th Guards Rifle Division in the Berezovka—Noven'koe area on 11 July should be viewed, first of all, as an attempt to distract our command's attention from the Prokhorovka axis, along which they were striving to create a surprise situation for the subsequent unfolding of the offensive and, secondly, as the German command's desire to carry out its mission, which remained from 10 July—of cutting off our salient, the left flank of which was hanging over the main German group of forces.

The fighting west of Prokhorovka

By 0400 on 11 July units of the 5th Guards Army's 95th Guards Rifle Division had reached the 52nd Guards Rifle Division's sector and had begun to occupy the jumping-off positions for the forthcoming offensive. By this time the army's 9th Guards Airborne Division, which was somewhat late in occupying its designated defensive line, was coming up to the line Mikhailovka—October State Farm—Yamki—northern outskirts of Grushki, in the rear of the 183rd Rifle Division's right flank.

At dawn on 11 July the enemy's air force, in groups of 5-40 planes, continually bombed the combat formations of the 183rd Rifle Division's right flank and the 2nd Tank Corps. At 0930, following a powerful air attack, up to 130 German tanks and two regiments of infantry attacked along a narrow front from the area of Komsomolets State Farm along the paved road and to the north toward Prokhorovka.

Up until 1230 our units successfully repelled several enemy attacks. At 1230 a group of up to 100 tanks and motorized infantry broke through the front of the 183rd Rifle Division and 2nd Tank Corps and began to develop the offensive along the paved road toward Prokhorovka.

The enemy shifted his air attacks to the 9th Guards Airborne Division's combat formations, throwing up to 100 planes against it. At 1400, following a massed aviation attack against the division's forward edge, the enemy attacked its combat formations with a regiment of infantry and 30 tanks in the direction of the October State Farm. The division's units had not had time to prepare a defense and at 1530 abandoned the October State Farm. The Germans continued attacking with part of their forces along the road to Prokhorovka, and with part of their forces from Mikhailovka to Prelestnoe, where up until then the enemy attacks had remained unsuccessful. The enemy, having committed up to 60 tanks into the fighting, pushed back the division's right flank to Prelestnoe. A small group of tanks, which had broken through to Petrovka, was destroyed. By the close of the day the division, as a result of stubborn resistance and counterattacks, had halted the enemy's advance in front of the line Prelestnoe—Lutovo—Grushki, along which it consolidated.

The 183rd Rifle Division's right-flank units were partially merged into the 9th Airborne Division's combat formations, while another part fell back to the line of the southern edge of the grove north of Storozhevoe—the railroad booth east of Yasnaya Polyana.

The 2nd Tank Corps fell back to the line of the northern outskirts of Mikhailovka—the northern outskirts of Yamki, where it merged into the 9th Guards Airborne Division's combat formations.

At 1655 a group of enemy infantry and tanks attempted to force the Psel River in the area of the village of Krasnyi Oktyabr'; all his attempts were beaten back by fire and counterattacks by the 52nd Guards Rifle Division.

The fighting south of Prokhorovka

On 10 July the German command did not undertake any offensive operations in the 69th Army's zone. On this day the Germans were regrouping their forces and bringing up replacements and fresh reserves. In particular, the reinforced 7th Panzer Division, which up to 9 July had been operating along the front Solov'ev Collective Farm—Polyana State Farm, was concentrated in the Melekhovo area.

Upon completing the concentration (during the night of 10-11 July) of up to 250 tanks in the Melekhovo area, the enemy launched an attack at dawn on 11 July, simultaneously along two axes: one group (about 100 tanks and infantry) attacked from the Dal'nyaya Igumenka—Melekhovo area toward Khokhlovo and Kiselevo, while another group (about 200 tanks) launched an attack from the Melekhovo area to the north toward Ol'khovatka and Verkhnii Ol'shanets. Besides this, German infantry, supported by 20-60 tanks, attacked the 94th Guards Rifle Division's front in the direction of Myasoedovo, attempting to break through it and throw back the division's units toward the Koren' River; by these actions the enemy was striving to widen the pocket here to the east.

In the second half of the day, following a series of repeated and unsuccessful attacks, the enemy nevertheless seized Khokhlovo and Kiselevo and pushed back elements of the of the 89th Guards Rifle Division's reinforced forward outposts, which had been defending Khokhlovo, to the eastern bank of the Severskii Donets River. With the onset of darkness these elements crossed over to the river's western bank.

The 92nd Guards Rifle Division's right flank, which was defending Kiselevo, fell back to the northern outskirts of the village and continued to withstand the enemy's pressure.

In the first half of the day, as a result of a massive attack by a tank ram from the Melekhovo area to the north, the enemy broke through the 305th Rifle Division's front and seized Shlyakhovo and Ol'khovatka. By the onset of darkness a significant group of German tanks reached the Verkhnii Ol'shanets area and had spread in individual groups toward Novo-Oskochnoe and Kazach'e.

The rifle units of the 92nd Guards and 305th divisions remained along their occupied lines and were fighting with the enemy infantry, which had been cut off from its tanks by our defensive fire. The fighting along this line continued until the onset of darkness.

As a result of repeated attacks, the enemy threw our units out of Myasoedovo and captured it. The enemy's attempts to advance to the grove east of Myasoedovo were beaten back by fire and counterattacks from the 94th Guards Rifle Division.

Results of the 11 July fighting

11 July may be viewed as the beginning day of the large battle for Prokhorovka.

The Germans continued to attack with part of their forces along the Dragunskoe axis and achieved an insignificant territorial success here; having pushed back units of the 90th Guards

Rifle Division and the 6th Tank Corps to the Chapaev—Krasnyi Uzliv—Noven'koe—Kruglik line. The enemy took up the defensive along the Oboyan' axis.

The enemy attacked along the Prokhorovka axis, had in mind the seizure of Prokhorovka. At the same time, he sought to employ to the maximum degree the element of surprise, operating with those forces that he managed to concentrate here—up to one infantry division, not tied down in fighting, and about two panzer divisions (up to 150-200 tanks). On the morning of 11 July the enemy simultaneously continued to develop the offensive with the forces of the III Panzer Corps from the Melekhovo area to the north, striving to break through to Prokhorovka from the south.

As a result of the stubborn fighting that unfolded toward the west of Prokhorovka, the Germans' shock group, consisting of more than 150 tanks and infantry, by the middle of the day had broken through our defense and by the close of the day had reached the October State Farm—Stalin State Farm (two kilometers northeast of Storozhevoi) area. Here, opposite the 9th Guards Airborne Division's front, approximately two kilometers west of Prokhorovka, the enemy was halted. Units of the III Panzer Corps, which had been attacking from the Melekhovo area, reached the Verkhnii Ol'shanets area.

Thus, on 11 July the enemy was not able to capture Prokhorovka, although it nearly reached it from the west; with just a little luck, his further offensive on Prokhorovka, a very important road hub that would have enabled the enemy to maneuver subsequently to the north, could have been in his hands.

The command's measures

The commander of the 6th Guards Army decided to organize an offensive with two groups of forces: with the 22nd Guards Rifle Corps, in conjunction with the 1st Tank Army, from the line Chapaev—Kruglik in the general direction of Syrtsevo and Yakovlevo, and the 23rd Guards Rifle Corps from the line Kruglik—Malinovoe woods (two kilometers southwest of height 244.8) in the general direction of Krasnaya Dubrava (one kilometer north of Gremuchii). By dawn on 12 July the 22nd Guards Rifle Corps' divisions had not occupied their jumping-off positions. The 184th and 219th rifle divisions had been delayed along their previous lines by the commander of the 40th Army, and it was only at 0400 on 12 July that they began the movement to the jumping-off positions.

Before the 184th and 219th rifle divisions' arrival at their designated lines, the 90th Guards Rifle Division continued to occupy its former line. At 0400 the 23rd Guards Rifle Corps (204th, 67th Guards and 309th rifle divisions) occupied jumping-off positions along the line Kruglik—Kalinovka—Malinovoe woods. The 51st Guards Rifle Division, following its relief by units of the 5th Guards Army, reached the army commander's reserve in the Alisovka area.

The 1st Tank Army, consisting of the 5th Guards and 10th tank corps, concentrated in the 1st Aleksandrovka (three kilometers north of Melovoe)—Yablonovo woods (three kilometers northwest of Noven'koe)—2nd Novoselovka area, in readiness to attack, in conjunction with the 22nd Guards Rifle Corps, in the general direction of Yakovlevo.

The commander of the 5th Guards Army, for the purposes of better cooperation with the 5th Guards Tank Army, decided to launch his main attack along his left flank—with the 33rd Guards Rifle Corps, which consisted of five divisions (97th, 95th, 42nd, 52nd, and 9th Guards Airborne divisions), from the Persyp'—Mikhailovka—Grushki line in the general direction of Pokrovka. On the night of 11-12 July the 52nd Guards Rifle Division was resubordinated to the commander of the 5th Guards Army. A supporting attack was to be launched by the 32nd Guards Rifle Corps (13th and 66th guards rifle divisions) from the line Melovoe woods—height 207.8 in the general direction of Krasnaya Polyana. The 6th Guards Airborne Division, which comprised the army commander's reserve, was to concentrate in the Kotovo—Pselets—Vyshnyaya Kotova area.

By the morning of 12 July the 5th Guards Army's forces had occupied their designated lines, with the exception of the 42nd Guards Rifle Division, which was late in arriving at its jumping-off position.

The commander of the 5th Guards Tank Army decided to launch his main attack with the forces of the 18th, 29th and 2nd Guards tank corps in the general direction along the railroad and then toward Pokrovka and Yakovlevo.

The 18th Tank Corps, which had been reinforced with a guards mortar regiment; its jumping-off position was the line Petrovka—the gully two kilometers north of Oktyabr'skii State Farm, had the task of destroying the enemy in the Krasnaya Dubrava—Bol'shie Mayachki—Krasnaya Polyana area and then, upon shifting its front to the north, to secure the offensive by the army's remaining formations toward the south.

The 29th Tank Corps, with one guards mortar regiment and a regiment of self-propelled artillery, operating from the line of the gully two kilometers northeast of October State Farm—the northern outskirts of Lutovo, was to destroy the enemy group of forces in the Luchki—Bol'shie Mayachki—Pokrovka area, and be ready for further operations to the south.

The 2nd Guards Tank Corps, with a guards mortar regiment, while attacking from the line Vinogradovka—Ivanovka, had the task of destroying the enemy's group of forces in the area Yakovlevo—the woods to the east and then be ready for operations to the south.

The army commander assigned the 2nd Tank and 5th Guards Mechanized corps and Major General Trufanov's detachment the following tasks: the 2nd Tank Corps, while remaining in its previous defensive position, was to cover the army's arrival in its jumping-off position for the offensive, and with the start of the tank corps' attack to support the latter with all its firepower; the 5th Guards Mechanized Corps, which had concentrated in the Dranyi—Krasnoe—Kamyshevka area, comprised the army reserve in readiness to develop the 29th and 2nd Guards tank corps' success in the general direction of Luchki and Smorodino.

Major General Trufanov's detachment, consisting of the 1st Guards Motorized, 53rd Guards Tank, 57th Howitzer, and the 689th Anti-Tank Artillery regiments, which was to support the army's march to the Prokhorovka area as a forward detachment, was also to be transferred to the army commander's reserve and concentrated in the Pravorot' area, with the task of securing the army's left flank.

The 5th Guards Tank Army's overall tank strength (minus the 2nd Tank and 5th Guards Mechanized corps, which did not directly participate in the 12 July fighting west of Prokhorovka) was 533 vehicles. During the night of 11-12 July the army's formations reached their designated jumping-off areas.

On the evening of 11 July the 69th Army's commander, in order to eliminate the breach that had arisen and to halt the enemy's further offensive from the Verkhnii Ol'shanets area to the north, made the decision to regroup his units on the night of 11-12 July and to withdraw them to new defensive lines.

Following this regrouping, by the dawn of 12 July the army's formations had taken up the following positions:

- the 93rd Guards Rifle Division continued to defend the Rozhdestvenka—Druzhnyi line;
- the 89th Guards Rifle Division, having left along the front Kalinino—Petropavlovka no more than two battalions with anti-tank guns, had taken up defensive positions along the front excluding Kiseleva—Krivtsovo;
- the 81st Guards Rifle Division was along the western bank of the Severskii Donets River (the Krivtsovo—Ryndinka sector);
- a regiment of the 375th Rifle Division in the Shipy area;

the 92nd Guards Rifle Division, with the 96th Tank Brigade, was along a previously prepared line along the front Vypolzovka—Novo-Alekseevksii Vyselok;
the 305th Rifle Division occupied the line excluding Novo Alekseevskii Vyselok—along the Razumnaya gully to Veselyi gully;
the 107th Rifle Division occupied the line excluding Veselyi gully—Shukhovtsevo—Gremyach'e—excluding Ploskoe;
the 94th Guards Rifle Division, with the 31st Anti-Tank Brigade, occupied the line excluding Shukhovtsevo—Mazikino—Sheino—Ushakova (one of the division's regiments, along with a regiment from the 31st Anti-Tank Brigade, was in the second echelon along the line Ploskoe—Novoselovka, along the eastern bank of the Koren' River).

To the left, along the line excluding Sheino—Solov'ev Collective Farm, the 7th Guards Army's 15th Guards Rifle Division continued to defend.

The Fighting on 12 July. The Tank Battle in the Prokhorovka Area

The Germans' group of forces along the Prokhorovka axis

Having pushed back our units from the line Prelestnoe—Lutovo—Grushki (west of Prokhorovka) and reached the Verkhnii Ol'shanets (south of Prokhorovka) area, the Germans planned on the morning of 12 July to renew the offensive with an attack from the west and south, capture Prokhorovka and subsequently, while developing their attack to the north, reach the Kursk area from the east.

In preparing at attack on Kursk from the west, the German command on the night of 11-12 July completed concentrating west of Prokhorovka a major group of forces, consisting of three divisions of the SS Panzer Corps (*Adolph Hitler*, *Totenkopf* and *Das Reich*) and units of the 17th Panzer Division, as well as the 167th Infantry Division. More than 700 tanks were in this group of forces, including more than 100 heavy "Tiger" tanks and heavy "Ferdinand" self-propelled guns. The main mass of tanks, as subsequent events showed, were operating in the zone of the railroad and roads leading to Prokhorovka.

About 100 tanks, with part of the *Adolph Hitler* Panzer Division's infantry, were operating to the north, along the Krasnyi Oktyabr'—Kozlovka sector.

All the available German aviation operating against the Voronezh Front supported this group of forces on 12 July.

Simultaneously, on the night of 11-12 July the German command brought up the main forces of the III Panzer Corps to the Novo-Oskochnoe—Kazach'e area to develop the attack on Prokhorovka from the south.

The 18th and 29th tank corps' battle in the area of the October State Farm

The 5th Guards Tank Army's offensive was initially set by the *front* commander for 1000. However, wishing to preempt the Germans' probable attack, he shifted the attack's start to 0830.

Following a 15-minute artillery onslaught, the 18th and 29th tank corps attacked at the appointed time. The enemy met our tank formations with fire from anti-tank artillery and attacks by heavy tanks, operating in groups of 30-40 vehicles, in conjunction with heavy self-propelled guns. The German tank attacks were supported by constant attacks from German aircraft, which literally hung over our combat formations throughout the entire battle. A fierce tank battle in the area of the October State Farm lasted the entire first half of the day. The counterattacking German tank units were defeated. At 1300 two brigades of the 29th Tank Corps, having undertaken a turning movement, occupied the southern part of the October State Farm and height 252.2 (one kilometer south of the October State Farm), from which they began to develop the attack on height 242.5.

The 18th Tank Corps, taking advantage of the 29th Tank Corps' successful maneuver, crushed the resistance of the enemy defending north and northeast of the October State Farm, and by 1430 part of its forces had broken into its northern part. Outflanking height 242.5 from the north, the corps began to develop the attack toward Andreevka and Vasil'evka.

At 1200, while fierce fighting was going on for the October State Farm, up to 100 enemy tanks, with motorized infantry and supported by assault guns, attacked along the Krasnyi Oktyabr'—Kozlovka sector. The enemy broke through the 52nd Guards Rifle Division's front and by 1300 had taken height 226.6.

The 18th Tank Corps, which was at this time developing the offensive toward Andreevka and Vasil'evka, upon reaching the area of height 224.9, came under heavy artillery fire from assault guns in the area of heights 226.6, 217.9 and 231.3. Besides this, the corps was continuously attacked by German aviation in groups of 15-20 planes. The corps, having routed several enemy tank groups along its route of advance, by 1730 broke into Andreevka. Here the corps' 181st Tank Brigade attacked on the march an enemy tank column of 30-40 vehicles advancing on Mikhailovka and routed it, throwing the remnants of the column back on Vasil'evka.

At 1800 the corps, while pursuing the retreating enemy, captured Vasil'evka and reached Kozlovka. Here it encountered powerful fire from tanks buried in the ground and was counterattacked by a major enemy tank group. Along with this, heavy fire continued to rain down on the corps from the northern bank of the Psel River, from the direction of heights 226.6 and 217.9. By the close of the day the corps had cleared the enemy out of Vasil'evka, Andreevka and Mikhailovka and had taken up a perimeter defense in the Vasil'evka—Prelestnoe—Beregovoe area, shooting up counterattacking groups of German tanks on the spot.

The 29th Tank Corps, which had reached height 242.5, was met with heavy fire from tanks buried in the ground. The corps fought all day against attacking groups of German tanks numbering 20-40 vehicles, which were operating together with self-propelled artillery. With the onset of darkness the corps' units went over to the defense in the area of this height.

During the corps' fight for height 242.5 its 53rd Motorized Rifle Brigade, having outflanked the height from the south, dashed forward and at 1730 it broke into the Komsomolets State Farm. Having routed the enemy defending here, the brigade, in order to restore coordination with the corps' remaining units, which were continuing to fight in the area of height 242.5, fell back to the area of the Stalin State Farm by the end of the day, where it took up defensive positions. The corps' 25th Tank Brigade, which was attacking the enemy in the area of the Stalin State Farm, encountered heavy artillery fire from the northern outskirts of this locale and was forced to fall back to the area of height 221. Here it also went over to the defense, with its front facing to the northwest.

The 2nd Guards Tank Corps' battle in the Kalinin area

The 2nd Guards Tank Corps, simultaneously with the army's remaining corps, attacked toward Kalinin. By 1430 units of the corps had reached a line east of Kalinin, where it entered into a meeting engagement with German tanks. Following a stubborn battle with a numerically superior enemy, the corps fell back to its jumping-off position with the onset of darkness.

The fighting along the northern bank of the Psel River

When by 1200 it was clear that the main German group of forces had not been able to break through to the Prokhorovka area in the area of the railroad and paved road, the German command decided to assist it by breaking through with part of its forces to the northern bank of the Psel River, to turn our attacking group's right flank and subsequently reach the area north of Prokhorovka, in the rear of the 5th Guards Tank Army.

For this, the enemy concentrated in the Krasnyi Oktyabr'—Kozlovka area a group consisting of 100 tanks, a regiment of motorized infantry and 200 motorcyclists, with several asault guns. This group, supported by aviation, attacked at 1200, broke through the 52nd Guards Rifle Division's defense, and by 1300 had captured height 226.6. On the height's northern slopes the enemy encountered stubborn resistance by units of the 95th Guards Rifle Division, which had prepared a defense in this area. The Germans' tanks, infantry and motorcyclists repeatedly attempted to break through our defense. Units of the 95th Guards Rifle Division successfully beat off the enemy's attacks with fire and counterattacks until 1800. At 1800 the Germans halted their attack and began to regroup and bring up fresh reserves.

At 2000 the enemy, following a massed air raid, again attacked the 95th Guards Rifle Division's combat formations. By the onset of darkness he had pushed back our units, reached height 236.7 and captured the village of Polezhaev with part of his forces. The enemy was unable to advance further along this axis.

During the second part of the day the army commander ordered the 5th Guards Mechanized Corps' 10th Guards Tank Brigade to move up to the Ostren'kii area, and the 24th Guards Tank Brigade to the area of the Voroshilov State Farm, against the enemy group of forces trying to break into the rear of the 5th Guards Tank Army.

The fighting in the area of Rzhavets and Ryndinka

At 0400 on 12 July the Germans' III Panzer Corps renewed its attack. The attack was directed at Prokhorovka from the south out of the Novo-Oskochnoe—Kazach'e area. Following heavy fighting, our units were forced to abandon the villages of Rzhavets and Ryndinka. A group of German tanks broke through the 92nd Guards Rifle Division's combat formation and began to advance on Avdeevka.

At 0600 on 12 July the *front* commander ordered the commander of the 5th Guards Tank Army to hurriedly move powerful mobile detachments into the Ryndinka—Avdeevka—Bol'shie Pod"yarugi area, with the mission of halting the Germans' attack and throwing them out of the villages of Ryndinka, Rzhavets and Vypolzovka.

On the orders of the army commander, two detachments were formed, the command of which he entrusted to his deputy, General Trufanov.

The right-flank detachment consisted of the 5th Guards Mechanized Corps' 11th and 12th mechanized brigades and the 2nd Guards Tank Corps' 26th Tank Brigade. With the detachment's arrival in the Ryndinka—Alekseevka area, it was joined by units of the 92nd Guards Rifle Division and a regiment from the 375th Rifle Division.

The left-flank detachment—the army's former forward detachment—consisted of the 1st Independent Guards Motorcycle, 53rd Guards Tank, 689th Anti-Tank Artillery, and 678th Guards Howitzer regiments.

The right-flank detachment, which had arrived with two guards brigades (11th Mechanized and 26th Tank) in the Pokrovka area, and the remaining forces in the Avdeevka area, attacked the enemy at 1800 simultaneously in the direction of Ryndinka and height 222.1, south of Avdeevka. A fierce tank meeting engagement broke out. The enemy was thrown out of Avdeevka with heavy losses and thrown back to the eastern bank of the Severskii Donets River in the Rzhavets area. Our units completely routed the German 19th Panzer Division's 73rd and 74th grenadier motorized regiments.

The 12th Guards Mechanized Brigade, which was attacking from the Avdeevka area toward height 222.1, routed the enemy here and, developing the success, reached height 216.

By the end of the day the right-flank detachment, with part of the 92nd Guards Rifle Division's forces, had consolidated along the Ryndinka—height 216 line. The enemy sought to break through to the north all night, but was unsuccessful.

On the morning of 12 July the enemy also attacked with part of his forces from the Kazach'e area toward Novo-Alekseevksii Vyselok and captured the latter locale. The enemy's subsequent advance on Aleksandrovka was halted by counterattacks by the 96th Tank Brigade and General Trufanov's left-flank detachment, which reached the Novo-Khmelevoi area during the second half of the day.

Upon reaching its objective, the left-flank detachment fell back to the Bol'shie Pod"yarugi area with the onset of darkness.

The 6th Guards and 1st Tank armies' offensive battle

The beginning of the 22nd Guards Rifle Corps' attack was greatly delayed because of the late arrival of the 184th and 219th rifle divisions to the jumping-off positions. These divisions attacked only at 1300 from the march, without preliminary preparation.

The 90th Guards Rifle Division, following the passage of the 184th and 219th rifle divisions through its combat formations, was left in the second echelon along the Chapaev—Krasnyi Uzliv line.

The enemy met the attack by the tank corps and the 22nd Guards Rifle Corps with fierce resistance. The Germans, fearing our attack against their main group's left flank, had by the morning of 12 July withdrawn the 3rd Panzer Division, reinforced and refitted, back to the line Sukhodol woods—Tolstoe woods. This division, along with units of the 332nd Infantry Division and the remnants of two panzer divisions (*Grossdeutschland* and 11th Panzer), was stubbornly defending its positions.

By the close of the day, following fierce fighting, units of the 22nd Guards Rifle and the 10th and 5th Guards tank corps reached the line of the western outskirts of Rakovo—Kubasovskii gully.

The 71st Guards Rifle Division, which was supporting the 22nd Guards Rifle Corps' right flank, attacked at 1100 and by the close of the day was fighting for the inhabited locales of Mikhailovka, Krasnyi Pochinok and Korovino.

The attack by the 23rd Guards Rifle Corps, along with units of the 3rd Mechanized and 31st Tank corps, began at 0830. By 1700 the 204th and 309th rifle divisions had reached the line of the branch of the gully one kilometer west of the burial mound and two kilometers southwest of Novoselovka—the pond 0.75 kilometers northwest of Novoselovka—excluding the southern edge of the Melovoe woods one kilometer north of height 248.3. They beat off fierce enemy tank and infantry attacks and consolidated along the occupied line. Attempts by our units to develop the attack further to the south were unsuccessful.

The 5th Guards Army's offensive battles

At 0830 the 32nd Guards Rifle Corps attacked. Its left-flank 66th Guards Rifle Division had to overcome fierce resistance by the enemy defending opposite it. By evening the division had consolidated along the northern outskirts of Kochetovka. Throughout the day the 13th Guards Rifle Division did not advance. The 33rd Guards Rifle Corps' 97th Guards Rifle Division, which was attacking from the line Peresyp'—Ol'khovskii, by the end of the day had reached the line of the northern outskirts of Kochetovka—Krasnyi Oktyabr', where it consolidated.

The 95th Guards Rifle Division, in conjunction with the 52nd Guards Rifle Division, was engaged throughout the day in fierce defensive battles along the northern bank of the Psel River. By the close of the day the division had halted the German offensive and occupied defensive positions along the line northern outskirts of Krasnyi Oktyabr'—height 226.6—the eastern outskirts of Polezhaev.

The 42nd Guards Rifle Division, on conjunction with the 5th Guards Tank Army's attacking formations, cleared the inhabited locales of Mikhailovka (one kilometer east of Andreevka) and Andreevka of the enemy.

By 1700 the 9th Guards Airborne Division had again occupied defensive positions which it had previously held along the line October State Farm—Stalin State Farm.

As a result of the daytime fighting, the 183rd Rifle Division's right flank fell back a little and consolidated along the line of the eastern outskirts of Storozhevoe—the railroad booth two kilometers east of Yasnaya Polyana. By the close of the day units of the 2nd Tank Corps, which had arrived in the Storozhevoe area, had been fed into the division's right-flank combat formation.

The offensive fighting by the 7th Guards Army's 49th Rifle Corps

According to the *front* commander's plan, at 0900 on 12 July the 7th Guards Army's 49th Rifle Corps (73rd Guards, 270th and 111th rifle divisions) attacked along the Batratskaya Dacha—Polyana State Farm sector. As a result of stubborn fighting, by the end of the day the corps had advanced 1½-2 kilometers and reached the line heights 207.9—191.2—Polyana State Farm, where it consolidated.

Results of the 11-12 July Fighting Along the Prokhorovka Axis

During 11-12 July the enemy, having ended active operations along the Oboyan' axis, directed all his efforts toward achieving a decisive success along the Prokhorovka axis. For this purpose the Germans carried out two powerful attacks on Prokhorovka, from the west and south. The battle for Prokhorovka reached its culminating point on 12 July. The enemy, having concentrated west of Prokhorovka up to four panzer divisions and as much as one infantry division, threw them to the east along the road.

Besides this, the III Panzer Corps, consisting of 300 tanks, was to attack from the south.

On 12 July two tank battles unfolded—one in the area to the west of Prokhorovka, in which the main forces of the 5th Guards Tank Army took part on our side, against the main enemy group of forces, consisting of three divisions from the SS Panzer Corps and the 17th Panzer Division; the other—in the Ryndinka—Rzhavets—Vypolzovka area, where the 5th Guards Tank Army's units—General Trufanov's detachment (three tank brigades)—clashed with the main forces of the enemy's III Panzer Corps (three panzer divisions).

This battle, in which more than 1,500 tanks took part simultaneously on both sides, was characterized by its great fierceness and great diversity of combat forms, which developed almost simultaneously along a comparatively limited territory. Offensive and defensive fighting, operations against the enemy's flanks, and fierce meeting encounters between major tank forces broke out and unfolded throughout the day along various sectors of the front.

Fierce air battles simultaneously occurred above the battlefield. Our aviation carried out about 600 sorties in the area of the tank battle west of Prokhorovka alone that day, and fought 12 air battles, in which our pilots shot down 18 enemy planes.

During the fighting west of Prokhorovka the enemy lost about 300 tanks and about 500 motor vehicles knocked out and destroyed, and more than 4,500 officers and men killed.

Our units' losses were also significant. The battle was lost by the enemy. As a result of the 5th Guards Tank Army's meeting attack, the main German group of forces attacking toward Prokhorovka from the west suffered enormous losses. By the close of the day it was forced to go over to the defensive, thus renouncing further attempts to renew active operations.

The enemy's attempt to break through to Prokhorovka from the south out of the Ryndinka—Rzhavets area also ended in complete failure. By the close of 12 July units of the German III Panzer Corps had advanced in fighting to the area of the village of Rzhavets; their further advance was halted by our forces' powerful counterattacks.

Thus on 12 July the enemy along this axis was forced to renounce further attempts to continue the offensive to the north.

The German forces suffered extremely heavy losses during the period of their offensive along the Oboyan' and Korocha axes. Finally, the main German tank groups suffered enormous losses from the 5th Guards Tank Army's powerful attack. Thanks to this, the enemy finally exhausted his offensive capabilities.

After 12 July the Germans went over to the defensive in front of the entire Voronezh Front, with the exception of the 69th Army's sector.

This day was the day of the German offensive's final crisis, the day that the enemy completely renounced efforts to achieve his objective—the capture of Kursk from the south. From this day the initiative passed completely into the hands of the Red Army command.

It's worth noting that on 12 July the forces of the Western, Bryansk and Central fronts launched a decisive offensive for the purpose of eliminating the enemy's Orel group of forces.

The Battle of Kursk was finally won in the fierce tank battles of 12 July.

The 69th and 5th Guards Tank Armies' Battles in the Rzhavets—Leski—Gostishchevo Area (13-15 July)

Having suffered a failure in his final attempt to break the Voronezh Front's defense along the Prokhorovka axis, as well as having suffered enormous losses in the desperate fighting of 11-12 July, which finally undermined the German army's offensive capabilities, the enemy was forced to renounce active operations along this axis as well. By 13 July the enemy, who had been seriously bled white, went over to the defense opposite the entire Voronezh Front, with the exception of the 69th Army's zone, where he continued to wage fierce combat.

The German command, having renounced the continuation of operations for the decisive goal of reaching the Kursk area, issued a local task to the III Panzer and SS Panzer corps—to encircle five of the 69th Army's divisions defending in the narrow salient between the Lipovyi Donets and Severskii Donets rivers and to eliminate the salient. In this way the enemy counted on somewhat shortening his defensive front and to expand to the west the pocket that had formed as a result of the failed German attack and to ensure favorable conditions for withdrawing the German Fourth Panzer Army's main forces from this pocket.

On 14 July the German command tried to widen the pocket to the west as well. At the same time it sought to parry the counteroffensive by the forces of the 6th Guards and 1st Tank armies, which, beginning on 12 July threatened to reach the main German group of forces' communications. For this purpose, the Germans undertook a local offensive along the Berezovka—Kubasovskii gully sector.

Finally, on 15 July the German forces were completely exhausted and ended their active operations.

On the basis of the evaluation of the 22 July battles, the *front* commander still allowed for the possibility of the enemy's active operations along the Prokhorovka axis. Thus on 13 July the *front* commander set forth the following objectives:

- to prevent the enemy's further advance on Prokhorovka, from both the west and south;
- through joint operations by the 5th Guards Army (95th, 52nd and 60th guards rifle divisions) and the 5th Guards Mechanized Corps' 24th and 10th tank brigades, to eliminate the enemy group of forces that had broken through to the northern bank of the Psel River;
- to eliminate the units of the III Panzer Corps that had broken through to the Rzhavets area, and;
- to continue the attacks by the 1st Tank and 6th Guards armies and the 5th Guards Army's right flank.

The Fighting on 13 July

The German attack toward Shakhovo

It was planned to carry out the German command's plan, which consisted of encircling five of the 69th Army's divisions defending in the salient between the Lipovyi Donets and Severskii Donets rivers, through concentric attacks from the Yasnaya Polyana—Ozerovskii area toward Shakhovo, and from the Shchelokovo—Rzhavets area toward Shakhovo.

The enemy spent the day of 13 July on preparing for this operation and the necessary regroupings were carried out.

In the Yasnaya Polyana—Ozerovskii area the Germans had concentrated the *Das Reich* SS Panzer Division, which had been brought up to strength from the SS Corp's other divisions. On the night of 12-13 July and during the day of 13 July, the enemy concentrated part of the corps' forces in the Pokrovka—Yakovlevo area for carrying out a 14 July attack against the 6th Guards Army's right flank.

In order to create favorable conditions for developing the attack from the Shchelokovo area toward Shakhovo, the enemy sought to throw back units of the 69th and 5th Guards Tank armies, which were operating in the Vypolzovka area, to the north and to thus pin down our reserves in that area. Thus the Germans continued their attacks throughout 13 July from the Rzhavets area to the north. Our units beat off all of these attacks and held on to the positions of the previous evening. The enemy lost 86 tanks damaged and destroyed on this day.

Simultaneously, the enemy launched attacks from the Visloe area to the northeast and from the Kiselevo area to the northwest; the Germans sought to encircle with these attacks the 89th Guards Rifle Division, which was defending in the salient's southern part. However, by this time the division's main forces had already been withdrawn and were occupying defensive positions along the sector Kiselevo—excluding Krivtsovo. The enemy's attacks hit empty space and he could not break through further to the north.

The attacks on Gostishchevo were beaten back by the joint efforts of the 89th and 93rd guards rifle divisions' second echelons. By the close of 13 July these divisions had organized a defense along the line Druzhnyi—height 223.2—excluding Krivtsovo.

The Germans were carrying out defensive works along the entire front and along individual sectors were carrying out reconnaissance with powerful detachments.

The enemy's units that had broken through to the northern bank of the Psel River were beaten back from height 236.7 and from Polezhaev village through the joint counterattacks by our forces—the 95th, 42nd and 52nd guards divisions, and the 24th Tank and 10th Mechanized guards brigades. By the onset of darkness our units' front ran along the line Klyuchi—height 226.6—the western outskirts of Polezhaev.

The command's measures

According to the *front* commander's decision, the *front's* forces on 14 July were to securely hold their defensive lines and continue attacking along the axes indicated earlier. The 5th Guards Army's attention was focused on eliminating the enemy's group of forces that had broken through to the northern bank of the Psel River.

In order to parry the enemy's attempts to break through to the north from the Rzhavets area and to reinforce the 69th Army's units that were defending along this axis, the *front* commander at 2000 on 13 July ordered that the army be reinforced. Additional reinforcements were to be transferred to the 69th Army from the 38th, 40th, 5th Guards Tank, and 7th Guards armies: one anti-tank brigade, one anti-aircraft division, one guards mortar regiment, and one mortar battalion.

The 69th Army commander, in his turn, reinforced the formations operating along the Rzhavets—Avdeevka axis, moving an additional eight anti-tank artillery regiments, a cannon brigade, a guards mortar regiment, a mortar battalion, and a tank regiment here. These were units received from other armies and freed up by regroupings within the army.

On the night of 13-14 July the commander of the 5th Guards Tank Army moved up the 25th Guards Tank Brigade (2nd Guards Tank Corps) to the base of the salient in the Maloe Yablonovo—Plota area, as a mobile reserve.

The 2nd Guards and 2nd Tank corps' mission was confirmed to in no way allow the enemy to break through to the east from the Teterevino farm—Yasnaya Polyana—Ozerovskii area.

The Fighting on 14-15 July

The fighting for Shakhovo

In order to encircle units of the 69th Army's 48th Rifle Corps, which were defending in the Vinogradovka—Gostishchevo—Plota triangle, the enemy attacked on the morning of 14 July in two groups, which operated as follows: the first consisted of the *Das Reich* SS Panzer Division, with infantry, from the Ozerovskii area toward Leski and Shakhovo, with another part of its forces attacking toward Maloe Yablonovo; the second, consisting of the 19th and 7th panzer divisions, with infantry, attacked from the Shchelokovo area toward Shakhovo.

Following fierce daytime fighting, the group attacking from the west captured Belenikhino, Ivanovka (two kilometers northwest of Leski) and Leski and reached Maloe Yablonovo. At the end of the day units of the 19th and 7th panzer divisions continued to be stubbornly engaged north of the woods one kilometer west of Shchelokovo. The enemy, in order to secure this group's right flank, simultaneously continued attacking to the north from the Rzhavets area toward Avdeevka, as well as from the Kazach'e area toward Aleksandrovka.

The enemy threw more than 100 tanks at Avdeevka. By midday he managed to capture Vypolzovka and Krasnoe Znamya. The enemy tanks' further advance was halted by concentrated anti-tank fire, which was concentrated along this axis, as well as by counterattacks by General Trufanov's detachment. By the evening of 14 July the enemy, at the cost of heavy losses, captured Aleksandrovka.

There was a danger that the 48th Rifle Corps' divisions might be surrounded. The corps commander, lacking communications with the army commander, ordered on the morning of 15 July that the divisions be withdrawn from the pocket under the cover of rear guards. On this day the corps' formations withdrew in stubborn fighting to a new defensive line: the grove two kilometers east of the line Vinogradovka—Zhilomestnoe—Novoselovka—Verin—excluding Shipy. The divisions' withdrawal was carried out in the following order: 89th, 81st and 93rd Guards rifle division and units of the 375th Rifle Division.

At dawn on 15 July the enemy continued his attacks, attempting to close the encirclement ring around the 48th Rifle Corps in the Shakhovo area. The Germans managed to capture Shakhovo only during the latter half of the day by attacks from the Shchelokovo area, after they committed about 150 tanks simultaneously into the battle. The enemy was unable to break through to Shakhovo from the Leski area and to close the escape route from the pocket before the onset of darkness. By the close of 15 July all the 48th Rifle Corps' divisions had occupied their designated positions.

Thus the enemy's stubborn and costly attempts to encircle the 48th Rifle Corps' divisions suffered a complete collapse. This ended the Germans' active operations along the 69th Army's front. During the night of 15-16 July the enemy here also went over to the defensive.

The 6th Guards and 1st Tank armies' fighting in the Berezovka area

On the morning of 14 July the enemy attacked with an infantry division and 100 tanks from the Rakovo—Berezovka area against the 184th Rifle Division and the 5th Guards Rifle and 10th Tank corps. Following stubborn resistance, our units fell back to the line Sukhodol woods (two kilometers north of Chapaev)—Platovaya woods (two kilometers southeast of Noven'koe). The enemy simultaneously carried out attacks with an infantry regiment and 20 tanks toward the Kubasovskii gully from the Verkhopen'e area. Our forces beat off these attacks.

As a result of the 184th Rifle Division's withdrawal, the 219th Rifle Division pulled back its right flank to the line of the western slopes of height 240.2—Kubasovskii gully.

The offensive battles of the 6th Guards Army's 23rd Guards Rifle Corps and the 5th Guards Army on 14 July yielded no definite result. Units of the 32nd Guards Rifle Corps advanced somewhat, reaching the line height 248.3—the northwestern outskirts of Kochetovka.

On the morning of 15 July the 6th and 5th guards armies, according to the *front* commander's decision, temporarily halted their offensive operations and went over to a static defense along their previous lines.

On 15 July the 1st and 5th Guards tank armies were pulled back into the *front* commander's reserve for refitting and preparation for the forthcoming offensive operations.

The Offensive by the Voronezh and Steppe Fronts to Restore the Situation (17-23 July 1943)

The overall situation by the start of the offensive

On 15 July the enemy had exhausted his offensive capabilities; bled white as a result of the stubborn resistance of the Voronezh Front's forces, the enemy was forced to halt active operations and go over to the offensive along the entire front.

The defense of the salient that had formed as the result of the failed German offensive, presented very great difficulties. In the case of a counterstroke by our forces against the flanks of the extended group of forces, its condition would be rendered very difficult. These considerations forced the German command to begin pulling back its main forces from the resulting pocket to the line that the enemy had occupied before the beginning of the offensive. It was decided to go over to a static defense there. The Germans were also forced to adopt this decision by the difficult situation that had arisen for the Orel group of forces as a result of the offensive by the forces of the Western, Bryansk and Central fronts. It was already necessary to shift part of the forces from the Belgorod—Khar'kov group of forces to help out the Orel group of forces, and the Germans dispatched the *Grossdeutschland* SS Panzer division there. Besides this, the Germans had to reinforce their units operating against the Southwestern Front, which had also gone over to the offensive, for which the 17th Panzer Division was transferred.

On 16 July the enemy, under cover of powerful rearguards that clung to the broadly developed system of the various defensive structures that the area of combat operations was so rich in, began to pull back his main forces.

During the latter half of 16 July our aviation observed the intensive movement of motor vehicles and tanks from the area of Komsomolets State Farm toward Bol'shie Mayachki and Pokrovka, and this movement continued all night. On 17 July the movement to the south became even more intensive. From 0700 to 1400 our air reconnaissance uncovered the movement of 12 enemy columns from the Verkhopen'e—Pokrovka—Komsomolets State Farm area, numbering up to 550 tanks and 1,000 motor vehicles. All of the detected enemy columns on 16-17 July were subjected to attacks by our bomber and assault aviation.

Fighting by the forward detachments on 17-18 July

The *front* commander, on the basis of reconnaissance data, as early as the morning of 17 July had assumed the possibility of the enemy's withdrawal from the pocket. In connection with this, he issued orders to immediately organize reconnaissance by powerful forward and reconnaissance detachments. By the close of 17 July the 6th Guards and 5th Guards Tank armies' forward detachments, while pushing aside the enemy's covering units, had advanced 2-5 kilometers along some axes and had occupied Sitnoe woods, the Komsomolets State Farm and Storozhevoe.

On the night of 17-18 July the *front* commander ordered the commanders of the 1st and 5th Guards tank armies to attack with part of their forces on the morning of 18 July. The 1st Tank Army was to move in the general direction of Tomarovka, while the 5th Guards Tank Army, on the left, was to advance toward Luchki and Krapivenskie Dvory. The remaining armies were to continue carrying out reconnaissance.

The 1st Tank Army, attacking with two tank brigades, in conjunction with two of the 6th Guards Army's rifle divisions, reached the line Korovino—Rakovo after stubborn fighting.

By the close of the day detachments of the 5th Guards Tank and 5th Guards armies, as a result of their joint operations, occupied the line Teterevino farm—Yasnaya Polyana—Vinogradovka.

Besides this, the 5th Guards Army's forward detachments captured Krasnyi Oktyabr', Bogoroditskoe (one kilometer northwest of Kozlovka) and Kozlovka.

The enemy put up fierce resistance everywhere.

The Voronezh and Steppe fronts' offensive on 20-23 July

On 18 July the *Stavka* of the Supreme High Command ordered a general offensive for the purpose of eliminating the forward forces, having in mind the further development of the offensive to defeat the Germans' Belgorod—Khar'kov group of forces.

On the basis of the *Stavka's* directive of 16 July, at 2300 on 18 July the Steppe Front, consisting of the 53rd, 47th and 4th Guards armies, as well as the 69th and 7th Guards armies transferred from the Voronezh Front, was to be committed.

On 19 July the forces of both *fronts*, while continuing to carry out reconnaissance, regrouped and prepared for assuming the offensive.

On the morning of 20 July the Voronezh Front's 6th Guards Army, part of the 1st Tank Army, and the 5th Guards and 5th Guards Tank armies, as well as part of the Steppe Front's 53rd Army, attacked. Units of the 53rd Army were committed into the battle in the 69th Army's center, along the Dal'nii Dolzhik—Gnezdilovka sector.

By the close of 20 July the forces of the Voronezh Front, following fierce fighting with the enemy's covering units, which were putting up desperate resistance, reached the line Berezovka—Yakovlevo—Luchki (southern). They advanced an average of 10-12 kilometers. The Steppe Front's forces reached the line Leski—Shakhovo—the northern outskirts of Shakhovo—the eastern outskirts of Novo-Oskochnoe—Verkhnii Ol'shanets—Shlyakhovo. The enemy put up stubborn resistance along this line throughout 21 July. Our forces advanced only insignificantly along individual sectors.

On the morning of 22 July the Red Army crushed the resistance of the Germans trying to delay our advance and the forces of both *fronts* attacked and by the close of 23 July reached the line Novaya Goryanka (seven kilometers south of Novo-Ivanovka)—Gertsovka (four kilometers south of Korovino)—Cherkasskoe—Trirechnoe—Kamennyi Log (1.5 kilometers northeast of Zadel'noe)—Druzhnyi—Kiselevo—Khokhlovo—Melekhovo—Yastrebovo—Razumnoe and then along the eastern bank of the Severskii Donets River. This was basically the line which had been occupied by our forces before the start of the German offensive. Along individual sectors of the front, where our forces did not reach this line, offensive fighting continued until early August. The Steppe Front's forces cleared the eastern bank of the Severskii Donets River of the enemy.

Main Conclusions

The defensive battle around Kursk in July of 1943, much the same as the Red Army's heroic struggle in July-November 1942 in the Stalingrad area, confirmed with complete clarity that a correctly organized defense, given the presence of combat-capable forces, can not only delay, but halt an offensive by superior enemy forces, plentifully armed with the latest combat equipment. Such a defense may also so exhaust and bleed white the attacking forces to such an extent during the battle that they completely lose their offensive capabilities. At the same time, the defending forces have favorable conditions for a subsequent decisive offensive.

In the fighting around Kursk the forces of the Central and Voronezh fronts met the main forces of the German groups of forces and, in the defensive fighting of 5-15 July, inflicted enormous losses in men and equipment on them. The Germans' Orel and Belgorod—Khar'kov groups of forces, which were attacking toward Kursk, lost 70,000 men killed and wounded, 2,952 tanks, 195 assault guns, 844 field guns, 1,392 planes, and more than 5,000 motor vehicles damaged or destroyed.

The Germans eloquently speak of their own losses. For example, prisoners from the 3rd Panzer Division testified that by the beginning of the offensive their division had more than 300 tanks, while the motorized regiments' rifle companies had 180 officers and men each; by the end of the operation there remained only 30 tanks in the division and no more than 40 soldiers in the companies.

Under interrogation a company commander of the 167th Infantry Division's 315th Regiment testified that by the end of the battle there remained only 42 soldiers in his company, including service personnel; the 315th Regiment's remaining companies contained approximately the same number.

The 17th Panzer Division, which the Germans committed into the battle only on 11 July (by the end of the battle of Kursk), was soon transferred to a sector opposite our Southwestern Front and numbered only 60 tanks.

General Schmidt, the commander of the 19th Panzer Division, wrote in his report that by 11 July there remained no more than 400 infantrymen in each of his division's grenadier (motorized rifle) regiments and only 17 combat-ready tanks in the division.

As a result of such great losses, the Germans' Orel group of forces, as early as 9 July, finally lost the capability of continuing the offensive and was forced to go over to the defensive. Actually, the

Belgorod—Khar'kov group's offensive capabilities proved exhausted by as early as 13 July, when this group of forces, with the exception of the 69th Army's sector, also went over to the defensive along the entire front.

Of significance for the defensive phase of the battle of Kursk was the fact that the Red Army's forces eliminated the entire offensive power of the German forces during the course of eight days.

The crisis situation into which the German army fell as the result of irs extremely heavy losses, enabled the Central Front command to begin a counteroffensive on 15 July for the purpose of restoring the situation, and by 17 July our troops had done so. The same sort of operation was successfully carried out by the Voronezh Front's forces during 17-23 July.

As a result of the defeat of the Orel and Belgorod—Khar'kov German groups of forces in the defensive battle around Kursk, extremely favorable conditions were created for the Red Army's subsequent major offensive operations.

The significance of forecasting in the defensive operation

The ability to guess the enemy's plans and to foresee the approximate course of combat developments is an important, often decisive factor, in preparing and conducting any operation. This factor acquires extreme importance in preparing for a major defensive operation—particularly along a major strategic direction—an operation, undertaken for the purpose of repelling an offensive by the main enemy group of forces.

In these conditions, when the enemy has the initiative, to guess his plan and to determine the axes of his main attacks ahead of time, as well as the date of the start of the offensive, means to achieve the opportunity to forcefully organize a defense accordingly and to avoid dispersing men and materiel along a broad front.

As early as March 1943 the *Stavka* of the Supreme High Command had not only made an extremely precise forecast concerning the overall character of the enemy's forthcoming operations, but had also concretely determined the deployment areas of his main shock groups and the likely axes of the enemy attacks. On the basis of this correct strategic forecast the Red Army organized the defense of the Kursk salient.

The Supreme High Command oriented the *front* commands beforehand as to the time of the enemy offensive, which deprived the German command of the advantage of surprise from the very start of the operation.

The structure of modern defense

The experience of the defensive fighting around Stalingrad and Kursk shows that in conditions of modern war, when the attacking group of forces disposes of a significant amount of equipment and has great penetrating power (tanks, aviation, artillery), the defense, in order to successfully withstand the attacker's blow, must be maximally deep and echeloned.

The depth of our forces' defense around Stalingrad exceeded 100 kilometers, counting the distance from the 62nd Army's forward defensive zone, which was organized along the western bank of the Don River along the Kletskoe—Surovikino—Verkhnyaya Kurmoyarskaya line to the Stalingrad urban position. Five defensive lines were created to cover the Stalingrad axis, including the so-called urban position.

The battle around Kursk unfolded in conditions of both sides having an abundance of modern military equipment. The attack against the Kursk salient from the north, which was delivered along a 32-kilometer front, was carried out by a group of forces consisting of 13 divisions, among which were six panzer divisions. This group of forces numbered 1,455 tanks and 4,264 guns, not counting mortars. Each kilometer of attack front contained, on the average, 45 tanks and more than 70 guns.

The Germans' Belgorod—Khar'kov group of forces, which was attacking Kursk from the south along a 70-kilometer front, consisted of 14 divisions, including nine panzer. This group of forces numbered 1,700 tanks and 2,500 guns. The density of the attack front along the axes of the main attacks amounted to 42 tanks per kilometer and 47 guns. Opposite the 6th Guards Army's front, where the main attack was made, the density reached up to 100 tanks per kilometer.

Both German groups of forces were supported by powerful aviation forces—about 2,000 combat aircraft.

Based upon the correct knowledge of the character of the modern battle, which was confirmed by data regarding the composition of the groups of forces being created by the enemy, the supreme high command of the Red Army assigned the forces of the Central and Voronezh fronts the task of creating a deeply-echeloned defense. Such a defense was created on the territory of the Kursk salient. Its overall depth, taking including the army and *front* defensive lines, reached 110 kilometers.

The forces of both *fronts* defending the Kursk salient prepared six lines (three army and three *front*). In order to reach Kursk by attacks from the north and south, the enemy would have to successively overcome no less than five defensive lines along any axis. Along the most threatened axes, our forces occupied 3-4 defensive lines beforehand. The depth of the defense occupied by our forces reached 60 kilometers.

The Germans, during their offensive, managed to overcome only one first defensive line along the Central Front; along the Voronezh Front they were able to overcome two army defensive lines and, along separate sectors, reach the rear army zone. The enemy completely exhausted his offensive capabilities in overcoming these lines.

Features of preparing the defensive zones

Each defensive line consisted mainly of a broadly developed trench system. Such a system included a significant number of anti-tank strong points (PTOP), prepared for all-round defense.

The trenches were the basis for stationing the infantry's combat formations and weapons. A thick network of trenches and communications trenches eased the creation of a firm and tenacious fire system, enabling us to broadly maneuver our weapons and personnel along the front and in depth during the battle. Besides this, the forces, employing a developed network of trenches, were able to dodge the massed fire onslaughts by the enemy's artillery and aviation. At the same time, the trenches served as a good cover against tanks and enabled the infantry to allow the tanks to pass through their combat formations and then cut off the enemy infantry, following behind the tanks, with their fire. Each rifle division, defending along the main zone, had an average of up to 60-70 kilometers of trenches.

The anti-tank strong points were stationed along the tank-accessible axes and represented powerful fire concentrations. They were mainly created by employing artillery weapons, and also including anti-tank rifles, automatic riflemen and, sometimes, tanks buried in the ground. All sorts of obstacles, particularly anti-tank ones, were set up around the anti-tank strong points.

In the Voronezh Front's main defensive sector, about 150 anti-tank strong points were outfitted; that is, one strong point for every 2.5 kilometers of defensive front. During the defensive fighting their role was extremely important. The strong points held up the attacking enemy tank groups for a long time and inflicted significant losses on them. As a general rule, the enemy tanks, following a series of unsuccessful and costly attempts to eliminate an anti-tank strong point, would end their attacks against it and seek to bypass it. Thus the anti-tank strong points served as something like powerful "wave breakers," which broke up major attacking tank groups into separate small groups. This significantly eased the subsequent fight with them.

The firmness of modern defense depends, to a significant degree, on how much the defending forces' personnel and equipment are covered (dug in), as well as on the number of various and sundry anti-tank and anti-personnel obstacles covering the defense. In this sense, the defense of the Kursk salient approached the ideal of modern field defense. Not only did our personnel defending along the main defensive zone dig in, but also all of our equipment, including artillery and tanks, as well as the operational reserves located along the rear defensive lines. In order to bring the defense to such a condition, in conditions of direct contact with the enemy, our forces needed about three months of intensive work.

It's completely natural that in conditions of maneuver warfare the troops will rarely have such a significant amount of time to prepare a defense in active theaters. Thus along particularly important, in the operational sense, axes, it is necessary to outfit beforehand a series of defensive lines in the troops' rear with the forces of the rear organizations and local population, for the purpose of securely covering them, regardless of the type of operations unfolding.

The disposition of forces in defense

The distribution of men and materiel along the defensive front cannot be even. It is necessary to create the greatest concentration of forces immediately occupying defensive lines along the most operationally important and threatened axes.

Naturally, such a disposition of forces can be achieved only as a result of the scrupulous and continuous study of the enemy and by observing his regroupings. This will enable us to make a relatively correct forecast as to the enemy's forthcoming intentions.

The defense of the Kursk salient is a classic example of the grouping of men and materiel, carried out on the basis of the supreme high command's forecast as to the enemy's intentions. The main forces of men and materiel were concentrated along the axes of the Germans' anticipated main attacks.

Along the Central Front a single division defending along a secondary axis occupied a front of up to 26 kilometers in width; the 13th Army's divisions defending along the axis of the enemy's main attack were assigned defensive sectors of no more than 6-8 kilometers. The 13th Army contained 37 percent of all the *front's* reinforcement artillery units, 50 percent of the independent tank brigades, and 33 percent of the tank regiments, as well as 37 percent of the mortar regiments and 55 percent of the guards mortar regiments.

The *front's* main reserves were grouped chiefly in the Ol'khovatka—Gnezdilovo—Berezovets—Mikhailovo area. As the enemy's offensive along the Orel—Kursk railroad unfolded, the *front* reserves had the opportunity to launch counterblows along both flanks of the attacking enemy group of forces, without the necessity of carrying out preliminary complex maneuvers.

Along the Voronezh Front each division defending along a secondary axis had, on the average, a front up to 22 kilometers to defend. Along the zone of the 6th and 7th guards armies, which were defending along the anticipated main attack axis of the Germans' Belgorod—Khar'kov group of forces, the divisions were assigned defensive sectors of no more than 14 kilometers. Up to 63 perecent of all the *front* reinforcement artillery regiments, 50 percent of the tank regiments and brigades, and 73 percent of the guards mortar regiments were included in the 6th and 7th guards armies.

All of the *front* reserves were also concentrated along the axis of the main attack. Thus the greatest defensive density and the disposition of both *fronts'* reserves were created at the base of the Kursk salient. The tip of the salient was comparatively weakly held by our troops, who were defending along a broad front.

In order to parry the enemy's attempts to attack toward Kursk from the west, from the area of Ryl'sk and Vorozhba, both *fronts'* reserves were oriented beforehand as to their possible employment in the direction of the Kursk salient's tip.

As a result of the fact that the enemy's attacks were launched against the most densely occupied sectors of the front, containing the highest concentration of men and materiel in the latter's depth, the enemy was unable to not only break through the entire operational defense, but the depth of the army defense as well.

Maneuver in defense

In the defensive battle's first stage (before the enemy group of forces had lost his offensive capabilities) the defending side had to try to deprive the enemy of the opportunity of carrying out maneuver in the depth of his defense. This is achieved, first of all, by the "envelopment" of the enemy breakthrough force by reserves brought up from the defensive depth. These reserves occupy defensive lines along the axis of the enemy's attack. The forces occupying the defensive line along the breakthrough sector have to undertake all measures for preventing the breach's broadening toward the flanks. For this purpose, one must widely employ previously prepared switch positions and zones.

During the defensive fighting around Kursk, second echelons and mobile reserves from the first *front* echelon, as well as units and formations set aside from the *front* reserve and transferred from the front's passive sectors, were employed to carry out this assignment.

As an example of maneuvering reserves in a defensive battle, one may point to the regrouping carrying out by the Voronezh Front commander. During the fighting along the Oboyan' axis during 5-9 July, the armies operating here received:

6th Guards Army—two tank corps (2nd and 5th guards) from the *front* reserve and two artillery regiments (111th Artillery and 12th Anti-Tank) from the 40th Army;

1st Tank Army—two tank corps: one (10th) from the *front* reserve and one (5th Guards) from the 6th Guards Army; three tank brigades—86th and 192nd from the 40th Army, and the 18th from the 38th Army; one anti-tank brigade (29th) and four anti-tank regiments—869th, 1244th and 4th from the 40th Army, and one (222nd) from the 38th Army; one anti-aircraft division (9th) from the 40th Army, and; one guards mortar regiment (66th) from the 40th Army and two rifle divisions—the 204th from the 38th Army and the 309th from the 40th Army.

40th Army—the 192nd Tank Brigade from the 38th Army (for reinforcing the army's left flank).

During the most intense fighting along the Korocha axis (5-7 July), the 7th Guards Army was reinforced from the 6th Guards Army by one tank brigade (96th) and an anti-tank brigade (31st) from the *front* reserve, and three rifle divisions (the 35th Guards Rifle Corps' 94th Guards Rifle Division, and the 69th Army's 111th and 270th rifle divisions).

During 9-15 July, when fierce fighting unfolded in the 69th Army's defensive zone, which was covering the Prokhorovka area from the south and southwest, the army was reinforced with two tank corps: one (2nd) from the *front* reserve and one (2nd Guards) from the 6th Guards Army, a mechanized corps (5th Guards) from the *front* reserve, three anti-tank brigades—the 32nd from the 40th Army, the 31st from the 7th Guards Army, and the 10th from the *front* reserve, an anti-aircraft division (36th) from the *front* reserve (from the 5th Guards Tank Army), an independent guards mortar battalion (441st) from the 38th Army, and a rifle corps (35th Guards) from the *front* reserve.

On 11 July, while preparing to carry out a counterstroke against the enemy' group's flanks, the 6th Guards Army was additionally reinforced with three rifle divisions: two (184th and 219th) from the 40th Army and one (309th) from the 1st Tank Army.

Thus, during the defensive battle the Voronezh Front commander carried out a regrouping, in which seven tank and mechanized corps, seven tank brigades, five anti-tank brigades, nine artillery regiments, two anti-aircraft divisions, and ten rifle divisions took part.[9]

As a result of the skillful and flexible maneuver of reserves during all phases of the defensive fighting, the enemy was not able to break through into the depth of our operational defense along a single sector of either *front*, and thus was unable to achieve freedom to broadly maneuver his mobile formations. No matter how deeply the enemy penetrated into our defense, he everywhere encountered newer and newer defensive lines that enveloped him, already occupied by forces ready to repulse the enemy's attacks.

The *Stavka* of the Supreme High Command's movement of strategic reserves played an extremely important role in strengthening the firmness of the Kursk salient's defense. The movement of the 2nd and 10th tank corps significantly eased the situation of the Voronezh Front's forces, which were engaged in heavy fighting along the second defensive zone against the main German group of forces trying to break through to Oboyan'.

With the participation of the newly-arrived 5th Guards and 5th Guards Tank armies with the Voronezh Front, our forces finally stopped the enemy, repelling his final attempt to break through the *front's* defense toward Prokhorovka. During the 12 July tank battle in the Prokhorovka area, when the 5th Guards Tank Army entered the fighting against the main German group of forces, the enemy's offensive capabilities were completely exhausted: the enemy was forced to renounce continuing the offensive for the decisive purpose of breaking through to the Kursk area.

Finally, the timely reinforcement of the Voronezh Front with formations moved up from the *Stavka* reserve enabled the *front's* forces to go over to a counteroffensive (without a pause) and to restore the situation at the moment the Germans were forced to renounce the continuation of their offensive.

The Central Front halted the enemy offensive and restored the situation without the assistance and participation of the strategic reserves.

A forecast, correctly determining the enemy command's immediate intentions and the pace of his regroupings, has great significance when battling an enemy possessing great mobility. The enveloping of the Germans' breakthrough tank groups with reserves was carried out in a timely manner, because the *front* commanders correctly determined beforehand the axes of the planned enemy attacks and quickly carried out the necessary regroupings. Thus the development of the enemy' main tank attack from the south toward Kursk was opposed by a powerful screen, consisting of the 1st Tank Army and the 5th Guards Tank Corps, which by the close of 5 July had occupied the second defensive zone, behind the 6th Guards Army' second echelon. The Germans' final attack along the road to Oboyan' on 9 July was met by the 19th Tank Corps and the 309th Rifle Division, which had been moved up beforehand to the line Kruglik—Melovoe woods—Ol'shanka and had formed a second defensive echelon here.

On 11 July the enemy attempted to break through our defensive front along the Dragunskoe axis, but this attempt also failed, because the line Chapaev—excluding Kruglik had been occupied beforehand by the 184th Rifle Division in the capacity of a second echelon.

The enemy's 11-12 July attacks on Prokhorovka were repulsed by formations of the 5th Guards Tank Army and part of the 5th Guards Army's forces, which had been moved up here. The enemy, while striving to break through to Prokhorovka from the south (through Rzhavets) was unable to

9 These figures do not include the 1st Tank Army's full-strength formations that were moved up on 5 July to the second defensive line from the *front* reserve, as well as three divisions from the 69th Army, which on 9 July was assigned its own defensive zone.

overcome the resistance by the 5th Guards Tank Army's detachments (General Trufanov's detachment) that he encountered and the powerful artillery concentration in the Avdeevka area.

The experience of two major defensive battles—around Stalingrad and Kursk—shows that the successful conduct of the defense demands a high degree of activity from the latter. For example, the offensive by the German group of forces streaming toward Stalingrad was delayed for an entire month along the western bank of the Don River. The reason for this was the counterstroke by the formations of the 1st and 4th tank armies. In September and October of 1942 the German command, by launching a crushing attack against the 62nd Army with all the power of its main group of forces, sought to capture Stalingrad from the march. However, the active operations of the Stalingrad (later the Don) Front's left flank, which was hanging over the flank and rear of the main German group of forces, invariably foiled all such attempts.

The Voronezh Front's offensive operations along the flanks of the main enemy group of forces forced the German command to peel off significant forces to secure its flanks, which excluded the possibility of employing them along the main attack axis. The 40th Army's left-flank offensive operations (8-10 July) also forced the enemy to hold up to two infantry divisions and one panzer division along this sector of the front. The counterstrokes by the 2nd and 5th guards tank corps toward Kalinin and Nechaevka, undertaken on 8 July, forced the enemy to dispatch up to 100 tanks there at a critical moment in the fighting along the axis of the main attack (along the Oboyan' road). Taken from the main shock group, they were designated for parrying the 5th Guards Tank Corps' counterstroke. A significant number of tanks were also dispatched against the 2nd Guards Tank Corps. Finally, the Germans' decisive attempt on 12 July to break through the Voronezh Front's defense along the Prokhorovka axis also collapsed completely as the result of the counterstrokes by the 6th Guards, 1st Tank, 5th Guards, and 5th Guards Tank armies. Our troops' active operations forced the Geman command to not only call off the offensive along the Prokhorovka axis, but to renounce in general all further attempts to break through to Kursk from the south.

Features of the Combat Employment of the Combat Arms

Artillery

The presence of large amounts of equipment that took part in the fighting around Kursk, also determined the features of employing the combat arms there.

The breakthrough of our defensive positions along the axes of the main enemy attack, and the development of the enemy's offensive in the defensive depth, was primarily accomplished by tanks, with the support of major aviation groups and self-propelled artillery. The Germans' field artillery, for the most part, only prepared the breakthrough during the artillery preparation. The infantry, moving behind the tanks in echelons, was mainly concerned with eliminating of the individual centers of resistance, which had not been suppressed by the tanks, and securing the flanks of the tank groups.

In these conditions, our very powerful artillery groups were prepared for encountering the enemy, and which was the main force that met the attack by the enemy's attacking tank units.

The artillery's role in the modern defensive operation, according to the experience of the Battle of Kursk, is most vividly characterized by the amount of expended shells and the losses inflicted on the enemy by artillery fire. Thus during 5-12 July the Central Front's artillery expended 1,198 rail cars of shells, of which 213 were for the artillery operating in the 13th Army's sector alone. The Voronezh Front's 6th Guards Army's artillery expended 236 cars of shells in 11 days of defensive fighting. All of the Voronezh Front's artillery during this period expended more than 1.5 million rounds and shells.

During 5-12 July both *fronts'* artillery destroyed and knocked out 1,861 enemy tanks and self-propelled guns (812 along the Central Front and 1,049 along the Voronezh Front), which accounted for 61 percent of the overall amount of tanks and self-propelled guns lost by the enemy.

The correct grouping of the artillery in accordance with the situation is very important in defeating attacking enemy tank groups. This grouping should foresee the creation of the greatest artillery densities in the defending forces' combat formations along the axes of the main enemy attack, as well as the concentration of the main artillery reserves along these axes.

The experience of the defensive fighting shows that a deeply-echeloned anti-tank defense, built according to a single plan by the *front* command, employing all anti-tank weapons and all artillery sizes and designations, may successfully withstand powerful attacks by the enemy attacking tank groups. In a number of cases, attacks by significant groups of German tanks were beaten off by artillery fire alone.

However, the greatest effect is achieved in that case, when the artillery does not work in isolation, but rather in close coordination with all the other combat arms and with engineering obstacles.

In modern battle conditions, which are characterized by great maneuver, the artillery must skillfully maneuver not only by fire, but by wheels as well. Besides this, mobile artillery reserves, which enable us to quickly create powerful artillery concentrations along any threatened axis, are particularly important. In order to more expediently employ them during the battle, the maneuver of such reserves was primarily carried out by order of the *front* commander. The Voronezh Front had for this purpose 49 anti-tank artillery regiments, a part of which were periodically transferred to this or that army.

Intelligence data about the enemy's groups of forces, which had been detected during the day, usually reached the *front* headquarters every day by 1800. In accordance with this data, the *front* command would regroup its anti-tank regiments for the next day's fighting. As a result of such regroupings, artillery "shields", consisting of 8-12 artillery regiments, were be created along the most important axes. For example, on 13 July, in order to parry the Germans' attempt to break through from the Rzhavets area to the north, the commander of the 69th Army ordered the movement of a mobile artillery concentration, consisting of eight anti-tank artillery regiments, a cannon brigade, and a guards mortar regiment, to the Avdeevka area.

It is necessary for all commanders to have such anti-tank reserves, beginning with rifle division commanders. The commander of the Voronezh Front had a reserve consisting of five anti-tank artillery regiments and eight battalions of anti-tank rifles. The commander of the 6th Guards Army had in his mobile reserve two anti-tank brigades, two independent anti-tank regiments, and a battalion of anti-tank rifles.

The chief method in the artillery's battle with enemy tanks was firing over open sights by anti-tank artillery units. They met the enemy tank attacks first, supported the maneuver by our tanks and, with their fire, covered, if necessary, our units' withdrawal to the next defensive line. These units' role was especially vividly revealed in the heavy defensive battles that the 3rd Mechanized and 31st Tank corps waged on 7-9 July.

Firing over open sights is supplemented by massed fire from artillery and mortar units in concealed positions. This fire was is directed against concentrations of enemy tanks and infantry, and its cooperation is mandatory with assault air strikes against the enemy's combat formations before the latter arrive immediately at the forward edge of our defense. The continuity of artillery pressure on the enemy is achieved by the coordination of firing over open sights and artillery and mortar fire from concealed positions.

In a number of cases, guards mortar units were successfully employed for combating tank attacks, particularly with infantry mounted on them. On 6 July the 23rd Guards Mortar Brigade foiled an attack by a large group of enemy tanks in the vicinity of height 255.1. Salvos by two battalions of M-30s[10] destroyed seven German tanks and up to two battalions of enemy infantry. The enemy attack was foiled. In a number of cases, the enemy's tank units that came under the combined fire of artillery and guards mortars, cut short their attack and returned to their jumping-off positions, because during the attack the enemy tank crews could not distinguish the explosions of our artillery shells from the mortar explosions.

The artillery counterpreparation is an important link in the overall chain of defensive measures. It, as the experience of the fighting showed, severely disrupts the planned character of the preparation and organization of the offensive, and also lowers the state of the attacking troops' morale. The most successful and effective was the counterpreparation conducted by the Voronezh Front's artillery. The artillery chose concentrations of enemy troops as its main target, particularly tanks, command and observation posts, and only the most actively operating artillery batteries. As opposed to this method, the Central Front's artillery basically directed the full might of its fire only against the enemy's artillery.

In conditions of an intense and extended battle, the timely restoration of the artillery units, which have been carrying the brunt of the fighting against the enemy's tanks, is very important from the point of view of maintaining the firmness of the defense; it's natural that during the battle they will suffer significant losses.

The Voronezh Front command pulled out of the battle almost every day up to 3-4 anti-tank artillery regiments, in which up to 75 percent of the equipment had been put out of action. These regiments were refitted with equipment and personnel from the *front's* resources and within 2-3 days were once again thrown into the fighting.

Tanks

The fighting around Kursk affirms with complete clarity the correctness of the proposition that when enemy tanks appear on the battlefield the main battle against them is waged by the artillery. Tanks fight the enemy's tanks only in circumstances of our obvious numerical superiority and a favorable situation.

The specificity of the situation in the fighting around Kursk was that our defense had to encounter attacks by large tank masses, including a large number of T-VI and T-V[11] heavy tanks, as well as heavy self-propelled guns and a large number of mobile anti-tank artillery.

Under these conditions the most expedient and profitable method of employing tank formations was using them for carrying out defensive tasks. The tank formations, in conjunction with the combined-arms formations, occupied defensive lines in the operational depth and repelled attacks by enemy tank groups in place. The most characteristic example of a similar employment of tank formations was the employment of the Voronezh Front's 1st Tank Army and 2nd and 5th guards tank corps. These formations, having occupied on the battle's second day the 6th Guards Army's second defensive zone, were chiefly involved in defensive fighting together with the army's second echelon throughout the entire battle.

The tank formations' occupation of defensive lines, together with the infantry, increases the operational depth of the defense, sharply increases the firmness of these lines and the density of their artillery saturation. The 1st Tank Army's arrival at the 6th Guards Army's defensive line increased the latter's artillery equipment (including tank guns and the tank army's artillery units'

10 Editor's note. This was one of several models of Soviet rocket-propelled artillery during the Great Patriotic War. The M-30 consisted of four launch tubes mounted on a truck and firing 300mm rockets.

11 Editor's note. The T-V ("Panther") was a German medium tank that appeared in the latter half of the Second World War. It weighed 44.8 tons and carried a crew of five. It was armed with a 75mm gun and two 7.92mm machine guns.

guns) by 85.5 percent. The army's arrival at the second defensive zone and its subsequent defensive actions, which had the purpose of covering the Oboyan' axis, as early as 10 July, forced the German command to renounce the development of the main attack along this axis. The attack was shifted toward Prokhorovka.

Such a method of employing tank formations was the most economic one. The static fighting by tank formations from outfitted positions resulted in a significant reduction of losses both from the enemy's artillery fire, as well as from attacks by aircraft in coordination with the attacking tank groups. In reporting to the Supreme Commander-in-Chief on the 1st Tank Army's fight for the second defensive zone, the commander of the Voronezh Front, General Vatutin, reported: "On 7 July the enemy suffered enormous losses and enjoyed almost no success. We lost only about 50 tanks during the day's fighting."

Our tank formations suffered the greatest losses as a result of meeting counterattacks, which they undertook against the superior forces of the Germans' attacking tanks. Characteristic of this are the actions on 6 July of the 16th Tank Corps' 107th and 164th tank brigades of the Central Front. On this day the brigades carried out a meeting counterstroke against an attacking enemy tank group, during the course of which they lost more equipment than in all the remaining days of the battle.

The tank formations (in cooperation with the combined-arms formations) fought for the defensive lines by means of combining the fire from tanks buried in the ground with the maneuver of units from the rear for the destruction of the enemy's tank groups that had broken through. Such, for example, was the fighting by the 1st Tank Army's 3rd Mechanized Corps on 7 July in the Syrtsev—Pokrovka—Verkhopen'e area. The corps' units employed a mobile defense, making wide use of ambushes; they held the attack by the Germans' main tank group throughout the day along the area of the Oboyan' road; the enemy managed to advance that day only 5-7 kilometers. The 6th Tank Corps' 112th Tank Brigade, which had been transferred to the commander of the 3rd Mechanized Corps, successfully attacked the Germans tank group that had broken through in the area of height 230.1 (1.5-2 kilometers north of Syrtsev) and destroyed up to 15 tanks. With this it held up the enemy's further advanced toward Verkhopen'e for a considerable time.

Infantry

Despite the abundance of modern equipment employed during the Battle of Kursk, one can state that modern infantry, equipped with anti-tank weapons and coordinating with the other combat arms, is in a condition to successfully fight attacking enemy tanks, even under conditions of the latter's massed employment. The infantry's chief task in the defense is fighting the attacker's infantry echelons and cutting them off from the tanks that have broken through into the defensive depth. A necessary condition for the successful employment of infantry in the modern defensive operation is its ability to bravely (by completely suppressing feelings of "tankophobia") battle the enemy tanks by employing all types of weapons.

These demands were met in the Battle of Kursk as a result of the skillful organization of combat training during the period preceding the German offensive (April-June 1943).

As a result of the inevitable losses that the infantry suffers, the factor of "mutual replaceability" acquires particular significance. A large part of the infantrymen must know how to employ several types of weapons systems available to it in battle. Both *fronts* resolved this problem satisfactorily.

Correctly employed infantry, making broad use of trenches and skillfully maneuvering, even under the most difficult battle conditions against massed tank and air attacks, can maintain its combat capability over an extended period. Not one of the Central and Voronezh fronts' rifle division lost its combat capability during the defensive battle. This is supported by the fact that in the subsequent offensive battles all the divisions took part without any kind of extended break.

Even the rifle divisions of the first army echelon, which received the brunt of the enemy attack by tank masses, lost during the entire period of the defensive battle no more than 50-60 percent of their personnel. For example, the 6th Guards Army's 52nd Guards Rifle Division, which was defending along the axis of the SS Panzer Corps' main attack and which was continually involved in fighting, lost during the 5-23 July period 4,085 men. The 6th Guards Army's 90th Guards Rifle Division, which was involved in extremely heavy fighting, lost during the same period 4,479 men. The losses of the 92nd Guards Rifle Division of the 35th Guards Rifle Corps, against which the Germans' III Panzer Corps was directed on 8 July in the Bol'shaya Igumenka—Myasoedovo area, were approximately the same: its losses in the defensive fighting of 5-18 July were 4,560 men. The losses of the 7th Guards Army's 81st Guards Rifle Division, which was defending Staryi Gorod and which repelled massed German attacks from the Mikhailovka bridgehead, were almost the same by 18 July—4,300 men.

Engineering troops

The engineering troops did a colossal amount of work in preparing the defense of the Kursk salient. The broad employment of mobile sapper anti-tank reserves is typical and instructive in employing engineering troops in a defensive battle. Modern defense, which is designed for fighting major enemy tank groups of forces, for the most part, cannot securely cover beforehand all the possible attack axes by enemy tanks in the defensive depth with anti-tank obstacles. Under these conditions, the skillfully organized maneuver of obstacle equipment acquires great significance. In order to carry out this work in all the formations in both *fronts*, special mobile reserves were created. Besides this, groups of minelayers were included in the mobile artillery anti-tank reserves.

The demand for special mobile reserves is typified by the following comparison: if by the beginning of the defensive battle, six engineering companies were used in the 13th Army to form such reserves, then during the battle three engineering battalions were used for the same purposes.

Based on the experience of the defensive battle under consideration, one may conclude that each army should have a mobile reserve for maneuvering obstacles, consisting of a subunit of sappers and minelayers and 20 motor vehicles, with 2,500 anti-tank mines; in a rifle corps such a reserve might consist of ten sappers, with ten motor vehicles and 1,000 mines; a division may limit itself to a group of sappers, 3-5 motor vehicles, and 500-600 anti-tank mines; a rifle regiment's mobile reserve wil include 1-2 motor vehicles and 300-400 mines.

Aviation

The Battle of Kursk was also characterized by the participation of a large number of aircraft and their intensive employment. In all, 4,303 aircraft (2,453 Soviet and 1,850 enemy aircraft) operated in the battle on both sides, which carried out 44,313 sorties (26,020 Soviet and 18,293 enemy sorties). Our aviation engaged in 1,022 air battles and shot down more than 1,000 enemy planes.

A typical feature of the battle was the concentration of aviation efforts almost exclusively over the battlefield. For example, our aviation carried out 13,539 plane attacks (6,484 during the day and 7,055 at night) against the enemy forces located directly on the battlefield, while at the same time only 139 night aircraft attacks were made against the enemy's communications. 80 percent of the enemy's air sorties were limited to the same area of the battlefield.

Both sides waged a fierce battle for air superiority. Our aviation carried out 11,380 sorties for the purpose of gaining air superiority. However, air superiority was achieved by the Central Front's aviation only on 7 July, and over the Voronezh Front still later—10 July, although the correlation of forces by the start of the battle was 1:3.1 in our favor. This is explained by the fact that in the first days' fighting both *fronts'* fighter aviation was limited to the passive tasks of covering our troops, while at the same time the enemy's aviation employed active methods of fighting.

In order to achieve air superiority, fighter aviation must shift its activities from the very start of the battle to the enemy's territory; broadly employ the method of free searching, and the blockading and destruction of the enemy's planes on their airfields. Fighter aviation, operating over the battlefield in large groups, strives to fully clear the air of enemy planes. After our aviation adopted these methods the enemy air force suffered serious losses and we gained air superiority.

Undoubtedly, a greater effect in foiling the enemy's offensive could have been achieved if our air efforts on the morning of 5 July (during the counterpreparation) had been directed at the suppression and destruction of the enemy's personnel and equipment in their jumping-off positions, as opposed to strikes against his airfields. However, by the beginning of our air attack, the enemy's aviation was already in the air.

One should note the high effectiveness of air operations employed for combating the enemy's tank groups. The greatest results were achieved from massed attacks against the enemy's tank groups by assault aircraft.

The assistance rendered by our aviation to the ground forces in defeating the attacking German groups of forces was enormous. The enemy's aviation suffered heavy losses during the battle, from which it could not recover for the duration of the entire period of the summer and fall campaigns.

Troop control

Our success in the defensive battle around Kursk was achieved, to a significant degree, thanks to the high quality of command and control at all levels. This quality was explained by the fact that a great deal of work had been carried out during the preparatory period.

During this period our command drew up a number of variations for the forthcoming operations. A number of command and staff games and staff rides were conducted against the background of the real situation. The command element at all levels, that took part in these exercises, became well acquainted with the terrain and the routes along the likely axes of their units' (formations') operations, established personal contact and mutual understanding with the representatives of the various combat arms, as well as neighboring units and formations.

During the preparation for the operation, a great deal of attention was devoted to providing the troops with reliable communications, as well as the inculcation of specialized command and control methods at all levels.

The *front* commander exercised command and control from his main command post. During the operation's most important times the commander's representatives were dispatched to the most important sectors of the front. For example, the member of the military council, General N.S. Khrushchev, was with the 6th Guards Army during the fighting along the Oboyan' axis; the *front's* chief of staff, Guards Lieutenant General S.P. Ivanov[12] was with the 69th Army during the fierce fighting with the German group of forces south of Prokhorovka. During the intensive fighting of 11-12 July the *Stavka's* representative, chief of the Red Army General Staff and Marshal of the Soviet Union A.M. Vasilevskii, who was with the Voronezh Front, traveled to the Prokhorovka axis.

12 Editor's note. Semyon Pavlovich Ivanov (1907-93) joined the Red Army in 1926. During the Great Patriotic War he served as chief of staff in various armies and *fronts*, including that of the Voronezh Front during the Battle of Kursk. He also served as chief of staff of the high command of Soviet forces in the Far East during the war with Japan. Following the war, Ivanov served as chief of staff of Soviet occupation forces in Germany and of a number of military districts.

The Voronezh Front's headquarters had 16 radio sets, mounted on motor vehicles, for maintaining continuous contact with those representatives who made trips to the troops. These mobile radio sets played a very large role.

The experience of the Voronezh Front shows that radio communications, organized according to the axis principle, and not by network, better provided for unbroken communications with the armies. Besides this, all of the tank corps in the *front* reserves, including those that were assigned to the armies, had direct radio communications with the *front* headquarters; the latter's radio center had special receivers that worked on the tank corps' wavelengths. As a result, the *front* command received information from them simultaneously with the armies; if necessary; it could actively and rapidly make the necessary corrections, based upon the demands of the overall situation along the front.

The army commanders correctly organized the work of their headquarters. When going out to the field, they systematically informed their headquarters about the situation and the orders issued by them on the spot. Well organized communications enabled the *front* and army commanders to rapidly receive the necessary information from the front and, rapidly react accordingly to all changes in the situation, while it also enabled us to carry out the necessary maneuver of reserves in a timely manner.

The commanders of those formations in the *front* reserve received systematic information from *front* headquarters on the situation; preliminary orders as to the likely employment of the reserves were issued in a timely manner. As a result, the commanders of the reserve formations could get in touch in time with the troop commander in whose zone they were slated to operate and to dispatch to that area his responsible representatives and establish technical communications with them.

As a general rule, the *front* commanders issued the majority of their orders over high-frequency communications, employing coded charts and prearranged message codes; the orders thus transmitted were then duplicated in code by telegraph or dispatched through communications officers.

A previously drawn up plan for the defensive battle, which calls for several variations of the troops' likely actions is necessary and useful from several points of view: for training troops, outfitting the defensive lines, the creation of reserve groupings, the deployment of communications, and the study and outfitting of march routes. But because in the course of the battle the real situation may not completely coincide with that which was imagined when drawing up the operational plan, its desirable to have, aside from the plan's main variations, a series of additional ones—foreseeing the possibility of maneuvering reserves along several axes.

Any, even the most insignificant, change of mission for major formations not foreseen by the plan, requires a significant amount of time for preparing the troops for carrying out the new tasks. For example, on 6 July the Central Front's 19th Tank Corps had its mission changed. Instead of operating along the Molotychi—Yasenok line, as called for by the defensive plan, the corps was to attack in the direction of Samodurovka. This led to a situation in which the formation could only set out to fulfill its mission ten hours late. Unforeseen obstacles were encountered; time was required not only for organizing the attack, but most of all, for clearing passages in the minefields that were covering the second defensive zone; because the corps' attack along this axis had not been foreseen, they had naturally not prepared passages through the minefields beforehand.

During the defensive battle part of the defender's forces will fall back from their forward positions and part of the reserves will be brought up from the depth, while other measures will be carried out as well. As a result, the concentration of a number of different units and formations will take place along one or another lines, or along individual sectors. This is a common and natural phenomenon for a defensive battle. For the purpose of the best coordination of the operations of all the formations and units slated for operations along the given axis or sector of the front, it is expedient to unite their command and control in the person of one senior commander. In this case, if we are not able, according to the situation, to unite them by order of the senior commander, the senior commander from among the formation commanders present along the particular sector of the front carries out this unification on his personal initiative.

There were instances when, under enemy pressure, the rifle and tank formations defending along one or another sector, fell back in an uncoordinated fashion, even along diverging axes. For example, during the night of 6-7 July the 5th Guards Tank Corps fell back from the line Yakovlevo—Luchki to the northeast to the Belenikhino area, while the 51st Guards Rifle Division fell back from the same line to the northwest to the Sukho-Solotino area. The commander of the 6th Tank Corps, as the result of incorrect and uncoordinated actions, pulled back his 10th Mechanized Brigade on the night of 10-11 July from the Berezovka area to the Noven'koe area, thus exposing the flank of the 90th Guards Rifle Division, which was half-surrounded as a result.

In some cases the battle plan was disrupted by the imprecise fulfillment of the senior command's directives. For example, as a result of the untimely transfer to the 6th Guards Army of the 184th and 219th rifle divisions by the commander of the 40th Army, and the 309th Rifle Division by the commander of the 1st Tank Army, the first two divisions were unable to take part in the 6th Guards Army's attack on 12 July, and when they arrived at their designated line they were thrown into the battle from the march, without preliminary preparation.

Coordination between the ground forces and our aviation was not always accomplished in a sufficiently precise manner. Sometimes the aviation was late in carrying out strikes or carried out attacks in a place not required by the ground forces. The reason for this was the insufficiently precise working of communications between the air representative, located with the combined-arms formation's headquarters, and the air force command.

By the start of the battle the 2nd Air Army had not delegated representatives to the headquarters of the combined-arms formations and the command and control of the air formations was exercised directly from the army headquarters; that is, completely divorced from the ground forces. On 9-10 July these representatives were delegated to the 1st and 5th Guards tank armies, but without communications equipment; this transformed them into simple reports to the army commander regarding the situation on the ground. This situation was subsequently righted.

The battle's experience showed that it's necessary to devote even more attention to the problem of the ground forces marking the front line. The obscuring of the battlefield with smoke and dust requires more reliable equipment for designating one's forces. It's obvious that such equipment can only be rockets—identification panels cannot be seen through the dust and smoke in the air, particularly from high-speed aircraft.

Conclusions

The defensive battle around Kursk, like the Battle of Stalingrad, will enter the treasure house of the history of military art and the history of the Great Patriotic War as one of the most important battles of the modern age. This battle, like the Battle of Stalingrad, had an enormous significance on the entire subsequent course of the Great Patriotic War. At the same time it was a new masterpiece of Stalinist strategic skill, new and brilliant evidence of the power, heroism and combat skill of the Red Army.

As a result of the successful completion of the battle by our forces, the German-Fascist high command's plan, which consisted of seizing Kursk and a new campaign against Moscow, collapsed. The German command, which dreamed of "getting revenge for Stalingrad," prepared to realize this plan for three months.

The Battle of Kursk eliminated the German command's final attempt to once again seize the strategic initiative, which had been won by the Red Army in the fighting at Stalingrad. The Germans not only could not manage to seize the strategic initiative, but as a result of the defeat of their Ninth and Fourth Panzer armies and the extremely heavy losses they endured, extremely favorable conditions were created for the Red Army's subsequent brilliant offensive operations in Ukraine in the summer and fall of 1943.

If in the battles of Leningrad, Smolensk, Kiev, and Odessa the plan for a lightning war collapsed, and during the Battle of Moscow the entire campaign plan for the war's first year came a cropper, and if in the Battle of Stalingrad the Germans' offensive strategy suffered a decisive defeat, then in the Battle of Kursk it suffered a final collapse.

As a result of the defeat at Kursk the German command was forced to go over to the strategic defense along the entire length of the Soviet-German front. In August 1943 the authors of the German offensive strategy had already begun to sing about an "elastic defense," about withdrawing in order to shorten the front, about "invincible eastern walls," and about the significance of space.

The rout of the German armies at Kursk was the beginning stage of the Red Army's new offensive operations, which subsequently unfolded throughout the entire summer, fall and winter of 1943 and which continued to the end of the war. As a result of these operations, the Red Army's forces cleared the Germans out of all Ukraine and a significant part of Belorussia. The Red Army's powerful blows threw back the German aggressors far to the west; the Red Army crossed the Soviet Union's state boundary and successfully carried the struggle with the German aggressors to the latter's own territory.

As a result of the Red Army's powerful blows in the summer of 1943 the Germans' defensive strategy suffered a defeat. In the Battle of Kursk the myth about our "seasonal" strategy was finally buried. The Red Army proved that it knows how to conduct victorious operations at any time of year. The Germans also proved incapable of achieving victory, whether attacking in the summer or winter.

In the defensive fighting around Kursk, just as during the battles of Moscow and Stalingrad, the mission of fighting the attacking enemy's major forces was brilliantly resolved. The main Stalinist principle of conducting a defensive operation—to exhaust, halt and rout—to an even greater extent than at Moscow and Stalingrad, justified itself during the Battle of Kursk. The fierce ten-day defensive battle completely swallowed up the offensive energy of the largest German groups of forces—Orel and Belgorod—Khar'kov. The drained German armies were forced to go over to the defense along all sectors of the front, and then, under the powerful and continuously increasing blows of the Red Army, to hurriedly retreat. Our forces' combat activities during this period were defined by the instructions of the Supreme Commander-in-Chief: "To exhaust the enemy along the prepared lines and prevent his breakthrough until we begin our active operations along the Western, Bryansk and other fronts."

The glorious traditions of the defense of Stalingrad once again came to life in the fighting for Kursk. The bearers of these traditions were the immediate participants of the Stalingrad battles, who so heroically and so skillfully and with self-sacrifice repelled the enemy's attack around Kursk. These were the glorious soldiers and officers of the 5th, 6th and 7th guards armies and the 2nd Tatsinskaya, 5th Stalingrad tank and 5th Zimovniki Mechanized corps.

Commanders of the Stalinist school, marshals of the Soviet Union Zhukov and Vasilevskii, army generals Vatutin and Rokossovskii, and other Red Army generals, were once again the talented executors of the high command's plan during the Battle of Kursk, as had been the case during the Battle of Stalingrad.

Once again the entire world was completely convinced of the defective nature of the German command's strategy. Its adventurous nature, the ignoring of a sober evaluation of the correlation of forces, and its failure to take into account its real capabilities was once again confirmed. The enemy continued to stand on his former fallacious position, overestimating its own forces and underestimating the Red Army's power and degree of resistance, as well as the skill of its commanders. Under the conditions of the modern battle the superiority of the Red Army's flexible maneuver tactics over the hackneyed tactics of the German forces, the power of Soviet combat equipment and its superiority over the enemy's equipment was once again demonstrated.

The defensive fighting around Kursk furnished extremely rich and valuable material, both for preparing the modern defense and command and control, as well as in the area of employing the various combat arms and the organization of coordination between them. The experience of this grandiose battle should be fully and in detail studied by the Red Army's entire command element.

BOOK TWO

THE DEFEAT OF THE GERMANS' OREL AND BELGOROD—KHAR'KOV GROUPS OF FORCES (JULY-AUGUST 1943)

PART ONE

THE DEFEAT OF THE GERMANS' OREL GROUP OF FORCES

The *Stavka* of the Supreme High Command, as early as the organization and planning of the defense of the Kursk salient in March 1943, was looking forward to going over to a general offensive by the forces of the Western Front's left wing, and the Bryansk and Central fronts, for the purpose of defeating the enemy group of forces operating along the Orel salient.

By 12 July, in connection with the collapse of the Germans' offensive on Kursk, a situation arose that favored such an offensive against the Orel group of forces—both that part that had unsuccessfully attempted to break through to Kursk, and that which was occupying defensive positions along the Bryansk Front's sector and that of the Western Front's left flank.

The offensive by the Western, Bryansk and Central fronts, which concluded in the defeat of the Germans' Orel group of forces and the elimination of the Orel strategic salient, took place in the period from 12 July to 18 August 1943.

Combat operations unfolded along a broad territory, bordered on the north by the line Plavsk—Belev—Zhizdra; from the south by the line Livny—Maloarkhangel'sk—Sevsk; from the east by the line Plavsk—Novosil'—Maloarkhangel'sk, and; from the west by the line of the Bolva and Desna rivers. The overall extent of this territory was 42,000 square kilometers.

A Description of the Orel Salient

A military-geographical description

The territory of the Germans' Orel strategic salient is very convenient for defense and made offensive operations extremely difficult. The rivers, the majority of which flow from south to north (Oka, Zusha, Neruch', Oleshnya, Optukha, Nugr', Vytebet', and Resseta) and north to south (Bolva and Desna), were a serious natural barrier against our forces' offensive to the west. The enemy broadly employed these rivers for organizing defensive lines and switch positions. Smaller rivers and streams (Fomina, Mashok, Nepolod', Ors, Mokhovitsa, Tskan', Orlik, Revna, and others) crossed the area of combat operations and favored the conduct of a defense and made an offensive by the Red Army's units difficult. The forward edge of the enemy's main defense zone generally ran along the banks of the Zhizdra, Oka, Zusha, and Neruch rivers. Our forces had to force these rivers in order to attack the main defensive zone.

The area's topography is slightly hilly and cut by a large number of gullies to a depth of up to 70 meters.

The southeastern part of the area as far as the Belev—Khotinets—Seredina Buda line has no forests; to the west and southwest of Orel small outcroppings of woods are encountered. This part of the area is the hilliest and is cut by a large number of gullies.

The area's northwestern part, on the other hand, is more level and almost completely covered with large wooded areas (the eastern half of the Bryansk woods) and quite swampy. In this part of the area the maneuver by our major combined-arms formations, tanks and artillery was made very difficult. The troops often had to operate along limited areas and hewed to the roads, of which there were extremely few in this area and which did not meet the demands of the attackers.

Large wooded areas, which were located northwest of Karachev and further to the west in the Bryansk area, created good conditions for the broad unfolding of partisan activities in the enemy's rear.

The area of combat operations, especially in its southeastern part, has thickly populated inhabited areas. Of these the largest are Orel, Bolkhov, Mtsensk, Karachev, Kromy, Khotynets, Zhizdra, Khvastovichi, Zikeevo, and Dmitrovsk-Orlovskii. These areas were important road and railroad junctions and served as the main centers of resistance in the German defensive system. The towns of Orel, Bolkhov, Mtsensk, Khotynets, Karachev, and Kromy, upon which the defense of the entire Orel salient was based, were especially important. The significance of these towns for the defense was increased in that they were located along rivers or along heights that commanded the area and offered the enemy significant advantages in organizing a defense.

The Bryansk—Orel railroad, from which branched the lines Bryansk—Zikeevo, Bryansk—Tereben', Orel—Mtsensk, Orel—Zalegosh', Orel—Kursk, and Bryansk—Navlya were a very important rail artery for the enemy. Of the paved roads, the most important were the Bryansk—Orel, Bolkhov—Orel—Kromy, and Orel—Mtsensk roads. The enemy also made use of convenient dirt roads that branched in various directions from such junctions as Orel, Bolkhov, Karachev, Kromy, Zhizdra, Zikeevo, Khvastovichi, Khotynets, Znamenskoe, Protasovo, Mokhovoe, Zmievka, Shablykino, and others. The thick road network in the area of combat operations enabled the German forces to widely maneuver on the battlefield and to supply their forces with food and munitions without interruption.

By the start of the offensive our forces had at their disposal only one lateral railroad: Tula—Yelets, and the branch lines Tula—Kozel'sk, Tula—Mtsensk, Volovo—Belev, and Yelets—Verkhov'e, as well as the Tula—Mtsensk automobile road. The limited road network hampered our forces' maneuver and made the work of the rear organs very difficult.

A Description of the German Defense

The forces of the Western Front's left wing and those of the Bryansk Front were faced with the enemy's well-fortified Orel strategic salient. This salient was very important in the German defensive system and served as the chief base for preparing an offensive on Moscow.

In the zone of the Western Front's left wing and the Bryansk Front's right wing and center as far as Vyazhi inclusively, the construction of a defensive line by the Germans had begun in August 1942, that is, nearly a year before the start of our offensive, while to the south, facing the Bryansk Front's left wing as far as the boundary line with the Central Front, construction had begun at the end of March 1943.

The enemy, while attaching great importance to the Orel salient, had created a firm defense here, with a developed system of field fortifications and had covered them with engineering obstacles. All the approaches to the enemy's positions were enfiladed by frontal, oblique and flanking multi-level fire. In the defensive depth the terrain had been well prepared for the maneuver of tanks and large troop formations and, in case of a breakthrough of the forward edge by our forces, it enabled the enemy to launch rapid and powerful counterstrokes. The majority of inhabited locales, which were located along the forward edge and road junctions in the depth, had been prepared by the Germans for stout perimeter defense. The enemy had created in his defensive system several pockets of fire, in case of a breakthrough by our forces, and had girded them with powerful strong points.

The main resistance zone consisted of well fortified strong points and centers of resistance, which had been configured for perimeter defense and connected with each other by a developed system of trenches and communications trenches. For example, the strong point in the Dudino area was built on powerfully fortified heights, which commanded the surrounding terrain, and which were thoroughly cut by trenches, the system of which included durable overhead covers, wooden and earth fortifications and all-metal machine gun firing points ("crabs"). All the approaches to the strong points were covered by a thick network of engineering obstacles and powerful artillery and machine gun fire. The defensive depth was 5-7 kilometers, and reached nine kilometers along some sectors.

The spaces between the strong points were covered by individual firing points. The first defensive zone consisted of three trenches, in which overhead covers and firing platforms for machine guns were located at a distance of 50-100 meters from each other. A part of the firing platforms had been advanced forward by 5-10 meters for conducting flanking fire. There were individual skirmisher's trenches every 5-6 meters in the trenches. A large number of reserve firing positions had been prepared in the trenches and strong points. Armored covers were encountered along a number of sectors.

There were 1-2 layers of barbed wire obstacles in front of the enemy trenches, mostly mobile (*cheval de frise*, a fence on metal stakes, etc.), and light and sound signals had been hung on the wire. The wire obstacles had been heavily mined and were saturated with all sorts of booby traps—air bombs and hand grenades, etc. Minefields from anti-tank and anti-personnel mines, which as a rule, were covered by machine gun and mortar fire, had been constructed between the wire obstacles and the first trench line, as well as along a number of sectors in the defensive depth. The depth of the mining reached ten kilometers in the rear from the forward edge of the defense. In places the enemy had laid hard-to-see obstacles between the wire obstacles and the first trench line.

The Germans had built solid barriers out of logs along the forested defensive sectors, 2-2.5 meters high and 2-4 meters wide. A clearing no less than 200 meters was usually made in front of these barriers and a wire fence set up. The edges of woods and groves were ringed with wire. Parapets out of logs and earth were erected along swampy sectors. In the main, the defense in the wooded areas and swampy sectors was organized just as in open terrain, with the difference that is was less deep and had a more developed obstacle system.

Intermediate and rear defensive lines had been prepared in the defensive depth, as well as switch positions, which had been outfitted like the main defensive zone. In the majority of cases, these lines were not occupied. The enemy had such lines and positions in the following areas:

- along the Oka River from Shashkino as far as Paslovo, and then along the Optukha River as far as Zmievka;
- along the Oka and Kroma rivers along the Paslovo—Orel—Kromy—Koros'kovo sector;
- along the Neruch' River from Vasil'evka to Pozdeevo;
- along the Nugr' River along the Krutogor'e—Znamenskoe sector;
- along the Mashok River from Nogaya to its mouth;
- along the Glinnaya—Dubna—Sorokino line;
- along the Shubnik—Khat'kovo—Ul'yanovo line, and;
- along the Resseta and Obel'na rivers, from Khat'kovo to Lyada; then to the east and south of Karachev, south and east of Goshcha, and; then along the Revna River to its confluence with the Desna.

The enemy was also able to broadly employ the line of the Vytebet', Bolva and Desna rivers for defensive lines and for organizing resistance in the depth of the Orel salient. By the start of the operation the Germans still did not have positions outfitted along these rivers.

The previously prepared defensive lines and the large number of rivers in the defensive depth were a serious obstacle to our forces' offensive.

Thus the Germans, employing favorable terrain conditions for organizing the defense and widely employing the local population for work, had created a firm and deeply echeloned defense, the breakthrough of which demanded a great intensity of effort from our troops and the wide employment of artillery, tanks and aviation in the offensive.

The Disposition of the Enemy's Forces by 12 July 1943

The Germans had created a powerful group of forces to defend the Orel salient. The German command, even during the intense fighting around Kursk, continued to hold large forces in front of the Western Front's left wing and in front of the Bryansk Front. It obviously feared our offensive against the Orel salient, in particular an attack from the northeast against the flank of the Orel—Bryansk group of forces.

Facing the Western Front's 10th Army north and west of the town of Kirov, units of the enemy Fourth Army's LVI Panzer Corps (131st and 321st infantry divisions, and others), as well as the German Second Panzer Army's 339th Infantry Division were defending.[1]

The units of the Western Front's left wing and the Bryansk Front were faced by the defending forces of the Second Panzer Army, which included the following:

110th Infantry Division: excluding Zaprudnoe—Paliki;
296th Infantry Division: excluding Paliki—Yasenok;
134th Infantry Division: excluding Yasenok—Rechitsa;
211th Infantry Division: excluding Rechitsa—Glinnaya;
293rd Infantry Division: excluding Glinnaya—excluding Gos'kova;
25th Motorized Division: Gos'kova—excluding Ulanova;
208th Infantry Division: Ulanova—Tolkachevo;
The 221st Security Division's 350th Infantry Regiment, which was subordinated to the 112th Infantry Division: excluding Tolkachevo—excluding Shashkino;
34th Infantry Division: Shashkino—Yadrino;
56th Infantry Division: excluding Yadrino—excluding Vyazhi, and;
206th Infantry Division: Vyazhi—Vasil'evka.

The 299th Infantry Division was defending along the boundary of the Bryansk and Central fronts. Further to the southwest and west units of the enemy's Ninth Army—292nd, 383rd, 216th, 78th, 86th, 31st, 7th, 258th, 102nd, 72nd, 45th, 137th, 251st, and 36th infantry divisions, the 18th, 9th and 2nd panzer divisions, and four *jaeger* battalions were operating.

The enemy's operational reserves were located as follows: the 5th Panzer Division in the Dudorovskii—Nogaya—Ul'yanovo area; units of the 12th Panzer and 112th Infantry divisions in the Bolkhov area; part of the 8th Panzer Division's forces, which was being transferred from the Vitebsk area, was moving through Bryansk, and; the Hungarian 120th and 1st security divisions were carrying out rear security in the areas of Kholmy and Krolevets. The 36th Infantry Division was concentrating in the area west of Zmievka, and the 292nd Infantry Division east of Tagino.

Units of the Hungarian VIII Army Corps (102nd, 105th and 108th infantry divisions, of which the 105th was in the Nezhin area) were operating against partisans in the Starodub—Novozybkov area. The 221st Security Division was in the Trubchevsk area and to the west.

The 707th Infantry Division was in the area northwest of Bryansk.

Besides this, our intelligence established the presence of the following forces: up to a division in the Lyudinovo—Dyat'kov area; small enemy troop concentrations in the areas of Khvastovichi and Karachev.

The enemy's main operational reserves, which were located in the Lyudinovo—Zhukovka—Bryansk and Ul'yanovo—Bolkhov areas, were covering the flanks and communications of the Orel group of forces from the north. The German command, fearing our forces' offensive from the north, as well as having information regarding the concentration of large forces along the left wing

1 General Schmidt commanded the Second Panzer Army up to 14 July, and from that day the command of the Ninth and Second Panzer armies was united under General Model. The Second Panzer Army included the LV Army Corps (339th, 110th, 296th, and 134th infantry divisions), the LIII Army Corps (211th, 293rd, 112th, and 208th infantry, and 25th Motorized divisions), and the XXXV Army Corps (34th, 56th, 262nd, and 299th infantry divisions).

of the Western Front, had grouped its reserves in order to occupy a flanking position in relation to the probable direction of the 50th and 11th Guards armies' offensive. In this manner, the Germans sought, in the event our forces' successful breakthrough, to be able to eliminate the breakthrough by powerful attacks along the bases of the wedge, and to restore the defense and cut off and destroy our forces that had penetrated into the depth of their defense.

The enemy's tactical reserves, which consisted, as a rule, of one battalion (only rarely, a weakened regiment) per division, were located 3-10 kilometers from the forward edge of the defense.

The German command, expecting our attack from the north, created their densest group of forces here.

Thus 27 German divisions were operating in the first line opposite the Western Front's left wing, and the Bryansk and Central fronts. Up to 13 divisions (of these, four were engaged in fighting the partisans and protecting the rear and communications) were in the reserve. The main reserves (more than six divisions) were concentrated against the Western Front's left flank. Thus even during the intensive fighting along the Belgorod—Kursk axis the enemy continued to hold no less than 40 divisions along the Orel salient.[2]

2 In computing the enemy's forces, individual units operating in the area of the Orel salient were counted. Of the above-enumerated Hungarian units, only three divisions (102nd and 108th infantry and the 201st Security divisions), which were directly securing the Orel salient's rear, were included in the total. The further removed Hungarian 105th Infantry and 1st Security divisions were not counted.

1

The Planning and Preparation of the Offensive Operation

The Operation's General Plan

In the summer of 1943, when the Germans were preparing for their latest general offensive in the Kursk area, the *Stavka* of the Supreme High Command, while adopting measures to strengthen the defense of the Kursk salient, was simultaneously preparing our forces for a decisive offensive on Orel for the purpose of defeating the enemy group of forces concentrated there and eliminating the Orel strategic salient.

Taking advantage of the operationally favorable situation of our forces, the *Stavka* of the Supreme High Command planned to launch powerful concentric offensive with three *fronts* (Western, Bryansk and Central) in the general direction of Orel, in order to encircle the enemy's Orel group of forces, cut it up into parts and destroy it. In its final form, the operational plan for defeating this group of forces consisted of the following:

The Bryansk Front's forces were to launch two turning attacks: the first from the Novosil' area, outflanking Orel from the south; the second from the area northeast of Bolkhov in the general direction of Bolkhov, was to, in conjunction with the Western Front, eliminate the enemy's Bolkhov group of forces and then advance on Orel from the north.

The Western Front's left wing had the following tasks:

a) upon breaking through the enemy's defense southwest of Kozel'sk and defeating, together with the forces of the Bryansk Front's right wing, the Germans' Bolkhov group of forces, to develop the attack in the general direction of Uzkoe and Khotynets;
b) to defeat the enemy's forces covering Orel from the north and northwest and, upon deeply outflanking the enemy's Orel group of forces from the west, to destroy it together with the forces of the Bryansk Front.

Besides this, it was foreseen that the forces of the Central Front, following the elimination of the enemy's attempt to break through to Kursk from the north, would go over to the offensive in the general direction of Kromy.

In order to realize this major offensive, it was decided to create four powerful shock groups: one along the Western Front's left wing, in the 11th Guards Army's sector in the area southwest of Kozel'sk; another in the sector of the Bryansk Front's 61st Army, in the area northeast of Bolkhov, and a third along the boundary between the 3rd and 63rd armies, in the area of the town of Novosil'. The forces of the Central Front's right wing were to operate as the fourth shock group. According to the *Stavka's* instructions, the operation would be supported by three air armies (1st, 15th and 16th).[1]

1 The 1st Air Army was subordinated to the Western Front, the 15th to the Bryansk Front, and the 16th to the Central Front.

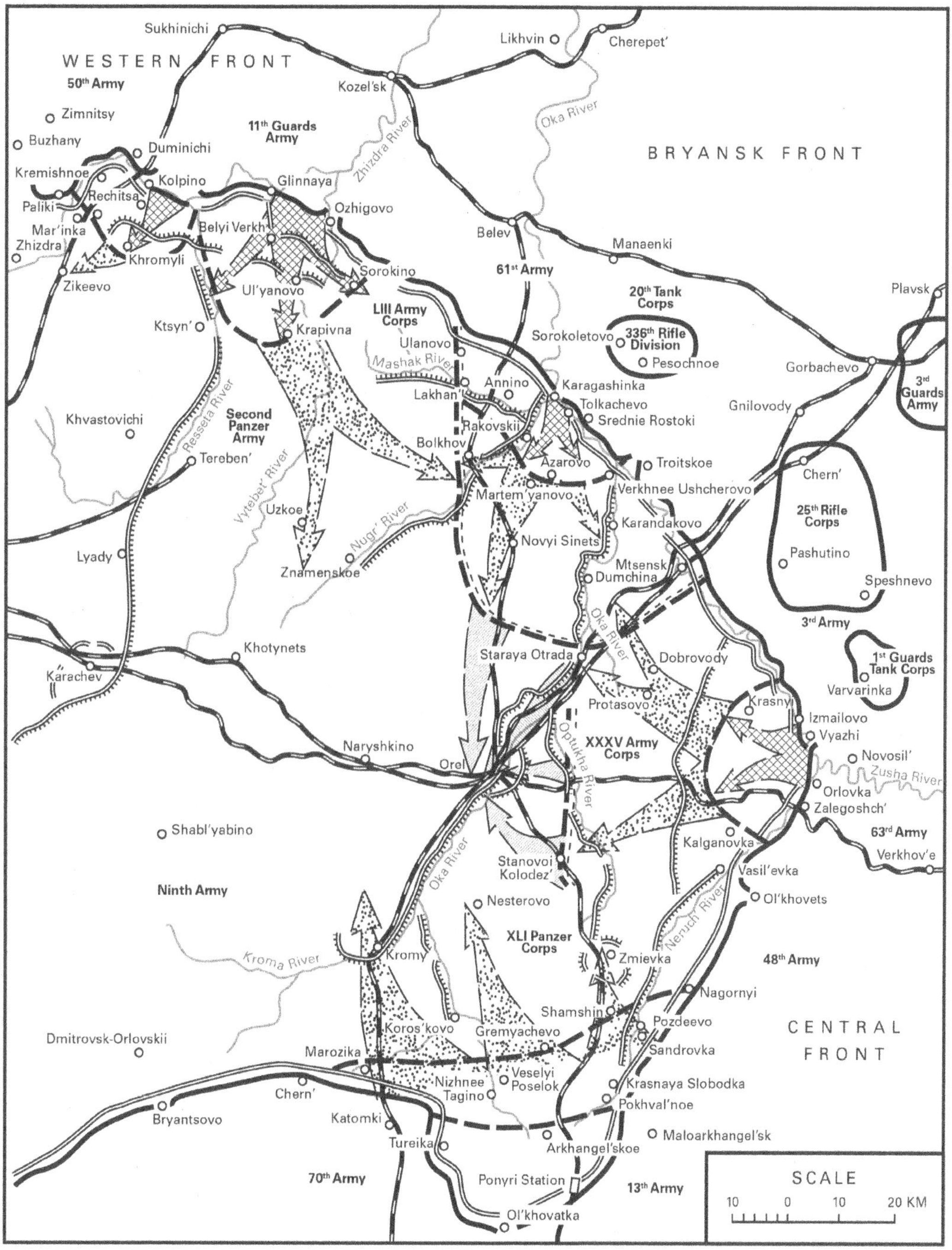

Map 4 The Plan of the Offensive Operation for Eliminating the Orel Salient.

The 11th Army, 3rd Guards and 4th tank armies, and the 2nd Guards Cavalry Corps were designated for developing the operation to defeat the Germans' Orel group of forces.

The reformed 11th Army, which it was planned to use for operations in the 11th Guards Army's zone, was concentrated in the Kaluga area; on 12 July this army was subordinated to the commander of the Western Front. The 4th Tank Army, which was also designated for operations in the 11th Guards Army's zone, was completing its formation in the Solnechnogorsk—Zagorsk—Kubinka area. On 18 July this army was also transferred to the Western Front; the 2nd Guards Cavalry Corps was completing its refitting in the Medyn' area and was to be transferred to the Western Front on 18 July.

The 3rd Guards Tank Army, which was designated for developing the operation's success along the Bryansk Front's left wing, was transferred to the Bryansk Front on 14 July, and having completed is formation in the Plavsk area, left for the area of the town of Novosil'.

The *Front* Commanders' Decisions for the Offensive

As early as April 1943 the *front* commanders began planning their offensive operations. They adopted their final decisions for the offensive in the beginning of July.

The Western Front commander's decision

By order of the commander of the Western Front, General (now Marshal of the Soviet Union) Sokolovskii,[2] the *front's* main shock group (11th Guards Army) was to break through the enemy's defense along the Glinnaya—Ozhigovo sector. Launching an attack in the general direction of Krapivna, on the operation's second day the shock group was to reach the line Resseta River (north of Ktsyn')—Krapivna—Sorokino. The army, in developing the attack subsequently to the southeast in the general direction of Bolkhov together with the Bryansk Front's 61st Army, was to encircle and destroy the Germans' Bolkhov group of forces. Moreover, the army was to attack to the south with part of its forces toward Uzkoe, in order to cut the Orel—Bryansk railroad and road in the Khotynets area, which was the main communications artery of the enemy's Orel group of forces.

The 50th Army (to the right of the 11th Guards Army) had the following tasks: a) to attack with part of its left-wing forces toward Zikeevo and to cut off the Germans' path of retreat to the west and southwest, and b) to secure the 11th Guards Army's flank against possible enemy counterstrokes from the west.

In launching the main attack, the 11th Guards Army, under the command of General Bagramyan,[3] had the following task: while defending a 22-kilometer front along the right flank with the forces of a single rifle division (217th), the main group along the left flank, consisting

2 Editor's note. Vasilii Danilovich Sokolovskii (1897-1968) joined the Red Army in 1918. During the Great Patriotic War he served in a variety of *front* staff positions and also commanded a *front*. During this period he served as chief of staff of the First Ukrainian Front. Following the war, Sokolovskii served as deputy commander and commander of the group of Soviet forces in Germany and the Soviet military administration in that country. He later served as chief of the General Staff.

3 Editor's note. Ivan Khristoforovich Bagramyan (1897-1982) served as a junior officer in the Russian imperial army during the First World War. He joined the Red Army in 1920 and served in a number of command, staff and teaching posts during the interwar period. During the Great Patriotic War he served chiefly in staff positions at the *front* level, before making the jump to army commander. He later commanded the First Baltic Front and the Samland operational group in East Prussia at the end of the war. Following the war, Bagramyan commanded a military district and held a number of positions within the central military apparatus.

of 11 rifle divisions,[4] two tank corps,[5] four tank brigades,[6] two tank breakthrough regiments, five artillery brigades, 38 artillery regiments, three mortar brigades, and ten mortar regiments, supported in the air by 150 planes from the 1st Air Army, were to break through the enemy's front along the 14-kilometer Glinnaya—Ozhigovo sector and, launching its main attack in the direction of Belyi Verkh, Ul'yanovo and Krapivna, by the close of the offensive's second day, was to reach the line Resseta River (from its mouth to the crossing near Ktsyn')—Vesniny—Krapivna—Sorokino. Subsequently, while covering with part of its forces along the Resseta River, the army was to develop the success with its main forces in the general direction of Bolkhov, for the purpose, in conjunction with the Bryansk Front's 61st Army, of encircling and destroying the enemy's Bolkhov group of forces.

The 11th Guards Army's combat formation was in three echelons. Six rifle divisions,[7] three tank brigades[8] and two tank breakthrough regiments were in the first echelon, supported by all the aviation and artillery (including the artillery of the second-echelon rifle divisions); four rifle divisions,[9] comprising the corps' second and third echelons, and one guards tank brigade,[10] were in the second echelon. The army's third echelon consisted of a breakthrough development echelon—the 5th and 1st tank corps and the 108th Rifle Division—were located in the army commander's reserve.

The 50th Army, under the command of General Boldin,[11] consisting of seven rifle divisions,[12] a tank brigade,[13] a tank regiment,[14] three artillery, one mortar and two guards mortar regiments, while securing the 11th Guards Army's right flank, was to launch an attack along its left flank, six kilometers in width, with the forces of the 212th and 324th rifle divisions, toward the Kolpino—marker 199.9 sector. These divisions' attack would be supported by the fire of three artillery regiments, artillery battalion, a mortar battalion, and two guards mortar regiments. The attack was to be in the direction of Budskie Vyselki, Mar'inskii and Khromyli. As a result of this attack, accomplished with the support of the 64th Rifle Division, which was to launch a supporting attack with part of its forces toward Kremishchnoe, it was planned to encircle and destroy units of the German 134th Infantry Division, and to subsequently attack toward Zikeevo and capture it.

In order to develop the attack on Zikeevo, it was planned to employ the 49th Rifle Division and the 233rd Tank Regiment, which were in the army commander's reserve.

The 38th Rifle Corps (along the 50th Army's right flank) had the following task: a) the 326th and 17th rifle divisions were to maintain their defense along the front excluding Zaprudnoe—marker 203 and support the army's shock group against a possible enemy counterstroke against

4 The 16th Guards Rifle Corps' 1st, 16th and 81st guards and 169th rifle divisions; the 8th Guards Rifle Corps' 11th, 26th and 83rd guards rifle divisions; the 36th Guards Rifle Corps' 5th, 18th and 84th guards rifle divisions, and; the 108th Rifle Division.

5 5th and 1st tank corps.

6 10th, 29th and 43rd guards, and 213th tank brigades.

7 169th Rifle, 16th, 31st, 11th, 83rd, and 18th guards rifle divisions.

8 29th and 43rd guards and 213th tank brigades.

9 1st, 26th, 84th, and 5th guards rifle divisions.

10 10th Guards Tank Brigade.

11 Editor's note. Ivan Vasil'evich Boldin (1892-1965) was drafted into the Russian imperial army in 1914 and joined the Red Army in 1919. During the Great Patriotic War he served as the deputy commander of two *fronts* and commanded armies, including the 50th Army during the Battle of Kursk. Following the war, Boldin commanded an army and military districts.

12 326th, 17th, 413th, 64th, 324th, 49th, and 212th rifle divisions.

13 196th Tank Brigade.

14 233rd Tank Regiment.

the flank in the direction of Bukan' and Zimnitsy; b) the 413th Rifle Division was to be ready to attack toward Mar'inka.

The Bryansk Front commander's decision

The commander of the Bryansk Front, General Popov,[15] decided to break through the enemy's defense along two axes: on the *front's* right wing with the forces of the 61st Army, and on the left, along the joint flanks of the 3rd and 63rd armies, and then, by committing powerful mobile groups into the battle along the breakthrough sectors, to encircle and destroy the enemy's group of forces defending east of Orel by concentric attacks from the north and south toward Orel. Upon taking the city, the forces of the Bryansk Front were to immediately and energetically develop the offensive to the west.

The 61st Army, commanded by General Belov,[16] and consisting of eight rifle divisions,[17] a tank corps,[18] a tank brigade,[19] a tank regiment,[20] two artillery divisions,[21] an anti-tank brigade, three independent artillery regiments, a self-propelled artillery regiment, a mortar brigade, a mortar regiment, a guards mortar division,[22] two guards mortar regiments, an independent guards mortar battalion, and two armored train battalions, was to launch its main attack with the forces of the 9th Guards Rifle Corps (12th, 76th and 77th guards rifle divisions) and the 68th Tank Brigade in the general direction of Tolkachevo and Bolkhov. The corps' attack would be supported by army' main artillery forces. The 9th Guards Rifle Corps had the assignment of reaching the line Rakovskii—Kishkino—Odnonitok—Martem'yanovo by the close of the offensive's first day, and then, having cut the Bolkhov—Orel road with part of its forces, to attack Bolkhov and capture it.

The 20th Tank Corps and the 336th Rifle Division were concentrated in the Sorokoletovo—Pesochnoe—Kuzmenki area to develop the breakthrough and the offensive in the direction of Novyi Sinets along the 9th Guards Rifle Corps' sector.

The widening of the breakthrough along the flanks and the securing of the shock group from the northwest and south was entrusted to the 97th and 110th rifle divisions, which were in the second echelon. The first was to attack in the direction of Kurasovo and Annino, with the task of reaching the Ulanova—Lakhan' line by the close of the operation's first day, together with the 356th Rifle Division; the second, while attacking in the direction of Kornilovo and Karandakovo, had the task of reaching the Azarovo—Verkhnee Ushcherevo line.

The 61st Army, having captured Bolkhov and secured it, was to subsequently attack as a mobile group on Orel from the north, for the purpose of getting in the rear of the enemy's Orel and

15 Editor's note. Markian Mikhailovich Popov (1902-69) joined the Red Army in 1920 and gradually rose through the ranks, despite a severe drinking problem. During the Great Patriotic War he commanded a number of *fronts* and armies, including the Bryansk Front during the Battle of Kursk, but never remained in the same command for long. Following the war, Popov commanded a number of military districts and served in the central army apparatus.

16 Editor's note. Pavel Alekseevich Belov (1897-1962) was drafted into the Russian imperial army in 1916 and joined the Red Army in 1918. During the Great Patriotic War he commanded a cavalry corps, and from 1942 until the end of the war the 61st Army. Following the war, Belov commanded a number of military districts.

17 The 46th Rifle Corps' 415th and 356th rifle divisions, the 9th Guards Rifle Corps' 12th, 76th and 77th guards rifle divisions, and the 336th, 97th and 110th rifle divisions.

18 20th Tank Corps.

19 68th Tank Brigade.

20 36th Tank Regiment.

21 The 7th Breakthrough Artillery Corps' 7th and 16th artillery divisions.

22 2nd Guards Mortar Division.

Mtsensk groups' path of retreat, and to support the 3rd and 63rd armies in completely routing the German's main forces defending the Orel salient.

Thus the 61st Army, along with the 11th Guards Army, had the task of encircling and destroying the enemy's Bolkhov group of forces; it was to subsequently develop the attack against the flank and rear of the German forces defending in the Orel area.

The army's combat formation was in two echelons: the first echelon contained three guards rifle divisions,[23] a tank brigade,[24] and reinforcements; in the second echelon were three rifle divisions,[25] one tank corps,[26] and a tank regiment,[27] was in the army commander's reserve.

The 3rd Army under General Gorbatov,[28] consisting of six rifle divisions,[29] two tanks regiments, a breakthrough artillery division,[30] six independent artillery regiments, two self-propelled artillery regiments, a mortar regiment, two guards mortar regiments, and two armored train battalions, was to make its main attack along the left flank with the forces of three rifle divisions[31] and two tank regiments, along with reinforcements. The army's mission was as follows: to force the Zusha River, to break through the enemy's defense along the 9-kilometer Izmailovo—Vyazhi sector and develop the offensive in the general direction of Staraya Otrada. With the troops' arrival at the line of the Lisitsa River, the army was to turn its main forces to the southwest, launch an attack toward Orel along the Oka River and, in conjunction with units of the 63rd Army, capture the city. Upon the shock group's reaching the line Dobrovody—Protasovo, part of its forces would turn north and, attacking toward Dumchina station, encircle and destroy the enemy's Mtsensk group of forces in conjunction with the 61st Army.

On the first day of the offensive the army was to break through the enemy's defense to a depth of 10-12 kilometers and reach the line Krasnyi—Zhelyabug, and on the second day reach the line Dobrovody—Titovo (24-26 kilometers), and on the third day reach the line of the Oka River (34-36 kilometers), cutting the Mtsensk—Orel paved road and railroad in the Staraya Otrada area.

The army's right wing—the 342nd, 283rd and 269th rifle divisions, reinforced by an anti-tank brigade and two armored train battalions—was to tie down the enemy's Mtsensk group of forces by means of a stubborn defense and active operations.

The army commander organized his shock group's combat formation in two echelons: the first echelon contained two rifle divisions (235th and 380th), with one rifle division (380th) in the second echelon. It was planned to commit the latter division into the battle on the morning of the offensive's second day. The first echelon was reinforced with two tank regiments, an anti-tank regiment, and two self-propelled artillery regiments.

The 20th Breakthrough Artillery Division and three independent artillery regiments supported the offensive.

23 12th, 76th and 77th guards rifle divisions.
24 68th Tank Brigade.
25 97th, 110th and 336th rifle divisions, with the latter short a regiment and a battalion.
26 20th Tank Corps.
27 36th Tank Regiment.
28 Editor's note. Aleksandr Vasil'evich Gorbatov (1891-1973) joined the Russian imperial army in 1912 and the Red Army in 1919. During the Great Patriotic War he commanded a division and a corps, and in 1943 he was appointed commander of the 3rd Army, a post he held to the end of the war. Following the war, Gorbatov commanded armies and a military district.
29 342nd, 283rd, 269th, 235th, 380th, and 308th rifle divisions.
30 20th Breakthrough Artillery Division.
31 235th, 380th and 308th rifle divisions.

The 25th Rifle Corps (362nd, 186th and 238th rifle divisions), which was designated for developing the success along the 3rd Army's sector, was located in the Chern'—Pashutino—Speshnevo area, in the *front* reserve.

General Kolpakchi's[32] 63rd Army, consisting of seven rifle divisions,[33] a guards tank corps,[34] four tank breakthrough regiments, two tank regiments, two artillery divisions,[35] a independent heavy cannon brigade, two anti-tank regiments, one guards mortar division,[36] one mortar and two guards mortar regiments, four self-propelled artillery regiments, and one armored train battalion, was given the following task: while closely cooperating with the 3rd Army's left wing, to break through the enemy's defense along the right flank along the 9-kilometer sector excluding Vyazhi—Orlovka and, while rapidly developing the offensive in the general direction of Stanovoi Kolodez', reach the line of the Orel—Zmievka paved road and railroad; subsequently, covering itself on the left with the Oka River, the army was to turn its main forces to the north and outflank Orel from the south.

Simultaneously, the army was to launch a supporting attack toward Orel from the east, from the line of the Optukha River.

The army's shock group consisted of six rifle divisions,[37] four tank breakthrough regiments, a tank regiment, the 1st Guards Don Tank Corps, four self-propelled artillery regiments, and two anti-tank and one mortar regiments. The 1st Guards Don Tank Corps was to be committed following the breakthrough into the depth of the enemy's tactical defense; developing the breakthrough's success, on the offensive's third day it was to reach the Stanovoi Kolodez' area.

It was planned that on the offensive's first day the army would reach the line Zhelyabug—Kalganovka (15-16 kilometers), on the second the line Mokhovoe—Neplyuevo—Kamenka (30-32 kilometers), and on the third day the line Yermolaevo—Pavlovo—Stanovoi Kolodez'—Novopetrovka (42-44 kilometers).

The combat formation of the army's shock group was organized in two echelons: the first echelon contained three rifle divisions (129th, 348th and 287th), with reinforcements; the second echelon contained three rifle divisions (5th, 397th and 250th, with the latter short one regiment) and the 1st Guards Don Tank Corps, which comprised the success development group. The operations of the shock group's first echelon would be supported by the 2nd Breakthrough Artillery Corps and the 15th Air Army's main forces, which were entrusted with the mission of securing the breakthrough of the enemy's defense along the 3rd and 63rd armies' adjoining flanks, having securely suppressed the enemy's centers of resistance and strong points in the Yevtekhov, Ivan', Matveevskii (four kilometers east of Khmelek), Progress, Malinovets, Khmelek, Setukha, and Kazar' areas.

Thus the 3rd and 63rd armies were to break through the enemy's defense along their adjoining flanks along an 18-kilometer front, and then, while energetically developing the success to the northwest and southwest, split the forces of the Germans' XXXV Army Corps and throw them back toward the flanks; the 3rd Army's right wing was to outflank the enemy's Mtsensk group of forces and, in conjunction with units of the 61st Army, encircle and destroy it; the 3rd and

32 Editor's note. Vladimir Yakovlevich Kolpakchi (1899-1961) was drafted into the Russian imperial army in 1916 and joined the Red Army in 1918. During the Great Patriotic War he served as chief of staff of an army and *front* and also commanded several armies, among them the 63rd during the Battle of Kursk. Following the war, Kolpakchi commanded military districts and armies.

33 129th, 348th, 287th, 250th, 41st, 5th, and 397th rifle divisions.

34 1st Guards Don Tank Corps.

35 The 2nd Breakthrough Artillery Corps' 13th and 15th artillery divisions.

36 3rd Guards Mortar Division.

37 129th, 348th, 187th, 5th, 397th, and 250th rifle divisions, with the latter short one regiment.

63rd armies' main forces were to destroy the German forces defending east of the Oka River and capture Orel.

The Central Front's commander's decision

In carrying out the *Stavka's* directive, the commander of the Central Front, General Rokossovskii, adopted his decision for the offensive on 12 July that is, following the completion of the battle's defensive stage.

In accordance with this decision, the *front's* right-flank armies (48th, 13th and 70th, supported by the 2nd Tank and 16th Air armies) were to first eliminate the enemy that had broken into our defenses, and then, developing the attack in the general direction of Kromy and then to the northwest, to outflank the Germans' Orel group of forces from the south and southwest and assist the forces of the Bryansk Front and the Western Front's left wing in destroying it.

In order to carry out this decision, the armies were given the following objectives:

The 48th Army, commanded by General Romanenko:[38] a) to hold the line along the right flank, and b) to attack the enemy with two rifle divisions along the Sandrovka—excluding Krasnaya Sloboda sector and, launching a blow in the direction of Shamshin, to reach by the close of 17 July the line Nagornyi—Shamshin, and to subsequently develop the success toward Zmievka.

The 13th Army, commanded by General Pukhov, consisting of the 15th and 29th rifle and the 17th and 18th guards rifle corps, was to attack on the morning of 15 July in the general direction of Gremyachevo, with the mission, in conjunction with the forces of the 48th and 70th armies, of destroying the opposing enemy and by the close of 17 July reach the line excluding Shamshin—Veselyi Poselok, and to subsequently develop the attack toward Nesterovo.

The 70th Army, commanded by General Galanin,[39] with the 19th Tank Corps, while firmly holding the line Katomki—Chern' with its left flank, with its right flank was to attack on the morning of 15 July in the general direction of Nizhnee Tagino, and by the close of 17 July the shock group's main forces were to reach the line Nizhnee Tagino—Morozikha and subsequently develop the attack toward Kromy.

Conclusions

Judging by the disposition of the forces and the location of the reserve, which had been created in accordance with the operational plan, it is clear that the Soviet command had prepared three powerful shock fists for breaking through the German defense and defeating the enemy's Orel group of forces: one on the Western Front's left flank and two in the Bryansk Front's zone.

The first and most powerful fist had been concentrated along the 11th Guards Army's left wing, where six rifle divisions, three tank brigades and two tank breakthrough regiments were in the first line along a 14-kilometer front. Behind them, in the army's second echelon, were four rifle divisions and a tank brigade, with two tank corps and a rifle division in reserve. The following forces had concentrated in the depth along this axis: Lieutenant General Fedyuninskii's[40] 11th Army,

38 Editor's note. Prokofii Longvinovich Romanenko (1897-1949) joined the Russian imperial army in 1914 and the Red Army in 1918. He later served in the Spanish civil war and in the 1939-40 war with Finland. During the Great Patriotic War he commanded a number of armies, including the 48th during the Battle of Kursk. Following the war, Romanenko commanded a military district.

39 Editor's note. Ivan Vasil'evich Galanin (1899-1958) joined the Red Army in 1918. During the Great Patriotic War he commanded a corps and a number of armies, including the 70th during the Battle of Kursk. Galanin commanded a rifle corps after the war.

40 Editor's note. Ivan Ivanovich Fedyuninskii (1900-77) joined the Red Army in1919. During the Great Patriotic

consisting of eight rifle divisions and three tank regiments, General Badanov's[41] 4th Tank Army, consisting of two tank and one mechanized corps, and the 2nd Guards Cavalry Corps.

The second powerful shock group was concentrated along the 3rd and 63rd armies' adjoining flanks. Here there were five rifle divisions and six tank breakthrough regiments along an 18-kilometer front; in the second echelon there were four rifle divisions (minus one rifle regiment) and two tank regiments. The 25th Rifle and 1st Guards Don Tank corps were in the Bryansk Front's reserve along this axis. Before the beginning of the operation, the latter corps was subordinated to the commander of the 63rd Army. General (now Marshal of Tank Forces) Rybalko's[42] 3rd Guards Tank Army, which consisted of two tank and one mechanized corps, was concentrated in the depth behind the Bryansk Front's left wing.

The third shock group, which was weaker than the two others, had been prepared along the 61st Army's left wing. Here three rifle divisions and a tank brigade were located along a 10-kilometer front; in the second echelon were three rifle divisions (minus a rifle regiment from the 336th Rifle Division, which was defending along the Polyany—Tashlykovo sector) and a tank breakthrough regiment. The 20th Tank Corps, which was transferred to the 61st Army at the start of the operation, was in the *front* reserve along this axis. The artillery units were distributed among the three axes accordingly. Our command concentrated an artillery breakthrough corps apiece along each of the three axes. The shock groups were reinforced with independent artillery and mortar units, which were included in the armies, *fronts* and High Command Reserve.

Besides this, in order to defeat the Germans' Orel group of forces, the participation of the Central Front's right-flank forces was also foreseen following the completion of the defensive battle, when they would launch an attack against the enemy's group of forces from the south.

Preparing the Offensive

Regrouping and concentrating the forces for the offensive

The troops' preparation for the offensive began in May 1943. For two months new formations and units flowed continuously to the front, while major artillery, tank and air forces were being concentrated. All of these were immediately dispatched to those sectors that had been set aside for them according to the plan, and they began to outfit jumping-off positions for the offensive.

Due to the front's great length and the plan's creation of four powerful groups of forces, which were located at a significant distance from each other, it was first necessary to carry out a large regrouping of men and materiel. The movement of forces and arrival of new formations and units to the front was carried out according to a plan that had been previously drawn up by the *front* and army headquarters and, as a rule, only at night. No less than two march routes were set aside for each rifle and artillery division. In those cases when several formations were assigned the same route, their passage was regulated according to time, and the interval between the first column's

War he commanded a corps and armies, including the 11th Army during the Battle of Kursk. Following the war, Fedyuninskii commanded an army and a number of military districts.

41 Editor's note. Vasilii Mikhailovich Badanov (1895-1971) was drafted into the Russian imperial army in 1916 and joined the Red Army in 1919. During the Great Patriotic War he commanded a tank brigade, division and corps, as well as the 4th Tank Army during 1943-44. Following the war, Badanov served in the central military apparatus.

42 Editor's note. Pavel Semyonovich Rybalko (1894-1948) joined the Russian imperial army in 1915 and the Red Army in 1919. During the interwar period he served mainly in the cavalry and intelligence branches. During the Great Patriotic War he served in the General Staff apparatus and the tank troops, becoming commander of the 3rd Tank Army in 1943. Following the war, Rybalko commanded the Red Army's armored forces.

tail and the second column's head was usually established as about a day's march (20-25 kilometers). In order to support the regroupings' planned course, each route was scrupulously reconnoitered with the participation of reconnoitering groups containing representatives from those units (formations) carrying out the march.

The engineering troops put all the roads and bridges in full order. Signposts and traffic control posts were established, and rest areas, feeding stations and potable water places were designated. The troops' movement, and particularly their rest areas, was heavily covered by anti-aircraft weapons.

Engineering preparation of the jumping-off position

During the preparatory period for the offensive, the *fronts'* and armies' engineering units carried out a great deal of engineering work. The work plan called for the preparation of jumping-off positions for the offensive, the outfitting of command and observation posts, the repair and building of new roads and bridges, and the preparation of crossings, etc. In order to carry out this work, the forces of the Bryansk Front were reinforced with three assault brigades and 20 engineering and pontoon battalions. Of these, the 63rd Army received 11, the 61st Army nine, and the 3rd Army three engineering battalions.

During the operation's preparatory period, the Western Front's 11th Guards Army was reinforced with seven engineering battalions. Besides this, by the start of the offensive (13 July), ten assault engineer-sapper brigades, each including five battalions, had arrived, as well as the 85th Pontoon-Bridge Battalion.

In order to support the timely arrival of our forces in the concentration areas and their later maneuver on the battlefield, the engineering troops' main forces mostly worked to build and repair roads and bridges. During the preparation for the operation, in the Bryansk Front's sector alone the troops built 250 kilometers of new roads, repaired 406 kilometers of old roads, laid down 47 kilometers of cross-country routes of march, built 75 bridges capable of handling 10-60 ton loads, repaired and restored 35 bridges, and prepared 39 fords.

By 15 July the sappers had built in the 11th Guards Army's sector 13 new heavy bridges for loads between 60-80 tons. Six bridges and fords apiece were prepared in each corps' sector over the Zhizdra and Vytebet' rivers.

Emergency stores of wood materials, up to 25-35 percent of the required amount, were to be created beforehand for the construction and repair of bridges in the armies, while ready prefabricated bridge parts were also stockpiled. All of these wooden materials were concentrated near the rivers and well camouflaged.

Representatives from the *fronts'* and armies' headquarters inspected the bridges' technical condition before the beginning of the offensive.

Country roads were prepared for two-way traffic. Low-lying and difficult areas along the roads were improved and covered and corduroyed. The dips toward the bridges and the rises from them were made gently sloping.

The command planned the massive removal of our minefields and those of the enemy during the final 3-4 nights before the offensive. Not long before the start of the general offensive, the sappers made 238 passages for the infantry and tanks through our minefields in the 11th Guards Army's sector, and removed 30,000 anti-tank and 12,000 anti-personnel mines. The work done by the sappers—making passages in the minefields—was attested to in documents presented to the combined-arms and tank commanders. A headquarters commandant's service was established for organizing the troops' passage through the minefields; a post consisting of three men was to be established for each passage, for guarding the minefield and regulating the troops' movement. The commanders of the rifle and tank subunits familiarized themselves with the location of the passages on the spot. The passages in the obstacles and the approaches to them were marked by special signs.

The formations and units were fully supplied with the necessary engineering equipment. In some armies (for example, the 63rd) the supply reached 130 percent of authorized strength. Aside from this, those armies designated for operations along the shock axes, were allocated engineering mobile installations from the military-technical depots, which supported the troops with the required equipment during the offensive.

Preparing the artillery offensive

After the artillery units arrived in the area of planned combat operations, these units' staffs and officers began studying the routes for the artillery's arrival to their position areas and determined the number of roads necessary for the simultaneous movement of the artillery to the designated areas.

Night test marches were carried out to check how realistic the compiled plans were. One battery was allotted for such a march from each brigade.

Work for outfitting observation posts and firing positions was hurried up. By the start of the offensive the armies had outfitted artillery observation posts (four posts per kilometer) and open firing positions (ten positions per kilometer of front). The preparation of such a large number of observation posts and firing positions prevented the enemy from determining beforehand the disposition of our artillery.

The stationing of artillery equipment in the position areas was carried out so as to secure the greatest range of fire of all systems, as well as to employ fire from heavy howitzers at the most favorable ranges for destroying the enemy's structures.

Light artillery brigades were designated for destroying the first and second lines' trenches, making passages in the enemy's wire obstacles, and accompanying infantry and tanks. Part of these systems' guns were employed for firing over open sights on trenches and embrasures. 122 mm howitzers were stationed at such firing positions from which they could support firing for adjustment against hidden approaches to the forward edge and destroy structures in the depth of the enemy's defense. 152mm howitzers were deployed along the front in accordance with the type of target to be suppressed; their positions were moved up to within 2-3 kilometers of the infantry's forward units, in order to achieve the greatest effectiveness and range of fire. Heavy artillery brigades and regiments were designated primarily for counterbattery work. Brigades of heavy caliber guns were to be used to destroy particularly powerful structures in the breakthrough zone.

The length of the offensive preparation enabled each battery commander to study his targets well and personally carry out registry of fire. Such a method of preparing for firing enabled us to achieve a high effectiveness of fire, even in conditions of smoke covering the targets. Target registration was carried out so as not to exceed the usual daily norm for expending shells along the given sector of the front and attract the enemy's attention.

The main mass of artillery was moved up to its firing positions two days before the start of the offensive. By this time the engineer outfitting of the firing positions had been completed. Guns for firing over open sights were rolled out to their firing positions on the eve of the offensive.

By the start of the offensive the artillery unit staffs had drawn up all the necessary documents: they had drawn up computations for the density of artillery along the shock axes, a plan for the requirements and expenditure of munitions for each day, a schedule for the artillery's occupation of its firing positions, and had prepared plans for destruction, fire registration, the artillery preparation, coordination with the infantry and tanks, maps of artillery fire along the shock axes, and the organization of shell delivery, etc.

Reconnaissance measures

The headquarters and troops continuously studied the enemy, and very scrupulously. All targets uncovered were noted on a map.

In May and June our reconnaissance aviation photographed the enemy's defensive lines along the axes designated for the breakthrough. The photographed zones were immediately deciphered and dispatched to the combined-arms headquarters. The aerial photographs enabled us to discover the character of the German defense in the Orel salient, the forward edge of the enemy's defense, the trench system, and the location of his artillery positions in sufficient detail.

All the aerial reconnaissance material and troop observation was organized by the *front* headquarters' topographical section and reflected on maps; maps with a detailed description of the German defense were issued to the troops.

The preparation of formation commanders and their staffs

During the preparation for the forthcoming offensive, the army commanders and the breakthrough corps and division commanders, the artillery commanders and chiefs of the army services carried out reconnaissance, during which they inspected and defined the routes of the troops' movement, their concentration areas and the jumping-off positions for the offensive.

Following this, the army commanders conducted war games on sand tables. Problems of the rifle corps' and divisions' attack, reinforced by a large amount of artillery in conditions of very broken terrain and the forcing of water barriers were worked out with the artillery commanders of the rifle corps and divisions and the commanders of the artillery regiments and their staffs.

During the preparation for offensive operations, the army and divisional artillery staffs drew up plans for the artillery offensive, the arrival of units at their firing positions and the fire support of the tank corps being committed into the breach. Calculations regarding the density of fire and the expenditure of shells were made, as well as calculating the number of guns for the suppression and destruction of unearthed targets along the forward edge and in the depth of the enemy's defense, and communications between the artillery headquarters and the combined-arms headquarters were drawn up, as well as with the artillery units and formations.

In order to work out problems of coordination with the infantry and tanks, the artillery commanders conducted reconnaissance together with the combined-arms chiefs.

The staffs of the tank units and formations studied the tank concentration areas, their movement routes and their waiting areas. They drew up a plan for coordinating with the infantry, artillery and aviation while forcing water obstacles and in breaking through the enemy's defense, and also resolved problems of materiel-technical supply.

Special staff exercises were conducted in the armies with the chiefs of the army and division staffs. The participants in these exercises worked out in detail problems of command and control of troops and communications in battle. Moreover, the staffs rehearsed on site the forcing of water lines by the troops, the breakthrough of the fortified zone and cooperation between the combat arms in the offensive. Exercises on a sand table showing the relief along the breakthrough sector usually preceded the exercises on the spot.

War games, staff exercises, and exercises with the troops enabled us to scrupulously work out coordination between the infantry, artillery and tanks.

The command and staffs oversaw each day the fulfillment of orders issued and rendered practical help to the troops in preparing for the forthcoming offensive. The *front* and army commanders were constantly among the troops and supervised their training on the spot and eliminated shortcomings that arose.

By the start of the offensive the staffs had worked up the combat documents in accordance with the command's plan, had deployed their men and materiel and organized unbroken and precisely operating communications. Main and secondary communications centers were created in the *fronts* and armies. All centers and users received special code names.

In preparing the troops for the operation, a great deal of attention was devoted to organizing communications using wire, radio and mobile equipment. The communications network in the troops' jumping-off position was sufficiently developed and fully guaranteed troop command and control.

The concentration in the armies of a significant number of radio sets (up to 5,000 in the 11th Guards Army) required the precise distribution of wavelengths between the networks and their proper usage.

A special radio communications network was created for the artillery support of the tank corps during their commitment into the breach. This included radio stations for the army commanders, artillery commanders, armored commanders, and the commanders of the corresponding artillery units and formations, as well as fire correctors.

By the start of the offensive communications with the Red Army General Staff were carried out over telegraph (Baudot,[43] signal telegraph-35), telephone (high frequency), radio, and mobile equipment. Communications were maintained between the *fronts* by telegraph (signal telegraph-35) and by radio with the headquarters' auxiliary command post, by telegraph (signal telegraph-35), telephone (high frequency) and mobile equipment.

The Western Front headquarters had a circuitous communications route with the auxiliary command post through the 10th, 50th and 11th Guards armies' communications centers, which guaranteed the reliability and uninterrupted nature of communications work.

The headquarters of the 10th, 50th and 11th Guards armies had a circuitous communications route over the Morse telegraph through the Western Front headquarters' secondary communications centers, which were located in Kaluga and Kozel'sk.

Communications between the *fronts'* headquarters and the armies' headquarters were established over the telegraph (Baudot, signal telegraph-35, by telephone (high frequency), radio, and mobile equipment.

Between the armies along the front, communications was organized through telegraph, radio and mobile equipment, and along the armies' boundaries between the flank divisions—through telephone and mobile equipment.

Such an organization of communications (wire and radio) not only guaranteed the command and control of troops in their jumping-off positions, but also allowed for the creation of new networks while regrouping forces as the result of new tasks assigned to them.

The troops' combat training

The orders of the Supreme Commander-in-Chief, comrade Stalin, the directives of the *fronts'* and armies' military councils, and the generalized experience of battle conducted previously formed the basis of the troops' combat training.

The defending troops were withdrawn into the rear for combat training, according to a specially prepared schedule. Here they conducted tactical exercises along terrain similar to the breakthrough sectors. Such themes as the control of the battle and the infantry's coordination with artillery and tanks at the company-battalion-regiment level were carefully studied in these exercises. The

43 Editor's note. The Baudot was a printing telegraph, invented by Jean Maurice-Emile Baudot (1845-1903) in 1870.

infantry trained to attack behind the explosions of their own artillery shells. In troop training particular attention was devoted to cooperation between the tank crews and infantry subunits and artillery. For example, in the 11th Guards Army the working out of cooperation between the infantry subunits and their attached tanks took up about a month.

In order to consolidate the skills acquired, regimental show exercises were organized, using live fire. In these exercises attention was mainly devoted to working out the theme of "Breaking through a fortified zone and developing the success in the depth." Problems of organizing combat formations in the offensive, troop control and the organization of cooperation between the infantry, tanks and artillery were studied. The infantry acquired habits of rapidly overcoming obstacles and trained to lunge forward in the attack.

Because assault groups and mine removal groups had the main burden in breaking through the enemy's defense, particular attention was devoted to their organization and combat training. In the regiments battalions were detached and trained for assault operations. By 12 July in the 11th Guards Army alone 404 assault groups of 8-10 men apiece had been trained.

For the organization of cooperation between the infantry and tanks and to eliminate the fear of tanks, joint exercises were conducted involving the practical working out of such themes as the offensive and the attack, passing tanks through one's own combat formations, communications between the infantry and tanks in battle, and the repulse of the enemy's infantry and armored counterattacks, etc.

The ground forces continually trained in laying out recognition signals for communicating with the air force.

The training of platoons, companies and battalions was conducted in accordance with the tasks assigned to them for the forthcoming operation.

Some subunits trained for breaking through the forward edge of the defense; others for joint operations with tanks in the depth of the enemy's defense; others for operations at night; others for blocking the enemy's strong points; others for fighting in the woods, and; others for forcing water obstacles, for operations in special conditions and for carrying out various special combat tasks, etc. Operations in special conditions, for example were characteristic of the Western Front's right-flank armies (11th Guards and 50th), the combat operations of which were to be conducted in wooded and swampy areas.

In working out problems of coordination between the infantry and tanks in joint exercises, a great deal of attention was paid to such units as the tank company and rifle battalion, the tank platoon and the rifle company, and the individual tank and the rifle platoon. During these exercises the coordination of tanks with the assault groups and mine clearing groups was worked out with special care.

During these show exercises the troops trained in methods of the tanks overcoming minefields and the creation of passages in the wire obstacles.

Materiel supply

The Western Front's 50th Army was based on the Tikhonova Pustin'—Sukhinichi—Duminichi railroad sector, and the 11th Guards Army, together with the Bryansk Front's 61st Army, on the Gorbachevo—Manaenki—Belev—Kozel'sk railroad sector. Its main supply bases were located along the Sukhinichi—Kozel'sk sector. The lateral position of the Kozel'sk—Sukhinichi railroad sector made it possible to supply the army's forces from both flanks.

The Bryansk Front's forces were based on the following railroad sectors: Tula—Uzlovaya—Volovo, Volovo—Yefremov, Tula—Gorbachevo, Volovo—Gorbachevo—Belev, as well as the Tula—Kozel'sk sector.

The *front's* regulating stations were Uzlovaya and Tula; freight was delivered by mobile detachments to the Likhvin, Kozel'sk, Manaenki, and Vypolzovo stations, from which it was delivered by auto transport to the divisional distribution points.

The distribution points for the first-echelon divisions were located 4-8 kilometers from the forward edge; army depot sections over the roads at 25-30 kilometers, and; army depots at 20-25 kilometers. *Front* depots were located in the areas of Tula, Stalinogorsk and Venev. Their remove from the forward edge did not exceed 180-200 kilometers.

The depots were located along the main railroad routes; being linked to the troops by a developed network of dirt roads, they guaranteed the uninterrupted supply of the troops with materiel.

In the troop formations, aside from the supplies available at the divisional distribution points, supplies were created on the ground. This had a definite object—to disperse the supplies in case of enemy air raids.

The railroads' capacity had increased considerably in comparison with the winter of 1942-43 and fully met the troops' needs. Cargoes were brought up closer to the troops, with the aid of mobile installations, to ease the work of the auto transport and increase the turnaround of supplies. We had to mainly use auto transport along short stretches of prepared army dirt roads. Aside from the main auto and graded roads (Tula—Belev, Tula—Mtsensk), by the beginning of the operation a broad network of army dirt roads had been prepared. These roads guaranteed the broad maneuver of supplies.

The shipment of freight to the depots and the troops was carried out according to a strict schedule. For this purpose, the forces of the Bryansk Front alone employed up to 1,000 motor vehicles daily.

The *front* auto battalions were chiefly engaged in delivering munitions, fuel and forage. At the same time, the auto battalions transported march parties to the armies and entire troop formations.

The army auto battalions delivered freight from the unloading stations to the army depots over dirt roads. In order to hide the direction of the cargo flow from the enemy and keep the enemy from discovering the concentration areas of our shock groups, supplies were delivered to the troops only at night. Only individual motor vehicles were allowed to move toward the front line during the day along the most important routes. Strict traffic control was established along the army and *front* roads.

In order to facilitate the evacuation of wounded from the battlefield and their passage through their first treatment stage, the army hospitals were concentrated along the axes of the forthcoming operations by the armies' shock groups. The first-echelon hospitals were located 7-15 kilometers from the forward edge, while the second-echelon hospitals were located 20-30 kilometers away. The *front* evacuation hospitals were mainly concentrated in the areas of Tula and Serpukhov.

Field surgical hospitals were set aside in the first line along the main axes, at the rate of one hospital per rifle division. One or two hospitals remained along the secondary axes as second-line hospitals and evacuation stations.

During the preparatory period, the army and troops rear organs coped with their mission: they created supplies among the troops and at the depots in such amounts that they guaranteed an unbroken supply of materiel during the major offensive operation.

The Central Front's forces continued to be based on the Kursk—Kastornoe—Yelets railroad. The main supply bases were located in the Yelets, Kastornoe and Shchigry areas.

Concealment and disinformation measures

As a rule, all fortification work was carried out by the troops only at night. Work was carried out during the day along the intermediate lines, although employing concealment means.

In order to disguise our troops' main attack axes and focus the enemy's attention on the secondary sectors, a large number of false and reserve trenches, artillery firing positions and other structures were built. Along the 50th, 3rd and 63rd armies' secondary sectors the artillery was moved up to its firing positions and the infantry and tanks were concentrated toward the forward edge. However, upon moving up to their jumping-off positions, the tanks and guns were immediately replaced by decoys and secretly moved to the rear. The increased movement of motor vehicles with switched-on lights was practiced along the roads leading to the forward edge. New false call signs were transmitted over the radio and telephone. We managed to fool the enemy with the aid of these measures.

Prisoners captured by our forces during the battle testified that the enemy knew about our offensive preparations, but did not know where and when it would begin and where the main attacks would be launched.

The Sides' Correlation of Forces on 11 July 1943

As a result of the regrouping and concentration of forces carried out according to the operational plan, the overall correlation of forces along the Western Front's left wing (50th and 11th Guards armies) and along the Bryansk Front's entire sector (overall length: 295 kilometers) was as follows:[44]

The Correlation of Forces Along the Left Flank of the Western Front and the Bryansk Front

The Enemy					
		Guns			
Tanks	All Tubes (not including anti-tank artillery and 50 mm mortars)	Divisional, High Command and Regimental Anti-Tank Artillery	Anti-Tank Artillery	Mortars	Battalions
Total in the First-Line Divisions					
234	1,730	668	563	1,062	84
Density per Kilometer of Front in the First-Line Divisions*					
0.8	5.9	2.3	1.9	3.6	0.3
Total, Including Army Reserves					
561	2,474	933	832	1,536	120
Density per Kilometer of Front, Including Army Reserves					
1.9	8.4	3.2	2.8	5.2	0.4

44 In this and the following tables, given the lack of information as to the number of battalions and weapons in this or that friendly unit, or that of the enemy, average strengths are assumed. Information from the Red Army General Staff's intelligence directorate is the basis for data on the enemy, while that concerning our forces is taken from the *front* and army replacement sections. The information on the 50th Army is as of the close of 12 July 1943.

			Soviet Forces			
			Guns			
Battalions	Mortars	Anti-Tank Artillery	Regimental Artillery	Divisional and High Command Artillery	All Tubes (not including anti-tank artillery and 50 mm mortars)	Tanks
			Total in the First-Line Divisions			
250	3,689	1,249	329	3,417	7,435	393
			Density per Kilometer of Front in the First-Line Divisions			
0.8	12.5	4.2	1.1	11.6	25.2	1.3
			Total, Including Army Reserves			
387	5,272	1,965	499	3,785	9,556	1,372
			Density per Kilometer of Front, Including Army Reserves			
1.3	17.9	6.7	1.7	12.8	32.4	4.6

* Counting reinforcement artillery and the second-echelon divisions' artillery that took part in the artillery offensive.

Our troops' operations were supported by 1,210 planes from the 1st and 15th air armies. The enemy's aviation, consisting of the "Ost" group, was based on airfields located in the Vitebsk—Dorogobuzh—Orel—Pochep—Bobruisk area. The enemy had more than 1,000 combat aircraft that could be employed along this sector of the front.

Thus our forces along the Western Front's left wing and along the Bryansk Front's entire sector were three times superior to the opposing enemy forces in infantry, almost 3.5 times in mortars, a little less than 2.5 times in anti-tank guns and tanks, 4.6 times in field artillery, and nearly four times in the overall number of artillery and mortar tubes, including medium and large calibers. If one takes into account only the forces within the first-echelon divisions, then our superiority declines somewhat in anti-tank artillery and tanks and increases in artillery density as the result of the concentration of the main mass of the field artillery for supporting the first echelon's offensive.

The tactical density along the sectors of the armies making the main attack (11th Guards Army, operating along a 35-kilometer front, and the 63rd Army, with a 42-kilometer front) was higher. The correlation of forces in the armies' zones is clear from the following numerical data:

The Correlation of Forces Along the 11th Guards Army's Fronts

The Enemy					
		Guns			
Tanks	All Tubes (not including anti-tank artillery and 50mm mortars)	Divisional, High Command and Regimental Anti-Tank Artillery	Anti-Tank Artillery	Mortars	Battalions
		Total in the First-Line Divisions			
53	300	125	125	175	8
		Density per Kilometer of Front in the First-Line Divisions			
1.5	8.6	3.6	3.6	5	0.2
		Total, Including Army Reserves			
200	540	220	170	320	18
		Density per Kilometer of Front, Including Army Reserves			
5.7	15.4	6.3	4.9	9.1	0.5

Soviet Forces						
			Guns			
Battalions	Mortars	Anti-Tank Artillery	Regimental Artillery	Divisional and High Command Artillery	All Tubes (not including anti-tank artillery and 50 mm mortars)	Tanks
			Total in the First-Line Divisions			
63	870	284	88	1,087	2,045	191
			Density per Kilometer of Front in the First-Line Divisions			
1.8	24.9	8.1	2.5	31.1	58.4	55
			Total, Including Army Reserves			
108	1,294	468	141	1,272	2,707	615
			Density per Kilometer of Front, Including Army Reserves			
3.1	37.0	13.4	4.3	36.3	77.3	17.6

The Correlation of Forces Along the 63rd Army's Front

The Enemy					
		Guns			
Tanks	All Tubes (not including anti-tank artillery and 50 mm mortars)	Divisional, High Command and Regimental Anti-Tank Artillery	Anti-Tank Artillery	Mortars	Battalions
Total in the First-Line Divisions					
40	193	68	65	125	12
Density per Kilometer of Front in the First-Line Divisions					
1.0	4.6	1.6	1.5	3	0.3
Total, Including Army Reserves*					
140	303	128	145	175	16
Density per Kilometer of Front, Including Army Reserves*					
3.3	7.2	3.0	3.5	4.2	0.4

Soviet Forces						
			Guns			
Battalions	Mortars	Anti-Tank Artillery	Regimental Artillery	Divisional and High Command Artillery	All Tubes (not including anti-tank artillery and 50 mm mortars)	Tanks
Total in the First-Line Divisions						
39	684	208	51	846	1,581	84
Density per Kilometer of Front in the First-Line Divisions						
0.9	16.3	5.0	1.2	20.1	37.6	2.0
Total, Including Army Reserves*						
63	1,044	358	83	795	1,922	341
Density per Kilometer of Front, Including Army Reserves*						
1.5	24.9	8.5	2.0	18.9	45.8	8.1

* Together with the 1st Guards Don Tank Corps, which was in the *front* reserve and designated for developing the breakthrough along the 63rd Army's sector.

The superiority over the enemy in the 11th Guards Army's zone was as follows: 3:1 in tanks, 5:1 in artillery, and 6:1 in infantry; in the 63rd Army's zone it was 6:1 in artillery and mortars, 4:1 in infantry, and almost 3:1 in tanks.

It should be noted that our superiority in artillery was achieved by creating an overwhelming superiority in heavy-caliber artillery, at the same time that we had a 2.5:1 superiority in anti-tank guns along these sectors.

In order to fully illustrate the sides' correlation of forces, it is necessary to view the correlation of forces along the sectors of the planned breakthroughs—14 kilometers along the 11th Guards Army's front, and 18 kilometers along the boundary of the 3rd and 63rd armies. Our command had concentrated along these narrow sectors major forces, which given a small superiority in men and materiel along the entire front, ensured an overwhelming superiority along the axes of the main attacks. Mighty army and *front* reserves, which were concentrated behind the shock groups' first-echelon divisions, were a powerful means of developing the breach and transforming a tactical success into an operational one.

The correlation of the sides' forces along the shock group's axes is clear from the following numerical data:

The Correlation of Forces Along the 11th Guards Army's Breakthrough Front

The Enemy					
		Guns			
Tanks	All Tubes (not including anti-tank artillery and 50 mm mortars)	Divisional, High Command and Regimental Anti-Tank Artillery	Anti-Tank Artillery	Mortars	Battalions
Total in the First-Line Divisions					
50	180	95	65	85	4
Density per Kilometer of Breakthrough Front in the First-Line Divisions					
3.8	12.9	6.8	4.6	6.1	0.3
Total Along the Breakthrough Front, Including Army Reserves					
200	434	174	137	260	9
Density per Kilometer of Breakthrough Front, Including Army Reserves					
14.3	31	12.4	9.8	18.6	0.6

Soviet Forces						
			Guns			
Battalions	Mortars	Anti-Tank Artillery	Regimental Artillery	Divisional and High Command Artillery	All Tubes (not including anti-tank artillery and 50 mm mortars)	Tanks
Total in the First-Line Divisions						
54	786	254	78	1,063	1,927	191
Density per Kilometer of Breakthrough Front in the First-Line Divisions						
3.9	56.1	18.1	5.6	75.9	137.6	13.6
Total Along the Breakthrough Front, Including Army Reserves						
99	1,210	438	131	1,248	2,589	615
Density per Kilometer of Breakthrough Front, Including Army Reserves						
7.1	86.4	31.3	9.4	39.1	184.9	43.9

The Correlation of Forces Along the 3rd and 63rd Armies' Breakthrough Front

The Enemy					
		Guns			
Tanks	All Tubes (not including anti-tank artillery and 50 mm mortars)	Divisional, High Command and Regimental Anti-Tank Artillery	Anti-Tank Artillery	Mortars	Battalions
Total in the First-Line Divisions					
40	97	45	30	52	7
Density per Kilometer of Breakthrough Front in the First-Line Divisions					
2.2	5.4	2.5	1.7	2.9	0.4
Total Along the Breakthrough Front, Including Army Reserves and the 1st Guards Don Tank Corps					
180	205	105	110	100	11
Density per Kilometer of Breakthrough Front, Including Army Reserves and the 1st Guards Don Tank Corps					
10	11.4	5.8	6.1	5.6	0.6
Total Along the Breakthrough Front, Including the 25th Rifle Corps					
180	205	105	110	100	11
Density per Kilometer of Breakthrough Front, Including the 25th Rifle Corps					
10	11.4	5.8	6.1	5.6	0.6

Soviet Forces						
			Guns			
Battalions	Mortars	Anti-Tank Artillery	Regimental Artillery	Divisional and High Command Artillery	All Tubes (not including anti-tank artillery and 50 mm mortars)	Tanks
Total in the First-Line Divisions						
45	897	238	60	1,219	2,176	154
Density per Kilometer of Breakthrough Front in the First-Line Divisions						
2.5	49.8	13.2	3.3	67.7	120.9	8.6
Total Along the Breakthrough Front, Including Army Reserves and the 1st Guards Don Tank Corps						
78	1,358	436	104	1,258	2,720	334
Density per Kilometer of Breakthrough Front, Including Army Reserves and the 1st Guards Don Tank Corps						
4.3	75.4	24.2	5.8	69.9	151.1	18.6
Total Along the Breakthrough Front, Including the 25th Rifle Corps						
105	1,672	580	140	1,354	3,166	334
Density per Kilometer of Breakthrough Front, Including the 25th Rifle Corps						
5.8	92.9	32.2	7.8	75.2	175.9	18.6

Along one of the main attack axes our forces had a more than 10:1 and along another 7:1 superiority in infantry, almost 3:1 in tanks along one sector and a 2:1 superiority along another. Our superiority in artillery along the 11th Guards Army's breakthrough sector was 6:1, and along the 3rd and 63rd armies' breakthrough sector 13:1. The density of artillery and mortars along the 11th Guards Army's was equal to 184.9 tubes per kilometer of front, and along the 3rd and 63rd armies'—151.1 tubes. If one counts all the guns and mortars supporting the infantry's attack in the center of the 11th Guards Army's shock group (along the 8th Guards Rifle Corps' sector), then the density is higher than 250 tubes per kilometer there.

Thus data on the correlation of forces testifies to the fact that our command created an overwhelming superiority over the enemy in men and materiel along the axes of the main attacks. Such a superiority fully guaranteed the success of the breakthrough of the enemy's defense and its development in the depth, as well as the mission of eliminating the enemy's Orel group of forces—missions assigned by the *Stavka* of the Supreme High Command to the Western Front's left wing and the Bryansk Front.

The Central Front's forces, having halted the German group of forces' offensive on Kursk, began to regroup its forces from 10 July, preparing to go over to the offensive.

2

A Brief Sketch of the Operation Along the Bolkhov Axis

On 12 July the forces of the Western Front's left wing and the Bryansk Front, and on 15 July the forces of the Central Front's right wing, attacked for the purpose of eliminating the enemy's Orel strategic salient and defeating the group of German forces defending it. This offensive chiefly developed along two main axes—Bolkhov and Orel—and consisted of four stages.

1. The Bolkhov operation (12-30 July) included the breakthrough of the enemy's defense by the forces of the 11th Guards and 61st armies, the development of the success in depth, and the outflanking and defeat of the Germans' Bolkhov group of forces.
2. The operations by the Western Front's left wing along the Karachev axis (20-30 July), the commitment of the 11th Army into the battle along the Khvastovichi axis, and the attack by General Kryukov's operational group along the Karachev axis.
3. The Orel operation (12 July-5 August), which concluded with the liberation of Orel. It was accomplished by the forces of the Bryansk Front's 3rd and 63rd armies, with the support of the Central Front's 48th, 13th, 70th, and 2nd Tank armies.
4. The pursuit of the enemy (6-17 August) by the forces of the Bryansk and Central fronts, including the major battles near Khotynets (6-11 August) and Karachev (12-16 August), and the arrival of our forces on the approaches to Bryansk.

The Breakthrough of the Enemy's Defense by the 11th Guards Army

The decision by the commander of the 11th Guards Army for the breakthrough

The commander of the 11th Guards Army, Lieutenant General (now General) Bagramyan, in carrying out the mission assigned to him of breaking through the enemy's defense along the Glinnaya—Ozhigovo sector, decided to concentrate his efforts in the center of the army's shock group, making his main attack in the direction of Belyi Verkh, Ul'yanovo and Krapivna. By the close of the offensive's first day the army was to destroy the opposing enemy and capture the line: the forester's house (three kilometers northeast of Ozerny)—Zhelyabovo—Medyntsevo—Ul'yanovo—Durnevo—Slobodka. The infantry's forward detachments, along with tank brigades, which were designated for developing the breakthrough, were given the task of reaching the line Resseta River—Dudorovskii—Vesniny—Krapivna—Krasnogor'e—Sorokino by this time, while the tank corps' main forces were to seize the Afonasovo—Strelenki—Melekhovo area. Subsequently, the infantry and tanks' main forces, covering themselves with part of their forces along the line of the Resseta River, were to develop the success in the general direction of Bolkhov and, in conjunction with the forces of the Bryansk Front's 61st Army, outflank the enemy's Bolkhov group of forces from two sides and destroy it.

The army commander formulated his decision and the troops' tasks in spoken orders.

The 8th Guards Rifle Corps, operating along the axis of the army's main attack, had the following task: to break through the enemy's defense along the sector Seraya—excluding Perestryazh and, by attacking to the south, by the end of the day to capture the line Obukhovo—Ul'yanovo—Krakhmal'nyi Zavod; the infantry's forward detachments, along with the 5th Tank Corps, were by this time to capture the line Vesniny—Krapivna—Krasnogor'e, for the purpose of preventing the arrival of the enemy's reserves from the south and southwest and securing the commitment of the corps' and army's second echelons; the corps was to subsequently develop the attack to the southeast.

The corps organized its combat formation in two echelons: the 111th and 83rd guards rifle divisions, 43rd Guards Tank Brigade, the 2nd Tank Breakthrough Regiment, and a self-propelled artillery regiment in the first echelon; the 26th Guards Rifle Division was in the second echelon. The corps' attack was to be supported by the 3rd Artillery Division, an artillery regiment, a guards mortar regiment and a heavy-calibre artillery brigade. The corps was to make its main attack along the right flank in the direction of Belyi Verkh and Obukhovo.

The 36th Guards Rifle Corps, which was also a part of the army's shock group, was to launch its main attack in the direction of height 162.3, Mar'ino and Sorokino, with the following task: to break through the enemy's defense along the front height 162.3—Ozhigovo and, by the close of the offensive's first day, reach the Vytebet' River along the sector excluding Krakhmal'nyi Zavod—Durnevo—Slobodka, while its forward detachments were by this time to capture the line Krasnogor'e—Sorokino and secure the commitment of the corps' second and third echelons and the army's success development group.

The corps' combat formation was organized in three echelons: the 18th Guards Rifle Division and the 213th Tank Brigade in the first, the 84th Guards Rifle Division in the second, and the 5th Guards Rifle Division in the third. The corps' operations were supported by two artillery and one guards mortar regiments.

The 5th Tank Corps was to be committed into the breach along the 8th Guards Rifle Corps' sector after the infantry's breakthrough of the enemy's second defensive line along the Fomina River. The corps' mission was as follows: to destroy the German forces in the Staritsa—Ul'yanovo—Rechitsa area and by the close of the first day reach the Afonasovo—Strelechki—Melekhovo area; by this time the corps' forward detachments were to seize Kharevka, Shvanova, Dvoriki, and Klyaginskii; on the morning of the next day the corps was to develop the attack in the general direction of Bolkhov.

The 1st Tank Corps and the 108th Rifle Division remained in the army commander's reserve along the axis of the main attack. According to the commander's decision, the 1st Tank Corps was designated for developing the success in the 8th Guards Rifle Corps' sector. It was planned to commit the corps into the breach on the operation's second day, behind the 5th Tank Corps. It was planned to employ the 108th Rifle Division along the Belyi Verkh—Ul'yanovo axis. Besides this, an anti-tank artillery regiment and a battalion of anti-tank rifles remained in the anti-tank reserve, concentrated in the woods south of Dretovo.

The 16th Guards Rifle Corps had orders to break through the enemy's defense along the Glinnaya—Seraya sector. Operating as part of the army's main group of forces, the corps was to attack along its left flank in the direction of Dudino, Dubna and Pustoi, and by the close of the first day was to reach the following line: the forester's house (three kilometers northeast of Ozerny)—Zhelyabovo—Medyntsevo, while its forward detachments were to occupy and hold the following line: the mouth of the Resseta River—the bridge over the Resseta east of Ktsyn'—Lyubovka. The corps' task was to prevent the arrival of the enemy's reserves from Ktsyn' to the right bank of the Resseta River and from Yelensk toward Dudorovskii, and thus to secure the arrival of the corps' main forces at that line. The corps was to subsequently secure the operations of the army's shock group along the Bolkhov axis from the west and southwest. The corps' attack was to be supported by the 6th Artillery Division, an artillery regiment, a guards mortar regiment, and two guards mortar brigades.

The corps' combat formation consisted of two echelons: the first included the 217th and 169th rifle and the 16th and 31st guards rifle divisions, the 4th Tank Breakthrough Regiment, the 29th Guards Tank Brigade, and a self-propelled artillery regiment; the second echelon included the 1st Guards Rifle Division and the 10th Guards Tank Brigade.

Thus the 11th Guards Army sought to accomplish its mission of breaking through the enemy's defensive zone with the main forces of three guards rifle corps (six divisions operating in the first echelon), reinforced with two tank breakthrough regiments, three tank brigades, a self-propelled artillery regiment, and eight engineering battalions. The first echelon's operations would be supported by the main mass of artillery (including that of the second echelon's divisions) and guards mortar units. It was planned to develop the breakthrough's success with the forces of two guards rifle corps (8th and 36th), consisting of six rifle divisions, and the commitment along their zone in the army reserve of the 108th Rifle Division, two tank corps, and a tank brigade.

The broadening of the breakthrough front and the securing of the army's main group of forces from the flanks was to be carried out, on the one hand, by the forces of the 16th Guards Rifle Corps and, on the other, by "rolling up" the enemy's combat formations facing the neighbor on the left with an attack against the enemy rear by the 36th Guards Rifle Corps' left-flank units.

Aside from this, the 11th Guards Army's flanks were to be secured by the operations of the neighboring 50th and 61st armies' units.

It was planned to accomplish the subsequent mission—an attack in the general direction of Bolkhov and the defeat of the enemy's Bolkhov group of forces—in conjunction with the main forces of the Bryansk Front's 61st Army. In order to carry out this task, the forces of two guards rifle corps and all the tank units under the army's control were to be set aside. During the attack on Bolkhov, part of the army's forces, attacking in the general direction of Uzkoe, was to support the main group of forces through active operations from the south.

The idea of concentrating the overwhelming mass of men and materiel along the main axis, while at the same time supporting the main attack through active operations by comparatively small forces along the secondary axes, is especially sharply revealed in this decision.

The great density of men and material, concentrated by the start of the offensive along the 11th Guards Army's sector, facilitated the achievement of a great success. The presence of powerful second and third echelons, possessing a large number of tanks, as well as the deep organization of the combat formations, increased the penetrating power of the attacking units and ensured the augmentation of the attacks from the depth.

The operational plan called for the rapid development of the attack for the purpose of rapidly expanding the breakthrough and the arrival of our forces in the rear of the enemy's defensive zone before the arrival of his operational reserves. In order to secure the most rapid commitment of the second and third echelons into the battle, as well as the reserves, the divisions, as a rule, were to attack in a single echelon. The regiments, in the majority of cases, organized their combat formations in three echelons, and only when operating along a comparatively broad front—in two echelons, with two battalions in the first echelon in this case. The breakthrough tank regiments were to support the infantry during the breakthrough of the forward edge only with individual heavy tanks, while the main forces were to be committed into the battle following the breakthrough of the forward edge, for the purpose, in conjunction with the infantry's forward detachments, of rapidly developing the breakthrough's success and overcoming the enemy's intermediate and rear line before the arrival of his reserves.

According to the operational plan, the tank corps were to be committed into the battle following the overcoming of the second defensive line by our units along the line Nikitskoe—Staritsa—Rechitsa;

their mission was to develop the breakthrough's success in the general direction of Bolkhov and to defeat the enemy's arriving reserves.

Simultaneous with the development of the success by the main forces, the army's flank units were to widen the breach with their own attack by "rolling up" the enemy's defense along the flanks of the breakthrough.

The reconnaissance battalions' actions on 11 July

The troops' regrouping and their arrival at their jumping-off positions, and the artillery's occupation of its firing positions, were carried out during the course of three nights before the attack. The preparations for the offensive were basically completed by 10 July.

A day before the start of the offensive, according to instructions from the *Stavka* of the Supreme High Command, our forces carried out a reconnaissance in force along all the sectors where the breakthrough was planned. The purpose of this reconnaissance was to uncover the enemy's fire system and to establish the true forward edge of his defense, as well as to create the impression among the Germans that our main forces were attacking and thus force the enemy command to pull his personnel and weapons out of their shelters for repulsing the attack.

The reinforced reconnaissance battalions, drawn from each division of the 11th Guards Army's first echelon, attacked at 0300 on 11 July, following a 10-minute artillery onslaught. The battalion's actions were supported by fire from a part of our artillery in their reserve positions.

As a result of this fighting, which lasted all day, our reconnaissance battalions overcame the obstacle zone along a number of sectors and captured the first trench line, which, as we had figured, was occupied only by small numbers of Germans. Our attacking battalions then reached the second line, where the enemy's main forces were located. As a result of these battalions' actions, the command exactly established the contours of the forward edge of the enemy's defense and his fire system. This enabled the army commander to refine the tasks for the artillery, aviation and tanks. Our artillery and aviation, having made the necessary corrections in the previously prepared plan for the artillery and air preparation, were thus able to avoid firing on the first trench line, which was weakly occupied by the enemy and which amounted to a sort of false forward edge.

The active and bold actions by our reconnaissance battalions not only helped us to uncover the enemy's fire system, but also created the impression along several axes of our unsuccessful attack. This somewhat weakened the Germans' attention and readiness for repulsing the offensive by our main forces, which began the following day.

The breakthrough of the Germans' defensive zone and the commitment of the tank corps on 12-13 July 1943

At 0300 on 12 July the reconnaissance battalions were relieved by fresh units, which had occupied their jumping-off positions for the offensive. At 0320 the artillery preparation began. Good target intelligence and the scrupulous preparation of the artillery offensive guaranteed our fire's high effectiveness.

The first powerful 5-minute fire onslaught covered the enemy's weapons and personnel that had left its shelters for the trenches and firing positions for repulsing the attack by our reconnaissance battalions. Following a break that lasted 15 minutes, the artillery once again opened a destructive and intensive fire. This maneuver was calculated on creating the impression with the enemy of the start of our attack and, once the Germans had prepared to repulse it, to suppress and destroy them with a surprise bombardment.

The calculation was justified. For an entire hour our artillery ravaged the enemy's main defensive zone, destroyed and suppressed his fire system and personnel, and then went over to destroying the enemy's firing points, strong points and obstacles. The destruction period lasted 55 minutes. At 0535 the artillery once again carried out a 25-minute fire onslaught against the enemy's main defensive zone, concentrating the greatest intensity of its fire on the forward trench and immediate depth of the German defense. This completed the suppression of the enemy's defense and the support for the attack by the infantry and breakthrough tanks. At 0600 the fire was switched 100 meters into the depth of the enemy's defense. Subsequently, a rolling barrage, anticipating the infantry's movement and clearing a path for it, made a jump of 100 meters every 2-3 minutes. The massive, powerful and highly accurate artillery fire lasted two hours and 40 minutes and completely paralyzed the Germans' defense to a depth of six kilometers.

The enemy's defensive structures (overhead covers, trenches, firing positions, minefields, and wire obstacles) were destroyed. His personnel and artillery (particularly anti-tank) were partially destroyed and partially so suppressed that they lost the capacity for organized resistance. The forward edge of the enemy defense was literally lifted into the air. As a result, our forces suffered paltry losses during the first half of the day.

At 0605 the 11th Guards Army's forces attacked the enemy's defensive positions. Staying close to the explosions of their artillery shells, the infantry, along with the breakthrough tanks, broke into the German trenches.

The Germans, crushed by the powerful artillery and aviation preparation, at first put up almost no fire resistance. Our infantry threw itself forward energetically and, moving at full height behind the artillery barrage, as early as 0700 broke through the forward edge of the enemy's defense. After this, the command committed into the battle the tank brigades that had been attached to the first-echelon rifle divisions. The tank brigades had the mission of preventing the enemy from clinging to the intermediate line's fortifications along the Fomina River. The offensive developed rapidly. As early as 1000 our forces occupied the enemy's powerful strong points in the Glinnaya, Belyi Verkh, Perestryazh, and Zhukovo areas, as well as a number of fortified heights that overlooked the terrain before them. All three of the enemy's trench lines along the front Glinnaya—Zhukovo were pierced. The main centers of resistance (Seraya, Perestryazh and others), on which the Germans' main resistance zone relied, quickly fell into our hands. By this time the tanks had broken through the intermediate defensive line.

During the second half of the day the enemy, having recovered from the first powerful blow, began to put up resistance in the defensive depth, relying on previously prepared positions and strong points. Units of the German 211th and 293rd infantry divisions and reserve units from the LIII Army Corps attempted to consolidate along the line Zhelyabova—Rechitsa and halt our attack in front of the rear defensive line. In places the Germans launched counterattacks, which were beaten off by our units with heavy losses for the enemy. The enemy aviation, supporting the operations of the ground forces, increased its activity. German planes repeatedly bombed our attacking forces in large groups. Units of the 5th Panzer Division, which had been transferred here by the German command, appeared opposite the breakthrough sector.

In these conditions, it was necessary for our forces to speed up the pace of the attack, in order to prevent the enemy from consolidating and organizing a firm defense along the rear line. Taking this into account, the army commander ordered the 5th Tank Corps committed into the breach along the 8th Guards Rifle Corps' sector and from the line of the Fomina River launch an attack in the general direction of Ul'yanovo and Afonasovo, for the purpose of breaking through the German defense throughout its entire depth; it was to subsequently develop the success toward Bolkhov.

At 1700 on 12 July the 5th Tank Corps entered the breach and raced to the south. By 2000 the corps' units, breaking the enemy's resistance, had already reached the northern outskirts of Ul'yanovo and Rechitsa. The onset of darkness and the lack of exact information about the anti-tank defense organized here by the Germans did not favor an attack by our units against this powerful line from the march. Thus the corps commander decided to carefully reconnoiter the enemy defense during the night and to bring up his forces and, having prepared for the attack, in the morning, in conjunction with units of the 8th Guards Rifle Corps, to renew the attack and break through the rear defense line along the Ul'yanovo—Rechitsa sector.

The fighting along the breakthrough sector continued with unrelenting force throughout 12 July. Our units, avoiding frontal attacks, bypassed the enemy's fortifications, got into his rear, and surrounded and destroyed the garrisons of the centers of resistance and strong points. The numerous outflanking and turning movements led to a situation in which the Germans, when threatened with encirclement, usually lost their resolve and ran, abandoning their fortifications, wounded, weapons, and other equipment. Those garrisons that sought to continue resistance were destroyed by our forces, operating from several directions.

As a result of our powerful attack and the rapid development of the breakthrough's success, particularly in the center of the army's shock group, by the close of 12 July the following situation had arisen.

The 217th Rifle Division, while continuing to defend along a broad front, attacked at 1500 with one regiment toward Ozerny and captured two lines of trenches.

The 16th Guards Rifle Corps, having broken through the enemy's defense along the Glinnaya—Seraya sector and, developing the success with its left flank to the southwest, reached the following line: the forester's house (three kilometers northeast of Ozerny)—Krasnyi Oktyabr' (two miles west of Nikitskoe), while its left flank had reached the area one kilometer north of Staritsa.

The 8th Guards Rifle Corps, having broken through the enemy's defense along the sector excluding Seraya—Perestryazh and developing the attack with its left flank to the south, reached the northeastern approaches to Staritsa and the northwestern outskirts of Rechitsa.

The 5th Tank Corps reached the northern outskirts of the Staritsa, Ul'yanovo and Rechitsa strong points.

The 36th Guards Rifle Corps, having broken through the enemy's defense along the sector excluding Perestryazh—Ozhigovo, and developing the attack to the southeast, reached the western outskirts of Brodok (four kilometers east of Belyi Verkh) with its right flank, bypassed it from the north, east and southeast, and occupied Zhukovo with its left flank.

Thus by the close of the offensive's first day the 11th Guards Army had broken through the enemy's defense along a 14-kilometer front and had penetrated to a depth of 10-12 kilometers. At the same time, the army not only overcame the enemy's first defensive zone, but also broke through the Germans' second defensive line along the Fomina River (well fortified by the Germans and representing a serious obstacle for our tanks) and had reached the rear defensive line.

On the night of 12-13 July our units carefully prepared to continue the attack, brought up their rear organs and reserves, put themselves in order and stocked up on ammunition. At the same time, individual small detachments carried out intensive reconnaissance of the enemy, made passages in the obstacles and minefields, and with fire and small attacks disrupted the Germans' rest and defensive preparations. Groups of our automatic riflemen, penetrating into the enemy rear, caused panic there, disrupted communications lines, and disorganized command and control and the delivery of food and munitions.

The breakthrough of the rear defensive line on 13 July 1943

On July 13 the most stubborn fighting broke out in the Medyntsevo—Ul'yanovo—Staritsa area. The enemy's units that had fallen back and, others that had been brought up, put up fierce resistance, relying on the strong fortifications of these main centers of the rear defensive line. Units of the 211th and 293rd infantry divisions, supported by the tanks of the 5th Panzer Division, sought to halt our offensive by heavy fire and repeated counterattacks and maintain their hold on the last fortified defensive line until the arrival of larger reserves.

On the morning of 13 July the 8th Guards Rifle Corps renewed its attack. The corps had the task of breaking through the Germans' rear defensive line along the Staritsa—Rechitsa sector, securing the commitment of the 5th Tank Corps into the breach and, in conjunction with the latter, to attack in the direction of Ul'yanovo and Krapivna. The corps' 11th Guards Rifle Division, along with the 43rd Guards Tank Brigade, attacked in the direction of Staritsa, bypassing it from the east and southeast. The 83rd Guards Rifle Division, along with the 2nd Guards Tank Breakthrough Regiment, was attacking toward Ul'yanovo, outflanking it from the west and east.

The Germans, taking advantage of previously prepared fortifications and folds in the terrain, met our units with powerful interlocking fire and repeatedly counterattacked our flanks in strength of up to 2-3 battalions of infantry and 15-30 tanks, including heavy ones. The fighting was very stubborn. Our units advanced slowly. The 11th Guards Rifle Division, maneuvering skillfully, outflanked Staritsa with part of its forces from the east, cut the highway between Staritsa and Ul'yanovo and, in conjunction with the 43rd Guards Tank Brigade, unexpectedly attacked Staritsa from the southeast and, having broken into the village, cleared the enemy out by 1300, following a brief but intense fight.

The remnants of the routed German garrison sought to fall back on Medyntsevo, but were met with and destroyed by units of the 1st Guards Rifle Division (the 16th Guards Rifle Corps' left-flank division), which, attacking together with the 10th Guards Tank Brigade, had outflanked Staritsa from the west and southwest.

The success of the neighbor on the right, which had seized Staritsa and thus weakened the defense of the approaches to Ul'yanovo from the northwest, was used by the 83rd Guards Rifle Division: one of its regiments reinforced with tanks, attacked the western outskirts of Ul'yanovo and broke into the village. The Germans, having brought their garrison's main forces here, tried in every way to throw the regiment out of Ul'yanovo. In the meantime, the division's main forces, together with the 2nd Guards Tank Breakthrough Regiment, launched a powerful attack against Ul'yanovo from the northeast. Outflanking the village from two sides, our units crushed the Germans' resistance and by 1430 captured Ul'yanovo, having almost completely destroyed the enemy garrison.

The breakthrough of the enemy's rear defensive line had been accomplished. The army commander, for the purposes of rapidly developing the success and the deep splitting of the enemy defense, committed the 5th Tank Corps into the breach, with the mission of attacking in the direction of Krapivna.

The tank corps, together with the 8th Guards Rifle Corps' forward detachments, while overthrowing the enemy with its rapid attack and pursuing the remnants of the enemy defeated in the Ul'yanovo area, captured Vesniny, Krapivna and Yagodnaya from the march.

Following the breakthrough of the rear defensive line, the Germans no longer had the forces to put up an organized resistance along this axis. Scattered remnants of enemy units were running away in panic toward the south, pursued by our forces. On this day the tank corps did not encounter any kind of serious enemy resistance anywhere. The corps' 70th Tank Brigade, reinforced with a battalion from the 83rd Rifle Division, valiantly and energetically pursued the Germans falling back in disorder. The brigade forced the Vytebet' River on the enemy's heels, broke into Yagodnaya and, having covered more than 30 kilometers in half a day of fighting, had inflicted heavy losses on the enemy.

The army commander believed that to leave the brigade in Yagodnaya, separated from the corps' remaining forces by more than 15 kilometers, was inexpedient and dangerous. Besides, the area, which contained few roads, enabled the enemy to comparatively easily cut it off from our main forces. Based on this, the commander ordered the brigade to fall back to the Krapivna area.

It should be noted that the abandonment of Yagodnaya later required two days of stubborn fighting with the newly-arrived enemy reserves, which lowered the rate of our forces' advance and increased their losses.

Units of the 8th Guards Rifle Corps, in conjunction with the 5th Tank Corps, taking advantage of the success achieved, developed the offensive to the south and by the end of the day had reached the line Senichkin—Krakhmal'nyi Zavod.

At 1430—simultaneously with the 5th Tank Corps—the army commander committed the 1st Tank Corps into the breach along the Staritsa—Ul'yanovo sector, giving it the mission of attacking toward Medyntsevo, in conjunction with the 16th Guards Rifle Corps' left-flank units, and completing the destruction of the Germans' 5th Panzer Division.

The 1st Tank Corps, along with the 1st Guards Rifle Division, crushed the enemy's resistance in the Medyntsevo—Dudorovo (six kilometers southwest of Ul'yanovo) area by the close of the day and captured both villages. The corps' forward detachments, reinforced with infantry, pursued the remnants of the routed German units in the general direction of Dudorovskii.

Units of the 36th Guards Rifle Corps, while continuing to attack to the southwest, were involved in heavy fighting with the 293rd Infantry Division, as well as with units of the Germans' 25th Motorized Division, which had been transferred to the line of the Vytebet' River. Taking advantage of his prepared positions, the enemy used all means to hold the bridgehead along the river's left bank. Powerful fire, repeated attacks and the terrain cut by gullies made it difficult for the Red Army's units to advance and maneuver. Our units, while skillfully employing artillery and expertly maneuvering in small groups of infantry and tanks, split up the enemy's defense by outflanking it, isolating individual enemy strong points and positions, and then successively destroying them. The artillery and mortars suppressed the enemy's fire system with concentrated fire; cut off the strong point slated for attack from support from the rear and flanks, and subjected the neighboring strong points, which could flank the approaches to it with fire, to a withering barrage. Small groups of infantry and tanks would flow around the strong point and eliminate it. During this time other groups blockade the enemy's defensive positions adjacent to the object of attack.

By the close of 13 July the corps' units had captured the enemy's powerful strong points of Dolgaya (two kilometers west of Durnevo), Durnevo, Debri (two kilometers north of Durnevo) and Slobodka and had reached the line of the Vytebet' River. The forward detachments had captured the crossings over the river south of Dolgaya and east of Durnevo and had crossed over to the eastern bank.

The 16th Guards Rifle Corps, attacking to the southwest, continued to widen the breach in the direction of the right flank and by the close of 13 July had reached in fighting the line Chernyshino—Dudorovo. Thus as the result of two days of fighting the 11th Guards Army, having overcome three powerful defensive lines, had broken through the enemy's defense throughout the entire tactical depth along a 23-kilometer front and had penetrated into his position to a depth of 12-25 kilometers.

During this time our units routed the 211th and 293rd infantry and 5th Panzer divisions and a number of other units that had been transferred to the breakthrough area by the German command. Two tank corps had been committed into the breach and were developing the offensive in the operational depth of the defense. Favorable conditions had been created for an attack by our forces to the southeast—toward Bolkhov—and to the south—toward Khotynets, for the purpose of cutting the Orel—Bryansk railroad and paved road.

The enemy was feeling the immediate threat of a deep envelopment of their Bolkhov and even Orel groups of forces, which had been created by our forces overhanging the rear, flank and main communications of their main forces operating in the Orel area. In order to halt the 11th Guards Army's further advance, the German command was hurriedly moving forces here from the depth and from other sectors of the front.

The neighbors' operations on 13 July

The 50th Army, having carried out a regrouping toward its left flank, following a short artillery preparation, on the morning of 13 July attacked with two rifle divisions (212th and 324th) along the Kolpino—marker 199.9 sector in the general direction of Khromyli. By 0700 both divisions had forced the Zhizdra River and broken into the German trenches north of Rechitsa. However, they did not manage to break through the enemy defense as a result of the insufficient density of their artillery fire (21 tubes per kilometer of front). The Germans had prepared an organized fire and, relying on a developed system of wire obstacles and nearly complete minefields, halted our attack along this sector. Seeing the failure of repeated attacks, the army commander called off further attacks and began to regroup for the purpose of breaking through the enemy front along a narrower sector (2.5 kilometers) between markers 152.8 and 199.9.

The commander concentrated two rifle divisions and the main mass of the army's artillery along this sector.

The 61st Army (to the left of the 11th Guards Army), while continuing to defend along its right flank, attacked on 12 July along its left flank. Having broken through the enemy's defense northeast of Bolkhov, it became engaged in heavy fighting with stubbornly resisting enemy units and by the close of 13 July its shock group had reached the line Pal'chikovo—excluding Krivtsovo—Kornilovo. As a result, the 61st Army created the threat of outflanking Bolkhov from the southeast and east and the encirclement (in conjunction with the 11th Guards Army) of the enemy forces operating in this area.

The Development and Widening of the Breach Along the 11th Guards Army's Sector

By the morning of 14 July a very serious situation had arisen for the enemy in the Bolkhov area. The 11th Guards Army, having reached the line Vesniny—Krapivna—Vytebet' River, was threatening to attack the left flank of his Bolkhov group of forces from the northwest. At the same time, the 61st Army, having broken through the enemy's defense along the Pal'chikovo—excluding Gorodishche sector, was attacking toward Bolkhov from the northeast and east.

Thus by the operation's third day there existed the threat of a two-sided envelopment and subsequent encirclement of the Germans' entire Bolkhov group of forces.

The successful development of our offensive and the absence of enemy reserves along the Bolkhov axis forced the German command to throw forces in here with feverish haste from the deep rear and other sectors of the front. As early as 12 July the Germans had brought up the 5th Panzer Division to the 11th Guards Army's breakthrough sector.

On 13 July they committed units of the 134th Infantry and 18th Panzer divisions to the fighting here, as well as a number of independent battalions and special subunits, and on 14 July transferred to this area units of the 20th Panzer, 183rd, 321st and 339th infantry divisions, which had been moved from other sectors of the front. During the succeeding days (15-19 July), while striving at all costs to halt the offensive by the 11th Guards Army, which was threatening the main routes connecting Orel and Bryansk, the German command threw here from its reserve, and from other sectors facing the Western and Central fronts, the 183rd, 707th and 253rd infantry, and the 9th, 18th and 20th panzer divisions, and the 10th Motorized Division, the 14th Jaeger, 630th and 745th engineering, the 222nd and 3rd construction, the 350th Security and 441st Independent battalions, and behind them, units of the 4th Panzer Division, the 50th Independent Infantry Regiment, and other independent units numbering up to a division in strength.

The enemy, taking advantage of all opportunities and by weakening other sectors of the front, reinforced the resistance to the 11th Guards Army. The remnants of the 211th and 293rd infantry and 5th Panzer divisions, which had been routed in the offensive's first two days, fell back into the woods and, together with the newly-arrived reserves, continued to put up fierce resistance to our attacking forces. The German command concentrated its main aviation forces along this axis to support the operations of its ground forces.

The enemy's resistance grew with each day. Striving to halt our attacking units along the line of the Vytebet' River and to cover Bolkhov from the northwest, the enemy was concentrating his main forces to the Melekhovo—Afonasovo—Yagodnaya area. Simultaneously, he was reinforcing the groups of forces along the breakthrough's flanks: one in the Khat'kovo—Moilovo area, and the other in the Sorokino—Ukolitsy area. The enemy intended to cut off the units that had punched a hole in his defense by means of powerful attacks against the base of the wedge and to restore the situation.

The 11th Guards Army continued to deepen the breach, launching its main attack to the southeast with the forces of the 8th and 36th guards rifle and the 1st and 5th tank corps. Operating in conjunction with the forces of the Bryansk Front's 61st Army, which were attacking on Bolkhov from the northeast and east, the 11th Guards Army had the mission of completely destroying the enemy's Bolkhov group of forces. Along its right flank, the army covered itself through the active operations of the 16th Guards Rifle Corps which, as a result of the 50th Army's unsuccessful offensive on 13 July, was forced to stretch its forces more and more along the front. In light of such a situation, the army command could not remove forces from its secondary right flank, in order to employ them along the axis of the main attack.

The fighting in the Yagodnaya area and the arrival of the 8th Guards Rifle and 5th Tank corps at the approaches to Bolkhov

The 8th Guards Rifle Corps, operating along the axis of the army's main attack, in conjunction with the 1st and 5th tank corps, attacked with its main forces to the southeast. Its goal was to outflank the Germans' Bolkhov group of forces from the southwest. The enemy, who attached great importance to the line of the Vytebet' River, which covered Bolkhov from the west and northwest, undertook all measures to maintain this line in his hands.

The main center of German resistance was Yagodnaya, in which all the roads to Bolkhov and Uzkoe converged. In order to delay our offensive and prevent the forcing of the Vytebet' River until the arrival of reserves from the depth, the enemy covered himself along the Afonasovo—Melekhovo line with the forces of the 350th Security Battalion, the 189th Repair and 262nd Road Transport companies, reinforced with artillery and tanks. By the morning of 14 July the 18th Panzer Division's 101st Motorized Regiment had arrived here. These units received orders to hold at any cost the approaches to the Vytebet' River until the concentration of the 18th and 20th panzer divisions.

On 14 July the 83rd and 26th guards rifle divisions, in conjunction with units of the 1st and 5th tank corps, launched a powerful attack against the enemy and completely destroyed the 350th Security Battalion, routed the enemy's remaining covering units, captured Afonasovo, Melekhovo, Shvanova, and Sopovo and seized crossings over the Vytebet' River east of Melekhovo.

On the night of 14-15 July the enemy hurriedly concentrated in the Yagodnaya area units of the 18th and 20th panzer divisions, the 3rd Engineer Battalion, and other units and elements from the reserve and other sectors of the front.

The commander of the 8th Guards Rifle Corps, knowing that Yagodnaya and the line of the Vytebet' River were heavily fortified and that the enemy was getting ready here for a stubborn defense, decided not to directly attack the Yagodnaya center of resistance, ordering his forces to force the Vytebet' River in the Shvanova area, where the Germans had not had time to create strong fortifications and did not expect our attack. Subsequently, having turned Yagodnaya from the flanks, he intended to capture this powerful center of resistance.

In order to carry out this order, the 83rd Guards Rifle Division and the 5th Tank Corps' main forces which were concentrating in the Shvanova—Sopovo area, with the mission of outflanking Yagodnaya from the south, while the 26th Guards Rifle Division and the 41st Tank Brigade, attacking from Melekhovo toward Nogaya, were to outflank Yagodnaya with part of its forces from the north.

On the morning of 15 July units of the 8th Guards Rifle Corps renewed their attack. The 83rd Guards Rifle Division, supported by massed artillery fire, forced the Vytebet' River in the Shvanova—Sopovo area in a powerful headlong attack. The main forces of the 5th Tank Corps crossed over to the river's right bank immediately behind the infantry. Then the division's main forces, with tanks, began the attack on Yagodnaya, outflanking it from the south and southwest. The 26th Guards Rifle Division, along with the 41st Tank Brigade, having crossed the Vytebet' River in the Melekhovo area and attacking further toward Nogaya, reached the Yagodnaya center of resistance with part of its forces from the north.

The enemy resisted stubbornly; he repeatedly counterattacked, striving with all means to hold Yagodnaya and the road to Bolkhov. Our units, while overcoming the enemy's resistance, continued to squeeze the ring around Yagodnaya and simultaneously began to deeply outflank the village from the southeast in the direction of Gorodok, in order to cut the Germans' sole path of retreat there. The threat of complete encirclement hung over the enemy; abandoning the wounded, weapons and other equipment, the enemy began to hurriedly fall back to the southeast.

The 1st Tank Corps, which had crossed the Vytebet' River behind the 83rd Guards Rifle Division and the 5th Tank Corps, and operating according to the operational plan, turned sharply to the south and, together with the 83rd Guards Rifle Division's 250th Regiment, moved along the woods in the direction of Uzkoe. The enemy did not expect such a maneuver and was almost incapable of putting up resistance to our tanks, whose main forces had secretly and rapidly reached the Kamenka area as early as 15 July, and their forward detachments seized Peshkovo and Uzkoe. On the following day our tanks reached the Studenka—Gnezdilovo—Selikhovo area. The 1st Tank Corps' swift arrival in this area created the serious threat of the left flank of the enemy's Bolkhov group of forces being turned and its complete loss of communications with Khotynets.

While pursuing the enemy, units of the 8th Guards Rifle Corps, reached the line Zhuevka—Mashok on 16 July. Here the Germans'18th and 20th panzer divisions, the 390th Infantry Division's 637th Regiment, a reconnaissance detachment and the 25th Motorized Division's 35th Regiment, the remains of the 293rd Infantry Division, and the 3rd Engineer and 350th Security battalions resisted them fiercely. During the following three days the enemy also transferred the 9th Panzer and parts of the 4th Panzer and 10th Motorized divisions to this sector. The enemy was being further reinforced and further consolidating along previously prepared positions, which covered the approaches to Bolkhov and the Bolkhov—Khotynets road. Stubborn fighting broke out with the Bolkhov group of forces.

The 8th Guards Rifle Corps, in conjunction with the 5th Tank Corps, attacked to the southeast, making its main attack along the right flank. Overcoming the enemy's fierce resistance, and beating back his repeated counterattacks, the 108th Rifle Division, which had been committed into the fighting from behind the 8th Guards Rifle Corps' right flank, along with units of the 5th Tank Corps, broke through the enemy's defense and on 19 July reached the line Shamyakino—Rudnevo—Vasil'evskoe, cutting the Bolkhov—Khotynets road. The Germans, having concentrated up to 150 tanks and a large number of infantry along this sector, were engaged in fierce fighting with units of the 8th Guards Rifle and 5th Tank corps. The enemy was striving at any cost to throw our units back from the Bolkhov—Khotynets road. The enemy's operations were supported by aviation, which had concentrated its main forces along this sector. The Germans carried out up to 1,500 aircraft sorties in the first half of 19 July alone against our attacking forces and their immediate rear.

The fighting in the area of Sorokino and Kireikovo

The 36th Guards Rifle Corps, which was also operating as part of the army's shock group along the Bolkhov axis, was attacking from the line Dolgaya—Slobodka toward the southwest.

The enemy, relying on the centers of resistance he had constructed in the Sorokino—Ukolitsy area, counted on cutting off our units that had broken into the defensive depth by launching a powerful counterstroke against the base of the breakthrough and restoring his defense. Simultaneously, according to the German command's plan, enemy units that had concentrated in the Khat'kovo area were to attack to meet this counterblow for the same purpose.

Having gathered a strike force from part of the 18th and 20th panzer[1] and 25th Motorized divisions and the remnants of units of the 293rd Infantry Division, which had been operating in this area, the Germans counterattacked on the morning of 14 July from the Sorokino area in the direction of Rechitsa. Having beaten off the Germans' counterattack and inflicted heavy losses on them, our units themselves attacked: supported by powerful artillery fire, two divisions and tanks launched a rapid attack and forced the Vytebet' River and continued to develop the success, outflanking Sorokino from the northeast with the 18th Guards Rifle Division and the 213th Tank Brigade, and from the southeast and south with the 84th Guards Rifle Division, together with the 43rd Tank Brigade and the 2nd Tank Breakthrough Regiment. Following a powerful artillery working over of the enemy's fortifications, Sorokino was attacked from the northeast and south. As a result of stubborn fighting, by 1100 on 15 July the German garrison had been completely destroyed and Sorokino cleared of the enemy.

The 5th Guards Rifle Division, which had been committed from behind the 84th Rifle Division's right flank, began its attack on Ukolitsy, outflanking it from the south. The Germans, who had not expected an attack against their rear, were expecting an attack by our forces from the Sorokino area. A powerful attack by units of the 5th Guards Rifle Division, which was launched against the Ukolitsy strong point from the south, proved unexpected for the enemy. The division's units cut the road to Kireikovo and at the same time enveloped the eastern outskirts of Ukolitsy. The 84th Guards Rifle Division was attacking Ukolitsy from the west and northwest. By the morning of 16 July our forces had crushed the resistance by units of the 25th Motorized and 293rd Infantry divisions and taken Ukolitsy. The remnants of the German units, which were attempting to resist, were destroyed. The 5th and 84th guards rifle divisions, while pursuing the enemy, continued to attack to the southeast—toward Kireikovo, while the 18th Guards Rifle Division, in connection with the offensive by the 61st Army's 46th Rifle Corps and the successes of the 36th Guards Rifle Corps' units, was pulled back into the reserve.

On 16 July the 84th Guards Rifle Division, along with the 213th Tank Brigade and, in conjunction with units of the 61st Army, outflanked Kireikovo from the north and east. Simultaneously, the 5th Guards Rifle Division and the 43rd Guards Tank Brigade turned the village from the west, south and southeast and, having seized Dubenka, linked up with the 84th Guards Rifle Division's left-flank units. The encirclement of Kireikovo was complete.

The Germans had heavily fortified Kireikovo, which was an important junction of dirt roads and a supply center for the German forces. Our units encountered the enemy's fierce resistance here. However, the rapidity of our forces' maneuver, which led to the complete encirclement of the German garrison, and the headlong attack from several axes, guaranteed their success. As a result of a brief but intense battle, our units completely destroyed the Germans and by the morning of 17 July had captured Kireikovo, seizing a large amount of goods. Pursuing the remnants of the

1 Another part of these divisions' forces was operating at this time in the Yagodnaya area against units of the 8th Guards Rifle and 5th Tank corps.

routed enemy, by the close of 18 July units of the 36th Guards Rifle Corps had reached the line of the Mashok River along the Seredichi—Ragozina—Arkhipovo sector.

The attack by the 36th Guards Rifle and the 1st and 25th tank corps on Uzkoe and Gnezdilovo

Due to the shortening of the front, which was a consequence of the attack by the 61st Army's right flank and the approach of the 8th Guards Rifle Corps to Bolkhov, the 36th Guards Rifle Corps, having transferred the 5th Guards Rifle Division, along with the corps sector, to the 8th Guards Rifle Corps, was moved to the wooded area north of Kamenka. The corps was to, along with the 25th and 1st tank corps, launch an attack in the direction of Gnezdilovo and Bogoroditskoe, for the purpose of cutting the Orel—Bryansk railroad and paved road and get into the flank and rear of the Germans' Orel group of forces, as well as to secure the attack by the 8th Guards Rifle and 5th Tank corps on Bolkhov from the west and southwest. The 36th Guards Rifle Corps also included the 217th Rifle Division, which had been transferred from the army's left wing.

The 1st Tank Corps, having crossed the Vytebet' River in the Shvanova area on 14 July, was developing the offensive in the direction of Gnezdilovo, and on 16 July its units reached the line Studenka—Gnezdilovo—Selikhovo and cut the Bolkhov—Khotynets road.

The German command, frightened by the rapid movement of our tanks in the flank and rear of the Bokhov group of forces, threw major air forces against the 1st Tank Corps and hurriedly began to concentrate tanks, motorized infantry and self-propelled artillery to this area. Having gathered a powerful mobile group of forces here, the Germans counterattacked. They sought to turn the flanks of the 1st Tank Corps, which had advanced to the south, and to encircle and then destroy it. The enemy's air force almost continually bombed and strafed our tanks for two days. Groups of German tanks, reinforced with self-propelled artillery and motorized infantry, as well as by aviation and artillery, systematically attacked units of the 1st Tank Corps, trying to outflank it and break it up.

The terrain was favorable to the enemy: an open plain, free of woods and cut by gullies and ravines, deprived our tanks of the possibility of taking cover against the enemy aviation. At the same time, the terrain offered the enemy a sufficient number of routes for the hidden approach and accumulation of tanks and motorized infantry and enabled him to carry out surprise attacks simultaneously from several directions.

While engaged in heavy fighting with superior enemy forces and beating off his innumerable attacks and air raids, by the close of 17 July the 1st Tank Corps was forced to fall back to the woods north of Kamenka. By this time the 55th Tank Corps, which had been transferred here from the *front* reserve, had concentrated. The 36th Guards Rifle Corps was also being transferred to this area from the army's left flank.

The center of operational gravity was obviously shifting from the 11th Guards Army's left flank to the center in the direction of Gnezdilovo and Khotynets. The army commander was concentrating the army's main forces along the flank of the enemy's Bolkhov group of forces, so as to launch his main attack here and then to reach the communications of the enemy's main forces defending the Orel salient, for the purpose of simultaneously outflanking and completing the defeat of the German's Bolkhov group of forces. In order no. 2 of 18 July, the army commander, in formulating the army's overall mission, pointed out that:

"The 11th Guards Army, with its main group of forces in the center, is to make its main attack along the front Peshkovo—Vasil'evskoe in the general direction of the south and southeast, in order to encircle and destroy, in conjunction with the armies of the Bryansk Front, the enemy's Orel—Bolkhov group of forces."

The 1st and 25th tank corps attacked on 18 July: the first toward Uzkoe, and the second toward Znamenskoe. By the close of 19 July our tanks, having broken through the enemy's defense along the front Peshkovo—Shamyakino and throwing the Germans back to the south, reached the line Myvrino—Bukino—Vysokaya—Proletarskii.

The 36th Guards Rifle Corps, which had quickly and secretly regrouped to the woods in the Kamenka area, also attacked on the morning of 19 July and by the close of the day had reached the line Peshkovo—Krasnikovo.

On the night of 17-18 July a group of tanks from the 162nd Tank Brigade broke through the combat formations of the defending German forces and, operating in the enemy's rear, reached the area of the village of Krasnaya Nov' (seven kilometers southeast of Khotynets). Having withstood a number of encounters and a serious battle with the enemy, our tanks damaged the Orel—Bryansk railroad, knocked out an armored train and routed a train with tanks. They destroyed 16 enemy tanks, several vehicles with cargo, killed more than 600 German officers and men and caused a panic in the enemy rear. Lacking sufficient forces to consolidate, the 162nd Brigade's tank crews again broke through the enemy front and linked up with our units in the Sorokino area.

The 11th Guards Rifle Division's attack along the Karachev axis

The 11th Guards Rifle Division, which was part of the 8th Guards Rifle Corps, was dispatched to the south following the breakthrough of the enemy's defense. The division had the following task: to reach the Dolina—Yelensk—Trosna line and secure the operations by the army's main group of forces from the southwest, as well as to ease the advance of the 16th Guards Rifle Corps' right flank, which was attacking along the Resseta River.

The wooded and marshy area between the Resseta and Vytebet' rivers has few roads, and the terrain here off the roads is difficult even for the infantry, and a result of almost continuous rain it had become completely impassable. The enemy did not have sufficient forces here to organize a solid front in the defensive depth, and thus while resisting he restricted himself to cutting the roads convenient for our forces' movement. The fulcrum of the enemy's defense here were the fortified inhabited areas, which were located along the road junctions or near the crossings over water lines. The Germans broadly employed obstacles and destruction, in particular mining, road blocks, and damaging bridges and roads.

The 11th Guards Rifle Division attacked in a single echelon along an 18-kilometer front. The division's operations were distinguished by a high level of maneuver and the division broadly employed turning and outflanking movements in its operations. Units of the division, supported by massed artillery fire, launched rapid and powerful attacks against the enemy's flanks and rear. As a result of such skillful maneuver, as early as 15 July the division, having split up and isolated the German garrisons from each other, had captured the powerful enemy strong points of Dolina, Yelensk, Trosna, and Klen. The division's mission had been successfully completed.

In the following days the 11th Guards Rifle Division continued to develop the offensive to the south and southeast, operating as before along a broad front and in difficult conditions of wooded terrain, as well as a small number of roads, and isolated from the army's other units. By the close of 19 July the division, with its left flank operating in conjunction with part of the 1st Tank Corps' forces, was fighting along the line of the Resseta River's right bank along the Kharitonovka—Novo-Fastovichi—excluding Tereben'—Kudryavets—Buki—the factory in Buki—Doktorovo—Zhudre—Il'inskoe—L'govo—Nizina sector.

The division was stretched along a very broad front (more than 50 kilometers). Encountering weak resistance from the enemy's isolated groups of forces; it sought to reach as quickly as possible the shortest route to the main railroad communications of the Germans' Orel group of forces along the Khotynets—Karachev sector. The resulting situation required the reinforcement of this axis, in order to launch a powerful attack for the purpose of cutting the railroad and road, which were in the rear of the German forces, and to thus begin the encirclement of the enemy's main group of forces in the Orel area. At the same time, the great distance from supply bases, the lack of useful roads, and the marshy and wooded terrain made it difficult for large groups of our forces to concentrate and operate in this area. The employment of tank formations and heavy artillery was completely excluded. Thus the army commander decided to reinforce this axis with the 16th Guards Rifle Division, having brought it over from the army's right flank to the Il'inskoe area and unified both divisions into a group under the command of Major General Fedyun'kin. The army commander dispatched the army's main forces to the east of the Vytebet' River, where the terrain and roads were more favorable and enabled us to employ large amounts of infantry and equipment.

The 16th Guards Rifle Corps' battle along the line of the Resseta River

On 14 July the 16th Guards Rifle Corps' right-flank units reached the line of the Resseta River and began fighting for the crossings and bridgeheads along its left bank, in order to expand the breach and support the operations of the army's shock group from the west. The enemy put up fierce resistance. Relying on a previously prepared line, the enemy sought to employ all opportunities to retain the crossings over the Resseta River, hoping to launch a counterstroke against us along the base of our wedge—toward the German forces that were also getting ready to launch an attack from the Sorokino area. The Germans calculated on such an attack to eliminate the breakthrough accomplished by the 11th Guards Army. They began to hurriedly transfer reserves and units, taken from other sectors of the front, to the Khat'kovo—Moilovo—Ktsyn' area. The following units appeared opposite the 50th Army's left flank and that of the 16th Guards Rifle Corps: units of the 183rd Infantry and 5th Panzer divisions and the 630th Sapper Battalion on 14 July; the 100th Artillery Battalion on 15 July; units of the 707th Infantry Division, the 50th Independent Infantry Regiment and the 14th Jaeger Battalion on 16 July; the 222nd Construction Battalion, 110th Reconnaissance Detachment and other units on 18 July, and; the 745th Sapper and 441st Independent battalions on 19 July.

The enemy was putting up the most determined resistance in the Kholmishchi—Khat'kovo—Moilovo—Ktsyn' area. The enemy continually threw his infantry and tanks into counterattacks. Particularly stubborn fighting broke out, in the course of which our forces had to temporarily fall back in places and abandon several recently captured enemy positions and inhabited locales. By 19 July the Germans had managed to hold out in Moilovo and Ktsyn', from which they continued to threaten the 11th Guards Army's right flank.

Units of the 16th Guards Rifle Corps were developing the attack in the general direction of the southwest, overcoming the enemy's stubborn resistance and repulsing numerous counterattacks by his infantry and tanks. The enemy was ruthlessly destroyed or was thrown back from positions along which he sought to consolidate. The corps' units, by rapid and powerful attacks, bypassing the enemy's strong points, getting into his rear, and cutting his routes of retreat, on 14 July captured Kholmishchi and Dudorovskii and crossed over to the left bank of the Resseta River from the march and occupied Moilovo. The garrisons of these strong points had been destroyed. Our forces seized a large amount of enemy equipment. On 15 July the corps' mission—to reach the line of the Resseta River and consolidate there—had been accomplished. The enemy undertook a series of attacks, as a result of which he once again seized Moilovo, and sought to throw our forces back to the Resseta River; the enemy's new counterattacks were repulsed.

On 17 July the 169th Rifle Division, following two days of fighting, cleared the enemy out of Khat'kovo and, continuing to develop the success, captured Suseya in a turning maneuver. On 19 July units of the 169th and 31st guards rifle divisions, supported by units of the 1st Guards Rifle Division, which was blocking Moilovo, captured the village of Brusny.

By the close of 19 July the 16th Guards Rifle Corps had reached the line of the woods two kilometers southeast of Chishche—Brusny—the northern outskirts of Moilovo, having seized crossings east of Ktsyn', and had crossed in small units over to the right bank of the Resseta River between Ktsyn' and Dolina.

The results of the 11th Guards Army's offensive by 19 July 1943

By 19 July the 11th Guards Army's forces had broken through the enemy's defense along the entire front and had deepened the breach to more than 70 kilometers. The army's main group of forces, consisting of the 1st and 25th tank corps and the 36th Guards Rifle Corps, while covering itself from the right (along the line of the Resseta River) with the forces of the 16th Guards Rifle Corps, was attacking toward the south in the general direction of Gnezdilovo and Bogoroditskoe. On this day the army reached the line Myvrino—Bukino—Proletarskii.

General Fedyun'kin's group (the 11th Guards Rifle Division and the arriving 16th Guards Rifle Division) had overcome the wooded expanse, which covered the Khotynets—Karachev railroad from the north, and reached its southern edge. Located 25 kilometers from Karachev and 15-20 kilometers from Khotynets, the group's units threatened to cut the main communications of the Germans' Orel group of forces.

The 8th Guards Rifle and the 5th Tank corps, continuing to attack Bolkhov for the purpose of outflanking it from the southwest, reached the line Shamyakino—Rudnevo—Vasil'evskoe—Ragozina.

By this time the 61st Army's forces, attacking toward Bolkhov from the north, northeast and east, reached the line Ragozina—Mel'shchino—Novolutovinovskii—Kolycheva—Azarovo—Gorodishche, outflanking the Germans' Bolkhov group of forces from the east and southeast.

Thus by 19 July the 11th Guards Army, having bypassed Bolkhov from the west and southwest and having deeply penetrated into the German lines, hung over the enemy's main communications linking Orel and Bryansk. Thus were created the conditions for an attack from both the southeast—for the purpose of encircling and routing the Bolkhov group of forces, in conjunction with the 61st Army, and from the south and southwest—for the purpose of cutting the railroad and road along the Khotynets—Karachev sector and reaching the withdrawal routes and rear of the Germans' Orel group of forces.

In eight days of fighting the army's forces had defeated the German 211th and 293rd infantry divisions, had attracted major enemy forces (more than nine divisions, of which up to five were panzer) on itself and inflicted heavy losses on them. The enemy lost alone more than 30,000 officers and men killed and up to 2,000 captured. During this period our forces destroyed about 1,000 machine guns, more than 500 guns and mortars, more than 200 tanks, and 27 planes, and captured large amounts of equipment and liberated territory of more than 2,000 square kilometers.

At the same time, as a result of the army's rapid advance, its front had lengthened and exceeded 150 kilometers. Only one division remained in reserve. The army's communications stretched up to 150-180 kilometers. The ceaseless rains had washed the roads away, which made not only supply, but the maneuver of our forces, more difficult. Given such an enormous stretching of the front and communications, the army's forces were already obviously insufficient for undertaking a decisive offensive for the purpose of getting into the rear of the Germans' Orel group of forces. The enemy, falling back on his communications, was hurriedly bringing up newer and newer forces to the breakthrough sector. As a result of this, the correlation of forces was gradually changing in his favor. The commitment on our part of new operational reserves was required for a decisive attack against the flank and rear of the main German forces defending in the Orel area.

The 50th Army's attack on Zikeevo

The 50th Army's left-flank units, following the unsuccessful attempt on 13 July to break through the enemy's defense, regrouped. The main forces of the 212th and 324th rifle divisions were concentrated along a 2.5-kilometer front. The breakthrough along this sector was to be supported by the main mass of the army's artillery. On 14 July, following a 30-minute artillery preparation, the army's units broke through the enemy's defense along the front marker 152.8—marker 199.9 (east of Rechitsa). On that day the 64th Rifle Division launched a supporting attack on Kremishchnoe. On the second day the 49th Rifle Division, which was in the army commander's reserve, was committed into the breach. On 17 July the 413th and 64th rifle divisions launched a general offensive.

While overcoming the enemy's resistance and beating off his counterattacks, the army's left-flank units reached the line Volevatka (three kilometers west of Paliki)—Nemetskii—Polyudovo—Pesochnya River in very difficult conditions of wooded and swampy terrain and lack of roads. Further attacks were unsuccessful. The enemy consolidated along this line and even recaptured Paliki by a local counterattack on 20 July.

There were no decisive operations along this sector in the following days. Units of the 50th Army, fighting local actions, were consolidating along the occupied lines and had began preparing for subsequent operations.

The 50th Army's offensive facilitated the success of the 16th Guards Rifle Corps' right wing; it played a major role in taking the Kat'kovo area (here the bold and enterprising actions of the 324th Rifle Division should be noted) and secured the 11th Guards Army's right flank during the time when the army was developing the success of the breakthrough. However, the 50th Army was unable to carry out its mission of taking Zikeevo. Its actions did not completely constrict the enemy's maneuver against the right flank of our successfully attacking forces. This could not but tell on the pace and course of the offensive by the 11th Guards Army, which was forced to stretch its front and expend forces along a secondary axis.

The 61st Army's Breakthrough of the German Defense and its Arrival at the Approaches to Bolkhov

The breakthrough of the German defense along the Karagashinka—Srednie Rostoki sector

On 12 July the 61st Army, simultaneously with the forces of the 11th Guards Army, went over to the offensive. Having carried out a reconnaissance in force the previous evening with designated battalions, the 61st Army's shock group, following a powerful air and artillery preparation, attacked the Germans' positions at 0505.

While overcoming the enemy's fire resistance and counterattacks, units of the 9th Guards Rifle Corps and tanks, supported by powerful artillery, broke into his trenches and, clearing them of Germans, by 0900 had reached the northeastern outskirts of Pal'chikovo, and by 1100 had taken Tolkachevo and the surrounding heights. The garrisons of the enemy's strong points, which sought to put up resistance in this area, were surrounded and completely destroyed. By this time the corps' left-flank units had taken Krivtsovo and Sivkovo and were developing the offensive to the southwest.

Thus as early as the first half of 12 July the 61st Army's shock group had broken through the enemy's defense to a depth of 2.5-4 kilometers, had driven a wedge into the German lines and deprived the enemy of important strong points in the main resistance zone.

The German command attached great significance to the Bolkhov salient, which covered his Orel group of forces from the north. Fearing the rapid development of our offensive, it hurriedly threw up to two regiments from the 112th Infantry Division and up to 40 tanks into the fighting here. During the second half of the day the Germans undertook a series of fierce counterattacks against the units of the 9th Guards Rifle Corps that had pierced their defense. In supporting the actions of its infantry and tanks, the German aviation, in groups of up to 40 planes, repeatedly bombed the combat formations of our forces and the crossings over the Oka River.

As a result of the fighting that continued all day, the Germans managed to push back our units in the Krivtsovo area a little bit and once again capture this locale. The enemy's counterattacks were beaten back with heavy losses along the remaining axes.

Despite the enemy's stubborn resistance and the increasing activity of his ground forces and aviation, units of the 9th Guards Rifle Division advanced in fighting. They captured a number of enemy strong points and by the close of 12 July were fighting east of Pal'chikovo, northeast and east of Krivtsovo, and north of Kornilovo.

By this time units of the 97th Rifle Division, which had been committed for widening the breach and supporting the shock group's flanks, were attacking Pal'chikovo from the north, while the 110th Rifle Division, which had crossed the Oka River along the 77th Guards Rifle Division's sector, had begun attacking toward Chegodaevo.

Thus as a result of the first day's fighting, the 61st Army's shock group had broken the enemy's main defensive line along an approximately 12-kilometer front and had driven a wedge into the German units' position to a depth of 3-7 kilometers.

The commitment of the 20th Tank Corps into the fighting

On 13 July the fighting along the breakthrough sector continued with undiminished force. The enemy sought in every way to halt our offensive and was bringing up fresh forces from the depth and was continuously increasing his resistance, relying on powerful strong points in the defensive depth and the fortifications of the intermediate line. As a result of this, the pace of our attack began to slow a little during the second half of 13 July.

In order to complete the breakthrough of the German defense, as well as to prevent our offensive from being halted along the intermediate defensive line, the army commander on 13 July decided to commit the 20th Tank Corps into the battle, without waiting for the infantry to complete the breakthrough of the enemy's defense throughout its entire tactical depth. The corps was ordered to launch its attack between Krivtsovo and Kornilovo, to break through the enemy's defense here throughout the entire depth and, developing the success to the southwest in the general direction of Chernogryazka, outflank Bolkhov from the south, cutting the Bolkhov—Orel paved road.

On the same day the 20th Tank Corps, pressing the enemy to the southwest, began to develop the offensive from Krivtsovo to Bagrinovo. The German command, fearing that our tanks might break through the rear defensive line, which ran along the line Rakovskii—Kishkino—Novomoskovskii—Korolevka, began to hurriedly fortify it. At the same time, the Germans threw significant aviation forces against our tanks that during the course of two days repeatedly bombed the combat formations of the tank corps, which slowed its advance. The corps, under continuous bombing from the air, was engaged in intensive fighting against the enemy's well-organized anti-tank defense, which our tanks were unable to break through due to a lack of forces.

Having failed to achieve a decisive success in the attack on Bagrinovo, the corps commander decided to halt his attacks along this axis and turn the corps' main forces for an attack on Anchakovo. On 18 July the corps began attacking along the new axis and by the close of the day, in conjunction with units of the 9th Guards Rifle Corps, had crushed the enemy's resistance and captured the villages of Odnonitok and Novomoskovskii. However, all subsequent attempts to develop the attack toward Makeevo were unsuccessful. On the approaches to this village the Germans met our tanks with a stubborn anti-tank defense, which was saturated with a large amount of artillery and support aviation. On 20 July the 20th Tank Corps was pulled back into the reserve and concentrated in the Khvoshchevo area, where it put itself in order until 23 July and prepared to attack toward Telyach'e.

While the 20th Tank Corps was fighting along the Bagrinovo axis, the intensity of the fighting grew continually along the entire attack sector of the 61st Army's shock group. For example, during 13 July alone the 9th Guards Rifle Corps repulsed nine fierce German infantry counterattacks, supported by tanks. Despite heavy losses, the Germans continued their insistent counterattacks, striving to halt our offensive at any cost and to throw our forces back across the Oka River. Particularly stubborn fighting broke out in the Khmelevaya and Krivtsovo areas. These locales changed hands several times.

By the close of 13 July the 97th Rifle Division and the 9th Guards Rifle Corps' right-flank units had occupied Pal'chikovo. The corps' remaining units while fighting for Khomyakovo, Khmelevaya and Krivtsovo, penetrated along their left flank into the enemy's intermediate defensive line and reached the line Fatnevo—Kornilovo. By this time the 110th Rifle Division, while securing the left flank of the army's shock group, had occupied the line Kornilovo—the northern outskirts of Gorodishche.

The breakthrough of the enemy's intermediate defensive line and the arrival at the approaches to Bolkhov

On the morning of 14 July the 61st Army's shock group resumed the attack. Straining all his efforts, the enemy was holding the intermediate defensive line, which had previously been prepared along the line Khomyakovo—Khmelevaya—Fatnevo—Dubrovskii. Having brought up all possible forces here from the neighboring sectors and reserve, the Germans were putting up stubborn resistance against our attacking forces with units from the 25th Motorized 208th, 112th and 34th infantry, and 12th Panzer divisions, and a number of independent units. The enemy continually launched fierce counterattacks with significant numbers of infantry and tanks.

Units of the 9th Guards Rifle Corps, in conjunction with the 20th Tank Corps, launched an attack against the enemy in the general direction of Kishkino. The Germans wanted to hang on to this intermediary defensive line at all costs and spared neither men nor materiel to do this. The fighting was extremely intense. Individual villages and heights changed hands several times. The enemy was sure he could beat back our attack; the Germans fought very stubbornly. Our forces took Gagrinovo after a fierce battle and captured the headquarters of the 112th Infantry' Division's 110th Regiment. The regimental commander, Colonel Wolfart, was killed.

While overcoming the Germans' fierce resistance and repulsing their numerous counterattacks, our units, supported by powerful aviation, advanced slowly. On 15 July they had completely broken through the enemy's intermediate defensive line. While continuing to develop the attack toward Bolkhov, by the close of 17 July the army's forces had reached the following line: 97th Rifle Division: Mel'shchino—the grove east of Morozovo; 9th Guards Rifle Corps: the grove east of Morozovo—Kolycheva—Odnonitok—excluding Azarovo. To the left, the 336th and 110th rifle divisions, while developing the breakthrough and securing the shock group from the left, were fighting along the line Azarovo—Slobodka—Gorodishche.

On 16 July the 46th Rifle Corps attacked. Taking advantage of the 11th Guards Army's left-flank units, which at this time had occupied Ukolitsy, as well as the 61st Army's shock group, which had broken through the Germans' main defensive zone, by the close of 17 July the corps, while pursuing the remains of the enemy's retreating 25th Motorized and 112th Infantry divisions, had reached the Mashok River along the Ragozino—Shcherbovo sector, while its left flank had captured Annino.

Thus by the close of 17 July the attacking forces of the 11th Guards and 61st armies had linked up in the area north of Ragozino. The breakthrough of the German defense along the northern side of the Orel salient had been expanded to nearly 110 kilometers—from Rechitsa to Gorodishche.

The Germans' Bolkhov group of forces, which had fallen back to its rear lines, and employing its powerful positions along the approaches to Bolkhov, continued its stubborn fighting. The group's actions were covering the main enemy forces defending the Orel salient.

The repulse of the German counteroffensive and the arrival at the approaches to Bolkhov (18-19 July)

By 17 July the enemy's Bolkhov group of forces, as a result of the successful offensive by our forces, had been outflanked from three sides. The 11th Guards Army's left-flank units were approaching Bolkhov from the west and northwest, threatening to cut the Bolkhov—Khotynets road and the Orel—Bryansk railroad and paved road. From the north the 46th Rifle Corps hung over Bolkhov. Units of the 9th Guards Rifle and 20th Tank corps were approaching Bolkhov from the northeast and east. This threatened to encircle the Bolkhov group of forces and cut the enemy's main communications.

The German command attached great importance to the Bolkhov salient, which covered the northern flank and rear of the entire Orel group of forces, and was undertaking emergency measures to ease the situation in the Bolkhov area. In order to organize the resistance along the approaches to Bolkhov, panzer and infantry divisions from other sectors of the front were being hurriedly thrown in here, as well as all available reserves. Large numbers of German planes were concentrated here as well.

It was shown above that the Germans had delayed the attack by the 11th Guards Army's left wing. Simultaneously, the enemy was trying to throw our forces back across the Oka River along the 61st Army's sector. For this purpose he had created a powerful force from the 12th Panzer, 112th and 26th infantry divisions, and from units of the 34th and 208th infantry divisions opposite the left flank of the army's shock group. On 18 July this group of forces launched a counteroffensive in the general direction of Anchakovo and Karagashinka.

The enemy's infantry and tanks continuously and insistently counterattacked our units for two days. The fighting was extremely fierce. Several strong points changed hands several times. The Germans' fierce counterattacks along all sectors immediately ran into our units' stubborn resistance and were beaten back almost everywhere. Only in the Odnonitok—Novomoskovskii area did the Germans, at the cost of heavy losses suffered in two days of intensive fighting, manage to push back our units a little bit, but their advance was halted here on 19 July. Along the other axes our forces not only successfully repulsed the German counterattacks, but along a number of sectors, having exhausted and bled the enemy, they even improved their position and advanced in the Novolutovinovskii—Azarovo—Slobodka area.

The results of the fighting along the 61st Army's sector during 12-19 July

As a result of eight days of intensive fighting, the 61st Army's forces broke through the enemy's defensive zone along a 70-kilometer front and repulsed the Germans' insistent attempts to thrown our forces back across the Oka River. Having advanced 20 kilometers into the depth of the Germans' position, they outflanked the enemy's Bolkhov group of forces from the north and east.

In this fighting our forces inflicted heavy losses on the 112th, 208th and 26th infantry, 25th Motorized, and 12th Panzer divisions, as well as a number of independent units that had been thrown in by the Germans for reinforcing this axis.

The chief result of the eight days of fighting was that the conditions for encircling and subsequent destruction of the Germans' Bolkhov group of forces had been created, which offered our forces the subsequent opportunity to attack the enemy's main forces defending the Orel salient from the north into the flank and rear.

The Elimination of the Enemy's Bolkhov Group of Forces and the Fighting Around Khotynets

The situation along the Western Front's left wing by 20 July and the *front* commander's decision

By 20 July the following situation prevailed along the Western Front's left wing. The 50th Army, having broken through the enemy's defense, had not been able, due to a shortage of forces, to completely carry out its assigned mission and had been halted along the line Paliki—Nemetskii—Alekseevskii.

The 11th Guards Army, while developing the breakthrough's success, had penetrated 70-75 kilometers into the depth of the enemy defense, having extended its front to 150 kilometers. The army's 16th Guards Rifle Corps, having captured Brusny, had reached the line Kholunya River—the northeastern outskirts of Moilovo, and then along the right bank of the Resseta River as far as Dolina; the corps was engaged in stubborn fighting along this line with the enemy who had gone over to the defensive.

General Fedyun'kin's group, which was attacking to the south with the mission of cutting the Khotynets—Karachev railroad, had reached the line Dolina—the crossings over the Resseta River near Krasnoe—the northeastern outskirts of Tereben'—Kudryavets—the factory in Buki—Kossy—Zhudre—Il'inskoe with units of its 11th Guards Rifle Division. The group was simultaneously continuing to hold the line L'govo—Bulatovo—Nizina with its left flank. The division's frontage reached 50 kilometers.

The 16th Guards Rifle Division, which was being transferred here from the army's right flank, was at this time approaching the Il'inskoe area. The army's main forces (1st, 25th and 5th tank, 36th and 8th guards rifle corps) were involved in stubborn fighting with the enemy along the line Myvrino—Bukino—Proletarskii—Krasnikovo—Rudneva—Vasil'evskoe—Ragozina.

By this time all of the 11th Guards Army's forces had been committed into the fighting. Only the 84th Guards Rifle Division remained in the army reserve. The ceaseless rains had washed away the roads and made it extremely difficult for the troops and transport to advance.

In order to halt the 11th Guards Army's offensive and maintain the Bolkhov salient, the enemy was moving up more and more new forces to the breakthrough sector, removing them from other sectors of the front. During 12-19 July the German command transferred no less than nine divisions here, of which up to five were panzer, as well as a number of independent units (including special ones), which were part of the Second Panzer and Fourth armies.[2] The enemy was concentrating his main efforts along the breakthrough's flanks, striving to prevent the further advance of our forces on Orel and Bryansk. The enemy designated the majority of the enemy reserves that had been transferred here for holding the Bolkhov—Khotynets road and covering the Orel—Bryansk railroad from the north. Following these regroupings, the enemy managed to achieve an equality

2 The Germans threw in the 9th, 18th, 20th, and 4th panzer and the 10th Motorized divisions from the Kromy area, the 253rd and 183rd infantry divisions from the Spas-Demensk area, and the 707th Infantry Division from the Bryansk area. The number of transferred special units and independent battalions reached up to 12; that is, they exceeded the strength of an average infantry division.

of forces along this sector of the front in infantry and tanks, and in artillery and mortars our superiority was reduced to 1:2 in our favor.

The following German units were fighting against the 50th and 11th Guards armies:

> along the line Volevatka—Pesochnya River—Brusny—Moilovo—Ktsyn'—Lovatyanka were units of the 296th, 134th and 183rd infantry divisions, and the remnants of the 5th Panzer and 211th Infantry divisions, the 50th Infantry Regiment, the 110th Reconnaissance Detachment, the 745th and 630th sapper, 222nd Construction and 741st Reconstruction battalions, and the 190th Assault Gun Battalion;
>
> along the line Lovatyanka—Tereben'—Pal'kevichi—Alekhino were units of the arriving 707th Infantry Division, along with the 441st and 446th reconstruction and 14th Jaeger battalions and a number of specialized units;
>
> along the line excluding Alekhino—Studenka were units of the 253rd Infantry Division and the 631st Auto Park;
>
> along the line Derlovo—Volobeeva—Uzkoe—Karen'tyaevo—Shemyakino—Otrada were units of the 4th, 9th, 20th, and 18th panzer, 25th and 10th motorized divisions, remnants of the 293rd Infantry Division and independent units.

Large enemy infantry and tank forces (up to approximately two infantry divisions and 200 tanks from the above-listed formations) were concentrating in the areas of Chupakhino, Shemyakino, and Voinovo.

The 61st Army's forces reached the line excluding Ragozina—Mel'shchino—Bolkhov from the north and east and simultaneously threatened to cut the Bolkhov—Orel roads.

The forces of the Western Front's left wing had two tasks: the first—to cut the railroad and road in the Khotynets—Karachev area, depriving the enemy of his main communications connecting his Orel group of forces with Bryansk; second—by attacking to the southeast, to outflank Bolkhov from the west and south and, together with the Bryansk Front's 61st Army, to complete the rout of the German's Bolkhov group of forces.

In order to strengthen the Western Front's left wing, the *Stavka* of the Supreme High Command transferred the 11th Army (General Fedyuninskii, commander) to the *front* as early as 12 July.

On 18 July, by a decision of the *Stavka* of the Supreme High Command, the 4th Tank Army (General Badanov, commander), which was moving at this time from the Naro-Fominsk area to the Kozel'sk area (the army arrived in its designated area on 23 July), was transferred to the Western Front, as well as the 2nd Guards Cavalry Corps, located in the Medyn' area.

The 11th Guards Army was ordered to launch an attack along its left wing to the south, in the general direction of Znamenskoe and Bogoroditskoe, for the purpose of cutting the Orel—Bryansk railroad and paved road, and with part of its forces to attack to the southeast for the purpose of, in conjunction with the 61st Army, surrounding and destroying the enemy's Bolkhov group of forces and subsequently, in conjunction with the forces of the Bryansk Front, to defeat the German's Orel group of forces.

The 11th Guards Army's attack front was reduced by approximately one-third, by turning over the right-flank 16th Guards Rifle Corps' sector, as far as the village of Dudorovskii, to the recently committed 11th Army from the *front* reserve.

On 14 July the commander of the Western Front ordered the 11th Army to move from the Kaluga area to the Kozel'sk area, and on 18 July, having made the decision to commit it along the boundary between the 50th and 11th Guards armies, ordered it on 20 July to attack from the line

Shubnik—Khat'kovo—Kholmishchi—Dudorovskii toward Khvastovichi. As was shown earlier, this pursued the aim of shortening the 11th Guards Army's overextended front and, by seizing the Khvastovichi road junction, to support the 11th Guards Army's operations along the Bolkhov and Karachev axes from the west and northwest.

The 4th Tank Army, in conjunction with the 11th Guards Army's left wing, was to break through the enemy's defense southwest of Bolkhov and, developing the attack to the south in the general direction of Naryshkino, to cut the Orel—Bryansk railroad and paved road. This would create conditions not only for completing the rout of the enemy's Bolkhov group of forces, but also for launching an attack in the flank and rear of the German forces defending in the Orel area.

The 2nd Guards Cavalry Corps was designated for operating along the Karachev axis, for the purpose of cutting in this area the railroad and highway connecting Orel and Bryansk.

The Fighting Along the 11th Guards Army's Sector, 20-25 July

The 11th Guards Army, having transferred on 20 July its right-flank sector as far as Dudorovskii to the 11th Army, shortened its front by nearly a third, which enabled it to regroup the 16th Guards Rifle Corps to the southern (Khotynets) axis and pull two divisions back into the reserve along the axis of the main attack.

The fighting along the approaches to Bolkhov (20-25 July)

From 20 July the Germans began to insistently and stubbornly counterattack our units along the sector Volobeevo—Voinovo, thus securing the flank and rear of the Bolkhov group of forces and the Bolkhov—Khotynets road. Employing bomber aviation and tanks, the enemy launched massed attacks against the flanks of our attacking forces.

On the night of 19-20 July the enemy, having brought up the 4th Panzer and 10th Motorized divisions, concentrated southeast of Krasnikovo (where units of the 9th Panzer Division were also operating) more than a division of infantry, with tanks, and in the Voinovo area (where the 20th Panzer Division had previously operated) and more than a regiment of infantry with 45 tanks. On the morning of 20 July the Germans, following an hour-long artillery and aviation preparation, launched a counteroffensive in order to encircle and destroy units of the 108th Rifle Division and the 5th Tank Corps with a double enveloping attack.

Having achieved a two to one superiority in tanks and infantry along this axis, and also having launched a series of massed air attacks, the Germans, following fierce fighting, once again seized the Bolkhov—Khotynets road and captured the strong points southeast of Stolbchee, which had been captured the previous evening by our forces. They tried to encircle and destroy units of the 108th Rifle Division and the 5th Tank Corps that had advanced here, but they were unsuccessful. Repulsing the enemy's attacks and inflicting heavy losses on him,[3] our units fell back and consolidated along the approaches to Stolbchee.

During 21-22 July the counterattacks by German forces continued in strength. Trying to throw our units back to the woods north and northwest of the Bolkhov—Khotynets highway, the enemy counterattacked: from the Studenka area toward Il'inskoe with the 253rd Infantry Division, from the Uzkoe area toward Senki with units of the 9th and 4th panzer divisions; from the Shemyakino and Vetrovo areas toward Karen'tyaevo and Stolbchee with units of the 10th Motorized and 20th and 18th panzer divisions. The counterattacks were supported by large numbers of planes. As a

3 In the Vetrovo—Rudchevo area the Germans lost on 20 July 3,000 officers and men, 64 tanks, 18 assault guns, and 20 armored cars.

result of these fierce German counterattacks, by the close of 22 July our units had been forced to fall back along a series of sectors.

However, despite the concentration of large forces along the Bolkhov axis, the Germans did not manage to seize the initiative. Units of the 36th and 8th guards rifle and 25th Tank corps, by inflicting heavy losses on the enemy, halted his advance. By going over to the offensive on 23 July, the Western Front's left wing crushed the Germans' resistance and by the close of 25 July had reached the jumping-off point for a decisive offensive for the purpose, in conjunction with the Bryansk Front's 61st Army, of completing the elimination of the enemy's Bolkhov group of forces.

By this time the 36th Guards Rifle and 25th Tank corps had occupied the line Derlovo—Karen'tyaevo, while the 8th Guards Rifle Corps, having regrouped its forces, had reached the line Stolbchee—Kozyul'kina—Krivchee. The 5th Tank Corps, which had been pulled back into the reserve, had been concentrated in the Podlesnaya Sloboda—Gorodok—Yagodnaya area. To the left the forces of the 61st Army were engaged in fierce fighting along the northern and northeastern outskirts of Bolkhov and along the approaches to Lutovinovo.

The 16th Guards Rifle Corps' battle along the Karachev and Khotynets axes

On 20 July the 11th Guards Rifle Division, together with a regiment from the 16th Guards Rifle Division, continued to successfully attack to the south. By the close of the day our units had reached the line Kossy—Alekhino—Yur'evo—Umrikhino and had cut the railroad communications between Khotynets and Karachev.

The 16th Guards Rifle Corps, having turned over its sector to units of the 11th Army on 20 July, transferred the 31st Guards Rifle Division to the army reserve, the 169th Rifle Division to the 36th Guards Rifle Corps and, along with the 16th and 1st guards rifle divisions,[4] had by 21 July regrouped to the south with the following task: having assumed control of the 11th Guards Rifle Division, to hold the line Dolina—Kudryavets with part of its forces, while the main forces would attack to the south to reach the Khotynets area and cut the Bryansk—Orel railroad and paved road.

With the arrival of our units at the Bryansk—Orel railroad in the area to the west of Khotynets, there arose the threat of the complete loss of communications between the Orel group of German forces and Bryansk. As early as the middle of July the German command had begun concentrating forces here, in order to cover the Bryansk—Orel railroad and road from the north. By 20 July the enemy had concentrated along the Lovatyanka—Studenka sector up to two infantry divisions, as well as the 441st and 446th independent, 631st Auto Park and 14th Jaeger battalions.

In the following days, as the threat of cutting the Orel—Bryansk railroad and paved road was becoming more and more tangible, the enemy, while continuing to throw troops into this area, brought up here the 45th Independent Security Battalion, the 569th Reconstruction Battalion and the 634th and 646th auto park battalions, the "Werze" Battalion, more than 50 tanks and a number of other units, including units of the 95th Infantry Division and the *Grossdeutschland* SS Panzer Division. By launching decisive counterattacks, the Germans sought to encircle and destroy our units threatening to cut the railroad and road, or to throw them back to the woods north of Khotynets and thus secure for themselves the Orel—Bryansk railroad.

On 21 July major enemy infantry and tank forces counterattacked along the corps' entire front. Our units were, on the whole, successful in beating back this counterattack and the Germans suffered heavy losses, and it was only along the right flank that they managed to penetrate our

4 From 21 July General Fedyunkin's group, along with the 16th Guards Rifle Corps' divisions that comprised it, began to be known as the 16th Guards Rifle Corps.

position and seize Kudryavets and Buki. The Germans' penetration into the Kudryavets area threatened the flank and rear of the 11th and 16th guards rifle divisions. The army commander immediately transferred to the commander of the 16th Guards Rifle Corps the 31st Guards Rifle Division, which was located in the army reserve, and also ordered the 4th Rifle Division, which had temporarily been transferred to him from the 11th Army, to attack from Yelensk toward Tereben', in order to, in conjunction with units of the 31st and 11th guards rifle divisions operating here, defeat the German units in the Tereben'—the factory in Buki—Kudryavets area and to firmly secure: a) the corps' right flank, and b) the attack by the corps' right-flank units to the south.

During the fierce fighting here, by the close of 24 July the corps' units not only held their positions, but had even improved their situation, having thrown the Germans back along the right flank beyond the Resseta River and occupied the following line: the crossing near Krasnoe—the Buki passing track—Kossy.

On 25 July the enemy, having created a significant superiority in forces along the corps' sector, launched a counteroffensive, which was supported by powerful artillery fire and air strikes. A force up to an infantry division in strength, supported by 50 tanks and two armored trains, attacked from Bashmakovo and Abolmasovo, trying to outflank the right-flank regiment of the 16th Guards Rifle Division along both flanks. At the same time, a force of up to two regiments of infantry, with ten tanks, attacked in the Alekhino area.

Following stubborn fighting which lasted the entire day, our units, under pressure from superior enemy forces, were forced to fall back a little in this area to the north. At the same time, the corps' right-flank units, together with the 11th Army's 4th Rifle Division, captured Tereben'. By the close of 25 July the corps was fighting along the line Shishkov—the crossing near Krasnoe—the Buki passing track—Kossy—Alisovo—Il'inskoe—L'gov.

The results of the 11th Guards Army's battles during 20-25 July

During the course of six days of fighting (20-25 July) the forces of the 11th Guards Army beat back a series of fierce counterattacks by the enemy, who had concentrated large forces here, in order to hold the Bolkhov salient and cover the main communications of his Orel group of forces from the north. Althoguh the army's units fell back a little in the Khotynets area; on the whole, they halted the Germans' offensive.

By 25 July the 61st Army's right wing had reached the northern and eastern outskirts of Bolkhov, while the left wing, attacking to the west and southwest, was threatening to cut the Bolkhov—Orel paved road.

Thus the Bolkhov group of enemy forces faced the immediate threat of being completely encircled and defeated. In order to carry this out, one more powerful blow against the enemy was required.

The Commitment of the 4th Tank Army and the 2nd Guards Cavalry Corps

On 25 July the 4th Tank Army and the 2nd Guards Cavalry Corps had concentrated in the 11th Guards Army's sector.

The 4th Tank Army had arrived from the Naro-Fominsk area, having carried out a combined march from there to the Kozel'sk area, and then had concentrated in the Shvanova—Serdichi—Peredel'—Ukolitsy area, and included the 11th and 30th tank and 6th Guards Mechanized corps. Subsequently, the 11th Guards Army's 5th and 25th tank corps, which had been operating in this area, were included in the tank army.

The 2nd Guards Cavalry Corps had concentrated in the Trosna—Klen area, having carried out a 250-kilometer march from the Medyn' area along country roads that had been washed away by the continuous rains. The horses were worn out and the command afforded the corps two days for putting itself in order.

At the same time, the enemy, while undertaking all measures for holding the Orel—Bryansk railroad and paved road, and covering the flank of his Bolkhov group of forces, continued to hurriedly throw forces into this sector. On 25 July the entire 95th Infantry Division appeared, while as early as July 23 units of the *Grossdeutschland* SS Panzer Division had begun to arrive from the Belgorod area. By the end of the month the German command had committed more than 12 new divisions, six of them panzer, along the Western Front's left-wing sector.

Along the Karachev axis, the enemy, with the forces of the 296th, 134th, 183rd, 211th, 96th, 707th, and 253rd infantry, and the 5th Panzer divisions, the *Grossdeutschland* SS Panzer Division, as well as various independent units and subunits, were holding our forces' offensive and had been able to push back our units a little bit along some sectors and once again seize the Khotynets—Karachev railroad.

Along the Orel—Bolkhov axis units of the German 10th and 25th motorized, 4th, 9th, 18th, and 20th panzer divisions, while engaged in active defensive fighting, were able to consolidate along the line Volobeeva—Vysokaya—Karen'tyaevo—Luchki—the northwestern outskirts of Bolkhov. Having created a firm and deep field defense along this line, reinforced with tanks buried in the ground, the Germans were putting up a stubborn resistance, covering the left flank and rear of the Bolkhov group of forces.

Further to the east and southeast, having consolidated along the approaches to Bolkhov and covering the Orel—Bolkhov paved road, units of the enemy's 112th, 208th, 26th, and 34th infantry, and 12th Panzer divisions were defending.

The delay in the arrival of the 4th Tank Army and the 2nd Guards Cavalry Corps, as well as the slow advance by the 11th Army, gave the enemy the opportunity to concentrate major forces to the breakthrough sector and consolidate. The 4th Tank Army and the 2nd Guards Cavalry Corps were transferred by the *Stavka* of the Supreme High Command to the Western Front on 18 July. They reached the area of combat operations on 25-26 July.

The troops of the left wing of the 11th Guards and 4th Tank armies received the following orders: they were to break through the enemy's front in a joint effort and, developing the offensive to the south, cut the Orel—Bryansk railroad and paved road along the Naryshkino—Khotynets sector. At the same time, part of their forces, in conjunction with the Bryansk Front, were to encircle and destroy the Germans' Bolkhov group of forces.

The 2nd Guards Cavalry Corps, operating together with the 16th Guards Rifle Corps, was to seize Karachev, cut the communications of the enemy's Orel group of forces, and then, by an energetic offensive to the west, capture the Bryansk railroad junction.

The 61st Army was given the mission of launching its main attack along its left wing and to cut the Bolkhov—Orel paved road and, together with 11th Guards Army's left-wing units, encircle and destroy the Germans' Bolkhov group of forces.

The 11th Guards Army was to break through the enemy's defense with the main forces of its 36th and 8th guards rifle corps along the Per'kovo—Luchki sector and secure the commitment of the 4th Tank Army into the breach here, and subsequently, while developing the offensive together with the tank army, to launch its main attack to the south and, outflanking Khotynets from the east, and against the flank of the Germans' Orel group of forces. An attack to the south and southwest would at the same time guarantee the complete isolation and defeat of the Germans' Bolkhov group of forces. Part of the 11th Guards Army's forces, following the breakthrough of the German defense and the commitment of the 4th Tank Army into the breach, was to turn to the east in the general direction of Borilovo and, in conjunction with the 61st Army's forces, to encircle and destroy the enemy's Bolkhov group of forces.

The 4th Tank Army, having entered the breach along the Per'kovo—Luchki sector, was to launch a vigorous attack in the general direction of Naryshkino and cut the main communications of the Orel group of German forces—the Orel—Bryansk railroad—and at the same time complete the isolation of the German units trying to stubbornly hold the Bolkhov salient.

The commander of the 4th Tank Army, in carrying out his assignment, decided to launch his main attack along his left flank and, upon entering the breach along the 8th Guards Rifle Corps' sector, to attack in the general direction of Znamenskoe and Samoryadovo, rolling up the enemy's combat formations opposite the 36th Guards Rifle Corps and, by the close of the day to reach the Naryshkino—Khotynets area and cut the Orel—Karachev railroad and paved road here.

According to this decision, the 11th Tank Corps was ordered, in conjunction with the 8th Guards Rifle Corps, to attack in the direction of Krasnikovo, Znamenskoe and Konevka and reach the Konevka area. The 5th Tank Corps was ordered to attack behind the 11th Tank Corps, in readiness to operate from behind the latter's right flank and, by the close of the day to reach the Krasnaya Polyana—Khotynets area.

The 6th Guards Mechanized Corps had the task of attacking in the direction of Borovoe, Sur'yanino and Bol'shaya Chern', so as to reach the Oboleshevo—Naryshkino area. The 30th Tank Corps was to attack behind the 6th Guards Mechanized Corps and by the close of the day reach the Bol'shie Ryabinki—Krasnye Ryabinki area.

The enemy's main defensive line ran along the line Volobeeva—Borovoe—the northwestern outskirts of Bolkhov. Three more powerful lines had been prepared for stubborn defense in the rear of the main defensive line, and which ran along favorable natural lines—along the banks of the Ors, Tskan', Nugr', and Mokhovitsa rivers, along the crests of the commanding heights, and locales favorable for defense.

The offensive by the 4th Tank Army and the 11th Guards Army's left wing southwest of Bolkhov

On 26 July, following a powerful hour-long artillery preparation, the forces of the 11th Guards Army's left wing (36th and 8th guards rifle corps) went over to the offensive.

The attacking units encountered a stubborn defense by the enemy, who had managed to consolidate and organize a firm anti-tank and anti-personnel defense, which relied on buried tanks, minefields and a system of anti-tank and automatic rifle fire. The absence of precise data on the location of the enemy's firing points led to a situation whereby the powerful artillery preparation that preceded the attack was mainly directed against area targets and did not suppress the enemy's weapons and personnel.

Units of the 36th and 8th guards rifle corps, met by the enemy's powerful fire, were not able to break through the enemy's defense and only in places were they able to penetrate insignificantly into the defensive zone. The delay in the infantry's advance forced our command to commit the 4th Tank Army's 11th Tank and 6th Guards Mechanized corps in order to speed up the breakthrough of the enemy defense. The first of these launched an attack in the direction of Krasnikovo and Znamenskoe, with the second attacking toward Borovoe and Sur'yanino. Instead of the planned commitment of the 4th Tank Army into the breach, it had to break through the stout German defense by itself, along with units of the 11th Guards Army.

The Germans' powerful anti-tank defense delayed the attack by our tanks, which that day were unable to achieve a decisive success. It was only in the Voinovo area that our units penetrated up to three kilometers into the enemy's defense. Stubborn fighting for the forward edge continued all day along the remainder of the front.

At the cost of heavy losses, the Germans managed to hold back our offensive that day, but their defense had been shaken. Despite the comparatively insignificant advance by our forces, the

German command was afraid the Red Army would repeat its attack, break through the defense and completely encircle the Bolkhov group of forces, and thus as early as the evening of 26 July it issued orders to evacuate Bolkhov. At the same time, the Germans continued to hold the attack by the 11th Guards and 4th Tank armies with all their forces, thus retaining the Bolkhov—Khotynets highway.

On 27 July intense fighting continued along the Germans' main defensive line. Striving to hold the Bolkhov—Khotynets road at all costs and to thus secure the evacuation of Bolkhov, the enemy put up fierce resistance. The Germans carried out insistent and numerous counterattacks along a number of sectors with forces of no less than a regiment of infantry each time, and with 20-30 tanks. The heavily cut terrain, which hindered our troops' maneuver and movement, aided the enemy's defense. The German air force, in large groups of up to 70 planes, bombed and strafed our forces almost continuously.

Our units advanced slowly, overcoming the enemy's stubborn resistance. At 1800 on 27 July the commander of the 4th Tank Army committed the 30th Urals Volunteer Tank Corps into the fighting to speed up the breakthrough of the German defense. The corps deployed from behind the 6th Guards Mechanized Corps' left flank and, together with units of the 11th Guards and 4th Tank armies, which had been operating here earlier, broke through the first position of the enemy's deeply-echeloned defense. By the close of 27 July our units, developing and broadening the breach thus created, had reached the line Vetrovo—Voinovo—Luchki and had begun fighting with the German units defending along the line of the Ors River and the northwestern outskirts of Bolkhov.

On 28 July the forces of the 11th Guards and 4th Tank armies were engaged in stubborn fighting with the enemy, who was seeking to hold on along the Ors and Tskan' rivers. On this same day units of the 61st Army seized Lutovinovo—an important German center of resistance covering the southeastern outskirts of Bolkhov and the Bolkhov—Orel paved road.

On 29 July units of the 11th Guards Army broke through the enemy's defense and raced to the south. By the evening of the same day the 61st Army finished clearing Bolkhov. The remnants of the routed German units, waging fierce rearguard battles, were retreating to the south and southwest.

As a result of five days of stubborn fighting, the enemy's resistance was crushed. The 36th Guards Rifle Corps, in conjunction with the 25th Tank Corps, was slowly advancing; by the close of 30 July the corps' units were fighting along the line excluding Brezhnevskii—Plekhanovo—excluding Proletarskii.

The 8th Guards Rifle Corps, while coordinating closely with units of the 4th Tank Army, was pursuing the enemy and, at the same time reached the line Proletarskii—Bol'shaya Chern'—excluding Krivchevskii.

The 4th Tank Army, while pursuing the enemy, reached the line Lokna—Krivchevskii.

To the left, the 61st Army, routing the remnants of the Germans' Bolkhov group of forces, reached the line Borilovo—Lunevka—Podchernevo.

The 61st Army's operations to capture the town of Bolkhov (20-30 July)

The 61st Army, while cooperating with the forces of the 11th Guards Army in routing the Germans' Bolkhov group of forces, beat back the enemy's attempts to go over to the offensive for the purpose of throwing our units beyond the Oka River, and on 20 July it resumed the offensive itself. Launching attacks from the north, northeast and east, on 22 July the army's right wing reached Bolkhov and became engaged in fighting along the town's northern and eastern outskirts. We were not able to capture the town from the march.

The Germans attached great significance to Bolkhov, which was a powerful center of resistance upon which the entire defense of the northern face of the Orel salient was based. At the same time, Bolkhov played an enormous role as a major road junction and an important supply base for the German forces. The enemy had transformed the town, its suburbs and the surrounding villages into a powerful defensive area. The Nugr' River, which covered Bolkhov from the east and south, was a serious obstacle for the attackers. From the heights located in the Bolkhov area, the enemy could observe and enfilade all the approaches to the town. Gullies with steep sides and the sturdy defensive structures built by the enemy, and the continuous engineering obstacles further strengthened the German defense and made our troops' operations more difficult.

The commander of the 61st Army decided to capture Bolkhov by means of an outflanking attack in conjunction with the forces of the 11th Guards Army and to cut the town off from the Orel group of forces by an attack from the rear and flanks and destroy the defending enemy forces here.

In accordance with this decision, the formations of the 46th Guards Rifle Corps received orders to attack Bolkhov: the 356th Rifle Division from the north from Skupshinino; the 97th from the northeast from Morozovo, and; the 415th toward the town's southwestern outskirts from the line Novolutovinovskii—Beketovo.

In order to complete the encirclement the Germans' Bolkhov group of forces and completely isolate it from the enemy forces operating in the Orel area, a group under the command of General Khalyuzin was formed along the army's left wing, consisting of the 76th Guards Rifle and the 110th and 336th rifle divisions, reinforced by the 37th Light Artillery Brigade and the 311th Guards Mortar Regiment. General Khalyuzin's group was to attack from the line Anchakovo—Tel'ch'e in the general direction of Petrishchevo and Samarka, get into the rear of the enemy south of Bolkhov, cut the communications between Bolkhov and Orel, and then, in conjunction with the 46th Rifle Corps and the 11th Guards Army's left wing, destroy the enemy's Bolkhov group of forces. With the group's arrival at the Bolkhov—Orel paved road, it would be reinforced with the 20th Tank Corps. Following the destruction of the enemy in the Bolkhov area, General Khalyuzin's group would be directed toward the outflanking of the enemy's Orel group of forces from the northwest, for which it was to turn to the south and develop the offensive in the general direction of Shcherbachevo.

The 9th Guards Rifle Corps, which had been worn out by the extended and intense fighting, was ordered to transfer the 76th Guards Rifle Division to General Khalyuzin's group and consolidate along the line achieved with the remainder of its forces.

The threat to the Germans' Bolkhov group of forces from not only the 61st Army, but also from the forces of the 11th Guards Army's left wing, which were continuing to attack, while outflanking Bolkhov from the southwest, forced the German command to take emergency measures to reinforce the defense of the Orel salient's northern face. The enemy still hoped to hold onto the Bolkhov fortified area. The Germans were throwing new forces to the area. Bolkhov was being defended by General Schlieffen's group, which consisted of units from the 25th Motorized, 18th Panzer and 208th Infantry divisions. This group, according to prisoner testimony, had the mission of preventing the cutting of the Bolkhov—Khotynets road—the main communications artery and chief path of retreat for the German forces operating in the Bolkhov area.

Besides this, the German command created a group under General Vize, which consisted of units from the 112th, 26th and 34th infantry divisions, which were operating southeast of Bolkhov. The group was designated for launching a counterstroke against the 61st Army's attacking units and covering the Bolkhov—Orel paved road.

On 22 July, after the enemy in the Bolkhov area and the surrounding heights had been subjected to a powerful artillery barrage and a massive air raid, the forces of the 61st Army began to storm the Bolkhov fortifications. On this day the 97th Rifle Division broke into the northeastern, and the 415th Rifle Division into the southeastern outskirts of the town, while the 356th Rifle Division reached the town from the north. Stubborn fighting broke out in the suburbs and along the town's streets. The enemy, taking advantage of previously prepared positions and buildings that had been configured for perimeter defense, put up fierce resistance. Some quarters of town changed hands several times. On 23 July the enemy managed to push units of the 415th Rifle Division out of Zaretskaya in a powerful counterstroke, but the division threw the enemy back again and, having inflicted heavy casualties on him, forced him to abandon Zaretskaya and fall back to the town.

In the following days the fighting for Bolkhov continued with unremitting force and reached its apogee on 27 July, when the forces of the 11th Guards Army's left wing and those of the 4th Tank Army broke through the enemy's main defensive line along the southwestern approaches to Bolkhov. On that day the Germans, having gathered all of their forces together, counterattacked in order to drive units of the 97th and 415th rifle divisions out of the town. The enemy was unable to accomplish this. Our units beat back all the enemy counterattacks and broke into Bolkhov on the enemy's heels and, having crushed the enemy's resistance, began to advance toward the town center, step by step. By 29 July Bolkhov had been completely cleared of the enemy.

At the same time the 61st Army's right-wing forces were engaged in intense fighting to capture Bolkhov, the army's left-wing units continued to attack and, overcoming the enemy's stubborn resistance, advanced to the southwest.

By the close of 30 July, as a result of the intensive fighting, the 61st Army, having captured the town of Bolkhov, reached the line Borilovo—Lunevka—Pavlovskii—Podchernevo.

Results of the Bolkhov Operation

As a result of 19 days of stubborn fighting (12-30 July) the forces of the 11th Guards, 4th Tank and 61st armies eliminated the enemy's Bolkhov fortified area, defeated the German group of forces defending it, and created the serious threat of completely encircling the enemy's main forces in the Orel area.

The Germans suffered heavy losses in the fighting for the Bolkhov area. The 211th, 293rd, 112th, and 208th infantry divisions were thoroughly defeated, as were a number of independent units that the German command had thrown into the Bolkhov area for securing the Orel salient from the north. Besides this, the 26th and 34th infantry, 10th and 25th motorized, and the 4th, 5th, 12th, 18th, 19th, and 20th panzer divisions suffered heavy losses.

Our forces captured more than 5,000 enemy officers and men, captured 100 tanks, more than 600 guns, about 900 motor vehicles, and up to 230 depots of various kinds.

The victory achieved in the Bolkhov area made it easier for our forces to capture Orel and had a significant influence on the success of eliminating the Orel strategic salient.

The German command, facing the threat of complete encirclement of its forces in the Orel area, was forced to begin withdrawing its force from the Orel salient, which was becoming an operational trap for them, while dispatching its main forces to cover its major group of forces from the north, and then to secure its withdrawal.

The forces of the 11th Guards, 4th Tank and 61st armies, successfully developing the offensive, attracted to themselves more than 14 divisions from other sectors of the front and the reserve, of which seven were panzer (4th, 5th, 9th, 12th, 18th, 20th, and *Grossdeutschland* SS), as well as a number of independent units with an overall strength of up to three divisions, thus bringing about his weakening along the other sectors of the front, which thus made it easier for our forces to go over to the offensive along other axes.

3

The Western Front's Left-Wing Forces' Battle Along the Karachev Axis (20-30 July 1943)

At the same time that the 11th Guards Army's main group of forces, along with the 4th Tank Army and the 61st Army, were engaged in intensive fighting along the Bolkhov axis, part of the Western Front's forces, consisting of the 11th Army and the 2nd Guards Cavalry and 16th Guards Rifle corps, was fighting along the Karachev axis, for the purpose of reaching the deep rear of the enemy's Orel group of forces and cutting the Orel—Bryansk railroad and paved road.

The Commitment of the 11th Army and its Offensive Along the Khvastovichi Axis

The 11th Army, having completed a 160-kilometer march in six days, occupied its jumping-off position by 1100 on 22 July along the line Chishche—excluding the northern outskirts of Moilovo, and further to the southeast along the Resseta River as far as the crossing near Ktsyn'. The army was to be committed into the battle from the march, without having completed its concentration and preparation for the offensive, because the situation required the immediate reduction of the 11th Guards Army's front and the securing of its right flank. Only four of eight divisions reached their designated areas. The remainder were still on the march to their concentration areas and was to reach them before 22 July.

Due to a shortage of transport, the army could take with it less than 0.7 of a combat load of artillery rounds. The infantry was worn out by the lengthy march along bad roads that had been washed away by rains. Besides this, the infantry had to drag along almost all of its heavy guns and ammunition. The artillery became stretched out. The rear organs fell behind. There was no time for carrying out additional reconnaissance, organizing coordination on site, registering artillery, putting the units in order, and bringing up straggling units.

The commander of the 11th Army, Lieutenant General Fedyuninskii, decided to launch his main attack in the direction of Brusny and Khvastovichi, with four rifle divisions (260th, 273rd, 135th, and 369th) and a tank regiment in the first echelon. Three rifle divisions (4th, 96th and 197th) were to operate in the second echelon. A rifle division (323rd) and a tank regiment were left in the reserve.

The artillery supporting the offensive had a density of no more than 63 tubes per kilometer of front, because a significant part of the artillery units were still on the march.

The enemy's 134th, 211th and 183rd infantry, and 5th Panzer divisions, and the 50th Independent Regiment were facing the army.

At 1230 on 20 July, following a 30-minute artillery preparation, the 11th Army's forces moved into the attack. The offensive's first day did not yield decisive results. Our tanks and infantry were halted by powerful fire and counterattacks by the enemy, who had consolidated along terrain favorable to the defense. Only along the army's left flank, the 369th Rifle Division, which was decisively and boldly operating in the wooded and swampy area southeast of Moilovo, forced the Resseta River in a vigorous attack along the Moilovo—Ktsyn' sector, cut the road between these two locales, and reached the eastern outskirts of Ktsyn'.

The failure of the offensive's first day was the result of the fact that the army, worn out by extended and difficult marches and committed into the fighting from the march without sufficient preparation, and having along a 25-kilometer front only four rifle divisions and two tank regiments, was not in a condition to break through the Germans' well-organized defense. The absence of precise data on the enemy's defense and his fire system, the incomplete readiness of the artillery, which fired at area targets, without having had time to put itself in order, organize artillery reconnaissance and observation, and its insufficient supply of ammunition—all of this taken together led to a situation in which we were unable to suppress the enemy's fire system during the artillery preparation, which is why our infantry and tanks encountered organized fire. During the subsequent days our units' advance developed slowly; they had to overcome the enemy's stubborn defense and literally gnaw their way through the enemy defense. The Germans launched powerful counterattacks more than once, striving to hold on to Zikeevo and Khvastovichi—very important road junctions that would enable them to maneuver along the front—at any cost. However, all of these counterattacks were invariably beaten back by our units.

On 21 July units of the 11th Army occupied Moilovo and Ktsyn' the next day. As a result of a number of powerful and insistent counterattacks, the enemy once again broke into these villages, but could not hold on to them. Our units threw the Germans out of Moilovo the same day and out of the Ktsyn' strong point, where the enemy had managed to consolidate, a little over two days later, having threatened to completely surround the enemy garrison (our units outflanked Ktsyn' from the south and southwest).

On 23 July the commander of the 11th Army concentrated two second-echelon rifle divisions (197th and 323rd), which had arrived in the battle area, behind his left flank. The army broke through the enemy's defense with an attack on Kolodyaztsy, forcing the Germans to fall back from Moilovo and Ktsyn'.

By the close of 25 July the army reached the line north of Granki, Mekhovaya, Katunovka and Kharitonovka. The army's 4th Rifle Division, which was operationally subordinated to the 11th Guards Army, was at this time fighting along the line excluding Sevastopol'—excluding Gnezdnoe.

On 26 and 27 July the enemy committed along this sector fresh units of the 707th and 95th infantry divisions, which had been completely brought up into this area, as well as a number of independent units. The army's further offensive halted and before 30 July it did not make any significant advance.

The army's main tasks—to develop the success of the 11th Guards Army's offensive and capture Khvastovichi—remained unfulfilled. The reasons for this are as follows:

- the insufficient training and organization of the troops, which had spent a long time in marches and on defensive works and did not have time for combat training;
- the army's commitment into the fighting from the march, following a 160-kilometer march, as a result of which the rank and file were very worn out, the rifle formations and the artillery and rear organs were strung out on the march and had not fully arrived by the start of the offensive;
- the troops did not know their area of operations or the enemy; having arrived at their designated area, they did not have time to organize reconnaissance and command and control, to organize cooperation between the combat arms, carry out artillery registration, and to bring up their rear organs and put their units in order;

- the operation's insufficient materiel-equipment support, which was a consequence of the fact that the army, having a serious shortage of transport, was forced to leave its main mass of supplies in Kaluga.

On 23 July 1943 the deputy chief of the General Staff, General Antonov,[1] noting the shortcomings in the offensive by the Western Front's left wing, pointed out that along the axis of the 11th Guards Army's main attack an insufficient number of rifle divisions had been allotted and that the Khvastovichi axis from the area of the Resseta River had been poorly covered, which enabled the enemy to seize the villages of Tereben' and Kudryavets. The tank corps in the Myvrino—Gnezdilovo area were engaged in heavy fighting from 17 July; lacking sufficient support from the combined-arms formations and having suffered losses, they were forced to go over to the defensive.

General Antonov recommended directing the 11th Army's main attack from Ktsyn' to the south toward Khvastovichi, and that of the 11th Guards Army on Khotynets and to employ the tank corps along the axis of the 11th Guards Army's main attack, in order to cut the Orel—Bryansk railroad and paved road as quickly as possible.

The chief result of the commitment of the 11th Army into the fighting was the shortening of the 11th Guards Army's front and the release of its forces for operations along the Bolkhov and Khotynets axes, as well as the support of these operations from the west.

The Attack by General Kryukov's Group Along the Karachev Axis

On 25-26 July the 2nd Guards Cavalry Corps' main forces concentrated in the Trosna—Klen area. According to the decision of the commander of the Western Front, an operational group under the command of General Kryukov was created out of the 2nd Guards Cavalry, 16th Guards Rifle and 1st Tank corps. The operational group had the task of breaking through the enemy's defense along the Pal'kevichi—Obel'na sector; part of the 2nd Guards Cavalry Corps was to capture Karachev and consolidate it until the arrival of the infantry; the group's main forces received orders to vigorously attack to the west for the purpose of seizing and holding the Bryansk railroad junction, while individual detachments would operate against the enemy's rear in a northeasterly direction.

This decision was affirmed by the *front* commander as early as 20 July; that is, at a time when the enemy had weak forces along the Karachev axis and the commitment of the cavalry corps here could have led to tangible results: cutting the Orel—Bryansk rail communications and laying the basis for the deep envelopment of the Germans' entire Orel group of forces.

However, only by the morning of 27 July was our command able to concentrate the 16th Guards Rifle Corps' three divisions (1st, 11th and 31st guards) and the 1st Tank and 2nd Guards Cavalry corps in the Buki—Zhudre—Kudryavets area. Moreover, the cavalry corps was worn out by the 250-kilometer march along roads washed out by the rain, while the remaining units, following 15 days of fighting, had been seriously weakened. The enemy, by using the railroad and dirt roads, was hurriedly throwing fresh forces into this area for covering the Orel—Kursk railroad and the approaches to Karachev from the northeast. A developed network of good roads and shortened communications, as a result of his retreat, gave the enemy the opportunity to win time. Having brought up the 95th, 707th and 253rd infantry divisions and the *Grossdeutschland* SS Panzer

1 Editor's note. Aleksei Innokent'evich Antonov (1896-1962) served as a junior officer in the Russian imperial army during World War I. He joined the Red Army in 1918 and took part in the civil war. During the Great Patriotic War he served in various front-line staff assignments, before being appointed chief of the General Staff's operational directorate in 1942 and deputy chief of staff the following year. Antonov was appointed chief of the General Staff in 1945, although he held that post for less than a year. Following the war, Antonov commanded a military district and served as chief of staff of the Warsaw Pact forces.

Division, as well as more than five independent battalions, the Germans preempted our units' arrival.

On the morning of 25 July, when the 16th Guards Rifle Corps had not yet finished its preparations for the offensive and the 2nd Guards Cavalry Corps was only arriving at the concentration area, the Germans suddenly launched a counterattack with major infantry and tank forces. As a result of a number of powerful attacks, by the close of July 26 they had pushed back our units a little and occupied Alisovo and Izmorozn', and seized Alekhino on the morning of 27 July.

As a result of the powerful pressure from fresh enemy units, the 16th Guards Rifle Corps was not able to organize the breakthrough of the enemy's defense and secure the commitment of the 2nd Guards Cavalry Corps into the breach. The corps' divisions had been drawn into intensive fighting with the enemy who was insistently attacking our units and they could not allot sufficient forces for breaking through the enemy's defense.

Despite this, General Kryukov decided to break through the enemy's defense with just his cavalry. On 27 July the group, consisting of the 2nd Guards Cavalry Corps and part of the 16th Guards Rifle Corps' right-flank units, began attacking along the Pal'kevichi—Obel'na sector in the general direction of the southwest.

The fighting was very intense. The enemy put up powerful fire resistance and took advantage of local conditions that favored the defense. Blocking the road of our attacking forces, the Germans cut all the axes along which the roads were suitable for movement in this difficult area, and they mined the corduroy roads through the swamps.

The enemy air force, in groups of 20-100 planes, bombed and strafed our units, delaying their advance and supporting at the same time the continuous and powerful counterattacks by their infantry and tanks.

The group began its attack when the tank regiments and part of the cavalry corps' divisional artillery was still on the march. Units of the 16th Guards Rifle Corps, which had on an average only 10-20 men per company, were very worn out by the preceding uninterrupted fighting. The 1st Tank Corps, which had also been weakened by the several days of fighting, could not be effectively employed along this swampy sector. The main burden of the breakthrough and offensive lay on the cavalry.

On the morning of 27 July units of the 4th and 3rd guards cavalry divisions broke through the enemy defense with a bold attack along the Pal'kevichi—Obel'na sector, destroyed a series of enemy strong points and, developing the breakthrough's success, drove to the west and southwest, defeating and throwing back the defending units of the 707th Infantry Division, the "Werze" group, the forward detachments of the *Grossdeutschland* Division, and elements of individual battalions thrown in here.

Boldly and decisively operating in a difficult wooded and swampy area, the cavalry units successfully advanced. To their right the 1st Guards Rifle Division was attacking, securing the cavalry's actions from the north.

At this time as many as two regiments of German infantry, with 65 tanks, attacked in the Alekhino area. At the same time, the enemy began attacking from the south toward Zhudre. The attack by a large group of infantry, motorized infantry and tanks in the Alekhino—Izmorozn' area would have created a threat to the flank of the cavalry corps advancing to the west.

However, as a result of the stubborn defense by the 16th Guards Rifle Corps' 31st and 11th guards rifle divisions, which were operating along with the 43rd and 29th guards and 117th tank brigades, the Germans, despite the quantitative superiority they had achieved along a number of sectors, were nowhere able to achieve any kind of significant successes.

The German command, frightened by our cavalry's advance, hurriedly reinforced the Karachev area with newer and newer units and concentrated here a major air group. The enemy's air force, in groups of 40-60 planes, bombed our forces almost continuously.

On 28 July stubborn fighting broke out with major enemy infantry and tanks forces, which following a powerful air preparation, counterattacked from the Alekhino area toward Zhudre and Pyryatinka. The villages of Bol'shoe Naryshkino, Pyryatinka, Klyuch-Kolodez' (one kilometer east of Bol'shoe Naryshkino) changed hands repeatedly.

As a result of the intensive fighting the Germans, at the cost of heavy losses, managed to delay the development of our offensive along the Karachev axis, but all their attempts to throw our units back into the Kudryavtsev woods were unsuccessful.

Stubborn fighting by General Kryukov's group lasted four days against the enemy's superior forces. As a result of this fighting, the group's forces inflicted heavy losses on the enemy, cut the Khvastovichi—Karachev road and, threatening Karachev from the north, by the close of 30 July had reached the line marker 174.2—excluding the Gutovskii timber mill—Moskovskii—the bend in the road between the villages of Zheltovod'e and Zhirkiny Dvory—Pyryatinka—Khotiml'—the northwestern outskirts of Il'inskoe, and then further to the northeast as far as the Gnezdilovo—L'govo road.

The enemy, reinforcing his group of forces operating along the Karachev axis and covering the Orel—Bryansk railroad, continued to throw newer and newer units into the fighting along this sector. The enemy's resistance increased with each day. Lacking forces for the further development of a decisive offensive, General Kryukov's group was forced to go over to the defensive and, while engaging in local offensive fighting with limited aims, remained along its occupied line.

On 30 July two regiments from the 4th Guards Cavalry Division carried out a bold raid in the enemy rear for the purpose of cutting the Karachev—Bryansk railroad along the Filosofskii Zavod—Slava sector and disrupting railroad communications in the German rear.

The cavalry broke through to the railroad in two separate detachments, carried out their assignment and, upon returning from the raid, on 3 August rejoined their division. On 4 August units of the 2nd Guards Cavalry Corps began turning over their defensive zone to the rifle units and, by the morning of August 7, having gone into the *front* reserve, concentrated in the Trosna—Butyrki—Klen area.

By a decision of the *Stavka* of the Supreme High Command, on 30 July the 11th Guards, 4th Tank and 11th armies and the 2nd Guards Cavalry Corps were transferred to the Bryansk Front for closer cooperation with the forces attacking toward Orel.

The Results of Combat Activities Along the Western Front's Left Wing, 12-30 July

As a result of the fighting along the Western Front's left wing, our attacking units, having created the threat of encirclement for the enemy's Bolkhov group of forces, carried out their main mission for eliminating it and essentially decided the fate of Bolkhov. The remnants of the defeated German units, pursued by our forces, were forced to abandon the Bolkhov position and fall back to the south and southwest.

The attack by the left wing of the 11th Guards Army and the 4th Tank army was the main reason for the German forces' retreat along this sector.

On 29 July the 61st Army, with the active support of units from the left wing of the 11th Guards Army and the 4th Tank Army, had completely cleared the Bolkhov area of the enemy.

However, the remnants of the enemy's Bolkhov group of forces managed to slip away from being completely encircled. The enemy also managed to hinder the encirclement of his entire Orel group of forces.

The main reason for this was the late arrival of our operational reserves—especially the 4th Tank Army and the 2nd Guards Cavalry Corps. These forces could have and should have developed the success of the 11th Guards Army, which had broken through the enemy's defense throughout its entire depth in two days; to bring about the destruction of the German defense along the entire

Orel salient through a headlong offensive to the southeast, south and southwest and, together with the forces of the Bryansk and Central fronts, to complete the encirclement of the large enemy group of forces operating here.

The great distance of the 4th Tank Army and the 2nd Guards Cavalry Corps from the front, the small number of roads (which had also been seriously damaged by the constant rains) required too much time for their movement to the front, while at the same time the 11th Guards Army's offensive during the first days developed at a high rate of speed that significantly exceeded the usual speed of an offensive operation against a heavily fortified enemy.

The conditions for committing powerful operational reserves along the 11th Guards Army's sector in the direction of Khotynets and Karachev were most favorable during the 17-23 July time period. At this time the enemy lacked sufficient forces for resisting our offensive. However, neither did the 11th Guards Army during this time possess sufficient forces for an attack on Khotynets.

Only two rifle divisions were operating along the Khotynets axis, which was supposed to become the main attack axis, while the army's main forces were attacking along the Znamenskoe axis. Here the enemy, employing the favorable terrain, was able to delay our offensive by powerful air attacks, artillery fire and counterattacks by mobile units, and even forced the army's shock group (including three tank corps) to temporarily go over to the defensive. In this the enemy was aided by the fact that cooperation between the infantry, tanks, artillery, and aviation, which had been well organized at the start of the offensive, had by this time been disrupted to a significant degree: the tanks operated without sufficient support from the combined-arms formations and the air force.

The commitment of the 11th Army along the Khvastovichi axis did not have decisive significance for the course of the operation. The army's forces were spread out and committed piecemeal into the fighting. The army got bogged down in the enemy's organized defense and could only push the enemy back somewhat.

By 26 July, when the 4th Tank Army and 2nd Guards Cavalry Corps arrived, the enemy had already managed to bring up major forces to the 11th Guards Army's sector and consolidate.

However, despite the fact that we were not able to carry out the encirclement of the enemy, the offensive by the left wing of the Western Front and the right wing of the Bryansk Front yielded major operational results.

In the Bolkhov area, which was covering Orel from the north, our forces defeated the Germans' most powerful group of forces, and at the same time eliminated the Bolkhov fortified area. The forces of the 11th Guards, 4th Tank and 61st armies, while continuing to attack to the south and southwest, had created an immediate threat of outflanking Orel from the northwest and the encirclement of the entire Orel group of forces. This subsequently forced the German troops, defending opposite the Bryansk Front's left wing, to hurriedly fall back to the west.

Besides this, another result of the operations by the Western Front's left-wing forces was that the German command, while trying to delay the advance by our attacking forces and to cover its main communications—the Orel—Bryansk railroad—was forced to transfer to this sector more than 12 divisions (including six panzer), a large part of which were routed during the course of the fighting. Thus the active operations of the Western Front's left-wing forces pinned down major enemy forces, forcing him to removed entire divisions and independent units from other axes and throw them into the Bolkhov and Karachev areas. This significantly aided our forces' operations in the areas of Orel and Belgorod, and later in the Smolensk area.

4

The Orel Operation

The Breakthrough of the Enemy's Defense and the Arrival of the 3rd and 63rd Armies to the Line of the Oleshnya River (12-16 July)

On 10 July 1943 the forces of the Bryansk Front's 3rd and 63rd armies completed their preparations and occupied their jumping-off positions for the offensive set for the morning of 11 July.

The 3rd Army, as was shown earlier, had the following mission: by launching its main attack along the left flank in the general direction of Staraya Otrada, to break through the enemy's defense along the Izmailovo—Vyazhi sector and reach the Lisitsa River, and then, turning its main forces to the southwest, to attack along the Oka River in conjunction with the 63rd Army and capture Orel. Part of the army's forces was to encircle and destroy the Germans' Mtsensk group of forces together with the 61st Army.

The 63rd Army was to attack along its right flank along the Vyazhi—Orlovka sector and break through the enemy's defense and, attacking toward Stanovoi Kolodez', reach the line of the Orel—Zmievka railroad and paved road, and subsequently turning to the north and outflanking Orel from the south, capture the city in conjunction with the 3rd Army; the army was also to launch a supporting attack from the line of the Optukha River toward Orel from the east.

On the night of 10-11 July, while the final preparations were being made, an order was received from the *front* commander, which contained the following:

> The offensive planned for 11 July is delayed until 12 July. On 11 July the 3rd and 63rd armies are to carry out reconnaissance activities along the planned breakthrough sector, for the purpose of seizing the enemy's first trench line along the forward edge and, while holding this position, to secure the main forces' attack the following morning. The attack is to determine whether or not the enemy has shifted his forward edge of the defense back to the depth at the last minute and, if he has, to what line.

In order to carry out the assignment, the most prepared rifle battalions rifle battalions were immediately singled out from each of both armies' first-echelon divisions (one from each division, plus 3-5 tanks in each battalion), which moved forward under the cover of darkness to our forces first trenches and made ready to attack.

At 1150 on 11 July, following a powerful fire onslaught by our artillery and a salvo by guards mortar units, the battalions crossed over the Zusha River and attacked the enemy's first trenches. Having discovered the infantry attack, the Germans opened a powerful rifle and machine gun fire. A battalion from the 235th Rifle Division, which was attacking south of Maloe Izmailovo, having suffered heavy losses from the enemy's flanking fire from this strong point, called off the attack and before long had fallen back to its jumping-off position. Under the cover of powerful artillery fire, a battalion from the 380th Rifle Division advanced energetically behind its tanks and broke into the enemy's trench 300 meters west of Vyazhi and, following a short hand-to-hand skirmish, seized it. At the same time, a battalion from the 129th Rifle Division broke into the enemy position. To the south, battalions from the 63rd Army's 348th and 287th rifle divisions were not able to reach the German trenches and were forced to fall back to their jumping-off position.

The commanders of the 380th and 129th rifle divisions, taking advantage of their battalions' success, immediately threw in fresh subunits to assist them. Artillery and mortars, edging the battalions' position with a dense wall of fire, continuously bombarded the enemy's position. Before long, anti-tank guns, anti-tank rifles and mortars were brought up to the captured trenches and both battalions securely consolidated their positions.

In general, both armies' reconnaissance battalions, despite the powerful support rendered by artillery and mortar fire, were unable to completely carry out their assignment. However, the reconnaissance in force confirmed that the German forces were occupying and securely defending the first trench and had not changed their forces' dispositions. Before the start of the general offensive this information played a major role in effectively employing artillery and mortar fire.

At 0200 on 12 July the 3rd and 63rd armies' artillery began the artillery offensive. More than 4,000 guns and mortars opened up a powerful fire against the enemy's first and second trench lines. Before long the air force arrived, and while continuously dive-bombing the enemy's combat formation, dropped bombs. Columns of flame from the explosions covered the German trenches with a thick wall of smoke.

Our infantry, covered by artillery fire and aviation, energetically advanced and forded the Zusha River and by 0530 arrived at the enemy trenches.

Within ten minutes (0540) a salvo by the guard mortar units followed, which also served as the signal for the attack. The infantry, supported by tanks, attacked the enemy and broke into the first trench. Stunned by the powerful fire, the German forces put up weak resistance. Units of the 235th Rifle Division, despite the fact that the attached 114th Tank Regiment could not cross the river near Izmailovo (one kilometer west of Maloe Izmailovo) at the same time and was forced to cross near Vyazhi, broke through the enemy defense along the Izmailovo—Vyazhi line and by 1100 had captured height 246.7 (one kilometer north of Ivan').

To the left the 380th Rifle Division, taking advantage of its neighbor's—the 235th Rifle Division—success, rapidly moved forward along its right flank and, capturing Ivan', began fighting for Grachevka.

The most stubborn fighting unfolded in the 63rd Army's offensive zone. The enemy, employing a large number of favorably situated heights, had heavily fortified them. Our offensive met immediate and stubborn resistance. In spite of the fact that four tank regiments were operating here, as well as a large amount of artillery, the infantry fought for four hours along the forward edge of the enemy's defense, and only after the army commander had concentrated the army's entire artillery fire against the Bol'shoi Malinovets area and heights 244.9 and 254.9, did the infantry and tanks break through the German defense. Developing the offensive to the west, units of the 129th Rifle Division had by 1200 captured the enemy's Bol'shoi Malinovets strong point and had begun stubborn fighting for the grove to the west. The 348th Rifle Division, having thrown the enemy out of his first trenches, was not able to break into height 254.9 on his heels and was engaged in heavy fighting on its eastern slopes. While continuing to clear the enemy out of the first trenches, the division advanced insignificantly.

Following the enemy's loss of such important defensive strong points as Maloe Izmailovo, Bol'shoi Malinovets and height 244.9, the German command began to take measures to delay our forces' advance at any price. At 1000 a large number of German planes appeared above the battlefield. In groups of 40-50 aircraft, they continuously dive bombed our infantry and tanks, bombed the crossings over the Zusha River, and strafed the artillery's firing positions. Before 1200 over 600 enemy aircraft had been sighted over our forces' position. Fresh German infantry and tank forces were hurriedly moved to the breakthrough area. Our aviation, which was engaged in intensive air battles, observed the concentration of the enemy's reserves in the Medyn'—Kochety area and also in the woods south of Grachevka. That same day the 12th Panzer Division's assault and training battalions arrived in the Zhelyabug area from Orel and which were thrown into the fighting against the 380th Rifle Division in the Grachevka area from the march. Units of the 235th Rifle Division east of Yevtekhovo were subjected to repeated counterattacks from several directions.

On the offensive's first day the forces of the 3rd and 63rd armies, despite the powerful support rendered by air and artillery, were not able to completely break through the Germans' main defensive zone and were forced to wage a difficult struggle to destroy the strong points that had been erected in large numbers in the defensive depth. The greatest advance was made by the 235th and 380th rifle divisions, attacking along the armies' boundary. On this day they penetrated 5-7 kilometers into the enemy's position and reached the line Yevtekhovo—Grachevka—Zatish'e.

The 1st Guards Tank Corps' commitment into the breach

The *front* commander decided to take advantage of the impending breakthrough along the 235th and 380th rifle divisions' sector, and at 2115 on 12 July issued an order by which the 1st Guards Tank Corps was given the following mission: during the night of 12-13 July the corps was to cross to the western bank of the Zusha River and concentrate in the Ivan'—Zatish'e—Vyazhi area. The following morning, as soon as the infantry occupied the Yevtekhovo—Grachevka line, the corps was to immediately enter the breach along the 235th and 380th rifle divisions' sector and, developing the success, capture the Mokhovoe area by the end of the day. The commitment of the tank corps into the breach was to be supported by the main forces of the 15th Air Army and the 2nd Artillery Corps.

At 0800 on 13 July units of the 3rd and 63rd armies resumed the offensive. The 235th Rifle Division, taking advantage of the powerful fire of bomber aviation and artillery directed against the Yevtekhovo strong point, enveloped it from the flanks and, following a short but stubborn battle, completely destroyed the German garrison and captured the village. Pursuing the subunits of the 171st Infantry Regiment, which were retreating in disorder, by midday the division reached the southern outskirts of Krasnyi. To the left the 308th Rifle Division, which had been committed into the fighting on 13 July and was attacking to the south of Yevtekhovo, destroyed the enemy in the woods west of Yevtekhevo and captured the village of Veselaya. The 380th Rifle Division, while developing the success toward Zhelyabug, completely destroyed an assault battalion from the Second Panzer Army in the area of the village of Kazinka and occupied the villages of Kochety and Kolbaevka. On this day the forces of the 63rd Army achieved great successes. The 129th Rifle Division, having defeated the German 262nd Infantry Division's 484th Regiment, captured the powerful enemy strong point of Setukha. Along the left flank the 250th Rifle Division, which had gone over to the offensive on 13 July, seized Berezovets, while the 348th and 287th rifle divisions, which had moved forward significantly, had begun fighting along the approaches to Arkhangel'skoe.

Thus on 13 July the forces of the 3rd and 63rd armies carried out their assignments and captured not only the Yevtekhovo and Grachevka enemy strong points along the axis of the main attack, but the Setukha and Berezovets strong points along the breakthrough's flank, thus creating the necessary conditions for the commitment of the 1st Guards Tank Corps into the fighting.

However, the tank corps was not able to fully take advantage of these conditions. Having completed its crossing over the Zusha River at 0500 on 13 July, the corps, which was insufficiently masked, was subjected to a powerful enemy air raid and suffered heavy losses in its concentration areas east of Yevtekhovo. It was only at 1400 that we were able to put the corps' brigades in order, after which it began its attack in three columns. However, despite the increased cover by our fighter aviation, the corps' movement was constantly under enemy air attack and forced to move very slowly. The tanks passed the infantry only at 1600 along the line Voskresensk—Rzhavets

State Farm and attacked along three axes: the right column in the general direction of Suvorova, the middle on Zhabino, and the left on Zhelyabug (south).

The right column, having reached Obraztsovka, destroyed the enemy's strong point in this village and by the end of the day had reached Trekhonetovo (two kilometers west of Obraztsovka). The middle column immediately encountered the enemy's powerful anti-tank defense in the Kochety area and fell back on its infantry. Nor did the left column achieve any success and became involved in heavy fighting with the enemy along the approaches to Kolbaevka.

Thus although the necessary conditions had been created for the commitment of the 1st Guards Tank Corps, it was unable to develop the infantry's success and its main forces remained behind the infantry formations. Despite this, the 3rd and 63rd armies' divisions, making wide use of infantry support tanks in the offensive, continued to energetically advance and by the close of 13 July reached the line Krasnyi—Kochety—Kolbaevka, having broken through the German defense throughout its entire tactical depth.

The arrival of the 3rd and 63rd armies' units at the Oleshnya River (14-17 July)

The enemy's resistance continued to increase as our forces advanced to the west. The German command, in spite of the serious threat that had arisen by this time for its Bolkhov group of forces, threw a significant part of its reserves against the 3rd and 63rd armies' breakthrough sector. On 13 July the 36th Infantry Division, which had earlier been operating along the Central Front's sector, arrived. Besides this, the 8th Panzer Division, which had been transferred from the Vitebsk area, began to arrive by rail. On the following day units of the 8th Panzer Division were committed into the fighting in the Arkhangel'skoe area. Units of the enemy's 36th Infantry Division were moved into this same area. On 16 July the 2nd Panzer Division, which had earlier been operating along the Kromy axis, concentrated in the area of the village of Suvorova. The German air force's operations increased considerably.

However, the German command did not have the opportunity to employ the newly arrived divisions for launching a powerful counterstroke. Our forces had deeply penetrated into the enemy defense and had widened the breach toward the flanks, securely maintaining the initiative in their hands. The Germans were forced to throw their reserves into the fighting piecemeal along the most varied axes, striving at whatever cost to halt the advance of our forces and to win the time necessary for occupying the defensive line along the western bank of the Oleshnya River.

On 14 July two infantry battalions with tanks launched a powerful attack against the 235th Rifle Division's flank from the north. On that same day up to a regiment of infantry, with tanks, counterattacked the 308th Rifle Division, which had been occupying up to this time the Suvorova strong point. Units of the 63rd Army's 5th Rifle Division, which had been committed into the fighting on 14 July near the village of Kazinka, were subjected to powerful attacks from the Zhelyabug area. The enemy repeatedly counterattacked the 63rd Army's other divisions. However, all the German forces' counterattacks, despite their powerful support by artillery and aviation, were successfully repulsed by our forces with heavy losses for the enemy.

Energetically developing the offensive to the northwest, units of the 3rd Army inflicted heavy losses on the 56th Infantry Division and by 16 July had reached the line of the Oleshnya River along the entire front. To the right, while rolling up the enemy's position along the western bank of the Zusha River, the 269th Rifle Division's 1018th and 1022nd regiments occupied the villages of Yelizavetinka and Leninskii, and continued clearing out the eastern bank. The 235th Rifle Division, overcoming the enemy's stubborn resistance, reached Leninskii farm (one kilometer south of Leninskii) with its right flank, while its left flank consolidated near the grove northwest of height 245.3. The 308th Rifle Division, beating back the enemy's continuous counterattacks, captured the village of Borodinskii and was slowly advancing on Borodinka. The 380th Rifle

Division, having defeated the enemy's powerful strong points of Pobednoe and Zhelyabug, crossed the Oleshnya River with its right-flank forces on the heels of the retreating German garrison, and seized a small bridgehead along the line Bol'shoe Ochkasovo—Aleksandrovka.

The 63rd Army's force advanced significantly slower during these days. The 1st Guards Tank Corps, which had once again been committed into the fighting on 15 July, with the mission of taking Mokhovoe, could not break through the enemy's defense along the front Podmaslovo—Tsarevka and, on orders of the 63rd Army commander, was withdrawn into the Zhelyabug—Zhelyabug farm area. The rifle divisions, having advanced insignificantly, reached the line Tsarevka—Dal'novidovo—Arkhangel'skoe—height 261.3 and encountering the enemy's stubborn resistance here along previously prepared positions, went over to the defensive.

The Central Front's counteroffensive

As a result of stubborn resistance along the northern face of the Kursk salient by the Central Front's forces, the enemy offensive that began on 5 July was halted. The exhausted and bled-white German forces were forced to assume the defensive.

The successful offensive by the Western and Bryansk fronts' forces, which had drawn off part of the strength of the enemy's Orel group of forces and almost all his air strength from the Kursk direction, had created a favorable situation for the Central Front's right wing to assume the offensive.

In carrying out the *front* commander's order, which was issued to the troops on 12 July, the *front's* right wing armies immediately set about regrouping their forces and preparing for the offensive. Over the course of three days a shock group was created in the Ponyri—Ol'khovatka area, consisting of the 18th Rifle and 16th Tank corps.

On 15 July the 48th (left wing), 13th and 70th armies went from the defensive to the offensive. The 13th Army launched a powerful attack in the direction of Gremyachevo and split the enemy forces into two parts. Simultaneously, units of the 48th and 70th armies launched attacks from the flanks. In order to avoid complete encirclement, the German forces began to fall back to the north, suffering huge losses and abandoning a large amount of equipment and munitions on the battlefield.

Pursuing the retreating enemy, the forces of the Central Front's right wing completely eliminated the salient along the Ol'khovatka axis by 18 July and completely restored the former situation.

The success achieved by our forces could not but cause concern within the German command. A new and serious danger hung over their Orel group of forces—the Central Front's outflanking of the Orel group of forces from the south, which would inevitably lead to the complete encirclement of the defending forces here. The commander of the German Ninth Army demanded that his officers and men maintain the positions they had been defending before 5 July, no matter what the cost. However, the German troops did not carry out this order. The Central Front's right-wing armies, without halting their offensive, on 21 July broke through the enemy's defense along the Ochka River and energetically developed the success toward Kamenets and Kromy.

Thus the 3rd and 63rd armies, closely cooperating with the Central Front's forces, reached the line of the Oleshnya River with their main forces and carried out their mission. On 16 July the operation's first stage was completed.

In five days of offensive fighting the Bryansk Front's left-wing forces had broken through the enemy's defense to a depth of 17-22 kilometers and had widened the breakthrough front to 36 kilometers. Having routed the enemy between the Zusha and Oleshnya rivers, they had created the necessary conditions for developing the 3rd Army's success to the northwest and outflanking Mtsensk from the southwest, and the 63rd Army to the southwest in the general direction of Stanovoi Kolodez'. The gates formed by our armies' offensive along eccentric axes, enabled the *front* commander to commit major tank and motorized formations from the line of the Oleshnya River in the space between the armies, for the purpose of speeding up the complete defeat of the German forces defending east of Orel and the subsequent envelopment of the German's Orel group of forces from the north and south.

The Breakthrough of the Enemy's Intermediate Defensive Line Along the Oleshnya River and the Arrival of Our Forces at the Oka and Optukha Rivers

The enemy's defensive line along the Oleshnya River had been prepared beforehand and was a powerful intermediate line between the main defensive line, which had been built along the Zusha River, and the third (rear) line, which ran along the western bank of the Oka and Optukha rivers. Taking into account the difficult situation that had arisen east of Orel, the German command threw all its reserves (2nd and 8th panzer, 36th Infantry and 12th Anti-Aircraft divisions) into the intermediate line, which were defending here. The line Golovinka—Zabrody—Podmaslovo—Arkhangel'skoe was especially strong fortified, and where the enemy had concentrated all his tank and main artillery forces. Minefields had been hurriedly laid on the approaches to this line, all the crossings over the Oleshnya River had been blown up, and specially-selected teams of incendiarists were burning the villages.

The breakthrough of the enemy's defense along the line of the Oleshnya River

The commander of the 3rd Army decided to attack the enemy on the morning of 17 July. In accordance with this decision, the newly-arrived 25th Rifle Corps (362nd and 186th rifle divisions) was to launch its main attack along the front Panama—Aleksandrovka in the direction of Kobyakovo, height 260.0 and Kruglitsa. The corps was to break through the enemy's defense toward the Oleshnya River and by the close of the day reach the line Yadrino—Dobrovody—Protasovo.

The 269th Rifle Division, which was operating along the right flank, received the following orders: while securing the shock group's operations from the north, to attack in the direction of Bratskii and Pyatovo and, rolling up the enemy's line toward the north and northwest, expand the breach in the direction of the right flank.

The 235th Rifle Division had the mission of tying down the enemy with active operations along the Leninskii—Avvakumovskii sector with one rifle battalion, while the remaining forces launched an attack along the front Avvakumovskii—height 245.3 in the general direction of Dobrovody, and by the close of 17 July to capture Verkhnii Gavrilits and Grachiki.

The 308th Rifle Division, while holding its line, had the mission of securing along its sector the commitment of the 25th Rifle Corps' units; following the corps' breakthrough of the enemy's defense, the division would go into the army's reserve.

The 380th Rifle Division, having regrouped its forces to the south, was to securely defend the line southern outskirts of Aleksandrovka—Gogol' and cover the shock group's left flank.

The 1st Guards Tank Corps was ordered to concentrate on the night of 16-17 July in the Suvorova—Kochety—Baranovo area, in readiness to enter the breach in the 25th Rifle Corps' zone. Once the infantry took the line of the Arsen'evo—Golubok road, the corps was to attack to the south in the direction of Merkulovo and Golubok and by the end of the day reach the area Oleshnya—Kazinka—Gusevo, with the task of securing the army's left flank from the direction of Zolotarevo and Mokhovoe.

The 63rd Army commander, leaving the army's previous tasks unchanged, committed the 5th Rifle Division into the battle along his right flank, in order to continue the the right flank's offensive, which had begun on 17 July, in the general direction of Mokhovoe.

By the close of 16 July units of the 3rd and 63rd armies had reached the Oleshnya River and, not having completely cleared the eastern bank of small groups of the enemy, intensely prepared for the offensive during the night and regrouped and conducted reconnaissance of the enemy.

During the night our aviation continuously launched raids against the enemy's reserves, the crossings over the Oka River and road junctions. The road junction near Protasovo, the Arsen'evo, Kobyakovo, Sychi, Podmaslovo, and Mokhovoe strong points were subjected to particularly heavy bombardment.

During the night the Germans fired along the eastern bank of the Oleshnya River with artillery and mortars. Groups of scouts along several sectors of the front sought to penetrate our lines. At dawn on 17 July the German air force launched powerful raids against the positions of the 25th Rifle Corps, which had occupied its jumping-off positions for the attack, as well as the position of the left-flank 380th Rifle Division. At the same time, units of the 63rd Army's 129th and 348th rifle divisions, which were ready to attack the enemy's Arkhangel'skoe strong point, were subjected to intensive air attack.

At 1130 on 17 July, following a 10-minute artillery and aviation onslaught, the 3rd and 63rd armies' forces attacked. The enemy put up stubborn resistance. The German artillery and mortars, which had not been suppressed during the artillery preparation, fired intensively, keeping the infantry and tanks from advancing. Units of the 269th and 235th rifle divisions twice attempted to break through the enemy's defense, but each time were forced to fall back to their starting positions.

The 25th Rifle Corps, along with the 253rd and 82nd tank and 1538th self-propelled artillery regiments, broke through the enemy's defense with an attack along their left flank along the Panama—Alekseevka sector, and at 1200 captured the eastern outskirts of Arsen'evo and the fork in the road one kilometer east of Kobyakovo and height 247.4.

Seeking to prevent the development of the breakthrough, the German command threw its main reserves and air strength against the 25th Rifle Corps' units. Throughout the day the 362nd and 186th rifle divisions were continuously subjected to counterattacks and powerful air raids.

At 1300 up to two battalions of infantry, with 30 tanks, launched an attack against the 362nd Rifle Division's right flank and forced its 1210th Regiment to abandon Arsen'evo.

Within an hour up to a battalion of infantry, with tanks, from the Kobyakovo—Novaya Zhizn' area, and up to a regiment of infantry from the woods southeast of the village of Bortnoe, counterattacked units of the 186th Rifle Division, which were forced to abandon height 247.4 and fall back 200-300 meters to the east. The German planes hung continuously over the battlefield until 1900, dropping bombs on the 25th Rifle Corps' units. More than 600 enemy aircraft flights were registered over this sector during the day's fighting.

Our units successfully beat back all counterattacks by the enemy, who suffered heavy losses. However, on 17 July the corps was forced to halt its attack and temporarily go over to the defensive along the line reached, having failed to completely carry out its mission.

The 1st Guards Tank Corps, having entered the breach along the 25th Rifle Corps' left flank between Alekseevka and Aleksandrovka, was attacked west of Aleksandrovka by a large number of enemy tanks, supported by aviation and, having suffered losses; fell back on its infantry.

Having begun the attack simultaneously with the 3rd Army, the 63rd Army's forces also failed to break through the enemy's defense on this day and continued fighting along its previous line.

The decision by the commander of the Bryansk Front to commit the 3rd Tank Army into the breach

The situation that obtained by 17 July in the Orel area required that the Bryansk Front's forces speed up the arrival of their left wing to the line of the Oka River, so that, together with General

Bagramyan's forces, which by this time had arrived at Khotynets, they could complete the defeat of the enemy's Orel group of forces and simultaneously, together with the Central Front's forces that had gone over to the attack on 15 July, assist with their left flank the destruction of the German's Orel—Kromy group of forces.

The commander of the Bryansk Front decided to commit his reserve—General Rybalko's 3rd Guards Tank Army—into the fighting. The tank army, by launching a decisive attack from the line Bogdanovo—Arsen'evo—Izotkino—Bortnoe—Podmaslovo in the general direction of Spasskoe and Otrada, was to cut the Orel—Mtsensk railroad and paved road and capture the western bank of the Oka River. The *front's* left-wing forces were ordered to launch a decisive offensive on the morning of 19 July, following an air and artillery preparation. By launching their main attack along the boundary between the 3rd and 63rd armies, they were to secure the commitment of the 3rd Guards Tank Army into the breach and, by the close of the day, reach the line Dobrovody—Protasovo—Oleshnya—Mokhovoe—Arkhangel'skoe.

The 3rd Army was to launch an attack along the Arsen'evo—Aleksandrovka sector, defeat the opposing enemy units and, having secured the commitment of the 3rd Guards Tank Army into the breach along this sector, reach the line Dobrovody—Protasovo—Oleshnya.

The 1st Guards Tank Corps, attacking from this line, was to reach the Staraya Otrada area and by the end of the day cut the Mtsensk—Orel railroad and paved road.

In order to support the commitment of the 3rd Guards Tank Army into the breach and its crossing of the Oleshnya River, it was decided to bring in the 15th and 20th artillery divisions and all the army's artillery. Subsequently, the army's main forces had the mission of attacking in the general direction of Orel, while another two divisions would attack to the northwest, so that in conjunction with the 61st Army, they would destroy the Germans' Mtsensk group of forces.

The 63rd Army was ordered to launch a decisive offensive along the entire front on the morning of 19 July and, launching its main attack along the right flank, defeat the enemy forces and reach the Podmaslovo—Mokhovoe—Arkhangel'skoe area; the army was to subsequently attack with its main forces toward Stanovoi Kolodez', securely guarding the *front's* left flank.

During the 3rd Guards Tank Army's commitment into the breach, the 63rd Army was to support its left flank with artillery fire.

The 15th Air Army, in conjunction with Colonel General Golovanov's[1] Long-Range Aviation, on the night of 18-19 July was to bomb the concentration and deployment areas of the enemy's artillery in the 3rd and 63rd armies' attack zone, and also to support with bomber and assault aviation the 3rd Guards Tank Army's commitment into the breach and attack.

Throughout 18 July our units made ready to carry out their mission. The artillery and mortars, concentrating their fire opposite the front of the 25th Rifle Corps, which was continuing to hold the line it had seized on 17 July, were destroying the enemy's fortifications and suppressing his artillery. The officers of the tank army, which had reached the area of the woods west of Yevtekhovo on the night of 17-18 July, carried out reconnaissance with the combined-arms commanders, indicated routes of passage through their combat formations and elaborated their mission. The 15th Air Army's planes systematically launched bombing raids against concentrations of the enemy's infantry and tanks. The area of Sychi, Novaya Zhizn' and the woods south of Bortnoe, as well as the Protasovo area, where a newly arrived column of German tanks had been spotted, were subjected to heavy air attacks.

1 Editor's note. Aleksandr Yevgen'evich Golovanov (1904-75) joined the Red Army in 1919 and later served in the secret police (OGPU-NKVD) and became a pilot. During the Great Patriotic War he commanded an air regiment and division and in 1942 was appointed commander of Long-Range Aviation (18th Air Army). Following the Great Patriotic War, Golovanov continued to occupy high administrative posts, but his career went into steep decline after Stalin's death.

The 3rd Guards Tank Army's commitment into the fighting on 19 July 1943

General Rybalko, the commander of the 3rd Guards Tank Army, decided to enter the breach with two tank corps (12th and 15th) in the first echelon; he gave these corps the following assignment: by launching a powerful blow against the enemy's rear, to defeat the Germans' units located east of the Oka River and to capture the crossings over the river along the Naryshkino—Ivanovskaya Optukha sector. The army's forward detachments were to cut the Bolkhov—Orel paved road along the Polozovskie Dvory—Nepolod' sector.

According to this decision, the corps received the following missions:

> The 12th Guards Tank Corps, having begun its advance from the line Krasnyi—Veselaya, was to enter the breach along the 3rd Army's sector and attack in the direction of Dobrovody and Yarygino; by the close of the offensive's first day the corps' main forces were to capture the crossings over the Oka River along the Naryshkino—Staraya Otrada sector, while its forward detachments were to cut the Bolkhov—Orel paved road along the Polozovskie Dvory—Dubovaya Roshcha sector.
>
> The 15th Guards Tank Corps was to attack from its jumping-off point along the line Rzhavets State Farm—Setukha in the direction of Kolbaevka, Bortnoe and Kaznacheevo, and by the close of the offensive's first day capture the crossings over the Oka River with its main forces along the sector Staraya Otrada—Ivanovskaya Optukha, while its forward detachments would cut the Bolkhov—Orel paved road along the sector Dubovaya Roshcha—Nepolod'.

The 2nd Mechanized Corps was to follow in the army's second echelon and by the close of 19 July was to concentrate in the Dobrovody area, supporting the army's first-echelon operations against the enemy's attacks from the direction of Mtsensk and Orel.

Along the 3rd Army's entire front the Germans were very active. During 18 July German infantry and tanks repeatedly counterattacked, while their artillery and mortars systematically laid heavy fire along the eastern bank of the Oleshnya River. At 0500 two battalions of enemy infantry, supported by 20 tanks, counterattacked units of the 186th Rifle Division from the Novaya Zhizn' area in the direction of height 247.4. At 1020 a battalion of infantry counterattacked from the Bortnoe area eastward, but was scattered by our artillery fire. With the onset of darkness, our aviation uncovered a large concentration of enemy infantry and tanks in the area of Sychi and Bortnoe, which, to judge by the signs, was preparing to counterattack on the morning of 19 July against units of the 25th Rifle Corps.

During the daylight hours of 18 July; that is, when the 3rd Guards Tank Army was intensively preparing for the offensive, an order was received from the *front* commander, in which he laid out new tasks:

> The 3rd Guards Tank Army, by taking advantage of the success of the 3rd and 63rd armies' offensive, is to attack on the morning of 19 July in the direction of Bortnoe, Stanovaya, Stanovoi Kolodez', and Kromy and, operating against the rear of the enemy facing the Central Front, to destroy him in conjunction with the latter. The army's immediate task is to cut the Orel—Kursk railroad and seize crossings over the Rybnitsa River along the sector Lyubanovo—Zmievo.[2]

2 14 kilometers south of Lyubanovo.

The commander of the 3rd Guards Tank Army, taking into account that an extremely small amount of time (less than 24 hours) remained for preparing his tank formations for an offensive along a new axis, decided to keep the existing organization of forces and, instead of committing the army into the breach in accordance with the order issued on 17 July, he ordered it to begin advancing its corps along the new axis from the line Arsen'evo—Bortnoe. The corps' missions were as follows.

The 12th Guards Tank Corps was to attack from the line Arsen'evo—Kobyakovo in the direction of Sychi, Bychki, Plautino, and Stanovoi Kolodez' (northern) and by the close of 19 July to capture the area Pugachevka—Stanovoi Kolodez' (northern)—Il'inskii, while its forward detachments were to seize crossings over the Rybnitsa River near Lyubanovo and Stupino.

The 15th Guards Tank Corps was to attack in the direction of Bortnoe, 1st Zybino, Aleksandrovka, and Stanovoi Kolodez' (southern) and by the close of 19 July capture the Kuleshevka—Olovyannikovo—Khotetovo area.

At 0800 on 19 July, following a 10-minute artillery onslaught, units of the 3rd and 63rd armies resumed their attack.

Supported by powerful air strikes, the 3rd Army's infantry and tanks attacked the enemy in an energetic rush and broke through his defense. Units of the 362nd Rifle Division, following stubborn fighting for the enemy's powerful strong point of Izotkino, captured it at 1100. Before long we had captured the second strong point of Kobyakovo.

Units of the Germans' 8th and 2nd panzer divisions, while suffering heavy losses, fell back in fighting to the west. To the left, units of the 186th Rifle Division, advancing quickly, threw the enemy out of the strong points of Novaya Zhizn' and Bortnoe and were developing the success on height 260.0, bypassing Sychi from the south. Units of the enemy's 8th Panzer Division attempted to halt our advance with numerous counterattacks, but each time they were thrown back with heavy losses. To the right, units of the 269th and 235th rifle divisions, having broken through the forward edge of the defense of the 56th Infantry and units of the 2nd Panzer divisions, and overcoming their stubborn resistance, captured the villages of Bugry and Avvakumovskii.

To the left, units of the 63rd Army's 5th Rifle Division, while breaking the 36th Infantry Division's defense in intensive fighting, captured the strong points of Alisovo and Podmaslovo. The army's remaining divisions were not able to break through the heavily fortified German defense on 19 July and remained in their previous positions.

Thus as a result of the energetic actions of the 25th Rifle Corps' divisions, as early as three hours after the start of the 19 July offensive, the enemy's defense along the Oleshnya River had been completely broken. The 362nd and 186th rifle divisions penetrated into the enemy's lines to a depth of 3-4 kilometers and widened the breach along the flanks to a width of 8-10 kilometers. This created the conditions necessary for the 3rd Guards Tank Army's commitment into the fighting.

At 1040 on 19 July the 3rd Guards Tank Army's 12th and 15th guards tank corps, on the orders of the *front* commander, delivered by radio, left their jumping-off areas and began their attack to the west. At the same time, a large number of our fighters appeared in the air, which, while patrolling, covered the army's operations. Having discovered the movement of our tanks, the German command threw its air force against them. Numerous air battles broke out, as a result of which our fighters shot down 13 planes and forced a significant number of enemy bombers to abandon the battlefield without having dropped their bombs. The tank army continued to advance without losses.

At 1130 units of the 3rd Guards Tank Army, while advancing along an 8-10 kilometer front, overtook our infantry along the Arsen'evo—Bortnoe line and, while destroying pockets of enemy resistance along the way began to rapidly advance. In the Sychi area the Germans attempted to resist, but were quickly crushed by the mass of attacking tanks.

Taking advantage of the tank army's attack, units of the 25th Rifle Corps captured Sychi, height 260.0 and Pokrovka and continued attacking toward Protasovo. From the Sychi—Kobyakovo area both tank corps turned to the southwest and, overcoming the enemy's increasing resistance, attacked Stanovoi Kolodez'. The German planes systematically attacked our tanks, attempting to delay their advance to the south and defeat them. In the Bychki—Pokrovka area units of the 15th Guards Tank Corps were unexpectedly counterattacked in the flank by a large number of enemy tanks, among which were many heavy T-VI ("Tiger") tanks. The counterattack was beaten back. About 30 knocked-out and burnt German tanks remained on the field.

While holding the 3rd Army's attack along the right flank, at 1400 the Germans threw into the fighting near Sychi up to 100 of their tanks against the 12th Guards Tank Corps, as well as a large number of motorized infantry. The enemy's counterattack was beaten back. The German command hurriedly threw into the breakthrough area units of the 36th Infantry Division from the Mokhovoe area, chiefly anti-tank artillery, which as early as 1300 had entered the fighting with the 12th Guards Tank Corps' forward detachments along the line Bychki—Kruglitsa.

At the same time the enemy in the Protasovo area was hurriedly carrying out defensive works and his tanks and artillery were occupying their positions. The enemy strengthened his bombardment of the tank army's formations with artillery fire from the Dobrovody area. The Germans repeatedly counterattacked in small groups of tanks the 12th Guards Tank Corps' combat formations and unloaded from their tanks small groups of tank-destroyers, who laid mines and fired from anti-tank rifles and guns, which had been hauled forward by the tanks to the breakthrough area.

The enemy's strengthened artillery fire and air raids and the continuous counterattacks by his infantry and tanks significantly slowed the pace of the tank army's advance. By the close of 19 July its formations were forced to temporarily halt their attack and go over to the defensive. The 12th Guards Tank Corps went over to the defensive in the Bychki area and the 15th Guards Tank Corps in the Oleshnya area. The 25th Rifle Corps, following the tank army's turn to the south, encountered stubborn enemy resistance east of Protasovo and became involved in heavy fighting here.

The 1st Guards Tank Corps, taking advantage of the 3rd Guards Tank Army's success, entered the breach and from the Bortnoe area was attacking to the northwest in the general direction of Protasovo.

Taking advantage of the 25th Rifle Corps' success, the 308th Rifle Division's left flank also broke through the enemy's defense and by midday on 19 July one of its regiments had captured Gorbuntsovo and the northern slopes of height 250.1. South of Gorbuntsovo, by order of the commander of the 3rd Army, the 283rd Rifle Division, which had been preparing from the morning of 20 July to develop the success of the 308th Rifle Division, entered the breach.

Thus the tank army, which was committed into the fighting on 19 July, significantly sped up the breakthrough of the enemy's intermediate defensive zone. By the close of 19 July units of the 25th Rifle Corps and the 308th Rifle Division, along with the 3rd Guards Tank Army, had penetrated 8-10 kilometers into the enemy lines and, having arrived in the Protasovo area with their main forces, had created, along with the 61st Army's units, a serious threat to encircle the enemy's Mtsensk group of forces. At the same time, units of the 3rd Guards Tank Army, which had moved to the south, although they had not completely carried out their assigned mission, occupied a favorable flanking position in relation to the powerful group of German forces, which over the course of several days had been delaying the 63rd Army's attack.

The rout of the enemy's Mtsensk group of forces

As a result of the breakthrough of the defensive line along the Oleshnya River by our forces, a serious threat had arisen to the enemy's Mtsensk group of forces and his forces defending between

Oleshnya and the Oka and Optukha rivers. Considering this threat, the German command decided on the night of 19-20 July to pull back its forces from the Mtsensk area and from the area between the Oka and Optukha rivers. While leaving behind a small covering force along the western bank of the Zusha River, the German forces, under cover of darkness, abandoned their positions and began to rapidly fall back to the west and southwest.

However, the enemy did not manage to completely hide this maneuver. The units of the 342nd Rifle Division, which were defending north of Mtsensk, discovered the enemy's withdrawal, which began at night, and immediately began to pursue. Having forced the river north of 1st Somovo and energetically destroying the enemy's covering detachments, the division broke into Mtsensk on the morning of 20 July and, following a short battle, captured the town, while its remaining units reached the line Volobuevo—Farafonovo.

The commander of the 3rd Army, while trying to prevent the Germans' withdrawal behind the Oka River, decided to destroy the Germans' Mtsensk group of forces by encircling it east of the Oka River. He ordered the commander of the 342nd Rifle Division to launch an attack in the general direction of Drobyshevo and to capture the village. Subsequently, while attacking along the eastern bank of the Oka River toward Zheleznitsa, the division was to deny the enemy the opportunity to fall back toward the crossings, and was to seize them or destroy them by artillery fire. On the morning of 21 July part of the division's forces was to attack toward Podmokrovo and, in conjunction with the 235th Rifle Division, to encircle and destroy the Germans' Mtsensk group of forces.

The 235th Rifle Division, which on 20 July had broken through the enemy's defense and had begun pursuing the retreating enemy units to the northwest, was given the following assignment: to attack toward 1st Voin on 21 July, in order to cut off the Germans' path of retreat toward the Oka River.

Throughout 20 July the 342nd and 235th rifle divisions did not let up their pursuit of the retreating enemy. Energetically advancing, units of the 235th Rifle Division cut the Orel—Mtsensk paved road at 0400 on 21 July along the Il'kovo—1st Voin sector. Small groups of unsupervised German soldiers stretched along the road to the southwest, as well as individual vehicles and supply trains. Having left a powerful screen facing to the north along the line Il'kovo—Golovlevo, the division commander dispatched the division's main forces toward Naryshkino, which they captured during the latter half of 21 July, having got into a fight with the enemy who was putting up resistance from the western bank.

The 342nd Rifle Division, developing the success to the south, was attacking toward Podmokrovo. By this time its main forces had reached the line Rassvet—Schastlivka, having pushed its forward detachments as far as the Oka River, while its remaining units were destroying the enemy's remnants in the woods west of Mtsensk.

On 21 July a significant part of the Germans' Mtsensk group of forces had been surrounded by units of the 61st and 3rd armies and destroyed. Throughout 21-22 July the 342nd and 235th rifle divisions were fighting to clear the occupied territory of the enemy. However, the fighting was already not as stubborn. The subunits and groups of German soldiers, deprived of command and control, were quickly destroyed by our forces; a large part of them, seeing the hopelessness of the situation, were surrendering.

By the close of 22 July both divisions had completely cleared the Oka River's eastern bank and occupied the line Drobyshevo—Storozhevoe—Naryshkino and to the south and were preparing to attack further.

As a result of the energetic actions by the 342nd and 235th rifle divisions in the Mtsensk area, in only two days about 200 German officers and men were killed and a large amount of equipment and prisoners taken.

The pursuit of the enemy and the arrival of the 3rd Army's main forces at the Oka River

On 20 July the German forces also began to fall back opposite the 3rd Army's left wing. Putting up stubborn resistance with their rearguards, the enemy's main forces were seeking to get beyond the Oka River. Columns of infantry and vehicles stretched out along the roads to Otrada, Vysokoe and Optukha were crossing the river and immediately occupying defensive positions along its western bank.

Having detected the enemy's withdrawal, the *front* command immediately threw all the 15th Air Army's main bomber forces to the line of the Oka River. Our planes launched powerful attacks against the enemy's crossings, which had been built near the villages of Naryshkino and Khrynki, heavily damaging them. The enemy's columns retreating along the roads were systematically subjected to attacks by our bombers, which continuously strafed the columns, delayed their advance and caused heavy losses in personnel and equipment.

Our tanks, which were operating among the infantry, rapidly came out on the enemy's path of withdrawal and destroyed his retreating groups of forces. Especially heavy fighting broke out for the major village of Dobrovody. Units of the 283rd Rifle Division outflanked the village, but were not able to break into it immediately. At the height of the fighting for Dobrovody tanks from the 1st Guards Tank Corps, which had deeply outflanked the village, arrived to the division and broke into it from the rear. Before long the enemy garrison had been completely destroyed.

In falling back to the west, the German forces burned villages, mined roads, planted delayed-reaction mines in the surviving structures, and blew up all the crossings.

Having received information that the enemy facing the 3rd Army had begun withdrawing, the *front* commander once again changed the 3rd Guards Tank Army's mission and ordered it to immediately attack to the northwest in the general direction of Otrada, in order to cut the Orel—Mtsensk paved road and by the close of 20 July seize the crossings over the Oka River.

Because the tank army's formations had already advanced far to the southwest (by the morning of 12 July the 12th Guards Tank Corps was fighting in the Zolotarevo area), the army commander, General Rybalko, seeking to speed up the process of regrouping his forces for the attack along the new axis, decided to pull the 12th Guards Tank Corps back to the second echelon and to carry out the assigned task with the forces of the 15th Guards Tank and 2nd Mechanized corps. For this purpose, he ordered the commander of the 2nd Mechanized Corps to begin his attack at 0920 on 20 July from the line Golovinka—Merkulovo—Bol'shoe Ochkasovo in the direction of Bogoroditskoe and Otrada, and by the close of 20 July to capture the area Zhukova—Novaya Slobodka—Kamenevo.

The 15th Guards Tank Corps was ordered to attack from the Oleshnya area in the direction of Klinovoe and Vysokoe, and at the same time to capture the area Paslovo—Ivanovskaya Optukha—Mozalevka.

The 12th Guards Tank Corps was to abandon the Zolotarevo area and attack behind the 15th Guards Tank Corps, and by the close of 20 July to concentrate in the Protasovo area.

In carrying out the army commander's order, the 2nd Mechanized and 15th Guards Tank corps moved out of their jumping-off positions at 0920 on 20 July. The tanks overtook their infantry, which was rapidly advancing behind the retreating enemy and, having deployed along a broad front, moved forward at a high speed. Destroying small and scattered groups of enemy troops along the way, by 1900 on 20 July the tank corps' main forces had reached the highway, along which the German forces' supply trains, artillery and columns of vehicles stretched out in a solid line to the south. Having cut the highway in several places (the 2nd Mechanized Corps near Kamenevo, and the 15th Guards Tank Corps along the line Vysokoe—Ivanovskaya Optukha), our tanks routed several enemy columns along this sector and seized the eastern bank of the Oka River along the line Otrada—Ivanovskaya Optukha.

Taking advantage of the tanks' success, the 3rd Army's forces, which had been closely pursuing the enemy throughout 20 July, completely finished clearing the German forces out of the territory between the Oleshnya and Oka rivers, and during the day of 21 July its main forces reached the eastern bank of the Oka River along the front Staraya Otrada—Ivanovskaya Optukha, and along the line of the Optukha River from the mouth as far as Deryuzhkino.

The 342nd Rifle Division was fighting along the line Volobuevo—Tarkunovka, while the 269th Rifle Division was engaged to the left, and the 235th and 283rd rifle divisions were along the sector between Naryshkino and Otrada. The 308th Rifle Division was operating south of Otrada as far as Vysokoe. The 25th Rifle Corps' divisions were deployed as follows: the 362nd Rifle Division along the eastern bank of the Oka River from Stanovoe to Ivanovskaya Optukha, and the 186th Rifle Division from Zolotilovo to Khitrovo.

On the evening of 20 July the 3rd Guards Tank Army had carried out its mission and had received new orders from the *front* commander, according to which the army was to shift its operations to the south from dawn on 21 July to the 63rd Army's zone and there attack in the general direction of Sukharevka, Zolotarevo and Stanovoi Kolodez' and get into the rear of the enemy group of forces operating south and southwest of Orel, and by the close of 21 July capture the area Malaya Kulikovka—Ivanovka—Khotetevo—Stanovoi Kolodez'. At 0300 on 21 July, having turned over its sectors to the 3rd Army's rifle formations, the 3rd Guards Tank Army shut down its operations in the 3rd Army's sector and set about regrouping its forces.

The 3rd Army commander's decision to take Orel (21 July)

At the same time the 3rd Army was energetically pursuing the remnants of the German forces to the Oka River, the army commander decided to employ the success achieved by his forces to force the Oka on the heels of the retreating enemy and, outflanking Orel from the north and northwest, to capture the city.

The army's formations received the following order on the evening of 20 July.

On 21 July the 283rd Rifle Division, along with the 13th Tank Regiment, was to force the Oka River along the Zhukova—Lomovets sector and, upon seizing a bridgehead on the western bank, to attack in the direction of Bornyakovo and Balduevo;

The 308th Rifle Division, along with the 114th Tank Regiment, was to force the Oka along the Lomovets—Kakurinka sector and attack in the direction of Paslovo, Zamezenskii and the northwestern outskirts of Orel;

The 25th Rifle Corps, together with the 253rd and 82nd tank regiments, was to seize a bridgehead along the western bank of the Oka in the Khryki area, as well as crossings over the Optukha River in the Snetskaya Luka—Kalinovka—Lunev—Yermolaevo area; the corps was to have its main forces along the front Khryki—Parakhino for the attack on Orel from the northeast;

The 380th Rifle Division was to force the Optukha River from the line Yermolaevo—Deryuzhkino and attack Orel from the east and southeast, through Razuvaevo and Luzhki.

The major water barrier of the Oka River lay across the 3rd Army's path of attack, the forcing of which was made difficult due to the lack of preliminary preparation and the absence of the necessary crossing equipment. Within the confines of the Orel strategic salient, this was the enemy's last defensive line, the loss of which would make the defense of the salient by the enemy's forces impossible. Naturally, it was necessary to expect serious enemy resistance along this water line.

In carrying out the commander's orders, on the morning of 22 July the 3rd Army's forces attacked. The 342nd Rifle Division forced the Oka River in two places and seized two bridgeheads along the western bank: one along the right flank, in the area of the machine-tractor station, and the other on the left flank, near Chizhovka. However, repeated attempts by the division's units to expand the bridgeheads were unsuccessful. The Germans were solidly blocking the division's elements that had crossed over to the western bank and had inflicted heavy losses on them through continuous counterattacks.

Units of the 235th Rifle Division were also unable to make use of their bridgehead, seized in the Bogatishchevo area. The 283rd Rifle Division, which had crossed over in part to the Oka's western bank, captured the enemy's Lomovets strong point and had begun fighting for Plautino. Before long the enemy counterattacked the division's units from the area of height 207.5 and forced them to abandon Lomovets and fall back to their jumping-off positions. The 308th Rifle Division abandoned its bridgehead west of Novaya Slobodka.

Throughout the day the enemy bombarded our forces along the river's eastern bank with powerful artillery and mortar fire. His aviation incessantly subjected the road junctions and our artillery positions to bombardment. On 21 July alone German aviation carried out more than 1,000 sorties.

Reconnaissance, which was organized by the divisions' headquarters, reported the presence of previously-prepared enemy positions along the western bank of the Oka, as well as new units and formations that had been transferred her from other sectors of the front.

All of, this clearly indicated that the 3rd Army's forces would once again encounter enemy resistance along the river line, which could not be successfully overcome without serious preliminary preparation.

Because of this, the 3rd Army commander decided to temporarily consolidate along the line achieved, to bring up his artillery as far as possible, uncover the enemy's troop dispositions, put his units in order, bring them up to strength, prepare his crossing equipment, and then attack the enemy. On 22 July the army's forces consolidated along the eastern bank of the Oka River and began immediately to prepare for a new offensive.

The pursuit of the enemy by the 63rd Army's forces and their arrival at the Optukha River (19-23 July)

At the same time that the 3rd Army's forces, on orders of the *front* commander, had attacked and on 19 July had broken through the enemy defense, the enemy continued to stubbornly defend his positions opposite the 63rd Army and to delay their advance. Only the 5th Rifle Division on that day managed to capture the enemy's fortified strong points in Podmaslovo and to the northwest. The remaining divisions had no success.

On the night of 19-20 July the 5th Rifle Division sent out a reinforced reconnaissance detachment to the Prilep area. Upon discovering that the enemy had abandoned this village, the detachment occupied it at dawn. Before long reports of the enemy's withdrawal arrived from the 129th and 348th rifle divisions' reconnaissance detachments.

The 63rd Army's right-wing units immediately attacked. Pursuing the enemy closely and destroying his rearguards, on 20 July they captured the powerful Mokhovoe strong point. On 23 July the army's main forces reached the eastern bank of the Optukha River (where by this time the 3rd Guards Tank Army had concentrated). Upon encountering here the enemy's stubborn resistance, the army began preparing to break through the enemy's last (rear) defensive zone along the approaches to Orel.

To the left, the Central Front's 48th Army, while taking advantage of the 63rd Army's success, resumed its attack along the right flank on 22 July and, upon forcing the Neruch' River, on 24 July captured the town of Bogodukhov, while the army's left flank and center reached the line Glazunovka—Gremyachevo.

Thus on 23 July the Bryansk Front's left wing completed the operation's second stage by breaking through the enemy's powerful intermediate defensive zone along the Oleshnya River, defeated the

Germans' Mtsensk group of forces, and inflicted heavy losses on the enemy forces operating to the east of Orel.

However, the enemy managed to bring up fresh forces (the 12th Panzer Division, units of the 95th Infantry and 78th Assault divisions, and others) to the line of the Oka and Optukha rivers and also avoid complete encirclement, having withdrawn part of his forces from the Oleshnya River and organized a defense along the western bank of the Oka.

Despite the serious threat that hung over Orel from the north and northwest, due to the arrival of the 11th Guards Army's units at the Orel—Bryansk railroad west of Khotynets, the German forces continued to stubbornly resist along the line of the Oka River, attempting to hold the advance of the Bryansk Front's left-wing units to the west.

In order to deny the enemy the opportunity of consolidating along the western bank of the Oka and organizing a secure defense here, the 3rd and 63rd armies' forces were to regroup their forces as quickly as possible and begin a new offensive on Orel.

The Breakthrough of the Enemy's Defense Along the Western Bank of the Oka River and the Capture of the City of Orel (25 July-5 August)

On the night of 23-24 July the *front* commander issued orders to the 3rd and 63rd armies to regroup their forces as quickly as possible and capture Orel by concentric attacks from the north and south. The 3rd Army was to launch a powerful attack in the direction of Orel from the north and northwest, while the 63rd Army would attack from the south and southeast. Both armies, having deeply outflanked the Germans' Orel group of forces, were to destroy them. The start of the offensive was set for 25 July. A new boundary line was established between the armies (Luk'yanchikovo—Orel and then along the Orlik River), while the city of Orel was in the 63rd Army's sector. The 3rd Guards Tank Army and the 1st Guards Tank Corps were to be pulled into the rear to the *front* commander's reserve in the Novosil' area. In their place, the 3rd Army received the 17th Tank Brigade, and the 63rd Army the 87th Tank Brigade.

The 3rd and 63rd army commanders' decision

The commander of the 3rd Army decided to tie down the enemy along the front Kikino—Luk'yanchikovo (with the 308th and 380th rifle divisions) with an active defense and to launch a powerful attack along the army's right flank (with the 269th, 283rd and 235th rifle divisions, the 25th Rifle Corps, and the 17th Tank Brigade) in the general direction of Andrianovo, Nel'bova and Raspopovskie Dvoriki, and then to then to the southwest and south, deeply outflanking Orel from the north and northwest. The 342nd Rifle Division, along with the 584th Anti-Tank Artillery Regiment and the 253rd Tank and 14th Self-Propelled Artillery regiments, was ordered to force the Oka along the Pakhomovo—Naryshkino sector and, upon breaking through the enemy defense, capture the line Zhilyaevo—Kholodkovskii; subsequently, while attacking in the direction of Polozovskie Dvory and Sakharnyi, the division was to secure the army's right flank.

The 269th Rifle Division, along with the 114th and 13th tank and 1452nd Self-Propelled Artillery regiments, received the following assignment: to break through the Germans' defense along the front Naryshkino—Kikino and capture the inhabited locale of Khutor and height 239.7, after which it would attack in the direction of Mertsalovo and reach the line Mertsalovo—Lukovskii Poselok.

The 283rd Rifle Division, along with the 82nd Tank and 1538th Self-Propelled Artillery regiments, upon the 342nd and 269th rifle divisions reaching the line Khvatnevo—Andrianovo, was to enter the breach along the boundary between these two divisions and, upon deploying in the Gost'ino area, attack in the direction of Khutor and Kashirino. By the close of 25 July the division was ordered to capture the line Kholodkovskii—Khutor, and then to attack toward Dubovaya Roshcha.

The 235th Rifle Division was ordered to defend the front Kikino—Novaya Slobodka, with the 81st Regiment behind the right flank in the Kikino—Zaroshchinskii area, ready to commit it into the breach behind the 269th Rifle Division's left flank for operations in the direction of Plautina and Paslovo.

The 308th and 380th rifle divisions were to securely defend the front Novaya Slobodka—Luk'yanchikovo, preventing the enemy from crossing over to the eastern bank of the Oka River. The 308th Rifle Division, upon the arrival of the 235th Rifle Division along the line Paslovo—Ivanovskaya Optukha, was to launch an attack along the front Shinaki—Narimanovskii and attack along the railroad toward Orel.

The 25th Rifle Corps, along with the 17th Tank Brigade, received orders to concentrate in the Dumchino station—Golovlevo—Il'kovo area, in readiness to develop the success in the 342nd and 269th rifle divisions' zone.

Thus the 3rd Army commander decided to launch the attack along his army's right flank. He created a powerful shock group (five rifle divisions and a tank brigade) along his wheeling flank, having organized these forces in three echelons: the 342nd and 269th rifle divisions were to attack in the first echelon, the 283rd Rifle Division in the second, and the 25th Rifle Corps' 362nd and 186th rifle divisions in the third.

Such an organization secured for the army all the necessary conditions, both for the successful forcing of the Oka River, as well as for the continuous augmentation of its efforts while developing the success in the depth of the enemy's defense.

The commander of the 63rd Army, while striving to organize close coordination with his neighbor to the right (3rd Army) and thus ensure the complete encirclement of the enemy in the Orel area, decided to launch his main attack along the left flank. This attack was to be made by three divisions and a tank brigade along the front Novaya Derevnya—Nikol'skoe, with the mission of capturing the Stanovoi Kolodez' (northern) area, and then, firmly securing itself from the west, to launch an attack on Orel from the south along the Rybnitsa River.

The 287th Rifle Division, along with the 12th Tank Regiment, was to break through the enemy's defense along the following line: the gully 1.5 kilometers southeast of the line Novaya Derevnya—Bogoroditskoe. Upon capturing height 242.5 and the gully west of it, the division was to then develop the attack in the direction of Malaya Kulikovka.

The 250th Rifle Division, along with the 26th Tank Regiment, was ordered to turn over the Novaya Derevnya—Bogoroditskoe sector to the 287th Rifle Division, to attack the enemy along the line southern outskirts of Bogoroditskoe—Domnino and capture the line Kryukovka—height 252.7, and then attack toward Tikhonovka.

The 41st Rifle Division received orders to break through the enemy's defense along the line southern outskirts of Domnino—Nikol'skoe and capture the Khotetovo area; it was then to attack toward Stanovoe.

The commander of the 35th Rifle Corps took control of the shock groups. The 5th, 129th and 348th rifle divisions were entrusted with the defense of the line Deryuzhkino—Semendyaevo—Novaya Derevnya. The 63rd Army commander's reserve was the 397th Rifle Division.

As opposed to the 3rd Army, the army was organized into a single echelon along the 63rd Army's main attack, along a comparatively narrow sector of the front. This is explained to a certain degree by the fact that the army commander did not have at his disposal the corresponding reserves, the overwhelming majority of which had been expended in breaking through the Germans' intermediate defensive line along the Oleshnya River.

Preparing for the offensive

During 23-24 July the regrouping of forces and preparation for the forthcoming offensive was carried out in the *front's* left-wing armies (3rd and 63rd).

Despite the fact that the enemy during these days was continually bombarding the eastern bank of the Oka and Optukha rivers with artillery and mortar fire, the 3rd and 63rd armies' forces quickly completed their regrouping and by dawn on 25 July were completely ready for the offensive.

During the preparatory period for the offensive the armies' headquarters devoted their main attention to reconnoitering the enemy and preparing their forces for forcing the Oka. Army sappers, along with infantry reconnaissance, sought out day and night places for building crossings and destroyed numerous enemy minefields, which he had left along the river's eastern bank. In only three days along the 3rd Army's front our sappers took up 13,127 anti-tank and anti-personnel mines, disarmed them, and prepared 113 kilometers of roads for two-way traffic. By the close of 24 July the sapper units had completely prepared several crossings over the Oka, of which one was south of Pakhomovo, another near Naryshkino, and a third near Kikino.

The artillery, having occupied its firing positions by the close of 23 July, immediately set about destroying the enemy's defensive structures, which had been built along the river's eastern bank, and suppressing the enemy's artillery and mortars.

On 24 July the *front's* aviation carried out massive raids against the German strong points of Kamenka, Volobuevo, Tsurikova, and Orel. On 23-24 July reconnaissance planes observed the continuous movement of supply trains and automobile supply columns, stretching from the Oka to the west and southwest.

The German command's measures for defending Orel

The German command, in attempting to delay the advance by our troops to the west and, if only temporarily, to stabilize the front along the line of the Oka River, moved from the Central Front part of the 12th Panzer Division, which had earlier been operating in the Bolkhov area, to the Orel area. A hurried regrouping of German forces was underway along the western bank of the Oka, with their main forces concentrating east of Orel along the Lomovets—Stanovoi Kolodez' sector. Here the 56th Infantry Division, which had been reinforced during the fighting, the 2nd, 8th and 12th panzer divisions, as well as a number of independent units (including units of the 36th and 299th infantry and 78th Assault divisions) occupied defensive positions here. In the city and the areas adjacent to Orel all the soldiers from the rear organs and police units were gathered up quickly and dispatched to the front. Guns and machine guns, removed from Orel's anti-aircraft defense were being moved to the Oka, while barbed wire, mines and other engineering equipment were being delivered.

Along the line of the Nepolod' and Oka rivers, as well as around Orel itself, the German forces were carrying out defensive works around the clock. The German artillery and mortars bombarded our lines day and night, while his air force carried out frequent raids against our communications, road junctions and artillery firing positions, while the 269th and 235th rifle divisions were subjected to powerful attacks from the air.

Upon the first attempts by our reconnaissance subunits to penetrate into their lines, the German forces opened a powerful mortar and machine gun fire.

Despite all these measures, the German command was not fully sure that its forces could hold Orel and thus simultaneously with the strengthening of the front, the evacuation of the city and neighboring villages began. All the subsidiary military establishments, rear organs, hospitals, as well as valuables belonging to the Soviet state and the local population, were moved to the west.

The breakthrough of the German defense along the 3rd Army's sector

On the night of 24-25 July units of the 3rd Army were completing their preparations for the offensive. The sappers, with the aid of the infantry, were completing the assembly of parts of a floating bridge not far from the river bank, preparing assault bridges and rafts. Under the cover of their artillery, the minesweepers made passages in the enemy's minefields and cleaned up the mined sectors of the river.

Our aviation (including Po-2 aircraft) bombed the German lines all night. The artillery methodically fired against previously registered targets and the German's fortifications, inflicting heavy losses on them.

The enemy, in turn, systematically illuminated the area with rockets and frequent salvos from mortars and sought to comb the eastern bank of the Oka River with machine gun fire.

At 0800 on 25 July, under the cover of artillery fire and aviation, the infantry from the 3rd Army's shock group went over to the attack. Employing the materials at hand (boards, small rafts and logs), it crossed its main forces over to the western bank of the river in 20-30 minutes and, with the first shift in the artillery's fire into the depth, attacked the enemy defense.

Stunned by the sudden and powerful fire of our artillery, the German troops put up weak resistance along the bank, and our infantry consolidated this position almost without loss.

At 0930 the sappers had laid down two crossings (near Pakhomovo and Naryshkino), along which the tanks and artillery began to rapidly cross. The infantry, reinforced with tanks and escort guns, increased the pace of the attack.

The 342nd Rifle Division launched a powerful attack along its right flank and destroyed an enemy pocket of resistance that had been heavily fortified near the grove south of Kamenka and, vigorously developing the attack, by the close of the day had captured Luzanovo and Khvatnevo. In this battle the division destroyed more than 500 enemy officers and men, two batteries, and several tanks.

The 269th Rifle Division, having successfully forced the Oka in the Savenkovo area and the grove to the north, encountered powerful fire resistance from the enemy. Repelling the enemy's constant infantry and tank counterattacks from the woods southeast of Gost'ino, the division advanced very slowly and by the close of the day had only captured the line Savenkovo—height 214.2. Three enemy tanks and four self-propelled guns were captured and more than 300 enemy officers and men were killed in the fighting.

The 283rd Rifle Division, following up in the second echelon, had concentrated in the woods east of Chizhovka, to where the 17th Tank Brigade arrived by the close of the day.

The resistance of the Germans, who had brought up fresh reserves to the breakthrough sector, was becoming more stubborn. Units of the German 20th Motorized Division launched a powerful counterstroke at 2330 from the Gost'ino area against the left flank of the 269th Rifle Division and forced it to abandon Savenkovo.

The commander of the 3rd Army decided to take advantage of the success achieved by the 342nd Rifle Division and ordered it on 26 July to capture the line Apal'kovo—Chupakhina, consolidate here and support the commitment of the 25th Rifle Corps into the fighting. The 25th Rifle Corps received the following orders: upon moving up to the area of the woods east of Narykovo at night, to cross the Oka on the morning of 26 July in the 342nd Rifle Division's attack zone, and attack from the line Gorka—Gorodishche in the direction of height 234.1 and Polyana. The commander ordered the 283rd Rifle Division, along with the 17th Tank Brigade, to be ready to attack from the Khvatnevo—Volobuevo line toward Chupakhina and Zhilyaevskii.

On 26 July the army's shock group resumed the attack. The 342nd Rifle Division, overcoming the enemy's stubborn resistance, advanced slowly in heavy fighting. Units of the Germans' 34th Infantry and 20th Motorized divisions counterattacked the division's flanks three times. Having suffered heavy losses, the 342nd Rifle Division captured the enemy's Shumovo strong point by midday and was forced to consolidate along the line Shumovo—Khvatnevo, without carrying out its assignment.

Units of the 25th Rifle Corps, having rapidly crossed over the Oka at dawn, deployed along its western bank and under cover of heavy artillery fire and aviation, began to attack toward Kamenka, but immediately ran into the enemy's powerful fire resistance. The German command, having discovered the corps' deployment near Gorka, threw about 100 dive bombers against this sector, which in the course of three hours continually bombed the corps' units. Our infantry, which had been met by intensive enemy machine gun and mortar fire from the front, despite the support from our tanks, began to cling to the ground more and more. At 1400 the right-flank 362nd Rifle Division was subjected to a powerful enemy counterattack, which was supported by tanks, from the Yul'evka area and was forced to consolidate in the Savenka area. By the close of the day the 186th Rifle Division had captured Kamenka and was also unable to advance further.

The 283rd Rifle Division, which had been committed into the battle along the boundary between the 342nd and 269th rifle divisions, also failed to achieve success. By the close of the day the division had gotten into heavy fighting for the powerful enemy strong point of Chupakhina.

Thus in two days of intensive offensive fighting along the western bank of the Oka, the 3rd Army achieved meager results, having only slightly dented the enemy's defense along its right flank. The army commander, seeking at all cost to break through the Germans' defense and to reach Orel as soon as possible, committed all his reserves—the second and third echelons—into the fighting in the offensive's first two days.

On 27 July the army resumed the offensive, but once again was unable to crush the enemy's resistance. Then the 3rd Army commander ordered his division commanders to securely dig in along their present line and prepare to attack on the morning of 30 July.

The 63rd Army's breakthrough of the enemy's defense along the line of the Optukha River

Simultaneous with the 3rd Army, the 63rd Army's left flank went over to the offensive. On the offensive's first day its units encountered heavy enemy resistance along the western bank of the Optukha River and, upon forcing the river, were only able to penetrate slightly the enemy's defense. As a result of fierce fighting, by the close of 25 July the 287th, 250th and 41st rifle divisions had captured the line running along line of the height 228.5—the nameless heights 1.5 kilometers west of Dadurovo—the eastern slopes of height 241.3.

The German forces, the defense of which had not been seriously disrupted by our artillery fire, were stubbornly resisting not only during the day, but during the night of 25-26 July, when the army commander made an attempt to renew the offensive.

On the following day, following a powerful artillery onslaught against the enemy's defense, the army's left wing resumed the attack. However, on this day only the 287th Rifle Division managed to achieve some results and capture the line Naumovo—height 242.5.

Lacking the necessary reserves, the army commander was deprived of the opportunity to develop the division's success and ordered the army's formations on 26 July to temporarily dig in along the line reached, in order to prepare to renew the offensive on the morning of 28 July.

After the 63rd Army's units were put in order, it once again attacked along its left flank on 28 July. On this day the 287th Rifle Division managed to push back units of the enemy's 36th Motorized Division to the northwest and capture the line height 225.8—Gremyachii. The 250th and 41st rifle divisions also achieved great success on this day. The former captured a number of strong points on heights 241.0 and 234.2 and had gotten involved in heavy fighting for Stanovoi Kolodez'. The latter seized height 252.3 and Olovyannikovo.

However, on the following day the enemy, taking advantage of his previously prepared positions along the line Gremyachii—Kozinovka, once again put up stubborn resistance. All the attempts by both divisions to break through to Orel were unsuccessful. The Germans had built a powerful intermediate switch position along the line Stanovoi Kolodez'—Zmievo (seven kilometers southwest of Olovyannikovo), the piercing of which required that the army once again regroup its forces and prepare them for a further attack.

On 28 July the 63rd Army called off the attack and dug in along the line reached.

The 3rd Army's breakthrough of the enemy's intermediate defensive zone and the arrival of its main forces along the line of the Nepolod' River (30 July-2 August)

Having regrouped its forces to the right flank, on 30 July the 3rd Army renewed the attack in the general direction of Polozovskie Dvory. However, on this day they were unable to break through the enemy's defense along the line Shumovo—Chupakhina. Only the 362nd Rifle Division, in conjunction with the 61st Army's left-flank units, which had arrived from the north in the Podchernovo area, following the elimination of the Bolkhov group of forces, captured the line Kalugino—Razinkina.

Fierce fighting continued throughout 31 July along this line. The Germans, employing large forces, repeatedly counterattacked, particularly in the center against units of the 283rd Rifle Division; artillery and mortars laid down a heavy fire on our forces. With the onset of darkness on 31 July the enemy's fire grew stronger and small groups of automatic riflemen repeatedly counterattacked, penetrating into our lines and attacking our individual firing points, while the terrain was heavily illuminated with rockets.

The enemy's extreme activity that night raised the suspicions of the commander of the 362nd Rifle Division, and he decided to strengthen his reconnaissance along the front, dispatching the division's reconnaissance battalion. The commander's supposition was justified. At 0200 the scouts uncovered the enemy's withdrawal and, upon reporting this to the division commander, began to immediately pursue the retreating enemy units. By the morning of 1 August the reconnaissance battalion captured the villages of Polyana and Malaya Kruglitsa. Before long the 362nd Rifle Division's main units began the pursuit, encountering the German rearguards' insignificant resistance; by the close of the day they had reached the line Tatinka—Zhilyaevskii.

Having received word of the Germans' withdrawal, the commander of the 3rd Army threw the army's main forces into the pursuit.

In carrying out the commander's order, the divisions began immediately to attack. The 186th Rifle Division, having crushed the resistance of the enemy covering detachments, began to advance quickly to the southwest and by the close of 1 August had reached the line Polozovskie Dvory—Nikol'skii.

To the left, the 342nd Rifle Division, having relieved units of the 283rd Rifle Division, which had been pulled back into the reserve, was successfully advancing and its main forces reached the line Aleksandrovka—Polzovo.

The 269th Rifle Division, in pursuing the enemy, reached the line Bornyakovo—Trufanovo, where it was fighting the German rearguard that had dug in here.

The 308th Rifle Division, which the army commander had ordered to prepare to attack along the south bank of the Oka toward Orel, had concentrated its main forces in the area Ivanovskaya Optukha—Parakhino—Kaznacheevo.

As the result of the pursuit, on 1 August the 3rd Army's units advanced 12-14 kilometers to the south and southwest and deeply outflanked Orel from the northwest.

By midday on 2 August the army's main forces had reached the Nepolod' River along the following sectors:

the 362nd Rifle Division—along the line Zarya Svobody—Red'kino;
the 186th Rifle Division—Koryakina—Zhitkaya;
the 342nd Rifle Division was fighting in the Mertsalovo area;
the 269th Rifle Division had captured Zamatino and reached the line Lukovskii Poselok—Tsvetyn';
the 283rd Rifle Division, advancing to the south behind the main forces, had concentrated in the area of Bol'shoe Durakovo.

The Germans hurriedly dug in along the southern bank of the Nepolod' River and, having thrown a large number of planes into the fighting, once again put up stubborn resistance to our forces along this line. Our units' attempts to force the river on the march did not meet with success. The remnants of the 34th, 20th Motorized and 12th Panzer divisions, which had fallen back here, did not give our units the opportunity to cross over to the south bank and resisted with powerful fire and fierce counterattacks.

The fighting along the Central Front's right wing

Taking advantage of the 63rd Army's success, the 48th Army's right-flank forces sped up their advance to the northwest from the line of the Zmievka—Ponyri railroad. By launching an energetic attack in the general direction of Nesterovo, they advanced more than 60 kilometers and by 1 August had reached the line Ploskoe—Gutorovo and had captured these villages.

To the left, the 13th and 70th armies, overcoming the enemy's stubborn resistance, advanced continuously. The German troops, striving to delay our attack, carried out desperate counterattacks. Despite this, by the close of 1 August the 13th and 70th armies had reached the line Nadezhda—Krasnikovo and, having captured these villages, continued to develop the success toward Kromy.

The fighting for Orel

At the same time that the 3rd Army's forces, having arrived at the line of the Nepolod' River, were engaged in fighting along the immediate approaches to Orel, the 63rd Army was continuing its intensive offensive battles, overcoming the enemy's intermediate defensive zone along the line Stanovoi Kolodez'—Olovyannikovo.

The resulting conditions required the immediate elimination of the enemy's resistance, by taking advantage of flanking position of the 3rd Army's forces over Orel from the north, in order to seize Orel and completely encircle the enemy units that had fallen back here.

The commander of the 3rd Army decided to attack with the forces of the 308th Rifle Division, which was completing its concentration in the area Ivanovskaya Optukha—Parakhino. It was planned to launch a powerful attack from the east, along the right bank of the Oka, in order to ease the situation of the divisions attacking from the north, and to break through the enemy's defensive line along the Nepolod' River.

At 1200 on 2 August units of the 308th Rifle Division, following a short artillery onslaught, forced the Optukha River in several places and began to attack along the railroad leading to Orel. The division encountered the Germans' stubborn resistance and was immediately forced to dig in, having advanced only 400 meters from the bank. At dawn on 3 August the 308th Rifle Division once again renewed the attack and, having broken through the enemy's defense along the line Shinaki—Kalinovka, by the close of the day captured the large inhabited locale of Vyazki along the southern bank of the Oka.

Taking advantage of its neighbor's success on the right, the 380th Rifle Division attacked on the morning of 3 August. Upon forcing the Optukha River, it broke through the defense with a powerful attack along the river's western bank and, overcoming the enemy's powerful resistance, threw back his remnants to the line Bol'shoe Bulgakovo—height 198.3—height 239.1. The 3rd Army's remaining forces continued to engage in fierce fighting with the German forces defending along the Nepolod' River.

At dawn on 3 August the 63rd Army attacked. The enemy, who put up stubborn resistance in the beginning, could not withstand our attacks and began to quickly fall back to Orel, coming under attack from the 380th Rifle Division from the east. As early as 1300 on 3 August the 5th Rifle Division had begun fighting along the eastern outskirts of Razuvaevo. The 348th Rifle Division was fighting in the southern outskirts of Grachevka. The 287th Rifle Division, while pursuing the enemy retreating toward Orel, encountered stubborn resistance by the Germans who had dug in along the heights in the Mikhailovka area, which slowed down the division's advance to the north. The 41st Rifle Division, securing the main forces against an enemy attack from the west, forced the Rybnitsa River and was attacking along its left bank, outflanking Orel from the south.

Thus by the close of 3 August Orel and the enemy's Orel group of forces had been outflanked in a half-ring by the Bryansk Front's left wing. The systematic destruction of the Orel group of forces began. Our aviation, closely cooperating with the ground forces, observed on 3 August in the Orel area a large concentration of German forces, stretching to the city from the east. German forces, which were falling back to the west, were crossing to the Oka's left bank along hurriedly constructed bridges to the north and south of the city. Subjected to powerful air attacks, they suffered enormous losses. The roads, wooded areas and villages in which the Germans sought sanctuary from our air and artillery fire, were filled with the corpses of enemy officers and men, smashed equipment and abandoned weapons.

Despite the difficult situation that had arisen in the Orel area, the German forces continued to resist fiercely. By concentrating toward the city individual units that had avoided complete defeat, the Germans fortified all the villages and individual heights and mined the approaches to them.

Hundreds of enemy guns and mortars rained down intensive fire on the Red Army's attacking units. Groups of enemy patrol bombers continuously arrived at the front and dropped their bombs on our forces and strafed them with machine guns and cannons.

On 3 August powerful explosions were heard from Orel. The German sappers were blowing up the city's buildings, depots and industrial plants.

At 1430 the 3rd Army's military council issued combat order no. 0050, in which it appealed to the army's soldiers and officers with the following words:

> The enemy, covering himself with mine obstacles and rear guards, is striving to slow down our offensive and win time to evacuate stolen property, drive out the local population and destroy the ancient Russian city of Orel.
>
> The army's military council calls upon the army's entire rank and file to bend all their efforts toward launching an energetic attack and liberating the city of Orel from the German occupiers and saving tens of thousands of Soviet people from German slavery and the city from complete destruction.
>
> Soldiers and commanders—before your eyes the city of Orel is being destroyed by the Hitlerite bands. You are 6-10 kilometers from the city. 2-3 hours of rapid attack will not only save you from excessive losses, but will prevent the enemy from completely destroying our native city.
>
> Forward, to the city's rapid liberation!

The army's formations were given the following missions:

The 25th Rifle Corps was to attack in the general direction of Yevdokimovo, Vorob'evka and Lopukhino and by the close of 3 August it was to reach the Izvekovo—Antsifrovo—Telegino area, cutting the Orel—Bryansk paved road and railroad; upon completing this task, it was to reconnoiter and send a forward detachment to Naryshkino.

The 342nd Rifle Division was to continue attacking toward Maloe Spitsino and Nekrasovo and reach the factory area west of Orel.

The 283rd Rifle Division was to attack along the paved road to Orel and by the close of the day capture the city's southwestern outskirts and the rail bridge over the Oka.

The 269th Rifle Division was to capture the northern part of the city, and the 308th and 380th rifle divisions the eastern part.

The 63rd Army commander did not change his decision and left in force the missions assigned earlier.

At 2300 on 3 August the forces of the 63rd Army suddenly went over to the offensive and attacked the enemy along the entire front. The Germans, who had evidently begun to fall back to the west during these hours, were caught off guard and, almost without putting up resistance, fled to the city. However, at dawn the enemy's resistance increased once again. Having dug in along the city's outskirts, the Germans opened a powerful machine gun and mortar fire. Units of the 5th Rifle Division, energetically advancing, linked up with units of the 380th Rifle Division, which was attacking Orel from the east and, supported by our powerful artillery fire, at 0440 on 4 August broke into the city. Several minutes later a powerful "Hurrah!" could be heard to the south—the 129th Rifle Division had opened its attack on the city's southern outskirts.

German automatic riflemen, who had dug in the buildings and basements, put up stubborn resistance to our units.

Fierce street fighting broke out in the city. By broadly employing fire from tanks and artillery, our infantry subunits cleared out one building after another. The German sappers, in falling back to the city center, blew up buildings and planted delayed-action mines in them.

Throughout 4 August bloody fighting raged in the eastern part of the city. Only by 1900 were our forces able to completely crush the enemy's resistance and, having captured the eastern outskirts of Orel, reach the Oka.

Hundreds of enemy corpses, smashed equipment and weapons lay scattered on the city streets.

Covered by thick smoke from the fires, our forward subunits crossed the river on the enemy's heels and began fighting in the western part of the city. Here the fighting eased considerably, thanks to the fact that the 3rd Army's 269th and 308th rifle divisions had arrived at the city from the north and northeast and by 1600 were fighting along the line of the Pleshcheevo State Farm—Rabochii Poselok. The remnants of the defeated 20th Motorized and 12th Panzer divisions were falling back in front of these divisions.

Seeing the hopelessness of further struggle, the German forces began to abandon the city in panic, throwing away their weapons and ammunition.

At dawn on 5 August Orel had been completely cleared of German-Fascist troops and the red flag waved from the building of the city council of workers' deputies.

At the same time as fierce street battles were raging in the city, the forces of the 3rd Army's shock group had broken through the enemy's intermediate defensive zone along the Nepolod' River and had advanced to the south, deeply outflanking Orel from the west. The 25th Rifle Corps' 362nd Rifle Division, which was operating along the turning flank, routed several columns of enemy infantry falling back from Orel, and by the close of 5 August had reached the Orlik River. The 342nd Rifle Division, which was attacking in echelon behind the 362nd Rifle Division, destroying small groups of the enemy, reached the testing field with its main forces, while its forward detachments forced the Orlik River and captured Obraztsovo, cutting the Orel—Bryansk paved road.

Units of the 63rd Army's 397th Rifle Division, attacking to the south of Orel, forced the Tson River and captured the Sakhanskii rail halt (four kilometers north of Lopukhino), linking up here with units of the 342nd Rifle Division advancing from the north. As a result of these divisions' energetic offensive actions, on 5 August the complete encirclement of the enemy remnants still fighting in the city was completed.

The further attack by the 3rd and 63rd armies' remaining divisions toward Orel, as called for in the plan, was no longer expedient, and the army commanders began regrouping their forces, in order to organize the pursuit of the retreating enemy.

By order of the Supreme Commander-in-Chief, comrade Stalin, the 5th, 129th and 380th rifle divisions, which were the first to break into the city of Orel and liberate it, were given the honorary title of "Orel" divisions.

In commemoration of the victory gained, Moscow, the capital of our motherland, on 5 August 1943 saluted the forces that had liberated the city of Orel with 19 artillery salvos from 120 guns.

5

The Pursuit of the Remnants of the Germans' Orel Group of Forces. The Capture of the Towns of Khotynets and Karachev

At the same time the forces of the Bryansk Front's left wing were fighting for Orel, the enemy's Orel group of forces, fearing encirclement, began to fall back to the west under pressure from our forces. The enemy was seeking to hold on to the Orel—Bryansk railroad and paved road, in order to secure the withdrawal of the remnants of the Orel group of forces and to simultaneously cover its flank and rear against the threat by the 11th Guards and 4th Tank armies hanging from the north.

The German command continually reinforced its units operating against the 11th Guards Army, and more than once tried to organize a counteroffensive for the purpose of throwing our forces back from the Orel—Bryansk railroad. As a result of these insistent attacks, the Germans managed to somewhat push back our units and seize the Karachev—Khvastovichi road, as well as to capture Alisovo (three kilometers west of the village of Izmorozn') and the woods north of Izmorozn'. All of the German's subsequent attempts to push back our units to the north and north-east were beaten back by the forces of the 11th Guards Army.

The Fighting for Khotynets

From 31 July through 5 August, when the Bryansk Front's left-wing forces were waging successful operations against the enemy's Orel group of forces, which concluded with the capture of the city of Orel, stubborn fighting was going on along the Bryansk Front's right wing against German forces covering the Orel—Bryansk railroad and paved road.

The 11th Guards and 4th Tank armies, while beating off the enemy's counterattacks, slowly advanced to the southwest along the left wing. Simultaneously, they were regrouping their forces, bringing them up to strength, supplying them with ammunition, food, forage, and fuel, in preparation for an attack on Khotynets.

By the morning of 6 August the 11th Army, having extended its front to the south as far as Paseka, was fighting along its previous line and repelling the enemy's frequent counterattacks. From 8 August the army began to create a shock group along its left flank, for the purpose of launching an attack along its left wing in the general direction of Karachev.

The 11th Guards Army, having turned over its right-flank sector to the 11th Army's units and having carried out a regrouping, had taken up starting positions for an offensive on Khotynets. The 16th Guards Rifle Corps had consolidated along the line excluding Paseka—excluding the woods to the north of Izmorozn'. The 36th Guards Rifle Corps had occupied its starting point along a 7-kilometer zone from the Vytebet' River west of Il'inskoe to the northern outskirts of the village of Brezhnevskii. The 8th Guards Rifle Corps, having a 5-kilometer front, was occupying its jumping-off position along the line excluding Brezhnevskii—excluding Uspenskii. The army commander's reserves were concentrated as follows: the 217th Rifle Division in the Glotovo area and the 1st Guards Rifle Division in the Nizina area.

The 1st Tank Corps in the Bulatovo area and the 25th Tank Corps in the Annikovo area were prepared for developing the breakthrough's success behind the 36th and 8th guards rifle corps.

The 4th Tank Army, consisting of the 6th Motorized and the 11th and 30th tank corps, had concentrated in the Peshkovo area.

Defending against the 11th Guards Army's forces were the following: the 10th Motorized Division, remnants of the 112th Infantry Division, the 8th Panzer, 253rd Infantry, and the 18th and 9th panzer divisions. To the left, facing the 61st Army's right flank, were the 20th Panzer and 25th Motorized divisions, which during the fighting were transferred to the 11th Guards Army's sector.

In accordance with the decision by the commander of the Bryansk Front, the 11th Guards Army was to break through the enemy's defense along the sector Il'inskoe—Gnezdilovo and support the commitment of the 4th Tank Army into the breach and, together with the latter, by developing the success to the southeast, capture the town of Khotynets and to subsequently attack toward Karachev.

Khotynets was the German troops' base, an important dirt road junction and a major station along the railroad connecting Orel with Bryansk.

The Germans attached great importance to the defense of Khotynets. The approaches to the town were covered by powerful defensive lines, one of which ran along the line Il'inskoe—Brezhnevskii—Bel'dino, and the other the line Studenka—Gnezdilovo. Moreover, the town and the surrounding heights had been prepared for stubborn defense.

The army commander decided to make his main attack with the forces of his 36th and 8th guards rifle corps and the 1st and 25th tank corps.

The 36th Guards Rifle and the 1st Tank corps received orders to attack in the direction of Studenka and Obraztsovo, outflanking Khotynets from the northwest and east. The 8th Guards Rifle and the 25th Tank corps were to attack in the direction of Androsovo and Bol'shie Ryabinki and, by securing the 11th Guards Army's main shock group and the 4th Tank Army from the east, bypass Khotynets from the southeast and south. The corps were reinforced with the following: 36th Guards Rifle Corps—a tank brigade, a tank regiment, two self-propelled artillery regiments, two artillery divisions, two artillery regiments, and a guards mortar brigade; 8th Guards Rifle Corps—two tank regiments, two self-propelled artillery regiments, an artillery division, an anti-tank brigade, three regiments and one guards mortar brigade.

The 16th Guards Rifle Corps had the mission of covering the shock group's operations along the Khotynets axis from the northwest; with the arrival of the 36th Guards Rifle Corps at the Moshenka River, the 16th Guards Rifle Corps was to launch a supporting attack to the southwest and reach the line northern outskirts of Karachev—Dolgii.

The attack was to be supported by the 15th Air Army, for which the plan for the aviation attack on the enemy called for 760 bomber sorties and 36 group assault air sorties.

The 4th Tank Army, following the breakthrough of the enemy's defense by units of the 11th Guards Army, was ordered to enter the breach along the sector Il'inskoe—Gnezdilovo and destroy the opposing enemy with an energetic attack and reach the area Yakhontovo—Shakhovo—Dubrovo, cut the Orel—Karachev railroad and paved road southeast of Khotynets and, in conjunction with the 11th Guards Army, encircle and destroy the Germans' Khotynets group of forces.

Moreover, the army's units, upon arriving to the southeast of Khotynets, were to cut off the escape route to the west of the remnants of the Germans' Bolkhov and Orel groups of forces.

At 0600 on 6 August, along the sector designated for the breakthrough, the reconnaissance companies, which had been allotted from each first-echelon division, began to operate. The reconnaissance companies' battle continued to 1200. During this period the forward edge of the enemy's defensive zone was fixed and our artillerists uncovered the main enemy firing points and positions and registered them. In order to repulse the attack by the reconnaissance companies, the enemy units occupied their forward trenches. At 1200 our artillery and aviation preparation began without any pause. A hail of fire covered the enemy that had ventured out into his trenches and shook his entire defense. At 1300 the artillery preparation ended and units of the 36th and 8th guards rifle corps, along with breakthrough tanks, moved into the attack and quickly broke through the forward edge of the enemy defense, bypassing and destroying strong points and centers of resistance. The Germans, shaken by the artillery and aviation preparation, were falling back in disorder to the intermediate defensive line, which had been built along the line Studenka—Gnezdilovo. The Il'inskoe garrison wanted to delay our attack, but units of the 169th and 18th Guards rifle divisions began to outflank Il'inskoe from both flanks. Fearing encirclement, the Germans ran away, leaving up to 1,000 corpses and a lot of weaponry on the battlefield.

At 1530, following the breakthrough of the forward edge along the entire attack zone, and following the infantry's penetration of the enemy's lines to a depth of three kilometers, the 1st and 30th tank corps were committed into the battle, followed by the 25th Tank Corps at 1700. Having dug in along the intermediate line, the Germans met our tanks with heavy fire—but the tank crews, in conjunction with the rifle units, outflanked the enemy strong points and crushed this defensive line. The fighting became drawn out and continued during the night. On the following day the 4th Tank Army's main forces were committed into the fighting.

At 1700 on 6 August the 11th Guards Rifle Division—the 16th Guards Rifle Division's left-flank division—attacked. However, encountering the enemy's strong resistance, it could not advance on this or the succeeding days. A firefight broke out with German units that had consolidated in the Izmorozn' area.

At the same time that the 36th Guards Rifle Corps' right-flank units were successfully advancing and reached the approaches to Klemenovo on 7 August, the 11th Guards Division's attack was delayed. This not only gave the Germans the opportunity to flank our units with fire from the Izmorozn' area, but at the same time created a threat to the flank of the 11th Guards Army's shock group. For this reason, the army commander on 7 August moved the reserve 217th Rifle Division to the line of the Vytebet' River, with the task of securing the 36th Guards Rifle Corps' right flank. The division took up defensive positions along the right bank of the Vytebet' River from the crossing northwest of Il'inskoe to the village of Il'inskii.

The enemy put up fierce resistance to the units of the 11th Guards and 4th Tank armies. By employing the broken ground and the large number of villages, the German units sought to delay our attack through fire and insistent counterattacks. Forced to fall back to the southwest under our forces' attacks, the Germans broadly employed the mining of and destruction of roads. Along the army's entire attack zone, the Germans did not leave a single working bridge. At the same time, the German command was throwing in new units from neighboring sectors and was drawing major air forces into the battle. Planes, in groups of up to 50 machines, insistently bombed the forces of the 11th Guards and 4th Tank armies.

On 8 August units of the German 25th Motorized Division appeared along the approaches to Khotynets. On this day the German air force carried out more than 1,000 sorties against our lines. On 9 August units of the German 34th and 26th infantry divisions, which had been reinforced with artillery and tanks, arrived in the Khotynets area. Two German armored trains were coursing along the railroad.

While overcoming the enemy's fierce resistance and his obstacles and beating back numerous counterattacks, our units continued to inexorably advance in continuous fighting toward

Khotynets. The closer our units approached the town, the more the resistance by the Germans' Khotynets group of forces grew. On 9 August fighting began on the immediate approaches to the town. Individual strong points, at Abolmasovo, Voeikovo, Khokhlovka, and the northeastern outskirts of Khotynets, for example, changed hands several times. By the close of the day units of the 36th Guards Rifle Corps and the 1st Tank Corps were fighting the enemy along the outskirts of Abolmasovo, Voeikovo, the village of Khotynets (one kilometer north of Khokhlovka), and Khokhlovka. At the same time units of the 8th Guards Rifle and 25th Tank corps, outflanking Khotynets form the south, cut the railroad and were one kilometer east of Khotynets station, and also reached the line of the eastern outskirts of Obraztsovo—Kopytets—Konevka.

The 4th Tank Army, operating along with the 8th Guards Rifle Corps and the 3rd Army's right flank, advanced its 6th Guards Mechanized Corps to the line Kopytets—Konevka—excluding Melovoe. The 30th Tank Corps reached the line Melovoe—Chalishchevo. The 11th Tank Corps reached the front excluding Chalishchevo—Telyakovo.

Thus by the close of 9 August the Khotynets center of resistance had been outflanked on three sides.

On the morning of 10 August our units, having crushed the resistance of the enemy's Khotynets group of forces, completely liberated Khotynets. The remnants of the German units, covered by strong rearguards, hurriedly fell back to the west. In the fighting for the town the Germans' Khotynets group of forces lost more than 7,500 officers and men, 70 tanks, 176 guns and mortars, and much other equipment.

Pursuing the enemy, the 16th Guards Rifle Corps (the 197th and 108th rifle divisions had been transferred to the 11th Army) were by the close of 11 August fighting along the line eastern outskirts of Alekhino—Shishkino.

The 36th Guards Rifle Corps, while pursuing the enemy, had reached the eastern outskirts of Yur'evo and straddled the Khotynets—Karachev paved road southeast of Yakovlevo.

The 8th Guards Rifle Corps reached the line excluding the southern outskirts of Yakovlevo—Dronovo.

The 169th Rifle Division, which was in the army commander's reserve, concentrated in the Moshchenoe area, while the 1st Guards Rifle Division was in the Vorotyntsevo area.

The 4th Tank Army, in conjunction with the left wing of the 11th Guards Army and the right wing of the 3rd Army, reached the line Dunaevskii—Krivosheevo.

In six days of intense fighting the forces of the 11th Guards and 4th Tank armies, having broken through the enemy's defense, advanced 40 kilometers, liberated the town of Khotynets, inflicted heavy losses on the enemy, and opened the gates for an offensive by our forces on Karachev.

The pursuit of the enemy by the Bryansk Front's left wing and the Central Front's right wing

At the same time the forces of the 11th Guards and 4th Tank armies were liberating the Khotynets area in stubborn fighting, the forces of the Bryansk Front's left wing and the Central Front's right wing were energetically advancing, pursuing the remnants of the Germans' defeated Orel group of forces and preventing it from consolidating along prepared lines. Falling back from one line to another, the Germans were trying to exhaust and bleed our attacking forces. Covering themselves with selected detachments, they were counting on pulling back their forces to previously prepared lines. The enemy often mined and destroyed roads, blew up bridges, mined favorable approaches and, in places, sought to halt our units' advance by frequent counterattacks against our flanks. However, none of the German command's measures were able to delay our unit's attack.

Crushing the resistance of the enemy's rearguards, overcoming, and in places simply bypassing his obstacles, by the close of 11 August the units of the Bryansk Front's left wing (3rd and 63rd armies)[1] reached the line excluding Dronovo—Kreml'—Shakhovtsy. The Central Front's right-wing forces, having captured Kromy on 6 August, by the close of 11 August reached the line Mytskoe—excluding Dmitrovsk-Orlovskii.

The Fighting for Karachev

The situation along the Bryansk Front's right flank

As a result of the 11th Guards and 4th Tank armies' successful offensive, favorable conditions were created for developing the success in the direction of Karachev and Bryansk, for the purpose of seizing the Bryansk railroad junction and further splitting the enemy's front. As early as 8 August the commander of the Bryansk Front made the following decision: developing the offensive by the forces of the 11th Guards Army toward Karachev from the east, the 11th Army's left wing was to launch an attack from the northeast, outflanking the Germans' Karachev group of forces and, through concentric attacks by the two armies' adjoining flanks, capture Karachev, an important road junction and powerful center of resistance covering the approaches to Bryansk.

In carrying out this decision, the 11th Army's forces carried out a regrouping of forces to their left flank from 9 through 11 August, and by the morning of 12 August they occupied the following positions:

- the 53rd Rifle Corps was operating along the line Granki—Mekhovaya—Katunovka—height 164.5;
- the 273rd Rifle Division was defending a broad front along the line height excluding 164.5—Sukhanka;
- units of the 25th Rifle Corps held jumping-off positions for an attack along the line Sukhanka—the woods east of Malaya Semenovka;
- the 46th Rifle Corps held jumping-off positions along the line of the woods west of excluding Bol'shoe Naryshkino—the woods north of Alekhino.

The 11th Army's forces were opposed by the 211th and 183rd infantry divisions, the remnants of the 5th Panzer Division, the 50th Sapper Battalion, the 95th and 707th infantry divisions, the 14th Jaeger and 441st Repair battalions, the 129th Infantry Division, the 45th Security Regiment, units of the 20th Motorized Division, remnants of the 293rd Infantry, and units of the 8th Panzer divisions.

The 11th Guards Army, having captured the area around Khotynets, continued to attack to the west and by the close of 11 August had reached the following lines: 16th Guards Rifle Corps—the eastern outskirts of Alekhino—excluding Mertvoe—Shishkino; 36th Guards Rifle Corps had reached the line Yur'evo—Yakovlevo; the 8th Guards Rifle Corps had reached the line excluding Yakovlevo—Dronovo; the 169th and 1st Guards rifle divisions, which composed the army reserve, had concentrated as follows: the former in the Moshchenoe area, and the latter in the Vorotyntsevo area.

Facing the 11th Guards Army and attempting to delay its offensive during its fighting retreat to the west were units of the German 8th Panzer Division, the 253rd Infantry, 10th Motorized, 18th Panzer, and the 26th and 34th infantry divisions.

1 The 61st Army, due to the contraction of the front, turned over its sector to the 3rd Army on 9 August and was put into the *Stavka* reserve.

To the left, units of the 4th Tank Army, in conjunction with the 3rd Army's right flank, had reached the line Dunaevskii—Krivosheevo.

To the right of the Bryansk Front's forces, the Western Front's 50th Army was continuing to defend along its previous line and was preparing to go over to the offensive on 16 August along with the 11th Army's right wing.

The attack by the 11th Army's left wing

At 0200 on 12 August the reconnaissance battalions of the 25th and 46th rifle corps' divisions began their attack. Battling the defending enemy, the battalions broke through his forward screen and reached the forward edge of the defensive zone and in places penetrated into the German units' main zone of resistance. The results of the reconnaissance detachment's actions were taken into account by all the combat arms. At 1200 the artillery opened up a powerful bombardment against the enemy's defensive zone, destroying the unearthed targets and suppressing the Germans' defense.

The artillery preparation continued for half an hour. At 1230 the main forces of the 25th and 46th rifle corps attacked. The fighting was waged for each village and each line behind which the German units could dig in. The enemy, seeking to delay our offensive, put up powerful fire resistance and often launched counterattacks.

By the close of 14 August our forces had completely broken through the Germans' defensive zone and reached the approaches to Karachev.

Units of the 11th Guards Army's right wing, having opened their attack on the morning of 12 August, broke through the enemy's defense along the Mertvoe—Kocherzhinka sector. On 12 August and the succeeding days the Germans put up fierce resistance. Bringing up new forces to the Karachev area, they repeatedly counterattacked our units. However, despite the steadily increasing enemy resistance, our forces continued to purposefully advance. Routing and throwing back the counterattacking and defending German units, by the close of 14 August they had reached Karachev from the east and southeast.

The capture of Karachev

At 0300 on 15 August the immediate fighting for Karachev began. The Germans put up fierce resistance. Attaching great significance to Karachev as a road junction, a supply base and the last major center of resistance along the approaches to Bryansk, the German command had gathered large forces in the Karachev area. In order to hold the town, the German command concentrated in this area units of the 78th, and 34th infantry and the remnants of the 253rd and 293rd infantry divisions, the 18th and 8th panzer divisions, the 45th Security Regiment, and a number of independent special units, as well as artillery and armored trains.

Overcoming the enemy's resistance, the 11th Army's 369th and 238th rifle divisions outflanked the town from the northeast and north. At the same time, the 11th Guards Army's 16th and 84th rifle divisions launched a powerful attack against Karachev from the east and southeast.

The 11th Guards Army's remaining forces powerfully assisted the success of these units' attack on Karachev. The 16th Guards Rifle Corps, having outflanked the enemy, captured the enemy's important strong point of height 209.2. The 83rd Rifle Division, which was attacking Karachev from the southeast, captured the strong points of height 246.1 and Glybochka, while the 8th Guards Rifle Corps' left-wing forces, which had outflanked Karachev from the south, forced the Snezhet' River. Units of the 11th Army (197th, 323rd and 110th rifle divisions), which had bypassed the town from the north and northwest, thereby creating the threat of completely encircling the German forces, also assisted in the capture of Karachev.

The enemy defended stubbornly, but he could not withstand our units' energetic concentric attack. Having crushed the German' resistance along the heights and in the villages surrounding the town, our forces broke into Karachev at 0830 and completely occupied it.

The Germans suffered enormous losses in personnel and equipment (no less than 4,000 killed and wounded in the fighting along the approaches to Karachev alone) and were deprived of all their main strong points, which they had built along the approaches to Karachev. The enemy began to fall back to the west, covering his retreat in stubborn rearguard actions and broadly employing obstacles (mainly mining) and destruction.

To note the success achieved by our forces around Karachev, an order by the Supreme Commander-in-Chief, comrade Stalin, bestowed the honorary name of "Karachev" on the 16th and 84th guards and 238th and 369th rifle divisions, which had crushed the Germans' resistance in the stubborn fighting and liberated the town of Karachev.

Pursuing the enemy along the Bryansk Front's right flank

As a result of our forces' advance along the Karachev axis and the successful attack by the Western Front's left wing in the Spas-Demensk area, a difficult situation had arisen for the German units defending east of the Bolva River.

Fearing that his main communications would be cut and that he would be surrounded, the enemy began pulling back his Zhizdra group of forces to the west on the night of 13-14 August. Having noticed the enemy's withdrawal, the 50th Army and the 11th Army's right wing attacked on the morning of 14 August.

On 15 August the 2nd Guards Cavalry Corps was committed along the boundary between the 50th and 11th armies for pursuing the enemy, with the mission of cutting the Bryansk—Sukhinichi railroad.

Pursuing the retreating German units and overcoming the resistance of their rearguards, the forces of the Bryansk Front captured the important road junction of Khvastovichi on 15 August, and on August 16 captured the town of Zhizdra.

By August 18 the *front's* forces reached the following line:

50th Army—Yasenok—Inochka—Orlya;[2]
2nd Guards Cavalry Corps—Orlya—excluding Kalinino;[3]
11th Army—Krasnoe—excluding Zhurinichi—Velim'ya;
11th Guards Army—Malye Luki—Kuprina.

The pursuit of the enemy by the forces of the Bryansk Front's left wing and the Central Front's right wing

To the left of the 11th Guards Army, the Bryansk Front's left wing and the Central Front's right wing continued to closely pursue the enemy's units that had been defeated in the area of Orel and Kromy. By launching powerful attacks against the Germans' retreating forces, pushing aside their rearguards and getting across their main forces lines of retreat, our units captured the town of Dmitrovsk-Orlovskii on 12 August and by 17-18 August had reached the line Glybochka—Nizhnii Gorodets—excluding Terekhovka—Domakha—Uporoi.

2 On 17 August the 50th Army was subordinated to the Bryansk Front.
3 The 2nd Guards Cavalry Corps was operationally subordinated to the 50th Army.

In the succeeding days our forces advanced only slightly in places. The enemy consolidated along his previously prepared positions, which consisted of three lines of fully-outfitted trenches and a developed obstacle system, and gone over to a fixed defense, covering the approaches to Bryansk. The elimination of the Germans' Orel strategic salient was complete. Our forces began preparing an operation to liberate Bryansk.

The Results of Our Forces' Offensive Along the Orel—Karachev Axis (12 July-17 August 1943)

By 18 August the Bryansk Front's forces (50th, 11th, 11th Guards, 3rd, and 63rd armies)[4] and the Central Front's right wing had completed the elimination of the Orel strategic salient, to which the Germans attached huge significance. For them this was the main bridgehead for an offensive on Moscow. The Germans had spent 22 months fortifying it. Upon our forces going over to the offensive, they sought to hold it at all costs, throwing all available forces into its defense and not stopping at stripping their other axes of troops.

Having lost the Orel strategic salient, the Germans also lost their favorable operational situation *vis a vis* the forces of the Western and Central fronts, which in turn made it easier for them to successfully attack in the western direction.

The German forces, having suffered a heavy defeat in the Orel area, were no longer in a condition to put up organized resistance. Their attempts to go over to the defense along the Karachev line were unsuccessful. Subsequently, the Bryansk Front's forces, while developing the offensive along a broad front, outflanked these positions and on 17 September captured the city of Bryansk.

During the fighting, which lasted more than a month, our forces completely routed 21 enemy divisions, of which 13 were infantry (7th, 31st, 34th, 36th, 56th, 112th, 208th, 211th, 253rd, 258th, 262nd, 293rd, and 383rd), two motorized (10th and 25th) and six panzer (2nd, 5th, 8th, 9th, 18th, and 20th). Heavy losses were inflicted on three panzer, one motorized and eighteen infantry divisions, as well as a number of independent units, which the German command transferred to this axis during the fighting, in order to delay our offensive.

According to the Bryansk Front's figures alone, more than 180,000 enemy officers and men were killed in these battles, with 281 planes, about 1,500 tanks, more than 3,000 guns and mortars, 2,330 motor vehicles, and much other equipment destroyed.

According to the same data, our forces captured: 5,765 prisoners, 243 tanks, about 1,700 guns and mortars, 88 locomotives, and 255 depots.

Besides this, much other weaponry, military equipment and ammunition was also captured, part of which was used by our forces during the fighting.

During this period our forces liberated a territory of more than 12,000 square kilometers and about 2,500 inhabited areas, including the cities of Orel, Bolkhov, Mtsensk, Khotynets, Karachev, Zhizdra, Kromy, and Dmitrovsk-Orlovskii.

The Germans' defensive strategy was subjected to the latest crushing blow by the Red Army, after which followed one blow after another, which led to the complete collapse of their defense along the Soviet front.

4 This includes the armies of the Western Front's left wing, which had been transferred to the Bryansk Front in accordance with the *Stavka* orders—the 11th Guards and 11th armies on 30 July, and the 50th Army on 17 August.

PART TWO

THE DEFEAT OF THE GERMANS' BELGOROD—KHAR'KOV GROUP OF FORCES

By the start of the Belgorod—Khar'kov offensive operation, the overall operational-strategic situation that had arisen for the Voronezh and Steppe fronts was characterized by the complete collapse of the German's July offensive on Kursk and the beginning of the defeat of the enemy's Orel group of forces.

The forces of the Western and Bryansk front had already begun fighting on the direct approaches to Orel at the beginning of August.

The forces of the Central Front, while assisting the Bryansk Front with part of its forces, had gone over to the offensive along the Kromy axis.

The offensive by the Fourth Panzer Army and army group "Kempf" against the forces of the Voronezh Front from the Belgorod—Khar'kov bridgehead had been halted. In ten days of fierce fighting and at the cost of enormous losses, the enemy along this axis had managed only to penetrate into our defense to a depth of 15-35 kilometers. Having lost their shock force in these battles, the Germans were forced on 15 July to go over to the defensive along this axis. The Voronezh Front's forces, along with the forces of the Steppe Front, restored the situation along this sector through powerful counterblows during the 17-23 July period, throwing back the Germans to the line they held before the start of their offensive.

On the orders of the *Stavka*, by the end of July the forces of the Steppe Front had reached the area of the fighting north of Belgorod in full strength, which decisively changed the correlation of forces along the Belgorod—Khar'kov axis in our favor. In the middle of July the Southwestern and Southern fronts also went over to the offensive with part of their forces. Thus our forces not only beat back the German offensive on Kursk, but had themselves gone over to the offensive along a broad front from Orel to the Sea of Azov and by the end of July had completely seized the strategic initiative.

The offensive by the forces of the Western and Bryansk fronts against the enemy's Orel group of forces, and that of the Southwestern and Southern fronts in the Donbass had created a favorable situation for launching a counteroffensive along the Belgorod—Khar'kov axis by the forces of the Voronezh and Steppe fronts.

The German command was forced to hurriedly remove a number of divisions from the Khar'kov axis and throw them into the areas of Orel and the Donbass.

For example, during 15-25 July the following units were removed and transferred from the Khar'kov axis:

- the 26th Infantry and the *Grossdeutschland* Panzer divisions to the Orel salient for operations against the Western Front;
- the *Adolph Hitler*, *Totenkopf*, *Das Reich*, and 3rd panzer divisions to the Makeevka axis for operations against the Southern Front;
- the *Wiking* Panzer Division to the area southwest of Izyum, against the forces of the Southwestern Front that had gone over to the offensive.

Thus by the end of July the enemy's Belgorod—Khar'kov group of forces had been significantly weakened, while our forces, in connection with the arrival of the Steppe Front to the front line, were, on the other hand, significantly stronger.

The conduct of such an offensive operation was brought about by the necessity of eliminating the Germans' Belgorod—Khar'kov bridgehead (which, according to the German generals' expression, was the gate barring the Red Army's offensive path to Ukraine), as well as the necessity for eliminating as quickly as possible the German group of forces defending the bridgehead. Besides this, it was necessary to deprive the enemy of the capability of maneuvering his reserves and then transferring them from the Khar'kov axis to Orel and the Donbass.

The counteroffensive by the forces of the Voronezh and Steppe fronts, which ended with the defeat of the German Fourth Panzer Army and army group "Kempf," as well as the elimination of the Belgorod—Khar'kov bridgehead, took place during 3-23 August 1943.

The fighting unfolded along a broad expanse of territory, delineated as follows: from the line Sumy—Belgorod to the north; the Psel River to the west; the line Zen'kov—Khar'kov to the south, and; the Severskii Donets River from the east. The extent of this territory reached 13,000 square kilometers.

Features of the Belgorod—Khar'kov Bridgehead

Even following the collapse of the German adventure—the offensive on Kursk—the Belgorod—Khar'kov bridgehead had no less strategic significance for the German command than did the Orel salient. According to one of the representatives of the fascist command, the bridgehead was the most powerful "bastion of the German defense in the East, the gates blocking the Russian armies' road to Ukraine." At the same time the Khar'kov area was the key to the Donbass, which continued to remain in German hands.

Within the bounds of this bridgehead was located the city of Khar'kov—a very important economic and political center of the Soviet Union, a very important railroad junction, and the second capital of Ukraine. Besides this, other large towns—Sumy, Belgorod, Akhtyrka, Lebedin, Bogodukhov, and Chuguev—were located here.

Military-geographical description

The area of the Voronezh and Steppe fronts' offensive operations has moderately hilly terrain, which is cut by a significant number of rivers, creeks, gullies, and washed out areas. This terrain made the offensive operations of our forces considerably more difficult and made the organization of the enemy's defense easier.

The eastern part of this area is almost without woods. There are woods only in the Khar'kov area and along the Severskii Donets River.

A significant territory in the western part of the area, in the area between the Psel and Vorskla rivers, is covered by large wooded expanses.

A large part of the rivers—the Vorsklitsa, Vorskla, Merla, Udy, Lopan', and Khar'kov—flows mainly to the southwest, creating significant natural obstacles for our forces' offensive to the south; when attacking to the southwest, these rivers limited maneuver toward the flanks and created favorable switch positions for the enemy reserves.

The Psel River, which flows in the western part of the area, represented a barrier for an offensive from the Miropol'e—Krasnopol'e area to the west, but at the same time served as a cover for the right flank of forces attacking to the south toward Bogodukhov.

The Severskii Donets River represented a natural defensive line for the Germans, which protected the enemy's Belgorod—Khar'kov group of forces from the east.

The battle area is heavily populated. There is, on the average, an inhabited area every ten square kilometers. The largest inhabited areas—Khar'kov, Sumy, Belgorod, Chuguev, Lyubotin, Bogodukhov, Akhtyrka, Kotel'va, Lebedin, and Tomarovka—had great tactical significance as major road junctions, as well as locales favorable for creating centers of resistance. The fact that the cities and some large towns were located along rivers and commanding heights increased their actual role even more.

The most important of these towns was Khar'kov, a powerful center of resistance of operational significance. It is also a very major railroad and road junction. The main paved roads and railroads here run from north to south and a large portion of them come together in the Khar'kov area. Such a road net facilitated the organization and support of a major offensive operation.

The main rail routes upon which our forces could be based during an offensive were: Kursk—Khar'kov, Sudzha—Khar'kov, Kupyansk—Khar'kov, and Kupyansk—Volchansk.

For the enemy, the most important railroads were the Khar'kov—Poltava, Khar'kov—Dnepropetrovsk, Khar'kov—Lozovaya, and Khar'kov—Sumy lines. Relying on these routes, the enemy had good communications with the rear and broad opportunities for the operational maneuver of reserves, both from the depth and along the front.

Description of the German defense

The Hitlerite command devoted a great deal of attention to the prior preparation of the Belgorod—Khar'kov bridgehead for a lengthy and stubborn defense.

The Germans had more than four months to prepare their defense along the northern face of the bridgehead (from Sumy to Belgorod). The defense of the line of the Severskii Donets River had been prepared and strengthened for a year and a half—since the fall of 1941.

The Germans' main defensive line ran through the villages of Komarovka, Alekseevka (north of Sumy), Krasnopol'e, Soldatskoe, Butovo, Visloe, and Khokhlova, and then along the western bank of the Severskii Donets River. Along the bridgehead's northern face it was based on a series of well fortified inhabited areas—Sumy, Krasnopol'e, Zybino, Dragunskoe, Visloe, and Belgorod.

The second defensive line, which covered the Belgorod axis, ran along the line Streletskoe—Shopino.

The third defensive line had been prepared along the line Bol'shoi Bobrik—Dorogoshch—Khotmyzhsk—Borisovka—Tomarovka—Belgorod. The enemy had transformed all of these inhabited areas into powerful centers of resistance.

The fourth and fifth defensive lines were intermediate ones and covered the far approaches to Khar'kov.

A sixth defensive line (the rear operational line) had been prepared along the Akhtyrka—Bogodukhov—Kazach'ya Lopan'—Zhuravlevka—Krasnyi—Veseloe—Nepokrytaya—Bol'shaya Babka—Novo-Pokrovskoe line.

Aside from these zones, the German command had created a seventh defensive line, which ran along the line Bezrukovka—Russko-Lozovoe—Russkie Tishki, and then south along the western bank of the Roganka River, as well as a number of switch positions, using the rivers and large inhabited areas for this purpose.

The enemy devoted special attention to preparing the defense of Khar'kov. Suffice it to say, he had prepared seven defensive lines for covering Khar'kov from the north alone, and three lines for covering it from the east. Aside from this, Khar'kov was immediately girded by still two more powerful ring lines, which were connected among themselves by a series of switch positions. The city itself had been prepared to wage stubborn street fighting. Thus the overall depth of the previously-prepared defense along the Khar'kov axis reached 85-90 kilometers.

The Germans' main defensive zone consisted of a series of strong points and resistance centers, which were in mutual fire communications and linked to each other by 3-4 continuous trench lines, echeloned in depth. By the start of our offensive, the defensive zone had been prepared from the engineering point of view—there was a developed network of fully-realized trenches, with communications trenches, and a significant number of wood and earth pillboxes and blinds.

In the majority of cases, the forward edge of the main defensive zone ran along the crests of the heights and the outskirts of the inhabited areas, which guaranteed the enemy sufficient observation of the area terrain lying in front of him, as well as the opportunity of organizing a fire system of all types.

The Germans had set up 3-4 lines of wire obstacles along the forward edge of the defense along the most important sectors, and had strengthened them with hard-to-spot obstacles and minefields. They were also creating a security position along some sectors, which represented a trench with individual pockets of resistance. Behind this position minefields and strengthened wire fence were usually set up. At a distance of 25 kilometers from the forward trench ran the forward edge of the defense's combat trench, in front of which were deployed pockets of resistance and open firing emplacements for machine guns.

Dugouts for the garrison were constructed 20-25 kilometers behind the main trench, which were connected with the trench by communications trenches.

A second combat trench was usually prepared along the reverse slopes of heights, at a distance of 100-120 meters from the main combat trench. Both trench lines were connected by communications trenches.

The Group of German Forces at the Time of Their Withdrawal to Their Former Defensive Line

By 23 July 1943 the German forces, under the pressure of the Red Army's counterblows, had fallen back to the line Zybino—Butovo—Dragunskoe—Zhuravlinyi—Visloe—Petropavlovka—Dal'nyaya Igumenka—Blizhnyaya Igumenka, and then to the south along the western bank of the Razumnaya and Severskii Donets rivers. Thus the enemy had mainly been thrown back to that line that he had occupied before his offensive.

Taking into account the extremely important strategic significance of the Belgorod—Khar'kov bridgehead, the German command was determined to organize a stubborn defense along this line.

As a result of the successfully developing offensive by the Red Army in the Orel area, as well as the start of the Southwestern and Southern fronts' operations, the German command was forced by this time to remove from the Fourth Panzer Army the *Grossdeutschland* Panzer Division to the Orel area, and the SS *Das Reich*, *Totenkopf* and *Adolph Hitler* panzer divisions, and the 3rd Panzer Division to the Mius River. Along with these divisions, the headquarters of the SS Panzer Corps and the III Panzer Corps from army group "Kempf" were also transferred to the south to the Makeevka area.

On 23 July all of the Fourth Panzer Army's main forces, as well as those of army group "Kempf," which were chiefly grouped in the area Borisovka—Tomarovka—Belgorod, had been drawn into the fighting.

The German forces facing the Voronezh and Steppe fronts on 23 July were defending along the following lines:

- units of the XIII and VII army corps (Second Army) along the line Komarovka—Samotoevka;
- the LII Army and XLVIII Panzer corps (Fourth Panzer Army) along the line Krasnopol'e—Visloe;
- the XI and XLII army corps (army group "Kempf") along the line excluding Visloe—Blizhnyaya Igumenka, and then south along the Severskii Donets River to Zmiev.

By this time the XLVIII Panzer Corps' 11th and 19th panzer divisions had been pulled into the Fourth Panzer Army's reserve. The 19th Panzer Division was located in the area northeast of Borisovka; the 11th Panzer Division northeast of Tomarovka, and the 7th Panzer Division in Boromlya.

The Disposition of the Red Army's Forces by 23 July 1943

As a result of their successful counterblows, the forces of the Voronezh and Steppe fronts had by the close of 23 July mainly restored their previous position.

The Voronezh Front, under the command of General Vatutin, by the close of 23 July occupied the line Snagost'—Uspenskoe—Glushinskii.

The disposition of the Voronezh Front's forces was as follows:

the 38th Army (Lieutenant General Chibisov[1]) occupied the line Snagost'—Alekseevka—excluding Uspenskoe;
the 40th Army (Lieutenant General Moskalenko[2]) occupied the line Uspenskoe—Bubny;
the 6th Guards Army (Lieutenant General Chistyakov[3]) occupied the line Gertsovka—Trirechnoe;
the 5th Guards Army (Lieutenant General Zhadov) and the 5th Guards Tank Army (Lieutenant General of Tank Troops Rotmistrov) occupied the line excluding Trirechnoe—Glushinskii.[4]

The Voronezh Front's reserve consisted of the 27th Army (Lieutenant General Trofimenko[5]) and the 1st Tank Army (Lieutenant General of Tank Troops Katukov), which were concentrated as follows: the first in the area Beloe—Bobrava—Peny, and the second in the area Ivnya—Melovoe (17 kilometers southwest of Ivnya)—Vladimirovka.

The Steppe Front, under the command of Colonel General (now marshal of the Soviet Union) Konev,[6] had by the close of 23 July reached the front excluding Glushinskii—Melekhovo—Myasoedovo—Razumnoe, and then along the eastern bank of the Severskii Donets as far as Volchansk.

1 Editor's note. Nikandr Yevlampievich Chibisov (1892-1959) joined the Russian imperial army in 1913 and the Red Army in 1918. During the Great Patriotic War he commanded a military district, a *front* and a number of armies, including the 38th Army during the Battle of Kursk. Following the war, Chibisov headed the Frunze Military Academy and was deputy military district commander.

2 Editor's note. Kirill Semyonovich Moskalenko (1902-85) joined the Red Army in 1920. During the Great Patriotic War he commanded an anti-tank artillery brigade, a rifle corps, a cavalry corps, a cavalry-mechanized group, and a number of armies, including the 40th Army during the Battle of Kursk. Following the war, Moskalenko commanded a military district and the Strategic Rocket Forces.

3 Editor's note. Ivan Mikhailovich Chistyakov (1900-79) joined the Red Army in 1918. During the Great Patriotic War he commanded a rifle brigade, division and corps, as well as a number of armies, including the 6th Guards Army during the Battle of Kursk. Following the war, spent his time in the Far East and was a deputy military district commander.

4 The 5th Guards Tank Army was preparing to enter the *front* reserve.

5 Editor's note. Sergei Georgievich Trofimenko (1899-1953) joined the Red Army in 1919. During the Great Patriotic War he commanded a military district and a number of armies, including the 27th Army during the Battle of Kursk. Following the war, Trofimenko commanded a number of military districts.

6 Editor's note. Ivan Stepanovich Konev (1897-1973) joined the Russian imperial army in 1916 and the Red Army in 1918. During the Great Patriotic War he commanded an army and a number of *fronts*, including the Steppe Front during the Battle of Kursk. Following the war, Konev was the commander-in-chief of the Central Group of Forces, the USSR Ground Forces and commander-in-chief of the Warsaw Pact Forces.

The disposition of the Steppe Front's forces was as follows:

- the 53rd Army (Major General Managarov[7]) occupied the line excluding Glushinskii—excluding Kiselevo (nine kilometers east of Visloe;
- the 69th Army (Lieutenant General Kryuchenkin[8]) occupied the line Kiselevo—excluding Myasoedovo;
- the 7th Guards Army (Lieutenant General Shumilov) occupied the line Myasoedovo—Razumnoe—Volchansk.

The *Stavka* reserve—4th Guards Army under Lieutenant General Kulik[9]—was concentrating in the Chernyanka—Orlik—Loznoe area. Lieutenant General Korzun's[10] 47th Army, which also formed part of the *Stavka* reserve, was in the Korocha—Novaya Sloboda—Alekseevka area.

To the left of the Steppe Front, along the eastern bank of the Severskii Donets River south of Volchansk, were the forces of General Malinovskii's Southwestern Front. Its right-flank 57th Army (Lieutenant General Gagen) occupied the sector excluding Volchansk—Malinovka.

---

7 Editor's note. Ivan Mefod'evich Managarov (1898-1981) joined the Russian imperial army in 1914 and the Red Army in 1918. During the Great Patriotic War commanded a cavalry division and a rifle and cavalry corps and armies, including the 53rd Army during the Battle of Kursk. Following the war, Managarov commanded an army and served in the National Air Defense Forces.

8 Editor's note. Vasilii Dmitrievich Kryuchenkin (1894-1976) joined the Russian imperial army in 1915 and the Red Army in 1918. During the Great Patriotic War he commanded a cavalry division and a corps and a number of armies, including the 69th Army during the Battle of Kursk. Following the war, Kryuchenkin served as a deputy military district commander.

9 Editor's note. Grigorii Ivanovich Kulik (1890-1950) joined the Russian imperial army in 1912 and the Red Army in 1918, where he allied himself early on with Stalin. During the interwar period Kulik headed the Red Army's Artillery Directorate and was made a marshal of the Soviet Union. During the Great Patriotic War he served as a *Stavka* representative and army commander, although he failed at these tasks and was demoted. He commanded the 4th Guards Army durng the Battle of Kursk, but was relieved shortly afterwards. Kulik was arrested in 1947 and executed in 1950, although he was rehabilitated in 1957.

10 Editor's note. Pavel Petrovich Korzun (1892-1943) joined the Russian imperial army in 1913 and the Red Army in 1918. During the Great Patriotic War he commanded a rifle division, a cavalry corps and armies, including the 47th Army during the Battle of Kursk. He was killed in action.

1

The Planning and Preparation of the Offensive Operation

The Operational Plan

The planning of the operation for the destruction of the Germans' Belgorod—Khar'kov group of forces began as early as the time of the defensive battle. On orders of the *Stavka* of the Supreme High Command, the staff of the Voronezh Front prepared a plan for an offensive operation.

The first variant of this plan called for the encirclement of the entire Belgorod—Khar'kov group of German forces by means of a breakthrough of the enemy front by two powerful shock groups: one in the area of Krasnopol'e, and another in the Chuguev area. Then both groups of forces were to advance: the first to the south to envelop the enemy group of forces from the west, and the second to the west, for the purpose of outflanking Khar'kov and the entire German group of forces from the south. In the event of the successful accomplishment of this operational variant, the entire German Belgorod—Khar'kov group of forces would fall into the encirclement ring.

According to a second variation, the encirclement of the enemy group of forces was to be carried out by means of concentric attacks from the areas of Krasnaya Yaruga and Chuguev. According to this variation, upon the successful completion of the offensive operation, the Germans' Belgorod—Khar'kov group of forces would be split into two parts, and that part of the German group of forces operating in the area of Belgorod and Khar'kov—that is; the main forces of the Fourth Panzer Army and army group "Kempf," would be surrounded.

In order to accomplish the first variation, it required the creation of major shock groups along the external flanks of the Voronezh and Steppe fronts, capable of completing the operation to a depth of up to 250 kilometers without slowing down. Of course, this would be possible only following very complex regroupings, which would take up a lot of time, as a result of which it would be necessary to shift our offensive to a later time.

In order to realize the second variation of the offensive operation, significant regroupings would also be required, as well as a great deal of time to carry them out. Besides this, during the course of the operation the forces of the Voronezh Front had to consecutively force several significant water lines, which had previously been prepared by the enemy for defense—the Vorsklitsa, Vorskla, Merla, and Merchik rivers. This would require a large amount of crossing equipment and threatened to reduce the speed of the offensive.

The resulting situation demanded that the Voronezh and Steppe fronts go over to the offensive as quickly as possible, before the German forces, which had fallen back under the Red Army's blows, succeeded in organizing a defense and put themselves in order following their unsuccessful offensive, and before they created reserves by the transfer of forces from the depth and others sectors of the front. It should be noted that by this time the Germans' Belgorod—Khar'kov group of forces had been significantly weakened, because its SS Panzer Corps had been shifted to the Donbass, and the *Grossdeutschland* Panzer Division to the Orel salient. This had been caused, on the one hand, by the successful development of the offensive by the forces of the Western and

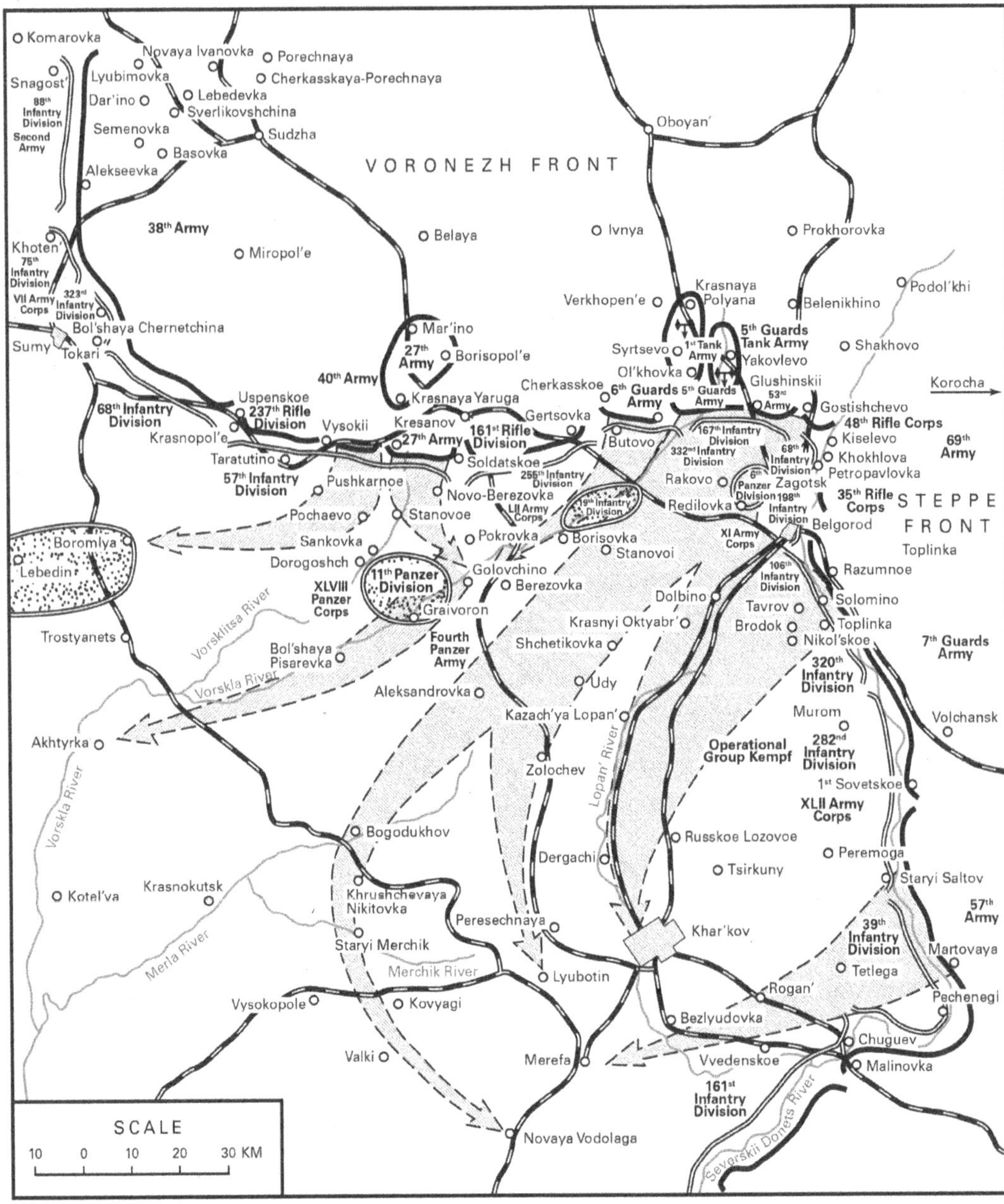

Map 5 The Soviet Command's Plan for Carrying out the Belgorod—Khar'kov Operation.

Bryansk fronts against the Germans' Orel group of forces, and on the other, by the offensive by the forces of the Southwestern and Southern fronts in the Donbass.

The final form of the offensive plan was drawn up on the basis of instructions issued by the *Stavka* on 22 July 1943.

In accordance with this plan, it was decided that the main attack, for the purpose of splitting the entire German group of forces into parts, followed by its subsequent defeat, would be launched by the adjacent flanks of the Voronezh and Steppe fronts from the area Yakovlevo—Trirechnoe—Gostishchevo in the general direction of Zolochev and Valki, bypassing Khar'kov from the west. Simultaneously, the center formations of the Voronezh (by means of an offensive from the area of Krasnaya Yaruga to the southwest, in the general direction of Graivoron and Akhtyrka) and Steppe (by means of an offensive to the south along the western bank of the Severskii Donets River) fronts were to "roll up" the German defense to the west and south.

This final variation, which was confirmed by the *Stavka* of the Supreme High Command, enabled us to save a great deal of time, because there was no need to carry out major regroupings. The group of forces along the left wing of the Voronezh Front and the right wing of the Steppe Front, which had arisen during the course of the fighting, basically corresponded to this variation of the offensive plan. The main group of forces (6th and 5th guards armies, 53rd Army, and the 1st and 5th Guards tank armies) was concentrated in the area Belenikhino—Verkhopen'e—Cherkasskoe—Gostishchevo; that is, along the axis of the planned main attack.

The planned attacks were directed along the rivers, which would significantly reduce the latters' significance as powerful natural barriers. Finally, the main attack was planned against the boundary of the Fourth Panzer Army and army group "Kempf"; that is, against those enemy formations that had been the most worn out and demoralized in the preceding unsuccessful enemy offensive and the withdrawal from the resulting pocket under the crushing pressure of our forces.

According to this plan, the Voronezh Front's left wing, consisting of the 5th Guards, 1st Tank and 5th Guards Tank armies, was to break through the enemy's defensive front along the 14-kilometer sector Trirechnoe—excluding Glushinskii, defeat the opposing German group of forces, and then develop the attack with mobile formations in the general direction of Zolochev and Valki, outflanking Khar'kov from the west.

The 6th Guards Army had the mission of breaking through the enemy front along the 10-kilometer Butovo—Trirechnoe sector and, by attacking to the southwest along the Vorskla River, to "roll up" the enemy's defensive front toward the west and to secure the main group of forces' right flank.

The 53rd and 69th armies, which comprised the Steppe Front's right flank, in conjunction with part of the 7th Guards Army's forces, were to launch concentric attacks from the north and east and encircle and defeat the Germans' Belgorod group of forces and, following the capture of Belgorod, to attack toward Khar'kov, "rolling up" the enemy's defense along the western bank of the Severskii Donets River.

Besides this, it was planned to employ the Southwestern Front's 57th Army to launch an attack from the Staryi Saltov—Martovaya area to the west, in the general direction of Merefa, for the purpose of reaching the area south of Khar'kov and assisting the forces attacking the city from the north. Our command assumed that the fight for Khar'kov would be fierce and that the enemy would ignore any losses in order to keep this very important strategic strong point in his hands.

In order to maximally and quickly broaden the breach of the enemy's defense and to securely protect the right flank of the main shock group of forces, it was decided to envelop both flanks of the Germans' Tomarovka group of forces and defeat it. For this purpose, the 6th Guards Army was to launch an attack from the Butovo—Trirechnoe sector in the general direction of Borisovka, while the 27th Army would attack from the Kresanov—Soldatskoe sector in the general direction of Golovchino.

The 40th Army, while making its main attack along the left flank from the Vysokii area, was to break through the German defense and subsequently develop the offensive on Dorogoshch, thus securing the operation by the 6th Guards and 27th armies for destroying the Tomarovka—Belgorod group of forces. Following the completion of the immediate task, it was planned that the 27th Army would develop the offensive on Akhtyrka, and the 40th Army toward Boromlya.

The operation's depth along the axis of the main attack was to reach 120 kilometers. The operation was planned to last 10-12 days, with an average daily rate of advance of 10-12 kilometers.

The Decisions by the *Front* Commanders and the Disposition of Forces

The decision by the commander of the Voronezh Front

The *front's* main shock group, which consisted of the 6th and 5th guards armies and the 1st and 5th Guards tank armies, was to attack on 3 August from the 24-kilometer line Butovo—Trirechnoe—excluding Glushinskii, in the general direction of Bogodukhov and Valki.

The 6th Guards Army, consisting of six rifle divisions,[1] a tank corps,[2] two independent breakthrough tank regiments, a heavy howitzer brigade, heavy cannon brigade, and an anti-tank artillery brigade, three howitzer, one cannon and seven anti-tank artillery regiments, a mortar regiment, two guards mortar regiments, seven independent anti-tank rifle battalions, and one anti-aircraft artillery division[3] were deployed along the 11-kilometer front Cherkasskoe—Trirechnoe.

In launching the main attack along its left flank from the Novo-Cherkasskoe area along a 5-kilometer front, the army was to break through the enemy defense along the Butovo—Dragunskoe sector and, developing the offensive in the general direction of Golovchino, in conjunction with the 27th Army, defeat the Germans' Tomarovka—Borisovka group of forces.

According to the commander's decision, by the close of the offensive's first day the army was to capture the line Yamnoe—Tomarovka; developing the offensive subsequently to the southwest along the Vorskla River, the army's rifle formations were to reach the line Trefilovka—Borisovka by the close of the second day, and by the close of the third day link up with the 27th Army's units in the Golovchino area.

The 5th Guards Stalingrad Tank Corps had the task, following its commitment into the breach at the close of the offensive's fourth day, of capturing Akhtyrka.

The army's combat formation was organized into two echelons: there were four rifle divisions in the first echelon,[4] along with reinforcements, two rifle divisions in the second echelon,[5] and the 5th Guards Stalingrad Tank Corps.

The army was to make its main attack with the guards corps—the 23rd Guards Rifle and 5th Guards Stalingrad Tank corps.

The 5th Guards Army, which consisted of seven rifle divisions,[6] two independent tank breakthrough regiments, the 13th Artillery Division (five artillery and one mortar brigades), two cannon, one howitzer and five anti-tank artillery regiments, one anti-tank artillery brigade, one regiment of self-propelled artillery, one mortar and four guards mortar regiments, the 8th Guards

1 22nd Guards Rifle Corps' 67th, 71st and 90th guards rifle divisions, and the 23rd Guards Rifle Corps' 51st and 52nd guards and 309th Rifle divisions.
2 5th Guards Stalingrad Tank Corps.
3 9th Anti-Aircraft Artillery Division.
4 67th, 71st, 51st, and 52nd guards rifle divisions.
5 90th Guards and 309th rifle divisions.
6 32nd Guards Rifle Corps' 66th, 97th and 13th guards rifle divisions, the 33rd Guards Rifle Corps' 6th, 95th and 9th guards rifle divisions, and the 42nd Guards Rifle Division.

Mortar Division (three brigades), the 29th Anti-Aircraft Artillery Division (four regiments), and a battalion of anti-tank rifles deployed along the 16-kilometer front excluding Trirechnoe—excluding Glushinskii. The army had the task of launching its main attack along the left flank along a 6-kilometer front excluding Zadel'noe—excluding Glushinskii, breaking through the enemy's front along the sector excluding Trirechnoe—Glushinskii and, developing the offensive in the general direction of Zolochev and by the close of the first day to capture the line Tomarovka—Rakovo. By the close of the second day the army was to reach the line excluding Borisovka—Bessonovka—excluding Dolbino.

One of the army's most important tasks was to secure the commitment of the 1st and 5th Guards tank armies into the breach.

The army's combat formation was organized into two echelons: there were five rifle divisions,[7] with reinforcements in the first echelon, with one division (9th Guards Rifle) in the second, and another division (42nd Guards Rifle) in the army commander's reserve. The army would make its main attack with the forces of the 33rd Guards Rifle Corps and the 42nd Guards Rifle Division.

The 1st Tank Army, which consisted of the 3rd Mechanized and the 6th and 31st tank corps, two regiments of self-propelled artillery, three anti-tank artillery regiments, two mortar regiments, one guards mortar regiment, one guards mortar battalion, two battalions of anti-tank rifles, and six anti-aircraft artillery regiments, was to enter the breach, created by the 5th Guards Army, from the area Krasnaya Polyana—Syrtsev—Ol'khovka. The 1st Tank Army, by developing the offensive in the general direction of Ol'khovka, Kalinina, Aleksandrovka, Bogodukhov, and Valki, and defeating the enemy's tactical reserves and retreating units, by the close of the offensive's first day was to reach the area Borisovka—Gonovka, and by the close of the offensive's second day the Bairak—Lyutovka area, the Bogodukhov area on the third day, and on the offensive's fourth day, while securely holding the Bogodukhov area with the 6th Tank Corps and defeating the enemy's arriving operational reserves and the Fourth Panzer Army's rear, the 3rd Mechanized Corps wa to reach the Kovyagi—Valki area, and the 31st Tank Corps the Novaya Vodolaga area.

The army's combat formation was organized in two echelons: the 6th Tank and 3rd Mechanized corps in the first echelon, and the 31st Tank Corps in the second, behind the 3rd Mechanized Corps.

The 5th Guards Tank Army, which consisted of the 5th Guards Mechanized and the 18th and 29th guards tank corps, a tank and a motorcycle regiments, four regiments of self-propelled artillery, one howitzer and four anti-tank artillery regiments, three mortar and one guards mortar regiments, two guards mortar battalions, and the 6th Anti-Aircraft Division (five anti-aircraft artillery regiments), was to enter the breach, created by the 5th Guards Army, from the area Pokrovka—Yakovlevo and, attacking in the general direction of Yakovlevo, Bykovka, Bessonovka, Zolochev, and Ol'shany, reach by the close of the offensive's first day the area Bessonovka—Shchetinovka—Kobelevka, and on the third day, while defeating the enemy's arriving operational reserves and the rear of army group "Kempf," reach the area Ol'shany—Lyubotin and cut the roads leading from Khar'kov to the west.

Air support of the main shock group was entrusted to the 2nd Air Army.

The 27th Army, consisting of six rifle divisions,[8] the 4th Guards and 10th tank corps, a tank brigade, an independent breakthrough tank regiment, the 17th Breakthrough Artillery Division, two self-propelled tank regiments, five anti-tank artillery regiments, one mortar and two guards mortar regiments, the 23rd Anti-Aircraft Artillery Division (four regiments), and an anti-aircraft

7 66th, 97th, 13th, 6th, and 95th guards rifle divisions.

8 147th, 241st, 163rd, 166th, 155th, and 71st rifle divisions.

artillery regiment, was concentrated behind the 40th Army's center in the Mar'ino—Krasnaya Yaruga—Borisopol'e area.

On the night of the operation's third day the army was to deploy along the 11-kilometer front Kresanov—excluding Soldatskoe. The army's main group of forces, located in the center, was to break through the enemy's defense along the 6-kilometer sector Kasilovo—Novo-Berezovka and, developing the offensive in the general direction of Kazach'ya Lisitsa and Golovchino, by the close of the offensive's first day its rifle formations were to capture the line excluding Sankovka—Ivanovskaya Lisitsa—Pokrovka, while its tank corps were to reach the area Graivoron—Golovchino. By the close of the offensive's second day the army was to capture the line Graivoron—Berezovka with its rifle formations and with its tank formations reach the following areas: the 10th Tank Corps the Aleksandrovka area, and the 4th Guards Tank Corps the Udy area.

The army's combat formation was organized into two echelons: four rifle divisions, a tank brigade, a tank breakthrough regiment, and other reinforcements in the first echelon; two rifle divisions and two tank corps in the second echelon. The shock group consisted of two first-echelon divisions (241st and 163rd), two second-echelon divisions (155th and 71st), the tank corps and the greater part of the reinforcements.

The 40th Army[9] was to attack with its shock group, consisting of two of the 47th Rifle Corps' rifle divisions (206th and 100th), the 2nd Tank Corps, a tank breakthrough regiment, two cannon, one howitzer and four anti-tank artillery regiments, one anti-tank artillery brigade, four mortar and two guards mortar regiments, three battalions of anti-tank rifles, and two anti-aircraft artillery regiments, was to operate from the morning of the offensive's third day. Deploying along the 8-kilometer front excluding Vysokii—excluding Kresanov, the army was to break through the enemy's defense along the sector Terebreno—excluding Lipovye Balki and attack along the Vorsklitsa River for the purpose of securing the 27th Army's right flank. By the close of the offensive's first day the rifle divisions were to reach the line Pushkarnoe—Pochaevo, and the 2nd Tank Corps the area Dorogoshch—Sankovka; by the close of the second day the rifle divisions were to reach the line Tarutino—Ryasnoe—Dorogoshch.

The 237th Rifle Division, operating along the army's right flank, had the mission of tying down the enemy along the front Uspenskoe—Vysokii. The 161st Rifle Division, operating to the left of the 27th Army along the 24-kilometer front Soldatskoe—Gertsovka, was entrusted with the task of supporting through stubborn defense the offensive by the 27th Army; by the close of its attack on the second day (6 August), the division was to link up with the army's other formations in the area Pushkarnoe—Starosel'e.

The 38th Army, consisting of five rifle divisions,[10] two anti-tank regiments, two mortar regiments, three battalions of anti-tank rifles, and an anti-aircraft artillery regiment, while continuing to occupy its 72-kilometer former line—Snagost'—excluding Uspenskoe and carrying out combat reconnaissance, was to tie down the opposing enemy during the course of the offensive. The army was also entrusted with the task of carrying out a masking maneuver during the offensive's preparatory phase, in order to distract the enemy's reserves from the axis of the *front's* main attack.

By the close of the operation's ninth day the *front's* armies were to reach the line Bol'shaya Chernetchina—Trostyanets—Staryi Merchik—Dergachi.

9 47th Rifle Corps' 237th, 206th and 100th rifle divisions, and the 161st Rifle Division.
10 240th, 180th, 167th, 232nd, and 340th rifle divisions.

The Steppe Front commander's decision

The Steppe Front's main shock group, consisting of the 53rd Army and the 69th Army's 48th Corps, according to the commander's decision, was to attack on 3 August from the line Glushinskii—Visloe, along an 11-kilometer front.

The 53rd Army, consisting of seven rifle divisions,[11] a mechanized corps,[12] three independent tank breakthrough regiments, 28 artillery regiments, 15 artillery battalions, four mortar and three guards mortar regiments, the 30th Anti-Aircraft Artillery Division, the 5th Anti-Aircraft Artillery Battalion, and an anti-aircraft artillery regiment, was deployed along the following 7-kilometer front: marker 244 (two kilometers southwest of Glushinskii)—excluding Visloe. Launching its main attack along the right flank along a 4-kilometer front (marker 244—the grove two kilometers east of Glushinskii), it was to break through the enemy's defense along the sector Zhuravlinyi—excluding Visloe and, developing the offensive in the general direction of Novo-Nikolaevka, by the close of the first day its rifle formations were to reach the line Rakovo—Zagotskot, and the 1st Mechanized Corps the Novo-Nikolaevka area; by the close of the second day it was planned that the rifle formations reach the line Redilovka—Arkhangel'skoe, while part of the mechanized corps's forces attacking from the Novo-Nikolaevka area, was to reach the Repnoe area, for the purpose of encircling the Germans' Belgorod group of forces along with units of the 69th and 7th Guards armies; it was planned that by the close of the fourth day the army's main forces would reach the line Vodyanoe—Novo-Nikolaevka.

The army's combat formation was organized in two echelons: three divisions with reinforcements in the first echelon, and four divisions and the mechanized corps in the second echelon. The army would make its main attack with the forces of six divisions and the mechanized corps.

The 69th Army's 48th Rifle Corps, consisting of four rifle divisions,[13] a tank brigade, eight artillery regiments, three mortar and one guards mortar regiments, and two guards mortar battalions, was to deploy along the 8-kilometer front Visloe—Kiselevo. Making its main attack along the right flank along the 4-kilometer front Visloe—excluding Dacha (east of Visloe), the corps was to break through the enemy's defense here and, developing the offensive in the general direction of Belgorod, by the close of the operation's first day was to reach the line Zagotskot—Belomestnaya. With part of its forces (89th Guards Division), the corps, in conjunction with part of the forces of the 69th Army's 35th Guards Rifle Corps, was to encircle and defeat by the close of the operation's third day the enemy group of forces defending in the Dacha area; by the close of the fourth day it was planned that the corps, together with the 69th Army's remaining formations, would reach the line Novo-Nikolaevka—excluding Novaya Nelidovka (four kilometers northwest of Nikol'skoe).

The corps' combat formation was organized in one echelon. The main attack was to be made by the forces of three divisions and a tank brigade.

The 69th Army's 35th Guards Rifle Corps, consisting of three rifle divisions[14] and acting as a pinning group, having deployed along the 13-kilometer front excluding Kiselevo—the center of Staryi Gorod, was to force the Severskii Donets River in the Khokhlova area and on the operation's first day, in conjunction with the 48th Rifle Corps' 89th Guards Rifle Division, encircle the Germans' group of forces in the Dacha area (east of Visloe), and by the close of the second day reach the area Belomestnaya—Petropavlovka and comprise the 69th Army's second echelon.

11 252nd, 28th Guards, 116th, 233rd, 299th, 214th, and 84th rifle divisions.
12 1st Mechanized Corps.
13 305th, 375th, 89th Guards, and 183rd rifle divisions.
14 107th Rifle and 93rd and 94th guards rifle divisions.

The 7th Guards Army, consisting of eight rifle divisions,[15] two artillery brigades, two independent tank breakthrough regiments, two independent tank brigades, ten artillery regiments, one mortar regiment, and one anti-aircraft artillery division, deployed along the 40-kilometer front the center of Staryi Gorod—1st Sovetskoe and, having its main group of forces (five divisions) in the center, was to cross over to the western bank of the Severskii Donets River with its main forces during the operation's first day along the Solomino—Pulyaevka sector and broaden the bridgeheads already there; by the close of the second day, with two of its divisions attacking from the Solomino—excluding Toplinka area in the general direction of Koloniya Dubovoe, reach the line Koloniya Dubovoe—Tavrovo and, in conjunction with units of the 69th Army and the 1st Mechanized Corps, encircle the German's Belgorod group of forces. The operation to encircle the Belgorod group of forces would be supported from the south by two divisions, which, while attacking from the area of Toplinka—Pulyaevka in the general direction of Brodok, were to reach the Brodok—Pulyaevka line; by the close of the offensive's fourth day it was planned that the army's shock group would reach the line Nikol'skoe—Pulyaevka.

The combat formation of the army's shock group was organized in two echelons, with four divisions and reinforcements in the first and one division in the second.

Following the elimination of the Germans' Belgorod group of forces, the *front's* forces were to engage in the operational pursuit of the enemy, which would conclude with the capture of the city of Khar'kov.

It was planned that on the fifth day of the operation the *front's* armies would reach the line Kazach'ya Lopan'—Murom; by the close of the seventh day they were to reach the line Dergachi—Tsirkuny—Peremoga, and by the close of the tenth day the *front's* armies would capture Khar'kov.

Thus the plan for the Voronezh and Steppe fronts' offensive operation called for the unfolding of active operations along a broad front, stretching up to 200 kilometers, with the simultaneous launching of attacks along four axes. If one takes into account the fact that the plan called for a subsequent attack by the Southwestern Front's 57th Army, then the overall width of the active front would grow to 260 kilometers, and the number of attacks to five.

Such an organization of the operation enabled us to simultaneously split up the entire system of the enemy's defense into a series of individual pieces, which would ease their subsequent destruction.

The attack by our main group of forces from the front Cherkasskoe—Gostishchevo would split the German defense; the subsequent movement of the Voronezh Front's shock group into the area Ol'shany—Valki—Novaya Vodolaga would enable us to split the Germans' entire Belgorod—Khar'kov group of forces into two isolated parts.

It should be emphasized that the main attack by the adjacent flanks of the Voronezh and Steppe fronts was to be launched against the main and most dense German group of forces. The defeat of this group of forces would undermine the stability of the Germans' entire defensive system along the Belgorod—Khar'kov bridgehead, and in the operation's first days the main and most powerful centers of resistance (Tomarovka—Borisovka and Belgorod), which blocked the route to Khar'kov from the north, would be put out of action.

The operational plan foresaw the rapid widening of the breakthrough front in the direction of both flanks. The widening of the breach to the west would be achieved by an attack by the 27th and 40th armies from the front excluding Vysokii—excluding Soldatskoe, as well as the "rolling up" of the enemy's front with attacks by the 6th Guards Army to the southwest.

15 111th and 15th Guards rifle divisions (49th Rifle Corps), 73rd, 78th and 81st guards rifle divisions (25th Guards Rifle Corps), and the 72nd Guards, 213th and 36th Guards rifle divisions (24th Guards Rifle Corps).

The widening of the breach to the south would be achieved by an offensive by the 69th and 7th Guards armies along the western bank of the Severskii Donets River.

Powerful groups of forces, created along both *fronts'* main attack axes, would secure the rapid crushing of the Germans' defensive system and the defeat of their main group of forces in the area of Tomarovka and Belgorod, as well as the rapid completion of the maneuver for the purpose of splitting into parts the entire Belgorod—Khar'kov group of forces.

Suffice it to say that given an average divisional frontage of six kilometers (counting only the first-echelon divisions) along the axes of the main attacks, the divisions were given attack sectors 1.8-2.5 kilometers in width, which enabled them to be echeloned deeply. If one takes into account the corps' second-echelon divisions, then the troop density along the main attack sectors increased to 1-2 kilometers per division.

The Voronezh Front's mobile formations—1st and 5th Guards tank armies—were concentrated in the 5th Guards Army's main attack zone, which yielded a tank density along this axis of up to 70 tanks per kilometer of front.

Given an average artillery density of 28 guns per kilometer of front, then along the main attack axis; that is, along the sector Cherkasskoe—Gostishchevo, it was 100 guns per kilometer of front. Along the main attack axes of the 5th Guards and 53rd armies, which were operating in the area of the main attack, the artillery density reached up to 230 tubes per kilometer.

The Enemy's Group of Forces

The Germans maintained a powerful group of forces for defending the Belgorod—Khar'kov bridgehead, consisting of 15 infantry and four panzer divisions, which formed part of the Second and Fourth Panzer armies and army group "Kempf." By the start of the Red Army's offensive, this group of forces was as follows.

Defending against the Voronezh Front were the 88th, 75th, 323rd, 68th, 57th, 255th, and 332nd infantry divisions. In reserve there was the 7th Panzer Division in the Boromlya area, the 11th Panzer Division in the Graivoron—Dorogoshch area, and the 19th Panzer Division northeast of Borisov.

The density of the German group of forces along various sectors of the front can be illustrated by data presented in the following tables.

The Density of the Germans' Group of Forces Along the Butovo—Zhuravlinyi Sector[16]

	Men and Materiel	Density per Kilometer of Front
Men	16,500	634
Rifles	8,900	342
Automatic Rifles	759	30
Machine Guns	969	37
Guns	306	12
Mortars	245	9.4
Tanks	155	6

16 The front of the Voronezh Front's planned attack.

The Density of the Germans' Group of Forces Along the Terebreno—Novo-Berezovka Sector[17]

	Men and Materiel	Density per Kilometer of Front
Men	22,740	1,033
Rifles	11,800	536
Automatic Rifles	820	37
Machine Guns	640	27
Guns	277	13
Mortars	130	6
Tanks	100	5

The Density of the Germans' Group of Forces Along the Zhuravlinyi—Visloe Sector[18]

	Men and Materiel	Density per Kilometer of Front
Men	4,000	360
Rifles	3,000	270
Automatic Rifles	300	27
Machine Guns	160	14
Guns	65	6
Mortars	58	5
Tanks	20	2

The Germans were defending opposite the Steppe Front with the 167th, 168th, 198th, 106th 320th, 282nd, 39th, and 161st infantry divisions, while the 6th Panzer Division was in reserve in the Redilovka area.

Besides this, as subsequent events would show, during the battle itself the German command, while striving to hold the Belgorod—Khar'kov bridgehead in its hands at any price, transferred to this area during the 7-23 August time period five panzer divisions (the SS panzer divisions *Grossdeutschland*, *Totenkopf*, *Das Reich*, *Wiking*, and the 3rd Panzer Division) from other sectors of the front or from the depth, as well as one motorized (10th) and four infantry (223rd, 355th, 34th, and 112th) divisions. More than ten various independent units and subunits—training courses, construction battalions, repair units and special subunits (the 55th Repair Regiment, 217th Sapper Battalion from the high command reserve, a training motorized battalion, the 357th, 637th and 332nd independent infantry battalions, the 48th Independent Sapper Battalion from the high command reserve, the 410th Independent Construction Battalion, the 28th Auto Battalion, the 616th Anti-Aircraft Battalion, minus equipment, the 1st Heavy Projectile Training Regiment, and the Khar'kov training courses for tank technicians, together with their equipment—tanks, self-propelled guns, etc.)—were transferred here from various sectors of the front.

The enormous losses inflicted on the enemy during the course of the defensive battle, as well as the major groups of forces expediently created by our command for attacking along the axes of the main attack, resulted in our superiority of force, which insured the successful conduct of the planned operation.

17 The 27th and 40th armies' attack front.

18 The attack front of the Steppe Front's main group of forces.

Along the Voronezh Front's main attack axis; that is, along the 27-kilometer sector Cherkasskoe—excluding Glushinskii, our forces outnumbered the enemy in men by ten times, six times in artillery, six times in mortars, and 6.5 times in tanks.

Along the axis of the Steppe Front's main attack; that is, along the 11-kilometer Zhuravlinyi—Visloe sector, our forces outnumbered the enemy 18 times in men, ten times in artillery, and seven times in tanks.

Along the axis of the Voronezh Front's auxiliary attack; that is, along the 22-kilometer excluding Vysokii—excluding Soldatskoe sector, our forces outnumbered the enemy in men by 3.6 times, 4.8 times in artillery, and five times in tanks.

The correlation of forces in the air was also in our favor.

The correlation of the opposing air forces (in the Voronezh Front's 2nd Air Army and the Steppe Front's 5th Air Army) is evident from the following table.

The Correlation of Aviation Forces

	2nd Air Army	5th Air Army	Total	Enemy	Correlation of Forces
Aircraft	753	501	1,254	About 1,000	1.2:1

The Voronezh Front's Masking Maneuver

In order to distract the enemy's attention from the attack area being prepared by the main forces of the Voronezh and Steppe fronts, on orders by the *Stavka* of the Supreme High Command, a deception maneuver was undertaken along the 38th Army's right wing in the Lyubimovka—Yunakovka—Sudzha area. This maneuver, carried out during 26 July-6 August, using the equipment of the Voronezh Front, was supposed to imitate the concentration of a large operational group of forces, which was preparing to attack along the Sumy axis.

The detailed plan for the deception operation, which was drawn up by the headquarters of the Voronezh Front, was approved on 25 July by the *front's* military council. In accordance with this plan, it was decided to imitate in the Sudzha area the concentration of two armies (one of them a tank army), consisting of two rifle, two tank and one mechanized corps.

It was planned to "concentrate" the rifle corps as follows: one corps in the area Lyubimovka—Dar'ino—Sverlikovshchina, and the other in the Semenovka—Yunakovka—Basovka area. The tank army was to be concentrated with one tank corps in the Novaya Ivanovka area, the second in the Sverlikovshchina—Lebedevka area, and the mechanized corps in the Russkaya Porechnaya—Cherkasskaya Porechnaya area. It was planned to deploy the headquarters of the fake group in the town of Sudzha.

In order to carry out this operation, they allotted a rifle division from the 38th Army, a machine gun battalion, an engineer-mortar company and a deception company, seven radio stations (RAF), eight tanks, 18 trucks, and one railroad flying column consisting of 20 rail cars. Besides this, the engineering units built 450 fake tanks and 500 fake artillery pieces of various types.

The overall control of the operation was entrusted to the 38th Army headquarters.

The deception operation consisted, first of all, in carrying out radio deception maneuver by means of unfolding the work of two networks and two axes. These networks worked for nine days (from 28 July through 5 August) and transmitted 35 radiograms and received 55 (1,638 transmitted and 3,744 received groups). The intensity of the networks' work continually increased. Transmissions were carried out using code PT-42. The subject of these transmissions consisted of requests and reports on the pace of the concentration and supplying the tank units with fuels, oils and lubricants.

In order to fix the location of the fake group's command post, a landing strip was deployed near Sudzha, on which three planes a day landed during 29-31 July.

The second measure called for by the plan was the reconnaissance of concentration and deployment areas for the fake formations. Data about forthcoming transfers by means of purposefully careless conversations was leaked to the local population. Apartments were vacated and prepared for the expected arrival of generals and their staffs in the town of Sudzha and the surrounding area, while quarters for combat units were prepared; railway workers received instructions to prepare stations for the arrival and detraining of major formations and a large amount of equipment; these instructions also called for the construction of additional unloading platforms and other structures.

Guards were placed near the apartments slated for the quartering of generals and their staffs; public access to some blocks was blocked. Trenches were dug along all the roads leading to the concentration area of the fake group of forces.

A group of officers, including one general, arrived from *front* headquarters to carry out reconnoitering and control over all of the preparatory measures in the Sudzha area.

It was suggested that the 38th Army headquarters draw up a plan for the army's offensive operation, in conjunction with the fake group of forces, while the operation's deception character was not known to the staff officers, with the exception of the leadership. The plan was transmitted to the subordinate headquarters. Measures to prepare for the forthcoming offensive were carried out in the troop units and a jumping-off area was prepared, while corresponding sets were distributed in the units. Rations for three days were distributed to the entire rank and file.

The plan called for a third measure—the fixing of the fake group of forces. For this purpose, units of the division, in platoon and company sized columns, marched each day along roads leading to the concentration area. At night these units once again returned to their initial positions.

The concentration of tanks was denoted by fake ones. The noise produced by tanks was imitated by the existing eight tanks; they laid down 450 tank tracks leading to the area where the fake tanks were concentrated. 500 fake artillery pieces were scattered among fake firing points alongside fake gun crews.

All of these measures yielded the desired effect. The enemy's attention was distracted to the fake concentration area. The enemy's air activities are the chief evidence of this. Following a series of reconnaissance flights, which began on 27 July, the enemy switched over to bombing attacks, which continued with increasing intensity from 28 July through 6 August.

The chief effect of the operation was that the enemy, fearing our attacking along the Sumy axis, despite the evidence of the attack by our main group of forces, which began on 3 August, continued to hold the 7th Panzer Division in the Boromlya area. The enemy carried out his most intensive bombing raid against the fake group of forces on 5 August, that is, on the third day of our offensive.

During 24 July-2 August the forces of the Voronezh Front, while preparing for the offensive, carried out local actions in order to improve their jumping-off position. During this period the forces of the Steppe Front, as a result of a local operation carried out by the forces of the 69th Army and the right flank of the 7th Guards Army, eliminated the Germans' bridgeheads on the eastern bank of the Severskii Donets River, and on the night of 2-3 August, in accordance with the plan for the offensive operation, occupied their jumping-off positions.

On 1 August, at the 5th Guards Army's command post, the *Stavka* representative, Marshal of the Soviet Union Zhukov, in the presence of the Voronezh Front's military council, transmitted to the army and corps commanders the latest *Stavka* instructions in regards to the forthcoming offensive.

2

The Course of the Battle

The offensive operation is divided into three stages, according to the character of its actions.

Stage One—3-7 August. The breakthrough of the German defense and the elimination of the main enemy centers of resistance along the Khar'kov axis.

Stage Two—8-11 August. The development of the offensive, the splitting of the Germans' Belgorod—Khar'kov group of forces and the arrival of the Voronezh Front's mobile formations at the communications of the Germans' Khar'kov group of forces in the Bogodukhov—Vysokopol'e—Kovyaga area. The development of the Steppe Front's offensive on Khar'kov, the arrival at the Khar'kov external defensive line, and the beginning of the fighting on the approaches to Khar'kov.

Stage Three—12-23 August. The repulse of the enemy's counterblows toward Bogodukhov and the maneuver by the Voronezh Front's right wing. The fighting for Khar'kov.

I. The Breakthrough of the German Defense and the Elimination of the Main Enemy Centers of Resistance Along the Khar'kov Axis (3-7 August)

The fighting on 3 August. The breakthrough of the main enemy defensive zone

On 3 August the Voronezh Front's 6th and 5th guards armies and the 1st and 5th Guards tank armies attacked, as well as the Steppe Front's 53rd Army, and the 69th Army's 48th Rifle Corps.

A powerful artillery-mortar and aviation preparation preceded the offensive. The artillery offensive along both *fronts* began with a common signal at 0500 on 3 August.

The artillery preparation for the Voronezh and Steppe fronts' offensive was organized as follows. It opened with a powerful 5-minute onslaught by all weapons against the forward edge of the enemy's defense. The onslaught continued from 0500 to 0505 on 3 August, that is, before it dawned fully. The onslaught proved completely unexpected for the Germans and caught them off guard, inflicting heavy losses on the enemy. In expectation of full dawn, from 0505 to 0535 there was a pause. At 0535 a controlled registration and checking of sights began, which continued for an hour—until 0635. From 0635 to 0750 both *fronts'* artillery carried out methodical fire to destroy the enemy's weapons and defensive structures. From 0743 to 0750 a barrage was also launched against the enemy's defensive position by all the guards mortar units. From 0755 to 0815 all of our weapons carried out increasing fire against the enemy's forward trenches, and at 0755 the infantry began to close to and arrive at the enemy's first trenches. According to the signals of the infantry subunits, the fire from the heavy-caliber guns gradually shifted ("crawled") from the forward edge to the depth of the German defense.

The artillery preparation unfolded in close cooperation with the air force, which in groups of 20-30 planes continuously bombed and strafed with artillery and machine gun fire the enemy's combat formations, as well as the locations of his reserves and artillery. Particularly powerful was the final artillery onslaught, which continued for five minutes; following this, the Germans were not able to come to and open fire for another 30 minutes. Individual German artillery batteries in various places, which tried to reply to our fire, were immediately suppressed or destroyed.

At 0800, according to a signal transmitted by radio, the artillery shifted its fire to the depths of the enemy position, and our breakthrough tanks and infantry, clinging to the rolling barrage, threw themselves into the attack. While overcoming the resistance of individual unsuppressed German firing points and strong points, and destroying their garrisons, our infantry and the breakthrough tanks rapidly advanced into the depth of the enemy defense.

At 0815, when the infantry and breakthrough tanks, following behind the rolling barrage, broke into the forward trenches, the artillery fired for 45 minutes according to a previously drawn up schedule, in order to suppress the most important strong points in the depth of the enemy's defense.

In the first half of the day the forward elements of 5th Guards Army's units, for the most part, reached the line Dragunskoe—Berezov, where they were bypassed by the forward units of the 1st and 5th Guards tank armies, which had been committed into the breach and were continuing to rapidly develop the resulting breach in depth. By 1400 the command committed the main forces of the tank armies into the breach. Both tank armies entered the breach along a narrow sector of front along the Zadel'noe—Zhuravlinyi sector. The width of the sector did not exceed five kilometers.

The 1st Tank Army was committed into the breach in the following manner. The 6th Tank Corps' 200th Tank Brigade and the 3rd Mechanized Corps' 49th Tank Brigade advanced in the vanguard directly behind the 5th Guards Army's infantry.

The 200th Tank Brigade, having forced the Vorskla River at 0700 in the area of Veselyi farm, passed the infantry at 1140 in the Zadel'noe area and began to pursue the enemy. At 1400 the main forces of the 6th Tank Corps finished crossing the Vorskla River and by 1500, moving in three columns, entered the breach behind the 200th Tank Brigade.

The 49th Tank Brigade, attacking behind the 97th Guards Rifle Division's formations, passed the infantry at 1330 in the Zadel'noe area and began to pursue the retreating enemy groups. By 1600 the corps' main forces had crossed the Vorskla River and, advancing in three columns, were also committed into the breach.

The 31st Tank Corps, the army's second echelon, having crossed the Vorskla River, was following behind the 3rd Mechanized Corps.

The 5th Guards Tank Army also allotted from the first echelon (29th and 18th corps) one tank brigade apiece as forward detachments, which advanced immediately behind the infantry formations.

At 1300, as soon as the 5th Guards Army's infantry had penetrated into the Germans' defensive zone, both corps, without waiting for the infantry to complete the breakthrough of the entire tactical depth of the enemy's defense, were deployed and committed into the battle.

The tank corps' forward brigades, and then their main forces, rapidly developed the offensive's opening success. The tank corps, having passed through the infantry's combat formations, completed the breakthrough of the second defensive zone.

The 5th Guards Mechanized Corps followed in the army's second echelon.

The 6th Guards Army, which had broken into the Germans' main defensive zone and, taking advantage of its neighbor's success to the left—the 5th Guards Army and the tank armies—continued to develop the offensive with particular intensity along its left flank, and during the first half of the day captured the important Dragunskoe—Kazatskoe center of resistance in the enemy's defensive system.

Along the sector of the 53rd Army and the 69th Army's 48th Rifle Corps, where the enemy was relying on a powerfully fortified line and was putting up particularly stubborn resistance, our forces were engaged in fierce trench fighting to 1500. In order to speed up the breakthrough of the enemy's defense, the 1st Mechanized Corps was committed into the battle, passed the infantry and, having crushed the enemy's resistance, completed the breakthrough of his main defensive zone.

By the close of 3 August units of the 1st Tank Army, while defeating the enemy's tactical reserves, had penetrated into his defense to a depth of 12 kilometers, while its forward units had reached the line eastern outskirts of Tomarovka—Dominin, while continuing to develop the offensive toward the villages of Kalinina and Kuleshovka.

Thus by the close of the first day of fighting, units of the 1st Tank Army had cut the main road connecting the Germans' Belgorod and Tomarovka groups of forces.

Units of the 5th Guards Tank Army, which had broken into the depth of the German defense to a depth of 26 kilometers, had reached the Saenkov—Dobraya Volya area by the close of the day.

Units of the Voronezh Front's 6th and 5th guards armies, having completed by the end of the day the breakthrough of the Germans' main defensive zone and having advanced 8-12 kilometers, reached the following lines: 6th Guards Army—Butovo—Krasnyi Ostrozhek, and 5th Guards Army—excluding Krasnyi Ostrozhek—northern outskirts of Rakovo.

Units of the Steppe Front's 53rd Army and the 69th Army's 48th Rifle Corps, consecutively blocking and eliminating the enemy's centers of resistance and strong points, by this time had reached the line height 218—Ternovka—the northern outskirts of Petropavlovka, having advanced 7-9 kilometers that day.

In the fighting on the offensive's first day our forces inflicted heavy losses on the 332nd and 167th infantry divisions. On this day, the German command committed the main part of its operational reserves—19th, 11th and 6th panzer divisions—into the fighting in the Tomarovka—Kazatskoe area.

The forces of both *fronts* carried out their assignments for the offensive's first day brilliantly. Such an offensive success was achieved not only thanks to the scrupulously prepared and skillfully conducted breakthrough, but also due to the fact that the attack proved to be a surprise for the enemy.

For example, our forces' offensive in the Butovo area caught units of the Germans' 332nd and 57th infantry divisions off guard at the same momement they were carrying out a partial regrouping.

The *front* commanders' measures

As the result of the successful development of the offensive by both *fronts*, by the close of the battle's first day the enemy's defensive front along the Butovo—Visloe sector had been broken throughout its entire tactical depth. The Voronezh Front's tank formations, having reached the area of Dobraya Volya (at a depth of 26 kilometers from the forward edge of the defense), had driven a powerful wedge into the Germans' defense. The main centers of resistance (Tomarovka and Belgorod), which covered Khar'kov from the north, had been divided.

Relying on these two centers of resistance, which were on the breakthrough's flanks, the German command could, by means of counterattacks by powerful groups of forces concentrated in the areas of the centers, if not parry our offensive, at least delay it significantly. Thus one of the most important tasks for our forces on 4-5 August was to eliminate these centers.

On the evening of 3 August the commanders of both *fronts* issued instructions to their forces to continue the offensive on the morning of 4 August, in accordance with the plan adopted.

Besides this, the commander of the Voronezh Front ordered the 27th Army on 4 August to organize along its entire front a powerful combat reconnaissance and prepare for attacking with its main forces. In order to support the breakthrough of the enemy's defense, on 4 August a large part of the High Command Reserve's artillery, which had earlier supported the 6th and 5th guards armies' offensive, was shifted to this army's zone.

The commander of the 5th Guards Tank Army was ordered to employ the 5th Guards Zimovniki Corps for developing the offensive from the Dobraya Volya area toward Gryaznoe and Tavrovo and, in conjunction with the forces of the Steppe Front, to encircle the Germans' Belgorod group of forces.

The fighting on 4 August

During 4 August stubborn fighting continued along the entire left flank of the Voronezh Front and the Steppe Front's right flank.

Both *fronts'* main shock group, flowing around the Germans' Tomarovka and Belgorod centers of resistance, continued to develop the offensive to the south.

The 6th Guards Army, attacking along the right bank of the Vorskla River, eliminated several enemy strong points and by the close of the day had reached the line of the northern outskirts of Novaya Glinka—the northern outskirts of Tomarovka.

The 5th Guards Army, covering with part of its forces from the west against likely enemy counterattacks from the Tomarovka area, by the close of a day of fighting had reached the line eastern outskirts of Tomarovka—Kozychev—Redilovka—Rakovo.

The 1st Tank Army's main forces, continuing to defeat the enemy's reserves and rear units, covered up to 20 kilometers that day and reached the area Kuleshovka—Klemenki.

The 5th Guards Tank Army was engaged in stubborn fighting all day with units of the 6th Panzer Division, which were defending the area of the groves south of Dobraya Volya.

On this day the 27th Army conducted reconnaissance with reinforced reconnaissance detachments, and along a number of sectors had penetrated into the German defense to a depth of 2-3 kilometers.

The forces of the Steppe Front's 53rd and 69th armies, which also were involved in fierce fighting all day, broke through the enemy's second and third defensive zones, which covered Belgorod from the north. Beating off the Germans' multiple attacks, by the end of the day the armies had reached the line northern outskirts of Kazatskoe—Oskochnoe—Chernaya Polyana.

The 7th Guards Army eliminated the Mikhailovka bridgehead along the eastern bank of the Severskii Donets River, having destroyed the enemy garrison there. During the second half of the day the army's forward units forced the river in several places along the sector Mikhailovka—Toplinka and began fierce fighting along the western bank. Such a major success by our forces forced the German command to make the decision to transfer reserves from the Donbass to the Khar'kov axis. On 4 August the movement of the III Panzer Corps and the SS Tank Corps from the Donbass (the Makeevka—Gorlovka area) in the direction of Khar'kov began. On 4 August the headquarters of both these corps had arrived in Khar'kov.

The instruction of the *Stavka* of the Supreme High Command

On 4 August Marshal of the Soviet Union Zhukov transmitted the following instructions from the *Stavka* of the Supreme High Command:

1. For the purpose of widening the breach toward the west, on the morning of 5 August the 27th and 40th armies are to begin their offensive in the general direction of Graivoron.
2. On 5 August the 6th Guards Army is to capture Tomarovka and by a subsequent offensive to the southwest decisively "roll up" the enemy's defensive front from east to west.

3. The 1st and 5th Guards tank armies, through rapid and decisive operations, are to reach the line Graivoron—Zolochev—Kazach'ya Lopan'.
4. The Steppe Front is to take Belgorod, after which it is to attack to the south and "roll up" the German defense along the western bank of the Severskii Donets River.
5. The 53rd Army and the 1st Mechanized Corps are to speed up the offensive in the general direction of Mikoyanovka.

The *front* commanders' instructions

On the basis of the *Stavka's* instructions, the corresponding directives were issued to the *front* commanders. In particular, the commander of the Steppe Front, Colonel General Konev, ordered:

1. The 53rd Army, along with the 1st Mechanized Corps, was to defeat units of the 6th Panzer Division and develop the offensive toward Mikoyanovka; the 1st Mechanized Corps was to attack from behind the army's right flank and reach the Gryaznoe—Repnoe area and cut off the Germans' Belgorod group of forces' line of retreat to the southwest.
2. The 69th Army, in conjunction with the 7th Guards Army, was to take Belgorod.
3. The 7th Guards Army was to break through the enemy defense and reach the line Tavrovo—Brodok, for the purpose of encircling, in conjunction with the 69th and 53rd armies, the Germans' Belgorod group of forces.

The Fighting on 5 August

The Voronezh Front's Offensive

On the morning of 5 August the 27th Army and the 40th Army's shock group attacked. The 40th Army began its operations at 0715, following a two-hour artillery preparation. The 27th Army, as a result of the fact that its reconnaissance detachments as early as 4 August had disrupted the enemy's defensive system, limited itself prior to the attack to a 15-minute powerful artillery onslaught.

Having crushed the resistance of the 57th Infantry Division and having inflicted heavy losses on it, both armies broke through the enemy's defensive front along a 26-kilometer sector and by the close of the day had advanced in fighting 8-20 kilometers and reached the line Starosel'e—Kasilovo—Ivanovskaya Lisitsa—Nikitskoe.

The enemy sought to pull out his units from under the 27th and 40th armies' attack. During the day the 11th Panzer Division continually counterattacked our attacking units. However, all of these counterattacks were beaten back successfully. The 11th Panzer Division suffered serious losses.

By the close of the day the 6th Guards Army had reached the line Zybino—Moshchenoe—Tomarovka and, as a result of two days of fierce fighting, captured the Germans' major center of resistance—the Tomarovka area. This center of resistance consisted of five powerful strong points: Kazatskoe, the woods southwest of Kazatskoe, Novaya Glinka, Staraya Glinka, and Moshchenoe. The strong point in Kazatskoe had been most completely prepared for defense. The garrison of the Tomarovka center of resistance consisted of units from the 332nd and 57th infantry and 19th Panzer divisions.

The fighting for the Tomarovka center of resistance occurred on 4-5 August. Having carried out a turning movement, the forces of the 6th Guards Army and the right flank of the 5th Guards Army, with help from units of the 1st Tank Army, half-encircled the Germans' Tomarovka group of forces in the second half of the day. Only the road to Borisovka remained in enemy hands.

The enemy, fearing complete encirclement and abandoning the wounded and combat equipment, began to hurriedly fall back under cover of darkness toward Borisovka. The fighting continued throughout the night of 5-6 August in Tomarovka against the individual German groups that had taken refuge there. By the morning of 6 August the Tomarovka center of resistance had been completely cleared of Germans.

By the close of the day the 5th Guards Army had reached the line Striguny—Gomzino—Step'. The 1st Tank Army, while rapidly developing the offensive and destroying the enemy's retreating units and rear troops, advanced another 30 kilometers that day and by the close of the day its forward units had reached the line Berezovka—Aleksandrovka—Gorodok, covering its right flank and rear against the Germans' Borisovka group of forces with the 31st Tank Corps.

During the fighting the 5th Guards Tank Corps, which had earlier been part of the 6th Guards Army, was subordinated to the commander of the 1st Tank Army.

The 5th Guards Tank Army, having bypassed the Germans' Bessonovka center of resistance from the west and taking advantage of the 1st Tank Army's success, made a fighting advance during the day of up to 15 kilometers, and by the close of the day had reached the area Vorozhbity—Verzunki.

The Steppe Front's offensive. The defeat of the Germans' Belgorod group of forces

On 5 August the 53rd Army, having pushed the Germans out of the Streletskoe and Bolkhovets strong points, broke through the enemy's fourth defensive line along the Vozolka River and by the close of the day reached the line Vodyanoe—Krasnoe in fighting.

The 1st Mechanized Corps, while carrying out its mission, by the close of the day had broken through in the Gryaznoe area, cut the Belgorod—Khar'kov paved road and railroad, thus depriving the Germans' Belgorod group of forces of its main communications.

On 5 August the forces of the 69th Army and the flank formations of the 7th Guards Army took Belgorod by storm and defeated the Germans' Belgorod group of forces. The enemy, who had transformed Belgorod into a powerful center of resistance, had built a large number of defensive structures in the area. Around the city, blocking the near approaches to it ran a ring-shaped defensive line, which had been built by the Germans as early as the winter of 1941-42.

By the beginning of our offensive the enemy had significantly strengthened this line. Besides this, immediately along the city's outskirts ran a thick network of wooden and earthen pillboxes, while all the stone structures had been transformed into powerful strong points. The city's inner quarters had also been configured for waging stubborn street battles. Along the street intersections the enemy had constructed barricades and wooden and earthen pillboxes, and they had mined a significant part of the streets and buildings in the city. The northern and eastern parts of the city were covered by powerful zones of minefields. Suffice it to say, that during the fighting our sappers removed 16,333 enemy mines from the Belgorod area.

From the east the city was covered by a broad water line—the Severskii Donets River, along the eastern bank of which, in the Mikhailovka area, the Germans had a small but powerfully fortified bridgehead.

The Belgorod center of resistance was defended by units of the 198th Infantry Division, which had been reinforced with a significant amount of artillery, mortars and tanks.

The 69th Army's 89th Guards and 305th rifle divisions, following stubborn fighting in Belgorod's northern outskirts, began even fiercer street fighting within the city.

At the same time that the 69th Army's units were attacking the city from the north, it was also being attacked from the east by the right-flank 111th Rifle Division of the 7th Guards Army's 49th Rifle Corps. The enemy, while putting up stubborn resistance, was striving at all costs to hold the Belgorod center of resistance. The battle was waged for every block and often for individual buildings, which had been transformed by the Germans into strong points. As evidence of the ferocity of the street fighting is the fact that the Germans left 3,200 officers and men on the city streets in killed alone.

By 1800 the city had been completely cleared of German forces and the 89th Guards and 305th rifle divisions, which had been the first to break into Belgorod, were awarded with the honorary title of "Belgorod" on 5 August, by an order of the Supreme Commander-in-Chief comrade Stalin.

By the close of 5 August the 69th Army and the 7th Guards Army's right-flank units had reached the line Krasnoe—Suprunovka. The 7th Guards Army, having penetrated into the Germans' defensive zone along the entire front along the western bank of the Severskii Donets River, was engaged in heavy fighting throughout the entire day, repelling numerous attacks by German infantry and tanks.

On 5 August, with the fall of the enemy's Tomarovka and Belgorod centers of resistance, our forces gained freedom for the subsequent offensive. By this time the overall width of the breakthrough front reached 90 kilometers; the Voronezh Front's mobile formations along the axis of the main attack had penetrated into the enemy defense to a depth of 40 kilometers.

The 1st and 5th Guards tank armies, having arrived in the Berezovka—Aleksandrovka—Gomzino area, had created an immediate threat to split into isolated parts the entire German group of forces, which was defending the Belgorod—Khar'kov bridgehead.

The garrison of the Borisovka center of resistance, as well as part of the Germans' Tomarovka group of forces, which had fallen back here as a result of the successful advance by the 1st Tank Army and the arrival of the 27th Army's units in the area of Ivanovskaya Lisitsa, was half-surrounded.

The enemy committed his closest operational reserve along this axis—the 7th Panzer Division. Besides this, the 11th Panzer Division, which had been committed from the reserve into the fighting on 4 August in the Tomarovka area, was transferred here.

Our units inflicted heavy losses on the 57th, 255th, 167th, 168th, and 198th infantry, and the 11th, 19th and 6th panzer divisions. Despite the difficult situation of the German forces around Orel, the enemy command was nevertheless forced to begin the transfer of reserves from the Orel axis to the Khar'kov axis. On 5 August the German command began to transfer from the area northwest of Karachev to the Khar'kov axis the *Grossdeutschland* Panzer Division, which at the end of June had been removed from the Khar'kov axis and transferred to the Orel area. By the close of 5 August the forward units of the *Das Reich* and *Totenkopf* panzer divisions, which had been transferred from the Donbass, had already arrived in the Khar'kov area, while the 3rd Panzer Division was already on the way.

Measures by the *Stavka* of the Supreme High Command

In accordance with the plan for subsequent operations to eliminate the Germans' Belgorod—Khar'kov group of forces, which had been approved on 5 August by the Supreme High Command, the 40th Army, along with the 2nd and 10th tank corps, was to develop the offensive toward Boromlya and reach the front Lebedin—Zen'kov, consolidate along this line and prepare an attack in the area between the Psel and Vorskla rivers.

The 27th Army, along with the 4th Guards Tank Corps, was to attack with its main forces to the southwest toward Akhtyrka and reach the front Oposhnya—Bol'shaya Rublevka—Kachalovka; it was subsequently planned to attack along both banks of the Vorskla River in the general direction of Poltava, while part of the army's forces would assist the 6th Guards Army in destroying the Germans' Tomarovka—Borisovka group of forces.

The 5th Guards Army was to reach the front Murafa—Dergachi, for the purpose of isolating the Germans' Khar'kov group of forces.

It was planned to pull the 6th Guards Army back into the *front* reserve following the capture of Borisovka and the destruction of the Tomarovka—Borisovka group of forces.

It was planned to employ the *front's* mobile formations for developing the subsequent offensive to the south in the general direction of Valki. It was planned for the 1st Tank Army to reach the Murafa—Alekseevka—Kovyagi area, in order to cut the Khar'kov—Poltava railroad and paved road; the 5th Guards Tank Army was to reach the Ogul'tsy—Staryi Merchik area, in order to launch an attack on Khar'kov from the west and southwest.

According to this plan, the tank corps were to reach the following lines: 5th Guards Tank Corps the area Parkhomovka (20 kilometers southeast of Akhtyrka); the 2nd Tank Corps the Lebedin area; the 10th Tank Corps the Zen'kov area, and; the 4th Guards Tank Corps the Oposhnya area.

The 38th Army, taking advantage of the 40th Army's success, was to break through the enemy's defense with its three left-flank divisions and reach the Psel River along the sector Bol'shaya Chernetchina—Pashkov. The 47th Army, while remaining in the *front* reserve, was to move behind the 40th Army in the general direction of Trostyanets. The forces of the Steppe Front were charged with the task of continuing to attack for the purpose of capturing Khar'kov.

The fighting on 6-7 August. The destruction of the Germans' Borisovka group of forces and the breakthrough of the enemy's rear operational line

On 6-7 August the forces of the Voronezh and Steppe fronts, while defeating the retreating units of the enemy's Belgorod—Khar'kov group of forces and crushing his rearguards' resistance, continued to develop the offensive in the depth of the enemy's defense.

While attempting to delay our attacking forces along its rear defensive line, which ran through Krasnokutsk—Bogodukhov—Zolochev—Kazach'ya Lopan'—Zhuravlevka—Veseloe, the German command began to hurriedly occupy the line with the remnants of its retreating and defeated units, as well as with special units, subunits and commands, which had been hurriedly formed from various rear units and organizations. Besides this, the enemy continued to bring up reserves from other sectors of the front and threw them into the fighting from the march.

On 6 August the 323rd Infantry Division, which had been transferred from its defensive sector in the Bol'shaya Chernetchina (northeast of the town of Sumy), took part in the fighting against the 40th Army in the Dorogoshch area. On that same day the 3rd Panzer Division concentrated in the Zolochev area. On 7 August units of the *Grossdeutschland* SS Panzer Division, which had been transferred here along with the 51st Independent Battalion of Mark-VI tanks from the Karachev area along the Orel salient, took part in the fighting against the 27th Army in the Bol'shaya Pisarevka area. Finally, on that same day the *Das Reich* SS Panzer Division, part of whose forces took part in the fighting with the 1st Tank Army to the east of Bogodukhov, appeared in the Ol'shany area. The approach of the *Wiking* Panzer Division toward Khar'kov was also noted.

The Voronezh Front's offensive

On 6-7 August the Voronezh Front's shock group attacked in a particularly forceful manner. Despite the fact that the enemy continued to hold such powerful resistance centers as Borisovka, Golovchino and Graivoron, the 1st Tank Army's formations, having covered more than 100 kilometers in five days of fighting, and having forged 25-40 kilometers ahead of the rifle formations, by the close of 7 August had captured one of the Germans' most important centers of resistance and road junction in the operational rear—the town of Bogodukhov.

The 5th Guards Tank Army, having crushed the stubborn resistance of the German garrisons in Shchetinovka and Udy, and having eliminated these centers of resistance, continued to develop the offensive in the area between the Udy and Lopan' rivers. The German command, while striving to delay our offensive at any cost, threw the 3rd Panzer Division into the area of Zolochev and Kazach'ya Lopan'. However, the army's formations inflicted heavy losses on the division and by the close of 7 August had captured both towns, which were important enemy centers of resistance covering Khar'kov from the northwest.

The 5th Guards Army, in conjunction with the 5th Guards Tank Army, had by the close of 7 August reached with part of its forces the Naumovka—Ol'khovatka area, thus firmly securing the Voronezh Front's left flank from the Khar'kov area.

The 40th Army, having crushed the enemy's resistance along its front, and while rolling up the German defense toward the west, reached the line Krasnopol'e—Popovka—Slavgorodok.

Following the elimination of the enemy's group of forces in the Borisovka—Golovchino area, the 27th Army continued to attack to the southwest along the Vorskla River. Here it captured the area of Bol'shaya Pisarevka, an important paved road junction and a powerful enemy center of resistance.

For the purpose of strengthening the resistance to the 40th and 27th armies, the enemy, beginning on 6 August, committed against these armies, besides the 7th Panzer Division, the 323rd Infantry and *Grossdeutschland* SS Panzer divisions as well.

On 6-7 August the 6th Guards Army was fighting to eliminate the Germans' Tomarovka—Borisovka group of forces.

The destruction of the Germans' Borisovka group of forces

At the same time that the Voronezh Front's main forces were developing the offensive to the south and southwest and had already broken through 60-65 kilometers into the depth of the enemy position, fierce fighting was taking place in the Borisovka—Golovchino area against the half-encircled group of German forces. As a result of the fighting of 4-5 August, units of the 27th Army had reached the Ivanovskaya Lisitsa—Kazach'ya Lisitsa—Nikitksoe area, while the 6th Guards Army captured the line Zybino—Moshchenoe—Tomarovka, the 1st and 5th Guards tank armies had broken through into the Berezovka—Aleksandrovka—Gomzino area, and the 5th Guards Army's right-flank units occupied the line southern outskirts of Striguny—Kuleshovka—Gomzino—Step' (five kilometers northeast of Bessonovka). A large German group of forces was now squeezed between these armies. This group of forces consisted of units, which had been thrown back from the main defensive zone—the 332nd, 57th and 255th infantry divisions, as well as the 19th and 11th panzer divisions, and other reinforcements, which had been committed by the German command into the fighting from the reserve.

In order to eliminate the enemy's Borisovka—Golovchino group of forces, the commander of the Voronezh Front decided to employ the 32nd Guards Rifle Corps (5th Guards Army), reinforced by the 1st Tank Army, as well as the 6th Guards Army and the 27th Army's 23rd Rifle Corps.

As a result of the offensive fighting, by the close of 6 August units of the 23rd Rifle Corps occupied Khotmyzhsk. Forces of the 6th Guards Army, attacking from the line Zybino—Tomarovka, by the close of the day had reached the line Kryukov—the northeastern edge of the Zapovednik woods—the northern part of Borisovka. Part of the army's forces, attacking along the Vorskla River, occupied Berezovka and reached the northeastern outskirts of Borisovka.

The 66th Guards Rifle Division, attacking to the left of the 6th Guards Army, had reached with part of its forces the eastern outskirts of Borisovka.

By the close of the day the 97th Guards Rifle Division's right flank was blocking Borisovka from the southeast and south, while its left flank had cut the Borisovka—Golovchino road south of Novoborisovka.

Thus the enemy, defending the Borisovka center of resistance, was encircled by our units.

Besides this, in order to securely cut the enemy's path of retreat to the southwest, the 13th Guards Rifle Division, which was carrying out a march from the Gomzino area to the west, was to reach the Golovchino area after a forced march and prevent the enemy from breaking through to the southwest in the area of the Borisovka—Graivoron railroad and paved road.

For the purpose of speeding up the completion of his assignment, the division commander threw into Golovchino a detachment of 11 tanks and a battalion of automatic riflemen, which by 1800 on 6 August had captured the Khotmyzhsk station. Having destroyed a battalion of the 255th Infantry Division, which had been defending the station, this detachment seized five trains (315 cars) and several major depots with ammunition and food. One of the captured trains contained 500 men in reinforcements. 11 German tanks were destroyed in the fighting for Khotmyzhsk station.

By the close of the day, under this detachment's cover, units of the 13th Guards Rifle Division had reached the line height 191.8—Berezovka—height 141.3—the southern and western outskirts of Golovchino.

At 0200 on 7 August units of the 66th and 97th guards rifle divisions attacked Borisovka from the east, southeast and south and threw the enemy out of the inhabited locale.

Stunned by this sudden attack, part of the German force ran away in panic to the Kuroedovo woods, and part to Zapovednik. However, upon encountering there fire and attacks by the 6th Guards Army, they were forced to turn back and, while losing hundreds of men and officers killed and wounded, flowed back to the south again and during the second half of the night had concentrated in the Zozuli—Nikol'skii—Golovchino area, having infiltrated into the spaces not occupied by our forces.

The Germans' subsequent movement to the south and southwest was halted by units of the 13th Guards Rifle Division. Then the enemy decided to attempt to break out of the encirclement in small groups of infantry, reinforced with mortars and tanks. From 0300 to 1300 on 7 August units of the 13th Guards Rifle Division repulsed six enemy attacks, which sought to break through our forces' defensive front. The enemy attacks were conducted in groups of 300-1,200 men and officers, reinforced with 5-20 tanks. Despite the fact that the enemy managed to achieve a significant superiority in men and materiel along the attack axes, not one of his attempts met with success. By the close of the day the encircled German group of forces had been completely eliminated.

Units of the 57th, 255th and 332nd infantry and 19th Panzer divisions were defeated in the Borisovka area. The enemy lost in killed alone more than 5,000 officers and men, with another 450 taken prisoner. Among the equipment captured were 92 heavy Mark-VI heavy tanks, of which 20 were in working order, as well as 17 medium tanks, 100 motor vehicles, 3,000 rifles, and a large number of guns of various calibers. Among the Germans killed was the commander of the 19th Panzer Division, General Schmidt.

The Steppe Front's battles

On 6-7 August the Steppe Front's forces continued to attack in extremely difficult conditions. The Germans were putting up fierce resistance, relying on defensive lines echeloned in depth, and numerous villages, which had been transformed into powerful strong points.

On 6 August the 53rd and 69th armies' formations cleared the enemy out of Belgorod and, developing the offensive to the south and beating back fierce German counterattacks, often supported by tanks, by the close of the day had captured Repnoe and Koloniya Dubovoe and had reached the Germans' fifth defensive zone along the line Dolbino—Tavrovo.

Part of the 7th Guards Army's forces broke through the Germans' defense along the western bank of the Severskii Donets River, had broken into the villages of Solomino and Toplinka and had begun street fighting to eliminate these enemy centers of resistance.

On the morning of 7 August the Steppe Front's forces renewed the offensive and broke through the enemy's fifth defensive line. Having beaten back several fierce enemy counterattacks, by the close of the day units of the 53rd and 69th armies reached the line Mikoyanovka—Nikol'skoe, captured these towns and destroyed the garrisons defending them.

The 7th Guards Army, while continuing to eliminate the enemy strong points along the western bank of the Severskii Donets River had by the close of the day captured Solomino, Toplinka and Volkovo.

Thus by the close of 7 August our forces, having broadened the breakthrough to 120 kilometers and penetrated into the enemy's position to a depth of 60-65 kilometers, reached the Germans' rear operational line and broken through it with the 1st Tank Army's formations, which captured the Bogodukhov area.

By 7 August our forces had overcome all of the German defense's prepared zones along the Bogodukhov axis; the Fourth Panzer Army and army group "Kempf," which were defending the Belgorod—Khar'kov bridgehead, had been split into two parts.

With the arrival of the 1st Tank Army in the Bogodukhov area, one of the main communications lines of the Germans' Khar'kov group of forces—the Khar'kov—Sumy railroad—had been cut. Having lost Bogodukhov, the enemy was deprived of a major junction of dirt roads.

II. The Offensive's Development Along the Voronezh Front's Left Wing and the Arrival of Our Forces at the Khar'kov—Poltava Railroad (8-11 August)

On 8-11 August the forces of the Voronezh Front continued to develop the offensive to the southwest and west, striving, on the one hand, to cut the main routes leading from the Khar'kov area to the west, and on the other, to broaden as much as possible the breakthrough of the enemy front to the west. Thanks to this, the possibility of German counterblows against the open right flank of our group of forces attacking toward Khar'kov was excluded.

In connection with the developing offensive by the Voronezh Front to the southwest, the German command, evidently having realized the full extent of the difficult situation of its Khar'kov group of forces, began to hurriedly adopt measures to create major groups of forces, for the purpose of carrying out counterblows against the flanks of the Voronezh Front's shock group.

The German command continued to bring reserves from other sectors of the front to the area west of Khar'kov. Aside from the divisions already listed, during the 8-11 August time period there appeared two more panzer divisions. The *Totenkopf* SS Panzer Division arrived on 9-10 August in the area south of Bogodukhov, where as early as 10 August part of its forces was already taking part in battles against the 1st Tank Army; on 10 August the *Wiking* SS Panzer Division, with a battalion of heavy Mark-VI tanks (30 vehicles), and the *Narva* Infantry Battalion arrived in the Staryi Merchik area.

The 355th Infantry Division arrived in the Poltava area from the Crimea.

The 8-9 August fighting along the Voronezh Front's left flank

Following the capture of Bogodukhov on 7 August, the 1st Tank Army continued to develop the offensive to the south in the general direction of Kovyagi, with the mission of cutting the Khar'kov—Poltava railroad as quickly as possible.

On 8 August the 1st Tank Army's formations were engaged in fierce fighting with units from the enemy's *Das Reich* and *Totenkopf* SS panzer divisions and the remnants of the 19th Panzer Division, which had been concentrated by the German command in the area southeast of Bogodukhov, and could no longer advance.

The enemy carried out a series of counterattacks, which, however, were all beaten back by our tank troops, with heavy German losses.

Part of the 1st Tank Army's forces were fighting in the area north of Bogodukhov; here they destroyed individual major enemy groups, which had been defeated near Tomarovka, Borisovka and Golovchino. The enemy groups tried to break through to the south. In the Novo-Sofievka area our tank troops destroyed a German column, consisting of 35 tanks and 200 motor vehicles with motorized infantry, which was trying to break through toward Kup'evakha.

The 5th Guards Tank and 5th Guards armies, which on 6-7 August had crushed the enemy's resistance in the Zolochev—Kazach'ya Lopan' area, continued to attack to the south and by the close of August 8 reached the line Bol'shaya Rogozyanka—Mironovka. The 6th Guards Army, which had been pulled back into the *front* reserve upon the elimination of the Germans' Borisovka group of forces, was concentrating in the Zolochev area.

On 9 August, having crushed the enemy's stubborn resistance south of Bogodukhov, the 1st Tank Army forced the Merla River and occupied the villages of Murafa, Khrushchevaya Nikitovka, Aleksandrovka, and Kiyany. By employing the line of the Merchik River, the Germans were able to organize a new defensive line and halt the tank army's further advance.

By taking advantage of his system of powerful centers of resistance (Ol'shany, Polevoe, Dergachi, Peresechnaya, and others), the enemy also halted the 5th Guards Tank and 5th Guards armies' advance. It was only by taking advantage of the 1st Tank Army's success that the 5th Guards Tank Army was able to advance somewhat along its right flank and reached the line northern outskirts of Krysino—Kadnitsa—Gurinovka.

On the evening of 9 August, on orders of the *Stavka* of the Supreme High Command, the 5th Guards Tank Army was pulled into the reserve in the Sennoe area and subordinated to the commander of the Steppe Front.

The fighting on 10-11 August

On the morning of 10 August the commander of the Voronezh Front received by high-frequency telephone the following message from the Supreme Commander-in-Chief, Marshal of the Soviet Union comrade Stalin:

> The *Stavka* of the Supreme High Command considers it necessary to isolate Khar'kov by immediately cutting the main railroad and road communications in the direction of Poltava, Krasnograd and Lozovaya, thus speeding up the liberation of Khar'kov. For this purpose, Katukov's 1st Tank Army is to cut the main routes in the Kovyagi—Valki area, while Rotmistrov's 5th Tank Army, by outflanking Khar'kov from the southwest, is to cut the routes in the Merefa area.

On the basis of these instructions, the commander of the Voronezh Front assigned the 5th Guards Army the following task: by the close of 11 August it was to reach the front Krasnyi Yar—Alekseevka—Vysokopol'e—Kovyagi—Ogul'tsyi station—excluding Ogul'tsyi village. The commander of the 1st Tank Army was ordered to capture the Murafa—Alekseevka—Kovyagi area by the close of 10 August, and with a detachment seize Valki, cutting the Khar'kov—Poltava railroad.

The 1st Tank Army, in carrying out the assigned task, resumed its attack on the morning of 10 August, and throughout the entire day was involved in fierce fighting along the line of the Merchik River, in which units of the *Totenkopf* SS Panzer Division, with which the German command had reinforced its group of forces along this direction, took part.

During the second half of the day our units captured the crossings over the Merchik River and seized small bridgeheads on the southern bank in the areas of 10th Sotnya, 11th Sotnya, Sharovka, and Aleksandrovka.

Having completed the crossing to the southern bank of the Merchik River at night, our tank units renewed their attack on the morning of 11 August. The enemy sought to halt it, having occupied the Chervonyi Prapor—Mar'ino line with part of his forces. This attempt was unsuccessful and at 0600 this line was pierced by our tanks.

At 0900 the 6th Tank Corps' 6th Motorized Rifle Brigade and the 3rd Mechanized Corps' 1st Guards Tank Brigade broke into Vysokopol'e and Kovyagi station, cutting the Khar'kov—Poltava railroad. The brigades' subsequent advance was unsuccessful, due to the Germans' growing resistance. During the latter half of 11 August fierce fighting broke out along this line with the enemy, who was attempting to launch a counterattack. The 1st Tank Army's main forces (6th and 31st tank and 3rd Mechanized corps), while holding the line Murafa—Aleksandrovka—Sukhiny, beat off the enemy's fierce tank attacks along this front.

During 10-11 August the 5th Guards Army did not advance and was engaged in stubborn fighting, beating back enemy counterattacks along the line Krysino—Gurinovka—Mironovka.

Thus by the close of 11 August the Voronezh Front's shock group had cut the main communications of the enemy's Khar'kov group of forces and was threatening to isolate it completely. However, by this time the enemy had brought up reserves here and created a group of forces sufficiently powerful to halt the further advance by the 1st Tank and 5th Guards armies—the panzer divisions (*Wiking*, *Das Reich* and *Totenkopf*), as well as a number of independent units and subunits.

At the same time, the Steppe Front's right-flank 53rd and 69th armies had reached in stubborn fighting the outer Khar'kov defensive line along the Dergachi—Cherkasskoe-Lozovoe—Tsirkuny sector and had begun to overcome them.

III. The Offensive by the Voronezh Front's Right Wing and the Widening of the Breakthrough to the West. The Fighting Around Akhtyrka and Kotel'va (8-11 August)

During 8-11 August the Voronezh Front's right wing developed the offensive along two axes: the 40th Army attacked toward Boromlya, and the 27th Army toward Akhtyrka.

The 40th Army, which had by the close of 7 August reached the line Krasnopol'e—Popovka—Slavgorodok in fighting, resumed its attack on the morning of 8 August. Throwing back the remnants of the 57th and 332nd infantry and 11th Panzer divisions, which were trying to put up resistance by hanging on to individual wooded areas and creeks, by the close of the day the army had captured the area Zhigailovka—Pechiny—Nitsakha.

On 9 August the 40th Army was involved in stubborn fighting against the enemy's increasing resistance. The army's right-flank units advanced 4-5 kilometers in fighting and captured the enemy's important center of resistance in Chernetchina.

The 10th Tank Corps, which was operating along with the forces of the 40th Army, broke through the enemy's defense and by the close of the day, having covered up to 20 kilometers, captured Trostyanets, a major road junction.

The junction's capture meant that the enemy's Sumy—Boromlya—Akhtyrka lateral paved road and railroad had been cut.

On 10 August, having thrown back the remnants of the 57th Infantry Division to the west and crushed the 7th and 11th panzer divisions' resistance, the 40th Army once again advanced 10-12 kilometers and captured Grebennikovka and Boromlya. Along the left flank the army's units were engaged in stubborn fighting in Trostyanets, beating back fierce counterattacks by the

Grossdeutschland SS Panzer Division, which had been transferred by the German command into the fighting from the Akhtyrka area. On 11 August stubborn fighting continued in the area of Boromlya station and the village of Trostyanets.

The 38th Army's left-flank forces, in order to secure the 40th Army's right flank, received orders on 8 August: to attack from the area northwest of Krasnopol'e in the general direction of Verkhnyaya Syrovatka. An attempt to break through the enemy's front that day did not meet with success.

Having penetrated on 9 August 3-5 kilometers into the depth of the enemy's defense, the 38th Army's units on the following day broke through the entire depth of his defense along a 20-kilometer front, and by the close of 10 August reached in fighting the line Zheleznyak—Bol'shoi Bobrik and had begun fighting for the important center of the enemy defense of Verkhnyaya Syrovatka.

The forces of the 27th Army achieved the greatest success in the fighting of 8-11 August. Continuing on the morning of 8 August to pursue units of the 323rd and remnants of the 255th infantry divisions along the Vorskla River and both its banks, and throwing back units of the *Grossdeutschland* SS Panzer Division, which had been transferred by the German command to cover the Akhtyrka axis, by the close of 9 August the army's units had reached the line Kirikovka—the northern and eastern outskirts of Staraya Ryabina—Kup'evakha. On 10 August the 27th Army outflanked the Staraya Ryabina and Yablochnoe strong points from the northwest and south, defeated their garrisons and opened the path for the subsequent development of the offensive on Akhtyrka and Kotel'va.

On 11 August the 4th Tank Corps, which was operating with the 27th Army, broke into the eastern outskirts of Akhtyrka and began fierce fighting on the town's streets. On that same day the 1st Tank Army's 5th Guards Tank Corps, which was operating along with the 27th Army, broke into Kotel'va and, having destroyed the garrison, completely captured this village.

By the close of 11 August the 27th Army's divisions reached the line Petrovskii—Vysokoe—Parkhomovka—Krasnokutsk, having covered more than 50 kilometers in four days.

The 47th Army, while remaining in the *front* reserve, had by the close of 11 August concentrated in the area Krasnopol'e—Brantsovka—Pozhnya—Slavgorodok—Ryasnoe, in readiness to develop the 40th Army's success in the direction of Trostyanets.

Thus by 11 August the forces of the Voronezh Front had reached along their right wing the strong points of Boromlya, Akhtyrka and Kotel'va, while the left flank had cut the Khar'kov—Poltava railroad in the Vysokopol'e—Kovyagi area. This created, on the one hand, a serious threat to the enemy group of forces that was continuing to stubbornly defend the Khar'kov area, and on the other, favorable prerequisites for the subsequent development of our forces' offensive along the Poltava and Gadyachii axes.

A particular threat to the enemy was presented by our group of forces, which consisted of the 27th and 1st Tank armies; it was slicing into the enemy's position with sharp wedges and cutting up his front into separate pieces.

In the 3-11 August fighting the Voronezh Front's forces inflicted heavy losses on the enemy. They defeated the 19th Panzer, 255th, 323rd, and 332nd infantry divisions, while the 3rd, 7th and 11th panzer, and 57th Infantry divisions suffered heavy losses.

The enemy lost about 50,000 officers and men killed and wounded, and 3,742 captured.

Besides the enemy equipment destroyed in the fighting, our forces captured 320 tanks, 524 guns, 850 machine guns, 6,000 rifles, 1,830 automobiles, and 40 aircraft.

IV. The Repulse of the Germans' Counterblows and the Maneuver by the Voronezh Front's Right Wing (12-13 August)

As was mentioned earlier, from the earliest days of our offensive the enemy had begun to move reserves from the other sectors of the Soviet-German front and to concentrate them against the Voronezh Front's forces. The enemy was preparing a counterblow, in order to defeat the Voronezh Front's shock group, which was attacking to the southwest, and to subsequently develop the attack against the flank of the Steppe Front's shock group, which was advancing on Khar'kov.

The enemy took into account the fact that the further offensive to the southwest by our group of forces, which had reached the Akhtyrka—Kotel'va—Bogodukhov area was particular dangerous, and therefore directed all his main counterblows from the Akhtyrka and Staryi Merchik areas toward Bogodukhov.

The Fighting South of Bogodukhov on 11-17 August

By 11 August the German command had concentrated the SS panzer divisions—*Das Reich*, *Totenkopf* and *Wiking*, a motorized regiment from the 6th Panzer Division, an independent battalion of heavy Mark VI tanks, a mortar training and the 55th Mixed Mortar regiments, and a number of other auxiliary element in the Vysokopol'e—Valki area.[1]

As a result of this, the enemy managed to somewhat change the correlation of forces in the area south of Bogodukhov along the front Bol'shaya Rublevka—Ol'shany and achieve a superiority in tanks over us.[2]

The fighting on 11 August

The Germans' counterattacks against the 1st Tank Army's units began during the second half of 11 August, simultaneously along two converging axes. One motorized regiment, with 30 tanks from the *Totenkopf* SS Panzer Division, attacked from the area of Konstantinovka in the general direction of Murafa. The enemy launched another counterattack with the forces of a motorized regiment, with 50 tanks from the *Das Reich* SS Panzer Division, from the Staryi Merchik area toward Sharovka.

As a result of the fierce fighting with the 1st Tank Army's forward units, the Germans broke through to the Sharovka—11th Sotnya area to the Merchik River, thus getting into the rear of the 6th Guards Tank Corps' 6th Motorized Rifle Brigade and the 3rd Mechanized Corps' 1st Guards Tank Brigade, which had occupied Vysokopol'e and Kovyagi. A counterattack by units of the *Totenkopf* Panzer Division, launched form the Perekop area toward Vysokopol'e was not successful.

Throughout the day the 5th Guards Army was engaged in stubborn fighting along the line Krysino—Gurinovka and did not advance.

The 6th Guards Army was finishing its concentration in the Polkovaya Nikitovka—Gubarovka—Pavlovka area.

The 5th Guards Tank Army, which had been operationally subordinated as early as 9 August to the Steppe Front, had by the close of 11 August completed its concentration in the Sennoe area. It was planned that the army would further develop the offensive on Kovyagi, Valki and Novaya Vodolaga, for the purpose of cutting the Khar'kov—Poltava and Khar'kov—Krasnograd railroads

1 This counts the SS *Das Reich*, *Totenkopf* and *Wiking* panzer divisions, the 6th Panzer Division's motorized regiment, an independent battalion of heavy tanks, the 223rd Infantry Division, and two mortar regiments.

2 This counts the 6th Guards, 1st Tank and 5th Guards Tank armies.

and cutting the German group of forces' routes of retreat from the Khar'kov area to the west and southwest.

The command's measures

Due to the situation that had arisen along the 1st Tank Army's front, at 0420 on 12 August the commander of the Voronezh Front, in carrying out the *Stavka's* instructions, decided to launch an attack with the forces of one of the 6th Guards Army's corps, in conjunction with the 1st Tank Army, in the direction of Murafa, Kitchinkovka and Konstantinovka and to destroy the German group of forces that had broken through to the Merchik River and, upon reaching the line Slobodka—Konstantinovka—Shelestovo, to firmly secure the right flank of the Voronezh Front's main shock group.

For the purpose of eliminating the Germans' group of forces, which had broken through into the 11th Sotnya—Sharovka area, the commander of the 1st Tank Army decided on the morning of 12 August to destroy this group with part of the 6th Tank and 3rd Mechanized corps' forces and restore communications with the army's forward units, defending in the Vysokopol'e—Kovyagi area.

Taking into account the ongoing concentration of enemy tank units on 11 August in the Staryi Merchik—Petropavlovka area and their likely counterblow from this area toward Bogodukhov against the army's left flank, the army commander ordered units of the 31st Tank Corps to occupy the line Aleksandrovka—Sukhiny on the night of 11-12 August, in order to securely cover this axis.

The fighting on 12 August

On 12 August fierce fighting unfolded along the Bogodukhov axis. The Germans, while striving to defeat the 1st Tank Army, which had reached the area south of Merchik and cut the Khar'kov—Poltava railroad, renewed their attacks on the morning of 12 August. Three SS panzer divisions—*Totenkopf*, *Das Reich* and *Wiking*—were operating along the Bogodukhov axis.

The 6th Guards Army's 163rd Rifle Division, which was operationally subordinated to the 1st Tank Army, along with the 6th Tank Corps' 200th and 22nd tank brigades, having gone over to the attack on the morning of 12 August, had by 1300 destroyed the German group of forces in the 11th Sotnya—Sharovka area, after which the 200th Tank Brigade, for the purpose of reinforcing the 6th Motorized Rifle Brigade, reached the Vysokopol'e area after fighting.

Both brigades, which had gone over to a perimeter defense, spent the entire day beating back continuous attacks by the *Totenkopf* SS Panzer Division's units.

The 3rd Mechanized Corps' 1st Guards Tank Brigade, which had broken through on 11 August in the area of Kovyagi station, conducted a fighting retreat under the pressure of superior enemy forces to the area of the Comintern State Farm, which it went over to a stubborn perimeter defense.

On the morning of 12 August the enemy, consisting of the forces of the *Totenkopf*, *Das Reich* and *Wiking* SS panzer divisions, and having up to 200 tanks in the first echelon, went over to the offensive from the Staryi Merchik—Petropavlovka area in the general direction of Kiyany and Bogodukhov. About 100 tanks and motorized infantry attacked the 31st Tank Corps' right flank in the Pavlovo area, while the main enemy group developed its attack toward Babynki farm (north of Sukhiny), along the boundary between the 3rd Mechanized Corps and the 6th Guards Army. By the close of the day the enemy had managed to push back units of the 1st Tank Army and capture Pavlovo, Kiyany and Sukhiny, although by the morning of 14 August the enemy offensive was halted here.

The 5th Guards Army's right-flank units, which were operating along with the 1st Tank Army, abandoned Krysino under enemy pressure and went over to the defense along its northern outskirts.

By the morning of 12 August the 5th Guards Tank Army had occupied the following areas as jumping-off positions for its attack on Kovyagi and Valki:

18th Tank Corps—Khrushchevaya Nikitovka;
29th Tank Corps—Gavrishi State Farm;
5th Guards Zimovniki Mechanized Corps (the army's second echelon)—Sennoe; that is, behind the 3rd Mechanized and 31st Tank corps' combat formations.

As a result of the fact that the 1st Tank Army's left-flank units had fallen back to the northwest under enemy pressure, the 18th and 29th tank corps, in conjunction with the 1st Tank Army's units, entered into battle with the attacking enemy, inflicted significant losses on him, and by the close of the day had halted the Germans' offensive along the line Aleksandrovka—the western outskirts of Kiyany—Gavrishi station (two kilometers southeast of Gavrishi State Farm)—the northwestern outskirts of Krysino.[3]

With the onset of darkness the 6th Guards Army reached the line Lyubovka—Karaikozovka—the northern outskirts of Kachalovka—the southern edge of the woods north of Murafa, in readiness to attack on the morning of 13 August in the general direction of Krasnyi Yar.

Despite the fact that the enemy had concentrated for his attack on Bogodukhov from the southeast a powerful group of forces, numbering up to 400 tanks, neither on 11 or 12 August was he able to break the 1st Tank Army's front and reach the Bogodukhov area.

The enemy offensive was halted as a result of the joint efforts by the 1st and 5th Guards tank armies.

Part of the 1st Tank Army's forces continued to hold the Vysokopol'e area, preventing the enemy from using the Khar'kov—Poltava railroad.

The fighting on 13 August

On 13 August stubborn fighting continued in the area south of Bogodukhov.

The 6th Guards Army, having gone over to the offensive, threw back the opposing enemy units to the south and by the close of the day reached the line Kovalevka—Blagodatnaya—11th Sotnya. During the night of 12-13 August the army turned over two of its divisions (71st and 97th) to reinforce the 1st Tank Army.

The 1st Tank Army's 6th Motorized Rifle and 200th Tank brigades continued to fight while encircled and, beating back the Germans' numerous attacks, held the Vysokopol'e area.

In the morning the enemy renewed his attack and, following a stubborn battle, pushed the 1st Tank and 5th Guards Tank armies out of Aleksandrovka and Khrushchevaya Nikitovka and also captured Gavrishi station. The Germans also managed to penetrate 1.5-2 kilometers into the 5th Guards Army's defense along the right-flank 32nd Guards Rifle Corps' sector north of Krysino.

Thus on 13 August, despite his powerful pressure, the enemy was unable to break through our defense and reach the Bogodukhov area and, at the cost of heavy losses, he was only able to slightly push back the 1st Tank and 5th Guards armies' units.

However, the enemy penetration into our defense along the boundary between the 1st Tank and 5th Guards armies and his arrival in the Kiyany and Krysino areas created a threat to the rear of the 1st Tank Army and the Voronezh Front shock group's entire left flank. The further withdrawal

3 By 12 August the 5th Guards Tank Army disposed of 115 tanks.

by our units along this axis could lead to our loss of Bogodukhov, which was a very important road junction connecting the Voronezh Front's flanks.

The command's measures

Taking into account the situation that had arisen by the middle of day on 13 August, the *front* commander made the decision to strengthen his position in the Bogodukhov area and defeat the German group of forces, which was pushing toward Bogodukhov, by concentrating along this axis reserves from the 6th and 5th guards armies and the main mass of reinforcement artillery.

In a directive issued at 1445 on 13 August, the *front* commander, General Vatutin, laid down the following tasks for his left-wing forces:

> The enemy group of forces, which is striving to break through along the front Aleksandrovka—Babynki farm in the direction of Bogodukhov, is to be destroyed by the joint efforts of the 5th and 6th guards and 1st Tank armies, for which they are ordered to do the following:
>
> 1. The commander of the 6th Guards Army, while rapidly developing the offensive along his right flank with the forces of the 67th and 71st guards rifle divisions, in order to reach the line Berezovka—Kolomak, is to firmly secure the line eastern edge of the woods immediately to the west of Khrushchevaya Nikitovka—height 197.1—height 183.2—height 202.4 (4.5 kilometers east of Bogodukhov). In no way is the enemy's breakthrough to be permitted along this sector.
> 2. The commander of the 5th Guards Army is to immediately concentrate all of his anti-tank artillery and anti-tank rifle battalions and employ them along the Bogodukhov axis. Demand the most stubborn defense from Rodimtsev,[4] in order to prevent the enemy's breakthrough in any way; the enemy attempting to break through is to be destroyed and the situation restored. All of the reinforcement artillery is to be concentrated to the Bogodukhov axis, while the 66th Guards Rifle Division is to organize and launch a counterblow from the north against the attacking enemy's flank, with the mission of destroying the enemy, restoring the situation and attacking further.
> 3. The commander of the 1st Tank Army is to hold those captured areas along the Khar'kov—Poltava railroad at any cost, while part of his left-flank forces is to destroy the enemy penetration.
>
> The army's overall task remains as before.

Besides this, General Rotmistrov, the commander of the 5th Guards Tank Army, was instructed that he was responsible for ensuring that the enemy did not advance. A retreat by the 5th Guards Tank Army was categorically forbidden.

The fighting on 15-16 August

On 14-15 August the Voronezh Front's left-wing forces, following fierce battles, halted the Germans' offensive on Bogodukhov from the southeast.

The enemy was forced to go over to the defensive along this axis, shifting his attacks further south along the Merchik River toward Kachalovka, against the 1st Tank Army's left-flank units.

4 The commander of the 32nd Guards Rifle Corps.

On 14 August the 6th Guards Army, developing the offensive, reached in heavy fighting the line Berezovka—Otrada—Vyazovaya—Shelestovo—Alekseevka, having advanced 10-12 kilometers that day.

The 1st Tank Army and the 5th Guards Army's right flank, along with units of the 5th Guards Tank Army, were stubbornly holding the line Vysokopol'e—Sharovka—the woods to the west of Khrushchevaya Nikitovka—Semenov Yar; they beat back all the enemy's attacks, which already lacked their previous intensity. The 5th Guards Army's left-flank formations, while continuing to wage offensive battles, by the close of the day reached the line Malaya Rogozyanka—Korobki (eight kilometers east of Malaya Rogozyanka).

The enemy, having suffered a complete lack of success in his attempts to break through to Bogodukhov from the southeast from the Staryi Merchik—Ol'shany area, decided to shift his attacks to the south, in order to parry the 6th Guards Army's offensive, the rapid advance to the south of which was increasing the threat of isolating the German group of forces in the Khar'kov area.

For this purpose, as early as 14 August the German command began to regroup its forces to create a powerful shock group in the Kovyagi—Novyi Merchik area. By the morning of 15 August the enemy had brought in the *Das Reich* and *Totenkopf* SS panzer divisions here.

On the morning of 15 August this group of forces attacked in the general direction of Kachalovka and launched a powerful attack against the units of the 6th Tank Corps, which were operating in the Vysokopol'e—Sharovka area, broke through their front and reached the rear of the 6th Guards Army.

By the close of 15 August the 6th Guards Army had fallen back in heavy fighting to the Merla River and during the night of 15-16 August had occupied defensive positions along the line Berezovka—Kachalovka—Mirnoe—Gavrishi State Farm. The 6th Tank Corps' main forces, which were operating within the 6th Guards Army's combat formations, fell back with the latter to the above-mentioned line. The 6th Motorized Rifle and 200th Tank brigades, being encircled, continued to wage fierce battles throughout the day in the Vysokopol'e area.

To the north of the Merchik River along the front Mirnoe—Krysino, our units successfully beat back all of the enemy's attacks and held their position.

On 16-17 August the enemy continued attacking the 6th Guards and 1st Tank armies, but all their attacks were beaten back.

On 16 August the 6th Motorized Rifle and 200th Tank brigades, having broken through the encirclement ring, abandoned the Vysokopol'e area and linked up with the 1st Tank Army's main forces.

By 17 August the Germans concluded their active operations along this axis and went over to the defensive. This situation along this sector of the front remained unchanged until the conclusion of the Belgorod—Khar'kov operation.

On 13 August the Steppe Front's forces broke through the Khar'kov external defensive line and following fierce fighting in the Dergachi—Cherkasskoe-Lozovoe—Bol'shaya Danilovka area, by the close of 17 August had come up against the internal line and had begun fighting in the northern outskirts of Khar'kov.

As a result of the fierce fighting, which took place on 11-17 August south of Bogodukhov, the German command was unable to break through to the Bogodukhov area and reach the rear of the Voronezh Front's shock group, in order to defeat it and decisively change the entire operational situation along the Belgorod—Khar'kov axis.

However, the enemy managed to temporarily halt the offensive by the *front's* main shock group on Kolomak and Valki. In connection with our units' withdrawal from the Vysokopol'e area to the north, the enemy again had the possibility of partially employing the Khar'kov—Poltava railroad.

The Fighting in the Area of Akhtyrka and Kaplunovka, 12-23 August

The 27th Army's battle along the line of the Vorskla River, 12-17 August

The 27th Army, in carrying out the mission of reaching the line Shilovka—Oposhnya—Artemovka (11 kilometers southeast of Bol'shaya Rublevka), during 12-17 August was engaged in stubborn fighting along the line of the Vorskla River. The fighting was particularly stubborn along the army's right flank in the Akhtyrka area.

On 12 August the army's right-flank formations continued to be involved in street fighting for Akhtyrka. The army's left wing, having crushed the Germans' resistance and thrown back the remnants of the defeated enemy units from the line of the Vorskla River, reached its eastern bank along the sector Khukhrya—Kotel'na—Kolontaev (along the Merla River).

On 14 August the army continued to wage fierce battles in the Akhtyrka area, beating back the Germans' counterattacks. On the army's left flank the 71st Rifle Division's forward detachment forced the Vorskla River and occupied Bel'sk.

During the second half of the day (14 August) the *front* commander gave the 27th Army its mission for the following day: to destroy the Germans' Akhtyrka group of forces, capture the bridgehead along the western bank of the Vorskla River and reach the line Dobroslovovka (five kilometers west of Akhtyrka)—Grun'—Oposhnya.

The 5th Guards Tank Corps, which was operationally subordinated to the 27th Army, was ordered to force the Merla River and seize Bol'shaya Rublevka, along the river's southern bank.

In carrying out this assignment, the army's left-flank formations (71st Rifle Division and 4th Tank Corps) were advancing in heavy fighting to the west and on 15 August reached the eastern outskirts of Grun', captured Budy and Bat'ki and had begun fighting for Oposhnya.

During the latter half of the day the enemy brought up additional reserves to this sector (a reserve battalion from the *Grossdeutschland* SS Panzer Division, with its equipment, a sapper battalion from the XLVIII Panzer Corps, and other subunits) and launched a counterattack along the front Grun'—Bel'sk. The 27th Army's further advance was halted.

The 5th Guards Tank Corps captured Bol'shaya Rublevka.

During the second half of the day, due to the difficult situation along the front of the 6th Guards Army, which was forced to fall back from the line Berezovka—Shelestovo—Alekseevka to the north, the 27th Army was ordered, in order to secure its left flank, to occupy with part of its forces the crossings over the Merla River along the sector Bol'shaya Rublevka—Krasnokutsk—Koz'evka. This was carried out by the 5th Guards Tank Corps and the 241st Rifle Division.

On 16-17 August the enemy's resistance along the 27th Army's front increased sharply. With the support of significant air groups, he repeatedly counterattacked the army's units. The villages of Grun', Bel'sk and Budy changed hands several times. Nonetheless, on 16 August the 4th Guards Tank Corps, together with the 71st Rifle Division, threw the Germans out of Oposhnya after heavy fighting and captured the village.

On 17 August the army, which had dispersed its forces along a 170-kilometer front, was not able to advance along a single sector. Despite the fact that our units attempted to throw the Germans out of Akhtyrka, the town remained in the enemy's hands, and following the transfer of the 241st Rifle Division to the army's left flank to the Merla River, only the 166th Rifle Division remained here along a 25-kilometer front.

At the same time the 27th Army was fighting along the Vorskla River during 12-16 August, the 38th and 40th armies were fighting along the line Verkhnyaya Syrovatka—Trostyanets and were unable to advance. The German command, in order to strengthen its forces operating against the 40th Army, on 15 August committed the 112th Infantry Division, which had been transferred from around Bryansk.

On the morning of 17 August the 38th and 40th armies renewed the offensive. In order to develop their offensive from the Boromlya area in the general direction of Malyi Istorop and Kostev, the 47th Army was committed into the battle from the *front* reserve. On 17 August, having broken through the Germans' defensive line along the line Verkhnyaya Syrovatka—Petrovskii and advancing 10-12 kilometers, by the close of the day the armies had reached the front Bezdrik—Nizhnyaya Syrovatka—Velikii Istorop.

By his time the 4th Guards Army, which had been transferred by the *Stavka* to the commander of the Voronezh Front, had concentrated in the area Yamnoe—Novaya Ryabina—Yablochnoe.

The Germans' counterblow from the Akhtyrka area. The fighting in the Kaplunovka and Kolontaev areas on 18-20 August

Having been unable to simultaneously launch counterblows against our forces' flanks (from the north toward Akhtyrka and Kotel'va, and from the south toward Bogodukhov) and having suffered a defeat in his attempts to break through to Bogodukhov from the Staryi Merchik—Ol'shany area, in the middle of August the enemy belatedly began preparing an attack on Bogodukhov from the northwest, from the Akhtyrka area.

For this purpose, the German command concentrated in the Akhtyrka area and to the west the *Grossdeutschland* SS Panzer Division, the 7th and part of the 19th panzer divisions, the 10th Motorized Division, the 51st and 52nd independent Mark-VI heavy tank battalions, and four artillery regiments. All of these units, with the exception of the 7th and 19th panzer divisions and the artillery, had been transferred from the Bryansk area. At the same time, the Germans concentrated the main forces of the *Totenkopf* SS Panzer Division in the area southeast of Bol'shaya Rublevka, for an attack on Kolontaev from the south. Besides this, by 14 August two infantry divisions—the 355th and 223rd (the latter from the Idritsa area)—had concentrated in the Poltava area.

As a result of this regrouping, as well as the significant expansion of the 27th Army's front, the Germans managed to achieve a significant superiority of force by the middle of August along the front Akhtyrka—Oposhnya—Krasnokutsk.

Without taking into account the overall situation along the Belgorod—Khar'kov bridgehead, which had developed quite unfavorably for the Germans (in particular, despite the danger hanging over the flank of the entire Akhtyrka group of forces in connection with the resumption of the offensive by the Voronezh Front's right-flank armies), and being content with only a local superiority of force along a limited portion of the front in the Akhtyrka area, the German command on 18 August began an attack along the Akhtyrka axis against the 27th Army's right flank.

At 0830, following a powerful artillery preparation and massed air attacks against the 155th and 166th rifle divisions, the enemy simultaneously committed into the battle up to 200 tanks and motorized infantry along the Pologii—Moshenki sector, supported from the air by a large number of aircraft. The 166th Rifle Division's front was pierced and by the close of the day the enemy had penetrated our defense to a depth of 24 kilometers, creating a narrow pocket up to seven kilometers in width and bordered by the line Akhtyrka—Verbovyi—Vysokoe—Kudryavyi—Zaporozhets—Novaya Odessa—Kaplunovka—Ivanovka—Moshenki.

During the first half of the day the 4th Guards Army's 7th and 8th guards rifle divisions, which had deployed along the line Vysokoe—Novaya Odessa entered the battle against the enemy's breakthrough units. During the course of the fighting for the forward edge of our defense alone, the 166th Rifle Division's artillery put more than 30 enemy tanks out of action.

That same day the *Totenkopf* SS Panzer Division attacked from the Kovalevka—Konstantinovka area in the direction of Kolontaev and Lyubovka. The Germans' attacks were beaten back by the defending 241st Rifle Division and units of the 5th Guards Stalingrad Tank Corps.

With the enemy's arrival in the Kaplunovka area, the situation along the 27th Army's left flank quickly became more difficult and there arose the danger of encirclement of the 71st and 241st rifle divisions and the 4th and 5th guards tank corps, which were operating in the area Khukhrya—Budy—Oposhnya—Kotel'va—Kolontaev.

The supreme commander-in-chief, comrade Stalin, personally instructed the *Stavka* representative, Marshal Zhukov, who was at the Voronezh Front headquarters, as to the necessity of eliminating the Germans' Akhtyrka group of forces as quickly as possible and also to adopt emergency measures to ward off the possible isolation of the 27th Army's left-flank formations.

At 1650 the *front* commander issued the following orders to the 27th, 6th Guards, 4th Guards, and 1st Tank armies: to defeat the German group of forces through joint attacks and to restore the situation in the Akhtyrka area.

The 38th Army was to securely hold the eastern bank of the Psel River along the sector Bol'shaya Chernetchina—Nizy, securing the right flank of the armies attacking to the southwest.

Besides this, on the basis of the supreme commander-in-chief's instructions, during the night of 18-19 August an order was issued to withdraw the 71st Rifle Division's main forces from the western bank of the Vorskla River in the Parkhomovka area; a single regiment was to remain to cover the Kotel'va—Likhachevka area.

The 4th Guards Tank Corps was ordered to concentrate in the Mikhailovo area (northeast of Kotel'va), in order to destroy the enemy breakthrough group together with units of the 5th Guards Stalingrad Tank Corps and the 166th Rifle Division and 93rd Tank Brigade. The corps left the 3rd Guards Motorized Rifle Brigade as a screen along the Lutishche—Zarech'e sector for covering the axis Lutishche—the northern outskirts of Kotel'va.

The 5th Guards Stalingrad Tank Corps had the following mission: while leaving part of its forces behind to strengthen the 241st Rifle Division, which had been operationally subordinated to the 6th Guards Army and was defending along the Merchik River, it was to concentrate its main forces in the Parkhomovka area for joint operations with the 4th Guards Tank Corps.

On 19 August the 27th Army's forces, along with the 1st Tank Army's 3rd and 6th tank corps and the 4th Guards Army's two divisions and its 3rd Mechanized Corps, were engaged in heavy fighting with the enemy breakthrough group.

By the close of the day the 3rd and 6th tank corps, which were operating along with the 4th Guards Army's 7th and 8th guards rifle divisions and the 27th Army's 147th Rifle Division, occupied Verbovyi, Vysokoe, Veselyi Gai, Kudryavyi, the Komsomolets State Farm, and Zaporozhets, following heavy fighting, and deprived the enemy of all his convenient strong points covering the left flank of his Akhtyrka group of forces from the north.

The enemy's attempts to deepen the breakthrough through repeated attacks to the east and to take Novaya Odessa and Koz'evka concluded in complete failure. Striving to broaden the sack to the south, the Germans repeatedly attacked from the Veliko-Ozerskii area toward Moshenki and Mikhailovo. By the close of the day, having captured these villages, they reached the line northern outskirts of Sidoryach'e—Parkhomovka, but were halted here by the 5th Guards Tank Corps and units of the 71st Rifle Division, which had fallen back here from the Vorskla River. During the fighting our units destroyed 40 enemy tanks, including several heavy "Tiger" types.

The 241st Rifle Division, which was defending along the Merla River, fought off all the German attacks during the day and held its position.

On 20 August the German command, having suffered a defeat in its attempts to break through to Bogodukhov by an attack from the Akhtyrka area and forced to renounce the continuation of the offensive along this axis, dispatched its main forces to eliminate our salient that had formed in the Kotel'va area. The German command tried to encircle our forces defending in this area (4th and 5th guards tank corps). For this, the Germans launched two concentric attacks: one from the Parkhomovka area toward Krasnokutsk, and the second from the Konstantinovka area toward Lyubovka and Krasnokutsk. Stubborn fighting continued throughout the day in the Parkhomovka—Mikhailovo—Khukhrya—Kolontaev—Lyubovka area.

By the close of the day the enemy offensive was halted along the line Kaplunovka—the eastern outskirts of Parkhomovka—Lyubovka.

During the course of three days of fierce battles the enemy suffered major losses. The 27th Army's forces alone destroyed 180 tanks, 50 guns, four batteries of six-barreled mortars, nearly completely destroyed two regiments of motorized infantry, with 30 planes shot down in air battles or by our anti-aircraft artillery. By 20 August the Germans' Akhtyrka group of forces had been bled white and lost all of its offensive capabilities.

On 20 August the German command's attempts to break through to the Bogodukhov area, so that following the defeat of our forces attacking to the southwest they could uncover the flank of our group of forces attacking along the Khar'kov axis, had collapsed completely.

On 20 August *Stavka* representative Marshal Zhukov reported to comrade Stalin that in the Akhtyrka area:

> The enemy wanted to break through our front, cut off the Kotel'va salient and attack the rear of our Khar'kov group of forces, and possibly, at the same time attack the rear of Moskalenko[5] and Korzun[6] with an attack toward Trostyanets. Up until now the enemy has been unable to break through our front, and the enemy in the Akhtyrka area has gone over to an active defense. Nor did he manage to cut off the Kotel'va salient, because following your warning the 71st Rifle Division and Kravchenko's[7] units had already been pulled back to the Parkhomovka area and one of the 71st Rifle Division's regiments, two regiments from the 166th Rifle Division, and part of Poluboyarov's[8] forces are being pulled back.

Thus all the German command's attempts to foil our forces' offensive to the southwest and retain Khar'kov through attacks on Bogodukhov from the north and south collapsed.

The insignificant tactical successes achieved by the Germans in the area south of Bogodukhov and around Akhtyrka could not appreciably influence the overall situation that had arisen by that time along the Belgorod—Khar'kov bridgehead.

The Voronezh Front's forces had not only destroyed all the Germans' plans, but by defeating the enemy's Akhtyrka group of forces had opened the road for a subsequent offensive to the west and southwest.

The enemy, in his fruitless attempts to halt our offensive, suffered heavy losses. During 11-20 August alone the Voronezh Front's forces killed 34,600 German officers and men and destroyed 521 tanks, 530 guns, 140 mortars, 2,327 motor vehicles, and 140 planes. During this same period our forces captured 1,736 prisoners, 485 guns, 60 mortars, and much other military equipment.

The Maneuver by the Voronezh Front's Right Wing (17-27 August)

Operations north of Akhtyrka, 17-18 August

As early as 15 August it became apparent to the Voronezh Front command that the enemy was striving, by means of counterblows against the flanks of our group of forces attacking to the

5 Commander of the 40th Army.
6 Commander of the 47th Army.
7 Commander of the 5th Guards Stalingrad Tank Corps.
8 Commander of the 4th Guards Tank Corps.

southwest, to foil the general offensive by the Voronezh and Steppe fronts and to win time for organizing a defense along the line of the Boromlya, Vorskla and Merla rivers. For this reason, the German command created powerful tank groups in the Staryi Merchik—Ol'shany and Akhtyrka areas, and that as early as 11 August the Germans' southern group of forces had gone over to active operations against the 1st Tank Army.

In order to foil the Germans' planned counterblow with powerful forces from the Akhtyrka area toward Bogodukhov and to destroy this group of forces, the *front* commander decided: "by committing additional forces, to launch an attack against the flank and rear of the enemy's force operating opposite Boromlya and to the east of Poltava, to encircle and destroy him in the Trostyanets—Oleshnya—Akhtyrka area."

The *front* commander laid out the following tasks in his operational directive of 15 August:

The 47th Army, along with the 10th Tank and 3rd Guards Mechanized corps, which was to be committed along the 40th Army's sector, was to launch an attack along its right flank and then, taking advantage of the 40th Army's advance, was to attack on the morning of 17 August from the line excluding Grebennikovka—Boromlya in the general direction of Velikii Istorop—Lebedin—Bol'shaya Pavlovka—Borki—Shishaki—Batrak, for the purpose of breaking through the enemy's defense and to reach the flank and rear of the enemy defending south of Boromlya, to roll up his front to the south, destroying his forces and preventing their withdrawal to the west; by the close of 19 August the army was to reach the Zen'kov area.

The 40th Army, together with the 2nd Tank Corps, was to attack simultaneously with the 47th Army and by the close of 19 August was to reach the Psel River along the sector Vorozhba—Svinarnaya (14 kilometers west of Veprika).

Before the start of the operation, the 27th Army was to support the seizure and retention of a bridgehead along the western bank of the Vorskla River in the Budy—Bel'sk—Laz'ki area, and on the morning of 17 August attack in the general direction of Kotel'va and Zen'kov and, in conjunction with the 47th Army, encircle the Germans' Akhtyrka group of forces in the Trostyanets—Akhtyrka area.

The 38th Army was to continue to carry out its previous assignment—to reach the Psel River along the sector Bol'shaya Chernetchina—Nizy.

The 2nd Air Army was to direct its main efforts toward supporting the 47th Army's offensive, while part of its forces would support the 27th Army.

For the purpose of committing the 47th Army into the battle, at 2300 on 16 August a corresponding regrouping was carried out. The 47th Army, upon relieving units of the 40th Army's 52nd Rifle Corps, occupied its jumping-off position along the sector Gaponovka—Batsaivshchina.

The 40th Army's 237th and 309th rifle divisions, along with the 2nd Tank Corps, occupied the line excluding the Kamennoe State Farm (west of Bol'shaya Bobrika)—Bratskii, while the 161st and 100th rifle divisions occupied their jumping-off positions along the line excluding Batsaivshchina—Boromlya—Kamenka. Thus following the regrouping, the 40th Army was cut into two groups, which subsequently operated independently along the 47th Army's flanks.

The offensive by the 38th, 40th and 47th armies began at 0700 on 17 August, following an intensive 50-minute artillery and aviation preparation.

The 88th, 75th, 68th, 57th, and 112th infantry divisions, and the 11th Panzer Division were defending opposite the Voronezh Front's right-flank armies along the sector Bititsa—Trostyanets.

The 38th Army, having broken through the enemy's defense and having eliminated the powerful resistance centers of Verkhnyaya Syrovatka and Nizhnyaya Syrovatka, by the end of the day had reached the line Bezdrik—Nizhnyaya Syrovatka; the army advanced 12-15 kilometers into the depth of the enemy position during the day.

By 1000 the 40th and 47th armies' right-flank groups had broken through the enemy's defense and, having also advanced 12 kilometers, by the close of the day reached in heavy fighting the front southern outskirts of Nizhnyaya Syrovatka—Supronov—the eastern outskirts of the village of Malyi Istorop. The 40th Army's left-flank group, having attacked at 1000, encountered the enemy's stubborn resistance and fought all day along its start line.

Thus on 17 August the main group of the Voronezh Front's right-flank armies had broken through the Germans' defense along the Verkhnyaya Syrovatka—Petrovskii sector throughout the entire tactical depth and had pressed the enemy against the Psel River.

The *front* commander, striving as quickly as possible to reach the communications of the Germans' Akhtyrka group of forces, as early as the evening of 17 August, demanded that the commander of the 40th Army capture the town of Lebedin as quickly as possible. For this purpose, he ordered the employment of a brigade from the 2nd Tank Corps, along with a detachment of automatic riflemen, two anti-tank artillery regiments, a mortar regiment, and a guards mortar battalion. In order to consolidate the detachment's success, it was to be followed by a rifle division. The 38th Army was ordered to maximally speed up the pace of its attack and by the close of 18 August to reach the Psel River along the entire front, having destroyed the enemy defending along the river's eastern bank.

On 18 August the groups of the Voronezh Front's right-flank armies continued their offensive, despite the Germans' fierce resistance, particularly along the front Belka—Trostyanets. Simultaneously with the resumption of the offensive by our armies, on the morning of 18 August the Germans' Akhtyrka group of forces attacked along the 27th Army's front in the general direction of Akhtyrka and Kaplunovka.

The 38th Army, which was supported by part of the 2nd Tank Corps' forces, reached the Psel River in stubborn fighting by the close of the day along the Bititsa—Nizy sector, and had begun fighting in the eastern outskirts of the town of Sumy.

The 40th Army's right-wing divisions also reached in fighting the Psel River along the sector Pashkov—Bishkin'.

The 47th Army, having advanced 20 kilometers in fighting, by the close of the day reached the line Novoselovka—Fedorovka—Kostev—the northern outskirts of the village of Belka.

The 40th Army's left-wing divisions, upon encountering stubborn resistance by an enemy relying on the favorable defensive line along the Boromlya River, as well as the powerful strong points of Belka and Trostyanets, did not advance during the day and was engaged in stubborn fighting for both centers of resistance.

Operations by the Voronezh Front's right flank, 19-20 August

As a result of the 18 August fighting along the Voronezh Front's right flank, a very difficult situation had developed.

The Germans' Akhtyrka group of forces had penetrated into the 27th Army's defense to a depth of 20 kilometers and reached the Kaplunovka area, which threatened the 27th Army's left flank, as well as the 6th Guards and 1st Tank armies.

On the other hand, the rapid advance to the south by the 47th Army and the 40th Army's right flank and their arrival in the Novoselovka—Kostev area had created favorable prerequisites for a subsequent maneuver in the direction of Chupakhovka and Grun', for the purpose of reaching the communications of the enemy's Akhtyrka group of forces and its deep envelopment.

In order to achieve this goal, as early as 1500 on 18 August the *front* commander demanded that the 47th Army commander maximally speed up the offensive by the 3rd Guards Mechanized Corps.

On the evening of 18 August, while assigning objectives for the following day, the *front* commander ordered the 38th Army to firmly secure the right flank of the attacking right-flank armies by going over to a fixed defense along the eastern bank of the Psel River.

The 40th Army's right-flank divisions were ordered by the close of 19 August to capture the Germans' powerful Lebedin center of resistance, as well as to reach the Psel River and organize a defense along its eastern bank along the Pashkov—Lebedin sector.

The 47th Army, along with the 40th Army's left-flank divisions, while developing the achieved success, was to cut the Lebedin—Akhtyrka road—one of the most important communications routes of the Germans' Akhtyrka group of forces—by the end of the day.

The 10th Tank Corps was given the task of launching an attack through Oleshnya to capture Akhtyrka.

The 3rd Guards Mechanized Corps was to attack toward Chupakhovka and reach the Yasenevoe area and support the 10th Tank Corps' operations from the west and southwest, and to be ready to attack toward Akhtyrka.

By 19 August the German command, having come to understand the threat hanging over its Akhtyrka group of forces, was forced to transfer part of its forces, designated for attacking from Akhtyrka toward Bogodukhov, for opposing the 40th and 47th armies' offensive. Thus the Germans' resistance to our offensive on 19 August was considerably strengthened.

As a result of heavy fighting, the 40th Army, with the forces of the 309th and 161st rifle divisions[9] and the 2nd Tank Corps, defeated the German group of forces defending the very important strong point of Lebedin and broke into the town.

The 47th Army, having reached the line Timofeevka—Zubovka, cut the Akhtyrka—Lebedin road.

The 40th Army's left-flank divisions (206th and 100th rifle), having crushed the Germans' resistance along the Boromlya River, captured the villages of Belka and Trostyanets and reached the line Zubovka—Stanova—Sosonka.

Thus as a result of the fighting on 19 August the 40th and 47th armies' forces reached the rear of the Germans' Akhtyrka group of forces and directly threatened it with encirclement. This was immediately reflected in the Germans' actions along the Akhtyrka—Bogodukhov axis and their attacks in the Kalpunovka area became less active.

On 20 August the 40th and 47th armies continued to develop the offensive. The 38th Army consolidated along the Psel River, while individual detachments had forced it.

The 40th Army's right-flank formations, having defeated the Germans' Lebedin group of forces and having gone over to an energetic offensive, pushing aside the enemy's rearguards, advanced during the day to the southwest along the Psel River to a depth of 35 kilometers and captured Veprik. With the onset of darkness, the army's units began to organize a defense along the eastern bank of the Psel River along the sector Bishkin'—Veprik.

The 47th Army and the 40th Army's left-flank divisions were engaged the entire day in heavy fighting with the enemy, who had increased his resistance by means of forces transferred from the Akhtyrka area.

By the close of the day the army, having advanced 5-10 kilometers, reached the line Berezovyi—Rossokhovatyi—Oleshnya—Sosonka.

The conclusion of the fighting around Akhtyrka (21-27 August)

With the capture of the village of Veprik by the 40th Army, the last road leading from Akhtyrka to the west had been cut. The Akhtyrka group of forces had one final road remaining to the rear—the

9 On 18 August the 161st Rifle Division was transferred to the army's right flank and subordinated to the 52nd Rifle Corps.

Akhtyrka—Zen'kov road, running to the southwest, but Zen'kov was also threatened by the 40th Army.

Besides this, units of the 47th Army and the 40th Army's left-flank formations had almost completely reached Akhtyrka from the north and northwest. Thus on 20 August the German command was forced to finally renounce all attempts to break through from the Kaplunovka area to Bogodukhov, and the enemy in this area went over to the defensive along the entire front.

In order to complete the defeat of the Germans' Akhtyrka group of forces, on 20 August the *front* commander, in carrying out the *Stavka's* instructions, laid out tasks for the *front's* right-wing armies for the following day.

For the purpose of simplifying control over the 40th Army, the 47th Army's 29th Rifle Division was to be transferred to the 40th Army, while the 40th Army's 206th and 100th rifle divisions were to be subordinated to the 47th Army. As a result of this regrouping, the 40th Army was regrouped completely to the right of the 47th Army.

The 40th Army was to firmly consolidate along the line of the Psel River along the front Pashkov—Veprik, in readiness to attack further.

The 2nd Tank Corps received orders to cut the Akhtyrka—Zen'kov road, for which it was to reach the Kamyshi area and to dispatch forward detachments to Zen'kov and Veprik to hold the crossings over the Psel River.

Upon resuming the offensive on the morning of 21 August, the 47th Army was by the end of the day to reach the line Pashkino—Alenina—Shevchenki—Bidany, for the purpose of enveloping the Akhtyrka area from the west and southwest.

The 3rd Mechanized and 10th Tank corps were ordered to reach the Shevchenki—Yasenovoe—Chernetchina area for a subsequent attack against Akhtyrka from the west.

The 27th Army received orders to attack toward Akhtyrka from the east and reach the line Yasenovoe—Khukhrya, completing the defeat of the Germans' Akhtyrka group of forces in conjunction with the 47th Army.

The 4th Guards Army was entrusted with the mission of attacking from the line Veselyi Gai—Kaplunovka toward Kotel'va, and by the close of the first day to defeat the opposing enemy and reach the line Khukhrya—Kotel'va.

The 6th Guards Army was to firmly hold its present position along the line Parkhomovka—Lyubovka—Khrushchevaya Nikitovka—Gavrishi State Farm.

The 1st Tank Army was to attack and capture the area Sidoryach'e—Pioneer State Farm—Parkhomovka.

As a result of the successful completion of the offensive operation's concluding stage by the Voronezh Front's right wing, which took place during 21-24 August, our forces defeated the Germans' Akhtyrka group of forces and occupied Akhtyrka. By 27 August the 4th Guards Army's forces reached the Vorskla River and captured the Kotel'va strong point. By the close of 27 August the front of the Voronezh Front's right-flank armies ran along the Psel River from Bezdrika to Veprik and then along the line Martynovka—Kamyshi—Grun'—Kuzemin—Kotel'va—Kolontaev.

The German command's attempt to foil our offensive by an attack from the Akhtyrka area ended not only in complete failure, but in the destruction of the enemy's entire Akhtyrka group of forces.

Due to the successful completion of this operation, favorable conditions had been created, on the one hand, for the Steppe Front's forces to eliminate the Germans' Khar'kov group of forces itself and, on the other, for the Voronezh Front's forces to undertake a new offensive both to the west toward Gadyach, and to the south toward Poltava.

V. The Steppe Front's Offensive. The Defeat of the Germans' Khar'kov Group of Forces and the Liberation of Khar'kov (8-23 August)

The fighting on 8-11 August and the arrival of our forces at the Khar'kov external line

Following the loss of the Belgorod center of resistance the Germans, striving to delay the offensive by the Steppe Front's forces on Khar'kov, went over to a mobile defense: they firmly held on to the numerous defensive lines that had been previously constructed along the road to Khar'kov. The enemy carried out a number of fierce counterattacks along a number of sectors, in battalion or regimental strength.

The Steppe Front's forces continued to develop the offensive in heavy fighting. By the close of 7 August the forces of the 53rd Army and the 69th Army's right flank broke through the Germans' fifth defensive line and reached the front Mikoyanovka—Nikol'skoe.

The 7th Guards Army, following the forcing of the Severskii Donets River, in taking advantage of the 69th Army's success, reached the Nikol'skoe—Volkovo area along its right flank.

The fierce battles continued the following day. The enemy was seeking to hold back our forces' offensive, rabidly defending the previously prepared strong points that covered the approaches to the sixth rear operational defensive line. However, by the close of the day the Steppe Front's forces had crushed the enemy's resistance and the right flank had reached this line.

By the close of the day the 53rd Army, with the 1st Mechanized Corps, had occupied the line Il'ich Collective Farm—the northern outskirts of Zhuravlevka. The 69th Army simultaneously reached the line height 219—the western outskirts of Revenek. The 7th Guards Army, having crushed the Germans' resistance, had broken through the fifth defensive line along its sector and captured the powerful resistance center of Ziborovka, having reached the line northern outskirts of Revenek—Korovino.

For 9 August the commander of the Steppe Front, comrade Konev, issued the following orders to the 53rd, 69th and 7th Guards armies: to break through the sixth (rear operational) defensive line and continue to develop the offensive to the south toward Khar'kov.

For the purpose of uniting the control of all the forces attacking toward Khar'kov in the hands of a single *front* command and to speed up the defeat of the Germans' Khar'kov group of forces, on 8 August the *Stavka* of the Supreme High Command included the Southwestern Front's right-flank 57th Army in the Steppe Front. The *front* commander gave this army the task of forcing the Severskii Donets River with its forward units on 9 August, to secure the bridgeheads and be ready to attack decisively with its main forces in the general direction of Rogan' and Osnova, outflanking Khar'kov from the south.

Simultaneously, in order to strengthen the Steppe Front's right wing, the *Stavka* of the Supreme High Command operationally subordinated to the *front* the 5th Guards Tank Army, which had been operating up to this time in tandem with the 5th Guards Army in the Zolochev—Kazach'ya Lopan' area, with the task of attacking toward Merefa.

On 9 August the forces of the 53rd, 69th and 7th Guards armies broke through the enemy's sixth defensive line. Vigorously pursuing the retreating enemy units, our forces advanced 14-20 kilometers on that day in fighting and by the close of the day reached the next seventh defensive line, which already formed a part of the forward security zone covering the Khar'kov outer line along the front Dolbino—Liptsy—the northern outskirts of Veseloe—excluding Peremoga.

On that day the 57th Army's right-flank formations forced the Severskii Donets River in the Rubezhnoe area and by the close of the day, having broken through the enemy's defense, reached the front Peremoga—Staryi Saltov. The forcing of the Severskii Donets River by the 57th Army was eased to a significant degree by the fact that the Steppe Front's forces, which had by this time reached the line Slatino—Liptsy—Veseloe—excluding Peremoga, had finished "rolling up" the enemy's defense along the river's western bank as far as Rubezhnoe, that is, right up to the 57th Army's right flank.

As the Steppe Front's forces approached Khar'kov, the enemy's resistance grew continuously.

Despite the enormous losses that the enemy suffered from our artillery fire, he stubbornly held on to his previously prepared defensive lines and strong points and strove, at any price, to delay our forces' arrival before Khar'kov.

The enemy based his defense on the maximum employment of all types of fire. In particular, he reinforced the group of forces that were defending the approaches to Khar'kov from the north, with artillery and a large number of mortar units, which numbered more than 600 guns and heavy mortars.

On 10 August the Steppe Front's right-flank forces were fighting in the defensive line's forward security zone. Having advanced 2-5 kilometers, they captured several powerful enemy strong points. On that day the 57th Army's main forces forced the Severskii Donets River and broke through the enemy's defense along the entire front, and took by storm the enemy's powerful resistance center of Pechenegi, cleared the enemy out of the large wooded expanse to the north, and by the close of the day had reached the line Nepokrytaya—Bol'shaya Babka—Kitsevka.

The forces of the Steppe Front were faced with a responsible task—to break through the external Khar'kov defensive position, which ran along the line Dergachi—Cherkasskoe-Lozovoe—Tsirkuny—the southern bank of the lake east of Tsirkuny—Prelestnyi—Losevo—Vasishchevo—Yakovlevka—Yuzhnyi—Korotich—Kuryazhanka.

On the night of 10-11 August the commander of the Steppe Front, comrade Konev, issued an order to attack and to break through the external defensive position and to subsequently develop the offensive for the purpose of taking Khar'kov.

The operation to take Khar'kov was to be carried out by launching several powerful attacks against the enemy's defense and to subsequently outflank Khar'kov with our forces from the northwest and southeast.

The 5th Guards Tank Army was ordered to reach the area Budy—Korotich—Ogul'tsy, for the purpose of cutting the Khar'kov—Poltava railroad.

The 53rd Army received orders to reach by the close of 11 August the front Peresechnaya—the western outskirts of Khar'kov; the 1st Mechanized Corps, operating in conjunction with the 53rd Army, was to reach the Gavrilovka area.

The remainder of the armies had the task of reaching the following lines by the close of the day: 69th Army—the northern outskirts of Khar'kov; 7th Guards Army—the city's eastern and south-eastern outskirts, and; the 57th Army—the city's southern outskirts.

In order to support the breakthrough of the external defensive position, the Steppe Front's forces were reinforced with 4,234 guns and mortars, yielding an overall correlation of forces of 6.5:1 in our favor.

Throughout 11 August our forces were engaged in bitter fighting with the enemy, who was stubbornly defending his strong points and centers of resistance, located north of the defensive position and covering the approaches to the position.

Especially stubborn fighting arose for Russkoe-Lozovoe, the 13 Years of the RKKA State Farm, Russkie Tishki, and Cherkasskie Tishki.

Units of the 69th Army's 305th Rifle Division, which were operating in conjunction with tanks, reached the immediate northern outskirts of Russkoe-Lozovoe following heavy fighting. Our units' repeated attempts to seize this village by a head-on attack were unsuccessful. The enemy, who attached great significance to the retention of Russkoe-Lozovoe, had concentrated a large garrison there and beat back our attacks with fire, repeatedly counterattacking in groups of infantry reinforced with tanks.

It was only after units of the 375th Rifle Division, which were attacking east of the 305th Rifle Division, passed through the large woods and eliminated the groups of enemy automatic riflemen who had ensconced themselves there and appeared in the area of height 215.8, did the enemy's resistance weaken somewhat. By the close of the day the 305th and 375th rifle divisions had seized Russkoe-Lozovoe through joint attacks from the north and east.

With the onset of darkness the 53rd and 69th armies reached the front Mishchenkov—the northern outskirts of Alekseevka—the northern outskirts of the village of Tsirkuny, in stubborn fighting. The 7th Guards Army, having broken through west of the lake, by this time reached with part of its forces the line northeast outskirts of Tsirkuny and had begun fighting for the village, while the remaining forces had reached the village of Klyuchkin and the Kutuzovka State Farm.

Thus by the close of 11 August the 53rd, 69th and 7th Guards armies along the entire front had reached the external Khar'kov defensive position.

The 57th Army, after it had overcome the enemy's second defensive line, which ran along the line Nepokrytaya—Bol'shaya Babka—Tetlega—Kamennaya Yaruga, seized the Germans' major centers of resistance in Zarozhnoe and Chuguev and reached the front Chervona Roganka—Kamennaya Yaruga. The army's right flank had reached the intermediate line covering Khar'kov from the east.

The 5th Guards Tank Army, which had been pulled back into the second echelon, had by the close of the day concentrated in the Sennoe area, six kilometers east of Bogodukhov, and was preparing to carry out its assignment.

By this time the forces of the Voronezh Front, developing the offensive from Bogodukhov to the south with the forces of the 1st Tank Army, had forced the Merla and Merchik rivers and reached the area Vysokopol'e—Kovyagi station, cutting the Khar'kov—Poltava railroad.

The overall course of the fighting for Khar'kov

During 12-23 August the forces of the Steppe Front were engaged in heavy fighting along the near approaches to Khar'kov and in the city itself, right up to its liberation.

Our forces were forced to operate in extremely difficult conditions, because the city was girded from all sides with a widely developed system of defensive structures. 8-14 kilometers from the city ran the external line, which was based on a series of resistance centers. The most important of them were Dergachi, Cherkasskoe-Lozovoe, Tsirkuny, Prelestnyi, Yuzhnyi (Losevo station), Vasishchevo, and others. The enemy had filled up the gaps between these centers with individual strong points, which had been prepared for all-round anti-tank defense and were all in mutual fire communication with each other.

The Germans had located the majority of the defensive structures along the reverse slopes of elevations, as a result of which the effectiveness of our artillery fire was reduced to a significant degree. The approaches to the resistance centers and strong points were covered by mine fields, anti-tank ditches and barbed wire obstacles.

All the roads to Khar'kov had been destroyed, the bridges burned, and along a number of sectors the road bed and possible bypass areas had been mined. The Germans widely used as booby traps here 50 and 100-kilogram air bombs.

The space between the external city positions had also been prepared for stubborn defense. Here there was a large amount of various intermediate and switch positions, as well as strong points and centers of resistance, which blocked the approaches to the city.

The city was covered from the north and west by large wooded areas, which the enemy had transformed into obstacle zones, making broad use of tree fellings and mine fields, among other things. The wooded areas were defended by detachments of automatic riflemen.

The city position was based on stone structures on the outskirts, which had been transformed into pillboxes of a kind. The buildings' lower stories were employed as medium-caliber artillery firing positions; the upper stories were occupied by automatic riflemen and machine gunners, while on the upper floors the Germans set up positions for anti-tank cannons and mortars.

All the approaches to the city, as well as the streets on the outskirts, had been completely mined and covered with barricades. The city's inner blocks, particularly in its northern and eastern parts, had also been prepared for defense.

In order to defend the Khar'kov area, the Germans had concentrated a powerful group of forces, consisting of the 167th, 168th, 106th, 198th, 320th, 282nd, 39th, and 161st infantry divisions, and units of the 3rd and 6th panzer divisions. Although these formations had suffered serious losses in the preceding fighting, they still maintained their combat capability. Besides this, during the course of the fighting the enemy repeatedly reinforced these divisions, pouring fresh units into them. On 19 August, south of Khar'kov, the Germans committed into the fighting against the 57th Army the fresh 355th Infantry Division, which had been transferred from Poltava.

Various SS detachments, security units, and detachments formed from the German police, etc., were brought in to defend the city and waging street fighting.

The enemy concentrated the main mass of his artillery for defending the northern and eastern faces of the external position, while strongly echeloned in depth. The Germans' resistance increased markedly from 11 August, which can be explained by the receipt of Hitler's order demanding that "Khar'kov be held at all costs," and that repressions be broadly employed against soldiers and officers displaying signs of cowardice and a lack of will to fight.

Thus, while liberating Khar'kov, our forces were forced to undertake a methodical breakthrough of a series of deeply echeloned German positions and eliminate his numerous strong points and centers of resistance.

The experience of the preceding fighting spoke to the insufficient effectiveness of artillery fire from hidden positions, given the great centralization of our artillery in conditions of limited observation and continuous fighting for numerous inhabited areas, and thus our command ordered the maximum employment of artillery of all calibers for firing over open sights. By this time, in some armies, the number of guns given over to firing over open sights reached 400 tubes (53rd Army).

The prisoners taken during this period testified that the German forces' greatest losses were suffered namely from guns firing over open sights.

In such conditions the tank units could operate, and operated, mainly in the infantry's combat formations.

The fighting along the external defensive position

The fighting along the external defensive position began on the evening of 11 August, when the 53rd, 69th and 7th Guards armies reached it. On 19 August the storming of the external position began.

Following a powerful artillery and air preparation, our units attacked the enemy positions. The attackers managed to break into the enemy's position along some sectors. Bitter fighting broke out in the trenches.

By the close of the day units of the 53rd Army seized Sheptushin and the northern part of Dergachi, having reached the creek that divided this village in two. In the Sheptushin area alone they killed 1,500 German soldiers and burned two heavy tanks.

As a result of bitter clashes, the 69th Army, having beaten back several infantry and tank counterattacks, reached the southern outskirts of Tsirkuny. The attacks by the 7th Guards Army on 12 August were not successful. Having completed the breakthrough of the enemy's second defensive position and eliminated the Kamennaya Yaruga center of resistance, the 57th Army continued to carry out successful attacks. By the close of the day the army had reached the intermediate defensive line that ran along the western bank of the Roganka River.

Taking advantage of the individual tactical successes achieved in the 12 August fighting, the *front's* forces on the following day continued to wage offensive battles along the entire front and completed the breakthrough of the external defensive position.

The 53rd Army eliminated the enemy group of forces, which was defending the resistance center in the Dergachi area. Having killed more than 500 Hitlerites here, by the onset of darkness the army had reached the front Polevoe—Severnyi Post. Here our forces encountered stubborn resistance: the Germans were vigorously defending the large wooded area; the entire northern edge of the woods had been prepared for stubborn defense, as were the villages of Semenovka and Zaichik, located along the main roads leading into the woods.

The 69th Army eliminated the major enemy centers of resistance in the areas of Cherkasskoe-Lozovoe and Bol'shaya Danilovka and, having destroyed up to 1,000 Germans, 12 guns and seven mortars, and having captured 13 guns and 37 machine guns, had closed up firmly to the city position along the northern outskirts of Khar'kov. The army's center had penetrated into the depth of the city position, having seized Sokol'niki, one of the strong points forming part of the system of the city's positions.

The 7th Guards Army, following the completion of the breakthrough of the external position along the Tsirkuny—Klyuchkin sector, was developing the offensive in the general direction of Losevo. Having outflanked Khar'kov from the northeast and launched attacks against the flank of the enemy units defending the eastern face of the external position, it eliminated it along the Klyuchkin—Zaiki sector and thus eased operations along the 57th Army's right flank. By evening the 7th Guards Army's right flank had reached the northeastern outskirts of the city in the Shevchenki area, while the left flank had begun fighting for Losevo.

The 57th Army forced the Roganka River and its right flank broke through the intermediate defensive line and external position on the march, having reached by the end of the day the front Gorbachev—Dedortsyi—Lyalyuki—Vvedenskoe.

Thus as a result of the 12-13 August fighting the *front's* forces, having broken through the external defensive position, had reached the city defensive position along a number of sectors and had begun fighting on the outskirts of Khar'kov.

Up to 17 August the *front's* forces were engaged in stubborn fighting along the lines reached, beating back intensive German attacks, which were attempting to delay our offensive. All of the enemy counterattacks were successfully beaten back and the 53rd and 5th Guards Tank and 57th armies were prepared to launch new attacks for the purpose of deeply turning Khar'kov from the west, east and south. By 17 August units of the 57th Army's left flank had successively captured the Ternovoe and Vasishchevo centers of resistance along the northern bank of the Udy River. Having completed the breakthrough of the defensive position opposite their entire front, they reached the line Lyalyuki—Vasishchevo.

The Germans resisted desperately along the northern approaches to Khar'kov. During 11-19 August they sought to defeat the main forces of the Voronezh Front's shock group by means of counterattacks by powerful groups of forces from the areas of Staryi Merchik and Akhtyrka, and thus achieve a decisive shift in the operational situation in their favor along the entire Belgorod—Khar'kov bridgehead. On 16 August the German high command renamed army group "Kempf" the Eighth Army.

The fighting on 18-22 August. The outflanking of Khar'kov from the west and southeast

During 18-22 August, particularly intensive fighting broke out along both of the Steppe Front's flanks. On the morning of 18 August the 53rd and 57th armies renewed their offensive, for the purpose of enveloping Khar'kov from the west and southeast.

Having gone over to the offensive, the 53rd Army waged prolonged battles during 18-19 August to clear the enemy out of the wooded area west of Khar'kov. Having bypassed this area with its main forces from the north, the army's units captured it, after which they had the opportunity to advance more rapidly.

By the close of 20 August the series of German resistance centers, which had been created along the Udy River—Peresechnaya, Gavrilovka and Kuryazhanka, had been captured. All of these centers blocked the path of our forces' attack along this sector toward the south.

The 69th Army, taking advantage of the success achieved during these days by the 53rd Army, had concentrated a large part of its forces along the right flank and had begun to rapidly lap around Khar'kov along the northwestern and western faces of the city defensive position.

In order to speed up the capture of Khar'kov, on 20 August the 5th Guards Tank Army was concentrated in the area of the woods south of Polevoe, with the assignment of attacking toward Korotich and cutting the enemy's path of retreat from Khar'kov to the west and southwest. On 21 August intensive fighting was being waged along the crossings over the Udy River in the area of Gavrilovka and Nadtochii. With the onset of darkness, our units crushed the Germans' resistance and at night captured a bridgehead along the river's southern bank.

Taking advantage of the crossings that had been laid down during the night, and having concentrated its tanks along the southern bank of the Udy River, the 5th Guards Tank Army attacked at dawn on 22 August and by the evening of the same day had captured Korotich, thus threatening to completely encircle the Germans' Khar'kov group of forces.

On 18 August the 57th Army resumed its attack. The army's main group of forces, consisting of five divisions, reinforced with tanks, was to develop the offensive in the general direction of Merefa. One division was to attack along the southern bank of the Udy River, for the purpose of supporting the left flank of the army's main group of forces.

The enemy, taking into account the threat to the entire German group of forces that had arisen as the result of the 57th Army's further advance to the west, began to take all measures to slow down our offensive. On 19 August it threw into the battle along this axis the fresh 355th Infantry Division, which had just been brought up from the Crimea.

Crushing the enemy's resistance, by the close of 22 August the 57th Army had completely reached the Germans' defensive position along the front eastern outskirts of Bezlyudovka—Konstantinovka (11 kilometers south of Bezlyudovka).

The storming of Khar'kov

With the 5th Guards Tank Army's breakthrough to the Korotich area and the arrival of the 67th Army in the Konstantinovka area, the immediate threat arose of the complete encirclement of the Germans' entire Khar'kov group of forces. The enemy retained only one railroad and road leading out of Khar'kov toward Merefa and Krasnograd, although these roads were already under constant bombardment from our aviation. Besides this, by this time the German command had finally lost all hope of successfully developing its counterblows by its units toward Bogodukhov from the Akhtyrka area; as early as 19 August the enemy had been forced to go over to the defensive in this area.

As a result of the successful maneuver carried out by the forces of the Voronezh Front's right wing and the arrival of the 40th and 47th armies in the Veprik and Zen'kov areas, the Germans' Akhtyrka group of forces was half surrounded.

All of this taken together led the German command to make the decision to withdraw the remnants of its group of forces from Khar'kov, in order to save it from complete destruction.

In the second half of 22 August our intelligence discovered enemy columns moving out of the city to the southwest. In order to deny the enemy the opportunity to carry out his intention and remove his forces defending Khar'kov from under our units' attacks, on the evening of 22 August the order was given to storm Khar'kov at night. The task of immediately taking the city was entrusted to the forces of the 69th and 7th Guards armies.

The 69th Army was to attack along its right flank from the area Kuryazhanka—October State Farm (five kilometers east of Kuryazhanka) in the general direction through Savchenko to Zalyutino, in order to encircle and destroy the German units defending in the northwestern part of the city. The 69th Army's left flank, attacking from the Alekseevka—Bol'shaya Danilovka area, was to operate through the city center and reach its southwestern outskirts.

The 7th Guards Army received orders to support the capture of Khar'kov by attacking in the general direction of Nemyshlya, Osnova and Zhikhor', while outflanking the city from the southeast.

By 1200 on 23 August, following stubborn fighting, Khar'kov had been completely cleared of German forces. A large part of the German group of forces, which had been defending the city, had been destroyed. Its remnants, being pursued by our tanks and air force, were running away in panic to the southwest beyond the Merefa and Mzha rivers. A large amount of military equipment had been abandoned.

The Germans' Khar'kov group of forces had ceased to exist. A large part of it had been destroyed during the course of the fighting for Khar'kov. In order to picture the losses of the enemy's Khar'kov group of forces, suffice it to say that during the 11-23 August fighting around Khar'kov, the 69th Army alone killed and captured about 22,000 German soldiers and officers, 249 guns, 900 machine guns, 78 tanks, and 340 motor vehicles.

Comrade Stalin, the supreme commander-in-chief, highly valued the combat activities of the Steppe Front's forces, which liberated the city of Khar'kov, the Ukraine's second capital, from the German occupiers, and which defeated, along with the Voronezh Front's forces, the Germans' Khar'kov group of forces and eliminated the Belgorod—Khar'kov bridgehead.

Ten divisions were given the honorary title of "Khar'kov." A number of units, a large number of generals, officers, sergeants, and Red Army enlisted men, received government medals.

The capital of our motherland, in the name of the motherland, saluted the valorous forces that had liberated Khar'kov, with 20 artillery salvos from 224 guns.

With the fall of Khar'kov the Germans' Belgorod—Khar'kov group of forces ceased to exist and this most important bridgehead had been eliminated.

The German army had been deprived of the most important pillar of its defense on the Soviet-German front. The Germans' defeat around Khar'kov not only enabled our forces to develop the offensive further to the west, but also played an important role in the Red Army's liberation of the Donbass.

Without interrupting military operations for a single day, the Red Army's forces developed the continuous pursuit of the retreating enemy, which later grew into a powerful offensive, which led our forces following the liberation of the Ukrainian left bank, to the shores of the Dnepr.

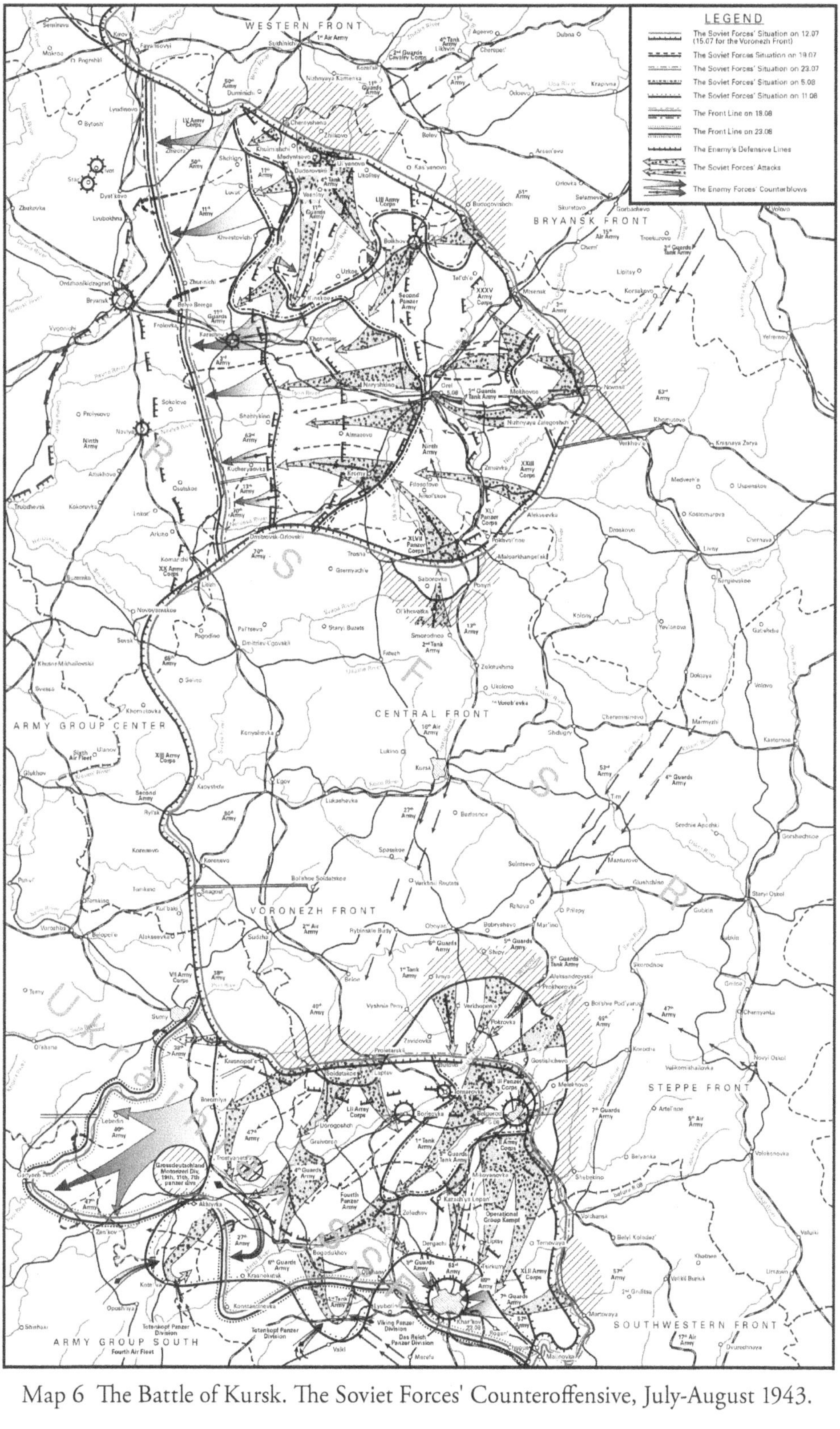

Map 6 The Battle of Kursk. The Soviet Forces' Counteroffensive, July-August 1943.

Lessons and Conclusions

The Red Army's offensive operations around Orel and Khar'kov are a very important and decisive stage of the Battle of Kursk. They represent a component organic part of the supreme commander-in-chief's, comrade Stalin, unified strategic plan to defeat the main enemy groups of forces in the 1943 summer campaign.

At Kursk the Red Army, for the third time during the course of the Great Patriotic War, accomplished a strategic counteroffensive with great success.

The strategic situation before the start of the 1943 summer campaign was immeasurably more favorable for us than before the start of the preceding campaigns. The correlation of forces along the Soviet-German front had firmly developed in our favor. Soviet forces had successfully incorporated the war's experience and had mastered all the forms of combat activity. This opened favorable opportunities for the unfolding of a strategic offensive along the most important directions in the summer of 1943.

However, the German command, hoping to change the situation in its favor, to seize the strategic initiative and unleash large-scale offensive operations, had still not renounced the desire to win the war. It counted on employing a number of factors favorable to it. First of all, the enemy, as before, enjoyed freedom in employing strategic reserves. He still had at his disposal the human and materiel resources of all of Europe and, thanks to this, could not only increase the number of his divisions operating along the Soviet-German front, but could come up with more powerful weapons.—new models of tanks and aircraft, primarily fighters. By taking advantage of all these factors, the German command, as is known, organized an enormously powerful attack along the Kursk axis from the Belgorod and Orel areas, in order to eliminate the Kursk strategic bridgehead and once again launch an offensive into the depths of our country.

This strategic plan was not unexpected for the Soviet high command, which made the decision to meet the enemy's attacks along previously prepared defensive lines and to exhaust and wear out his shock groups in defensive fighting, so that, by going over to a counteroffensive, completely defeat them and to subsequently launch a large-scale strategic offensive. A tried and true strategic system was employed here, but it was put into action in new forms, in accordance with the new conditions of the situation—of which the most decisive was the significantly more favorable correlation of forces for us.

First of all, the defensive period of the battle this time was short in comparison with the preceding campaigns. It did not exceed two weeks. On the other hand, our loss of territory during the course of an active defense was extremely small. The German forces' greatest advance did not exceed 35 kilometers; the enemy's breakthrough did not reach the operational scale. The enemy's losses during the course of our forces' defensive operations were enormous. The defense carried out by our forces, richly supplied with equipment and making wide use of fortified structures, particularly a trench system, forced the enemy to almost completely expend the shock force of his attacking groups of forces during a short period and in a limited area.

It's completely natural that in such conditions our strategic counteroffensive took on different operational forms than had been the case in the battles around Moscow and Stalingrad. It began as early as the defensive battle with attacks by the left wing of the Western Front and the Bryansk Front along the northern and eastern faces of the enemy's Orel salient, particularly as these attacks were operationally linked with our forces' defensive battle along the Orel and even Belgorod axes. There then followed a counterblow by the Central Front's forces along the Orel axis and, finally, a counterblow by the Voronezh Front along the Belgorod axis. In the course of a few days, as a result of the successfully developing counterblows, the enemy's breakthroughs were eliminated and the situation along the front was restored, while the Central and Voronezh fronts' counterblows grew into a strategic counteroffensive. As is known, this counteroffensive, in its turn, later grew into a strategic offensive of enormous scope, which embraced the area from Velikie Luki to the Black Sea.

In the Battle of Kursk three basic forms of battle were employed with great effect—concentrated both in relation to space and time—defense, the counteroffensive and the strategic offensive. At the same time the defensive was employed in its highest form and, from the point of view of its operational and tactical accomplishment, in its most rational form.

The shift to a strategic counteroffensive followed immediately upon the resolution of the defense's main tasks. This capability was secured by timely preparation. The counteroffensive itself, along the sectors of those *fronts* that had been subjected to the enemy's attack; that is, those *fronts* that began the battle in the defensive phase, had, if one may use the term, a developed form. It was begun by operational counterblows, which resolved the task of eliminating the enemy's breakthrough and restoring the previous operational situation. Then the operational counterblows grew into an already developed counteroffensive. It is also typical that the strategic counteroffensive during the battle of Kursk went beyond the bounds of the *fronts* that had been subjected to the enemy's attack—by including with the offensive operations the left wing of the Western Front and the Bryansk and Steppe fronts, which were operating in operational connection with the Central and Voronezh fronts.

The third accomplishment of a strategic counteroffensive in the course of the Great Patriotic War indicated the successive growth both of its scope, as well as of the skill shown in organizing and carrying it out. The strategic counteroffensive, as a form of combat, was becoming more refined from one campaign to the next, along with the overall growth of the Red Army's military art.

The chief feature of the Red Army's offensive operations was the decisiveness of the goals being pursued, which flowed from the missions assigned to the Red Army by the supreme high command.

Comrade Stalin, in his addresses repeatedly emphasized the decisive character of our struggle with Hitlerite Germany and its satellites. In his November 1941 address he stated: "The German aggressors want to have a war of destruction with the peoples of the USSR. Well, if the Germans want to have a war of destruction, they will get it."

In order no. 130 of May 1 1942, comrade Stalin once again emphasized that: "... we must defeat the German-fascist army and destroy the German occupiers to the last man, insofar as they will not surrender. We have no other choice."

Tasks of such magnitude naturally imparted all of the Red Army's operations the character of operations with a decisive goal—operations to crush and destroy the main and most important of the enemy's strategic groups of forces. Such were the Red Army's offensive operations against the Orel and Belgorod groups of German forces.

Tasks of such magnitude demand large-scale offensive operations, both in the sense of the size of the front embraced, as well as in the sense of the offensive's depth and speed.

The Red Army's offensive operations around Orel and Khar'kov unfolded along a front exceeding 600 kilometers and involving the forces of five *fronts*. The depth of the operations at the moment of completing the assigned tasks reached 180 kilometers.

The organization of offensive operations

A characteristic feature of Stalinist strategy and Soviet military art consists in the fact that in the organization and realization of these operations there is no room for hackneyed elements. An outstanding example of this is the conception and organization of the Red Army's offensive operations for destroying the Germans' Orel and Belgorod—Khar'kov groups of forces. According to the supreme high command's scheme, it was planned to conduct the offensive operation around

Orel as an envelopment of the main forces of the German Second Panzer and Ninth armies by launching three concentric attacks in the general direction of Orel.

1. by the Western Front's left wing from the Vosty—Ozhigovo—Pavlovo area;
2. by the Bryansk Front's main forces—from the Izmailovo—Zalegoshch'—Novosil' area;
3. by the Central Front's right wing—from the Ponyri—Arkhangel'skoe area.

Such an operational concept, first of all, is conditioned by the operationally favorable shape of the front, which hung over from the north and east the enemy's main group of forces; secondly, the supreme high command proceeded from the consideration that an offensive by the forces of the Western and Bryansk fronts, which were to launch the main attacks, must begin only after the main forces of the Germans' Orel group of forces were fully drawn into the fighting with the Central Front's forces along the southern face of the Kursk salient.

Finally, as a result of the fact that the offensive operation around Orel was being prepared beforehand, the Red Army command disposed of sufficient time to create the necessary groups of forces.

The operation to defeat the Germans' Belgorod—Khar'kov group of forces was conceived and planned in a completely different situation. This operation was prepared in conditions of extremely limited time and in the course of the defensive battle along the southern face of the Kursk salient. As early as the second half of July, following the collapse of the offensive toward Kursk and the assumption of the defensive along the old defensive line, the German command began to throw tank formations from the Belgorod—Khar'kov group of forces to the areas of the Donbass and Orel, in order to parry the Red Army's offensives that had begun there; the German forces, which had fallen back to their previous defensive line, immediately began to create there a solid defense through engineer means, and to create new lines in depth and operational reserves.

All of this demanded the immediate assumption of the offensive by the Voronezh and Steppe fronts.

At the same time, as a result of the completion of the operation for eliminating the salient, which had formed following the collapse of the Germans' July offensive, the main group of forces of both *fronts* naturally formed in the Oboyan'—Cherkasskoe—Gostishchevo area. By the end of July there were concentrated here two tank armies (1st and 5th Guards), the 6th and 5th guards and 53rd armies, plus a large part of the 69th Army's forces.

The most favorable axis for employing large tank and mechanized formations was the area between the Vorskla and Lopan' rivers.

The configuration of our front, which represented a broad bulge embracing the entire front of the German Fourth Panzer Army and army group "Kempf," the main mass of which was located in the Tomarovka—Golovchino—Belgorod area, reminded one, in general terms, of the configuration of the front around Stalingrad in the beginning of November 1942. This pushed us to adopt the decision to envelop the Germans' entire Belgorod—Khar'kov group of forces by means of concentric attacks from the Miropol'e—Ugroedy area toward Valki, and from the Martovaya—Pechenegi area toward Merefa.

However, the organization of an operation of such scope required the presence of very powerful groups of forces along the converging flanks of both *fronts*, which could be achieved only as a result of a complex regrouping, which would involve the transfer of our main forces located in the Oboyan'—Cherkasskoe—Gostishchevo area: partially—to the Voronezh Front's right flank and partially to the Steppe Front's left flank. Such a regrouping would have required a lot of time, which by no means corresponded to the developing situation.

Besides this, it should be noted that the area occupied by the enemy opposite the Voronezh Front's right flank, was cut by a significant number of rivers, which would interfere with the operations of large tank masses.

All of this taken together determined the character of employing the forces of the Voronezh and Steppe fronts in the forthcoming operation.

The mission of destroying the Germans' Belgorod—Khar'kov group of forces was to be accomplished in the following manner:

a) by splitting it into two parts with a powerful attack by our existing group of forces in the Kochetovka—Cherkasskoe—Gostishchevo area. Valki was designated as the attack's overall axis; at the same time, we would try to achieve the envelopment of the enemy's Khar'kov group of forces from the west.
b) by launching a supporting attack with part of our forces from the area Staryi Saltov—Martovaya toward Osnova.

It was planned to defeat the western part of the Belgorod—Khar'kov group of forces through a deep attack by part of the Voronezh Front's forces from the Krasnaya Yaruga—Kresanov—Soldatskoe area toward Akhtyrka, followed by the encirclement, by joint attacks by the 27th and 6th Guards armies, of the Germans' Tomarovka—Borisovka group of forces and the destruction of the German forces defending in the Bol'shoi Bobrik—Krasnopol'e area by a flank attack by the 40th Army from the Kresanov area toward Boromlya.

The conduct of offensive operations

The broad scope of offensive operations is to a significant extent conditioned by their high rate of speed.

The average rate of advance of the Western Front's main shock group—the 11th Guards Army, operating along the main axis—during the 12-16 July period reached 13 kilometers per day.

The average rate of advance for the mobile formations of the Voronezh Front's shock group during its move to the Bogodukhov area, and then to the Khar'kov—Poltava railroad, was 20 kilometers per day, with a maximum speed of 30 kilometers per day.

High offensive speeds were conditioned, in their turn, by the rapid overcoming of the enemy's positional defense, as well as the rapid advance into the operational depth of the enemy's defense.

The tactical defense of the Second and Fourth panzer armies and army group "Kempf" was overcome by our forces, for the most part, on the offensive's first day. By the close of the operation's first day the forces of the 11th Guards Army penetrated 12 kilometers into the depth of the enemy defense, while the Voronezh Front's shock group penetrated 25 kilometers.

By the close of the second day the forces of the 11th Guards Army reached the line Vesniny—Krapivna, to a depth of up to 25 kilometers, having overcome all zones of the enemy's defense.

The forces of the Voronezh Front's shock group overcame the operational depth of the German defense on the operation's fifth day, when the mobile formations reached the Bogodukhov area, having broken through the Germans' rear operational defensive zone. With the arrival of our forces in the Bogodukhov area, the entire enemy Belgorod—Khar'kov group of forces was cut into two parts.

It should be remembered that the problem of overcoming the positional front and the problem of transforming the tactical success into an operational one were the most hard-to-solve problems of the First World War. The forces of both sides repeatedly managed to more or less penetrate into the enemy's defense, but were almost never able to develop this penetration into a full-scale breakthrough of the entire depth of the enemy defense, in order to achieve broad wide-open "gates" through which so-called mobile formations (in the First World War this was primarily cavalry) could be committed for operations in the enemy's depth.

Up to the end of the First World War this problem essentially remained unresolved. The only results of the major offensive operations were the enormous losses and more or less deep salients in the front. These salients only made further defense more difficult, because the troops defending them were always under the threat of being encircled as a result of enemy attacks along the base of such a salient.

During the Great Patriotic War around Leningrad, around Moscow, around Stalingrad, and, finally, around Kursk, the Germans sought over a lengthy period of time to break through our defense. But all their attempts usually cost them colossal losses and ended in complete failure. The heroic defense by our forces of Sevastopol', to which the Germans broke through only after eight months of severe and bloody fighting, should also be remembered.

The rapid overcoming of the German defense and the defeat of the defending enemy groups of forces was achieved as the result of the organization and conduct of operations in accordance with the situation.

Offensive operations, both against the German Orel and the Belgorod—Khar'kov groups of forces, unfolded along a broad front; moreover in both cases several simultaneous or almost simultaneous attacks by powerful shock groups were launched against the enemy's defense, which broke through the enemy defense along comparatively narrow sectors of the front. The forces of the Western and Bryansk fronts, having attacked along a 300-kilometer front, launched simultaneous attacks against the enemy along four axes. The forces of the Voronezh and Steppe fronts, having attacked along a front more than 100 kilometers in width, launched attacks along four axes.

As has already been shown, the breakthrough of the enemy defense was accomplished along comparatively narrow sectors of the front. The 11th Guards Army was to break through the enemy's defense along a 14-kilometer sector, the 3rd and 63rd armies along an 18-kilometer sector, and the 27th Army along a 10-kilometer sector; the Voronezh Front's main shock group, consisting of the 6th and 5th guards and the 1st and 5th Guards tank armies were to break through the enemy front along a 27-kilometer sector.

From the examples cited here, it is clear that each army received an average breakthrough front of about 10-12 kilometers.

Such a method of conducting operations split up the Germans' defensive front from the first days of the offensive along a number of sectors, paralyzed his system of control and deprived the German command of the capability to create major shock groups from his operational reserves. The widening of the breakthroughs achieved by the initial blows was carried out by the subsequent eccentric attacks toward the breakthrough's flanks, which would lead to the rapid "rolling up" of the enemy defense. For example, the 11th Guards Army, following the breakthrough of the tactical depth of the enemy defense, launched an attack by the 36th Guards Rifle Corps along the front of the enemy (defending opposite the Bryansk Front's 61st Army to the left in the general direction of Kireikovo and Seredichi), which in the course of three days "rolled up" the Germans' combat formations along a sector more than 30 kilometers in width. As a result, the 61st Army's right-flank 46th Rifle Corps was completely freed from operating against the enemy defense; the corps, together with the 36th Rifle Corps, reached the immediate approaches to Bolkhov from the north.

The most illustrious example of the successful employment of the maneuver of "rolling up" the enemy's front on a large scale is the operations of the 69th and 7th Guards armies, which by attacking to the south along the western bank of the Severskii Donets River "rolled up" the Germans' entire defensive system along the Belgorod—Rubezhnoe sector, thus significantly easing the unfolding of the 57th Army's offensive. The rapid defeat of the enemy defense was also achieved by the employment of bold and decisive maneuver toward encircling the main and most powerful centers of resistance in the enemy's defensive system covering the most important axes.

As a result of the maneuver skillfully carried out by a part of the 61st and 3rd armies' (Bryansk Front) forces, which concluded in their arrival at the communications of the enemy group of forces defending a very important center of resistance in the Orel salient's system of defense, the German command was forced to hurriedly evacuate the Mtsensk area and thus open to our forces one of the most important axes toward Orel. Thus thanks to the fortunate flanking maneuver; it was not necessary for our forces to storm the very powerful previously-prepared Mtsensk defensive center.

As the result of these coordinated attacks by part of the Steppe Front's 69th and 7th Guards armies' forces, by the close of the offensive's third day that very important center of resistance in army group "Kempf"—the city of Belgorod, which covered the main routes to Khar'kov, was eliminated and the group of forces defending it was destroyed.

Units of the 27th and the 6th and 5th guards armies also launched coordinated attacks and on the offensive's fifth day encircled and eliminated the Tomarovka—Borisovka center of resistance, which was a major center of resistance in the enemy's defensive system along the Belgorod—Khar'kov bridgehead, and completely destroyed the German forces defending it.

The rapid elimination of the Belgorod and Tomarovka—Borisovka centers of resistance destroyed the German defense along an 80-kilometer front and opened for the forces of the Voronezh and Steppe fronts the prospect of unfolding broad offensive operations in the depth of the enemy defense, both directly upon Khar'kov and to the southwest.

The rapidity of overcoming the Germans' positional defense, as well as the rapidity of maneuvering in the depth of the enemy defense was, to a significant degree, conditioned by the strength and composition of the main shock groups of the *fronts* and armies. For example, the 11th Guards Army's main shock group, which had deployed along a 14-kilometer front (as against the army's overall 36-kilometer front), was composed of 11 rifle divisions, two tank corps, four independent tank brigades, two tank breakthrough regiments, five artillery brigades, 38 independent artillery reinforcement regiments, 19 mortar regiments, and 20 guards mortar battalions.

The average tank density along the breakthrough sector reached 44 tanks per kilometer of front, while the average artillery density was 185 guns and mortars per kilometer of front (not counting battalion and regimental artillery and light mortars), and if one takes into account the regimental and battalion artillery, along with the light mortars, then the density become 210 tubes per kilometer of front. The artillery density along the 8th Guards Rifle Corps' main attack sector reached 260 tubes per kilometer of front. The tank density along the axis of the main attack for the Bryansk Front's left wing (the adjacent flanks of the 3rd and 63rd armies) reached 19 tanks per kilometer of front, while the artillery density reached 176 tubes.

The Voronezh Front's shock group, which attacked along a 27-kilometer front, consisted of 30 divisions, five tank and two mechanized corps, four independent tank breakthrough regiments, nine artillery brigades, 34 artillery reinforcement regiments, a mortar brigade, seven mortar regiments, three guards mortar brigades, and eight guards mortar regiments.

The tank density along the shock group's attack sector reached 40 tanks per kilometer of front and 70 tanks per kilometer of front along the 5th Guards Army's sector; on the whole, the shock group's artillery density reached 135 guns per kilometer of front, and along the 5th Guards Army's sector—230 tubes. Thus a large number of weapons imparted to the *fronts'* and armies' shock groups a high penetrating power and a high degree of mobility to the major mobile formations.

The success of the breakthrough was achieved by the corresponding organization of the armies' combat formations, and here the absence of rote was especially noticeable.

The 11th Guards Army's combat formation was organized on the basis of the necessity of breaking through the enemy's powerfully fortified defensive zone.

The army organized its combat formation in two echelons. The first echelon consisted of the combat formations of three rifle corps. The second echelon, which was designated for developing the success, consisted of two tank corps and a rifle division, which had been concentrated behind the central corps (8th Guards), which was making the main attack. The rifle corps organized their combat formation in one, two or three echelons.

The 16th Guards Rifle Corps, which had deployed along a front about seven kilometers in width, had three divisions in one echelon, while each division received an attack sector of about two kilometers.

The 8th Guards Rifle Corps had an attack front of about 3.5 kilometers; there were two rifle divisions in the first echelon and one in the second. Each first-echelon division had an attack sector of about 1.5 kilometers.

The 36th Guards Rifle Corps, which was also operating along a front of about 3.5 kilometers, organized its combat formation in three echelons—each containing a single rifle division.

Divisions, as a rule, organized their combat formation in a single echelon, while the regiments did this in two or three echelons.

As the course of the battle showed, the first two lines of the enemy trenches were broken through in the first half of the first day of the offensive by the first-echelon battalions. The second and third echelons of the first-echelon regiments would overcome the remaining tactical depth of the enemy defense right up to the intermediate defensive line along the Fomina River.

The second-echelon divisions, as a rule, were committed on the second day of the offensive for breaking through the rear defensive zone. The third-echelon division (36th Guards Rifle Corps) was committed on the fourth day; it was to launch an attack in the direction of the flank, in order to "roll up" the enemy defense in the operational depth opposite its neighbor's front.

The tank corps were committed into the breach on the first day of the offensive, after the intermediate defensive line was broken through; at first they assisted the infantry in advancing to the rear defensive line.

After the piercing of this line by the infantry, the tank corps bypassed it, entered the resulting breach and subsequently operated independently, whle developing the success achieved. Thus the tank corps were essentially committed following the piercing of the entire depth of the enemy defense, for fighting the Germans' arriving operational reserves.

In organizing the 11th Guards Army's combat formation, it was planned that each individual echelon would independently overcome one line of enemy trenches. It actually transpired that in a number of cases the echelons broke through up to two trench lines.

The Voronezh Front's armies organized their combat formations in accordance with the task of breaking through the enemy's defense, which was less prepared and had only been occupied by the enemy forces as they fell back from the salient that had formed following the unsuccessful offensive on Kursk; moreover, in this case the enemy did not dispose of major reserves in the immediate operational depth.

The combat formation of the 5th Guards Army, which had the task of securing the commitment of the tank armies into the breach, consisted of one echelon, in which there were two rifle corps. As a reserve, the commander had a single rifle division at a distance of ten miles from the front line.

The mission of developing the success in this army's sector was entrusted to the *front's* success development group—the 1st and 5th Guards tank armies.

The right-flank 32nd Guards Rifle Corps, which deployed along a front of about nine kilometers, had all three divisions in one echelon, with each division having a frontage of about three kilometers.

The left-flank 33rd Guards Rifle Corps, which was operating along a 5-kilometer front, organized its combat formation in two echelons, having in the first echelon two rifle divisions, with one in the second. The first-echelon divisions deployed along a front of about 2.5 kilometers each.

All of the corps' first-echelon divisions, as a rule, organized their combat formation in two echelons, just like the first-echelon regiments.

The 33rd Guards Rifle Corps' second echelon and the reserve rifle division were committed into the fighting on the offensive's ninth day. They were designated for combating the enemy's arriving reserves in the rear defensive zone at a distance of 70 kilometers from the starting point, as well as for relieving divisions of the first corps echelons.

The experience of both the Orel and Belgorod—Khar'kov operations is instructive from the point of view of the possibility of employing armies for operations along one or two operational axes. In the operation under study, the armies, as a rule, received their orders and actually successfully attacked—each along a single axis.

Along the Western Front an attempt was made to employ the 11th Guards Army simultaneously along two axes—Bolkhov and Khotynets.

In planning the offensive operation, the 11th Guards Army received orders to operate along the Bolkhov axis, in order to encircle the Germans' Bolkhov group of forces in conjunction with the 61st Army.

Following the breakthrough of the enemy defense and the army's arrival on 18 July at the line Dudorovskii—excluding Kudryavets—Peshkova—Stolbchee—Ragozino, when success was noted along the Khotynets axis, where the 11th Guards Rifle Division was attacking, for the purpose of cutting the Orel—Bryansk railroad, this axis starts to be strengthened as the expense of the main shock group, which was operating along the Bolkhov axis (the 1st Tank Corps was taken), and at the expense of the army's right flank, from which direction the 16th Guards Rifle Corps was transferred. Besides this, on 18 July the 36th Guards Rifle Corps, which was operating along the left flank of the army's shock group along the Bolkhov axis, was shifted laterally from the Seredichi area to the Kamenki area for the purpose of attacking toward Gnezdilovo and then to outflank Khotynets from the east. The 25th Tank Corps, which had been transferred on 14 July from the *Stavka* reserve to the army, on 18 July, was also employed for operations together with the 36th Guards Corps along the Gnezdilovka axis for an attack on Khotynets.

Thus from 19 July the army was actually attacking along two axes; on neither of them did it have the necessary amount of men and materiel for the successful development of the offensive.

Subsequently, with the commitment of the 4th Tank Army (26 July), the main efforts of the Western Front's left wing were shifted to the Khotynets axis for the purpose of cutting the Orel—Bryansk railroad and paved road and reaching the flank and rear of the Germans' Orel group of forces. A part of the 11th Guards Army's forces (8th Guards Rifle and 5th Tank corps) was to launch a supporting attack toward Borilovo, in order to assist the 61st Army's forces in completing the defeat of the enemy's Bolkhov group of forces.

Simultaneously, the 16th Guards Rifle Corps and the 2nd Guards Cavalry Corps, the latter of which had joined the 11th Guards Army on 26 July, were ordered to attack toward Karachev.

It follows that during 12-18 July the 11th Guards Army was developing its main attack along the single Bolkhov axis. During 18-26 July the army's efforts were split: one part of it was operating along the Bolkhov axis, and the other along the Khotynets axis. Only after 26 July did the army once again concentrate is main efforts along the single Khotynets axis.

Thus in trying to carry out an offensive along two operational axes, the 11th Guards Army expanded its front by more than 150 kilometers and, having spread out its men and materiel, could not develop the success achieved along any one of these axes. Having lost time, the army was nevertheless forced to operate only along the Bolkhov axis, and then later along the Khotynets—Karachev axis. However, the delay in developing the army's success enabled the enemy to bring up major forces to the threatened sectors and consolidate. Thus the army's subsequent operations were significantly complicated by the necessity of breaking through the enemy's newly organized defense, which required expending time, men and materiel. All of this could not but be reflected on the overall course of the Orel operation.

Evidently, it would have been much more expedient following the breakthrough of the entire depth of the enemy's defense to concentrate the army's main efforts along the Khotynets axis and, by launching a massed attack with three tank and two rifle corps, supported by all our aviation, and to reach by the shortest route the communications of the Germans' Orel group of forces in the Khotynets area. This would have undoubtedly have led to the crushing of the German defense in the Bolkhov area, and would also have sped up the defeat of the entire enemy group of forces defending the Orel salient.

The employment of operational reserves

The experience of both offensive operations quite fully speaks to the importance of the timely commitment of operational reserves into the fighting, both for developing the success in the depth of the enemy's defense, and for eliminating crisis situations arising during the course of the operation, in which the enemy attempts to employ his reserves in order to foil our forces' successes.

The rapid development of the offensive by the 11th Guards Army, given the significant distance from the *front* reserves (120-150 kilometers), and given the absence of a satisfactory road network, finally completely ruined by the unceasing rains, led to a delay in the commitment of the operational reserves.

The most favorable time for committing the operational reserves in the 11th Guards Army's sector was the period between 15 and 20 July. By this time our forces had broken through the enemy's defense throughout its entire depth; the enemy opposing us did not have sufficient forces for organizing resistance. His reserves, which were being transferred from other fronts, had only begun to arrive in the Karachev and Bolkhov areas. At this time the 11th Guards Army, which had elongated its front to more than 100 kilometers (as a result of the rapid advance and widening of the breakthrough), was forced to use a significant part of its forces to secure operations along secondary axes.

It was only on the morning of 20 July that General Fedyuninskii's 11th Army reached the operational area with half of its forces. On that day, following a continuous six-day march, almost without artillery and ammunition and the necessary preparation, it was committed into the battle from the march. The *front* commander directed the army to attack along the Brusny—Ktsyn' sector, with the mission of attacking toward Khvastovichi. Lacking sufficient men and materiel for breaking through the Germans' defensive zone in the wooded and swampy area, where they had managed to consolidate and bring up reserves from the neighboring passive sector of the front, the army along this axis was only able to insignificantly penetrate into the enemy defense. The army did not carry out its mission of developing the 11th Guards Army's success or to secure the latter from the west.

The deputy chief of the General Staff, General Antonov, noted in a 23 July telegram that it would have been more expedient to employ the 11th Army to attack south of Ktsyn', for the purpose of seizing Khvastovichi and attacking toward Karachev along the shortest route. The commitment of the 11th Army along this axis would doubtlessly have led to a greater success, all the more so as the enemy here lacked an organized defense and large forces.

Besides this, the 11th Army's offensive along this axis would have enabled us to organize close cooperation with units of the 16th Guards Rifle Corps, and subsequently with the newly-arrived 2nd Guards Cavalry Corps.

The 2nd Guards Cavalry Corps arrived in the area of the fighting only by 26 July, when the enemy had managed to bring up more than five divisions to the Karachev axis and, having preempted our units in deploying, as early as 25 July had counterattacked along this axis.

As a result of the delayed commitment of General Kryukov's group, consisting of two corps (2nd Guards Cavalry and 16th Guards Rifle), into the battle, it was only able to achieve a relatively insignificant success, although just a few days before (20 July) a single rifle division (11th Guards), operating here along a 50-kilometer front, advanced successfully, without encountering the enemy's organized resistance.

The 4th Tank Army, which was committed into the fighting on 26 July along the Bolkhov axis, was not able to achieve a rapid and decisive success for the same reasons: the enemy, taking advantage of the time between 17 and 26 July, brought up here significant reserves and organized a strong field defense.

A completely different picture was encountered in those cases when the reserves were located close to the immediate battle area at the moment they were committed, and were committed into the fighting in a timely manner. For example, the timely arrival in the battle area of the Voronezh Front's 4th Guards Army, which at the moment it was committed into the battle was located in the Yamnoe—Yablochnoe area at a distance of 20 kilometers from the front line, enabled us, when a crisis situation in the Akhtyrka area arose, when the Germans' Akhtyrka group of forces broke through the 27th Army's front, to commit into the battle on the same day part of the 4th Guards Army and halt the attack by the enemy trying to break through to Bogodukhov.

By the start of the offensive the 47th Army—the Voronezh Front's operational reserve—was located in the Miropol'e area, ten kilometers behind the front line. During the operation the army was moved up behind the attacking forces, and by 11 August it had been concentrated in the Pushkarnoe—Brantsovka—Pozhnya area. This enabled us on the morning of 17 August, without any kind of difficulties, to commit the army into the battle for an attack on Lebedin, together with the 40th Army, for the purpose of widening the breach toward the southwest and to reach the rear of the German's Akhtyrka group of forces.

The rapid maneuver by the 4th Guards and 47th armies foiled the German command's attempt to achieve a significant change in the operational situation on the Belgorod—Khar'kov bridgehead.

Characteristic Features in Employing the Combat Arms

Employing the artillery

In both of the Red Army's offensives the artillery played an enormous role as the main means of breaking through the enemy's defense.

Thanks to the correct employment of large artillery masses, the effect of its fire in a number of cases proved to be so significant that we managed to achieve a "clean" breakthrough. The Western Front's 11th Guards Army and the Voronezh Front's 5th Guards Army were able to drive 10-12 kilometers into the depth of the enemy's defense, without encountering the enemy's organized resistance, because the Germans' entire defensive system to this depth had been paralyzed by a powerful artillery and air preparation.

The massed employment of artillery yielded good results. As was shown earlier, the artillery density along our forces' main attack axes reached 200-260 tubes per kilometer of front.

In preparing the breakthrough along the 5th Guards Army's sector, the density of artillery fire against the main centers of the Germans' defense reached one explosion per each 18-20 square meters of the enemy's defense.

The overall expenditure of shells to carry out the artillery preparation along the Steppe Front reached the following figures:

Artillery Expenditure by the Steppe Front

Artillery	Shells per Gun	Combat Loads	
		Not Counting Expenditures on Registration	Counting Expenditures on Registration
76mm divisional	175	1.25	1.5
122mm	100	1.25	1.5
152mm	90	1.5	1.75
203mm	60	1.5	1.75
120mm mortars	100	1.25	1.5

In organizing the artillery offensive, our command renounced the accepted routine in carrying out the artillery preparation, of which they enemy was generally already aware.

In the course of both offensive operations, particularly during the period of fighting in the depths of the enemy defense, the artillery of almost all calibers widely employed firing over open sights. For example, while storming the Khar'kov external position, the 53rd Army's forces employed 400 guns of various calibers for firing over open sights.

Of particular interest and value is the maneuver of reinforcement artillery, employed by the staff of the Voronezh Front. Following the successful accomplishment of the 3 August breakthrough along the front of the 6th and 5th guards armies, a significant portion of the reinforcement artillery was immediately transferred to the 27th Army's sector, where on 5 August it took part in preparing the breakthrough along this army's sector.

Both the *Stavka* and the *front* commanders devoted a good deal of time during the battle to the massed employment of artillery for parrying the enemy's counterblows. For example, on 13 August, when the enemy was heavily counterattacking our forces south of Bogodukhov, along with bringing up the 6th and 5th guards armies' reserves, measures were simultaneously adopted to bring up to the battle area the main mass of both armies' artillery, in order to parry the enemy's counterattacks.

Among the shortcomings committed in the employment of artillery, the following should be noted: sometimes the combined-arms commanders did not allow the artillery chiefs and staffs the necessary time for preparing the artillery offensive, and the artillery chiefs, failing to report this, sought to fit into the extremely tight timetables. Thus the artillery offensive in a number of cases was carried out without the necessary preparation.

This circumstance, as well as the not always satisfactory work of artillery intelligence, led to a situation in which in a number of cases fire was conducted by area, which lowered the effectiveness of our fire and resulted in a great expenditure of shells.

Particularly striking is the insignificant employment of 45mm guns in the fighting, while the employment of divisional and reinforcement artillery for firing over open sights was broadly employed. For example, the 69th Army's artillery in 27 days of fighting (3-30 August) expended 44,946 45mm cannon shells, that is, no more than nine shells per day per gun.

The employment of tanks

In both offensive operations the tank forces were widely employed and played a very large role. The massed employment of breakthrough tanks aided the rapid breakthrough of the Germans' positional defense. The employment of large tank formations as part of the *fronts'* main shock groups significantly sped up the pace of the offensive in the operational depth of the enemy's defense.

A powerful tank wedge, consisting of the 1st and 5th Guards tank armies, as early as the offensive's fifth day had broken through into the enemy's position to a depth of up to 100 kilometers and, having reached the Bogodukhov area, split the Germans' Belgorod—Khar'kov group of forces.

On 19 July the 3rd Tank Army, along with units of the 25th Rifle Corps, broke through the enemy's defense along the line Arsen'evo—Alekseevka, and then in the Staraya Otrada—Ivanovskaya Optukha area reached the Oka River. This forced the German command to abandon the Mtsensk area—a very important resistance center along the Orel salient—without a fight.

The tank formations' high rate of effectiveness was determined by the rapid pace of their offensive, as well as by the bold employment of maneuver. The 1st and 5th Guards tank armies' pace of attack during their advance on Bogodukhov reached 25 kilometers per day.

The 1st Tank Army boldly and rapidly carried out its maneuver to split the enemy group of forces. The maneuver was conducted 40 kilometers apart from the shock group's combined-arms echelon, while significant groups of German forces remained in the army's rear and continued to hold major centers of resistance (Borisovka and others).

During the offensive there were cases when the combined-arms formations were not able to break through the enemy's defense. Then major tank formations independently carried out the breakthrough of the powerful enemy defensive lines. This was exactly how the 2nd, 3rd Guards and 4th tank armies operated. During 15 July-2 August the 2nd Tank Army was employed for breaking through the enemy's defense eight times, the 4th Tank Army three times, and the 3rd Guards Tank Army six times.

It should be noted that in the majority of cases such an employment of tank formations did not yield the desired effect and only led to large and unjustified losses, depriving our forces of a powerful means for developing the success in the operational depth of the enemy defense.

This method may be employed only during the course of an operation, when the tank formation, operating apart from the main forces, encounters a defensive line, which as the result of these or other circumstances cannot be bypassed and does not represent a previously prepared and occupied zone.

Often major tank formations, during their commitment into the breach, had to operate alongside combined-arms formations in order to "finish off" the enemy's defensive zone, because the infantry was not always able to fully complete the breakthrough with its own forces. An example of this is the operations of the 20th Tank Corps on 13 July northeast of Bolkhov, and the 4th Tank Army on 6-7 August northeast of Khotynets.

It should be noted that during the course of operations individual cases were observed of frequent changes in the direction of the attacks by major tank formations, which were not justified by the situation. For example, the 3rd Guards Tank Army during 19 July-4 August changed the axis of its attack six times and was given new tasks, without having carried out the previous ones. Frequent and radical changes in the attack axes led to a situation in which the army, while carrying out such "maneuvers," was forced to cover more than 500 kilometers and, as a rule, did not have time for the necessary offensive preparation along the new axis.

Besides this, individual cases of "jerking around" major tank formations were observed. For example, in the employment of the 1st Tank Army in the fighting around Akhtyrka by the commander of the 4th Guards Army (General Kulik), the army's corps were split up by brigade, while individual brigades received orders to operate together with the rifle divisions along various axes as reinforcement tanks.

The employment of aviation

The offensive operations against both the Orel and the Belgorod—Khar'kov German groups of forces were characterized by the intensive activity of our air force. This is attested to by the number and results of the air battles conducted in August. In a month of fighting the 2nd Air Army alone carried out 572 air battles, having shot down 567 enemy planes (283 fighters and 284 bombers).

During the breakthrough period of the enemy's defense, the air force, as a rule, was employed *en masse*. Significant attention was devoted to the organization of cooperation between aviation and the attacking forces.

Artillery and aviation chiefs sought to achieve continuous coverage throughout the entire depth of the enemy's defense. The artillery usually fired to a depth of 2.5-3 kilometers along the enemy's position. Our aviation, operating at an altitude of 1,500-2,000 meters, attacked deeper targets, including the Germans' long-range artillery positions.

The plan for artillery and aviation cooperation was drawn up by the commanders of the air corps and divisions, along with artillery officers who would usually travel to the breakthrough area.

Air cooperation with the tank formations was established through responsible aviation officers, who were commandeered to the tank formations' (army and corps) headquarters. During the offensive there was a commander in the 1st Tank Army's headquarters, and in the 5th Guards Tank Army's headquarters was the chief of the 5th Air Assault Corps' operational section, which supported both tank armies.

The cooperation achieved during the first 2-3 days of the offense was the smoothest. Subsequently, when the tank formations' units encountered organized resistance in the operational depth of the enemy defense and adopted a broken combat formation, the aviation was no longer capable of precisely determining the position of our tanks, which sharply narrowed the intensity of its operations. In order to make communications between the forward tank units with the air force more effectual, it was expedient to have aviation representatives within the tank brigades' headquarters during the most intensive fighting.

The aviation rendered great service to the combined-arms echelons of the ground forces during the fighting in the depth of the enemy's defense. For example, when the enemy began his counterattacks on 16 August in the Akhtyrka area, the entire 2nd Air Army was thrown in to parry the enemy counteroffensive. As a result of the successful attacks by our bombers, which carried out four sorties during a short period, the first German counterattack was beaten back with great losses for them. Our aviation worked very effectively during the subsequent fighting in the Katukovka area, helping the ground forces parry the Germans' attempts to break out from the Katukovka area toward Bogodukhov.

The employment of infantry

The course of both operations showed that the infantry is capable, in cooperation with the other combat arms—artillery, tanks and aviation—of carrying out all its assigned objectives.

The chief shortcoming in the infantry's operations was the poor employment of its own fire, including mortars and 45mm guns, as well as the desire to shift the resolution of all fire tasks exclusively onto the artillery.

In a number of cases, the infantry did not know how to fully employ that assistance that our artillery rendered it during the artillery preparation in order to maximally close with the enemy's defense.

For example, the 15th Rifle Division's (70th Army) infantry, following the completion of the artillery preparation called for by the plan, turned out to be 500-1,000 meters from the forward enemy trench. Bringing up the infantry to this trench for its subsequent attack required additional time and the great expenditure of artillery shells not called for by the plan.

Cooperation with the partisans

In the fighting for Orel and during the pursuit of the enemy, who was trying to escape from out from under our blows to the west, the glorious partisans of the Orel *oblast'* rendered a great deal of assistance to our troops. During the intensive fighting for Bolkhov and Orel, when the German command was rapidly bringing up reserves to the Orel area from other sectors of the front, the people's avengers, on instructions from the *Stavka*, were waging a bitter "rail war" in the enemy rear. The partisans systematically damaged the railroad lines, blew up bridges along the railroad and roads, derailed tens of trains loaded with troops and troop supplies, and carried out incessant attacks on German transports and rear targets. This forced the enemy to allot a significant number of forces to guard his communications. Sentries assigned to guard the roads were spaced within sight of each other. Wide expanses of woods were cut on either side of the roads, in order to render sudden attacks on German convoys more difficult.

During the pursuit of the retreating German forces during the second half of August, the partisans supplied our pursuit detachments with experienced guides, which led them along forest roads and paths into the enemy rear. The partisans seized and held crossings over water lines until the arrival of our forces, preventing the enemy from destroying them. On the other hand, the partisans destroyed crossings and laid ambushes along the roads along the retreat routes of large German columns.

Finally, the partisans hindered the Germans from carrying off bread and other property from the areas they were abandoning, and also prevented them from carrying off Soviet citizens to hard labor in Germany.

Conclusions

The Red Army's victories around Orel, Kursk and Khar'kov during the Great Patriotic War had very great significance.

In the fighting in the Orel and Belgorod—Khar'kov salients were finally buried the mad plans of the Hitlerite command, which dreamed of a new advance on Moscow. During the fighting around Kursk, Orel and Khar'kov the defective nature of German strategy, which was based upon an overestimation of its strength and an underestimation of the Red Army's strength and capabilities, was once again demonstrated to the entire world. In the battle of Kursk the Red Army crushed the reputation of German arms, destroyed the plans of the German command, which was seeking to "get revenge for Stalingrad" and once again seize the strategic initiative lost at Stalingrad.

The Red Army did not only foil the Germans' plan for a summer offensive, but also placed Germany in a catastrophic position. The entire German military machine received a new crushing blow.

In the battle of Kursk the Hitlerite command expended all of its main reserves, which had been gathered with such difficulty for the summer campaign of 1943, and which, naturally, to a significant degree aided the subsequent victorious advance by our forces.

The following data are sufficiently eloquent in showing the scope of the catastrophe which struck the German armies at Kursk as the result of our attacks.

During the Soviet armies' offensive against the Germans' Orel and Belgorod—Khar'kov groups of forces, the latter included 77 divisions, including 57 infantry, 17 panzer and three motorized.

During the 12 July-23 August offensive our forces defeated 35 divisions, including 22 infantry, 11 panzer and two motorized. Besides this, all the remaining 42 divisions suffered heavy losses and lost their combat capability to a significant degree.

It is of interest to emphasize that in the battle of Kursk the German command employed 20 panzer and motorized divisions out of an overall number of 26 such divisions available at that time along the Soviet-German front, while, as has been shown, 13 divisions were completely routed.

The Germans were forced along the entire Soviet-German front to switch from an offensive strategy to the strategic defense.

It's necessary to note that the July-August operations around Kursk, Orel and Khar'kov, which were so brilliantly completed by the Red Army, and in which an enormous number of German forces and all available reserves were involved, to a significant degree assisted the successful development of landing operations by the Anglo-American forces in the Mediterranean Sea, just as the Red Army's operations along the Stalingrad axis in the winter of 1942-43 to a great degree facilitated the successful unfolding of operations by British forces in Africa against Rommel's group of forces.

The battles around Kursk, Orel and Khar'kov were a new triumph of Soviet strategy. In this colossal battle, the Red Army demonstrated its growing combat preparation, its ability to fight one on one with a powerful and perfidious enemy and to inflict crushing blows on him. In the battle of Kursk the propaganda myth, created by Hitlerite propaganda, as to the "seasonality" of the Red Army's strategy, was destroyed. The Red Army showed that it could beat the Germans at any time of year.

The battle of Kursk, just as the battle of Stalingrad, occupies an honorable place in military history as one of its most brilliant pages.

Index

INDEX OF PEOPLE

INDEX OF PLACES

INDEX OF GERMAN MILITARY FORMATIONS & UNITS

INDEX OF SOVIET MILITARY FORMATIONS & UNITS

INDEX OF GENERAL & MISCELLANEOUS TERMS